THE
EASTERN
EUROPE
COLLECTION

ALBANIA—
THE RISE OF A KINGDOM

J. Swire

ARNO PRESS & THE NEW YORK TIMES

New York - 1971

Reprint Edition 1971 by Arno Press Inc.

Reprinted from a copy in
The Harvard University Library

LC# 79-135835

ISBN 0-405-02777-X

The Eastern Europe Collection
ISBN for complete set: 0-405-02730-3

Manufactured in the United States of America

ALBANIA
THE RISE OF A KINGDOM

IN THE VALLEY OF THE DRIN (NEAR DIBRA), LOOKING SOUTH

ALBANIA

THE RISE OF A KINGDOM

By

J. SWIRE

F.R.G.S.

etc.

"J'ai trouvé quelquefois de pareilles contrariétés
dans les mémoires que l'on m'a confiés. En ce
cas, tout ce que doit faire un historien, c'est
de conter ingénument le fait, sans vouloir
pénétrer les motifs, et de se borner à dire
précisément ce qu'il sait, au lieu de
deviner ce qu'il ne sait pas."

VOLTAIRE: *Histoire de Charles XII*

WILLIAMS & NORGATE LTD
38 Great Ormond Street
London W.C.1

First Published in 1929

Printed in Great Britain by
UNWIN BROTHERS LIMITED, LONDON AND WOKING

CONTENTS

ILLUSTRATIONS

MAPS AND DIAGRAM

Note to Map 2.—The various frontiers shown are plotted after consultation of *The Map of Europe by Treaty; Political and Territorial Changes since the General Peace of* 1814, Vol. IV, 1875–91, by Sir Edward Hertslet, C.B., H.M. Stationery Office, London: 3,380 pp. The line denoting Albanian ethnographical limits has been plotted after consultation of a number of maps, and *roughly corresponds with the ethnographical map of Turkey in Europe by H. Kiepert*—cartographer and traveller—published in Berlin in 1876. Kiepert appears, however, to have been misled with regard to southern Albania; his map should be compared with: (i) Ethnographical map of Turkey in Europe, by G. Lejean, published in *Petermann's Mitteilungen*, Gotha, 1861, by Justus Perthes; (ii) Ethnographical map by F. Mirkovitch—a Russian, an ardent Pan-Slavist—published in Moscow in 1876; (iii) Map showing the distribution of Slavs in Turkey, by P. F. Bradaska of Agram, 1869, published in *Petermann's Mitteilungen* (Vol. XII), Gotha, Justus Perthes; (iv) Ethnographical map of Turkey in Europe, by C. Sax—for seventeen years Austro-Hungarian Consul in Macedonia—published by the *Journal of the Austrian R.G.S.*, Vienna, 1877; (v) Ethnographical map published in *Les Roumains Koutzovalaques*, by Constantin Noe, Bucharest, 1913; (vi) Ethnographical map of Macedonia, by Vasil Kentchoff, in *Makedoniza etnografija i statistika*, Sofia, 1900. All the above maps are reproduced in *Albanais et Slaves*, by "Lumo Skendo," published by the Librairie des Nationalités, Rue Caroline, Lausanne, 1919, and obtainable from Midhat bey Frasheri, Librarija Lumo Skendo, Tirana. Comparison should also be made with (vii) *Die ethnographische Abgrenzung der Völker auf der Balkanhalbinsel*, by Cvijic, reproduced in *Petermann's Mitteilungen*, 1913; (viii) *Osnove za gheografijou i gheologhijou Makedonije i Stara Serbije*, Belgrade, 1906; (ix) Maps accompanying articles in the *Encyclopædia Brittanica*, eleventh edition, Vol. III, p. 259, and Vol. XXX, p. 368—bearing in mind the purpose for which Cvijic drew his maps—and (x) Map on p. 300 of the text.

Note to Map 9.—The frontier has been plotted after consultation of the maps annexed to the *Rapport Général sur la marche des travaux et note sur le fonctionnement technique de la Commission* (1922–6); and *Protocole de Délimitation*, Florence, 1926.

General Note.—In order to avoid confusion, the pre-war nomenclature has been adhered to both in the maps and text.

INTRODUCTION

Fierce are Albania's children, yet they lack
   Not virtues, were those virtues more mature.
Where is the foe that ever saw their back?
   Who can so well the toil of war endure?
Their native fastnesses not more secure
   Than they in doubtful time of troublous need;
Their wrath how deadly! but their friendship sure,
   When gratitude or valour bids them bleed,
Unshaken rushing on where'er their chief may lead.
     Childe Harold's Pilgrimage: Canto the Second. Verse LXV.

So wrote Lord Byron of that stalwart race which inhabits the rugged but incomparably beautiful highlands, fertile valleys, and wooded uplands, of Albania. "It is a quick-witted race, with keen æsthetic perceptions, a feudal sense of honour and, above all, an individualism which shows itself in moral and intellectual originality. It is a race worth saving" (H. N. Brailsford, *Peace in the Balkans*, A.R., March, 1919).

An apology for the production of so large a book upon the subject of Albania—a country with a population of only 816,610—might have been necessary four years ago, when I began to write it. It is unnecessary to-day. Ever since the signature of the Treaty of Berlin the Albanian question has been of international importance, but it is only since the conclusion of the Pact of Tirana in November, 1926, that its importance has been generally acknowledged.

Throughout the century preceding the calamity of 1914, the main factors determining the course of Balkan history were the conflict for supremacy between Austria-Hungary and Russia, the decline of Turkish power, the reawakening of the subject races of Turkey in Europe to national self-consciousness, and the anxiety of those subject races (except the Albanians) to re-establish in the Peninsula the ascendancy which each in turn had held before the arrival of the Turks.

With the invasion of the Peninsula in the sixth and seventh centuries A.D. by the Slavonic hordes, the Illyrians—forbears of the Albanians—who had withstood the attraction of Roman civilization, retired to the Albanian mountains and were never conquered or Slavonized. Then came the Turks, and imposed their suzerainty upon Slavs and Greeks. But the exogamous Albanian tribes, similar in many respects to the Scottish clans, secure in their fastnesses, preserved their independence, traditions, and mode of living.

With the decline of the Turkish Empire there began the struggle for hegemony in the Peninsula in which Serbia has proved victorious. That struggle stirred the Albanians to reassert themselves as a nation; and it is only during the present century that they have succeeded in winning a reluctant acknowledgment of their right to an independent existence, and in preserving for themselves some small part of their birthright.

The War of 1914–18 led to the elimination of Austria-Hungary, and—temporarily—of Russia, as factors in Balkan affairs. But their place has been filled by Yugoslavia and France on the one hand (and to that group a rejuvenated Russia will probably belong in the future), and on the other hand, Italy.

On account of her strategic position Italy finds herself compelled to link with her own by the closest possible ties the destinies of the Albanian people. Her method of doing so has not been always commendable; but if we may believe in the sincerity of Fascism's admission of that fact, we may also accept Signor Mussolini's declaration that Italy's primary interest in Albania is to preserve that country for the Albanians and from their neighbours. That in maintaining that primary interest Italy has destroyed the neutrality of Albania as established by the Powers in 1913, a neutrality which the Powers themselves destroyed and never re-established, and which the League of Nations failed to reassert, is a declaration which need not be taken seriously. One trusts that Italy will continue to act towards Albania in the spirit of her treaties with that country, and will never infringe the actual sovereignty and independence of Albania, *which must be maintained both in theory and in fact.*

Albania, wrote Gibbon, "is a country within sight of Italy which is less known than the interior of America". It was scarcely better known five years ago, and it was that fact which first induced me to go there. I had been led to expect that I should find a wild and lawless race; instead, I found a very prepossessing, gallant, and law-abiding people, with a passion for independence of which their neighbours disapproved. Their history is epitomized in a story told by the late Colonel Aubrey Herbert of an Albanian who was a native of an Albanian district annexed by Montenegro. He fled before the invaders, to Turkey. The Albanians had been the first of the Balkan races to attack the Turks, and accordingly he was bastinadoed and cast into prison. He escaped to Egypt. When the Great War broke out he was arrested as a Turk. When in prison he was beaten constantly by his fellow-prisoners, who were Turks, and considered him a traitor.

It has been my aim in this book—for which I claim no literary merit whatever—to give a clear and comprehensive account of the vicissitudes through which the Albanians have passed during the last fifty years, and to disprove the many mischievous statements of propagandists who have striven to conceal facts; and if, in pursuing that aim, I have brought up again incidents which are better forgotten, I have done so only in order to provide material on which a true appreciation of the Albanian question may be based. That is all I hope to do. I certainly do not claim infallibility, or to have exhausted all available sources of reference, but merely to have provided a *point d'appui* from which further research may be made. I was prompted to write the book by the complete absence of any satisfactory work upon the subject—a subject which interested me and appeared to be of considerable importance—and have done my best to provide one, while believing that it is better to produce a fairly comprehensive one now than an exhaustive one years hence. There are many better qualified than I for this task, but they have not undertaken it. I possess no special personal knowledge of any particular period—which has proved, perhaps, an advantage, as I have been influenced by no personal prejudices—but have collated the knowledge of those who have, and weighed the relative values of their statements. I have no doubt that those who have special knowledge will find faults, and I shall welcome any criticisms which are made in a scientific and constructive manner (but not any which may be made for the purpose of giving publicity to the critic). I hope that anyone who can add anything to what I have written, or make the smallest correction, will do so, in order that I may, if I am able to write further upon the subject of Albania, correct my mistakes.

As footnotes both add to the cost of publication and—in my opinion—are tiresome to the reader, I have used a system of index letters which is fully explained on the first page of the Bibliography. The Bibliography does not include books to which I have referred only cursorily. Obviously it is impossible in a book of reasonable size to give a reference for every fact stated, especially when gathered verbally (or in confidence), or from the Press, and therefore only enough references have been given to enable those who wish to do so to open the principal sources of reference which I have used. References are necessarily thicker where the Press has been consulted than where a book was the source of reference.

With regard to the spelling of place names, I must confess that I have attempted to do no more than ensure as far as possible that it is uniform throughout the text. My difficulty will be clear when I mention that most place names appear to have some six different forms (for example: Korcha, Kortcha, Koritza, Koritsa, Coritza, Coritsa, and sometimes confused with Konitza).

As no suitable maps existed, and as the cost of having them prepared by professional cartographers was prohibitive I was obliged to draw them myself, and am painfully aware of their shortcomings. I am very grateful to Messrs. Wace & Co., notably to Mr. A. E. Watkins, for careful reproduction of both the maps and illustrations. For the photographs facing page 214 I am indebted to Mr. William Walford, for that of Prenk Pasha (facing page 354) to Major D. Heaton-Armstrong, and for that of King Zog to "Marubbi", photographer, of Skutari, to all of whom I take this opportunity of expressing my thanks. Those who have ever had the misfortune to make an index will, I think, forgive the shortcomings of mine! The italics throughout the text are my own.

In conclusion I must express my gratitude to all those who have so readily helped me by supplying information, by giving advice, and by reading the manuscript or proofs. Foremost among them are His Highness Prince William of Albania, Prince of Wied, who discussed the incidents of his reign with the utmost frankness and provided me with a mass of valuable notes: Miss M. E. Durham, the well-known Balkan traveller and writer, who spared no pains to give me information and advice: Mr. Morton F. Eden, British Representative in Albania in 1919: Sir Harry Eyres, K.C.M.G., British Representative and Minister in Albania from 1921 to 1925: Major D. Heaton-Armstrong, formerly Prince William's private secretary in Albania, who placed at my disposal his most valuable manuscript, *Albania, the Six Months Kingdom*: Mehmed bey Konitza, Albanian Minister in London from 1922 to 1924, and his secretary Mrs. Furzeland: Sir Harry Lamb, K.C.M.G., British Commissioner in Albania in 1914: Mr. C. A. Macartney, author of *The Social Revolution in Austria*, etc., who laboriously read and criticized the book both in manuscript and in proof: Monsignor Fan S. Noli, Prime Minister of Albania in 1924: M. Lef Nosi, Albanian Minister of Posts and Telegraphs in 1912–13, and Delegate at the Peace Conference: General Pariani, commanding the Italian Military Mission in Albania: Count de Salis, K.C.M.G., British Minister in Montenegro from 1912 to 1915: Colonel W. F. Stirling, D.S.O., Adviser to the Albanian Minister of the Interior since 1923, and Mrs. Stirling, to whom I am indebted for much kindness and hospitality: Prince Michel Sturdza, Councillor of the Roumanian Legation at Washington, and Attaché of the Roumanian Legation in Durazzo in 1914, who placed at my disposal his most valuable manuscript, *L'Aventure Albanaise*: Professor A. J. Toynbee: and the staff of the Royal Institute of International Affairs, without whose assistance I should have been unable to obtain access to many important documents: and Signor Luigi Villari, M.C., the well-known writer and historian.

I am also indebted to His Majesty King Zog for answering several questions concerning his early activities, to Raouf bey Fiço, present Albanian Minister for Foreign Affairs, who gave me all the assistance which his official position would allow, to Midhat bey Frasheri, Albanian Minister of Public Works in 1914, Delegate at the Peace Conference, and Representative at Geneva, for information and several books, to M. Constantine Chekrezi, author of *Albania, Past and Present*, who answered an extensive questionnaire, to Mr. A. J. Brayley for assistance with the proofs and index, and to my very good friend Edhèm Kémal bey Vlora, for innumerable kindnesses while I was in Albania. There are many others whose names I would like to add to this list, only space forbids it. I must, however, mention my wife, my mother, and father, without whose support I should have been unable to carry through a task which has proved very much more formidable than I anticipated.

J. SWIRE

DALTON HOLME, BEVERLEY, E. YORKS,
      September, 1929

CHRONOLOGY

MODERN ALBANIA

(International events affecting Albanian history are shown in italics.)

A*

ALBANIA: THE RISE OF A KINGDOM

CHAPTER I

ALBANIA BEFORE THE TREATY OF BERLIN

ON the 26th July, 1880, Mr. G. T. (afterwards Lord) Goschen, then British Ambassador at Constantinople, sent to Lord Granville, then Secretary of State for Foreign Affairs, a telegram in which were included the following remarks:

"As ancient and distinct a race as any by whom they are surrounded, they [the Albanians] have seen the nationality of these neighbouring races taken under the protection of various European Powers and gratified in their aspirations for a more independent existence. They have seen the Bulgarians completely emancipated in Bulgaria and made masters in eastern Roumelia. They have seen the ardent desire of Europe to liberate territory inhabited by Greeks, from Turkish rule. They have seen the Slavs in Montenegro protected by the great Slav Empire of the north with enthusiastic pertinacity. They have seen the Eastern Question being solved on the principle of nationality and the Balkan Peninsula being gradually divided, as it were, among various races on that principle. Meanwhile they see that they themselves do not receive similar treatment. Their nationality is ignored; and territory inhabited by Albanians handed over in the north to the Montenegrins to satisfy Montenegro, the protégé of Russia, and in the south to Greece, the protégé of England and France. . . .

"If a strong Albania should be formed, the excuse for occupation by a foreign Power in the case of the dissolution of the Ottoman Empire would be greatly weakened. A united Albania would bar the remaining entrances to the north, and the Balkan Peninsula would remain in the

B

hands and under the sway of the races who now inhabit it. Otherwise the Albanians might be an insuperable difficulty at a time when troubles should arise. A population in great part Mussulman would be a source of the greatest difficulty to the Slav or Greek countries round it. . . . I consider that, in proportion as the Albanian nationality could be established, the probability of European intervention in the Balkan Peninsula would be diminished" (Accounts and Papers, 1880, Turkey, No. 15, Vol. LXXXI).

The boundaries within which lives this race were defined in the same year by Lord E. Fitzmaurice, British representative upon the Eastern Roumelian Commission, who, on the 26th May, wrote to the Foreign Office:

"The district covered by this geographical expression [Albania] falls mainly within the two vilayets of Skutari and Janina, but extends also in an easterly direction beyond the watershed of the mountains dividing the streams which fall into the Adriatic from those which fall into the Ægean Sea, and includes portions of the vilayet of Bitolia or Monastir, and of the vilayet of Prishtina or Kossovo. The extension of the Albanian population in a north-easterly direction towards Prishtina and Vranje is especially marked, and is fully acknowledged, even upon maps such as that of Kiepert [map p. 48], generally regarded as unduly favourable to the Slav element, and that published by Messrs. Stanford in the interest of the claims of the Greek Christian population. . . . The vilayet of Kossovo, with the exception of the Serb district extending eastward from Mitrovitza, may be said to be Albanian."

And on the 22nd July he wrote:

"Every map that I have seen of those districts (the greater part not only of the Kossovopolje, but also of the Metoja, and indeed the whole country up to the line of the rivers Bistritza and Drin, and the district of Ljuma, including Ipek and Prizren) marks them as Albanian and not as Slavonic, always excepting the Kossovopolje. It is, no doubt, true that these districts at the end of the seventeenth century were still mainly inhabited by Serbs, and once did form part of the old Serbian Kingdom, though M. Hahn is inclined to think that the aboriginal inhabitants were Albanians whom the Serbs dispossessed at a still earlier period of history" (Accounts and Papers, 1880, Turkey, No. 15, Vol. LXXXI.)

Yet at the Congress of Berlin in 1878 Bismarck had declared impatiently: "There is no Albanian nationality."

When these statements were made, the people within the confines of that "geographical expression" were but beginning to awake to national consciousness. Since those days fifty years have passed. Freedom is theirs; and the little Albanian State, although attenuated to gratify her neighbours, weakened by the blood shed for freedom and mourning the loss of her most prosperous lands and towns, strives to take an honourable place among the States of Europe. And she is succeeding. The race from which sprang so many of the Roman Emperors, and in more recent years Mehmed Ali Pasha— a native of Voskop, near Korcha—Admirals Miaoulis and Condouriotis, Marco Bochari, Repoulis, Crispi, the Köprülü —who originated at Rrochnik, near Berat—and no less than twenty other Grand Viziers, Ferid pasha Vlora, and a host of other famous men (L.S. 24–7), cannot fail to rise to power and prominence in the future.

There are few, if any, races in Europe whose passage through the ages has been more stormy than that of the Albanians. Yet despite differences of religion, social system, dialect, a subdivision of race, historical events which seldom affected all alike, the machinations of their neighbours, conquests which never forced them into the same mould, geographical features which kept them apart, the suppression by the Turks of any movement of a national character, and the absence since the death of Skenderbeg of any leader who had been universally respected—in short, despite every conceivable obstacle to national unity—the Albanians have preserved their racial individuality, language, and love of freedom.

Although it is difficult to construct a continuous history of the Albanians,

"one fact clearly stands out through all the centuries. Sheltered by their impassable mountains and defended by their own indomitable courage and fierce spirit of local independence, the Albanians alone of all the peoples of the Balkan Peninsula have safely weathered the storms of invasion. The Celts, the Romans, the Goths, the Serbs, the Bulgars, and the Turks successively overwhelmed them; but, though in each case all or part of them were nominally conquered, they emerged with their peculiar national characteristics as strong as ever. They have always succeeded in preserving their singular individuality and language, and, if any foreign elements forced their way among them, have assimilated them to their own type and culture, or rather, perhaps, lack of culture" (F.O. 31).

The history of the Albanian State dates in theory from the 28th November, 1912, but before her history as a State can be understood, the vicissitudes through which the Albanians have passed, and their relations with their neighbours, must be studied.

The Albanian race is probably descended from the earliest Aryan immigrants, and is represented in historical times by the Thraco-Illyrians and Epirots or Pelasgians who originally inhabited the whole of the Balkan Peninsula between the Danube and the Ægean (E.B. 4: 779, etc.). The Epirots are described by early Greek writers as non-Hellenic and barbarous, which is important in view of Greek pretensions to southern Albania; and Strabo wrote that the inhabitants of Macedonia, Illyria, and Epirus, spoke the same language and had similar customs.

Undoubtedly some proportion of that ancient civilization which is wholly attributed to the Greeks of the classical epoch may be claimed by the Albanians. Moreover, the modern Greek, with the exception perhaps of the inhabitants of the Ægean and other Greek islands, has in his veins but a negligible quantity of the blood which made the name of Greece immortal. "Owing to the operation of various causes, historical social, and economic", the population of modern Greece is "composed of many heterogeneous elements, and" represents "in a very limited degree the race which repulsed the Persians and built the Parthenon" (E.B. 12: 429). Its presumed descent from the Ancient Greeks has, however, proved a national asset of great value of which it has not failed to take advantage (E.B. 12: 429).

"In spite of its diﬆance from the chief centres of Greek thought and aﬄion, and the barbarous repute of its inhabitants, Epirus (= mainland) was believed to have exerted at an early period no small influence in Greece, by means, more especially, of the oracle of Dodona. . . . The States of Greece proper founded a number of colonies on its coaﬆ which formed ﬆepping-ﬆones towards the Adriatic and the Weﬆ" (E.B. 9: 698).

But Greek influence, even upon the coaﬆ, was rapidly superseded by Latin civilization after the third century B.C. (E.B. 14: 326).

There is to-day a slight racial diﬆinﬄion between the Albanians of the north and of the south; those of the north, the reserved and warlike Ghegs, among whom, during the laﬆ twenty years, the piﬄuresque fuﬆanella has been discarded in favour of close-fitting trousers and short jackets, being, it is thought, descendants of the Illyrians; and those of the south, the affable and more progressive Tosks, who continue to wear the fuﬆanella, being descendants of the Epirots or Pelasgians.

The Albanian language is remarkable as the only surviving representative of the so-called Thraco-Illyrian group, which formed the primitive speech of the Peninsula.

"The ancient Illyrian languages fall into two groups, the northern, closely conneﬄed with Venetic, and the southern, perhaps allied to Messapian, and now probably represented by Albanian" (E.B. 14: 326. See also T.E. 379–81).

It is considered the only reasonable interpretation of the names of the ancient Greek Gods. Both Ghegs and Tosks speak the same language, although it is but natural that wide dialeﬄal differences exiﬆ in a land where means of communication are ﬆill extremely limited.

From about 1200 to 167 B.C. the northern and central Albania of to-day were parts of the Kingdom of Illyria (Albanian: "liria" = freedom), which had as its capital Shkodra (Skutari). The Illyrian tribes seem to have lived in a ﬆate of continuous warfare with their neighbours and each other, and the earlier hiﬆory of the Macedonian Kings is one conﬆant ﬆruggle againﬆ them.

In about 600 B.C. took place the great barbaric invasion of

the Celts. But their effect upon the Balkan Peninsula was transitory and negligible.

The Illyrian Kingdom rose to the zenith of its power early in the fourth century B.C. under the rule of Bardhyllus (Bardh = White; hylla = star), whose Kingdom at one time extended from Trieste (Albanian for market-place) to the Gulf of Arta. Bardhyllus almost succeeded in destroying the rising Kingdom of Macedonia; but the Illyrians were eventually defeated, and their territory as far as Lake Ochrida annexed by the Great Philip in 358.

King Kleitos, son of Bardhyllus, was induced to follow his kinsman Alexander the Great—son of Philip II of Macedon—in his expedition against the Persian Empire, in which the Illyrian troops played a prominent part.

The death of Alexander restored to Illyria her liberty of action, and in 312 the Illyrian King Glaucius drove from Durazzo the Corcyreans and Corinthians, who had founded the town at the end of the seventh century B.C. (E.B. 8: 695); but while she was under the rule of the enterprising Queen Teuta, widow of King Agron, the depredations of her navy upon Roman commerce brought down upon her the might of Rome. There followed the Illyrian Wars (229 and 219 B.C.), which terminated to the advantage of the Romans, who annexed certain parts of the country. Illyria remained, however, a powerful and extensive kingdom until 180 B.C., when the Dalmatians proclaimed themselves independent, and established a Republic which survived until finally subjugated by the Romans in A.D. 9 after many years of fierce warfare.

The Romans again attacked the reduced Illyria in 168 B.C., and three years later her King, Gentius, was defeated at Skutari and brought to Rome. Thereafter, Illyria became a Roman dependency divided between the three provinces of Dalmatia, Macedonia, and Epirus. She became Rome's foremost recruiting area, and her sons doubtless assisted to hold the Britons in subjection!

Meanwhile, from 1270 to 168 B.C. the southern Albania of to-day, inhabited by fourteen independent Epirot or Pelasgian tribes, formed part of the Kingdom of Molossia ruled by a line of Kings who claimed descent from Pyrrhus, son of Achilles. Plutarch states that Achilles was known as "Aspatus", which in Albanian means "swift". The most prominent of these Kings was the famous Pyrrhus of Epirus, who ruled from

295 to 272 B.C. He was a formidable opponent of Demetrius, "King of Macedonia and the leading man in the Greek world" (E.B. 22:697). In 273 he wrested most of Macedonia from Antigonus Gonatas, son of Demetrius. The latter at once recovered it, but was again temporarily driven from his kingdom by Alexander, son of Pyrrhus, between 263 and 255 B.C.

It is asserted that from a remark to Pyrrhus that his troops must be "sons of the Eagle", since they were so mobile, originated the name that the Albanians give to themselves— Shqipetare. The Molossian troops took part with the Illyrians in the expedition of Alexander the Great, nephew of Alexander King of Molossia, against Persia.

In 168 B.C. after the battle of Pydna, the kingdom became a Roman province. "The difficulty experienced by the Romans in subduing and incorporating into the Empire these brave tribes is well known", wrote J. B. Bury.

Although Albania proved an excellent recruiting area for the Roman legions, and although a large proportion of the Prætorian Guard were Illyrians, Roman supremacy in Albania was never firmly established. Although Durazzo (ancient Epidamnus; Roman, Dyrrachium) was the head of the Via Egnatia by which the Roman legions marched into Asia, and although there are traces of Roman occupation throughout the country, yet Roman influence upon the history and character of the Albanians was slight, though upon the language considerable. The Vlachs, however, of whom there are large numbers in Epirus and the Pindus mountains, preserving their distinctive nationality, customs, and Latin language, "apparently descend from the Latinized provincials of the Roman epoch, who took refuge in the higher mountains from the incursions of the barbarians and Slavs" (E.B. 12: 430.)

It was during the Roman occupation that Christianity was introduced into Albania by St. Paul, who visited, among other places, Durazzo. "Round about into Illyricum", he wrote, "I have fully preached the Gospel of Christ".

In A.D. 395, with the disruption of the Roman Empire, Albania became part of the eastern or Byzantine Empire, divided between the provinces of Dyrrachium (Durazzo) and Nicopolis. The Bishoprics of Skutari and Antivari seem to have been created at about this time.

Then swept down from the north the barbarian Goths, Huns, and Avars. Their ravages thinned the Illyrian population in those territories, now Yugoslav, which the Illyrians had occupied for centuries, and drove southwards the majority of the survivors, while the remainder sought refuge in the mountainous Dalmatian coastal regions.

In A.D. 535 the Emperor Justinian drove out the Goths, but in A.D. 640 the Serbs and Croats, who had first crossed the Danube in strength in A.D. 550, were invited by the Emperor Heraclius to assist him against the Avars. They overran the Peninsula, which had been to some extent depopulated by the previous barbarian invasions, and settled principally in the districts which are now North Serbia, Bosnia, the Hertzegovina, Croatia, Slavonia, and northern Montenegro. It seems improbable that they penetrated in strength into the southern part of the Peninsula, but many undoubtedly eventually fled southwards before the Bulgarians, who followed them. They were quickly subjugated by Byzantium.

After two centuries of almost continuous warfare with the Byzantine Empire, the Bulgarians, a Turanian race akin to the Tartars, who first crossed the Danube towards the end of the seventh century A.D., succeeded in overrunning, under their progressive Tzar Simeon the Great (893 to 927), most of the Peninsula. Their dominion extended from the Black Sea to the Adriatic, including the whole of the Albanian lowlands and Montenegro, and from the borders of Thessaly to the Save and the Carpathians (E.B. 4:780). The Serbs were crushed and either fled to remote parts of the Peninsula or intermarried with the conquerors; the still further reduced Illyrian population shared their fate. The Bulgarians firmly established themselves, and Simeon became the most powerful Monarch of eastern Europe. After his death, however, his Empire split in two and a fresh western Empire, including Albania and Macedonia, was founded at Ochrida by Shishman, a Bulgarian nobleman. Under Samuel, son of Shishman (976 to 1014), this Empire was extended to include the greater part of the Peninsula from the Danube to the Morea.

Bulgarian supremacy was crushed in 1014 by the Emperor Basil II at the battle of Kleidion, and Byzantine power re-established. Traces of the Bulgarian conquest still remain outside the boundaries of modern Bulgaria, especially around

Monastir and in South Serbia, where Bulgarians and Albanians comprise the bulk of the population.

In 1081 the Normans, under Robert Guiscard, captured Durazzo after a gallant defence by George Palaeologus, and invaded central and southern Albania in warfare against the Byzantine Empire. It is believed that they were the originators of the name Albania. During the Crusades, too, the country was frequently a thoroughfare for the Crusading armies. Durazzo, which had been treacherously surrendered, was again, but unsuccessfully, besieged by Guiscard's son, Bohemund, in 1107.

There were evolved from this period of invasions several independent Albanian principalities ruled by foreign Princes with the consent or by invitation of the people. In A.D. 1204 the Crusaders participating in the Fourth Crusade resolved, for their own private ends and in view of the schism which had arisen between Rome and the Eastern Church, that instead of proceeding to the Holy Land they would attack Constantinople. The city was captured largely owing to the skill of the Venetian forces which participated in the expedition, and Venice accordingly received as part of her spoil the eastern shores of the Adriatic. But a Prince of the overthrown rulers of Byzantium, Michael Comnenus, gathered around him the Albanian nobility, drove the Venetians from southern Albania, Acarnania, and Ætolia, and set up an independent principality with Janina as its capital—the Despotat of Epirus. The Comneni claimed Roman origin, but the earliest representatives of the family appear to have been landed proprietors in the district of Kastamuni in Asia Minor (E.B. 6 : 793).

It was at about this period that the Albanians of the south, who had hitherto adhered to the Patriarchate of Rome, seceded therefrom under Byzantine influence to the Orthodox Church, while the Catholics of the north remained faithful to Rome.

In 1169 Stefan Nemanya had succeeded in uniting most of the Serbian provinces in the north under his rule, and thereupon founded a dynasty. By 1180 the Serbs had brought northern Albania, including Skutari and Prizren, under their sway, slaughtering a large proportion of the Albanians who did not fly before them or successfully defy them in the mountains (A.S. 32, etc.).

But in 1205 the Bulgarians, who in 1186 had successfully

revolted against Byzantium, defeated Baldwin Count of Flanders, founder of the Latin Empire at Constantinople; and the second Bulgarian Empire shortly afterwards reached the zenith of its power. Belgrade, Nish, and Uskub were included within it, and between 1218 and 1241 Ivan Asen II established his suzerainty over Albania, Epirus, Macedonia, and Thrace. Shortly after his death, however, the Empire disintegrated. Tzar Asen seems to have governed his Balkan possessions with efficiency and moderation, and in marked contrast to the "hateful and abominable lordship of the Slavs".

In 1222 Theodore Comnenus had conquered Thessaly and overrun Macedonia, which he had ruled until defeated and captured by the Bulgarians in 1230. But Tzar Asen married his daughter, his brother and successor, Manuel, married Asen's daughter, and the Despotat continued to exist more or less as an independent principality, ruled by Comneni until 1318, and thereafter by the Orsini until 1358.

In the middle of the fourteenth century the Despotat was overrun by Albanians (Illyrians or Ghegs) under Jin Bua Spata and Peter Liosha, who were driven from the north by the Serbs under Stefan "Dushan". These Albanians took Janina and Arta, displacing Tosks, who thereupon moved south and established extensive settlements in Greece, which have never been absorbed. Finlay estimated in 1851 that of a total population of Greece of one million, 200,000 were Albanians (Greek: Arvanitæ. E.B. 12: 428 and 465); and in 1879 it was estimated that 58,858 persons spoke Albanian only (E.B. 12: 428; O.J. February, 1925).

"The Albanian population extends over all Attica and Megaris (except the towns of Athens, Peiræus, and Megara), the greater part of Bœotia, the eastern districts of Locris, the southern half of Eubœa, and the northern side of Andros, the whole of the islands of Salamis, Hydra, Spetsæ [L.S. 13] and Poros, and part of Ægina, the whole of Corinthia and Argolis, the northern districts of Arcadia, and the eastern portion of Achæa. There are also small Albanian groups in Laconia and Messenia. . . . The process of their Hellenization, which scarcely began till after the establishment of the [Greek] kingdom, has been somewhat slow; most of the men can now speak Greek, but Albanian is still the language of the household . . . they furnish the best soldiers in the Greek army and also make excellent sailors" (E.B. 12: 430).

In an article in the Greek monthly magazine, *Parnassos* (February, 1916: C.C. 206), it is stated that "the majority of our soldiers speak to one another in the Albanian language . . . a very deplorable habit. . . . It is expedient that this habit be destroyed by all necessary and vigorous means". Prince Lichnowsky wrote: "the so-called Greek national dress itself is of Albanian origin".

At the beginning of the fifteenth century Charles II Tocco, Lord of Cephalonia and Zante, assumed the title of Despot of Epirus, and was recognized by the Emperor Manuel Comnenus. But his family was deprived of its possessions in 1431 by Murad (Amurath) II.

In 1268 a ruler of the Despotat had ceded to Manfred, King of Sicily, Corfu, Durazzo, Valona, Tchamouria, Vutrinto, and Berat as part of the dowry of his daughter, whom he married to Manfred to secure his alliance. But the Pope, whose displeasure Manfred had incurred, thought fit to dispose of his crown, in 1266, to Charles of Anjou, by whom he was defeated and slain at Benevento. In 1271 Charles entered into negotiations with the Albanian chieftains, which resulted in the formation of the "Albanian Kingdom" of the Angevin princes, which lasted until 1368, despite constant warfare with Byzantium, the Bulgarians, and Serbs, against whom the chieftains loyally co-operated.

With the exception of Filippo, Prince of Taranto and grandson of Charles, the Angevin rulers spent little time in their Albanian Kingdom, and the country remained divided into small feudal estates under native chieftains, who regarded the Angevin princes as suzerain protectors rather than rulers. In 1294 Durazzo became an independent duchy under John— another grandson of Charles of Anjou—and thereafter under Filippo of Taranto until 1333, when it was annexed to Achæa and captured by the Serbs in 1336.

Under Tzar Stefan "Dushan" (1331–58) the Serbs had reasserted themselves and reached the zenith of their power. The Bulgarians had been defeated in 1330 at the battle of Velbuzhd, and for a brief period "Dushan" brought the whole of Albania nominally under his suzerainty. The Despotat owed him fealty. But upon his death his kingdom broke up and was divided among his provincial governors or feudal lords.

"That the Albanians were, when conquered by the Serbs, Catholic, is evident from contemporary accounts. In 1321 they appealed to Charles of Anjou and to Filippo of Taranto to force the Serb King Milutin to respect their religious rights. In 1332 the French friar, Père Brochard, described the land and people. 'It is inhabited', he said, 'by two peoples, the Albanians and the Latins, who both belong to the Church of Rome. The Albanians have a language quite other than Latin. . . . They have four Bishops under the Archbishop of Antivari. . . . Both these peoples are oppressed under the very hard servitude of the most hateful and abominable lordship of the Slavs.'

"That the friar did not exaggerate is shown by the extremely severe laws enacted against the Catholics by the great Tzar Stefan "Dushan" in 1349 in his celebrated canon. Here we find that those of the Latin heresy who refuse to be converted are punishable by death, as are also Latin priests who attempt to convert anyone to the Latin faith. And so forth" (A.Q.).

Upon the collapse of Stefan "Dushan's" ephemeral Empire, the Governor of the Serb principality of Zeta, which included the Hertzegovina, Montenegro, and northern Albania, assumed the title of Balsha I, and formed an independent Albanian State (1366–1421) with Skutari as its capital. Balsha was, it is alleged, a Norman (F.O. 60) knight who had entered the service of Stefan "Dushan".

From Alessio throughout the extreme north of Albania ruled the Dukaghin, while the northern part of the "Kingdom of Albania", including Durazzo and Kruja, was ruled by the Topia (1358–92), and thereafter by the Castriota, the Spani, and Dushmani; and the southern part by the Muzaki (1368–1476), Zaccaria, Gropa, and Bua Spata. It appears that the Balshas succeeded in uniting these chieftains and in driving out the Serbs and Bulgarians. Ochrida, Kastoria, Ipek, and Prizren were wrested from Marko Kraljevitch in 1373.

The power of the Balshas was short-lived, and towards the end of the fourteenth century the Venetians once more obtained possessions in Albania, including Durazzo (1394), Skutari, and Antivari, as the price of a defensive alliance against a fresh and formidable foe from the east, whose victory over the Serbs at Kossovo (1389) and capture of Trnovo, the Bulgarian capital (1393), had shaken Christendom. Fortunately, the Turkish armies were for the next thirty years too fully occupied by internal strife, and by repelling attempts to drive them from the lands they had already occupied, to undertake fresh conquests. In 1421 the Balsha dynasty came to an end with the death of Balsha III, and in the meantime there came the inevitable invasion. One by one the Albanian feudal chieftains, including John Castriota of Kruja, were forced to submission. The latter was allowed to retain his independence under Turkish suzerainty, but as proof of his good faith, so the story goes, was compelled to give as hostages his four sons, the youngest of whom was destined to win fame throughout Europe and to be immortalized as the national hero of his country. Janina was taken in 1431, Arta in 1449, and shortly afterwards the suzerainty of Murad II was established, although only nominally, throughout Albania.

The four young hostages were sent to the Turkish capital to be trained for the Ottoman service. George, the youngest, born in 1403, by his great ability and strength, soon won the Sultan's favour; he was promoted to high military rank and was entrusted with the administration of a sanjak. He became a nominal Mussulman, and so distinguished himself by his valour and strategy that he was named Iskender Bey (Albanian: Skenderbeg = Prince Alexander) in complimentary reference to Alexander the Great.

Upon the death of John Castriota, one of his four sons should have succeeded him. But Skenderbeg's elder brothers had been disposed of by poison; and Skenderbeg himself was considered by the Sultan to be sufficiently favoured, more useful, and less dangerous, in the Turkish service. Accordingly, a Turkish Governor, Sabel Pasha, was installed at Kruja. Skenderbeg concealed his indignation, but resolved to return to his home and religion at the first opportunity. In 1443 his patience was rewarded when the victorious John Hunyadi, at the head of a combined army of Hungarians and Serbs routed at Nish the Turkish army in which Skenderbeg held a command. During its flight Skenderbeg extorted from the Sultan's secretary an imperial order instructing Sabel Pasha to surrender to him the fortress and Governorship of Kruja. After a seven-day forced march Skenderbeg arrived at Kruja with a handful of loyal Albanians, the unsuspecting Pasha readily surrendered the fortress, and the red flag bearing the black double-headed eagle—the emblem of Skenderbeg—was hoisted above its battlements. Longfellow graphically related this stirring incident in *Tales of a Wayside Inn*.

Skenderbeg abjured the Moslem faith and embraced Roman Catholicism. On the 1st March, 1444, a gathering of Albanian chieftains in the Cathedral of Alessio, attended by the Prince of Montenegro—Stefan Crnoievich—and by delegates of the Venetian Republic, proclaimed Skenderbeg "Chief of the League of the Albanian People"; and the whole of Albania, including the greater part of Epirus, united under his leadership against the common aggressor.

The enraged Sultan now began a series of ruthless campaigns against Skenderbeg, which lasted, with brief interludes, until his death. Again and again the Moslems hurled themselves against Albania, the last bulwark of Christianity in the Balkans, only to be shattered by the little army of scarcely thirty thousand men, led by its resolute commander, and to roll back broken and powerless. Twice was Kruja unsuccessfully besieged. It is indeed a remarkable story of which any race might be proud, for beyond supplies of arms and money from Venice, Skenderbeg received no assistance. In 1449 Murad II himself was routed by the Albanians, and subsequently the Conqueror of Constantinople, Mohammed II, was driven from Albania and compelled to acknowledge Skenderbeg ruler of Albania and Epirus by a temporary truce. Thereupon, in 1461, Skenderbeg undertook an expedition to Italy to protect his friend Ferdinand, King of Naples, against the Angevin Kings of Sicily. Upon his return he was again attacked by the Turks; but again he was successful. He then attempted to go to the aid of John Hunyadi, but was opposed and delayed by the Serb Despot, George Brankovitch, who thus enabled the Turks to crush Hunyadi at Varna. Death overtook Skenderbeg in the year 1467 at Alessio, where he was buried in the Cathedral. When the news reached the Sultan, he exclaimed triumphantly: "Asia and Europe are mine at last. Woe to Christendom! She has lost her sword and shield" (A.Q.).

Upon his death-bed, Skenderbeg, who was succeeded by

his young son, Giovanni, placed Albania under the protection of Venice. But Giovanni was unable to hold the chieftains together, and being without resources adequate to continue the struggle against the aggressor, abandoned in 1474 his rights in favour of the Venetians. Four years later Kruja was captured by the Turks, and Skutari in 1479, after an heroic defence by 1,700 Albanians and Venetians against 40,000 Moslems. The siege of Skutari, which lasted for fifteen months, is remarkable both for the prominent part which women played in its defence and for the employment of incendiary shells by the Turks.

In 1479 peace was concluded between Venice and Turkey, but their conflicting interests soon brought about a renewal of hostilities. In 1501 Durazzo was lost, and Venice was obliged to renounce all claim to Albania, with the exception of Dulcigno and Antivari, which remained in her hands until 1571. One by one the Albanian chiefs were subjugated, or, as did the Dukaghin (Venetian: Duca = Dux = leader) sought refuge abroad in Sicily, Naples, Venice, or elsewhere; and with the fall of the last-mentioned ports the whole of Albania—with the exception of the mountainous districts—passed under the heel of the Turk. The tribes of the Albanian Alps, of the districts of Mirdita, Mati, Ljuma, and in the south of the Tchamouria, succeeded in retaining their internal independence throughout the four centuries of Turkish rule which followed, carrying on an intermittent guerilla warfare with the Turks, who never considered their subjugation worth while.

The defeat of the Turks at Lepanto in 1571 encouraged the Albanians (Turkish: Arnauts) to renew their efforts for freedom. An insurrection took place in the north, and the Crown was offered to Charles Emmanuel of Savoy and to the Duke of Parma; but neither felt inclined to undertake the task of evicting the Turks.

In 1623 a Turkish army retiring from Montenegro was cut to pieces in the northern highlands of Albania; but a punitive expedition crushed the insurrection.

Shortly after the defeat in 1683 of the Turkish armies besieging Vienna by John Sobieski, the army of the Holy Roman Empire under Piccolomini, in conjunction with the Venetians, invaded the Balkans, which encouraged the Albanians to revolt again. Piccolomini died while in the Peninsula, and was succeeded in command by the Duke of

Holstein, whose arrogant conduct alienated the Albanians, who withdrew their support. He retired into Hungary in 1690.

The Serbian population of Kossovo, under Turkish rule since 1389, and constantly harassed by the Albanians, who regarded the Slavs as intruders and usurpers of their lands, availed themselves of the protection of the retreating Austro-Hungarian army to retire across the Danube. Led by the Serbian Archbishop of Ipek, Arsen Crnoievich, some 37,000 Serbian family groups migrated at the invitation of the Emperor Leopold I into Austria-Hungary, where they settled in the Banat. The Emperor feared that the Serbs, if they remained, might come to terms with the Turks and establish a power in the path of Austrian expansion. The land evacuated by the Serbs was occupied by Moslem Albanians, and thus was restored to its original owners. But when during the present century the Serbs found that their claims to that land upon historical grounds carried little weight, and upon sentimental grounds no weight whatever, owing to the fierce hostility of the Moslem Albanians, M. Tomitch of the Belgrade National Library, ingeniously "discovered" that the above migration had never taken place and that those Moslem Albanians actually were Albanized descendants of the Serbs (D.F.)! Needless to say, this theory has made no headway against the mass of historical evidence to the contrary (A.S. 32. Also *Blgarite v' Makedoniza*: Jordan Ivanoff: Sofia, 1915).

Thus did the Albanians regain possession of that region which is now central Serbia, as the Serbs themselves acknowledged (A.Q.), although a few Serbs flowed back again as time went on. In a report upon the population of north-eastern Albania dated the 27th August, 1880, Mr. Alvarez, of the British Consulate at Constantinople, wrote:

"The races which inhabit this district, which politically comprises the greater part of the vilayet of Kossovo and part of that of Monastir and the whole of Old or Turkish Serbia, are the Albanian and the Serb. . . . Of the two, the Albanians are numerically far superior to the Serbians who are not numerous in the Kossovopolje and the Sanjak of Novibazar. . . . The Albanian element in the Kossovo vilayet has recently been further increased by the accession of many thousands of refugees from districts now, in virtue of the Treaty of Berlin, in Serbian possession, which, prior to the late war, were exclusively inhabited by the descendants of twelve Gheg tribes which at a remote period emigrated from Upper Albania. . . . The natural hatred existing between the Arnauts (Albanians) and the Serbians of the principality, fanned by the late war, has been intensified by the expulsion of Ghegs (north Albanians) in large numbers from the territory lately acquired by Serbia."

(See also: E.B. 1: 483; 3: 259, map, and 15: 916; F.O. 24; T. 22. 9. 25; A.R., October, 1918; G.J., July, 1918; C.C. 93; A.S. Statistics; A.S. refs. in footnotes on pp. 3, 5, 6, 15–21, 23, 33–4, 35–8, 40, 41; C.E. 194; P.D. 52: 2298; H. N. Brailsford's *Macedonia*; W.P.; etc.)

In 1718 Albania was again a battlefield for Turks and Venetians, and the latter sustained a crushing defeat at Dulcigno. Nineteen years later combined Austro-Hungarian and Russian armies invaded the Balkans, and the Albanians seized the opportunity to rise; but the Turks were eventually victorious and the Albanians again subjugated.

From the defeat of the Turks by John Sobieski in 1683 dates the decline of the Ottoman Empire. As it declined, bribery, corruption, and the power of its local governors increased, and an eleventh-hour attempt to stay the rot brought about its ultimate downfall.

In the middle of the eighteenth century an Albanian, Mehmed Bushati, of the Skutari district, had acquired more influence than the Porte thought desirable. But through the agency of the Sultan's emissary sent to suppress him he succeeded by bluff in obtaining the title of Hereditary Pasha of Skutari. Vested with this title Mehmed lost no time in imposing his authority upon the few surviving rival chieftains of the north, and shortly succeeded in uniting northern and central Albania under his leadership. He captured Dulcigno, which had become a pirate stronghold, and burnt the pirate fleet. He then negotiated with Vienna for arms and money with which to throw off Turkish suzerainty. He had accomplished what the Turks had striven to prevent, and had brought about a national union of tribes and chieftains in the most inaccessible part of the Empire. Ali Pasha was commissioned to suppress him, and contrived his assassination. But his son, Mahmoud "the Black", proved even more capable and

C

enterprising. He defeated his rival Kurd, the hereditary Pasha of Berat. In 1785 he defeated the Montenegrins and invaded the possessions of the Venetian Republic. Venice appealed to the Sultan, but Mahmoud routed the Turkish army sent against him in the Kossovopolje in 1786 and annexed that district. Another Turkish army in conjunction with Ali Pasha of Janina invested Skutari, but Ali's contingent deserted to Mahmoud with all the Turkish artillery. A third army was destroyed in Mirdita. Mahmoud was eventually slain by the Montenegrins.

In 1829 Mustafa pasha Bushati fought against the Turks during the Russo-Turkish War. With 35,000 men he entered Bulgaria and occupied Nish. In 1831, with 20,000 Albanians, Mustafa joined the Bosnian insurgents under Hussein Aga; the combined armies occupied Bulgaria and parts of Macedonia. But a dispute contrived by the Turks between the two leaders led to a dissolution of their partnership. Reshid Pasha then fell upon each in turn and the Albanians were defeated at Prilep. Mustafa was, after a four months' siege at Skutari, compelled to surrender. The Hereditary Pashalike ceased to exist, and a Turkish Governor was installed.

Ali Pasha, known as "the Lion of Janina", was born in 1740 of a Tepeleni family whose head had held the hereditary position of Bey of that town. Bold, cunning, and cruel, he began his career as a guerilla leader, for which profession he had been "educated" by his mother, Khamko. She had formed and led a band of irregulars with the object of avenging her husband, who had been killed by neighbouring chieftains, and of regaining the property and position which the family had lost. At last Ali secured power in and around his native town, and, to consolidate it, murdered his brother and imprisoned his mother on the charge of attempting to poison him. He then contracted a marriage tie with the leading family of Delvino, and thus widened the sphere of his influence. The next step was to remove his father-in-law and instal himself in his place; and this he did by denouncing him as a traitor. He succeeded in ingratiating himself with the Porte, and in recognition of his services against Mehmed Bushati was appointed Lieutenant to the Derwend-Pasha of Roumelia. By connivance with the brigands, whom it was his duty to suppress, he amassed considerable wealth. In recognition of the part he played in the war with Russia in 1787, he became

Pasha of Trikkala in Thessaly and Derwend-Pasha of Roumelia, and, a year later, Pasha of Janina. He then suppressed his brigand friends, and retained the confidence of the Porte by the cruel discipline he enforced and by tribute and bribes, meanwhile by the most unscrupulous methods eliminating other leading families which stood in the path of his ambition to form an Albanian Kingdom.

When the Venetian Republic was overthrown by Napoleon, the French occupied the Ionian Islands and certain coast towns held by the Venetians which Ali wished to possess. Russia, fearing that French influence in the Balkans would replace her own, especially as the French had entered into relations with Ali, concluded an alliance with the Sultan, whereupon Ali, once more becoming an ardent Turk, drove the French from the coast, and gained possession of Vutrinto, Prevesa, and Vonitza. He was created Pasha "of three tails" by the Sultan, and congratulated by Nelson. He was appointed Governor of the whole of Albania from the Gulf of Arta to Montenegro and of Thessaly, and, in 1799, Vali of Roumelia. He never succeeded, however, in subduing northern Albania, where the Bushati successfully defied him. He had previously married his two sons, Mouktar and Veli, who were subsequently appointed Governors of Lepanto and the Greek Peloponnesus respectively, to the two daughters of Ibrahim Pasha, head of the Vlora (Valona) family and Governor of Valona and Berat, by way of consolidating his power. But Ibrahim had now outlived his usefulness, Ali announced to the Porte that he was under French influence, attacked, defeated, and captured him, and imprisoned him at Janina, where he died twelve years later.

Ali always clothed his nefarious deeds with the justification that he was reducing disaffected districts or chieftains to obedience to the Sultan!

The Christian Albanians of Suli had defied Ali since 1788. They were descendants of emigrants from northern Albania in the fourteenth century: and with conspicuous bravery had repulsed his successive attempts to storm their crags. But in 1803 he suppressed them after a fierce struggle, and the last obstacle to his absolute power was removed. Thenceforward he negotiated with Russia, France, and Great Britain as suited his purpose, built ports along his coast, strengthened his castles in the interior, and consolidated his power, contemplating complete independence.

The Sultan, however, became alarmed at his growing power; and when, in 1820, he attempted to procure the assassination of a personal enemy, Pacho Bey, within the Palace at Stamboul, he was declared a rebel. An army under Khurshid Pasha was sent against him with which many dispossessed Albanian chieftains co-operated. After an eighteen months' siege at Janina Ali capitulated in 1822; and was treacherously assassinated. The State he had created then ceased to exist, but his example encouraged the Greeks to strike for independence (E.B. 1 : 659).

While the Turkish armies were besieging Janina, the Greeks struck their first blow. Ali Pasha had done much to foster Greek discontent in order to weaken Turkish power; and the precedent of the French Revolution, the decline of the Turkish Empire, a literary revival, and Russian intrigue since 1774—when Russia had claimed the right to protect the Orthodox Christian subjects of the Porte—had all combined to foster the spirit of nationalism. That success crowned the efforts of the insurgents was due principally (T.E. 299) to the Orthodox Albanian inhabitants of Greece, who fought for liberty with their co-religionists. "Where Orthodox Albanians and Greeks dwelt together", wrote Finlay (VI. 40) . . . "their common lot as Christians exposed them to the same exactions", and in consequence the distinction of race was effaced while they struggled against the common foe. Many of the principal leaders of the Greek insurrection such as Marco Bochari, the Suliot leader Djavella Andrucho, and Karaiskakis, had been military commanders under Ali Pasha (S.A. 9); and the commercial fleet of the Albanian islands, Hydra and Spetsæ, under Admiral Miaoulis, himself a descendant of Albanian immigrants, saved the insurrection from failure.

The crisis through which the Ottoman Empire passed during the Greek insurrection, the Russo-Turkish War of 1828-9, and the Albanian insurrections, coupled with the growth of nationalism in Serbia, accentuated the need for drastic reforms. As a preliminary measure, steps were taken by Turkey to tighten her grip upon her possessions and curtail the power of the local Governors. Especially in Albania, where the achievements of the Bushati and Ali Pasha, particularly the latter (T.E. 368), and the ties which existed between the Albanian leaders of the Greek insurrection and the principal Albanian families had tended to revive the spirit of nationalism, did the Porte endeavour to consolidate its authority. But although Ali's example had fired many Albanians with national enthusiasm, and although by breaking the power of local chieftains he had destroyed many petty rivalries which hitherto had kept the adherents of those chieftains apart, yet at the same time, by concentrating the power in his own hands and crushing the leading families, he had facilitated the task of the Porte in reducing southern Albania to submission, once he himself was removed. For example, with the subjugation by Ali of Tchamouria and Suli disappeared the last vestiges of the tribal organization in the south, and with Ali's fall those districts became subject to Turkish authority. Moreover, the natural sympathy of Christian Albanians with the Greek insurgents, founded upon a common creed which inspired a desire for a common culture as opposed to Turkish culture— or lack of it—tended to widen the breach between them and Albanian Moslems, of whom many fought for the Turks. Lastly, the rivalry between Ali and the Bushati had aroused a certain amount of jealousy and hostility between the Tosks and Ghegs, which was accentuated among the latter by a suspicion that the former were falling under Hellenic influence, a suspicion which was only mitigated by the outcome of the Tosk insurrection in 1854. In consequence of this jealousy, the growth of nationalism was retarded, and on several occasions one subdivision of the race co-operated with the Turks in suppressing an abortive insurrection by the other.

At the close of the Russo-Turkish War, Reshid Pasha was sent to Janina to re-establish order and strengthen the authority of the Sultan in Albania. Having defeated the Albanians under Silehdar Poda, Pasha of central Albania, and Veli Bey, Governor of Janina, he invited five hundred Albanian leaders to negotiate with him at Monastir and treacherously assassinated them. Men of obscure or foreign origin were thrust forward to administer the districts over which they had hitherto held sway under the suzerainty of the Sultan. Reshid Pasha then proceeded to crush the Bushati in northern Albania, where he pursued the same policy; but although Mustafa surrendered in 1831, the tribesmen, inspired by his example, revolted throughout the north no less than three times, in 1835, 1836, and 1842, and on several occasions locally, before Turkish authority was established. During 1849, 1851, and 1852, several of the northern tribes co-operated with the Montenegrins against the Turks, but during 1853 and 1856 the Mirdites supported the Turks against the Montenegrins. In 1862, two thousand Mirdites under Bib Doda again co-operated with the Turks under Omer Pasha against the Montenegrins, and it was only through the intervention of Russia that Cettinje was saved.

In 1847 an attempt was made to enforce further reforms in southern Albania, including direct taxation and compulsory military service. This resulted in a general rising of both Christians and Moslems under the leadership of Ghion Lek, Mahmoud Vlora, Selim Pasha, and others. Fierce fighting ensued and continued for several months; but the Albanians were outnumbered. Greek support which had been promised did not materialize, and although the Turks, supported by Mirdites, suffered several reverses, the insurrection was quelled. It was followed by the wholesale arrest and deportation of the leading families, while thousands of insurgents fled abroad. But the Turks soon realized that drastic measures in Albania would accelerate rather than retard the growth of nationalism. Accordingly, the stringent regulations which had been imposed were relaxed, the exiled chiefs were reinstated, and Upper and Lower Albania were placed under the administration of Ismail pasha Plassa, resident at Prizren, and Ismail Rahmy Pasha, resident at Janina. Both were Albanians, the latter being a grandson of Ali Pasha. In 1865 the country was split into the four vilayets of Skutari, Janina, Kossovo, and Monastir, each with its own Vali and garrison.

The effect of the Turkish occupation of Albania may be summarized in one word, namely, stagnation. Turkey gave her neither schools nor roads nor advantages of any description, and, with the exception of a few ramshackle barracks and custom houses, relinquished her in much the same condition as she found her. The intrepid highlanders of northern Albania were never subjugated, principally because the Turks never considered that the expenditure of blood and money which would have been necessary would be repaid by the conquest of the wild and rugged districts which they inhabited. Therefore, except that they rendered voluntary military service to Turkey in time of war and when so disposed, and occasionally so provoked the Turks that a punitive expedition was sent against them, Turkish suzerainty only affected them to the extent that it isolated them from the world; and, untrammelled by the march of "civilization", they preserved their mediæval laws, traditions, customs, and ignorance until the present century. Miss M. E. Durham, "Queen of the malissori", as she was called by them, has dealt exhaustively and graphically with their customs and social organization, but a few brief details here are necessary, that their part in Albanian history may be understood.

Each "fisse" (= family, i.e. all persons with a common male ancestor, who may not intermarry), tribe, or "bairak" (= standard; some of the larger tribes, i.e. "far" = group of families—are divided into two or more bairaks, each having a separate male ancestor) sank into obscurity among their mountains. The tribesman's country became his valley and his chief the hereditary military leader or "bairaktar" (standard-bearer); loyalty to country became loyalty to bairak; and between tribes there inevitably arose disputes which could be settled in one way only—by bloodshed.

Each bairak is divided into "mehalas", or groups of houses, presided over by the "krue" or "jobars", whose position and privileges, like those of the bairaktar, are hereditary. Each mehala is again subdivided into single houses (shpis) presided over by their house lord (Zoti i shpis). Supreme power rested with the assembly (Kuven) of the whole tribe.

The tribesmen recognized no law but that of Lek Dukaghin, administered within each bairak by a council of Elders (Plekniya) over which the bairaktar presided. Lek lived during the fourteenth century, and legislated minutely on all subjects. He was evidently

"of insistent individuality to have so influenced the people that 'Lek said so' obtains far more obedience than the Ten Commandments. The teachings of Islam and of Christianity, the Sheriat and Church Law, all have to yield to the Canon of Lek. . . . Lek possibly put together the then existing tribe law, but his own laws are probably those only that are designed to check or reform old usage by enforcing punishment (H.A. 25, 27). . . .

. . . "The Canon of Lek had but two punishments, fine and burning of property. Neither death nor imprisonment can be inflicted. Prison there is none. Death

would but start a new feud. And Lek's object appears to
have been to check feud" (H.A. 33), in which he failed;
and, the preservation of unblemished honour being the
principal aim of the tribesman's existence, feuds, originat-
ing in the merest trivialities such as a blow accidentally
struck, and involving the families of the principals, raged
throughout the highlands.

"Blood vengeance, slaying a man according to the
laws of honour, must not be confounded with murder.
Murder starts a blood feud. In blood vengeance, the rules
of the game are strictly observed. A man may not be shot
for vengeance when he is with a woman nor with a
child, nor when he is met in company, nor when *besa*
(oath of peace) has been given. The two parties may
swear such an oath for a few weeks if they choose for
business purposes"

or to repel the attacks of a common foe. To have shot four
men in defence of honour, and to have been burnt out four
times in consequence, was no exceptional record. Abduction
of a girl necessitated the taking of blood, as also did adultery,
but the latter offence was rarely committed, being contrary
to the Maltsor's (= Mountain man: plural, Maltsors or
Malissori) moral sense; and that his moral sense is high—
higher indeed than in many western countries—there is no
shadow of doubt. But lest anyone be inclined to exclaim that
blood vengeance is the custom of savages, let him remember
that it is not so long since the practice of duelling prevailed in
western Europe, whereas the malissori are only now emerging
from conditions of environment and existence which have in
no whit changed since the early Middle Ages, except that
modern weapons have replaced the pistol and yataghan. Many
tribesmen recognized that feuds were the curse of the land,
and to a competent incorruptible government and gendarmerie
were willing enough to lay down their arms, provided they
were assured of protection from the Slav, and to submit their
disputes to arbitration. But during the Turkish régime no
incorruptible administration or gendarmerie ever existed, and
therefore they thought themselves obliged to settle disputes
in their own way. It is not therefore surprising that when
their compatriots, of whom many had served in the Turkish
services, set up a National government and gendarmerie, the

malissori regarded them with suspicion, associating them with corruption and abuse.

The tribes and bairaks of northern Albania fall into various groups:

1. Roman Catholic Mirdita, which successfully preserved its unity, autonomy, and ruling family throughout the Turkish occupation, is the only tribe which does not include both Christians and Moslems (T.E. 353). It is divided into five bairaks—Oroshi, Spachi, Kushneni, Fandi, and Dibri. Its chiefs ruled also Kthela—divided into the three bairaks of Kthela, Selati, and Perlati—Zadrima, and the Alessio mountains.

2. The Mi-Shkodra (Upper Skutari) or Maltsia e madhe (Great Mountain land) group of five Christian tribes—Hoti, and Gruda, annexed by Montenegro in 1913, Kastrati, Shkreli, and Klementi—the latter subdivided into four bairaks, of Seltze, Vukli, Boga, and Nikshi. Owing to their proximity to Skutari, which in 1832 became the centre of Turkish authority in the north, these tribes were ultimately compelled to pay a nominal annual tribute.

When in 1856 Mustafa Pasha was sent with an army to Skutari in connection with the Jesuit seminary dispute, he instituted, with the approval of the tribesmen and as a means of maintaining relations with them, a "Djibal" (Council) at Skutari. Each of the five tribes of Maltsia e madhe had a representative (Krye t Malit) upon it, and the Government was represented by five (or less) Moslem officials or Bylykbashas. The Djibal was under the Presidency of a Sergherdé appointed by the Government.

One of the principal functions of the Djibal was to arbitrate and arrange the compounding of cases of blood feud.

"The penalty for murder is about £24 paid to the Sergherdé, and £12 to the Bylykbasha of the tribe. Twenty-four pounds is payable also to the Church if the murder be on Church land: twenty-four pounds also to the Zoti e Ghakut (Lord of Blood—that one of the deceased's family who has the right to demand blood, or its equivalent). Should he accept it, the feud ceases. But he usually prefers to shoot the offender himself, and the blood feud thus started is not compounded till several on either side have been killed" (H.A. 30).

"Sometimes the Ghaksur (taker of blood) flies and shelters with another tribe . . . or his relations take him in" and help to pay his fine by which he might compound the feud; "for the honour of them all is cleansed by the blood-taking. . . . Any house to which a Ghaksur flies for shelter is bound to give him food and protection; he is a guest, and as such sacred" (H.A. 34), hospitality to a stranger, whether friend or foe, being a sacred duty fulfilled at any cost. Those who sheltered the Ghaksur were exempt from attack by those to whom either he or they owed blood until he had been received as a guest by others.

"The Sergherdé and Bylykbashas have no other pay than the fees they can collect for 'blood', so are reported not to wish to stop the practice. They are called on sometimes for an opinion in other cases, and are said to require bribing. . . .

"Neither Sergherdé not Bylykbashas venture into the mountains save on rare occasions under promise of safe-conduct. If their fees are in arrears they arrest any man of the same tribe who comes down to market, and imprison him as hostage till paid. As a rule in Maltsia e madhe they are paid punctually, and all shooting cases are notified to Skutari by the tribes with surprising speed. They say Lek ordered a fine to be paid, and that they themselves accepted the Djibal—'It is the law, so must be obeyed'. What the tribesman resents to the uttermost is not the administration of law, but the attempt to force on him laws to which he has never assented" (H.A. 30).

3. The Postripa district, inhabited by the Mazreku, Temali, Drishti, Shlaku, and Dushmani tribes, and several bairaks. Owing to its proximity to Skutari, and being a lowland district, Postripa, like Maltsia e madhe, was ultimately compelled to pay tribute. The tribes of Postripa, for which three Catholic Bishops at one time contended, while the tribesmen were left without priests, are almost entirely Moslem.

4. Maltsia e Leshit, the mountainous district immediately to the east of Alessio, inhabited by four small Catholic tribes—the Buljeri, Manatia, Kruezez, and Velya (F.O. 15).

5. Lower Pulati, inhabited by the Catholic Kiri, Plani, Mgula, and Ghoanni tribes, each of one bairak.

6. Upper Pulati, inhabited by the Catholic Shala, Shoshi, Nikaj, Merturi, and Toplana tribes, subdivided into numerous bairaks. These tribes preserved complete independence, and never paid tribute to the Turkish Government. Toplana was reputed to have the highest death-rate by blood feud, at any rate among Christian tribes. Nikaj was notorious for thievishness, which is remarkable since theft—not to be confounded with the "honourable pastimes" of cattle-lifting and horse-stealing—is almost unknown and universally despised (F.O. 13; *Macedonia*: H. N. Brailsford; etc.) in Albania. The inhabitants of Pulati, Postripa, and Puka are known generally as Dukaghini. This name is derived from the Dukaghin family, although during the fourteenth and fifteenth centuries it ruled not only these districts, but also the whole of the northern mountains. The Canon of Lek Dukaghin was accepted by all the tribes of northern Albania, and was applied by Skenderbeg to all districts under his sway.

7. The Puka tribe, south of the Drin, divided into seven bairaks—Puka, Komain, Dushaj, Cheriti, Chiri, Berisha and Merturi-Gurit, and Kabashi. The tribe is partly Moslem and partly Christian. During the later stages of Turkish rule these bairaks were nominally administered by a Turkish kaimakam, but he was a "mere spectator of their proceedings" and they preserved absolute independence.

8. East of Pulati and surrounding the town of Djakova lie three large Moslem tribes—Krasnitch, Tropoja, and Gashi, and to the south of them Hashi, which is almost entirely Moslem. These tribesmen are known as Malissori e Djakove and maintained a representative at Djakova, although they were never subject to taxation or Turkish authority.

9. To the south of Hashi and beyond the White Drin is the land of the notoriously independent and war-like Moslem Ljuma tribe.

10. Below Ljuma lie the Moslem Dibra, Malizi, and Luria tribes—the "Tigers of Dibra" and the terror of the Slavs in the plains to the east. They were never subject to the Turkish Government nor did they ever recognize it except as an ally against the Slavs. Blood feuds within this group were never compounded, and continued until both parties were satisfied that honour was cleansed by blood.

11. To the west lies the Mati district which is divided into four regions, each governed by a hereditary chieftain; and

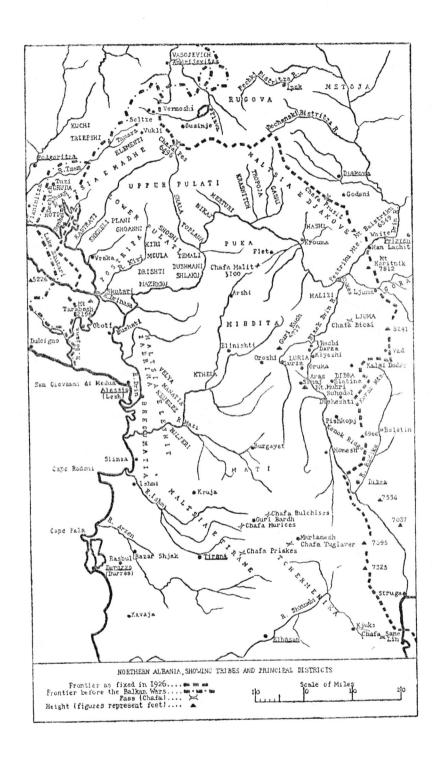

NORTHERN ALBANIA, SHOWING TRIBES AND PRINCIPAL DISTRICTS

Frontier as fixed in 1926....
Frontier before the Balkan Wars....
Pass (Chafa)....
Height (figures represent feet)....

Scale of Miles

from the foremost family, the Zogolli, sprang Ahmed Zogu. Mati never compounded blood feuds.

Perhaps the most striking characteristic of the Albanian tribesman, as indeed of every Albanian, is his respect for the *besa* or oath of peace. This is best illustrated by the following anecdotes:—

(i) "En allant sous la tente du Pacha [Prenk Bib Doda] . . . je trouve devant sa porte, comme d'habitude, le chef de ses gardes, le fidèle Noz Gureji. Noz est l'ennemi mortel de Prenk, il ne se fera pas faute de le tuer un jour, plus allègrement encore qu'il ne tuerait un chien; mais une *besa* générale unit aujourd'hui les tribus chrétiennes du nord, et Noz, au lieu de tuer, garde fidèlement. Pourtant nous dormirons au milieu des ruines du village dont les Gureji étaient les chefs, village brûlé et pillé par le père de Prenk. Quelles pensées, quels souvenirs tourmenteront le pauvre Noz cette nuit, sous la lune? Combien de fois sa main hésitante se portera-t-elle à la crosse de son revolver pendant que le gros Pacha ronflera tranquillement?" (S.m/s. 24, 115).

(ii) A guide, a Kastrati man, "was specially pressed to drink; his presence caused great mirth. The 'joke' was a peculiarly Albanian one. Not only was Kastrati at blood with Hoti, but Kastrati had blackened the honour of the very house in which he was sitting, so bitterly that the whole of both tribes was involved. Except with safe-conduct of a Hoti man—or under the protection of a stranger, as was the case—my gay young Kastrati could not have crossed the border-line save at the peril of his life. But he had chosen to come right into the lion's jaws, and the 'cheek' of him pleased every one immensely. All drank healths with him, he was the honoured guest, and they discussed pleasantly how many bloods would be required before peace could be made. The house-master was quite frank; five was the number he thought necessary. And the Kastrati thought five would satisfy them too" (H.A. 61).

Despite their complete subjection, women might traverse districts hostile to their men-folk without danger, being employed to carry messages between the belligerents. Their *besa* would protect the stranger. Their opinions upon all subjeċts are frequently asked and aċted upon, and their arbitration in disputes accepted. They were never liable for blood vengeance, female blood being of no account. Women may not be ſtruck, except by their husbands, or, if unmarried, by their parents. Violation of this law entailed blood. To their lot, however, falls much heavy work, as is usual in all countries which are not yet "weſternized". Throughout Albania they were generally betrothed in infancy or even before birth by the head of the house to which they belonged, and in consideration of the prospeċtive transfer of their services, a purchase-price agreed upon, part of which was paid on betrothal, and the balance when the bridegroom took possession of his bride. If the bridegroom refused her, which was seldom the case, a feud resulted. The bride could escape only by swearing lifelong virginity, in which case she was treated with the greateſt respeċt. This unhappy manner of betrothal was a fruitful cause of abduċtion and consequent feud between the abduċtor and his family on the one side, and the families of the betrothed couple on the other. Though the abduċtor and bride might escape abroad the feud continued, and twenty or thirty might be slain before the matter was settled.

By their feuds, and guerilla warfare with the Turks, the Albanians earned the reputation of being lawless savages; and should anyone wish to travel in the interior of Albania he was warned that it was dangerous to do so not only by the Turks, but in recent years by the Montenegrins and Auſtro-Hungarians also (B.T. 117, 110). Indeed, to prevent foreign intrigue the Turks eventually prohibited travel in the mountains upon this pretext (B.T. 181).

In *Visits to Monaſteries of the Levant*, the Hon. Robert Curzon, Junior, portrays in delightful ſtyle the myſtery which enshrouded Albania while under Turkish rule. He unwittingly explains how, through insurreċtion and guerilla warfare, Albania became notorious for brigandage, and bears teſtimony to the security which those "brigands" were able to afford to ſtrangers, where the authority of the Porte was non-exiſtent. Equipped with a pass from Mahmoud Pasha, the Governor of Janina, he unconsciously presented it to the very insurgent leader againſt whom it was intended to afford him proteċtion. The latter "being a good-natured fellow, gave us a note to the officer next in command ordering him to proteċt us as his friends and to provide us with an escort," otherwise "it would have been impossible for me to have travelled with safety through any one of the mountain passes of the Pindus."

That "brigandage", as distinct from petty theft, was regarded by many as an honourable profession is true enough. But in the first place, acts of brigandage were generally committed only against the Albanian's foes, namely, the Slav who had driven him from his "fat lands", and the Turk—who was an intruder —or his hireling, and never against a stranger travelling under protection of the *besa*. The highlander regarded both the Turk and the Ottomanized Albanian lowlander as "fair game", and in any case one to be excluded from his fastnesses; to this end many tribes always opposed the construction of roads in the mountains, knowing that with roads would come the Turk, and with them Ottomanization (T. 5.2.09; etc.). On the other hand, the lowlander who turned brigand generally did so either to escape military service or the payment of taxes by which he benefited nothing, or to be avenged for some injury suffered at the hands of a Turkish official or extortionate Ottomanized Albanian Bey. This "brigandage" was, during the nineteenth and beginning of the present century, made much of by neighbouring races in furtherance of their own political ends, and seriously prejudiced Europe against the Albanians during their struggle for independence. This propaganda, coupled with Turkish occupation, which was never precisely an inducement to tourists, completed the isolation of Albania, especially High Albania, from the march of western "civilization" and development.

In the lowland districts of Albania the Turks ruled through those leading families who embraced Islamism, allowing them to retain their privileges, feudal rights, and the conduct of local administration. From the Turkish point of view it was an admirable method, as it enabled the Porte to draw men for military service, or enforce the payment of taxes, by threatening to deprive the Beys of their privileges. Moreover, by encouraging rivalry between them the Porte secured its own authority (F.O. 33). National unity, so vital to the effective preparation and organization of a struggle for independence was thereby prevented, while feud and the resultant civil strife, high infant mortality, and general insanitary conditions sapped the strength of the people. Blood feuds in the lowland districts, however, where they did not concern the feudal Beys, were generally confined to the principals in the dispute, and during the later stages of Turkish rule tended to disappear.

Undoubtedly the most outstanding result of Turkish occupation was the conversion to Islamism of two-thirds of the population (69 per cent. of the Albanians within their country are Moslems). This occurred principally during the fifteenth and seventeenth centuries, that is to say, when the Turks first subjugated the land, and when subject peoples who were Moslems became generally eligible for official employment. The principal factors underlying this conversion were the regulations of Jihad, by which it was decreed that conquered "unbelievers" who would neither embrace Islam nor pay poll-tax must be put to the sword. If the "unbelievers" embraced Islam, their lives, property, and families were secure, and thenceforward they became part of the Moslem community by which they had been conquered, enjoyed its privileges, and lived on terms of equality with the conquerors. If on the other hand they elected to remain "unbelievers", the payment of poll-tax ensured religious liberty and personal safety up to a point, but they assumed the inferior status of subjects without technical citizenship or privileges; and, in fact, the peasants became mere "serfs" to Moslem overlords, who not infrequently proved cruel and extortionate. Moreover, the Christian peasants, being Christians, could obtain no redress for injuries through legal channels, and the reforms introduced during the nineteenth century mitigated, but never removed, the disabilities from which they suffered.

These conditions never affected the malissori of northern Albania, nor, until after their subjugation by Ali Pasha, the highlanders of the south. In the lowlands, however, matters were different. Once the lowlanders—especially the Tosks, whose lands were, generally speaking, more accessible, and to whom Turkish rule became more of a reality than it ever did to the Ghegs in the northern mountains—had become reconciled to the inevitability of Turkish rule, to which they remained reconciled until some fresh "reform" or dispute united them against their suzerain, they were quick to avail themselves of the few advantages which Turkish suzerainty presented to Moslem subjects. Thousands embraced Islamism either to retain their privileges, as in the case of the leading families, or to enter the Turkish service. They supplied Turkey with some of her ablest leaders and finest fighting material.

Many of these Albanians reached the highest standard of education and culture, and together with those few who had been educated by foreign tutors at home or had been able to afford an education in western Europe or America, piloted their country to independence. But while all those who entered the Ottoman service absorbed some measure of education, and modern as opposed to mediæval ideas, they inevitably acquired also the vices and failings of the Turk. There naturally existed a sharp distinction between those who had, principally by taking advantage of Turkish suzerainty, more or less kept abreast of the times, and those who had remained in their mountains, preserving undefiled the magnificent qualities and characteristics of their race, but at the same time permeated with superstition, and totally devoid of education or of progressive ideas. It will be readily understood that this distinction was the basis of endless misunderstandings between the mountaineers and their more educated compatriots, and explains the lamentable lack of co-operation between them. But once Albania obtained independence, the usefulness of these Ottomanized Albanians came to an end. Imbued with the slipshod methods and practices of the Turkish Empire, they are, with notable exceptions, more inclined to retard than accelerate the progress of the young State, and until their generation has disappeared Albania cannot resolutely set forth on the road to prosperity. Among them are the majority of landowners or "Beys", and the conduct of many of them towards the peasants has been deplorable.

Ismail Kemal Bey (1844–1918) gave an interesting account of conditions in the lowland districts from the point of view of the landowning Bey:

"The chief elements in the education of a young Albanian of the period were horse-riding, shooting, and hunting. At each of the four seasons I was sent to make a horseback tour in the interior of the country, accompanied by my two tutors and by young companions of my age, together with a numerous suite. On these occasions I visited the various villages and was the guest of the notables, and there were all kinds of festivities, especially the performance of the national dances, which formed a part of youthful education. In the hunting season I frequently rode to hounds, every man in com-

D

fortable circumstances in those days keeping a pack of dogs. Hare-hunting was carried on, especially with a view to exercise in horsemanship. Our principal sport with the gun was shooting wild duck and woodcock. Another sport was carried on in the month of May, when we went up in the mountains to catch partridges, with nets. Behind the nets, in cages, were placed female partridges, and these, when they called, attracted the male birds, which were separated from the females when sitting.

"My suite consisted of young men of the household service and professional hunters. There were no paid upper servants. Young men from the families of the notables were attached to the service of the chief family in the country in an entirely honorary capacity, as a part of their education or apprenticeship. The practice enabled them to take part in the events of the day, to learn manners and good breeding, and to get an acquaintance with public affairs. (Only grooms, coachmen, and cooks were paid and treated as servants.) All these young men were dressed in the national costume of rich embroidered cloth or velvet, and armed with pistols and yataghans in silver-gilt, which they carried in embroidered leather belts. Most of them possessed their own saddle horses, and the Beys, at fêtes and on other occasions, made gifts to them of arms and similar objects. The female servitors of the household were also young girls of the country, mostly peasants from the villages, and never from the families of notables. They received no wages, but remained in the service of the family until they married, their marriages being arranged and organized by the Beys, who bore all the cost, and continued later to interest themselves in the future of the couple" (I.K. 13–14).

Needless to say, this feudal system of administration was open to grave abuse, and in almost every case where the Bey held an appointment under the Turkish Government was abused. Moreover, advantage was taken of it by some of the Moslem peasantry, notably in the Malakastra district, to sell their daughters' services to the Beys for generally £T5 or £T6 for ten to fifteen years; and the girls, who received no wages, were entirely at the mercy of their masters, a state of affairs which was nothing less than slavery.

There was another outstanding cause which led to the conversion of many Albanians to Islamism. Ever since the Slav hordes drove the Albanians to the mountains in the west of the Balkan Peninsula, there has smouldered in Albanian breasts a hatred of the intruder—a racial hatred having individual exceptions—which time has in no way diminished. Indeed, rather was it accentuated in consequence of Russian intrigue, notably hatred of the Montenegrins. (A.S. 24–5: ref. to *Im Türkischen Kriegslager durch Albanien*: Dr. Jaekh: 1911; *Travels in the Slavonic Provinces of Turkey in Europe*: G. Muir Mackenzie and A. P. Irby: 1877. Also D.Z. 9: 97). As a Christian the Albanian had been held in subjection, and had suffered atrocities at the hands of the Slav in comparison with which Turkish brutalities were mere trifles. On the other hand, with the help of Islam the hated Slav could be driven back. As a Moslem the Albanian was the ally and equal of the Turk who protected him from the encroachments of the Slav, offered him employment, and paid him if he chose to render military service; in short, he enjoyed the advantages of Turkish rule while going his own way. But as a Christian he was treated as an inferior and ally of the Slav, which, in consequence, in certain cases he became. This explains the conversion to Islamism of many mountaineers, especially those of the north-eastern districts, who, secure on their crags, never had cause to seek by conversion the preservation of their privileges (map p. 300). With the connivance of the Turks, Albanian settlers from the tribes of the barren highlands, which were too sterile to support an increase of population, flowed back once more into the more fertile lands evacuated by the Serbs during the seventeenth century. This alliance with the Turks against the Slavs, by giving the Albanian a sense of security from his neighbours, largely contributed to the growth of jealousy and rivalry between chieftains and tribes and the submergence of national consciousness, a state of affairs which the Turks carefully fostered to secure their own position in Albania, on the principle of "divide et impera".

It is to be understood that any form of religious persecution in Albania was the exception rather than the rule, and occurred only when an exceptionally fanatical Turkish official held a local administrative appointment, and perhaps also during the earliest stages of the Turkish occupation of the country. Indeed, the Turks respected the religion of the Christians even

to the extent of granting in the seventeenth century to the
Catholic Archbishop of Skutari the fullest freedom and
privileges for his flock, and a salary, which were not withdrawn
until a successor became involved in intrigue against the
Empire. On the other hand, Islamism had many advantages
to offer, and kept up a steady propaganda, while Christianity
neglected its adherents. There never were schools for native
priests until Austria-Hungary interested herself in the matter
in the nineteenth century, foreign priests were frequently
ignorant of native language and customs, and, while the
Bishops strove to extend the limits of their respective Bishoprics, the spiritual welfare of those in the disputed districts
was neglected. This state of affairs appears to have recurred
with disgraceful frequency in Albania.

"That any Catholics now remain in north Albania is
mainly due to the efforts of the Franciscans, of whose
courage there can be no question, and who, through the
then darkest centuries, took Albania under their special
care" (H.A. 8).

Although Austria-Hungary had assumed, in the year 1689,
the right to protect the Catholic subjects of the Porte, and in
consequence the Catholic Albanians, the majority of these
Franciscans until the middle of the nineteenth century were
descendants of Albanian immigrants to Italy, who were
trained as priests in their adopted land. But during the nineteenth century Austria-Hungary reasserted herself (I.K. 280),
and in 1870 a Franciscan theological college was established
under Austrian auspices at Skutari. Thereafter, native Albanians
were trained for the priesthood at Skutari, generally by
Albanian teachers, their training being completed by a year
in Villach or, subsequently, in Bosnia.

The Jesuits also sent a few priests to Albania from time to
time, but they confined their activities principally to the
towns, where they were unpopular owing to the commercial
activities which they combined with their religious duties,
for, being endowed, they were able to undersell local trades-
men. Moreover, they were thought to be the agents of Austria-
Hungary, whose intentions with regard to Albania had been
regarded by the Albanians with suspicion for generations,
(although some Catholics, who looked to Austria-Hungary for
salvation, welcomed them as such). Indeed, an attempt by the

Jesuits at Skutari, with the concurrence of the Pasha, to establish a seminary, was the immediate cause of the insurrection in 1842. Although it began among the Moslems, the Catholics joined their compatriots, and the whole of northern Albania from Skutari to Prishtina rose. The insurrection was eventually suppressed by Omer Pasha, who defeated the Albanians at Caplan Han near Kalkandalen.

In 1855, the Jesuits again attempted to establish a seminary at Skutari, and for the purpose the Emperor Francis Joseph, having concluded on the 15th August a special concordat with the Vatican, placed at their disposal a considerable sum of money. But so strong was the resentment of the Albanians that the Pasha was obliged to permit its demolition on the 12th January, 1856. At the end of the year, however, Mustafa Pasha was dispatched to Skutari with ten thousand men to restore order, the Porte indemnified the Jesuits, the seminary was rebuilt, and still exists.

Although the Franciscan priests usually obtained considerable influence over their flocks, they were never able to overrule "adet" (traditional custom), and seldom succeeded in checking blood feuds, though they doubtless prevented many starting. There is something extremely romantic in the story of these gallant, hardy priests—sharing the vicissitudes of their parishioners, adhering to their customs in so far as it was compatible with the doctrine which they taught, ministering to them in the tiny chapels overshadowed by rugged peaks, and striving to stem the tide of Islamism. Being the only men who could read and write in that remote corner of Europe, they were called upon to act as "Parliamentary Secretaries" to their respective flocks, and to record, whether they approved of them or not, the deliberations of the Plekniya or Kuven. The Catholic malissori seldom grasped the doctrine of Christianity to any extent, and regarded the cross more or less as a charm. Heaven, they thought, was located upon the top of some very high mountain.

With the advent of the Turks in the fifteenth century, many Albanians, including the foremost families, fled to Italy and Sicily. During the nineteenth century many Christian Albanians emigrated to Greece, where they might live on terms of equality with their neighbours while remaining Christians; others went further afield, to Roumania or Egypt. And at the beginning of the present century, hundreds crossed to the

United States, where was subsequently formed the Pan-Albanian Federation "Vatra", of which more will be said in due course. All these Albanian emigrants and their descendants have preserved their national characteristics, customs, and traditions, and have never been absorbed by the races which surround them. In every case they have served the lands in which they dwell with loyalty, often with distinction, and have given many famous men to the countries in which they settled. Those in Italy (see *Old Calabria*; Norman Douglas, London, 1920: 151–92), who in 1901 numbered 208,410, mainly in Calabria, Apulia, and Sicily, annually commemorate their national hero, Skenderbeg, and the bonds which unite them with the land of their origin (C.C.). The most notable of them were Francisco Crispi, born at Ribera in 1819 and Prime Minister of Italy from 1887 to 1896 (E.B. 7: 467); and Girolamo di Rada, born at Macchia, near San Demetrio, in 1814—an Albanian Mazzini, who crystallized the aspirations of his countrymen and first drew to them the attention of Europe. A regiment of these Albanians served Napoleon from 1807 to 1814 (J.B.).

Many of those Albanians who became Moslems, became so in name only, and secretly adhered to their former faith. The Frasheris, for example, secretly remained Christians and celebrated mass for generations (S.m/s. 31). And, above all, never did they forget their native land, to which always they acknowledged the greater allegiance (F.O. 33; D.Z. 89–90; etc.). Monsieur Aubaret, the French Representative upon the Eastern Roumelian Commission, wrote in a Memorandum on the Sanjak of Skutari:

"The people live together in perfect harmony. They are Albanian before everything. If it be true to say that the Catholics are sincerely attached to their religion, it is, none the less, true that for them, as well as for their Mohammedan compatriots, national sentiment, love for their land, and respect for their ancient customs take the first place beyond all else. The spirit of dignity and independence, possessed alike by all Albanians, is strengthened among them by their markedly warlike characteristics. It is thanks to their indomitable vigour that in spite of the frequent endeavours of the Sublime Porte, these mountaineers have succeeded in preserving,

almoſt intaɛt, the privileges which they have enjoyed from
the earlieſt times" (A.Q.).

The Albanian is not a religious fanatic. To him religion
does not mean nationality; and his progress towards the
realization of his national aspirations has been greatly ham-
pered by the inability of the world to grasp the faɛt that a
Moslem Albanian is by no manner of means a Turk (D.Z.
89–90; etc.).

Although the majority of the Moslems of northern Albania

"belong to the usually ſtriɛt Sunnite seɛt, they are, with
few exceptions, not at all fanatical, and seldom perform
their daily prayers and ablutions except at a Mosque.
Many in the southern part of the diſtriɛt belong to the
almoſt pantheiſtic Bektashite confraternity, which is
notorious for its loose observance of the Moslem ordinances and traditions—even of the five canonical hours
of prayer. . . . Catholics and Moslems live side by side
in varying proportions; and, although quarrels between
tribes and individuals are only too common, religion is
rarely the matter in dispute. Ordinarily, in faɛt, toleration
goes so far that members of the same family profess
different religions; and it is said to be not uncommon
for parents to have the same child baptized one day as
a Chriſtian and circumcised another day as a Mussulman—with the result that a man uses two names, one
Chriſtian, the other Moslem, according to the circle in
which he happens to be moving" (F.O. 9).

In southern Albania, where, since Turkish rule was always
more of a reality than in the north, one would expeɛt that the
Moslem ordinances were more ſtriɛtly observed, it is significant
that the overwhelming majority of Moslem Albanians belong
to the Bektashite seɛt (F.O. 17). This is conclusive evidence
that national consciousness was placed before religion, and
that their conversion was superficial.

While in the south and centre the Albanians had become
converts to the Orthodox Church during the thirteenth
century, the Albanians of the north had remained adherents of
the Roman Catholic Church. As a result of Turkish occupation
the majority of the latter became converted to Islamism.
In religion, therefore, the Albanians within the present

frontiers of Albania fall into three groups, namely (1) Moslems (approximately 562,010), again subdivided into two sects, namely, Bektashite and Sunnite; they are strongly in the majority in central and southern Albania; (2) Roman Catholics (approximately 85,600), forming a strong minority in the north; and (3) Eastern Orthodox Catholics (approximately 159,000) constituting strong minorities in central and particularly in southern Albania. These latter remained under the spiritual jurisdiction of the Greek Patriarch who, from the first, held a privileged position in the Turkish Empire—the Greek having been the first Christian community to be recognized by the Porte (Q.K. Annex 16)—and was able to keep a closer hold upon the Christians of southern Albania than the Pope was able to do upon those of the north.

Unfortunately, the Eastern Orthodox Church (of Byzantium) is generally and inaccurately described as the "Greek" Orthodox Church in contradistinction from the Latin or Roman Catholic Church. This led to a confusion which has been deliberately promoted by Greece, who claimed as Greek nationals the Albanian adherents of the "Greek" Church; indeed, this formed the foundation for Greek claims to southern Albania, and proved a very effective means of gulling Europe.

Greece also contended that if adherents of the "Greek" Church were left within Albania they would be subjected to oppression, since Albania was a Moslem State. Incontestably, Moslems are in a majority in Albania, and there certainly were some grounds for this contention. But a large number of Christians shared the antipathy of the Moslems for Greece; and since the Moslems had embraced Islamism to avoid the disabilities which adherence to Christianity entailed, to gain greater freedom, and in the case of the aristocracy to safeguard their social position—many of the Slav aristocracy did likewise (C.E. 155)—and since the Albanian is not a religious fanatic, most Christians believed that once Albania had achieved independence, a central government would curtail the power of the Beys and assure them of equality within the State. In that case, they preferred to be Albanian subjects, and their choice is proving fully justified.

Religious strife in Albania was an almost unknown phenomenon (l'Illustration 7.4.17.—Q.K. Annex 4, etc.), although admittedly there have been disputes and misunderstandings between adherents of the three Churches, as was inevitable in a State which has for so long been shrouded in, and is only now emerging from, obscurity and mediæval gloom. Rather were religious differences deliberately overruled by custom, as is exemplified by the ceremony of cutting four locks of a child's hair during the first year of its life:

> "The father chooses a friend to do this—a Christian, if the father be a Mussulman, and vice versa. . . . This act is supposed to create a spiritual relationship between the family of the child and the friend, and by it they contract obligations towards each other of mutual aid or vengeance in case of outrage. This kind of alliance is held in especial honour among the mountaineers where Mussulmans and Christians both call it the Saint-Nicolo" (I.K. 359).

That Albania eventually succeeded in winning her independence is largely due to the co-operation of Moslems, Catholics, and Orthodox Christians in cultivating national consciousness.

CHAPTER II

THE NATIONAL AWAKENING

"Awake, Albanians, awake!
Let not mosques and churches divide you.
The true religion of the Albanian is his national ideal."
VASSA PASHA.

THE revival of Nationalism in Serbia, Greece, and Bulgaria inevitably reacted in Albania. That the Serbs had become autonomous and that the Greeks had thrown off the yoke of their suzerain gave food for discussion, but beyond that it signified little to the Albanian tribesmen who had never recognized that suzerainty. That it aroused grave anxiety in Turkey has been observed. But how was it regarded by educated Albanians?

For some years after the death of Skenderbeg, the Albanians had offered a desultory resistance to the Turks, punctuated by spasmodic national risings. But as the years passed, those risings became less national in character, and more of the nature of local struggles to preserve local privileges. The preservation by the Turks of the authority of the feudal Beys, and the fostering of jealousy between them to the extent that on occasions we even find one supporting the suzerain power against another, in pursuit of some local advantage: the discord between the tribes of the north: feuds and civil strife: the opportunities offered to Albanians in the Turkish service: the conversion of many Albanians to Mohammedanism: and the security provided by the Porte against the Slav and other foes: all these factors had combined to submerge the spirit of nationalism. They had not, however, drowned it.

The precedent of the Greek War of Independence, together with the drastic measures adopted in Albania by Reshid Pasha, resulted in the revolt of 1847 which, although suppressed, ultimately achieved its object in that Albania received a more liberal administration shortly afterwards. Then came the Crimean War, and with it an event of significance. The

Greeks had for some years threatened Thessaly and Epirus; and profiting by the diversion of the war in which Turkey was involved with Russia, and by the insurrection of a small section of the population which they had encouraged to rise by assurances of assistance, they invaded southern Albania under General Grivas, and seized Mezzovo (I.K. 15). But they were driven out by an Albanian force under Mahmoud Vlora, and Great Britain and France prevented them from making further incursions by a naval demonstration and occupation of the Peiræus. Nevertheless, the Albanians had found in their new neighbour a foe with a national policy in territory which they regarded as an integral part of their motherland. Thenceforth the intentions of Greece were regarded with suspicion, and phil-Hellenism was discredited (G.A. 221).

Not alone, however, upon military force did Greece rely for the furtherance of her ambitious projects. Directly her independence was assured, she had built up a system of public education through which she sought subsequently to Hellenize lands which she coveted, while her own lands cried for development. In this respect she was considerably in advance of Turkey, in which public education was not seriously taken in hand until 1860. In that year the Sublime Porte recognized that education throughout the Empire was an indispensable part of the programme of reform which had been undertaken. Apart from other considerations, it was appreciated that unless steps were taken by the State to provide the subject races which remained within the Empire with educational facilities, the subject races would take steps to provide themselves with these facilities, assisted by those who had already achieved independence and educational reform; and in view of the progress of the age, such steps could not be prohibited, unless in favour of a State-controlled system of education. Notably in southern Albania did this contingency threaten to occur as a result of the precedent and progress of public education in Greece, and if permitted would inevitably cause a national movement similar to that which had occurred in Serbia or Greece. In the latter countries, prompted by foreign, principally Russian, influences among the aristocracy, who had learnt to read and write in their homes, a literary revival had done much to prepare the way for the struggles for independence which had followed; and of this the Porte was fully aware. That Greece had obtained independence was very largely due to the literary achievements of her ancestors. The Serbs had enjoyed the support and encouragement of Russia for political and racial reasons. But the Albanians had not yet attracted the attention of Europe, and no Power had discovered any advantage which might accrue to it by the instigation of an Albanian national movement. "The Albanian, proud and silent on his crags, without even a disastrous battle to serve as a peg for advertisement, has through the centuries asked nothing of Europe and has been given it in ample measure" (W.P.). Consequently the Albanian language had never been reduced to writing for practical purposes, and Albanian literature was non-existent since there was no demand for it.

Throughout their European possessions the Turks had recognized only two divisions of the population, namely, Moslems, being to them synonymous with Turks, and "Christians, the latter being in common parlance synonymous with Greeks" (F.O. 18). Turkish had been, therefore, the official language in Moslem districts and in the mosques, while in districts inhabited by adherents of the Orthodox Church, Greek had been the language for official and commercial documents, correspondence, and in the church. Ali Pasha and the later Turkish Valis of southern Albania had issued their edicts in Greek. In consequence the majority of the Tosks were bilingual, the Moslem Albanians speaking Turkish in public, the Orthodox Albanians Greek, while the majority of both spoke their own language in their homes. In the circumstances, provided the progress of education was carefully controlled and directed, the Porte had every reason to suppose that it would be of inestimable value as a channel for Ottoman propaganda, and a means of consolidating Turkish authority in Albania by creating a barrier between Moslems and Christians.

In the year 1860 a number of inefficient State schools were established throughout the Empire. These schools were, however, only for Moslem children, and the Christians were left to provide their own schools. The Orthodox southern Albanians—among the Catholics of north Albania the demand for education in the Albanian language beyond that which could be obtained from the Franciscans, and in Austro-Hungarian and Italian schools at Skutari, did not become insistent until 1908—proposed therefore to establish Albanian Christian schools. But here the Porte made it clear, and with much plausibility, that Turkish was the language of the Empire, and that Moslems should be educated in the State schools in that language. If Orthodox Christians wished to attend Christian schools, the instruction therein must be in Greek, which was their official, commercial, and ecclesiastical language. In any case the printing of Albanian was prohibited (B.T. Chap. 9). It was even taught that Christ would not understand prayers in the Albanian language. In this attitude the Porte and the Greek Patriarch found themselves in agreement (D.Z. 113). The latter desired the union of Orthodox Christians, if not as a national, at any rate as far as possible as a linguistic entity (D.Z. 94), while the former was aware that education in the Albanian language would inevitably lead to the creation of a demand for Albanian literature, and the establishment of an Albanian national spirit, which was contrary to the wishes of both. On the other hand, the education of Christians in the Greek language would accentuate the difficulties which lay in the path of Albanian national unity (F.O. 63), while at the same time the Porte was aware that the Albanians would never acquiesce in the seizure of Epirus by Greece. Greek schools at once appeared in Epirus under the auspices of the Greek Patriarch, and were supported by the Orthodox Albanians, who were ready enough to avail themselves of any opportunity of gaining knowledge which presented itself (Q.K. 27–9). These Greek schools—M. Cassavetti stated (H.W.) that in 1913 there were in northern Epirus 250 of them—although they produced for Albania some of her most ardent patriots, subsequently created an extremely complicated situation—Greece claiming that their existence proved her right to the territory in which they existed—and were a channel for Greek propaganda. Nevertheless, a desire for Albanian national schools had been aroused.

In view of these differences of opinion between the Albanians and the Porte, it may seem inconsistent with their traditional policy that the Albanians did not seize the opportunity afforded by the Russo-Turkish War of 1877–8 to strike a blow for some measure of independence, but fought loyally and bravely, Catholic Mirdites, Moslems, and Orthodox Christians together, against the Slavs. It must, however, be admitted that in view of the absence of a sense of political unity in Albania, owing to the success of the policy pursued by the Turks, any concerted effort would depend entirely for its initiation upon those more or less enlightened Albanians of the south and upon Albanian statesmen in the Turkish service. These Albanians, however, were by no means insensible to the dangers to which an independent, but backward and disunited, Albania would be exposed from her more advanced neighbours. The designs of Montenegro, Serbia, and Greece upon Albanian territory were well known: designs which were partially realized at the close of the war. These States were the satellites, and the two latter largely the creations of Russia and France respectively, and the intentions of Russia with regard to Bulgaria were also known. To this extent, then, was Russia the enemy both of Turkey and of Albania, and for this reason the Albanians fought with the Turks. Moreover, the intervention of the Powers in Turkish affairs and the promulgation of the "Midhat Constitution" by Abdul Hamid in December, 1876, had aroused hopes of better days—hopes which were soon shattered.

To pretend that at this stage nationalism and a national policy, which in Serbia and Greece had been spoon-fed in infancy by Russia, had sprung into existence spontaneously in Albania or solely as a result of its success in those neighbouring States, would be absurd. On the other hand, it seemed to educated Albanian chieftains and statesmen that the power of the Turkish Empire was declining, that its very foundations were shaken, and supported only by interested Powers for political motives, and that once the tottering structure fell a disunited Albania would be partitioned. That patriotism and a sense of nationality were latent in the Albanians had been demonstrated by their desire for national schools, but that either some exterior influence or much careful preparation, or both, was required to unite them, was clear. On the other hand, premature independence would leave a mediæval Albania to the machinations of her neighbours, and this apprehension was fully justified by the demands which those neighbours subsequently made at the Congress of Berlin.

From these reflections sprang a national policy (B.T. 108) which has been misunderstood and woefully misconstrued by Europe as a religious attachment to Turkey. The Albanian leaders determined that the Ottoman Empire must be preserved as an unwilling foster-mother, while education was encouraged, and the national ideal surreptitiously propagated from without by Albanians resident in more liberal countries, assisted by those in the Turkish service; and while simultaneously every endeavour was made to obtain by constitutional means an autonomous administration for the country.

The bellicose policy of Serbia and Montenegro, who had attacked Turkey in the previous July, forced the hand of Russia, and war was declared by her, by Serbia, and by Montenegro against Turkey in April, 1877. The Montenegrins captured Nicsish. They attacked Dulcigno, and were repulsed by the Turks and Albanians only after some severe house-to-house fighting, in which a large part of the town was destroyed by fire.

The war, which was disastrous both for Turkey and for the Albanians, terminated with the abortive Treaty of San Stefano. But the intervention of Great Britain, whose traditional policy it was to preserve the Ottoman Empire as a barrier between Russia and the route to India, and the threatening attitude of Austria-Hungary, who feared that the great Bulgaria proposed by Russia would become a Russian dependency and render impossible the realization of her own projects in the Balkans, compelled that country to consent to a revision of this Treaty. Accordingly there followed the Congress of Berlin, which was concluded by the Treaty of Berlin, signed on the 13th July, 1878. Among the provisions which were made, Serbia and Montenegro became entirely independent of the shadowy suzerainty which the Porte had exercised over them as autonomous principalities, and obtained accessions of territory. But to the chagrin of Serbia, Bosnia and the Hertzegovina were handed over for administrative purposes to Austria-Hungary, with the proviso that they should be returned to Turkey when order and prosperity had been restored, and when the Porte had qualified as fit to administer them.

Austria-Hungary, by way of compensating Serbia, and wishing to bring Serbia within her sphere of influence, concluded a secret Treaty with Prince Milan Obrenovitch, on the 23rd June, 1881, by which Serbia agreed to negotiate or

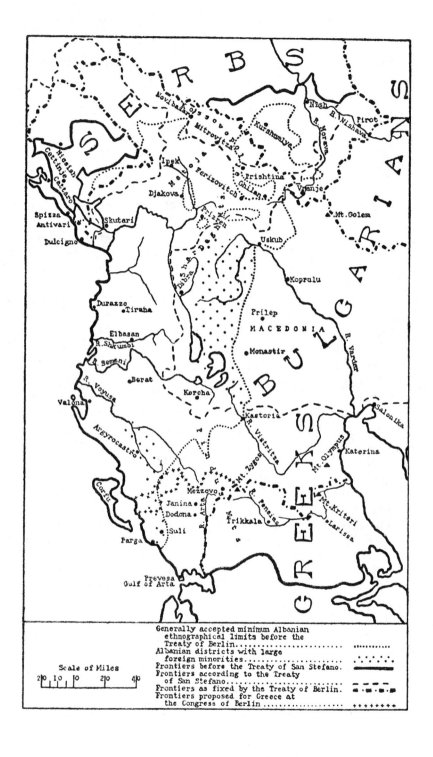

Generally accepted minimum Albanian
  ethnographical limits before the
  Treaty of Berlin..................... ·············
Albanian districts with large
  foreign minorities................... ·········
Frontiers before the Treaty of San Stefano. ▬▬▬▬
Frontiers according to the Treaty
  of San Stefano...................... ▬ ·▬ ·▬ ·▬
Frontiers as fixed by the Treaty of Berlin. ▬ ·▬ ·▬ ·▬
Frontiers proposed for Greece at
  the Congress of Berlin .... +++++++

Scale of Miles
2|0 1|0 |0   2|0   4|0

conclude no political treaties without the consent of Vienna, and in return Austria-Hungary guaranteed that no foreign troops or volunteers should be allowed to enter Serbian territory, agreed to recognize Milan as king whenever he wished to assume that title—which he did on the 6th March, 1882—to protect his dynasty from its rivals the Karageorgevitches, and not to oppose Serbia's acquisition of as much territory in the Valley of the Vardar as possible (Pribram. 51).

When this Treaty was renewed in 1889, Austria-Hungary agreed to support that expansion, "which may be carried in the direction of the Valley of the Vardar as far as the circumstances will permit" (Pribram, 137), always provided that Serbia renounced all dreams of expansion northwards or towards the Adriatic. The Serbs had, however, already looked southward, and in 1868 the Government had begun to subsidize the establishment of schools and churches in competition with Bulgaria (C.E. 25, 26, 39). The Turkish Government dared not interfere lest it should be accused of persecuting the Christians and give to the Powers a pretext for intervention.

Although Bismarck proposed to Italy that she should abandon her claim against Austria-Hungary for the *terre irredente* and seek territorial compensation in Albania, Italy was too preoccupied with the consolidation of national unity to indulge in foreign conquests, and considered her security in the Adriatic adequate so long as Albania remained under Turkish rule. Accordingly she pursued no independent policy with regard to Albania, and supported Austria-Hungary at the Congress of Berlin.

Russia's policy in the Peninsula as exposed by the Treaty of San Stefano had been to create an independent Serbia and Montenegro, emancipated as far as possible from Austrian influence, and a great and homogeneous Bulgaria, retaining therein her prestige by every possible means (C.E. 39). Bulgaria was to be bounded in the north by the Danube, in the south by the Ægean and by a very small Turkey-in-Europe, and in the west by the River Drin; but by the unfortunate Treaty of Berlin, which sowed the seeds of endless suffering and bloodshed (see also C.E. 40) Bulgaria's irredentist dreams were shattered, and the whole of Macedonia left in the possession of Turkey.

The failure of Bismarck to support Russia at this stage,

E

in return for her benevolent neutrality during the Franco-
Prussian War, marks the beginning of the struggle between
Austria-Hungary and Germany, subsequently supported by
Italy, on the one hand, and Russia, subsequently supported
by France, on the other. Russia's disregard of the aspirations
of Serbia, who had anticipated a very much more extensive
accession of territory than she obtained, temporarily alienated
the sympathies of Prince Milan and his following, and thenceforward the internal history of Serbia was an uninterrupted
struggle for political ascendancy between the protégés of
Austria-Hungary and the Panslavist adherents of Russia. The
prestige of the latter was not finally and definitely re-established until the annexation of Bosnia and the Hertzegovina
by Austria-Hungary in 1908.

By the Treaty of Berlin (T.B.) Serbia received accessions
of territory, including the Kurshumlye-Vranje districts which,
since the Serbian emigration in 1690, "had been occupied
under Turkish rule by Albanians, west of the Morava, and
by Bulgarians along the Nishava; but after 1878 the Albanians
withdrew and the Bulgarians were absorbed" (E.B. 24:689;
F.O. 38). The Serbs returned. Actually 100,000 Albanians in
these districts were dispossessed and driven over the frontier
(P.D. 52: 2305) with hideous brutality (B.T. 84). In view of
the subsequent pretensions of Serbia to northern Albania,
this should be borne in mind.

Montenegro also was well-nigh doubled in size by the provisions of the Treaty, although she was not permitted to
retain much of the territory ceded to her by the Treaty of
San Stefano. The latter Treaty had left a narrow Turkish
corridor of the Sanjak of Novibazar connecting Bosnia with
Albania, and separating Serbia from Montenegro. Upon
this Austria-Hungary insisted, in pursuance of her policy of
holding apart Serbia and Montenegro, and of controlling
the routes to Salonika to secure the *Drang nach Osten* (T.B.
422–4; 437–44). By the Treaty of Berlin this corridor was
enlarged. At the same time Montenegro was to receive the
Albanian towns of Podgoritza, Antivari, and the purely
Albanian districts of Plava, Gusinje, Kuchi, and Triepshi
(F.O. 24), which she has in no degree assimilated (F.O. 69).

Although Antivari was an Albanian town, one must admit
that in view of the attitude of Austria-Hungary, who sought
to prevent the Montenegrins and Serbs from obtaining free

access to the sea, and to this end held the whole Dalmatian seaboard to Spizza, the award of the port to Montenegro was justified upon economic grounds, especially since it entailed the surrender of an almost negligible area of Albanian-inhabited territory. The seaboard which Montenegro thus obtained was ample for her needs, and might have been developed to serve the needs of an united Serbia and Montenegro. Certainly, with the addition of Dulcigno, her seaboard was ample to serve the commercial needs of both, but provided no potential naval base.

Greece, too, had determined to have a finger in the pie. The fall of Plevna induced her to invade Thessaly. To her indignation, however, her claims were ignored at San Stefano, but the glamour of ancient Greece enabled her to obtain a hearing at the Congress of Berlin, where it was decided that the rectification of her frontier should be settled between herself and Turkey, with the mediation of the Powers if need be (T.B. 406). Greece claimed all territory south of a line from the valley of the Peneias in Thessaly to the north of the River Kalamas in the west, including a large slice of Albanian territory.

The above claims justified the fears entertained by the Albanian leaders. But the policy pursued by Turkey for four centuries had so effectively disrupted and prevented national unity that it required an exterior influence to re-unite the indignant tribesmen with their compatriots in the plains, and convert their latent patriotism and smouldering impotent resentment into an active national resistance. It seems, indeed, an irony of fate that the Porte itself should have provided this exterior influence which first united the Albanians in the name of patriotism.

The Porte realized that the wave of popular indignation which swept through Albania at the claims of her neighbours might be turned to advantage in opposing the separation of Albanian territory from the Ottoman Empire. Accordingly the Albanian leaders were encouraged to protest to the Congress of Berlin against these projects. But their protestations were brushed aside by Bismarck, who denied the existence of an Albanian nationality. Seeing that protestations were of no avail, the Sultan, through Hussein Pasha, the Vali of Skutari, and Abdul Frasheri, instigated a further step, and the northern Albanian tribesmen were advised to unite to resist the cession of Albanian territory to Montenegro, which accordingly they did. The restrictions which hitherto had been imposed in Albania to prevent national unity were removed; the ban on national schools and printing of the Albanian language was raised, and a national movement encouraged. The Albanians were not slow to respond; the movement spread with rapidity, and the embers of patriotism which had smouldered for centuries burst into flame.

While the Congress of Berlin was in session a Central Albanian Committee was formed under the leadership of Elias pasha Dibra, "Skender Bey" (Aladro Castriota: T. 27.12.78; 31.1.79), Prenk Bib Doda of Catholic Mirdita, and other chieftains, while local nationalist committees came into existence throughout the country. On the 30th May, 1878, the Committee issued a proclamation declaring its intention to defend the rights of the Albanian nation, and on the 13th June dispatched from Skutari a memorandum to this effect to Lord Beaconsfield. At the same time representatives from all parts of Albania were called upon to assemble at Prizren. Christians and Moslems alike hastened to respond to the summons, and on the 1st July was formed a "League for the Defence of the Rights of the Albanian Nation". Its policy was as follows:

(1) To maintain the sovereignty of the Sultan; and to resist until death any attempt by any State to annex Albanian territory;

(2) To obtain the union of all territory inhabited by Albanians in one province governed from Monastir by a Turkish Governor-General and Council of ten, who were to be advised by an Albanian Committee elected by universal suffrage.

(3) To ensure that Albanian should be the administrative language.

(4) To raise a national militia under officers of the Turkish army (F.O. 39).

For the first time for four centuries Albanians from Janina to Skutari were united for one purpose—the preservation of their country—and a general *besa* was proclaimed. There were, of course, discordant notes which were to be expected in a land where existed three religions, two subdivisions of race, two dialects, and two distinct social organizations again subdivided by local prejudices and inter-tribal rivalries: and the progress of nationalism was therefore slow. There was no national literature; 99 per cent. of the Albanians represented at Prizren on that eventful first day of July were wholly illiterate and four centuries behind the times. There was no national religion in the cause of which Albanians could be called to fight a holy war. They had no foreign support, and certain Powers even ignored their very existence as a nation. There was, however, one common factor, namely patriotism; by patriotism and loyal co-operation alone have Albanians achieved independence. By comparison with that of her neighbours who had enjoyed European support for a century, the unity of purpose which has characterized Albania's politics since 1879 is one of the most remarkable phenomena of national evolution, and has never yet been fully appreciated. (It is interesting to note that in the activities of the League a young Englishman, subsequently to win fame in the Boer War as Major George Paget, of Paget's Horse, played a part.)

In a dispatch to Lord Granville on the 26th May, 1880 (Accounts and Papers, 1880; Turkey, No. 15, Vol. LXXXI) Lord E. Fitzmaurice wrote, with reference to the formation of the Albanian League:

"It is generally believed here [Constantinople] that the recent Albanian movement *has a more vigorous hold on this eastern district than perhaps upon any other. Djakova, Ipek, Prishtina, are all centres of activity*, being in the neighbourhood not only of the territory of Montenegro, but also of that of Servia, against the latter quite as much as against the former of which two principalities, the Albanian population considers itself to have grievances connected with recent events."

And on the 27th July, writing from Buyukdéré, he said:

"In my dispatch of the 26th May last I expressed the opinion that the whole of the former vilayet of Prizren, which included Dibra, Djakova, Ipek, Kossovo, Prizren, and Prishtina, was distinct from the Slavonic countries lying east and south of it, and was predominantly Mohammedan and Albanian in character."

Mr. Goschen, writing from Therapia to Lord Granville on the 26th July, expressed his opinion as follows:

"The situation is complicated by the manner in which the fate of part of the inhabitants of Albanian territory has become involved in the pending cessions of territory to Montenegro, and also by the excitement produced among the Albanians by the proposed cession of the Janina diſtrict and other points claimed by the Albanians as being inhabited by men of their race, to Greece. . . . Whatever the hiſtory of the movement may be, I venture to submit to your Lordship, as I have done before, that *the Albanian excitement cannot be passed over as a mere manœuvre conducted by the Turks in order to mislead Europe and evade its will.* Nor can it be denied that the Albanian movement is perfectly natural (see text, pp. 1 and 2). . . . I am putting very roughly the case of the Albanians in order to illuſtrate the natural character of their resistance to the will of Europe. It does not appear to me to be an artificial or even a blameworthy attitude. It is one which is the natural outcome of the general movement in the Balkan Peninsula. Analogous considerations lead me to the conclusion . . . that the Albanian nationality is an element which ought not to be overlooked in any future political combinations. On the contrary, I believe it may be utilized with much advantage to general intereſts, and accordingly I should deprecate any partial measures which would be likely to impede the formation of one large Albanian province. If it is premature, or if it is impossible, to conſtruct such a province now, I would certainly abſtain from any measures which would make the impossibility permanent, or which would at leaſt cause future difficulties. I would recommend that the formation of a united Albanian province should at leaſt always be kept in view."

Unfortunately, this advice was not followed.

The Albanian League eſtablished its general headquarters at Berat—which was more or less central for both northern and southern Albania—with local headquarters at Prizren and Argyrocaſtro: and proceeded to show that it was not to be trifled with. The Porte was prevailed upon to permit the eſtablishment of a purely Albanian adminiſtration throughout the north, and Albanian authorities were inſtalled. A formal protest to Europe, and demand that Albanian territorial integrity should be respected, was, however, disregarded, and an International Commission sent out to delimit the Montenegrin frontier. A second protest was made to this Commission, but with similar results. In December, 1879, Montenegrin troops endeavoured to occupy Plava and Gusinje, but were so stubbornly opposed by the forces of the League that they were obliged to retire. Montenegro thereupon appealed to the Powers, and after prolonged negotiations and a Conference at Constantinople, a compromise proposed by Count Corti, the Italian Ambassador to Turkey, was adopted, and an agreement was signed on the 18th April, 1880. This was the first occasion upon which official Italy appeared on the Albanian stage.

By the provisions of the Corti Compromise, Plava and Gusinje were restored to Turkey, and in place of these districts the Hoti, Gruda, and the greater part of the Klementi lands were assigned to Montenegro. Having been obliged to agree to this arrangement, Turkey sent an official to supervise its execution. But the Albanians were indignant that Turkey should have accepted a compromise which was no less unjust than the original one, although she could not well have avoided doing otherwise. The unfortunate official, Mehmed Ali Pasha, and a detachment of troops, were annihilated by the tribesmen at Djakova on their way to the area in dispute. The Montenegrins were no more successful in Hoti and Gruda than they had been in Plava and Gusinje; and the Hoti tribesmen under Marash Hutzi successfully defended Tuzi. Thereupon Mukhtar Pasha was sent with a Turkish force to assist the Montenegrins, but their combined efforts failed to break the Albanian resistance, and the Powers were compelled again to reconsider their decision. The "Corti Compromise" was abrogated, Hoti and Gruda restored to Turkey, and Montenegro compensated with Dulcigno and a strip of seaboard extending to the Bojana—"a district which was just as much Albanian as the other" (F.O. 40; also B.T. 381). To this, however, Turkey refused to agree, and again found herself in accord with the Albanians. The Powers thereupon resorted to coercive measures, and the combined fleets of Great Britain, France, Germany, Austria-Hungary, and Russia appeared off Dulcigno on the 28th September, 1880, while Great Britain threatened to occupy Smyrna unless the Porte took steps to coerce its truculent subjects. On the 11th November the Porte yielded, but the Albanian mountaineers with an admirable obstinacy remained obdurate; but they were defeated and scattered by a Turkish army of 30,000 men under Dervish Pasha on the 22nd, and three days later the Albanian garrison was driven from Dulcigno, which was handed over to the Montenegrins. Since its surrender to Montenegro, the population of the town has steadily decreased (E.B. 8 : 652).

As Serbia had occupied and established herself in the Albanian districts allotted to her before its formation, the Porte now considered that the League had outlived its usefulness, and Dervish Pasha was instructed to reinstate Turkish authority in the north. This he did, although not without further bloodshed.

While the above events were in progress, the delimitation of the southern frontier was proceeding, though even more slowly. A Greco-Turkish Commission met in 1879; but the Turks, confident of the support of the Albanian League (T. 26.10.78; 24.2.79; 30.5.79; etc.), declined to consider the Greek proposals. Thereupon Greece sought the arbitration of the Powers, which task was entrusted to a Conference of Ambassadors at Berlin in the following year. The Ambassadors proposed, on the 25th June, a line following the River Kalamas which almost coincided with that proposed by Greece, and displayed thereby either a profound ignorance of essential ethnical facts or an unpardonable devotion to the illusion of Greek descent. The attitude of Turkey remained unchanged, the Albanians prepared to support her, and Greece mobilized. Five hundred Greek irregulars were landed at Santi Quaranta to lead an insurrection, but the Albanian population supported the Turks, and the Greeks were crushed by Ghion Lek.

"An International Commission went at this time to Preveza in order to effect the transfer of the district to His Hellenic Majesty. But the Commission found itself confronted by the opposition of the whole population, and was forced to retire without fulfilling its purpose. The population of Epirus rose like one man and opposed the cession of this Albanian district to Greece" (A.Q.).

The Powers thereupon decided that the coercion of Turkey, supported by the Albanians who had demonstrated their powers in the north, was a task not lightly to be undertaken, and the Greeks were certainly not prepared to undertake it unaided. Eventually a convention was signed at Constantinople in July, 1881, by which the demarcation of a frontier less favourable to Greece was entrusted to an International Commission. The new frontier followed a line from a point between the mouth of the River Peneias and Platamona to Mts. Kritiri and Zygos, thence following the River Arta to the Gulf of Arta. But Greece did not abandon her intention to invade southern Albania until a naval demonstration and blockade of her coast was carried out by the Powers. It is noteworthy that in the execution of these coercive measures France did not participate, and Russia only partially and very reluctantly. Thenceforward Greece took every possible step to detach southern Albania from Turkey by a gradual penetration, and Hellenization of the population (T.B. 406).

The foundation of an Albanian national movement was now laid, and the League continued to pursue its policy as unostentatiously as possible. But its power among the independent tribesmen was as yet slight, and isolated incidents which were no part of its policy continued therefore to occur between tribesmen and Turks or Montenegrins.

The precarious position of the Ottoman Empire precluded any immediate attempt to suppress the national movement; and since the Nationalists desired to avail themselves for the time being of Turkish protection, the quarrel between them and the Turks in consequence of the coercive measures applied by the Powers and the suppression of their authority in the north by Dervish Pasha, was temporarily patched up.

Prenk (= Peter) Bib Doda, however, hereditary chieftain of Mirdita, head of the only surviving ruling family of the Highlands which had preserved its mediæval rights, authority, and fief, and one of the principal leaders of the League, was suspected as a possible champion of Albanian independence. Dervish Pasha induced him to inspect a Turkish warship off Medua, and he was carried into exile in 1881. But his fief, in which the Porte, through the intervention of Austria-Hungary supported by France, had undertaken to make no change of status (T.B. 432) was held together principally by Primo Dochi, who, after spending some years in exile as a priest in Newfoundland and India (B.T. 107), became Abbot of Mirdita in 1888, and played a considerable part in the national movement. He invented an excellent system of spelling Albanian, which he persuaded the Austro-Hungarian authorities to use in their schools in Albania. His death during the Great War was an irreparable loss to his country.

In 1868 Prenk Bib Doda's father had died. For some years he had been planning to emulate Ali Pasha and the Bushati, but had dissipated his resources in fruitless wars (1853 and 1862) against the Montenegrins. Upon his death, therefore, the Turks, in an endeavour to curtail the authority of this powerful feudal family, under which Mirdita had successfully defied them for centuries, refused to allow young Prenk, who was being educated at Constantinople, to return. The Mirdites, numbering approximately 30,000 hardy Roman Catholic mountaineers, whose one obligation had been to supply contingents for the Turkish Army, thereupon refused to continue to do so, and it became clear that serious trouble would ensue unless Prenk was allowed to return. He was therefore created a Pasha and sent back to Mirdita. But in 1876 the Turkish authorities learnt that the Mirdites, who had refused to assist them against the Montenegrins as the other tribesmen had done, were again planning independence. When, therefore, Montenegro and Serbia signed an armistice with the Turks in November, a Turkish force, assisted by tribes which were "in blood" with the Mirdites, devastated the district and burnt Prenk's house. Prenk had escaped, and with his tribesmen not only played a prominent part in the activities of the League, but also against the Slav invaders during the Russo-Turkish War of 1877. (For art. on Mirdita, see T. 6.3.14.)

The occupation of Bosnia, the Hertzegovina, and the Sanjak of Novibazar by Austria-Hungary had brought that country into direct contact with the Albanians. The latter were regarded as a race which should be strengthened in such a way that they might, when eventually the Turkish Empire broke up, act as a barrier between the Serbs and the Adriatic sea. Austria-Hungary feared that Serbia would fall under the influence of Russia, and, as that country's protégé, threaten her position in the Adriatic if she acquired access to the sea and control of the Albanian coastline, and deny her commercial access to Salonika and the east. A strong Albania under Austro-Hungarian influence might counterbalance Serbia. Austro-Hungarian policy in Albania was clearly defined in the

Peſter Lloyd in June, 1880: "Les Albanais sont les alliés éven-
tuels dont il faut bien se garder d'affaiblir la force dissolvante
dans le milieu sud-slave: ils sont les Roumaines du sud-
ouest" (T.B. 421).

In May, 1883, the Kaſtrati, Hoti, Gruda, and Shkreli tribes,
inspired by promises of assiſtance given by a foreigner who
described himself as an Auſtro-Hungarian agent, revolted. A
Commission was then delimiting the Albano-Montenegrin
frontier, and the agent told the tribesmen that they muſt rise
to save their land, otherwise it would be ceded to Montenegro. The surrounding tribes did not support the insurgents,
and the promised assiſtance never materialized. The insurrection was ruthlessly suppressed by the Turks. An insurgent
leader, it is said, subsequently obtained an interview with
Baron Kallay, Auſtro-Hungarian adminiſtrator of Bosnia and
the Hertzegovina, through a card which the agent had given
him. He demanded and received compensation (H.A. 58).
That the tribesmen were the pawns in some political game
seems clear; such was the case in moſt of the minor diſtur-
bances in Albania since 1880. It was at this ſtage in her hiſtory
that Albania became the buffer between Auſtro-Hungarian
intereſts and those of the Slav in the Balkans; and the illiterate
but impetuous malissori (mountain men) were a fertile soil for
propaganda, and a means of creating a diversion, a pretext
for intervention, or aggression on the part of one or other
of the rivals or their satellites. Thus we find from 1880 onwards
a group of enlightened Albanian patriots ſtriving to prepare
the way for independence and widen the sphere of their
influence in the teeth of intensely hoſtile neighbours, while
frequently embarrassed by their unenlightened compatriots
who would recognize no law but that of Lek and regarded any
attempt to bring them into line as a fresh machination of the
Turk or Slav. Yet this intractability was principally the outcome of the very machinations which they sought to defy.
They loved their land, they resented the Turk, and they hated
the Slav. The firſt muſt be preserved, the other two deſtroyed.
There was no more to be said, and only the Mirdites had an
enlightened leader, their Abbot, to teach them otherwise. If
Auſtria-Hungary, or Montenegro, or Serbia promised arms
and told them the time was ripe for an attack upon the Turk,
they attacked him. If the Turk told them that Auſtria-Hungary
or the Slavs were about to invade Albania, they rallied round

him to resist the common foe. If they were told that a neighbouring tribe was in league with one of their foes they, credulous as children, attacked it. Thus were they the pawns in a game in which the very land and the very freedom which they sought to preserve were at stake. There is perhaps no more pathetic story than that of these magnificent tribesmen, instinctively law-abiding according to their lights, and rigidly adhering to their mediæval code, but stirred by their foes to strife in the cause of freedom, often even against their kith and kin who likewise strove in the selfsame cause, and ruthlessly sacrificed by the players of a game far beyond their comprehension. Cut off from the world for four centuries, defying alien authority from their crags and fastnesses, could they be expected to grasp in a year or even in a decade the principle of nationalism, the intricacies of diplomacy, the ethics of modern statesmanship? Is it surprising that at times they acted contrary to the subtle policy which guided their compatriots and smote their hereditary foes as they had done for centuries, on the slightest provocation: and later, regarded with suspicion and distrust their own central authority which sought to impose what was to them unintelligible legislation? Could they be expected at once to abandon the customs and traditions of remote antiquity, and follow an intricate policy contrary to their instincts? Tradition dies hard the world over.

CHAPTER III

THE STRUGGLE FOR AUTONOMY

THE resistance by the Albanian League against the cession of Albanian territory to Montenegro in 1879–80 was not unnoticed by Europe, and much correspondence upon the subject passed between Mr. (afterwards Lord) Goschen, British Ambassador at Constantinople, and Lord Granville, then Secretary of State for Foreign Affairs. The British and Austro-Hungarian Consuls-General at Skutari in 1880 proposed an autonomous administration for all those districts which had been under the authority of the League, and this proposal was submitted to the Eastern Roumelian Commission (E.P. 89–90) which had been constituted to organize the administration of eastern Roumelia (Macedonia), and recommend an organic law and reforms to the Porte. The Commission, with the exception of the Russian representative, approved the proposal and stated that it saw no objection to the union of all Albanian districts within one vilayet. Lord Edmund Fitzmaurice, the British Commissioner, supported by Mr. Goschen, accordingly recommended the formation of an autonomous Albania which should include the vilayets of Skutari and Janina and the greater parts of Kossovo and Monastir. Verbal assurances, too, were given to the Albanians that their rights and interests would be safeguarded. The correspondence doubtless "received attention" from those who docket and "pigeon hole"; and in a "pigeon hole" it and the matter rested.

The Porte had no doubt expected that with the *raison d'être* of the League would pass away its existence: and with its existence all traces of the national spirit which it had fomented. Its forces had been scattered and its power overthrown by Dervish Pasha. No doubt these considerations, combined with the transient interest displayed by Great Britain in Albanian affairs, and the embarrassing interest of the Powers in Turkish affairs in general, were the principal reasons why the Porte refrained from any immediate attempt to eradicate all traces of nationalism in Albania. Whatever the reasons, the ban upon Albanian schools and the printing of the language was not reimposed until 1886.

The Albanian nationalists made hay while the sun shone to the best of their ability. The principal difficulties with which they had to contend were the absence of national educational facilities and the primitive state of the language, and to the overtaking of Greece and Serbia in these respects they directed their energies. A number of national schools were established, financed by patriots; and both teachers and pupils were indiscriminately Moslems and Christians. Of religious animosity there was none; patriotism usurped the place of religion.

Hitherto, Albanians who were themselves unable to write had corresponded with each other through the medium of Turkish professional letter-writers or Greek Orthodox priests; and although Brocardus in the fourteenth century states that the Albanians used Latin characters, the Albanian language had never been reduced to writing for practical purposes. But in the middle of the seventeenth century a religious work published in Venice, and a dictionary, contained examples of the language, and at the end of the eighteenth century Theodore of Elbasan produced an Albanian dictionary. The Jesuits frequently printed it in Skutari in the eighteenth century, and reports to the Vatican were often written both in Latin and Albanian. In 1824 the Gospel of St. Matthew had been translated into Albanian by Evangeles Mexicos, and published in modern Greek and Tosk Albanian in Greek characters at Corfu, under the auspices of the British and Foreign Bible Society, which, after the suppression of the Albanian League in 1886, became of inestimable value to the Albanian nationalists. At the end of the nineteenth century the branch of that Society at Monastir was entirely in Albanian hands (B.T. 100).

"The Director of the Bible Depot in Monastir was an Albanian of high standing both as regards culture and energy. Grasping the fact that by means of these publications an immense national propaganda could be worked, he spared no pains, and by carefully selecting and training Albanian colporteurs, whose business it was to learn in which districts the officials were dangerous, where they were sympathetic, and where

THE STRUGGLE FOR AUTONOMY 63

there were nationalists willing themselves to risk re-
ceiving and distributing books, succeeded to a remarkable degree" (B.T. 108; also T. 15.8.08).

In 1827 the whole of the New Testament had been published
in modern Greek and Tosk Albanian under the auspices of
the Bible Society. An Albanian dictionary appeared dated
1866. Between 1860 and 1870 an Albanian patriot, Constantine Christophorides, translated large parts of the Bible,
and a volume containing the four Gospels and the Acts,
together with an alphabet to enable the illiterate to read it,
was published in the Latin characters, with minor alterations
to convey certain sounds necessary to the pronunciation of
the Albanian language (D.Z. 110–12). The Latin were considered more suitable than either the Arabic or Greek characters, and more readily learnt; moreover, there was an anxiety
among Albanians to avail themselves of every opportunity to
establish the individuality of their race, divorce themselves
from Orientalism, and bring themselves into closer contact
with the West (A.S. 16).

In 1877, at the instigation of Sami bey Frasheri, John Vreto
and Vassa Pasha—Moslem, Orthodox Christian, and Roman
Catholic respectively—an Albanian Committee was formed
at Constantinople under Sami's presidency for the purpose
of rehabilitating the Albanian language and building up an
Albanian literature. This Committee adopted a modified
form of the Latin as the national alphabet, and in it published
an Albanian school spelling-book in 1879. The adoption of
the Latin characters was an important step, as hitherto the
adherents of the Orthodox Church had been prejudiced
against them on religious grounds! There followed a *General
History*, by Sami Bey, who also published *Albania: Her Past,
Her Present, Her Future*, while his brother, Naim bey Frasheri,
wrote patriotic poems which did much to fan the flame of
nationalism. Branches of the Committee were established in
Albania and elsewhere, notably in Monastir, Elbasan, Korcha,
and Bucharest. In 1889 the Book of Genesis and Gospel of
St. Matthew were published at Bucharest under the direction of
Gerasim Kyrias (D.Z. 112).

But both the Porte and the Greek Patriarch became alarmed
at the progress made by popular education, especially in view
of the rapidity with which the religious barriers, which they

had striven to erect, were being broken down. In 1886 therefore the ban upon Albanian publications, and upon schools which were not under foreign protection, was reimposed. The Patriarch went a step farther, and threatened with excommunication anyone convicted of reading or writing the Albanian language. For twenty-two years this threat constituted a serious obstacle to the progress of popular national education. In the south, indeed, until the beginning of the present century, Korcha was the only town in which the Albanian language was taught openly. There, in 1888, under the auspices of the American mission, a school for boys was established by Gerasim and Sevasti Kyrias which continued to exist until 1903; and under the same auspices a girls' school was founded in 1891, in which Rev. P. Kennedy, of the mission, became a member of the staff. In both schools Albanian was taught. The pupils taught their relatives and friends, and the Turks hesitated to interfere with schools under such powerful patronage. Korcha became one of the principal headquarters of the Central Albanian Committee, gave to Albania some of her most ardent nationalists, and has been called the "cradle of Albanian nationalism" (Q.K. Annex. 17).

Although outwardly suppressed, the League continued to work clandestinely, principally among the more advanced patriots of southern Albania, and its efforts and accomplishments constitute one of the most remarkable stories in the history of Europe. It is a story of a nation, opposed on every hand, endeavouring without encouragement or assistance from any source to step, in a generation, from the obscure Middle Ages into the progressive world of the present century; and that it has succeeded in taking honourable place among the other Balkan States which had enjoyed foreign support for a century, is an astonishing achievement. Not only were the nationalists confronted with the hostility of the suzerain power, but also with the intrigues of neighbouring States which sought, basing their efforts upon their own well-established educational systems, to Hellenize or Slavize the portions of Albania which they respectively coveted. Throughout the south, Greek schools with Greek teachers were established, and Greek gymnasia at Janina and Korcha, while Greek propaganda inevitably wrought harm to the Albanian cause. Indeed, it would have been a miracle if the

Greeks had failed to Hellenize a considerable number of Albanians, and "in view of the fact that Albanian nationalism had always been suppressed under Turkish misrule, and that Greece had been given the upper hand with every opportunity to Hellenize the population by means of the Greek Orthodox Church and Greek schools teaching the Greek language, it is surprising that Albanian nationalism had made such headway as has been noted" (S.A. 104). "We have reared", confessed a Greek, "serpents! The Greek schools, instead of creating for us Greek partisans in Albania, have created our worst foes" (A.Q.). This is borne out by the fact that those inhabitants of southern Albania, of whichever religion, who emigrated, established for themselves not Greek but always Albanian schools.

Although on a much smaller scale, the Serbs pursued much the same policy in north-eastern Albania as did the Greeks in the south. Two Serb seminaries were established in Prizren, and schools and churches elsewhere. Nevertheless, the Albanian population remained almost solely Albanophone, and had it not been for support from without, it is probable that the scattered Serb element would have been absorbed by the Albanians (H.A. 294). The Serbs claimed that north-eastern Albania had been theirs before the advent of the Turks. True enough, but for how long? A mere two centuries as compared with Albanian possession through the ages. Even the most imperialistic Englishman would hesitate to claim Calais upon the grounds of former occupation, yet did he do so, his claim would be better founded than that of the Serbs to any territory which they have acquired beyond their south-eastern and south-western boundaries in 1879. When two races adjoin under one suzerain power there is inevitably an overflow, the one into the territory of the other. This overflow was liberally adjusted in favour of Serbia by the Treaty of Berlin. The Moslem Albanian population was expelled. But the Serbs were not satisfied, and set themselves to Serbize Albanian and Bulgarian lands, basing their claims largely upon their defeat at Kossovo, and oblivious of the many victories which the Albanians had won subsequently in that same region. Naturally the Albanians resented this, and being at a disadvantage in respect of education, retaliated by the only means in their power. The Serbs employed this as a further pretext for expansion—"in self-defence".

F

"Between the Albanian and the Slav there stand centuries of hatred and blood feud. The Albanian regards the Slav as an intruder and a robber; the Slav looks on the Albanian as an inconvenient person who, although occasionally beaten, has always refused to be conquered: and having the inestimable advantage of being more skilled in literature, he has consistently represented the silent Albanian as a brigand and a plunderer of Slav villages. As a matter of history the boot is on the other leg" (W.P.).

Austro-Hungarian interference in Albanian educational matters dates from 1870, when the first Austro-Hungarian-supported school was established at Skutari. It is an interesting fact that the Austro-Hungarians did not attempt to introduce German, but taught Albanian, and even, at first, Italian. Italy did not show political activity in Albania until the beginning of the present century, although she had previously established and supported three schools at Skutari, and others at Valona and Janina, largely, it seems, at the instigation of Crispi for sentimental reasons (*Journal of the R.I.I.A.*, Vol. 6 : 170). When she began to compete politically with Austria-Hungary, she strove, wishing to outbid that country, to offer better educational facilities than were obtainable in those schools under Austro-Hungarian auspices, and even bribed parents to send their children to them.

Austro-Hungarian interference complicated the task of the Nationalists. Austria-Hungary's object being to frustrate Pan-Slavism in the Balkans, and control the eastern shores of the Adriatic, she sought to take advantage of the right to protect the Catholic subjects of the Porte, which she had claimed—and which Kiamil Pasha had admitted—in order to establish her prestige in Albania by propaganda (D.Z. 90 : 92) among the Catholic malissori. Some thought even that she sought to create an incident between them and the Moslem element, and thereby a pretext for intervention and a further step towards Salonika. Her virtual monopoly of the coastal trade, and the provision of educational facilities for Albanian students, were subsidiary means of extending her influence. Her activities were resented by the Porte, which was provoked to adopt counter-measures. Through their *hodjas*, it strove to stir up among the Moslem tribes hostility towards Austria-

Hungary, justifiable suspicion of her intentions, and as a corollary hostility towards their Catholic compatriots. Hence there arose a certain amount of religious animosity in the north.

The Albanian Nationalists, whose efforts were co-ordinated by a Central Committee, carried the headquarters of their activities abroad. Centres of Nationalist activity were established in Bulgaria, Egypt, Roumania, Italy, and more recently in the United States. These centres published an astonishing number of books and newspapers, most of which were written or edited by patriots resident in Albania or Turkey, writing under assumed names, and which when printed were smuggled back into their country with the assistance of Moslem Albanians in the Turkish services. These publications were eagerly studied, in spite of the fact that anyone found in possession of them was liable to a term of fifteen years' imprisonment! Irrespective of their creed or class—and many of the most ardent patriots were of humble origin—Albanians from all parts of the country strove shoulder to shoulder in the cause of nationalism. Between 1880–1908, and without any encouragement by interested powers, more than thirty different newspapers and periodicals, together with a large number of books in the Albanian language were printed and published abroad. Of the most important newspapers, seven were published in Bulgaria, seven in Italy, four in Egypt, four in Roumania, three in Belgium, one in Austria-Hungary, one in Greece, one in the United States, and one in London, edited by Faik bey Konitza. All this the Albanian patriot accomplished in exile and unassisted (D.Z. 91). He purged his language of foreign words which had crept into use, and sought out Albanian words which had fallen into disuse with which to reconstruct it. And in his own land, despite the drastic penalties (Q.K. 25, etc.) which even the possession of the Albanian alphabet entailed, thousands of Albanians of all ages and occupations strove secretly and successfully to teach themselves to read and write their native language. All this was accomplished while Abdul Hamid, the "Red Sultan", reigned!

Of Albanians abroad, the emigrants to the United States have played the most conspicuous part in the growth of nationalism, although more recently; there are at least 60,000 of them in America. Important settlements exist in the New

England States, New York, Pennsylvania, Ohio, Michigan, Washington, and in Massachusetts, where there are some 10,000. Most of these Albanians entered the country since 1900, and there was a great influx as the result of the Greek devastations of southern Albania in the summer of 1914. Few of these emigrants, however, can be described as wealthy, judged by American standards, their lack of education having been a tremendous handicap to their prosperity.

In 1906 Sotir Petsi, an Orthodox Christian of Korcha, and graduate of the University of Athens, working in a gloomy basement in Boston, laid the foundation of the National Movement in America by the publication of the newspaper *Kombi* with the proceeds of his own manual labour. He was at the time a factory worker, having been unable to obtain other employment through ignorance of the English language. Of the 5,000 Albanians in the United States at that time, only about 20 could read and write, whereas the growth of the National Movement may be judged by the fact that in 1919, 15,000 could do so.

In the same year a number of more or less educated Albanians came from Roumania to Jamestown, N.Y., and founded the first Albanian Society in the States, called "Motherland".

These activities were, however, contrary to the policy of the Greek Patriarch at Constantinople, who threatened with excommunication the families in Albania of those in America who ignored him by using the Albanian language. The Albanians thereupon determined to bring to an end this interference with their affairs. In 1908 a Convention at Boston proclaimed religious independence, and instituted an Albanian Orthodox Church under the leadership of the Rev. S. Fan (Theophanes) Noli. A church was improvised, and a National Church Association founded.

The Rev. Noli, an ardent patriot who had worked unceasingly in the national cause, had been ordained priest by the Russian Metropolitan in New York, the Greek higher clergy having refused to ordain him for obvious political reasons; he was subsequently proclaimed a bishop by the community, since no one would accept the responsibility of investing him. He was born in 1882, at Ibrik Tepe, an Albanian village in eastern Thrace, was brought up in the United States, is a graduate of Harvard University, and in addition to his political activities has translated into Albanian works by Shakespeare, Ibsen, and Blasco Ibanez.

It was not until 1923 that, in agreement with the Patriarch, an Autocephalous Church was established in Albania, although in 1908 an Orthodox League was formed at Korcha to resist the policy of Hellenization and interference in Albanian affairs pursued by the Patriarchate. Branches were established at Elbasan and in Bucharest. This League did not favour the formation of an independent Church, but set itself rather to secure the agreement of the Patriarch to the reading of at least a part of the Liturgy in the Albanian language and the employment of Albanian in the Orthodox schools (D.Z. 94).

The threat of excommunication being removed by the determination of Fan Noli and his colleagues, a great impetus was given to the National Movement, and Orthodox Christian Albanians who had hitherto refrained, hastened to lend their aid. Many Moslem Albanians, profiting by the example of their Christian compatriots, dissociated themselves from the Sheik-ul-Islam at Constantinople, and hastened to the United States, where they swelled the ranks of Nationalists in that country, and liberally contributed to the Christian Albanian Church. Thenceforward progress was amazing. Numerous societies and clubs were founded, and between 1906 and 1918 fourteen newspapers appeared in America, ten of which were in the Albanian language and four in English and Albanian. The leading paper was the *Dielli* (*Sun*), first published by Fan Noli in 1909, which subsequently became the official organ of the Vatra, or Pan-Albanian Federation. The Vatra was founded in 1912, in collaboration with Fan Noli, by Faik bey Konitza, who brought about the amalgamation of already existing local societies into one powerful national association, with headquarters at Boston and branches throughout North America.

While the Albanian leaders strove to prepare their country for autonomy, events occurred in other parts of the Balkan Peninsula which justified both their anxiety and their policy of preserving for their own benefit Turkish suzerainty and power.

In 1886 Greece mobilized with the object of exacting territorial compensation for the aggrandisement of Bulgaria by her union with eastern Roumelia, and engagements between

Greek and Turkish troops took place on the frontier. Greece feared that Bulgaria, victorious against the Serbians, might attempt to come by her own in Macedonia, to the exclusion of Greek pretensions. The Powers—with the exception of France—blockaded the Peiræus for a month, before the Greeks agreed to demobilize. In 1897 Greece again attempted expansion, "the populace demanded war with Turkey and the annexation of Crete" (E.B. 12 : 468). "A Bulgarian proposal for joint pacific action with a view to obtaining reforms in Macedonia was rejected" (E.B. 3 : 261). The remonstrances of the Powers were disregarded, and "history records few more unjustifiable wars than that which Greece gratuitously provoked" (E.B. 12 : 425). Greece was soundly beaten, and sought the mediation of the Powers whose remonstrances she had ignored. "Thus ended an unfortunate enterprise which was undertaken in the hope that discord among the Powers would lead to a European war and the dismemberment of Turkey" (E.B. 12 : 469).

Upon each of these occasions the Albanian Committee adhered to its policy, and instead of taking advantage of Turkey's preoccupation to strike for freedom, supported the Turks against the common foe.

The designs of Russia, Austria-Hungary, and their protégés, the intrigues of their agents whose activities were carried on under the protection of the Capitulations or of diplomatic immunity, Austro-Hungarian propaganda among the Catholic tribesmen, and the activities of the Slavs among the Serbian minorities of Kossovo, caused alarm in northern Albania. Accordingly, in 1899, an assembly of Albanian leaders took place at Ipek to consider measures to secure the inviolability of their lands, and to revive the League in the north.

In the year 1897 negotiations between Austria-Hungary and Russia led to the conclusion of a secret agreement between those two Powers. The terms of this agreement were set forth in a dispatch from the Austro-Hungarian Government, dated the 8th May, to the Austro-Hungarian Ambassador in St. Petersburg (Pribram, 185).

"1. It was agreed that, in case the maintenance of the present *status quo* becomes impossible, Austria-Hungary and Russia discard in advance all idea of conquest in the Balkan Peninsula, and that they are decided to make this principle respected by every other Power which might manifest designs on the above-mentioned territory. . . .

"3. On the other hand, the establishment of a new order of things in the Balkan Peninsula, outside Constantinople and the Straits, would, in case it should occur, give rise to a special stipulation between Austria-Hungary and Russia, who, being chiefly interested in the settlement of this question, declare themselves disposed to act in common accord in fixing thenceforth the basis of their understanding, to wit:

"(a) The territorial advantages accorded to Austria-Hungary by the Treaty of Berlin are and remain acquired by her. In consequence, the possession of Bosnia, of the Hertzegovina, and of the Sanjak of Novibazar may not be made the object of any discussion whatsoever, the Government of His Imperial and Royal Apostolic Majesty reserving to itself the right of substituting, when the moment arrives, for the present status of occupation and of right of garrisoning, that of annexation.

"(b) The part comprised between Janina to the south, and the Lake of Skutari to the north, with a sufficient extension on the east side, shall form an independent State under the name of the Principality of Albania, to the exclusion of every foreign domination.

"(c) The rest of the territory to be disposed of shall be the object of an equitable partition between the different small existing Balkan States, a partition on the subject of which Austria-Hungary and Russia reserve the right of being heard in good time. While inclined to take into consideration as far as possible the legitimate interests of the participants, they are resolved, on the other hand, to safeguard the principle of the present equilibrium, and, if need be, by means of rectifications of frontiers, to exclude every combination which would favour the establishment of a marked preponderance of any particular Balkan principality to the detriment of the others."

Russia entered into the agreement solely in order that she might be free to concentrate upon the Far East, and develop her Far Eastern policy, but with no intention to adhere to the spirit of it for a moment longer than suited her purpose.

To the above clauses she adhered with considerable reservations. In his reply to Count Goluchowski's Note, Count Mouravieff wrote (Pribram, 191):

"In subscribing to this principle [a] we deem it necessary to observe that the Treaty of Berlin assures to Austria-Hungary the right of military occupation of Bosnia and the Hertzegovina. The annexation of these two provinces would raise a more extensive question, which would require special scrutiny at the proper times and places. As to the Sanjak of Novibazar, there would also be the necessity to specify its boundaries, which, indeed, have never been sufficiently defined.

"It seems to us that points b and c, having regard to the eventual formation of a Principality of Albania and to the equitable partition of all the territory to be disposed of between the different small Balkan States, touch upon questions of the future which it would be premature and very difficult to decide at present" (see also H.M. 219; B.T. 127).

The above agreement served merely as a cloak beneath which the two principals, while preserving peace between themselves, might intrigue against each other in furtherance of their respective interests in the Peninsula through their respective protégés; and indisputably, Russia derived the greater benefit from it, although while Serbia remained within the Austro-Hungarian sphere of influence, Austria-Hungary's position with regard to it was not disadvantageous. Its obvious insincerity is made clear by the following clause included in the secret Austro-Hungarian-Russian Promise of Mutual Neutrality of the 2nd October, 1904 (Pribram, 237):

"The engagement between Austria-Hungary and Russia stipulated in the above, naturally does not apply to the Balkan countries, whose destinies are obviously closely attached to the agreement established between the two neighbouring Empires. The said engagement is understood to remain valid so long as these two Great Powers shall pursue their policy of an understanding in the affairs of Turkey; it shall be kept secret and cannot be communicated to any other Government except after a previous understanding between the Cabinets of Vienna and St. Petersburg."

Nevertheless there was one foundation for co-operation between these two Powers inasmuch as both wished to interfere in the internal affairs of Turkey, and to this end combined in 1903 to draw up the "February" (H.M. 220) and Murzšteg (October, 1903; E.P. 276; H.M. 222) programmes of reform for Turkey in Europe. The Albanian Committee viewed with apprehension this infringement of Ottoman sovereignty, which threatened to give to Aušria-Hungary and Russia a measure of influence in Albanian territory, which would be derogatory to the national development of its Albanian inhabitants, and favourable to the Slav minorities. In the same year some thousands of Albanian malissori, širred by the National Movement and the aĉtivities of the Com-mittee, but impatient of delay in the realization of better con-ditions, alarmed by the possibility of Aušro-Hungarian-Russian intervention, and unable to grasp the subtle policy which guided the Nationališ leaders, rose in revolt in the Mitrovitsa dišriĉt. Partly by force and partly by concessions the revolt was suppressed, but it gave encouragement to the Bulgarians of Macedonia who, like the Albanians, resented the Turkish yoke. The insurreĉtion which followed was savagely sup-pressed by the Turks with the co-operation of the Greek party in Macedonia which feared that Bulgarian success might thwart Greek projeĉts (E.B. 12 : 469), while the Greek Government adopted a policy of friendship with Turkey. A few years later Greece sought to "liberate" the Chrišians of Macedonia!

In 1904 took place at Bucharešt the firš Albanian National Assembly (S.A. 14); a number of resolutions were passed, but the Assembly had no important consequences, except that it brought the synchronization of the policies of various Albanian political groups a šage nearer. In 1907 a memoran-dum was submitted to the Hague Conference, but this like-wise had no consequences.

That Serbia was less aĉtive than Greece during this period was principally due to violent party šrife and internal unreš. Nevertheless, she, too, feared that Bulgaria might attempt to gain possession of Macedonia, which hitherto had been regarded as Bulgarian, and seems to be Bulgarian in sentiment, language, and by nationality, and under the same pretext as that employed by Greece in the following year, attacked her in 1885. Although Russia withdrew at the eleventh hour, her officers who had filled all field rank appointments in the Bulgarian Army, and although taken by surprise, the latter country was victorious. The Serbs were routed at Slivnitza, Pirot was occupied, and the intervention of Austria-Hungary alone saved the Serbian Army. "Serbia escaped almost unpunished from her war of aggression" (E.B. 24 : 700). In 1903 she added still further to her unsavoury reputation by the assassination of King Alexander and Queen Draga, a deed which checked the growth of Austro-Hungarian prestige, powerful since 1885. The regicides received the unanimous thanks of the Shkupstina, and were rewarded with the highest administrative offices.

Between Austria-Hungary and Italy there existed grounds for collaboration in regard to Albania, in that both were opposed to the extension of influence or access of any third Power to the Adriatic. On this subject desultory negotiations had taken place, culminating in a secret verbal agreement reached during conversations on the 5th and 7th November, 1897, between the Marquis Visconti Venosta and Count Goluchowski regarding the intangibility of Albania, and confirmed three years later in an exchange of notes (Pribram, 197). The Italian Note, addressed to the Italian Ambassador in Vienna, for communication to the Austro-Hungarian Government, dated the 20th December, 1900, was as follows:

"I call the attention of Your Excellency to my reply to an interpellation recently addressed to me in the Chamber of Deputies on the subject of Albania. Here is the text of that reply:

" 'I am able to give the assurance that the Italian Government and the Austro-Hungarian Government have had occasion to consider their interests on the Ottoman coasts of the Adriatic, and to recognize that these interests find their safeguard in respect for, and in the maintenance of, the *status quo*.'

"I think it would be useful for you to bring my declarations to the knowledge of His Excellency Count Goluchowski. I have no doubt that the Imperial and Royal Minister of Foreign Affairs will find them in conformity with the understanding which was established between him and me on this subject on the occasion of the visit at Monza in 1897. In the exchange of views which took place during our conversations in respect to this question, we found ourselves agreed upon the following points:

"(i) To maintain the *status quo* as long as circumstances permitted;

"(ii) In case the present state of affairs could not be preserved, or in case changes should be imperative, to use our efforts to the end that the modifications relative thereto should be made in the direction of autonomy;

"(iii) In general, and as a mutual disposition on both sides, to seek in common, and as often as there is reason for it, the most appropriate ways and means to reconcile and to safeguard our reciprocal interests.

"I should appreciate being assured that Count Goluchowski, like myself, sees in the preceding the faithful summary of the substance of what was agreed between us upon this subject. In consequence I authorize Your Excellency to communicate this dispatch to him."

"*(Signed)* VISCONTI VENOSTA."

The assurance for which the Marquis Visconti Venosta asked was contained in a Note from Count Goluchowski, dated the 9th February, 1901, and the agreement was again confirmed in the second Final Protocol of the Fifth Treaty of the Triple Alliance (Pribram, 257).

Beyond this agreement, however, the interests of the two Powers ceased to coincide. Count Tittoni made the position clear when, on the 14th May, 1904, he said:

"The true value of Albania lies in her ports and in her sea coast, the possession of which would mean for either Italy or Austria-Hungary the incontestable supremacy of the Adriatic Sea. This is what Italy would never allow Austria-Hungary to obtain, nor Austria-Hungary Italy. In the event that either one of these States should seek to appropriate for itself that region, the other ought to oppose it by all available means."

Since southern Albania

"faces the extreme heel of Italy just below the narrowest point in the neck of the Adriatic, its possessor may control ingress to and egress from that sea. Its position, like that of Albania as a whole, would make it the natural means of entry into and exit from a large part of the western Balkans, *were it not for the topography of the country.* . . . The interior is mountainous; *the ranges run from north to south, thus rendering communication north and south easy, but east and west difficult*" (S.A. 1–2).

Italy subsequently led the way in supporting Albanian interests in the south in order to frustrate Greek aspirations, Greece being supported by France, who regarded Italy as a rival in the Mediterranean and sought to consolidate her own position by identifying herself with Greek interests. This conflict of interests centred round the roadstead of Corfu and the Bay of Valona, points of strategic importance which, in the hands of the protégé of a naval Power would constitute a threat to the security of Italy. Austria-Hungary, on the other hand, was principally interested in frustrating Slav aspirations in northern and eastern Albania (A.W.), fearing that a Slavonic wedge might be driven under Russian auspices, across the Peninsula, thus preventing an expansion southward of her zone of influence. But Italian and Austro-Hungarian interests were also conflicting, in that the latter Power sought to consolidate her prestige in Albania to the exclusion of Italian influence in order that Italy might not gain control of the Straits of Otranto, whereas the preservation of southern Albania from the sphere of influence of another Power was, and is (as explained below) a *sine qua non* of Italian security.

With this in view, Italy regarded with apprehension the extension of Austro-Hungarian influence, by propaganda, into northern Albania, and sought to counteract it partly by stimulating commercial relations with and providing educational facilities in that country; but principally by establishing cordial relations with Montenegro—a method which, in view of Albanian hatred of the Slav, tended to defeat the ends of Italian propaganda in Albania (B.B.).

Under the disastrous policy pursued by Abdul Hamid, the position of the Turkish Empire became worse and worse. His persistent refusal to adopt any reforms left his own absolute

power might be curtailed, brought his Empire to the brink
of destruction. The repeated intervention of the Powers was
resented by all patriotic Turks, and a determination to eliminate the causes of their interference gave rise to the formation
of the Young Turk Party. Meanwhile the Albanian leaders,
especially those in the Turkish services, and thus in the best
position to appreciate the dangers which threatened, viewed
with apprehension the approaching disintegration and premature downfall of the Power under whose protection they
sought to prepare their country, first for autonomy and then
for independence. Both Serbs and Greeks anxiously awaited
the downfall of the Empire to aggrandize themselves at the
expense of Albania. Albania was by no means prepared
for independence, and of this her leaders were fully aware.
Naturally enough, therefore, their policy tended to coincide
with that of the Young Turks.

While Abdul Hamid was opposed to any measure of
reform or to the recognition of the principle of nationality,
which might limit his absolutism, he favoured individual
Albanians. Ferid pasha Vlora, who was President of the
National Albanian Society in Constantinople, became his
Grand Vizier in 1903; and his bodyguard was recruited from
among the Albanian malissori. Those in a position to do so,
prominent among them being Marshal Redjeb Pasha and
Ismail Kemal bey Vlora, cousin of Ferid Pasha, sought to
press upon the Sultan counsels of prudence, but to no purpose, except that they incurred his displeasure. In 1900 Ismail
Bey was obliged to take refuge abroad, where he devoted himself to the preparation of his country for that independence
which he himself was destined to proclaim. The Sultan sent
agents throughout Albania to carry on propaganda against
him, which in most places signally failed, although Essad
pasha Toptani, who commanded the Turkish gendarmerie
at Janina, spared no efforts to assist these propagandists.

Essad Pasha was one of the most unscrupulous adventurers
who has ever achieved political notoriety. He owed his
successful career in the Turkish service to his brother, Ghani
Bey. The latter, after an adventurous early life in his native
land, went to Constantinople, where he became one of those
agents of terrorism whom the Sultan was wont to employ
to carry out the assassinations which formed part of his
policy. Ghani Bey had many crimes to his account, but was,

nevertheless, a favourite among many who were captivated by his prepossessing appearance. One day in 1878, however, while he was joking with a certain Hafriz Pasha, the latter shot him dead. Whether he was shot by accident or design is not known, as Hafriz mysteriously disappeared; the story goes that Ghani's servant avenged his master's death by shooting the culprit on the Galata Bridge. It has been said that Ghani was suspected of aspiring to the throne of Albania, and was accordingly assassinated by design of the Sultan: that Essad swore vengeance, and avenged himself by the part which he played in the subsequent deposition of Abdul Hamid. But one is more inclined to believe that Essad himself was the instigator of the deed. In any case, Ghani's death left him head of the Toptan family and in possession of their extensive property around Tirana. While in command of the Turkish gendarmerie at Janina he won unenviable notoriety by taking advantage of his position to enrich himself, and advance his personal ends, at the expense of his fellow-countrymen. After the revolution of 1908 he was sent to Skutari in the same capacity, and while there professed ardent nationalism; but he was universally disliked and distrusted even by his own tenants around Tirana. Foreign gold alone enabled him to play a part in Albanian history.

Ismail Bey meanwhile joined Faik bey Konitza at Brussels, and took over the management of his paper *Albania*, which he had published there for some years. It should be explained that Albanian families of importance derive their surname from their town or district of origin or, much less frequently, from a distinguished ancestor. The Konitza family, for example, hail from the town of Konitza, around which they possess extensive property, although the district has been ceded to Greece. Faik Bey, educated in France and at Harvard, is the most able Albanian writer, and one of the most prominent Albanian politicians of the present century. His pen caused much uneasiness among the Turks, as it has among his political opponents in Albania. He left Brussels with his paper shortly after Ismail Bey's arrival, and the latter thereupon began the publication of a paper of his own, *Le Salut de l'Albanie*. Ismail Bey was condemned to death *in contumaciam* by the Sultan, upon the charge that he had offered the crown of Albania to the brother of the Khedive of Egypt, which allegation the latter made without the slightest foundation, for the purpose of gaining personal advancement. The lie achieved its purpose.

Ismail Bey subsequently attempted to arrange, in conjunction with Redjeb Pasha (of Mati: T. 22.8.08) a *coup d'état* to force reforms upon the Sultan, and thereby avert the downfall of the Empire; and was assured of the protection, with reservations, of Great Britain against any attempt which Russia might make to thwart the enterprise. Redjeb Pasha was in command of the army in Tripoli, and was universally respected throughout the Turkish Army. Unfortunately the preliminary arrangements broke down and the project was abandoned.

At the end of 1907 Austria-Hungary abandoned her agreement of 1897 with Russia, who had taken advantage of it to intrigue among the Serbs, withdrew her support of Macedonian reform projects, and extracted from the Porte a concession to construct a railway through the Sanjak of Novibazar to Mitrovitza. This seemed to be a prelude to the annexation of the Sanjak, and any interference with the railway or its construction would provide a pretext. Accordingly, at the beginning of 1908, Russia, with the assent of Great Britain and with the object of frustrating Austro-Hungarian projects, announced her intention of imposing upon the Porte the "Reval programme" of reform (E.P. 286; H.M. 237) for Macedonia in place of the "Murzsteg programme", which had proved a fiasco. The Young Turks, who from their headquarters in Paris had been for some time preparing to overthrow the existing régime, were both alarmed and exasperated, fearing that the programme, which included the establishment of an autonomous government, would lead to the loss of the province. Their avowed aspirations were to unite the various ethnical elements as separate national entities within the Empire, under the Turkish flag, and to assure indiscriminate justice and equality for all its subjects, whether Christian or Moslem, thereby reconstituting the Empire upon a stable foundation, to the exclusion of foreign interference. But there were many who had grave misgivings as to their intention of adhering to this liberal programme.

The Albanian leaders were no less alarmed by the intentions of Russia, which appeared to threaten the realization of their projects. Their faith in Europe had been grievously shaken: their fear of their neighbours had been justified and increased: and they chafed under the oppression of Abdul Hamid, who denied them national schools or liberty to use their language. Since 1886 spasmodic local risings forming no part of the nationalist programme had taken place, the most formidable being in 1903, whereby the Albanian people had demonstrated to no purpose their impatience. On the other hand, the programme proposed by the Young Turks appeared to their leaders to offer a hope of better conditions, and in any case seemed to be the only hope of saving the Empire, and with it Albania, from dismemberment. Most of them therefore readily threw in their lot with the Young Turks (T. 24.7.08; 17.8.08) when approached by the latter, who had set up at Salonika a central body known as the Committee of Union and Progress. They stipulated, however, that in return for their support, Albania should be accorded a privileged position within the Empire as an autonomous State.

In the first week of July, 1908, Naizi Bey and Enver Bey (later Pasha) retired to the hills above Resna, the former's native town in Macedonia, and issued an appeal to the Army and Empire. The Young Turks had, however, decided that their *coup d'état* would not take place until the 1st September, the anniversary of Abdul Hamid's accession.

Both Albanians and Turks shared the apprehension that Austria-Hungary, whose attitude had led to the belief that she was working for, and anxiously awaited, a pretext for intervention in Macedonia, might seek to safeguard herself against a loss of prestige which would follow the enforcement of the "Reval programme" by the annexation of at all events the Sanjak of Novibazar, in which she had retained garrisons since 1879. This would have jeopardized Albanian projects to an even greater extent than the close European supervision of affairs proposed by the "Reval programme". The indignation of the Moslem Albanians had been aroused, largely by Turkish propaganda, against Austria-Hungary on account of that country's intrigues and endeavours to establish her prestige especially among their Catholic compatriots, and their indignation was still further aroused by the above apprehensions which were made known to them chiefly through Shemshi Pasha, a faithful supporter of Abdul Hamid (D.Z. 95). Then came the climax.

G

"In the neighbourhood of Uskub and Kossovo, which were largely inhabited by Albanians, the Albanian chiefs were greatly displeased with an Austrian Consul who sheltered under his flag gambling-houses, brothels, and other disorderly houses. The chiefs declared that their young men were robbed and demoralized by the debauchery protected under the Austrian flag. Under the Consul's auspices a great orgy, intended to last for a week, was arranged to take place" (E.P.),

at Ferizovitch, doubtless for the purpose of furthering Austro-Hungarian propaganda. Sheds and booths were erected, and special trains were to be run. This finally determined the Albanians of the surrounding districts to act. On the 10th July they gathered in the neighbourhood to the number of about 10,000, burnt the sheds, and determined once and for all to rid their soil of Austro-Hungarian propagandists. The Young Turks and the Albanian Nationalist leaders heard of their intentions, and at once realized that such action would inevitably precipitate the intervention of Austria-Hungary, bring down the Austro-Hungarian Army, and frustrate the proposed coup. They therefore hastily dispatched representatives to persuade these Albanians to refrain from adopting so dangerous a course, and instead to demand with their support the restoration of the Midhat Constitution. It seems doubtful whether the majority of the Albanians, assembled at Ferizovitch, had the remotest idea of what the Constitution was; but upon the assurance that it meant reforms, national schools, liberation from foreign intrigue, and the building of roads and railways for their benefit, they readily and unanimously acclaimed it.

On the 15th July they telegraphed to the Sultan demanding the immediate restoration of the Constitution, while Enver and Naizi, supported by the Albanian Nationalists, raised the standard of revolt at Resna. The Sultan ordered troops to march against the rebels, but they refused to do so. He consulted his Ministers, and they advised him to yield, as did Ismail Kemal Bey for whose advice he telegraphed, although he had previously condemned him to death. The Army of Macedonia declared for the Young Turks, and the troops at Adrianople did likewise. On the 23rd the Sultan yielded to the wishes of his people, and the restoration of the Midhat Constitution was proclaimed.

The Constitution was hailed throughout Albania, as indeed throughout the Empire, with the wildest enthusiasm. A general *besa* was proclaimed throughout the country, and for almost a year no private or inter-tribal feuds took place (F.O. 42). The acclamation of the Constitution was, of course, necessarily somewhat tardy in the northern highlands. Each bairak represented a separate self-governing unit, frequently in a state of war with its neighbour, and because the Moslems in the east had thought fit to demand the Constitution, and because their compatriots in the lowlands had supported it, it did not necessarily follow that it was desirable. Once more it must be emphasized that this was one of the principal difficulties which confronted the Nationalists and, subsequently, successive Albanian Governments. It equipped the enemies of Albania with a powerful argument against the formation of an independent Albanian State.

Skutari accepted the Constitution on the 2nd August, and the Skutarines gave vent to wild enthusiasm. But what of the malissori? The general *besa* which had been proclaimed throughout Albania was accepted in the highlands to celebrate and facilitate discussion of this mysterious thing. It appeared to be a panacea for all evils: there were rumours that Albania was free. Each tribe and bairak discussed it. And eventually all, with the exception of Mirdita, decided to accept it, provided the Sergherdé, an undesirable by name Shachir Bey, was dismissed. The Young Turks, aware that universal acceptance of the Constitution was essential, if the sympathy of Europe was to be retained, assented. Thereupon the malissori hastened to Skutari to acclaim it, and incidentally to hear what it meant.

From the 6th to the 10th August the malissori, Moslems and Christians, flocked to Skutari by tribes and bairaks to hear the official proclamation and celebrate the event in their own way. On the 10th came the Christian tribesmen of Pulati. Their arrival "was unrehearsed, undrilled, but no preparation could have made it more magnificent. Summoned by their chiefs, they came—chosen representatives from all the big tribes—1,500 strong, each tribe headed by its bairaktar with the bullet-riven banner, and led by its priest or Franciscan—sons of the Church militant (a revolver peeped from the habit of more than one)—riding or marching in front of their men, and marshalling them with a precision that called forth general admiration. Keeping neither line nor step, but in perfect order, they swung down the street with the peculiar stride of the sandal-shod mountaineer. . . . Through a cloud of dust, sweltering heat—to the continuous roar of fifteen hundred rifles and the applause and revolvers of the onlookers—singing and shouting, the mass swept into the drill-ground." The tribesman expresses joy, or welcomes a guest, by the discharge of rifle or revolver.

> "For two whole days and nights over two thousand heavily armed men were loose in the town—nor was there either military or police force sufficient to have coped with an outbreak—but not one incident occurred to mar the general joy. They rejoiced like children, too happy to be naughty. Even the representatives of two Consulates, who frankly detested the Albanians, said 'Mon Dieu, under a decent Government, what a people this would be!' " (H.A. 227-8).

But the Mirdites still hesitated to accept the Constitution, fearing it might mean curtailment of the absolute freedom which they had hitherto enjoyed. The Abbot of Mirdita, Mgr. Primo Dochi, was instructed by the authorities to bring them to Skutari formally to accept it. He replied that it was not his place to do so, but that Prenk Pasha, their hereditary chieftain, still lived in exile. Prenk, who had risen to the rank of Brigade Commander in the Sultan's Albanian Guards, was hastened back to his native land, where he arrived on the 30th September. The Constitution was accepted, and the abolition of blood vengeance agreed upon.

While the malissori were accepting the Constitution and awaiting results, the Nationalists in the lowlands hastily took advantage of the situation which the success of the Young Turks had created. The Committee of Union and Progress had proclaimed liberty and equality for all nationalities within the Empire, and had thus secured the support and co-operation of all educated Albanians and their followers. Now the latter sought to take advantage of the liberty for which they had given their support. Indeed, the promulgation of the Constitution was the signal for an explosion of Albanian national sentiment. The Albanian League abandoned clandestine methods, and once again for a brief space found itself in enjoyment of Turkish benevolence. The explanation of this benevolence is that the Young Turks appreciated the necessity of retaining Albanian support, which had so largely contributed to their success, in view of possible complications with neighbouring States, and to this end even distributed some 40,000 rifles among the Albanians of Kossovo and the north (D.Z. 97). But the Young Turks did not appreciate the extent to which Albanian national sentiment had grown since the formation of the League, and while they remained under the impression that it would prove but a safeguard against foreign interference, the Albanians took steps to safeguard themselves not only against foreign aggression, but also against any attempt which might be made by the Turks to suppress the League once more, or to curtail their new-found liberties. From Florina to Mitrovitza a series of Albanian clubs was established along the borders of Albanian territory, and throughout all Albania from Prevesa to Skutari, and Janina to Prizren (A.S. 25; also *Au jeune royaume d'Albanie; ce qu'il a été ce qu'il est*: G. L. Jaray) composed of Albanian patriots determined to defend their national rights and liberties. Albanian schools were at once opened; newspapers appeared—at Korcha alone three papers were published and numerous patriotic clubs and societies founded (Q.K. 24). Christians and Moslems vied with each other in their efforts to better the conditions of their compatriots (D.Z. 118).

Many exiles hastened back to their native land, and with them the organizations which had struggled for twenty-two years to propagate the national ideal from the shelter of more liberal countries; while those who remained abroad redoubled their efforts. Among those who returned was Ismail Kemal Bey, who was elected Deputy for Berat and Valona to the Turkish Parliament, despite the endeavours of the Young Turks to prevent his election. In theory he shared their ideals, but in practice he was too liberal for them.

In November, 1908, as the result of arrangements made at Korcha earlier in the year, an Albanian Congress was held at Monastir under the Presidency of Midhat bey Frasheri to discuss educational problems. The Young Turks did their utmost to prevent the Congress from being held, and subsequently to divert its course from Nationalist channels, but were unsuccessful. The Congress lasted for a week. Moslems, among them several hodjas, took a leading part. In the course of its deliberations it confirmed the decision of Sami Bey's Committee at Conſtantinople in 1878 to employ modified Latin charaƈters as the national alphabet (A.S. 25-6; D.Z. 114). Since 1878 this alphabet had been used almoſt exclusively in publishing books for circulation among the Ghegs. The national alphabet, with amendments, was appended to the report of the proceedings of the Congress, which included the passing of a resolution to the effeƈt that all Albanian clubs and societies should submit reports periodically to the *Bashkim* Club at Monaſtir, to enable that centre to keep in touch with, and co-ordinate, the work being carried on throughout Albania (D.Z. 114).

The apparent success of the Conſtitution caused grave misgivings in those countries which had so anxiously awaited the downfall of the Empire. Greece once again raised claims to southern Albania, but they were ignored. Bulgaria, over which the Porte had latterly exercised a purely nominal suzerainty, feared that Turkey might now attempt to reassert her authority, and therefore declared complete independence on the 5th Oƈtober, 1908. But the moſt outſtanding aƈt on the part of neighbouring States was committed by Auſtria-Hungary. Aƈting in accordance with the ſtipulation embodied in her agreement with Russia of 1897 (see above), claiming legitimacy for her aƈt under the terms of her agreement with that country and Germany of the 18th June, 1881 (Pribram, 43), which had been confirmed on the 27th March, 1889 (T. 17.3.20), but in violation of the terms of the Treaty of Berlin to which she, Germany, and Russia had been signatories, she proclaimed, on the 7th Oƈtober, 1908, the annexation of Bosnia and the Hertzegovina (which she had adminiſtered, greatly to their advantage, for twenty-eight years).

The hiſtory of the annexation crisis cannot be dealt with here; but it should be mentioned that the aƈtion of Auſtria-Hungary—to which Great Britain agreed with reluƈtance (P.D. 3 : 1507) and which was a primary cause of the Great War of 1914–18—caused exasperation in Russia. That country had concluded the agreement of 1881 before the emancipation of Bulgaria from her tutelage had been foreseen, and before Serbia had succeeded Bulgaria as her principal protégé and inſtrument of her Balkan policy. In 1889 Russia had wished to avoid possible complications in the west, that she might be free to pursue her Far Eastern policy. The Russo-Japanese War had wrecked that policy, shattered her prestige, and sapped her strength, and in 1908 she had not recovered sufficiently to denounce her agreements with Austria-Hungary and risk war in the interests of her Balkan policy. But from 1908 war between these two rival Powers was inevitable.

Having annexed Bosnia and the Hertzegovina before a rejuvenated Ottoman Empire could demand their restoration in accordance with the terms of the Treaty of Berlin and thus deprive her of the benefit of her efforts to develop them, Austria-Hungary adopted a conciliatory policy towards Turkey whom she resolved to support against Pan-Slavism. Accordingly she withdrew her troops from the Sanjak of Novibazar—where they were in a position of strategic insecurity—and renounced all rights therein, at the same time concluding an agreement with Turkey which was very favourable to that country. The removal thereby of the Austro-Hungarian menace probably encouraged both Turks and Albanians, the former to enforce reforms and the latter to resist them (T. 10.4.09).

It is interesting that as a prelude to the annexation Austria-Hungary appears to have armed the Catholic malissori (T. 21.7.11); but whether that signified that she anticipated war with Turkey, or the retaliation of one of the Balkan States or even Italy by attempting the annexation of Albania, it is difficult to say. The annexation did, however, provoke a storm of indignation in Italy, and relations between the two countries became strained; but despite the bellicose attitude of the military party in Austria-Hungary, the saner elements appreciated then, as they did during the Turko-Italian War three years later, that a breach with Italy would shatter the Triple Alliance and play into the hands of Russia. These considerations were among those which led to the evacuation of the Sanjak of Novibazar; and on the 30th November of the following year Austria-Hungary assured Italy that if

"in consequence of the impossibility of maintaining the status quo in the Balkans Austria-Hungary should be compelled by the force of circumstances to proceed to a temporary or permanent occupation of the Sanjak of Novibazar, that occupation shall be effected only after a previous agreement with Italy based on the principle of compensation" (Pribram, 241).

The Young Turks accepted the action of Bulgaria, and the annexation with financial compensation, as a means of ridding themselves and the Empire of foreign interference. They imagined that they would now be left free to carry out the programme which they adopted once they had secured power. But they were soon disillusioned.

The annexation was a blow to Pan-Slav projects; and Serbian aspirations to expansion northwards and westwards to the sea could be realized now only through a European war. Russia seized the opportunity provided by the wave of indignation which it created throughout the Balkans to propose the formation of a Balkan League against Austria-Hungary, and her Foreign Minister—Isvolski—supported by her Ambassador at Constantinople—Tcharykov—advocated the inclusion therein of Turkey, provided that country would agree to grant free access of the Russian fleet—through the Dardanelles—to the Mediterranean. But the support which this project enjoyed in the Balkan capitals was only transient. For many years the Balkan States had looked upon Turkey in Europe as their legitimate heritage, and were determined not to abandon their aspirations in this respect. Greece claimed Thrace and Epirus; Bulgaria coveted Macedonia; and Serbia desired to re-establish the ephemeral empire of Tsar Stefan "Dushan"—which would entail the annexation of north-eastern Albania (where Albanians were in an overwhelming majority: E.B. map 3 : 259; B.T. Chap. VIII, etc.)—and access to the sea through north-western Albania. Moreover, Serbia was encouraged by the conviction that in any eventuality Russia, to whom she had transferred her allegiance, would support her, and that in those circumstances her security was assured by the existence of the Triple Entente (Bogitchevitch: Annex XVI; B.T. 134, 159; etc.).

By closing the door to Serbian expansion northwards, Austria-Hungary threw Serbia into the arms of Russia; and the latter country thereupon began to exert pressure upon Montenegro—no longer her principal protégé—to modify her ambitious aspirations to hegemony in the Balkans and to revise her unfriendly attitude towards her rival Serbia, which had reached a climax with the "Cettinje bomb plot" in 1908. There had always existed in Montenegro a party in favour of the union of the two Slav States, but to this Austria-Hungary was strongly opposed—unless it should be effected under her suzerainty; and to prevent it she had retained garrisons in the Novibazar corridor until 1908 and encouraged Prince Nicholas to proclaim himself king—as an "opposition" to the Serbian dynasty—in 1910.

Russia continued to favour a Balkan League against Austria-Hungary which should include Turkey, until the beginning of 1912; but thereafter she adhered to the alternative policy advocated by her Minister in Belgrade, M. Hartwig, who advocated a League directed against Turkey as a means of achieving her purpose—a policy already under consideration in the Balkan capitals.

Excessive zeal is not infrequently more detrimental to a cause than apathy. During the old régime the Turkish administration in Albania had been apathetic. Albania had drifted; and Turkish lethargy had been overcome only during an insurrection. But constitution meant reforms, and accordingly the Turks set themselves to apply these reforms regardless of local customs, institutions or age-long traditions. They handled the Constitution almost as skilfully as would the average Cabinet Minister a plough. They blundered hopelessly, and floundered from one blunder to another, until pulled up by Albanian resentment.

No administration, however efficient, could possibly succeed in northern Albania unless liberally endowed with tact. The Turks possessed none (H.A. 230). Consequently dissatisfaction with the Constitution grew rapidly. Within a few weeks the tribesmen began to clamour for the roads and schools which had been promised; nor would they forego their ancient privileges or submit to taxation and compulsory military service. Tactfully handled, their confidence would have been retained. By tactlessness they were alienated and embittered. Moslems began to suspect that the Constitution was an attack upon their religion which was synonymous with freedom, for which they had accepted Islamism: perhaps it was a fresh machination of Austria-Hungary. Christians began to fear that they might lose their rights; they outnumbered the Moslems in the Skutari district, and accordingly were disqualified wholesale from voting at the election. Then appeared the hand of the Slav. The Montenegrins no less than the Serbs feared that a reconstituted Turkish Empire would prevent their expansion southward, and when a rift appeared they set themselves to widen the breach.

Before the close of 1908 the Committee of Union and Progress revealed its actual intentions; it set itself a "task to which the absolutism of the Sultan had never ventured" (C.E. 35). There was to be liberty and equality for all Ottomans who shared the views of the Committee, but not otherwise. All the subjects of the Empire were Ottomans. Allegiance to the Empire was not sufficient, and those who claimed racial distinction were to be forcibly "Ottomanized". For a while the Liberals, foremost among them being Kiamil Pasha, also Ismail Kemal Bey and other Albanians in Constantinople, held the Committee in check. But its arbitrary conduct was the negation of Constitutional Government. Kiamil Pasha, the Grand Vizier, was compelled by it to resign on the 14th February, 1909, and was succeeded by Hilmi Pasha. His Unionist Cabinet provoked popular indignation, and the Committee resorted to acts of intimidation. A climax was precipitated by the assassination on the 5th April of Hassan Fehmi, the Albanian editor of the *Serbesti*, the official organ of the Liberal Union.

On the 13th April the Sultan's Albanian bodyguard mutinied, and the mutineers gained possession of the capital almost without bloodshed. The Liberal Union, supported by Albanians in the city, was placed in power, while the Sultan was prevailed upon to grant a free pardon to those who had participated in the disturbance. But the Committee at Salonika refused to recognize the new Government which denied it absolute power, and an army under Mahmoud Shevkct Pasha invested Constantinople. Fighting ensued, culminating in the occupation of the capital and deposition of Abdul Hamid, who was succeeded by his brother, Mohammed Reshad. Essad Pasha was entrusted with the task of announcing to the Sultan that he was deposed. There were undoubtedly a few Albanians who had not as yet appreciated the difference between their ideals and those of the Committee, and still therefore supported it in the expectation that it would carry out its avowed programme. But it is improbable that Essad, who was an official of high rank, was unaware of the policy which it actually intended to pursue; rather was he a shrewd gambler. He had "gone abroad for his health", and had waited until the success of the Young Turk coup in 1908 was assured before declaring his allegiance to their cause, when he cowed Tirana into returning him as a Deputy to the

Turkish Parliament, with Mufid bey Libohova, Ismail Kemal
Bey, and other Albanians; and in April, 1909, he knew that
fortune, in the case of an armed conflict, must favour the
Committee's military superiority.

Almost the first act of Hussein Hilmi's Unionist Cabinet
had been to pass legislation against "bands" in European
Turkey, and also to authorize the bastinado as punishment for
certain offences such as vagrancy. It was chiefly this legislation which had provoked popular indignation and the subsequent mutiny. Once their supremacy was assured by the
success of Shevket Pasha, the Unionists proceeded to give
effect to these measures, both of which had been adopted in
order that the policy of Ottomanization might be carried out
with the utmost vigour. Both were expressly directed against
subject races, especially the Albanians. The Young Turks
recognized that the latter were the principal national entity
within the Empire and the most dangerous to their policy.
At the same time they imagined that by coercion and drastic
measures which no Turkish Government hitherto had been
sufficiently foolish to adopt, they might obliterate a nationality
which had survived four centuries of Turkish rule. Their
policy produced a very contrary effect.

The legislation against "bands" enacted that should one
member of a family join a "band", the whole family should
be exiled and its goods confiscated. Thus, should one member
of a family, which in Albania frequently comprises a village
or bairak, participate in guerilla warfare, the whole village
or bairak would be punished. Thus was provided a pretext
for drastic punitive measures against Albania; while the
authorization of the bastinado was perhaps more provocative
of trouble than any other conceivable measure (T. 27.7.12), in
that a blow, in Albania, is an insult, which could be avenged
only by blood. A Bulgarian will submit sullenly to being
beaten, but never an Albanian (T. 24.2.12).

Among the other steps taken by the Committee of Union
and Progress in pursuance of its insane and suicidal policy
were the abolition of the freedom of the newly emancipated
Press, the granting of unrestricted powers to the police to
suppress public meetings, the prohibition of the formation of
clubs upon a racial basis for any purpose whatever (August,
1909), and the curtailment of the internal autonomy of
Christian communities. Turkish was to be the only language of

instruction throughout the Empire, a uniform system of conscription, taxation, and administration was to be enforced irrespective of local customs and traditions; and all civilians were forbidden to carry arms.

The first step towards forcible Ottomanization of the Albanians was to deny their existence as such. But when in the Turkish Assembly the Minister of the Interior declared that there was no Albanian nationality, he was fiercely contradicted by cries of "Var, Efendim, var!" ("There is, Efendi, there is!") from the Albanian deputies present.

The next step was to establish Turkish schools—in conformity with a uniform system of education throughout the Empire—in place of the Albanian schools which were appearing everywhere, "in order to suppress the Albanian language" (P.D. 32 : 2571; F.O. 44); and to impose compulsory military service and regular taxation upon the tribesmen, who had never paid taxes from time immemorial, and whose only obligation had been to furnish voluntary contingents for service in time of war. The first Albanians upon whom the Turks attempted to impose these measures were the Moslems of north-eastern Albania, who had led the way in demanding the Constitution in 1908. They refused, however, to tolerate Turkish schools where Albanian were available—opposing not education, but Ottomanization. Nor were they prepared to forfeit their liberty by compulsory military service; nor to pay taxes unless they were assured that the money would be expended in their own districts; nor to surrender their arms or enlarge into windows the loopholes of their *kulas*, which would place them at the mercy of both local enemies and Slav raiders (T. 2 and 23.6.09).

To deal with the Albanians of Kossovo, with whom the Young Turks anticipated trouble, once their intentions were revealed, Djavid Pasha had been appointed military commandant of the Mitrovitza region, and entrusted with the task of "establishing schools" therein. His appointment was in itself provocative of trouble, since he had previously acquired an unenviable reputation in the district. His first act was to carry out operations in the mountainous region north of Mitrovitza, with the primary object of capturing the redoubtable Isa Boletin (B.K. 192, 198, 209–13), who possessed supreme authority among the Albanians of the Kossovo vilayet. Of a meeting with this great chieftain at Mitrovitza in August, 1912, Colonel A. Herbert gave the following account (B.K. 205–6):

"It was a perfect night outside, with an enormous full moon in a cloudless sky. Hadji Salih was waiting with an unnecessary lamp, and we walked quickly through the streets outside the town to a *han*, where Isa had come to meet me. He was surrounded by numbers of his wild Albanian mountaineers covered with weapons. They made a fine picture in the moonlight. I waited in the courtyard. One or two of them came up to talk to me; they were generally very aloof, but seemed to be tingling with excitement. Then I was shown upstairs, and outside on the landing was another crowd of be-weaponed Albanians. The walls were all hung round with arms. I went into a fair-sized room, where I found Isa Boletin, a very tall, lithe, well-made Albanian, aquiline, with restless eyes, and a handsome, fierce face, in the Gheg dress. . . . A couple of shots went off under the window. I was interested in the conversation and paid no attention. Isa pulled back a little curtain and looked out into the moonlight. As he did so a dozen shots rang out just outside. Instantly his clansmen swarmed into the room, taking arms down from the wall. They walked upon dancing feet, and their eyes glittered. Isa jumped up with a rifle in his hand and said to me, 'The house is surrounded by the Turks. I am going to fight my way out'. I said to him, 'This is not my quarrel, but I will come with you, as if you are taken the Turks will not shoot you if I am there'. He said, 'No, you are my guest. My honour will not allow this thing. You protect my son'. Isa and his men poured out. Some stayed and kept me in.

"They were back again almost at once. It had apparently been only a brawl outside—Turks, they said—and nobody was hurt I am very glad that I saw it. It was wonderful, the way in which the clansmen formed round Isa Boletin. They were like men on springs, active and lithe as panthers."

Although Djavid succeeded in burning Boletin's native village—Boletin—the chieftain himself escaped. At once this unsurpassed guerilla leader accepted Djavid's challenge, and during the winter of 1908-9 collected a force of Albanians with the intention of marching on Mitrovitza; but before his preparations were completed Djavid again took the initiative and destroyed the villages in which Boletin was organizing his resources.

But Boletin and his compatriots were not to be discouraged. Moreover, the innovations which the Young Turks were attempting to impose, especially the proposed levying of a super-tax for educational and military purposes, widened the disaffected area and swelled the ranks of those prepared to defend their liberty by force of arms. During the summer Ferizovitch became, once again, the centre of Albanian insurrectionary activity, but in August Djavid's troops advanced against the town and dispersed with artillery fire a large force of Albanians concentrated in and around it (T. 4.11.09). Fierce fighting against Isa Boletin, Bairam Tsuri of Hashi, Islam Sipahi of Ljuma, and other leaders ensued, and continued throughout August and September. Eventually Djavid succeeded in fighting and burning his way into the Ljuma district, disarming (the tribesmen generally surrendered only obsolete weapons; T. 6.6.10) and flogging the proud tribesmen (T. 3.2.11) as he went; and at the end of September, 1909, he fell back to Mitrovitza, congratulating himself that he had brought to an end the Albanian insurrection. It was, however, but beginning (D.Z. 98-9).

The whole of eastern Albania was now disaffected, and the Albanians were determined to be avenged for the manner in which Djavid had carried out the above operations. It needed but a spark to set the region ablaze once more. This was supplied by Mazhar Bey, the Vali of Uskub, who imposed an "Octroi" which affected the Albanian peasants bringing their produce to market. The proceeds were to be devoted to the improvement of the towns, about which the Albanian tribesmen cared nothing. In itself perhaps a trivial matter, it was regarded by the Albanians as "the last straw", and they rose in insurrection once more at the beginning of April, 1910 (D.Z. 103-4; also T. April, 1910).

The insurrection began at Prishtina, when several thousand Albanians attacked and drove out the Turkish garrison, capturing two guns. In the middle of April Shevket Torgut Pasha arrived at Ferizovitch, and assumed supreme command of the Turkish troops in northern and eastern Albania. Apart from troops on garrison duty, he had at his disposal 17,000 men, a force subsequently increased by various reinforce- ments (some 60,000 men in all: T. 17.5.10; 21.7.11). Half this army he concentrated at Ferizovitch, while the other half was dispatched to re-occupy Prishtina and subdue the surrounding district. Meanwhile a small force was sent from Ferizovitch to occupy Prizren, but was attacked and surrounded in the Tchernalova Pass and was only extricated upon the arrival of strong reinforcements from Ferizovitch. The Albanians then occupied the Katchanik Pass, thus cutting Shevket's communications with Uskub and Salonika, and further opera- tions were thus rendered impossible until communications had been reopened with the assistance of reinforcements from the south.

Once the Katchanik Pass was cleared, the Turkish troops, operating in three parallel columns, advanced upon Prizren, which was occupied after some heavy fighting, in the middle of May. Thence Shevket moved upon Djakova and Ipek, and although these towns were entered without opposition the operations of mobile columns, detached from the main line of advance to suppress the insurrection in outlying districts, were so fiercely opposed that the Turkish advance was con- siderably delayed. Eventually, however, the Albanians of the Kossovo vilayet were temporarily subdued once more (although severe fighting was reported from the Ghilan district in July; T. 29.7.10). Their defeat seems to have been due largely to their tactical inferiority to the Turks. Being generally obsessed with a fear of being surprised, taken in rear, or of occupying a position commanded by higher ground, they preferred to occupy bare hill-tops which pro- vided an excellent mark for the Turks, and seldom made use of cover (T. 24.5.10).

There were several considerations which had restrained the Albanians of the west and south from rising simul- taneously and going to the assistance of their compatriots in the east. In the first place the Catholic tribesmen of northern Albania (T. 14.5.10) had no reserve of ammunition, and although frenzied appeals were made to the Austro-Hungarian Consulate and to other possible sources of supply, it suited nobody's game at that stage to supply it. And the Moslems of the north feared that a rising might provoke Austro- Hungarian intervention. Secondly, the Albanian Nationalist leaders, whose influence was paramount in central and southern Albania, where national education had made progress, held their compatriots therein in check (except the Tchams, who made an abortive insurrection; T. 10.5.10) in the hope that the Young Turks might eventually relent, and thus enable them to adhere to their original policy of national consolidation under Turkish protection and suzerainty. Thus while the blood of their countrymen was flowing copiously in Kossovo, the Albanian leaders strove unceasingly, both in Parliament and without, to bring the Turkish Government to reason, and to emphasize the danger to the Empire of a senseless struggle: but to no purpose. Thirdly, as yet there existed no universally recognized Albanian authority which could coordinate and direct the efforts of Albanians throughout the whole country in the cause of nationalism: and the tribes continued to act independently, at their own discretion, and in defence of their own particular interests. Fourthly, Ismail Kemal Bey's honesty of purpose is not unchallenged. It is alleged that his ambition was stronger than his patriotism, and that he planned to strike only when sure that he would be regarded as the saviour of Albania; also that he took advantage of his position to enrich himself by accepting bribes from Greek sources to remain inactive.

Having temporarily subdued Kossovo, Djavid Pasha, who commanded a column detailed to reinforce Bedri Bey at Skutari, demanded of Prenk Bib Doda safe conduct through Mirdita. Prenk had, for political reasons, been made a member of the Committee of Union and Progress, and acceded to Djavid's demand. He could not well have done otherwise, since the Mirdites were without the means to resist, nor would it have been in accordance with the national policy of the more prudent Albanian leaders to do so. Djavid encountered, therefore, no resistance, although some of the passes had been blocked with trees and rocks (D.Z. 105), and arrived in Skutari on the 24th July. It had taken the Turkish army four months to fight its way from Uskub—a journey which, in normal circumstances, took five days. Djavid's arrival caused exasperation and dismay, although discretion prevailed and no resistance was offered. The Turks at once proceeded forcibly to disarm the inhabitants, and on the 25th martial law was proclaimed and a decree issued that all arms were to be surrendered throughout the Skutari district. Many of the malissori concealed their weapons, surrendering only obsolete ones, and the Klementi men were allowed to retain theirs, so that they might act as frontier guards. The latter were hereditary foes of the Montenegrins, and so recently as 1907 had assisted the Turks to defend a blockhouse against them, in one of the frequently recurring frontier incidents. The Plava and Gusinje Moslems openly defied the Turks, who accused the Montenegrins of encouraging them to do so (T. 30.11.10).

Once the disarmament was completed, troops were sent throughout the highlands to compile a register of those eligible for compulsory military service and to collect taxes. In Skutari a retrospective tax was even demanded to pay for the insurrection of 1903.

While these events were taking place in the north, forcible Ottomanization began everywhere, and the Albanians were finally convinced that the Young Turk régime threatened their national aspirations even more than that of Abdul Hamid had done. The Young Turks, however, realized that the suppression of national education, by prohibition of the teaching of the language, would present grave difficulties in central and southern Albania, where the educational movement was already established. They thereupon attempted at first to divert its course to their own advantage, and thus prevent the unity which the Nationalists were striving to achieve.

During the summer of 1909 the Young Turks ascertained that the Albanian Nationalist Committee proposed to hold another Conference to discuss problems of national importance. Thereupon they took the initiative, and convened at Dibra at the end of July a Congress to which they called representatives of all the races of European Turkey, with the intention so to manipulate the proceedings of the Congress that the representatives, among them the Albanians, might be persuaded to accept the programme of Ottomanization which the Young Turks had in view. A number of Young Turkish representatives, among them Naizi Bey, contrived to become elected as representatives to the Congress, and a list of resolutions was prepared, the adoption of which the Young Turks hoped to secure without discussion. But the latter once more had underestimated the strength of Albanian national feeling, and very shortly after the Congress opened, the Albanian element gained complete control of the proceedings.

H

The delegates, assembled at Dibra, elected eight of their
number to represent each of the five vilayets of Turkey in
Europe. These forty adopted the report which had been
prepared by the Turks, and then proceeded to introduce additional clauses and amendments which were by no means in
accordance with Young Turkish policy. Specifically, the
Albanians demanded that there should be justice in the courts
of law, that Albanian schools should be established in Albania,
that the power of the Councils-General of vilayets should be
wider, that the amount of the annual tithe levied by the
Government should be assessed, not annually, but on the
basis of an average taken over five years, that roads should
be constructed in Albania by the Government—hitherto not
one penny of the money collected by taxation in Albania had
been spent therein—and that the Turko-Montenegrin frontier
should be demarcated on the ground without further delay
(D.Z. 100–1; compare with T. 5.8.09). In short, whatever
was achieved at the Congress, it certainly emphasized once
more the determination of the Albanians to shape their own
destinies, and it certainly did nothing to further the ends
which the Young Turks had in view.

The Congress of Dibra was followed by another, a purely
Albanian Congress, held at Elbasan in September of the
same year, primarily for the purpose of devising a definite
educational system. All the Albanian Nationalist clubs, including even those at Caraferia, Katerina, and Drama, sent
representatives. The Albanians succeeded for a few months
in evading the legislation passed by the Turkish Government in August, 1909, against the formation of clubs upon a
racial or political basis, by declaring that their clubs were
social and non-political (D.Z. 118).

Before it dispersed, the Congress of Elbasan confirmed the
decisions taken at Monastir in the previous year. Moreover, it
agreed to reassemble at Janina in the following year, but
before it was able to do so the Young Turks discarded the
velvet glove in their dealings with Albanian nationalism
(D.Z. 114; A.S. 26).

One of the immediate consequences of the Congress of
Elbasan was the establishment in that town of a Normal
School to meet the demand for trained Albanian teachers.
The Principal, M. Louis Gurakuchi, was a Catholic, and the
remainder of the staff and pupils indiscriminately Moslems and

Chriftians. Within a few months of its eftablishment this school was attended by more than fifty pupils.

It now being clear to the Young Turks that the tide of Albanian nationalism was not to be ftemmed, they sought to divert it. To this end they attempted to subftitute Arabic charaƈters for the Latin charaƈters of the Albanian national alphabet (Q.K. 24; D.Z. 116; T. 28.2.10; etc.), at the same time proclaiming that the Latin charaƈters were the invention of foreigners whose objeƈt it was to pervert good Moslems from their faith, and that the Arabic charaƈters were sacred. This propaganda proved, however, a complete failure. Moslems and Chriftians of all classes combined in holding meetings of proteft againft it, and at Elbasan 7,000 Albanians gathered to declare their readiness to proteƈt their language with their lives. During February, 1910, regardless of the opposition of the Government, a great demonftration which began with a prayer recited by a Moslem *hodja*, took place at Korcha (T. 28.3.10); the assembled crowds unanimously agreed that the Latin charaƈters should be retained and that the queftion of the alphabet had no conneƈtion with religion (D.Z. 116). In the same town, which was a centre of the Albanian educational movement, thirty-eight pupils, by way of proteft, left the State High School and attended the school which had been eftablished by the Albanian Club. This example was followed by the majority of boys attending the local Turkish preparatory school (D.Z. 117). A quantity of books published by the Young Turks in the Albanian language with Arabic charaƈters at once became the objeƈt of ridicule, since these charaƈters not infrequently imparted a false meaning to the words which they were supposed to represent. Eventually these books were publicly burnt in the market-places throughout Albania.

Having failed to divert the course of national education, the Young Turks now decided to suppress it altogether. Albanian schools throughout the country, including the Normal School at Elbasan, were closed. The Albanian newspapers were suppressed, and the editors in many cases imprisoned without trial. Hundreds of prominent Nationalifts were either arrefted (T. 1.6.10; 10.6.10) or obliged to seek refuge abroad, many going to Cettinje, there to plan a general national insurreƈtion, while others travelled throughout Europe in an endeavour to win the support, or at leaft the sympathy, of the Powers. Even the printing of the words "Albania" and "Albanians" was prohibited! There were no Albanians! All were Ottomans! A more puerile policy it is difficult to imagine!

Then came the beginning of the end. A comet appeared in the sky. War, it signified; war was predicted. Albanian patience was exhausted. The old régime had been bad: the new one was insufferable. The Turks had violated their undertakings. Albania was treated as a conquered country; customs and traditions were disregarded as never before. Since autonomy could not be obtained by constitutional means it must be won by force of arms. Arrangements for a general insurrection were set on foot, and preparations made for a rising of all tribesmen, both Christians and Moslems, in conjunction with their compatriots of the south, directly instructions were received from the Nationalist leaders, the deputies, chief of whom was Ismail Kemal Bey, who were still endeavouring to bring the Young Turks to reason. The Albanian leaders were aware that unless their country at once obtained autonomy and liberty to continue national education, she would never be able to prepare herself for independence before the now inevitable disintegration of the Empire occurred, and would be partitioned among neighbouring States.

But the manner in which the troops and officials enforced reforms among the disarmed malissori drove some 3,000 of them to seek refuge in Montenegro. That country drew the attention of the Powers to the difficulty of maintaining them (T. 29.10.10), whereupon the Turks, anxious to avoid international complications, offered to moderate their policy upon the condition that the refugees would return (T. 3.11.10; 19.6.11). The majority accepted, but the Turkish promises remained a dead letter. The malissori were exasperated, resolved to resist the infringement of their immemorial rights, and sent their families across the border. Some 12,000 refugees poured into the territory of their hereditary foes—evidence (T. 3.7.11) enough to show that the Turks were adopting extreme measures—where they were received by the Albanian subjects of King Nicholas. Their plight provided an irresistible opportunity for the Montenegrins.

The possibility of joint action against Turkey by the Balkan States which desired aggrandizement at her expense was already under consideration in their respective capitals.

Like Serbia, Montenegro sought eagerly (C.E. 1 , 47) for means whereby she might prepare the way for the expansion she anticipated. As did Serbia, she sought expansion into Albanian territory; Ipek, Djakova, Gusinje, Plava, and above all Prizren and Skutari, were the towns and districts she desired to acquire. Indeed, to King Nicholas, who aspired to the throne of a Great Serbia which was to include all those territories which Stefan "Dushan" had included in his ephemeral Empire, the capture of Prizren, "Dushan's" ancient capital, became an obsession. Never did he doubt that his dreams would be realized, since he relied implicitly upon Russia, who had subsidized the Petrovitches since 1715 (B.T. 19), and was considered invincible. That Russia might give preference to the conflicting aspirations of Serbia, Montenegro's despised rival, was an eventuality quite unforeseen. While therefore Serbia acted strictly in accordance with Russian instructions, Montenegro forced the pace, eager to precipitate war and draw in Russia.

Since the population of Montenegro was acknowledged to be only 282,000 (official 1907, E.B. 18 : 768. Population, 1920, official, 435,000, E.B. 31 : 978), it is clear that she was not anxious to acquire with the districts she proposed to annex a large, warlike population almost equal to her own and essentially hostile to Slav rule. It was therefore to her advantage to encourage the warlike elements in these districts to revolt, expend their lives and energies in abortive struggles, and suffer reprisals in consequence from the Turks. Furthermore, a successful insurrection in Albania, and the creation of an autonomous State, was the last thing which either she or Serbia desired. On the other hand, the tribesmen might be employed to clear up the Turkish posts on the frontier, and unwittingly to play into the hands of their hereditary foes by opening the way to Skutari for the Montenegrin Army before war was declared. In any case, it was imperative to secure the assistance or neutrality of the survivors by appearing to support their cause, Montenegro remembering the opposition of the Albanian League which she had encountered in 1880.

There were, too, other considerations.

"Crueller and more calculating than the Turk, the rulers of the Balkan States deliberately and in cold blood

incited resistance, stirred up rebellion. For the aim and
hope of each was to advertise his cause upon a poster
bloody enough to justify war. . . . And behind each
petty ruler sat a Great Power with 'a sphere of influence'
in view, and restrained or egged him on accordingly as
it suited a yet larger game" (S.S. 88).

It was a case of "Europe divided, and her demoralizing
influence in the Balkans" (C.E. 19).

The Montenegrins urged the Catholic Maltsia e madhe
tribesmen to revolt, and upon the assurance that they would
be supplied with arms and ammunition they did so (T.
30.3.11) prematurely, in March, 1911. General Yanko Vukotitch, a cousin of the Queen of Montenegro, unofficially
directed operations. But he dealt out arms very sparingly, and
those which were issued were of a pattern discarded by the
Montenegrin Army, so that it might appear that they had
been sold surreptitiously to the insurgents by the peasants.
This revolt was regarded as premature by the Nationalist
leaders. The Albanian deputies still hoped to bring the Government to reason, while the forthcoming visit to Kossovo of the
Sultan (T. 19.6.11) towards whom the Albanians repeatedly
protested their loyalty (it was the policy of the C.U.P. to
which they objected), exercised a restraining influence in those
districts which in any case were disarmed and exhausted by
Djavid Pasha's ravages. With the exception therefore of
local outbreaks (T. 18 and 21.7.11) and a Mirdite rising,
the remainder of Albania remained passive but sympathetic.
This attitude was not, however, appreciated by the Maltsia e
madhe tribesmen.

Heavy fighting ensued (T. 11.4.11), but the tribesmen
carried all before them. Tuzi, a Turkish outpost, was surrounded and Skutari threatened. Had the revolt been postponed until the other tribes were armed, Skutari would undoubtedly have been captured. Torgut Shevket Pasha's
Division was scattered throughout the north (T. 13.5.11) on
garrison duty, and Bedri Bey, the Vali of Skutari, had only
about 1,000 men at his disposal for the defence of the town
until reinforcements arrived. But Bedri turned to his own
advantage the situation created by the isolated action of the
Maltsia e madhe tribes. He called upon the Moslems of
Skutari and the Postripa district to defend their town and

faith. The alarm was spread that the Catholic malissori were subsidized by, and the advanced guard of, the Montenegrin Army, which intended to seize the town, and that a massacre of Moslems was intended. Three thousand incensed Moslems thereupon flocked to receive arms (T. 31.3.11) and marched against the Catholics. The Maltsia e madhe tribesmen entreated the Poštripa men to remember that they were all Albanians, that they had undertaken to rise together against the Turks, and that the insurrection was directed solely against Ottoman authority with the object of freeing Albania of the alien yoke. But suspicion, distrust, and fear of the Montenegrins prevailed. Incited by the Turks, the Moslems persisted in attacking the Catholics, were trounced (T. 10.6.11), and compelled to retire whence they came. But reinforcements were rushed by sea to Skutari and the triumphant advance of the insurgents checked.

On the 1st May the Central Albanian Committee addressed to public opinion and the Young Turk Government an appeal (F.O. 93) in which it set forth its policy. It declared that for five centuries the Albanians, loyal to the Turkish Empire, had frequently been the means of preserving it, while perhaps too little conscious of their distinctive nationality. But thirty years of tyranny had compelled them to follow the example of their neighbours with regard to national development. They had supported the Young Turk movement, only to be rewarded by repression. In view of the gravity of the situation, the numerical inferiority of the Turkish element in Europe, and the unjustifiable propaganda carried on by foreign agency in their country, they insisted in order to preserve their national existence, that (1) Albania once more should be united in a single vilayet, (2) that Albanian schools should be supported by the State, and (3) that in time of peace Albanian soldiers should serve only in Albania. This appeal was, however, ignored.

Meantime active preparations for war were set on foot in Montenegro, who was openly and repeatedly charged by Turkey with responsibility for the revolt (T. 11 and 20.4.11); and the Turkish Minister for Foreign Affairs declared that unless she ceased to assist the rebels he would be obliged to call her to account (T. 27.4.11). But the Powers, including Austria-Hungary and Russia, exercised their influence to avert a crisis at this juncture, and expressed to Montenegro the "hope that she would not lose sight of her international obligations" (T. 15.4.11), similar representations being made in Constantinople (T. 29.5.11). Turkey thereupon declared that while she had no intention of attacking Montenegro, she insisted that the Montenegrins should disarm the refugees (T. 25.5.11).

The Montenegrins on their part indignantly disclaimed their complicity in promoting the insurrection.

> " 'We Montenegrins', said Prince Danilo, 'most sincerely desire peace. . . . It grieves my heart to see these brave, uncultured mountaineers suffer and die for the liberty of having their own schools for their own children.' These remarks, when his stout cousin Yanko was actively engaged in supplying arms, keeping up the revolt, and preparing for war, and when a Montenegrin officer and several men had been wounded, were so impudent as to border on the sublime" (S.S. 66).

He might have assuaged his grief at the prohibition of Albanian schools in Turkey by bringing about the removal of the prohibition which had been placed on Albanian schools in Montenegro.

Torgut Pasha now ordered the insurgents to return to their homes, otherwise all accessible villages would be burnt (T. 20.4.11). They refused to comply, and the threat was duly carried out throughout the lowland districts by reinforcements which had been poured into the low country along the Lake of Skutari. On the 11th May Torgut offered pardon to all insurgents who would return to their homes (or what remained of them) within five days, and an armistice was arranged. On the third day the Turks treacherously seized Dechich, a height commanding Tuzi, which was now relieved. Dechich also commanded the entrance to Maltsia e madhe and the road to Skutari.

Operations were now resumed and desperate fighting ensued. (For a detailed account of Turkish operations in Albania in 1910 and 1911, see the contemporary *Times*.) Torgut Pasha's troops, supported by adequate artillery, advanced in two columns, one from Skutari and the other from the east through Gusinje, destroying every village, house, or church in their path (P.D. 27 : 780; T. 30.6.11; 5.7.11). By the end of June, "after a gallant defence which, when the history of these times comes to be written, will rank among the most brilliant episodes of modern warfare" (T. 21.7.11), the mountaineers were enclosed, by the junction of the two Turkish columns, in an "iron circle", escape being possible only across the Montenegrin frontier.

At the beginning of June the Mirdites rose in insurrection, against the advice of both the Abbot and Prenk Pasha, proclaimed autonomy under Sig. Tocci, an Albanian from Calabria, and established a provisional Government (T. 5.6.11). It seems that the Abbot favoured adherence to the policy of the Central Committee. Prenk, it has been alleged, was planning to establish himself as prince of an autonomous Mirdita—under Serbian protection if complete independence proved impracticable—and may have considered that a premature rising jeopardized his plan.

Some 10,000 rifles had been purchased, it was reported, in Italy by the Central Committee. In order to divert the attention of the Turks a large body of Mirdites attacked Alessio and seized the citadel, but were driven out two days later by troops from Skutari. Meantime the arms had been landed safely (T. 7 and 9.6.11). A Turkish punitive expedition into Mirdita was defeated with heavy losses, and the Turks refrained from further interference with the Mirdites.

During June Ismail Kemal Bey and his secretary, M. Gurakuchi, arrived at Cettinje and called a meeting at Gertché of malissori leaders to discuss the situation and future action.

In view of the suspicions entertained by the national leaders of Montenegrin intentions, it was decided that a memorandum should be drawn up for the benefit of Europe in general, and Turkey and Great Britain in particular (P.D. 27 : 557), setting forth the national claims and aims of the insurgents. These were as follows:

"(1) To obtain an amnesty from the [Turkish] Government for all Albanians, Moslem and Christian, who have been sentenced for political reasons.

"(2) To secure the appointment by the Government of a commission formed from native Albanians to assess the damage caused by the disarmament of 1910, and to pay an indemnity in accordance with its report.

"(3) To obtain official recognition of the Albanian

nationality and language, together with the national alphabet (Latin letters).

"(4) To obtain from the Chamber of Deputies recognition of the Albanian Society of Progress as a moral and legal individual according to the decision of the Congress of Elbasan. (In order to enable it to purchase land, hold property, etc.)

"(5) To persuade the Government to bring to justice those who issued orders for the dishonour and flogging of the Albanians during the process of disarmament of 1910, as well as those who carried out these orders, and to sentence them in accordance with their deserts.

"(6) To obtain from the Government the concession that education in the Government primary schools be imparted in Albanian and Turkish without discrimination.

"(7) To demand from the Government that all employees of the State sent to Albania should possess a knowledge of the Albanian language.

"(8) To demand from the Government that all police agents and gendarmes in Albania be Albanians.

"(9) To secure a promise that all Albanian soldiers perform their service in Rumelia.

"(10) To demand from the Government that a portion of the taxes collected in Albania be devoted to the development of the country, in providing roads, railways, bridges, hospitals, schools, etc.

"(11) To have recourse to every means within the power of the nation to secure the above objects.

"The emphasis laid in these documents on the demand for education to be imparted in the Albanian language is noteworthy. It implies (1) a real desire for education both among the Ghegs and Tosks, of which recent travellers supply much independent evidence; (2) a desire, equally keen, to compete with Turkish, Bulgarian, Greek, and Serbian propaganda, which has principally worked by the institution of numerous schools corresponding with the different nationalities concerned" (F.O. 95).

It is also noteworthy that the policy hitherto pursued by the Nationalist leaders was rigidly adhered to (see T. 26.1.09 for an almost precisely similar memorandum addressed to the

Turkish Government in January, 1909, by the mountaineers of southern Albania). Independence was not sought, but the liberty to develop and prepare themselves and their country for independence at some future time. This is frequently misconstrued as indicating a reluctance to secede from the Turkish Empire. Actually it indicated a shrewd policy.

At the same time a letter was addressed to the principal newspapers of Europe setting forth the insurgents' demands and causes of the insurrection. Briefly the former, as enunciated in the letter, were that the Albanian nationality should be recognized, and the use of the language permitted in schools and local administration. Of the latter, the injustice with which the elections were carried out (Christians having been disfranchised to ensure a Moslem majority), the suppression of the language, the injustice of taxation of rich and poor alike enforced by corrupt officials, disarmament without compensation, the closing of national schools, and the failure to carry out the promised public works, were the principal points set forth (S.S. 56).

On the 20th June Torgut Pasha issued a manifesto to the insurgents declaring that if they laid down their arms and returned to their homes before the 1st August they would be pardoned and compensated for damages (T. 15, 20, 21.6.11). If they failed to do so they would be "pursued to the frontier, exterminated, and annihilated" (P.D. 27 : 415; T. 21.7.11). If they attacked him, he had been ordered, he added, to pursue them even across the Montenegrin frontier (T. 24 and 26.6.11). Meantime the Porte expressed the hope that Montenegro would encourage the mountaineers to make peace and that the Powers would press her to do so (T. 16.6.11).

The situation, which now assumed a grave international aspect, was viewed with great satisfaction in Montenegro (S.S.); but the remaining Balkan States were not then prepared for war, nor was an outbreak of hostilities at that juncture in accordance with the policy of any Great Power. Moreover, Turkey, whose relations with Italy were strained, was particularly anxious to avoid being drawn into a conflict with the Balkan States. Italy, on the other hand, desired to avoid, while involved with Turkey, any disturbance in the Balkans which might be turned to their advantage by Russia or Austria-Hungary; she did not therefore support either Montenegrin aggression or the Albanian insurrection which, in other circumstances, it would have been to her advantage to do. In Great Britain it was considered that although the Albanian revolt was a Turkish internal problem (P.D. 27 : 557), and while it so remained any intervention was undesirable (Mr. Lloyd George, P.D. 28 : 1834), there would be a grave threat to the peace of Europe if the situation was allowed to drift (P.D. 28 : 1835; 32 : 2574). On the 27th July, 1911, Mr. Noel Buxton said that the Albanian situation was "the most urgent matter before us" (P.D. 28 : 1835), and on the same day Sir Edward Grey, then Secretary of State for Foreign Affairs, spoke of the danger that the Albanian disturbances might spread and of the sensitiveness of neighbouring countries (P.D. 28 : 1864).

In Austria-Hungary the opinion was expressed that Albanian good will was essential to the very existence of the Turkish Empire (T. 3.7.11), that the Constitution could never have been restored had not the Albanians supported it (T. 5.6.11), and that Turkey ought to abandon her short-sighted policy. Moreover, in virtue of her right to protect the Albanian Catholics, she could not ignore the ruthless policy which Turkey was pursuing towards them, and urged the Porte to adopt a more reasonable attitude (T. 4.7.11). Italy supported her ally, while Russia led the Entente Powers in restraining Montenegro (T. 12.7.11), being then in no position to go to war. The attitude of Germany was influenced by her political interests in Turkey, and was very reserved (T. 10.6.11); nevertheless, she associated herself with the Powers in restraining (T. 21.6.11) Montenegro.

King Nicholas protested—with every justification—that he could not advise the Albanians to accept the terms offered by Turkey unless their fulfilment was guaranteed by the Powers (T. 22.7.11). This declaration, much secret support, and a rising in the Djakova district (T. 21.7.11) encouraged the tribesmen, who continued to demand the right to carry arms—to protect themselves—and other concessions which the Turks were not prepared to make, and above all, a European guarantee. Torgut Pasha ordered the Archbishop of Skutari, Mgr. Sereggi, to persuade them to submit (T. 7.7.11), although he protested that he had no authority to do so nor was it his business. His mission failed (T. 25.7.11). The Mayor of Skutari and other emissaries were also sent into Montenegro to treat with the malissori, but failed likewise. Finally,

at the end of July, Turkey agreed that in certain circumstances arms might be carried (T. 27.7.11; 1.8.11), at the same
time instructing her Minister at Cettinje to inform the Montenegrin Government that "if it continued to harbour the
malissori the troops, who were much excited, would be
obliged to pursue them as far as the frontier".

This declaration, equivalent to an ultimatum, brought
matters to a head. But Montenegro found herself alone
(P.D. 28 : 1793) in favouring defiance, and on the 2nd
August she yielded to the pressure of the Powers.

The terms offered to the malissori were, briefly (S.S. 72;
for full terms, T. 3.8.11) as follows: (1) A general amnesty
should be granted; (2) an Albanian-speaking and Christian
Kaimmakam should be appointed at Tuzi for Maltsia e
madhe, and native officials should administer the district in
accordance with local customs and traditions; (3) Albanian
schools should be opened by the Government; (4) roads
should be constructed in the mountains; (5) money for the
rebuilding of houses destroyed should be allotted; (6) maize
sufficient to live upon until the next harvest should be provided; (7) every male over fifteen years of age should receive
£T1 on returning home; (8) the right to carry arms should
be acknowledged except (as always before) in the towns and
bazaars; (9) the malissori should not be liable for military
service outside Albania, except in Roumelia and Constantinople, and (10) should be exempt from taxation for two
years; then subject to a reduced taxation, and the revenue
applied to local needs.

These terms were satisfactory enough provided they were
fulfilled, but of their fulfilment the insurgents were more than
doubtful, as indeed they had every cause to be. If they were
fulfilled, the malissori had achieved much by the insurrection,
while the Turks had sustained about 8,000 casualties, not to
mention financial losses. But the malissori refused to accept
them without a European guarantee, which the Montenegrins
had previously told them to insist upon. Now Montenegro
threatened to disarm them forcibly, and cut off all food
supplies unless they accepted; but if, on the other hand, they
did at once accept, to issue 6,000 rifles and a supply of
ammunition. Even so the malissori hesitated. Fortunately
Miss Durham, who by her unselfish devotion to their cause
had won their implicit confidence, was among them. Vuko-

titch entreated her to persuade them to accept the terms, which, she considered, was the only course. And, largely owing to her influence, they finally decided to return to their homes (T. 4 and 5.8.11); but she was obliged to reassure them by promising to spend the winter among them. She writes:

> "The Klementi men sent me a message that they went back entirely on my responsibility, and that if aught happened to them their blood was upon my soul. . . . I wondered how often in history a foreign female had been asked by a Commander-in-Chief, who was also a Queen's cousin, in the name of God and his Government to make terms for him with insurgents he had himself incited" (S.S. 80, 77).

Miss Durham may congratulate herself that she saved hundreds of lives, not only upon this occasion but also by the relief work which she has carried out from time to time in Albania.

On the 11th September, 1911, Italy declared war against Turkey. Hostilities continued for more than a year, and peace was not concluded until the 15th October, 1912, when Turkey decided to cut her losses in Tripoli that she might be free to face the Balkan League, and signed the Treaty of Ouchy. Throughout the war Italy was restrained by Austria-Hungary (P.D. 38 : 199) from extending hostilities even to the coasts of European Turkey (the bombardment of Prevesa and Medua brought forth a sharp protest from Vienna); and she made no attempt to promote disturbances in Albania—although from a strategic point of view it was her obvious course (P.D. 11 : 918)—fearing that a pretext for intervention therein might be created of which Austria-Hungary would take advantage. Meantime the Albanian leaders advocated (T. 11.5.12) adherence to their original policy, and at first refrained from embarrassing Turkey by encouraging insurrection. Events, however, proved too strong for them. On the other hand, it is significant that in response to a call for volunteers scarcely an Albanian offered his services (T. 9.11.11), although upon former occasions there had always been thousands of men prepared to serve the Empire.

In view of the Porte's anxiety to avoid further complications while at war with Italy, the terms of the agreement with

the malissori were, in part, fulfilled (T. 12, 25, 29.8.11;
20.9.11). But its dilatory methods, and a reluctance to go
farther towards the fulfilment of its obligations than was
absolutely necessary (T. 7.10.11; 9.11.11; 12.1.12) aroused
discontent to which other factors contributed.

Firstly, the Christian malissori were sore with the Moslems
of Skutari and Postripa who had attacked them at the instigation of Bedri Bey.

Secondly, they were exasperated by the damage wrought by
the Turks to their property, especially to their churches which
had been destroyed or desecrated, although the malissori
had been careful to respect all mosques during the struggle.
It is noteworthy that in all insurrections of Albanians, whether
Christian or Moslem, the Turks never charged the insurgents
with outrages of any description, and Turkish prisoners were
always as well treated as circumstances permitted; generally
they were merely disarmed and released.

Thirdly, the malissori who had not revolted were discontented because they did not receive the concessions
accorded to the tribesmen of Maltsia e madhe. They asserted
that they did not revolt through no fault of their own; had
they had arms they would have done so; and when they
obtained arms they would most assuredly revolt, and the
Turks would then be obliged to give them maize and money
likewise!

Fourthly, ignorance, coupled with the disunion produced
by the tribal system, prevented them from envisaging wider
issues than those which directly concerned them. The issue
with which they were then concerned was the ejection of
the Turks and the achievement of absolute freedom. The
Nationalist movement and propaganda stirred them to insurrection; but the Nationalist leaders failed to control them
when their policy appeared to be contrary to the immediate
issues with which the malissori were concerned.

Montenegro was not slow to take advantage of the discontent in northern Albania. Her policy was now to consolidate her position as the friend of the malissori whose districts
she hoped to annex, but not to precipitate war until the
political situation was such that her troops could follow
them to Skutari: in other words, until she was sure of the
support of the Balkan States or of Russia, who had failed
her in the previous year. She therefore carried on vigorous

propaganda against the Turks (B.K. 159), denounced the devastation they had wrought, although she subsequently excelled them in barbarity, and even succeeded in creating a dispute over the terms by which the malissori had been induced to cease hostilities by producing a faked copy of the agreement (S.S. 125). The British Consul in Skutari, however, held a copy which tallied with the Turkish and not with the Montenegrin version. Nevertheless, the heads of the tribes of the Skutari district met in the Cathedral on the 10th February, swore *besa*, prepared to revolt again, and demanded Austro-Hungarian intervention (T. 11.3.12).

The task of the Nationalists in northern Albania was an extremely difficult one. On the one hand they strove to propagate the national ideal and superimpose their influence upon the tribes: this naturally tended to add to the determination of the malissori to drive out the Turks. On the other hand, they strove to counteract Montenegrin propaganda, but since Montenegro was also avowedly working for the eviction of the Turks, their task became increasingly difficult. Despite this difficulty the great majority of the tribesmen were made aware of Montenegrin intentions, and were accordingly held in check, but some in Maltsia e madhe persisted in their blind hatred of the Turks to the exclusion of all other considerations.

Meantime the Albanian deputies had tried vainly to bring before the Turkish Chamber the demands formulated in all parts of Albania. Eventually even the most optimistic of them openly renounced their allegiance to the C.U.P. (T. 18.1.12), among them being Essad Pasha, who ardently espoused the cause of nationalism, which coincided with his own ambitions.

But the Porte was aware that further trouble with Montenegro was ahead. On the one hand, therefore, Hussein Riza Pasha, who had been appointed to command at Skutari, energetically began to strengthen the fortifications, construct military roads, and erect barbed wire entanglements; while large consignments of arms and ammunition were sent up to Prishtina, Ipek, and Djakova for distribution among the Moslems in the event of war (T. 13.5.12). On the other hand, a commission under the Presidency of Hadji Adil, Minister of the Interior—and including the French Colonel Foulon and Mr. (now Sir) R. W. Graves, C.M.G.—was constituted

(P.D. 35 : 169; T. 9 and 24.2.12) in the spring of 1912 to inquire into the demands which the Albanians had made. It seems that this step did signify that the Turks, apart from the fanatics of Union and Progress, had begun to realize that their policy in Albania was ill advised. It signified the decline of Chauvinism; and the Unionists had been returned to power only through their employment of violence and corruption.

The Commission was not well received. It was ambushed near Elbasan (T. 16.3.12). At Skutari the bairaktars refused to meet it, despite the concessions (T. 9.5.12) which Hadji Adil offered—an attitude which, in view of the treatment they had previously received, is not surprising, and in Kossovo the distribution of large sums of money (T. 13.5.12) was attributed to fear or duplicity (T. 20.5.12). Any improvement in the relations between Albanians and Turks which the Commission might have brought about was more than counteracted by the behaviour during the election in April of the C.U.P. officials, who again resorted to every possible measure of corruption and violence to secure the return of their candidates. In the Skutari district the Christians refused to vote, believing the result a foregone conclusion, but in Kossovo and elsewhere the Albanian candidates were rejected by the usual methods (T. 9 and 20.5.12). The exasperation aroused by this election, combined with the course of events beyond the control of either side, forced the issues.

Briefly the position was as follows: The policy of the Nationalist leaders had been to prepare their country for autonomy while supporting the Turkish Empire and taking advantage of its protection. In 1912 they knew that their country was not prepared, and for another twenty years would not be fully prepared for autonomy, much less for independence. They did not therefore seek independence, but liberty, to prepare for it. Under the régime of Abdul Hamid it had become increasingly difficult for them to adhere to their policy, owing to the suppression of the national schools and language. They had therefore espoused the cause of the Young Turks. But the Committee of Union and Progress, by its policy of Ottomanization, had made their position even more intolerable than it had been during the reign of the "Red Sultan". One autocrat was replaced by a swarm of corrupt and fanatical officials. On the other hand, Serbia, Greece, and Montenegro looked towards Albanian territory

I

for expansion. The Albanian leaders found themselves upon the horns of a dilemma: and their difficulties were accentuated by the ignorance of their compatriots, especially those of the highlands. Their only course had appeared to be to hold steadfastly to their purpose, while bringing pressure to bear upon the Turkish Government to relinquish its disastrous and Chauvinistic policy. But the Turks were deaf to their protestations, and the attitude of the Balkan States became increasingly menacing. Thus came the Turk and the Albanian to the parting of the ways.

The evolution of the Balkan League made rapid progress. The purpose for which Russia had instigated its formation, namely, the prevention of further Austro-Hungarian expansion in the Balkans, was not overlooked: and during negotiations between the Balkan States provision was made for combined defensive action against that country, should she attempt to interfere further in the Peninsula. But the motive which actually led to its formation was the desire for territorial aggrandizement. Each of the four States concerned was determined to expand, and this could only be accomplished by war with Turkey. The war which ensued was undertaken ostensibly to free their Christian co-nationals of European Turkey; but the only State which had any justification in claiming that this was its motive, was Bulgaria, although admittedly each of the four States was ethnically entitled to a small area therein. North and west of Uskub, Turkey in Europe was inhabited almost exclusively by Albanians, while hitherto the Macedonians had always been considered Bulgarian both by themselves and by their neighbours (C.E. 24, 26, 50–1, etc.). When a plebiscite was taken under Article 10 of the Firman of 1870 in the provinces of Uskub and Ochrida, the requisite two-thirds majority was easily obtained for the appointment of Bulgarian exarchist bishops. The existence of a Greek minority in southern Macedonia was generally admitted, but nothing was ever heard of Macedonians of Serbian nationality until Austria-Hungary insisted on the renunciation of Serbian expansion to the Adriatic, and agreed in return to support the latter's expansion southward. The Serbian statesman, Dr. Milovanovitch, admitted in 1908 that

"the Serbs did not begin to think about Macedonia till 1885. . . . When schoolmasters and priests failed to produce inhabitants of the required nationality in sufficient numbers to justify the political ambitions of their employers, new and fantastic theories had to be devised to prove that the inhabitants of Macedonia were anything but Bulgarian" (B.P. 27).

The first step towards a Balkan Alliance directed against Turkey was taken by M. Venizelos, who made overtures to Bulgaria in the winter of 1910–11. An alliance between these two States had never been regarded as possible, in view of their irreconcilable interests in Macedonia, which explains why both the Powers and Turkey were so slow to appreciate this fresh threat to the peace of Europe. Some months later overtures were made by Bulgaria to Serbia, which resulted in the conclusion, on the 13th March, 1912, of a Treaty of friendship and alliance, with a secret annex by which the prospective loot was divided. A secret Treaty to much the same effect was concluded between Bulgaria and Greece on the 29th May, 1912. Although this latter Treaty remained secret for two months, there were ample indications of its conclusion or approaching conclusion; and the attendance of the Crown Princes of Greece, Serbia, Montenegro, and Roumania at the celebration in Sofia in February, 1912, of the coming of age of Prince Boris, was widely recognized as an indication of increasing co-operation between the Christian States of the Peninsula. Serbia then entered into negotiations with Greece and Montenegro, and with the latter country a Treaty, which was little more than a military convention, was concluded in September, 1912. The delay in bringing Montenegro into the alliance was due to friction between Belgrade and Cettinje over dynastic problems (C.E. 47), and not to any reluctance on the part of Montenegro to make war (C.E. 1, 47). Military conventions co-ordinating military plans between the respective General Staffs were concluded between Serbia and Bulgaria on the 19th June, 1912, and with Greece on the 22nd September.

In the negotiations between Serbia and Bulgaria considerable difficulties presented themselves. Bulgaria favoured autonomy for the whole of Macedonia, and thereby showed a generosity which deserves recognition, although of course she was well aware that an autonomous Macedonia would eventually opt for union with her. Serbia, however, insisted

SANJAK OF
NOVIBAZAR
•Bijelopolje
•Mojkovatz
•Berane
Ipek
•Cettinje
Djakova
•Skutari
Prizren
(Tetovo)
Kalkandalen•
Gostivar
Krouchevo
Dibra
•Durazzo Tirana
Elbasan
•Ochrida
Resna
Florina
•Berat Korcha
•Valona
Santi Quaranta
EPIRUS
Kalamas
•Janina
Corfu
Paramythia•
Parga•
Louro
Prevesa•
Gulf of Arta

Nish
R. Nishava
Pirot
Slivnitza
Sofia
Mitrovitza
Prishtina
Ferizpvitch
Ghilan
Vranje
Mt. Golem
Katchanik
•Kumanovo
•Uskub
OVTCHE
POLYE
•Koprulu
(Veles)
R. Vardar
Prilep
Monastir
Brod
Banitza
Lake Ostrovo
Ostrovika
Ceghali
Lake Doiran
•Fort Rupel
Seres
SALONIKA
THRACE
•Laudli
Doganzi
•Vodena
•Langaza
•Salonika
Kastoria
Karaferia
Katerini
R. Vistritza
Mt. Olympus
9794
Platamona
Kalabaka
R. Arta
Trikkala
Larissa
THESSALY
Volo

Scale of Miles
20 10   0   20   40   60

Frontiers before the Balkan Wars..... ▬▬▬
Boundaries of Vilayets and Sanjak.... ....
Railways at the outbreak of War...... ┼┼┼┼
Line of partition agreed upon by
  Serbia and Bulgaria.............. + + + +
Maximum claims of the Albanian
  Provisional Government, Jan. 1913.... ▬ ▬ ▬
Frontier of Albania proposed by
  the Balkan Allies.................. ▬·▬·▬

upon "liberating the Christians of Macedonia" by imposing her rule upon them. Eventually, in the secret annex to the Treaty concluded, she agreed to recognize Bulgaria's claim to Turkish territory east of the Struma, possession of which would give that State access to the Ægean, in return for Bulgarian acknowledgment of her claim to all territory north and west of the Shar Mountains: in other words, to northern Albania. For the remainder of Turkey in Europe, including Macedonia after Greece had obtained her share, that is to say, for the predominantly Bulgarian area, autonomy was proposed. If, however, autonomy should prove impracticable, these two States agreed that, subject to the approval of the Tzar of Russia, a line south-west from Mt. Golem to Lake Ochrida should divide their respective portions. Albanian nationality was ignored, and the proposed aggrandizement of Serbia, although nominally at the expense of Turkey, was almost wholly at the expense of the Albanians.

"Confident in the ignorance and heedlessness of western Europe, the Allies proposed to deprive Albania of all that was distinctly Albanian. Albania was to be made into a State in name only, shorn of everything which could enable it to live as an independent and self-governing principality. . . ."

A glance at the ethnographical map of the western Balkans at this date (p. 48: also E.B. 3 : 259) makes it clear that almost the whole of the territory thus abortively allotted to Serbia was essentially Albanian. Of the comparatively small Serbian minority which existed therein, the majority had immigrated since 1878. Some had arrived in consequence of the deliberate policy which had been followed with the object of establishing a Serbian claim to the area; others, Moslems, had been driven from the territory annexed by Serbia in 1878 by their Orthodox co-nationals; the remainder had come to seek employment from Albanian landlords, since the Albanian population, reduced by constant military service, was inadequate to cultivate the land (A.S. 30; also *Blgarite v' Makedoniza*: Jordan Ivanoff, Sofia, 1915, p. 53; and *Grad Skopie*, Vassil Kentchoff, Sofia, 1898, p. 55).

Almost the only region to which the Serbs were entitled was the Novibazar corridor, and its annexation by either of the two Serb States would give Serbia access to the sea through Montenegro. The union of these two States was inevitable. The Montenegrin royal family was increasingly unpopular; while a large proportion of the population maintained that union with Serbia would be mutually beneficial, and lead to increased prosperity and security (E.B. 31 : 979). As early as 1865 an agreement had been reached which provided for the abdication of Prince Nicholas in favour of the Prince of Serbia, should the two States succeed in obtaining a common frontier. But domestic scandals and military disasters had discredited Serbia and its ruling house, and in consequence Prince Nicholas began himself to aspire to the throne of a Great Serbia. This difficulty might, however, have been overcome by a military, diplomatic, and economic union—to which end negotiations were actually in progress in 1914 (E.B. 32 : 404) when the Great War broke out—and legislation regarding the succession or a royal marriage. Serbia would thus have acquired the desired access to the sea through Montenegro, pending settlement of the dynastic problem, and without alienating neighbouring peoples. In any case it was for Serbia to justify by more creditable domestic conduct the claim which she made to the sympathy of Europe in her desire for an outlet to the sea and win support against Austro-Hungarian policy, rather than seek the achievement of this end by a fresh act of aggression against the original inhabitants of the Peninsula.

To the Albanian leaders, especially to Ismail Kemal Bey, who, as leader of the Liberal Opposition in the Turkish Parliament, was in the closest possible touch with the political situation, the intentions of the Balkan States daily became clearer; and in the spring of 1912 any doubts which they had previously entertained as to the possibility of a Balkan League, and any hopes which they had held that the C.U.P. would shortly assume a more reasonable attitude were dispelled. In addition, the reverses sustained by Turkey in the war with Italy gave them cause for misgivings as to her ability to protect their country, and were an additional inducement to her enemies to launch their attack.

These considerations convinced Ismail Kemal Bey that unless the principle of Albanian autonomy was recognized before the Balkan States began hostilities, his country would be partitioned. From Nice, whence he had retired after the election in April, he issued a circular to all Albanian centres

abroad and also to the Nationalists in his native land, setting
forth the critical position and recommending that steps should
be taken to meet the eventualities which threatened. His
colleagues who had likewise left Turkey and the Nationalist
leaders in Albania were also aware of the situation; accordingly steps were taken to organize a general insurrection, and
a *besa* was sworn throughout Albania (T. 20.5.12).

The Kossovo Moslems once again led the way (T. 9 and
10.5.12). Exasperated by the machinations of the C.U.P.
during the election in April, they had at once and independently
planned a rising. The *casus belli* appears to have occurred in
early May at Krouma, which was reported to have been
destroyed by the Kaimakam of Djakova in consequence of
a trifling dispute with the inhabitants over timber. Thereupon
his escort was attacked and cut up (T. 11.5.12); and a large
body of Albanians marched upon Djakova to seize the arms
depot.

Hostilities now broke out on the borders of Mirdita, and
a Turkish force with artillery was routed with considerable
losses (T. 9, 20, 25.5.12; 27.6.12). The outcome was that the
Turks offered, through Prenk Pasha, who on this occasion
supported his tribesmen, to extend to Mirdita the same privileges as had been accorded to Maltsia e madhe.

In southern Albania Mufid bey Libohova (T. 25.5.12) and
other ex-deputies began to collect forces, Aladro Castriota
sailed from Brindisi for Albania (T. 30.5.12), and Ismail
Kemal Bey arrived in Valona.

Maltsia e madhe did not rise until the end of July. There
was a great shortage of rifles and ammunition among all the
northern tribes who had not been fully rearmed since 1910
(S.S. 157), the Montenegrins having supplied them only as
suited their purpose; while both Austria-Hungary and Italy,
being opposed to any change in the *status quo* (T. 17 and 22.5.12),
had prohibited the exportation of arms to Albania. Moreover,
King Nicholas, by the support he had given them in the
previous year, had acquired considerable influence among the
tribesmen, and now restrained them, intending that they
should wait until the Kossovo Albanians and Turks had
exhausted each other before opening the way to Skutari for
the Montenegrin Army (S.S. 153). Further, the negotiations
between the Balkan States had not matured; and Russia had
failed him in 1911 and still refused to support him. When,

despite him, the tribesmen did rise to prove their solidarity with the Nationalist movement they were everywhere successful. The frontier posts were cleared up, a fortified encampment in Hoti besieged, a relief force routed, and Tuzi isolated (S.S. 163).

Meantime the insurrection spread throughout the whole of Kossovo vilayet, and tribesmen under Isa Boletin, Hassan bey Prishtina, Riza bey Djakova, Mehmed pasha Dralla, Redjeb Mitrovitza, Bedri Bey of Ipek, Salih Yuka, Idris Sefer, Bairam Tsuri, Islam Sipahi, and other leaders gathered to defy the C.U.P. They were, however, divided into three groups, namely, those who desired autonomy as a prelude to independence, those who were opposed to the absolutism of the C.U.P. and desired a privileged position within the Empire, and those who wished for a restoration of the old régime which had given them greater personal liberty. But all were united in demanding a dissolution of the unfairly elected Unionist Chamber and a fresh election.

The majority of the Turkish troops in Kossovo were concentrated at Ferizovitch (under Fadil Pasha), Uskub, and Monastir. The outlying detachments were driven in, and Djakova, Prizren, Ipek, Ghilan, and Prishtina soon fell entirely into the hands of the Albanians. A sharp engagement took place at Hass (near Prizren) on the 18th June (T. 29.7.12), in which the Turks were reported to have lost 300 killed, including the commandant, Hair-ed-Din Bey, who, on a charge of cruelty to Albanian women, was hanged on the spot where Shaban Binaku, the bairaktar of Krasnitch, had been executed in 1910 after surrendering on terms. The Albanians took 600 prisoners, 1,000 rifles, and 25 loads of ammunition. With these, in addition to the dumps and stores seized, they were fully equipped.

But in comparison with previous years there was little heavy fighting. Hadji Adil counselled moderation and conciliation (T. 25.5.12; good article on Adil's tour and proposals in T. 5.7.12), and did his best to restrain the C.U.P. Moreover, it was not only the Albanians who were exasperated with the Young Turk Committee; and this circumstance had been thoroughly exploited by the Albanian leaders who had carried on a great propaganda among the troops. In the middle of June a battalion at Monastir, composed largely of Albanians, took to the hills and declared for the insurgents (T. 27.6.12).

Mutiny now spread like wildfire (T. 29.6.12; 4.7.12) throughout the Army Corps at Uskub and Monastir. Troops refused
to fire on the Albanians, gendarmerie deserted to them
(T. 16.7.12), and the 1st (Ildiz) Division, sent to reinforce
Fadil Pasha, deposed its commander and joined the insurgents
(T. 29.7.12). Troops which remained amenable to discipline
were now withdrawn, first to Uskub, then to Koprulu and
Monastir. Throughout the remainder of Albania bands were
formed and arms depots seized, while the majority of the
scattered garrisons either did not oppose or connived at these
proceedings.

By the middle of July the Albanians found themselves
masters of the situation throughout Albania. Their organization was good, and complete harmony existed between the
various leaders, who possessed the confidence of both Moslems
and Christians (T. 20.7.12). The Serbian and Bulgarian minorities, incited by the agents of their respective fatherlands,
supported the Albanians as a means of weakening Turkish
power. Hassan Bey with (it was reported) some 50,000 men
installed himself at Prishtina as director of the movement.
The telegraph service was appropriated, the sending of
cypher telegrams forbidden, and Nationalist leaders throughout western Albania instructed to hold themselves in readiness for action (T. 26 and 29.7.12).

Meantime the Turkish Cabinet resigned. Its successor,
under Muktar Pasha, at once assured the Albanians that a
Parliamentary Committee under Ibrahim Pasha should be
constituted to investigate their grievances, treat with the
bairaktars, and inaugurate reforms, that the election of unfairly elected deputies should be nullified, and that no military
measures should be taken against the insurgent forces. The
Albanians, while accepting these assurances to the extent
that they agreed to suspend hostilities, still insisted upon the
execution of all their demands, especially the dissolution of
the Chamber. They continued their preparations, perfected
their organization (T. 3.8.12), and declared that if any Turkish
troop movements occurred they would at once resume
hostilities (T. 29.7.12). The southern Albanians began to
concentrate at Berat (T. 6.8.12). Isa Boletin, trusted alike by
Albanians and Serbs, who had occupied Novibazar, set
himself up as virtual dictator of the Sanjak. Idris Sefer assumed
command at Ghilan, and other leaders in their respective

localities (T. 3.8.12). No looting or disorders were countenanced, and excellent discipline was preserved.

In view of the procrastination of the Turkish Cabinet, 250 Albanian delegates from all parts of the country assembled at Prishtina on the 30th July and telegraphed to the Porte that unless the Chamber was dissolved within forty-eight hours the insurgent army under General Mehmed pasha Dralla would march on Uskub, and, if need be, on Salonika (T. 2.8.12). They also demanded that Kiamil Pasha, whom the C.U.P. had compelled to resign in February, 1909, should be appointed Grand Vizier.

The now impotent Government was forced to yield, and on the 5th, to the mortification of the Committee, their hardly won majority disappeared in the dissolution of the Chamber by imperial decree (T. 6.8.12). Kiamil Pasha formed a fresh Cabinet.

The Albanians now peremptorily set forth their demands on behalf of the four vilayets of Skutari, Kossovo, Janina, and Monastir. Briefly the main points (T. 12 and 13.8.12; S.A. 19; A.S. 27; etc.) were as follows:

(1) The appointment of a Governor-General for the four vilayets.
(2) The appointment of experienced native governors and officials therein.
(3) Albanian soldiers to perform their military service, in time of peace, within the four vilayets only.
(4) Inauguration therein of a fresh judicial system which would respect local laws, traditions, and customs; Albanians to be tried only before Albanian judges.
(5) The local language therein (it is not clear whether Albanian was definitely specified or not) to be the official language and the medium of instruction in all State schools.
(6) Absolute liberty therein to establish private schools.
(7) The establishment therein of technical schools (teaching agriculture, science, etc.).
(8) Local revenues to be expended locally; roads and railways to be built.
(9) Houses destroyed by the troops during the recent disturbances to be rebuilt at the expense of the Government.

(10) Recognition of the right of all (? Albanians) to bear arms; and the restoration of those confiscated.
(11) A general amnesty for all political offenders.
(12) The impeachment before the High Court of the Cabinets of Hakki Pasha and Said Pasha.

The Government demurred with regard to the impeachment, declared that it would acknowledge only the right of frontier villagers, shepherds, and forest workers to bear arms, and that the limitation of military service for Albanians to their own localities would create a precedent for a similar demand by all the other subject races of the Empire. Thereupon a large body of Albanians under Isa Boletin entered Uskub by rail, and the town was soon occupied by 20,000 tribesmen; but it is unanimously agreed (T. 19.8.12; etc.) that no disorders took place and that their conduct was exemplary. They encountered no opposition, and a detachment pushed on to Koprulu. It was reported that some even entered Salonika.

It was alleged (T. 19 and 23.8.12) that Boletin's action did not meet with the approval of Hassan Prishtina and the more moderate leaders, whose attitude encouraged the Government to take military measures to prevent the occupation of Koprulu. But it seems more probable that the political leaders tacitly approved, while assuming an attitude of disapproval, in order to preserve their freedom of action in negotiating with the Porte through Ibrahim Pasha's commission which had arrived at Prishtina; and that the military movements which took place were due to the threatening attitude of the Balkan States, an attitude which doubtless influenced both Turks and Albanians to adopt a conciliatory attitude towards each other. In any case, Boletin's action in duced the Government to yield with regard to the bearing of arms, whereupon the Albanians evacuated Uskub and dispersed to their homes. But they continued to demand a distribution of rifles (T. 23 and 27.8.12); and while negotiations continued the administration of the districts which had revolted remained entirely in their hands.

Meantime the Government, as an earnest of its intention to carry out the terms it had agreed upon, began to fill administrative posts in the four vilayets with Albanian leaders. Notably, Mehmed pasha Dralla was appointed Mutessarif of

Prizren and Hassan Tahsin Pasha Vali of Janina. The latter appointment called forth a storm of protest in the Greek Press (T. 27 and 30.8.12; 10.9.12), which declared that if the Albanians encroached upon territory which was regarded as Greek, "a spirit of solidarity would ultimately develop among the Balkan States whose interests are equally threatened by the action of the Albanians". Meanwhile Serbia and Bulgaria were assuring Turkey of their amiable intentions (T. 19.8.12) and denying the existence of an alliance (T. 21.9.12), while pressing forward their military preparations, Count Berchtold was advocating the initiation of "conversations" between the Powers with regard to the "friendly advice" which should be offered to Turkey (which threatened to deprive the Balkan Allies of even the most shadowy pretext for declaring war). M. Poincaré was visiting Russia, and the Montenegrins were straining at the Russian leash (T. 8.8.12, etc.).

At the beginning of September the Porte formally declared that while accepting the remainder of the Albanian demands, it could not impeach the Cabinets of Hakki and Said Pashas, such procedure being the prerogative of the Chamber (then dissolved), and could not agree to regional military service (T. 6.9.12). The Albanians, on the other hand, passively and suspiciously awaited the fulfilment of their terms. There, it seems, the dispute rested, for before any reconciliation between the two sides could be effected the Balkan Allies hastily intervened.

Thus ended the struggle between Turks and Albanians—a struggle which had sapped the strength of both. Moreover, Turks and Albanians had been alienated, and in consequence the former were deprived of Albanian support, which, hitherto, had been the source of their power in Europe. Had Turkey continued to enjoy the support of her Albanian subjects, it is doubtful whether the Balkan Allies would have ventured to go to war with her, and even more doubtful whether they would have proved victorious (*L'alliance balkanique*: I. E. Guechoff, Paris, 1915, p. 82; *Il nuovo Stato di Albania*, Antonio Baldacci, Rome, 1913, p. 16; A.S. 28).

"Mais une fatalité extraordinaire veut perdre la Turquie; par une folie étrange elle brise la seule force qui soutenait sa domination en Macédoine; le Turc combat l'Albanais; c'est la fin; le nationalisme turc a fait la révolution, le nationalisme turc a perdu la Turquie d'Europe; les Arnautes, quatre. années durant résistant, guerroient, reculent, reviennent et au jour favorable entrent victorieux sur cette place du Konak (à Uskub) où ils installent leur chef" (*Au jeune royaume d'Albanie*, G. L. Jaray, p. 189).

CHAPTER IV

INDEPENDENCE

THE success of the Albanians in attaining virtual autonomy within the Ottoman Empire was an event of momentous importance which was, however, eclipsed by its even more momentous consequences. Too late the Ottoman Government realized that the creation of an autonomous Albania was the surest means of winning the support of the Albanians against any attack by Serbia, Greece, Montenegro, and Bulgaria; and that autonomous Albania would create a barrier against further Austro-Hungarian or Slav expansion. Had not the Balkan Allies rushed to "liberate" Albania and Macedonia, the Turks would perforce have fulfilled their undertakings, and a strong autonomous Albania under Turkish suzerainty, a bulwark of the Turkish Empire, would have been created. But this was precisely what the Balkan Allies were determined to prevent (T. 18.12.12), being aware that once the Albanians were satisfied that the Turks intended to fulfil their obligations, they would unite with them in defending the frontiers.

The part played by Montenegro in inciting the Albanian malissori to revolt as a means of preparing the way for her armies has already been described. Serbia pursued precisely the same policy.

When Austria-Hungary annexed Bosnia and the Hertzegovina and Serbia definitely determined to expand southwards into Macedonia, the Narodna Odbrana and Black Hand Societies redoubled their efforts to stir up strife (T. 12.4.10) in that region. Comitadjis were recruited from Bosnia, the Hertzegovina, the Voivodina, and Turkish territory, and trained in schools founded for the purpose, the first being established at Chuprija in 1908. Major Tankositch, who subsequently trained the Archduke Francis Ferdinand's assassins, was the principal instructor.

The manner in which the Albanian insurrections in Kossovo prepared the way for, and indeed made possible the victory of the Balkan Allies over Turkey has not hitherto received the attention which it deserves. The following statements from Serbian sources are therefore illuminating:

Colonel Chedo A. Popovitch, who was subsequently condemned during the scandalous Salonika trial in 1917, but afterwards pardoned, wrote (*The Work of the Union or Death* [*Black Hand*] *Society in preparing for the Balkan War: Nova Europa*, XVI, 10 and 11. N.B. In this article members of the Black Hand endeavour to establish their patriotism, and, in consequence, right to existence—a right disputed by the White Hand, a rival organization no whit less nefarious, which brought about the Salonika trial on forged evidence):

"Most important of all were the revolts of the Albanians. These revolts were frequent and great. The victorious Albanians marched as far as Skoplje [Uskub] and returned after parleying with the Turkish Government. In these revolts the strongest and chief of the leaders was Isa Boletin.

"To suit the plans of Serbia, who, with her allies, was now preparing for war with Turkey, it was important to get into close contact with him and see if it were possible in any way to make use of his discontent. It was only possible to converse and parley with him on Turkish territory, so it was necessary to send persons to him from our side. The circumstances under which it was possible to do so, and enter Turkish territory, were very difficult. The Turkish Government, aware that its neighbours were preparing for war, concentrated its whole attention upon the frontiers. Confronted with this situation, the members of the Organization, especially the members of the central administration, thought themselves morally obliged to undertake the task themselves.

"In the first half of 1912 Major Tankositch volunteered to go and converse with Isa Boletin. It is natural that in the first talks with this cautious and suspicious Albanian, they could not come to a definite understanding. It was necessary to converse with him again.

"Immediately before the declaration of war, it was necessary for the Chief of the General Staff to have the question [of Isa Boletin's attitude] definitely settled, and obtain some facts about certain things along the principal routes upon which our army would operate. It was necessary for this purpose to send the most reliable persons. Dragutin Dimitrijevitch-Apis, Bogdan Radenkovitch, and Milan Zavadjil [now Lieutenant-Colonel, retired, General Staff] went for these fresh parleys with Isa Boletin. . . ."

Photographs of these officers in Albanian dress were reproduced in *Solunski Procec Ponuda Austrije za separatni mir*, December, 1916, to October, 1917 (Austria's proposal for a separate peace), reprinted from the *Glasnik*, Belgrade, 1923.

"After many difficulties", continued Popovitch, "the officers carried out their task successfully."

From the above it is clear that Isa Boletin for some time hesitated to come to any arrangement with the Serbs, regarding with suspicion their declaration that they desired only to liberate the subject races of European Turkey, and owing to this hesitation was described as "cautious and suspicious", an epithet which is indeed ironical! Eventually, however, Dimitrijevitch-Apis, the leader of the Black Hand movement, succeeded in allaying his suspicions, in raising doubt in his mind as to the advisability of satisfying himself with the concessions already wrung from the Turks, and in inducing him to believe that the Serbs and Albanians together should free the land from the Turks for their common benefit.

Again, "Marco" [Colonel Bozhin Simitch] wrote (*Nova Europa*, XVI, 10–11):

"It was at the beginning of August, 1912, the eve of the war with the Turks. *How would the frontier Albanians behave in regard to the Turks in this war was the great question.* In the early spring of 1912 Dr. Milan Milovanovitch, *the Prime Minister*, had sent as emissaries to Isa Boletin, Captain Bozhin Simitch, pope Andjelka from Mitrovitza in Kossovo, and Ognjan Radenkovitch [brother of Bogdan] to parley with Isa about the revolution which he was rapidly bringing to a success.

"*This revolution, as is well known, gave the death-blow to Turkish prestige both within and without Turkey.*

"*His unexpected and complete success* released Isa from all obligations with regard to Serbia, and left him with his hands free for fresh parleys.

"Serbia's interest in the revolution was to support Isa with both hands in his revolution against the Young Turk régime, for in an organized manner and by fixed plan the Young Turks were destroying our people [i.e. the Black Hand agents and those whom they incited to acts of violence] in Old Serbia and Macedonia.

"Therefore, for tactical and political reasons on our side, nothing else was asked of Isa in the name of Allied obligations towards Serbia than *that he should protect and shelter our people from tyranny. We saw that in all probability this Albanian rising would bring about great disorder in Turkey, and that this disorder would make the success of the Balkan War possible.* . . .

"Before the arrival of our emissaries there came from King Nicholas to Isa delegates specially begging that he would not work for Serbia. 'I tell you this in confidence', said Isa to our emissaries. 'Tell it to whom it is necessary. But I beg it may not appear in the newspapers, for I have eaten bread in King Nicholas's house'."

"From this it is plain", wrote Miss Durham, through whom these extracts were obtained, "that both Montenegro and Serbia", who in opposition to each other were striving to establish their ascendancy in the projected Great Serbia, "tried to enlist Isa as an ally. The terms offered by Serbia, so far as I know, have not been revealed. . . . But it is clear that the poor man trusted himself to Serbian promises. It is equally clear that these promises were void of all value, and the object of the Serbs was to obtain the territory themselves. It is a repulsive tale of treachery. The above shows that Isa protected the lives of the Serb minority in Kossovo, and as reward the lands were claimed as Serbian. Had he carried out the Young Turk system of expelling or exterminating them, the land would now be part of Albania."

Boletin's bodyguard included Serbs. At night he was guarded by two Serbs at his outer door, two at the second door, and ten Moslem Albanians within, a fact which proves that the Serbian minority were on excellent terms with the insurgent leaders. The latter maintained rigid discipline among their men; and Idris Sefer shot several of his followers for robbing Serb houses (T.

18.5.10). The same attitude was preserved towards the Turks; prisoners were disarmed and released unharmed, and no outrages upon isolated detachments were committed (T. 27.5.10).

"In August, 1912, therefore," continued Marco, "it was necessary to speak again with Isa on different grounds, for the question now was our war with the Turks. The situation now was not so favourable; the Young Turk régime was so weak that the revolutionaries, after easily capturing Novibazar and Mitrovitza carried their success to Skoplje [Uskub] by the railway. Skoplje they left after a few days, *but only after Constantinople had officially promised to fulfil all their wishes* at a time fixed upon. Thus the whole revolution came to an end without bloodshed, like any wedding. . . .

"As Inspector-General of the frontier region, Bozhin had already submitted a proposal, namely, that the Chief of the General Staff should send two General Staff officers across all Albania in order to ascertain the attitude of the Albanians—whether they would be our allies or our enemies in the coming war."

Briefly, then, the situation was as follows. The Balkan Allies, having employed the Albanians to prepare the way for their armies, had never expected the insurrection to succeed, and were determined that their plans should not be frustrated by the creation of an autonomous Albania (C.E. 47. Also S.A. 19). But Russia, who had been informed by the Allies of the negotiations between them, refused to approve of aggressive action, being herself unprepared for war, and well knowing that if such action was undertaken with her connivance, the immediate intervention of the Triple Alliance would be provoked. The Balkan Allies therefore set themselves to provoke "incidents" which would justify action. The Turks, exasperated by the reverses which they had sustained at the hands of the Albanians, and wearied by guerilla warfare in which they had been at a disadvantage, readily swallowed the bait cast by the Christian States. The Christians in European Turkey, incited by their co-nationals across the borders, threw bombs, raided, murdered (B.K. 199–202), or otherwise irritated the harassed Turks: and they retaliated ruthlessly. Then the Balkan Allies declared that the treatment of their co-national minorities was intolerable and that the Turks were compelling them to intervene. Their subsequent treatment of Albanian majorities was ſtill more intolerable, but of that more later. On the Montenegrin border, where there was a series of such incidents, the Slavs were invariably the originators of the trouble.

The reverses inflicted upon Turkish armies by both Italians and Albanians had encouraged the Balkan States to press forward their preparations for war; but when, to their dismay, Albania won virtual autonomy, they resolved to act at once, before she became reconciled with the Turks, organized her resources, and eſtablished her claim to consideration by weſtern ſtatesmen.

The Montenegrins were spoiling for war. They believed themselves invincible, and they knew that should they be defeated, Russia would never allow them to be subjugated or deprived of territory. But in view of the attitude of the Powers in general and Russia in particular they sought to make Turkey appear the aggressor (B.K. 160), confident that their invincible army would then sweep through northern Albania and the Kossovo vilayet and foreſtall the Serbs in Prizren. Nicholas believed that such a victory, and of victory he was confident, would lead to his acclamation as King of Great Serbia. And the frontier, never yet properly delimited, lent itself to the creation of "incidents". In July a Turko-Montenegrin frontier commission was actually appointed at the inſtigation of Turkey, but it never visited the frontier! It attempted to delimit it by maps, although no accurate maps exiſted.

Turkish frontier poſts, harassed by the conſtant threat of surprise attack, were easily provoked to fire upon Monte-negrins, especially where the frontier was in dispute. In the middle of July a skirmish between Turkish and Montenegrin troops took place on the frontier near Podgoritza. But it did not lead to war. On the 3rd Auguſt a sharp engagement took place at Mojkovatz (T. 8.8.12) near Bijelopolje, brought about by the grass-mowing trick which the Montenegrins employed upon several occasions. In this particular case, Montenegrin peasants, exhorted by gendarmes, had been sent to mow grass near a Turkish blockhouse, while troops, concentrated near by, awaited developments. The Turks fired, as anticipated. The blockhouse was then rushed and surrounded. A Montenegrin soldier pressed himself against the wall between the loop-holes, and with his shirt upon a stick ignited the roof. The small garrison rushed out and was shot down, while Turkish reinforcements were obliged to retire. "The Montenegrins were mad with rage; they cut the noses off their fallen foes, put them in their pockets, and followed the retreating Turks in a wild rush almost to Bijelopolje, fifteen kilometres over the frontier. They lost twenty-two killed and thirty-two wounded. . . . The Montenegrins had over three thousand men in the field" (S.S. 161) and four blockhouses were burnt. But Turkey did not declare war, although she would have been justified in so doing; and the Legations at Cettinje demanded the withdrawal of the Montenegrin troops.

In the middle of August the Montenegrins succeeded in stirring up trouble in the Serb villages near Berane (T. 19.8.12). In consequence, on the night of the 14th–15th a Turkish detachment fell upon the villagers, killed ten, and carried off thirty women and children as hostages. The Montenegrin troops, who had been ready as in the Mojkovatz affair, again crossed the frontier and burnt several blockhouses. Berane would have been taken had not the Legations again protested. In their report of the affair the Montenegrins made it appear that it had taken place on Montenegrin territory, which was untrue. Meanwhile, sniping along the frontier between Montenegrin and Turkish blockhouses became general, while Montenegrin troops and guns were moved into position and Serbs across the border armed (T. 21.8.12). Turkey, however, persisted in refraining from declaring war, and Russia refused her support if Montenegro took the initiative. Montenegro's only course was to seek the support of Serbia, whom she was anxious to forestall.

When Turkey granted virtual autonomy to Albania, the Archbishop of Skutari was sent to explain the fresh situation to the Maltsia e madhe tribes and to arrange a cessation of hostilities. The Turks agreed to withdraw all troops from the mountains except from frontier posts and from Dechich and Planinitza, points of strategic importance for the defence of Skutari. Peace was accordingly made, at Bukovitza, with all the tribes except Gruda and Shala, who refused to make peace until the Turks withdrew altogether (T. 14.8.12).

But peace between the Turks and the malissori was the last thing the Montenegrins desired (S.S. 164). Peace might be followed by reconciliation, now that autonomy was granted, and would result in co-operation to resist the projected Montenegrin invasion. Accordingly they urged the malissori to renew the struggle for complete independence. The tribesmen found it difficult to understand the meaning of "autonomy". They had fought for independence. Hatred of the Turks made them blind to the hypocrisy of Montenegro, who offered to help them, deaf to the warnings and entreaties of their compatriots, who sought to restrain them. Austria-Hungary refused to assist them. Accordingly, certain malissori leaders of Maltsia e madhe went to Cettinje in the middle of September; they agreed to fight with Montenegro upon the assurance of King Nicholas that he wished to take none of their land, merely to free his borders from Turks (P.D. 63: 1259; S.S. 177).

Maltsia e madhe rose. The malissori stormed Planinitza, capturing quantities of arms and ammunition, but were driven out again by artillery fire. They cut up a Turkish battalion near Nenhelm: and for a fortnight struggled desperately, despite heavy losses, to capture Dechich. But without the support of artillery it was impossible to dislodge the Turks. Meanwhile the Klementi tribesmen, under Ded Soko, pushed boldly south to Bregumatia to prevent the arrival of Turkish reinforcements and isolate Skutari. Ded Soko was a common tribesman of Seltze, who, by force of character and natural ability, had won the confidence and respect of his northern compatriots, and at the same time the hatred and jealousy of Essad Pasha. Turkey again appealed to the Powers to intervene at Cettinje (T. 20 and 24.9.12), at the same time constituting another commission to investigate the tribesmen's grievances.

Meanwhile, the Treaty between Serbia and Montenegro, by which the latter became a member of the Balkan League, had been signed; and the plans of the Allies were completed by the Greco-Bulgarian military convention of the 22nd September. The mine was laid which shattered Turkey and well-nigh Europe also.

Russia had refrained from informing her allies of the Entente of the negotiations between the Balkan States, and the Powers were unaware of the formation of the League until a few weeks before hostilities commenced. Even when aware of its existence, they failed to appreciate the Allies' determination for war and merely made vague and independent proposals for administrative reform. Further, Europe doubted the ability of the Allies, even should their co-operation be sustained, which was considered extremely unlikely, to overthrow the Turkish armies.

Before any collective steps had been taken, the Allies began to mobilize on the 30th September. They knew that Russia would neither allow them to sustain defeat by Turkey nor attack by Austria-Hungary. The Powers protested, warned the Balkan States that even should they be victorious "under no circumstances would they agree to any change in the *status quo* in south-east Europe" (P.D. 52: 498), and prepared a collective Note. Montenegro, whose troops had long ago "got set" and made several false starts, was determined to be first in the field. On the day upon which the Note was presented King Nicholas proclaimed that to preserve the integrity of his frontiers and to liberate his brethren across the border he was reluctantly, and as the only course, obliged to declare war. On the 8th October, 1912, began the scramble for aggrandizement. Montenegro proclaimed a holy war!

The Powers meanwhile presented their Note. Therein their previous warning was reiterated, together with an assurance that they themselves, "relying on article 23 of the Treaty of Berlin, would take in hand the restoration of administrative reforms in European Turkey, in the interest of the populations concerned, on the understanding that such reforms should not infringe the sovereignty of the Ottoman Empire". But Serbia, Bulgaria, and Greece ignored the Note and on the 13th October presented a joint ultimatum to the Porte, in which they demanded immediate and far-reaching reforms amounting to autonomy for all the subject races of European Turkey. Four days elapsed, during which the Powers might have intervened. But so much at variance were they that no further effective steps were taken, and Turkey was left to her own resources. Surrender or war were her only alternatives. On the 17th, therefore, she declared war upon Serbia and Bulgaria, while attempting to buy Greek neutrality by the cession of Crete and a railway concession. But Greece had in view larger acquisitions, and on the 18th declared war upon Turkey. The Powers now awaited events, anticipating the speedy overthrow and disruption of the League.

The outbreak of war found the Albanian Nationalists once again upon the horns of a dilemma (S.A. 19). Their hereditary foes were sweeping down upon land which was indisputably Albanian. But they were aware of a widespread ignorance which had led to their classification as Turks; and since 1880, interested States had encouraged this misconception which the Turks had done nothing to dispel. For four centuries their existence as a distinct nationality had been ignored. Their resistance in 1880 to the provisions of the Treaty of Berlin had been generally misconstrued as signifying allegiance to Turkey; and were they now to assist the Turks, this misconstruction would appear to be confirmed. Their compatriots, too, fresh from a struggle with the Turks, wearied of their perfidy and oppression, would find it difficult to understand a policy which now dictated co-operation with their foes of yesterday. Already the malissori of Maltsia e madhe were co-operating with the Montenegrins.

On the other hand, their struggle with Turkey was for the moment at an end: their patriotic aspirations were realized to the extent which they desired for the time being. They had no further cause for strife with Turkey until national unity had been consolidated, and were now free to pursue their original policy of preserving the Ottoman Empire for their own protection. To declare for the Balkan Allies would be contrary to that policy, and it would seem, too, as if they hailed the Christian States as their deliverers. They had, however delivered themselves, to the extent desired at the time. They sought no assistance; and the majority of their compatriots would never agree to co-operate with their hereditary foes. Already bands of Kossovo Albanians were resisting the advance of the Serbs (T. 31.10.12).

Another all-important consideration was that there existed no universally acknowledged Albanian central authority strong enough to override local independence and direct an intricate policy. The Albanian leaders were determined that such must be created without further delay, and a policy pursued which would unite the two extreme elements among their compatriots: namely, those whose hatred of the Turks led them to fight with the Balkan Allies, and those who resisted their hereditary foes, the Slavs or Greeks.

From every point of view, therefore, a policy of neutrality seemed to the Albanian Central Committee desirable. By following a distinctive policy the Albanians hoped to give tangible proof of their racial individuality, while relying for the preservation of their territorial integrity more upon the jealousy and rivalry of the Powers than upon their good will.

Thus did the situation appear to Ismail Kemal Bey. After the conclusion of hostilities between Albanians and Turks in the summer he had left Valona for Constantinople, there to confer with the new Cabinet. While on his way, he had been summoned to an interview with Prince Mirko of Montenegro at Porto Roso near Trieste. On behalf of his father, the Prince had invited Ismail Bey to discuss with the King the part which Albania might play with advantage in the impending war with Turkey. King Nicholas doubtless sought to secure the co-operation of the southern Albanians, perhaps by the proposal that Ismail Bey should proclaim himself King with Montenegrin support, and in return acknowledge Montenegrin claims to northern Albania: for it appears that a similar proposal was subsequently made to Essad Pasha. In any case the conference did not take place. Ismail Bey had adhered to the policy which had been pursued hitherto by the Nationalists, and had returned to Constantinople, to strive afresh for the welfare of his country and of her suzerain protector.

At the outbreak of war Ismail Bey shared the misgivings of his compatriots regarding the security of their country. And as the Turks, hopelessly outnumbered, fell back before the Allies, he considered that the time had arrived for the Albanians to abandon the sinking ship lest they should be drawn into the vortex, and at once take vigorous measures for their own salvation.

The Grand Vizier, Kiamil Pasha, pressed Ismail Bey to stand by him and offered him a Ministry, but the latter refused. He hurried to Bucharest and held a meeting of the large Albanian colony there, at which fifteen of his compatriots decided to go with him to Albania. He then telegraphed to all parts of Albania announcing his intended arrival, and convening a national congress at Valona. At Budapest he conferred with Andrassy and Berchtold; the latter approved his views on the national question, and arranged that a vessel should convey him to Durazzo—Valona being blockaded— before the arrival of the Serbs.

In Durazzo it was believed that the Turkish Army was everywhere victorious. The population was not even aware of the approach of the Serbs, and the Turkish element, joined

by some of the local population—moſtly Bosnian immigrants
—received Ismail Bey and his colleagues with hoſtility, declaring that they were "agents provocateurs". Nevertheless,
delegates from Durazzo and the dependent diſtriĉts joined the
little band of patriots, who set forth for Valona; and the
Turkish authorities, probably because they were aware that
Albania could be preserved from Serbia and Greece only by
a declaration of independence, did not intercept them. At
Valona, where eighty-three Moslem and Chriſtian delegates
from all parts of Albania had assembled, they were received
with enthusiasm.

The National Congress at once opened, and voted unanimously on the 28th November, 1912, the proclamation of
Albanian independence; and the flag of Skenderbeg, which
had remained wrapped in its folds for 445 years, was hoiſted
over the town.

The Congress then eleĉted a Cabinet of seven Miniſters,
Chriſtian and Moslem, Ismail Bey as President, and Dom
Nikol Kachiori as Vice-President.

The Cabinet was as follows:

MUFID BEY LIBOHOVA	Miniſter for Foreign Affairs.
MEHMED PASHA DRALLA	Miniſter for War.
PETER POGA	Miniſter of Juſtice.
LOUIS GURAKUCHI	Miniſter of Education.
ABDI BEY TOPTANI	Miniſter of Finance.
PANDELE TSALI	Miniſter of Agriculture.
LEF NOSI	Miniſter of Poſts and Telegraphs.

A senate of eighteen members was also formed. A telegram
was then addressed to the Powers and the Porte, announcing
the ſteps which had been taken to defend the rights of the
Albanian people, the oldeſt in eaſtern Europe, and asking for
recognition and proteĉtion (I.K. 370-3).

In a Memorandum subsequently presented to Sir Edward
Grey (at the second meeting of the Conference of Ambassadors) in which the Albanians claimed "the right to life,
and the possibility of orderly and peaceful development",
their exiſtence as a homogeneous ethnic group, whose
development had been retarded by unfavourable conditions,
was ſtressed. "To place territory where the Albanian population is in a majority under foreign domination", continued the
Memorandum, "would be to perpetuate germs of discord and

trouble" (S.A. 26), and (to quote B.P. 54) ". . . it is indeed certain that neither Serbia nor Greece could govern Albania except by a policy of extermination." The Albanians proposed that a mixed commission should be entrusted with the task of delimiting the frontier.

With the exception that they rendered assistance in the defence of Janina and Skutari, which were considered of vital importance to the existence of Albania (and indeed made it possible, by holding up the invading armies, for Europe to establish her as an independent State), and with the exception of a desultory resistance offered by Albanian bands in Kossovo and the east to the Serbs, and by southern Albanians to Greek detachments at Logora, fifteen miles south of Valona, the Albanians adhered to the policy advocated by the Nationalist leaders. Doubtless this observance of a national policy was largely due to the influence of the Provisional Government and Albanian leaders; but in part also to ignorance of the situation and of the intentions of the Allies. The individual Albanian was at first inclined to regard the struggle between the Turks and the Slavs, Bulgars, or Greeks as none of his business unless fought upon his own personal property. A "national frontier", to the average "man in the street", or perhaps more appropriately, "man in the hills", conveyed nothing. The belligerents were all foes, and if they cared to slaughter each other, so much the better for the Albanian.

The southern and central Albanians were more or less under the control of the Nationalist leaders, most of whom hailed from these districts. The Kossovo Albanians had always acted independently, although they had whole-heartedly espoused the cause of nationalism, and indeed borne the brunt of the struggle for autonomy. But diplomacy decreed that they were never to have the opportunity, with the exception of a handful, of declaring their allegiance to a national Government for which they had so bravely fought. The malissori of the extreme north were the victims of Montenegrin machinations, while the Mirdites, guided by their courageous Abbot, followed, in so far as they were able, the national policy (T. 31.10.12).

The outbreak of war found Skutari fortified. Field works and barbed wire entanglements had been constructed to augment its antiquated defences. The artillery was, however, defective, and there were at most seventy guns, the heaviest being 12-cm. naval howitzers. The perimeter of the defences was approximately twenty-eight miles.

Hussein Riza Pasha had at his disposal about 14,000 men of the 24th Division. But Essad Pasha, who was in central Albania and still apparently adhering to the Albanian national cause, appreciated the importance of the fortress. He therefore hastened to the assistance of Hussein Pasha with a reserve (Redif) Division of 10,000 men, which was under his command at Elbasan and Tirana. Ded Soko, with the Klementi tribesmen, lay across his route. Essad ordered them to recognize the obligations of autonomous Albania to Turkey and let him through. Probably he was tactless. In any case Essad and Ded Soko were foes; and Essad was supporting Turkey, against whom Ded Soko was fighting for independence. Essad was obliged to fight his way through, and arrived in Skutari.

The Montenegrin Army was a badly trained, badly disciplined, and shockingly equipped militia. Commissariat and medical arrangements were negligible. The Montenegrins thought that the war would be a "walk-over" for them, and did not expect many casualties. Operations were carried out by three armies, which were disposed at the outbreak of war as follows: (1) The main body, 13,000 strong, under the Crown Prince Danilo at Podgoritza; (2) General Martinovitch, with 8,000 men and the bulk of the Montenegrin artillery at Virpazar and Antivari; and (3) 10,000 men under General Vukotitch at Andrijevitza.

It was intended that Prince Danilo and Martinovitch should converge upon Skutari, carry the fortress by assault, in which no difficulty was anticipated, and then march upon Prizren, the objective also of Vukotitch.

Miss Durham witnessed and vividly described the opening of the campaign on the 9th October:

"We started for the little hill from which Podgoritza takes its name. The rain ceased; the sun came out and sparkled on the coarse, drenched grass. About three-quarters of the way up we were halted by the perianiks, and saw the King, in full Montenegrin costume, standing brilliantly white against the sky, on the summit with Prince Mirko and a small suite.

"The clouds lifted from the mountains with a won-

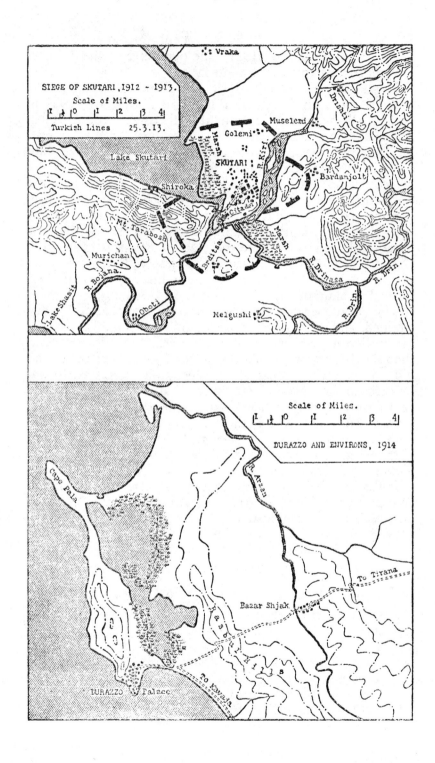

SIEGE OF SKUTARI, 1912 - 1913.

Scale of Miles.

Turkish Lines   25.3.13.

Vraka

Muselemi

Golemi

SKUTARI

Lake Skutari

Shiroka

Bardanjolt

Citadel

Mt. Tarabosh

Marsh

R. Drinasa

R. Drin

Murichan

Proditsa

R. Drin

R. Bojana

Lake Shasit

Oboti

Melgushi

Scale of Miles.

DURAZZO AND ENVIRONS, 1914

Cape Pala

Arzan

To Tirana

Bazar Shjak

To Kavaja

DURAZZO   Palace

derful play of light and shade. Not a sound was heard but the tinkle of sheep-bells from the wide plain below, across which ran the frontier line. Beyond it towered Dechich with its roughly fortified Turkish outposts. The air was crystal clear. An endless quarter of an hour dragged by. So peaceful was the scene, it was hard to realize that the long-talked-of *status quo* was about to be shattered and the map of Europe changed. In the strain of excitement all possible and impossible results of the approaching fall of the Turk whirled through my mind. Boom! The big gun roared from Gradina, on the height to our left, fired by Prince Petar. A great white puff of smoke showed where it struck Planinitza, the camp on the flank of Dechich. I had no field glasses, but, so clear was the air, I could see the walled camp with the naked eye.

"The bells rang out from the church below us; the band, which was with the King, struck up the national hymn. The few spectators, mostly little boys, and the perianiks joined in, and shouted 'Zhivio!'

"I looked at my watch; it was eight a.m." (S.S. 186).

Under fire from the Montenegrin artillery, the Turks evacuated Planinitza. Two days later they were driven from Dechich by the malissori, supported by the Montenegrins and artillery fire. During the next few days Tuzi, Vranji, Nenhelm, and Rogom surrendered, and the way to Skutari lay open. The Montenegrins burnt and looted as they advanced.

The wide distribution of the Montenegrin forces gave Hussein Pasha a most tempting opportunity for a bold manœuvre upon interior lines. Had Prince Danilo been held before Dechich or at some other point on the frontier, Hussein Pasha might have overwhelmed Martinovitch with ease, isolated as he was by Lake Skutari, and have destroyed the bulk of the Montenegrin artillery. Alternatively, but entailing greater risk owing to the co-operation of the malissori with the Montenegrins, he might have held Martinovitch, crushed Danilo, and then have fallen upon Martinovitch before Vukotitch could arrive. Unfortunately his troops were not of a very high standard of efficiency, although superior to the Montenegrins, and he passively awaited the Montenegrin attack. It is, however, difficult to understand why he did not adopt the former alternative plan. Doubtless he anticipated the ultimate victory of his country; and in the circumstances thought it wiser to avoid casualties or unnecessary risk of premature defeat, so that he might immobilize the Montenegrin armies before Skutari.

The Montenegrin advance was slow; and indeed it is doubtful whether there would have been any advance had it not been for the assistance of the Albanian tribesmen. The Montenegrins did not reach the Kiri until the 25th, and did not cross it until three days later. They carried Great Bardanjolt hill, without waiting until Martinovitch could launch a simultaneous attack upon the north-western defences. In consequence they were driven back with such heavy losses by a Turkish counter-attack that they withdrew, and made no further attempt against the fortress until February. They occupied a position between the Kiri and the Lake, some three thousand yards from the Turkish lines. Martinovitch, advancing from Antivari and Virpazar unopposed, carried the Turkish advanced positions with heavy loss and came to a standstill likewise before the main defensive line.

Vukotitch had proceeded energetically to stake out Montenegrin claims in the Sanjak of Novibazar, but without encountering serious opposition except from Moslem Albanians. Bijelopolje, Berane, Ipek, and Djakova had been occupied; but the Serbs had forestalled him in Prizren. He arrived at Skutari with 6,000 men on the 19th November, and took over the command of the besiegers.

A general armistice between the Allies and Turkey was signed on the 3rd December, but as the revictualling of the fortress while it lasted was not agreed upon, Hussein Pasha refused to recognize it. But nothing beyond desultory skirmishes took place until February.

Apart from their anxiety to oust the Turks, the malissori, who had joined the Montenegrins, had been anxious to avenge themselves upon the Moslem Albanians who had attacked them in the previous year at the instigation of Bedri Bey. Apart from operations against the Turks, they had anticipated nothing more than inter-tribal warfare, waged in the usual courteous manner and according to the rules of the game. But the atrocities committed by the Montenegrins upon their Moslem compatriots, the burning of houses, and the destruction of property, disgusted them; and they fed and sheltered hundreds of Moslem refugees during the winter.

The Montenegrins behaved in the country as conquerors, not as allies. They commandeered hay and cattle, plundered poultry, and generally helped themselves without payment. They had not made the promised issue of bread and shoes: and attempted to persuade the malissori to wear Montenegrin caps. The latter had expected the Albanian, not the Montenegrin, flag to be hoisted at Tuzi and Dechich. They began to suspect that Montenegrin assurances were as worthless as those of the Turks. And at the end of October they began to drift back to their homes. By the end of November there were no malissori in the field (T. 11.12.12.); indeed, the pendulum began to swing in the opposite direction. Then came news of the declaration of independence. Still the Montenegrins continued to loot and pillage; they even looted several Catholic churches. The Catholic malissori leaders then met to discuss the situation, and swore to resist any further outrages upon Albanians or Albanian property. A further Montenegrin attempt to commandeer hay at Mazreku ended with a skirmish in which the Montenegrins suffered seventeen casualties; fearing a general attack they paid damages, and thereafter refrained from interfering with the malissori. But relations between them continued to be strained.

Only in Martinovitch's army was mutilation forbidden and press correspondents allowed to move freely. Vukotitch met with but slight resistance, and only from peasants striving to defend their property, but "scarcely a nose was left on a corpse between Berane and Ipek" (S.S. 237, 176, 185). Prince Danilo had declared that the Rugova Moslems should be exterminated, and exterminated they were (S.S. 253).

Meantime the other Allies swept all before them. The Turks had less than 300,000 men to oppose at least 800,000 Bulgarians, Serbs, Greeks, and Montenegrins. In addition the troops of the three first-mentioned countries were very much better trained and equipped. The solidarity of the Turkish units had been seriously shaken by the conscription, under the Young Turk régime, of men of the same race and religion as the enemy. They were badly trained, badly equipped, and transport difficulties rendered the bringing of reinforcements from Asia Minor extremely slow.

On the 23rd October the Serbs won the decisive battle of Kumanovo, and the Turks retired precipitately southwards. This left the whole of northern Albania to the Serbs and

Montenegrins, and on the 31st the Serbian III Army, under General Yankovitch, was sent eastwards to subdue and occupy the territory which Serbia proposed to annex, and to secure access to the sea. In two columns the Serbs crossed the Drin, one moving upon Elbasan, and the other through Mirdita, and except at Flet, where they were held up for three days, they were almost unopposed (T. 22.11.12.). The Mirdites were short of ammunition, and their Abbot persuaded them to refrain from resistance, which would have led to a massacre. Moreover, Prenk planned a compromise with the Serbs. But although they had given to the Albanians "God's *besa*" that they came only as liberators, they burnt, looted, and executed anyone who dared to protect his property and women (T. 2.12.12; 5.2.13). For example, the Ljuma tribe was massacred because one Serb telegraphist was shot (S.S. 239), and at Kruja, where a local Provisional Government had been formed, which received them very hospitably, no less than fifty persons were summarily hanged. Everywhere Albanian patriots were killed or imprisoned without trial (B.T. 240-2).

The Montenegrins, who had captured Medua on the 17th November, arrived simultaneously with the Serbs at Alessio on the 19th, and in conjunction with them occupied the town after a sharp engagement (T. 22.11.12). On the 30th the Serbs occupied Durazzo. But the battles of Kirk-Kilesse, Monastir, and Lule Burgas had been won by the Allies, and the general armistice between Turkey and Bulgaria, Serbia, and Montenegro, signed on the 3rd December, brought operations to a close except at Skutari.

The Greeks, although they participated in the ensuing Conference of Ambassadors, did not subscribe to the armistice, as they had not at the time staked out their claims in southern Albania (S.A. 20), and were determined to take Janina, which Turkey refused to surrender. At the outbreak of war the main body of the Greek Army, under the Crown Prince Constantine, had operated entirely in a north-easterly direction, with the object of forestalling the other Allies in Salonika, which surrendered on the 9th November. The 8th and 9th Divisions, composed almost entirely of volunteers and reservists, constituted the Army of Epirus under General Sapundjakis. The army was opposed by two Turkish Divisions, and its progress was extremely slow. Not until the 3rd November did it succeed in clearing the Prevesa and Louro area, and did not arrive before Janina until the 10th. A Greek detachment, which landed at Santi Quaranta, and a column of irregulars from Mezzovo converged upon the fortress, and, in conjunction with Sapundjakis, established a loose blockade. The weather then precluded further operations until the spring.

When Ismail Bey proclaimed the independence of Albania he knew that he would be supported by Austria-Hungary and Italy, who would combine in opposing the access of a third Power to the Adriatic. When the Serbs marched into Albania the semi-official Austro-Hungarian *Fremdenblatt* remarked that their advance could have "no national or military reason" (T. 7.11.12). Pasitch, on the other hand, declared that "an independent Albania was neither desirable nor possible" (T. 9.11.12). But Russia warned Serbia that she would not go to war for the sake of a Serbian port on the Adriatic and counselled prudence; nevertheless, she began military preparations (T. 15.11.12). The Greek Press announced that "to allow the barbarous Albanians an independent existence amid Greek civilization was inconceivable" (T. 14.11.12).

On the 12th November the Austro-Hungarian Minister in Cettinje warned King Nicholas to refrain from operations against Alessio and Medua, a *démarche* which the King declared "null and void", and ignored. Italy supported Austria-Hungary (T. 15.11.12.). A *démarche* was made simultaneously in Belgrade. While Austria-Hungary maintained a moderate and reasonable attitude (T. 14.11.12; leading art.), she made it clear that she would not tolerate a Serbian military port on the Adriatic, it being considered that Serbian commercial access to the sea through Albania or Montenegro could be arranged by a convention; and she followed the example of Russia in regard to military preparations.

A European war now appeared imminent (A.H. 40–1). Great Britain alone of the Powers preserved a conciliatory attitude. Europe, a mass of inflammable material, threatened to explode, and Sir Edward Grey alone was in a position to save the situation by mediation. Russia and France pressed the Powers to make a declaration of "disinterestedeness": or, in other words, to accept the accomplished fact and allow the Allies to retain whatever they succeeded in obtaining. But Vienna indignantly refused to consider the proposal, and in this attitude was supported both by the Italian and British Governments (S.A. 21). For their intervention Ismail Bey

L

presented his thanks in person to the Austro-Hungarian and Italian Consuls at Valona, and by letter to Sir Edward Grey.

The solution of the problem was entrusted to the Ambassadors in London of the six Great Powers, who assembled at the Foreign Office under the presidency of Sir Edward Grey on the 17th December, 1912, as the "Conference of Ambassadors". Three days later the following announcement was made: "The Ambassadors have recommended to their Governments, and the latter have accepted in principle, Albanian autonomy, together with a provision guaranteeing to Serbia commercial access to the Adriatic Sea. All six Governments have agreed in principle on these points". Thus was an immediate conflagration averted.

Of the ensuing negotiations Prince Lichnowsky wrote:

"The British Statesman maintained from the beginning that England had no interest in Albania, and would therefore not go to war on the subject. In his rôle of 'honest broker' he would confine his efforts to mediation and an attempt to smooth away difficulties between the two groups. He therefore by no means placed himself on the side of the Entente Powers, and during the negotiations, which lasted about eight months, he lent his good will and powerful influence towards the establishment of an understanding.

"But we"—Germany—"instead of taking up a position such as England adopted, invariably accepted the views dictated to us by Vienna. Count Mensdorff led the Triple Alliance in London, and I acted as his second. My task consisted in supporting his proposals.

"On every point, including Albania, the Serbian harbours in the Adriatic, Skutari, and in the definition of the Albanian frontiers, we were on the side of Austria-Hungary and Italy, whilst Sir Edward Grey hardly ever took the French or Russian point of view. On the contrary, he nearly always took our part, in order to give no pretext for war. That pretext was supplied later by a dead Archduke".

During the winter of 1912–13 the main body of the Greek Army, which had easily completed its task in Macedonia after the defeat of the Turks by the Serbs at Monastir on the 18th November, was transferred by sea to Epirus. It had there a threefold purpose to fulfil: first, to reduce the fortress of Janina: secondly, to ſtake out as large a claim as possible in southern Albania; and thirdly, to round up the remnants of the Turkish Army under Djavid Pasha, which had escaped from the disaſter of Monaſtir and retired through Korcha (T. 15.1.13) to the area Fieri-Lushnja-Berat (T. 30.4.13; 2.5.13) to oppose the Serbian advance. Janina was defended by a garrison of 30,000, but these troops were demoralized by the defeat of their country in every other theatre. Many had fled thither from Monaſtir. On the other hand, the Crown Prince Conſtantine had at his disposal almoſt the entire army and material resources of Greece; and it is not therefore surprising that on the 5th March, 1913, he was able to deliver a successful assault upon the fortress. It was formally sur-rendered upon the following day (T. 7.3.13) by Vehid Bey, brother of Essad Pasha. Djavid was driven from Lushnja during March by the Serbs, and thereupon concluded an armiſtice.

Italy and Auſtria-Hungary had intimated to Greece that in no circumſtances would she be allowed to occupy Valona, and in that attitude were supported by Berlin. Communications between Valona and Europe were, however, interrupted on the 3rd December by a Greek squadron, which shelled the port (T. 6.12.12.)—an aćt which well-nigh precipitated Italian intervention—cut the cable which was the sole remaining link with the outside world, and eſtablished a blockade. This blockade was extended to Durazzo on the 27th February, raised between Prevesa and Palermo Bay on the 22nd March, and along the remainder of the coaſt on the 16th April; it corresponded with the rigid censorship which the Greek military authorities enforced in Epirus. "Never before, in any war, not even in the Japanese War, has a censorship been so severe, have war correspondents been kept so many miles behind and not allowed to see anything" (G.O. 4).

The blockade prevented the Provisional Government from communicating freely with its representatives at the Con-ference of Ambassadors—Mehmed bey Konitza, Rassik Dino, and P. Nogga. But towards the end of March Ferdinand de Bourbon, Duc de Montpensier, sailed into the bay on a yacht flying the British flag, and announced his candidature for the throne (I.K. 375). He was cordially received, and on the 1ſt April Ismail Bey, Louis Gurakuchi (Miniſter of Education), and Isa Boletin left Valona on board his yacht for Brindisi. They travelled to Rome, Vienna (T. 21.4.13), Paris, and London to win sympathy for Albanian claims; but they obtained little support, for "even after the reluctant recognition of the independence and the creation of the Albanian Principality, the new State was looked upon with holy horror as the illegitimate child of Austrian diplomacy, with Italy figuring as the midwife" (C.C. 84).

From the outset the Powers were indifferent to the welfare of the new State. She was created of expediency, not of spontaneity, and her vital interests were sacrificed that the peace of Europe might be preserved. She had no Diplomatic Corps, no Press to fight her cause; and public opinion, mistress of justice, was stifled by ignorance. On the other hand Serbia, Greece, and Montenegro strove by propaganda to discredit her and even deny the existence of the Albanian race. Powerless, she was obliged to remain a mere spectator while a million (P.D. 52: 2304) of her helpless countrymen who had fought fiercely for freedom from Moslem Turks were handed over to her *Christian* neighbours to be butchered or oppressed because they were neither Slavs nor Greeks, and dared to say so. "The nascent Albania is cut down to a minimum, and if Europe had wished to make the new State dependent on Austria or Italy, she could hardly have set about it more effectually" (W.P.; P. D. 52: 2298).

The Balkan Allies first sought the total dismemberment of Albania. The Serbs contended (*Die Albanesen und die Grossmächte*, Dr. V. Georgevitch, Leipzig, 1913; F.O. 70) that the Albanians, although possibly a distinct race, were incapable of uniting. Both Serbs and Montenegrins ignored ethnographical facts, relied largely upon irrelevant historical claims, and declared that a tiny Moslem State among the Christian States of Europe would be an anachronism. They ignored the existence of the large Christian Albanian populations of Epirus and North Albania, and the fact that the Albanians had never had an opportunity for self-government (n.b. T. 25, 26.11.12).

Total dismemberment being at once overruled, the Allies brought forward claims (map p. 116) which would have condemned Albania to speedy destruction (P.D. 52: 2304-6; 53: 411; 56: 2320). They sought to deprive her, in the north, of her most stalwart warriors, and in the south, of her most intellectual and enlightened elements, and to leave only those diStriĉts whose inhabitants had been rendered inert by the ravages of malaria and the demoralizing effeĉt of Turkish corruption. In the north a considerable Strip of the present Albanian coaSt would have been divided between Serbia and Montenegro, and in the south Valona commanded by Greek guns. M. Venizelos at firSt insiSted that the Greek frontier should begin at C. Glossa and should include a port in Valona Bay (S.A. 23). These proposals were at once rejeĉted, both Italy and AuStria-Hungary refusing to give their consent "to the delimitation which the Greek Government has in view, which tends to separate from Albania the territories which the two Governments consider essentially necessary for the vitality of the Albanian State". (Berchtold to Von Braun, 6th January, 1913; see S.A. 28). San Guiliano favoured the River Kalamas as the boundary, including Janina to Albania, reasoning that "this would give a basis for discussion, and one could then yield the case with Greece; so that Valona in no case would be left to the Greek kingdom" (S.A. 23). The Greeks thereupon modified their claim by proposing a frontier Starting from a point on the Albanian coaSt some ten miles south of Valona; beyond that they were determined to make no concessions, and Italy, supported by AuStria-Hungary, was equally determined to make none. Thus a deadlock was reached.

The frontier proposed by the Provisional Government (map p. 116) included all Albanian-inhabited territory, and in addition those regions which are ethnographically debatable, and might have been accepted had the Albanians been popular enough to command a propaganda such as was worked on behalf of the Balkan Allies (W.P.). It was by no means unreasonable either hiStorically or ethnographically (F.O. 24; E.B. 1 : 483; etc.). Moreover, it is probable that Ismail Bey claimed more territory than he thought his country would be allowed to retain, that there might be a margin for compromise.

In accordance with the agreement concluded between them in 1900, both Italy and AuStria-Hungary, neither of whom would allow the other to obtain or control the vital Albanian coaStline, were determined that no third Power should do so, and therefore insiSted upon the formation of an independent Albania. They did not, however, demand only for Albania a narrow Strip of land along the coaSt from Montenegro to Greece; they demanded also considerable depth of territory.

They were actuated partly, no doubt, by the knowledge that the larger Albania became, the wider would be the sphere of influence in the Balkans of whichever side gained the ascendancy in the country. But undoubtedly the principal motives which actuated the two Powers were, firstly, that the larger Albania became, the more quickly would she establish herself as a progressive and prosperous State, a "buffer" against Pan-Slavism, and a "buffer" between the two Powers themselves; and secondly, the frontiers, which they proposed, followed well-defined natural features, included natural obstacles between them and the sea, gave depth, and made it possible for Albania to defend herself and her coastline, with or without assistance, from aggression. A strip of coastline without proportionate depth is impossible to defend throughout its length, principally because a break-through by the aggressor at any point in its length threatens lateral communications, divides the country into two parts, and enables him to reduce each part in detail. Depth is an essential requirement of the defence, whether strategic or tactical.

But Austria-Hungary, having annexed Bosnia and the Hertzegovina, and thus denied to the Serbs the realization of their legitimate aspirations, considered it expedient to conciliate them, or more precisely Russia, by allowing them to obtain compensation in Macedonia in accordance with the policy formulated in the secret Treaty with Serbia of 1881 and 1889, in so far as was compatible with her own interests. She therefore agreed to the cession to Serbia of the Kossovopolje, and Uskub (D.Z. 96), Koprulu (F.O. 25), Prilep, and Monastir (P.D. 55: 1404), which were essentially Albanian or Bulgarian, but most certainly not Serbian towns. Moreover, she reluctantly agreed to the cession to Montenegro of the Catholic Albanian Hoti and Gruda tribes and the Moslem Albanians of the Plava-Gusinje district (F.O. 14). The inhabitants, who entreated the Powers to reconsider their decision (P.D. 63: 1259—petition to the International Commission of Control), were handed over to be butchered (P.D. 61: 1375; 63: 1259) like so many sheep, although the Montenegrins had failed to assimilate the inhabitants of the Albanian districts acquired in 1880 (F.O. 24).

Nevertheless, the frontier which Austria-Hungary proposed did give the new State a reasonable chance of achieving stability and prosperity. But this neither Russia and France nor the Balkan Allies desired; and Great Britain feared to adopt the Austro-Hungarian proposal lest she might jeopardize the solidarity of the Triple Entente. The frontier eventually decided upon was a violation of every ethnical, historical, economic, geographical, and, indeed, every relevant consideration.

Count Berchtold was eventually obliged to give way to the Russian proposal that Ipek, Prizren—the birth-place of the Albanian League—Struga, and Ochrida (towns which were overwhelmingly Albanian: F.O. 24; H. N. Brailsford—*Macedonia*—stated that in 1903 the Serbs of Prizren and Ipek numbered 5,000 householders against 20,000 to 25,000 Albanian householders, and that in the department of Prizren there were 100,000 Moslems, 13,000 Orthodox Christians, and 3,000 Catholics. See also E. B. 22: 375) should be excluded from Albania, whereupon Sazenov yielded with regard to the incorporation of Skutari in the new State. With regard to Dibra (E.B. 8: 176) and Djakova (E.B. 15: 130), purely Albanian towns, Berchtold proposed that a decision should be left to a special international committee; but Russia supported by France, demurred (A.W. 830-2), and as Berchtold did not consider it worth while to go to war on this, the last point to be settled, he gave way once again on the 20th March, upon the condition that the Albanians annexed by Serbia and Montenegro should be guaranteed internationally against religious or racial oppression (T. 24 and 31.3.13). Thus the northern and eastern frontiers of Albania (T. 28.3.13) were settled—the question of the southern frontier was the subject of further and protracted negotiations—and an International Boundary Commission, upon which Colonel Granet was the British representative, appointed to delimit it. The report of this Commission was never published, but it is known that the Commissioners failed to agree; they began operations in the autumn of 1913, were held up by the winter, recommenced in May, and a few days later returned to Skutari because of a dispute between the French and Italian Commissioners (T. 14.5.14)!

On the 7th April, 1913, in the House of Commons, Sir Edward Grey said:

"The agreement between the Powers respecting the [northern] frontiers of Albania was reached after a long and laborious diplomatic effort. It was decided that the littoral and Skutari should be Albanian, while Ipek, Prizren, Dibra, and (after much negotiation) Djakova should be excluded from Albania. This arrangement leaves a large tract of territory to be divided between Serbia and Montenegro as the fruits of victory. The making of the agreement was essential for the peace of Europe, and, in my opinion, it was accomplished only just in time to preserve that peace between Great Powers" (P.D. 51: 817).

On the 12th August Sir Edward Grey added:

"The difficulty of coming to an agreement about particular frontiers [of Albania] has been very great. Everyone will remember how difficult and how critical at some points were the questions raised in connection with the settlement of the northern and north-eastern frontiers of Albania. They were settled some time ago. We have now come to an agreement for the delimitation, under certain agreed conditions, of the southern and south-eastern frontiers of Albania, which will complete the whole frontiers of this State. I am quite aware that, when the whole comes to be stated, it will be open on many points to a great deal of criticism from anyone with local knowledge, who looks at it purely on the merits of the locality itself. It is to be borne in mind that in making that agreement the primary essential was to preserve agreement between the Great Powers themselves, and if the agreement about Albania has secured that, it has done the work which is most essential in the interests of the peace of Europe" (P.D. 56: 2285).

These words imply that Great Britain never maintained that the frontier of Albania was a just and equitable one. Indeed, by the northern and eastern frontiers as delimited in 1913, "half a million Albanians forming a compact ethno-graphical unit within the watershed which constitutes the natural geographical boundary of Albania were left, without appeal, to Montenegro and Serbia" (E.B. 30: 106). This figure does not include some 250,000 Albanians who inhabited districts farther east towards Prishtina and farther south towards Monastir. A creature deprived of a limb cannot thrive like one which is whole: nor can a State, if deprived of its most fertile lands and most exuberant manhood (A.S. 22). A race divided by a political frontier strives incessantly to overthrow the artificial boundary. Mountaineers struggle for unity with their lowland kinsmen, from whom alone they may obtain the necessaries of existence: peasants, to be united with their town-dwelling co-nationals, with whom alone they may barter their produce for the amenities of life. The frontier created in 1913 produced almost insuperable obstacles to the development of the new State, and brought famine and death to thousands of poverty-stricken peasantry. It deprived large rural populations of their market towns. Djakova, for example, was the market for the Nikaj, Merturi, Gashi, Krasnitch, Tropoja, and Puka tribesmen, who, when they attempted to go thither across the frontier, were either flogged or shot. A four days' tramp to Skutari was their only alternative (S.S.). The same state of affairs prevailed in the Dibra district, where the border line, instead of following the natural frontier provided by the range of mountains behind the town (see frontispiece), forms a loop into the Drin Valley to include Dibra. Either the peasants had to barter their goods in an open field or make a three days' journey (in the saddle) to Tirana over the most primitive mountain tracks (illustrations pp. 448, 482.). Again, farther south, another Serbian salient cut the natural line of communication between north-east and south-east Albania along the Drin Valley.

The only possible means of alleviating the suffering entailed by this iniquitous frontier was by the building of roads, but not until 1926 did Albania acquire adequate resources with which to undertake their construction amid such stupendous natural obstacles.

While the Conference of Ambassadors had been deliberating as to the fate of Albania, negotiations had been in progress, also in London, between Turkey and the Balkan Allies. Turkey, however, refused to submit to the terms upon which the Allies insisted, which included the surrender of Skutari, Janina, and Adrianople. The Allies broke off negotiations, and hostilities were resumed upon the 3rd February.

The Montenegrins at once redoubled their efforts to reduce Skutari. Considerable Serbian reinforcements with artillery, under General Boyovitch, had been sent to their assistance (T. 10.3.13), and to complete the investing line between the Drinasa and Bojana, for which the Montenegrins had not

sufficient men. From motives of pride their assistance was at
first refused, but was ultimately and reluctantly accepted. The
Montenegrins prepared for a general assault, and called for the
assistance of 4,000 malissori. No more than fifty presented
themselves, and these, when they had received the promised
supply of cartridges, retired again to their homes.

During the winter the Turks had strengthened their
positions at Muselimi, and on Great Bardanjolt. Against these
points the Montenegrin main attack was delivered on the
7th February, while the Serbs delivered a feint attack from the
south, which was repulsed, and a Montenegrin column
attacked Tarabosh, but broke down before the Turkish wire.
The Montenegrins met with slight resistance at Muselimi,
which they occupied: but on Great Bardanjolt they were held
up by wire. A second attempt upon the following day was no
more successful. But on the 9th, supported by a battery at
close range, they carried the position after a fierce struggle.
These operations cost them about 2,000 killed.

Hussein Riza Pasha had become aware of the rapidly
increasing ill feeling between the malissori and the Montenegrins. He was aware too of the reverses sustained elsewhere
by his country. He was determined to continue the defence of
the fortress despite the shortage of food supplies, and to this
end considered the possibility of creating a diversion which
might relieve the pressure upon Skutari, and possibly enable
Turkey to take the offensive in Thrace. He therefore proposed
to raise the Albanian flag at Skutari, declare the town Albanian,
and call upon the malissori to rally against the invaders
(see T. 24.4.13 for statement that Hussein Pasha opposed and
Essad favoured this course; also for account of Essad's
career).

This project did not, however, appeal to Essad Pasha,
who was second-in-command, and to whom the malissori
were fiercely hostile. Accordingly, on the 30th January,
while Hussein Pasha was leaving Essad's house after
dining with him, he was assassinated by Osman Bali and
Mehmed Kavaja, two of Essad's agents. By the Albanian laws
of hospitality Essad was in honour bound to avenge this deed,
but as he was undoubtedly the instigator, he naturally did not
do so, thereby irretrievably compromising his honour in the
eyes of his compatriots (J.B.).

The motive for this crime is not clearly established. It is, however, indisputable that Essad aspired to the throne of Albania; but he was probably aware that by abuse of his powers while commander of the gendarmerie first at Janina, and then at Skutari, he had incurred universal distrust, and that therefore he would never be acknowledged as their ruler, or allowed to play a leading rôle in the country by either the Nationalist leaders of the south or by the malissori. Only in central Albania was he powerful enough to establish himself among his tenants. There is no doubt that at a later stage of his career he sought to employ those hostile districts as bribes with which to buy the support of neighbouring States; but whether at this stage he planned to use Skutari as such, defending the town only until he could obtain the most advantageous terms for himself, or whether he sought to retrieve his popularity by distinguishing himself as the defender of Skutari is still obscure. Perhaps he was actuated by both motives.

The decision of the Powers that Skutari should be retained by Albania aroused the wildest indignation among both Montenegrins and Serbs. Cettinje, supported by Belgrade, was determined that Skutari should be occupied, with the object of confronting the Powers with an accomplished fact. It was therefore decided that a fresh assault should be made before the Powers could intervene.

Meantime the Montenegrins had been endeavouring to convert or expel the hostile populations of the regions they proposed to annex (P.D. 56: 1935). They boasted that they would simplify the racial problem by exterminating the inhabitants (P.D. 115: 1879); and while the passes were filled with snow during the winter, rendering isolation complete and escape for women and children well-nigh impossible, they had pursued a policy by which conversion to the Orthodox faith or death were the only alternatives. In the Plava-Gusinje area alone some five hundred persons were slaughtered (S.S. 301; D.F. 75), while conditions in the Djakova district were even worse. Eventually the *hodjas* advised the Moslems nominally to accept the Orthodox faith to escape death. Moslems and Catholics alike suffered. In the Djakova district a Bosnian Franciscan, Luigi Palitch, "refused to make the sign of the cross in Orthodox fashion and abjure his faith, and was stripped, beaten, and finally bayoneted to death" (S.S. 269). This last atrocity provoked, on the 20th March, the day upon which agreement regarding the frontier was reached by the Powers, a sharp Note of protest from Austria-Hungary to Cettinje (T. 21, 22, 24, 25, 26.3.13). At the same time Austria-Hungary urged that the Powers should make a collective demand for the cessation of hostilities, and withdrawal of the Serbian and Montenegrin troops from territory assigned to Albania. In this Great Britain supported her (P.D. 50: 1497) and the proposal was accepted. Austria-Hungary dispatched a squadron to the Montenegrin coast, intending to enforce this decision by a naval demonstration; but in this it was thought advisable that Italy should participate if a demonstration proved necessary, and eventually it was agreed that in order to prove the solidarity of the Powers it should be carried out by an international squadron of Austro-Hungarian, Italian, British, French, and German ships. Russia refused to participate (A.W.; T. 8.4.13).

On the 28th March a collective Note from the Powers was delivered at Belgrade and Cettinje. Serbia and Montenegro were ordered to withdraw their troops from Albania (T. 29 and 31.3.13; P.D. 51: 365). But they ignored the Note, and on the 31st launched an attack upon Tarabosh from the north-west and south-west, preceded by five hours' artillery preparation, and supported by feint attacks upon other parts of the line. Upon the latter side the assault was completely repulsed, but upon the north-west the Montenegrins penetrated the Turkish front line. Further progress was, however, prevented by enfilade machine-gun fire, and the Montenegrins driven back by counter-attacks.

Upon the following day a fresh attempt was made to storm the position, but without success. In two days the Montenegrins had lost 1,200 killed, and during the remainder of the siege confined their activities to a desultory bombardment of the civilian quarters and the Consulates (S.S. 281). The Slavs were under the impression that the Consuls were urging the garrison to continue its resistance. The British Consulate was hit and the Vice-Consul wounded.

The Montenegrins were exasperated by the failure of this assault, and on the 2nd April replied to the Powers, refusing to comply with their demands. Meantime the Serbian General Boyovitch took over the command of the besieging army (T. 11.4.13). On the 5th the international squadron, including H.M. ships *King Edward VII*, *Dartmouth*, and *Defence* (Rear-

Admiral Troubridge) arrived off Antivari; and Vice-Admiral Sir Cecil Burney, who was in command, dispatched a further Note to Cettinje demanding the immediate withdrawal of the Serbian and Montenegrin troops, adding that unless this demand was complied with the Montenegrin coast would be blockaded. As a "gesture" a blockade was excellent, and it satisfied Austria-Hungary that the Powers were determined to enforce their demands; but as a practical measure it was entirely ineffective, since Montenegro was in no way dependent for her existence upon her seaboard. The Slavs cared no more for "gestures" than for inadequate measures, and the demand was ignored (T. 7.4.13). They defied even Russia, who urged them to comply. A blockade was therefore established on the 10th April from Antivari to the mouth of the Drin, and to Durazzo on the 23rd April.

The international crisis now became acute. The Austro-Hungarian *Reichspost* declared that unless Montenegro accepted the decision of the Powers, Austria-Hungary and Italy would take action (T. 28.3.13). Indeed, so determined was the former country that her own point of view should be upheld, that on the 22nd April she had reached a compromise with Italy involving Valona. At one stage of the negotiations with regard to Skutari she had intimated that if Montenegro would cede to her Mt. Lovtchen, which commands the impregnable harbour of Cattaro (thus giving her potential control of the Montenegrin and north Albanian coastline), she would be willing to acquiesce in the annexation of Skutari by Montenegro; but the latter country, indirectly supported by Italy, had refused to consider the proposal (T. 27.3.13). It was now agreed between the two Allied Powers that if intervention became necessary Austria-Hungary should seize Mt. Lovtchen, while Italy, by way of compensation, should occupy Valona, Albania being divided by the River Shkumbi into Austro-Hungarian and Italian spheres of influence until such time as the security of Albania from the Slavs was assured, Austria-Hungary being confident of her power to secure the withdrawal of the Italians when the Slavs had been dealt with (H.M. 227–8; T. 1 and 5.5.13).

Russia, on the other hand, caused consternation by denying a statement which had appeared in the Russian Press to the effect that she would in no case make war (T. 28.3.13). The delay in instructing her Representative in Cettinje to collaborate with the Representatives of the other Powers—which had held up the Note finally presented on the 28th March— seems to have been intended to give the Montenegrins an opportunity to confront the Powers with an accomplished fact; while Austria-Hungary's insistence that the civil population should be allowed to withdraw from Skutari (T. 26 and 27.3.13) was probably intended to assist the garrison (in that its food supplies, etc., would be available for the troops). It may or may not be significant that Essad Pasha refused to allow the inhabitants to depart—so the Montenegrin envoy reported—upon the terms which the Montenegrins offered (which may have been that they should take supplies with them) until he was authorized to do so by the Porte. The authorization was received by the German Minister at Cettinje on the 7th April (T. 8.4.13), but as in the meantime the Powers had ordered the Montenegrins to withdraw, it does not seem to have been transmitted to Essad.

Although the Montenegrins had implicit faith both in Russian support and in the weight which the capture of Skutari would give to their claims to the town, there were, in addition to their desire to annex it, other considerations which weighed with King Nicholas, considerations which were made the weightier by the fall of Janina and Adrianople. He had promised Skutari to his people; and his prestige had become linked with victory. Defeat would mean not only the loss of that prestige, with which he had hoped to win the throne of Great Serbia, but perhaps also even the loss of his own throne and the extinction of his dynasty in favour of the victorious ruling house of Serbia (T. 8 and 10.4.13). If, after the fall of the town, he was obliged to bow to the will of the Powers, that was a different matter. There was also, of course, the question of "his operations on the Vienna Bourse" (S.S. 272)!

The Serbian troops (15,000) were withdrawn from before Skutari on the 16th (T. 12 and 15.4.13), and the Montenegrins took over the whole line under heavy fire from the Turkish batteries. The withdrawal of the Serbs must be ascribed to the strained relations between Serbia and Bulgaria rather than to a sense of obedience to the Powers, since Serbian troops remained at Durazzo until the 6th May, and in Mirdita until several months later.

While the Powers were considering the advisability of landing an international force to occupy Skutari, terms of

surrender were offered to Essad Pasha. On the 20th the
Montenegrins informed Admiral Burney (S.S.) that they had
lost his Note, and asked for another copy! Upon the 21st the
Montenegrin frontier was closed, and contrary to international
law foreign subjects were forbidden to leave or foreign
Representatives to send cipher telegrams to their Governments.
This high-handed proceeding called forth a sharp protest from
the Legations, and the frontier was reopened. On the 22nd
General Vukotitch went down to Skutari through the lines;
and on the same day Montenegrin Headquarters reported
(T. 23.4.13) that a desperate assault upon the fortress was in
progress (which was quite untrue). Early in the morning of
the 23rd Skutari surrendered.

By the terms of surrender Essad Pasha was allowed to
march out with all his troops, arms, and equipment, with the
exception of heavy guns. The Montenegrins agreed to give
him food supplies and provide for the wounded who were left
in the town. They also undertook to refrain from molesting
the civilian population and to respect their religious rights
(S.S. 277); in view of the proximity of the international
squadron they could not well have done otherwise, especially
since they hoped to be allowed to retain the town.

Essad Pasha's capitulation while the Powers were taking
action to secure the withdrawal of the Montenegrins, and when
the Serbs had withdrawn, is frequently described as treachery.
It is, however, widely believed that he was unaware of the
proximity of the international forces when he accepted the
Montenegrin terms. Moreover, it is doubtful whether he
could have held out much longer, for while there was no
actual starvation among the troops there was a shortage of
ammunition (T. 24.4.13); also the defence of an Albanian town
was no longer the concern of the Turkish units of the garrison.
In the circumstances Essad may perhaps be defended on the
grounds that since (presumably) capitulation would not effect
the decision of the Powers, it was better (from his point of
view) to satisfy Montenegrin honour, conciliate King Nicholas,
and retire with his army intact, than risk unconditional surrender or further bloodshed. What personal advantages he
gained thereby will probably never be known.

Once inside Skutari, the Montenegrins made frantic endeavours to retain it. King Nicholas claimed it upon the
pretext that the remains of his ancestors lay buried there (he

lamented the annexation by Austria-Hungary of the Hertzegovina for the same reason in 1908), although the Petrovitches
had not become a ruling family until two hundred years
after the Slavs had lost it! He protested that since the Albanians
had failed to keep clear the channel of the Bojana (thus
rendering the passage from the lake to the sea impossible for
all except very light craft, and raising the level of the lake
until it had inundated large tracts of fertile land now annexed
by Montenegro), the town and river should remain in Montenegrin hands.

The Montenegrins were unable to claim Skutari upon
ethnical grounds (T. 24.4.13. Art.; S.S.; P.D. 52: 236; etc.;
of its population of 50,000, two-thirds of whom were Moslems,
only 3,000 to 4,000 were Slavs); nor could they claim it upon
historical grounds. The Slavs held it for 210 years in all; for the
remainder of time it had been Albanian and was mentioned by
its native name (Shkodra) in 604 B.C., 1,154 years before
the Montenegrins crossed the Danube! They therefore
sought, since they could not change its ethnical features,
to coerce the population to sign petitions in favour of union
with Montenegro. But the inhabitants were now aware that
the international squadron was at hand, and, exhorted by the
Archbishop and others, refused. The Albanians were determined to retain the town. "We have fought for centuries",
they declared, "to keep the Slavs out of Skutari. If they
attempt to take it now, we shall go on fighting until none of
us are left."

Austria-Hungary was exasperated by the surrender of
Skutari (S.A. 29; T. 24 and 25.4.13), but refrained from
precipitating a conflict. She "reserved freedom of action" in
the event that the Powers did not at once order the Montenegrins to retire (T. 30.4.13), intimated that in that eventuality
coercive measures would be adopted, and moved troops
towards the Montenegrin frontier. The Montenegrins made
preparations to resist. "The menace to the general peace was
more serious than at any moment since the outbreak of the
Balkan War" (T. 1.5.13). But Russia advocated forbearance
and moderation; and she joined the other Powers in informing
Montenegro that their previous decision stood and that her
troops must be withdrawn immediately.

Cettinje and Belgrade were now compelled to give way.
Montenegro denied that she had "ever dreamed of defying

the decisions of Europe" (T. 2.5.13), and declared that she "placed the fate of the town of Skutari in the hands of the Powers" (T. 6.5.13)! On the 14th May the Montenegrin troops, to the relief of the inhabitants (S.S. 288; T. 10 and 12.5.13), evacuated the town, which was occupied by an international Naval Brigade. An international administration for the town and its immediate surroundings was constituted under the Presidency of Admiral Burney (T. 21 and 27.5.13).

The tribes were overjoyed by the intervention of the Powers. Their hatred of the Slavs, temporarily in abeyance while they were fighting the Turks, had been accentuated by Montenegrin and Serbian conduct since the outbreak of the Balkan War. A few days after Admiral Burney's arrival the bairaktars of Maltsia e madhe came down to pay their respects to him; his arrival they described as "the greatest day for the mountains since the day when Christ was born". They were, however, in despair at the news that their brothers of Hoti and Gruda had been allotted to Montenegro, submitted a petition (the first of many: T. 13.8.13) to the Admiral begging him to entreat the Powers to reconsider their decision (T. 29.5.13. Art.), and resolved to resist its execution. They did so fiercely, in conjunction with other annexed districts (see below) during the following August and September (T. 13.8.13) and captured Tuzi (T. 25.9.13), but eventually were overwhelmed.

It has been said that the creation of the Albanian State, which denied Serbia access to the sea, brought about the second Balkan War. This was not the case. M. Pašitch had talked of a revision of the Treaty—of the 13th March, 1912, dividing Macedonia and Albania between Serbia and Bulgaria—during October, 1912, that is a month before Ismail Kemal Bey proclaimed Albanian independence, and two months before the Powers agreed that an independent Albanian State should be created. In an official circular he proclaimed that Prilep and Ochrida, which were within the zone provisionally allotted to Bulgaria, belonged to Old Serbia. The military party, with Prince Alexander at its head, indulged in even more extravagant pretensions (C.E. 61), and while the Bulgarians, whose operations alone assured the success of the Allies (B.P. 39), and who had borne the brunt of the first Balkan War (they sustained 93,000, the Serbs 31,000, and the Greeks 29,000 casualties), were preoccupied in Thrace (C.E. 24, 26, 50–1,

M

58–9), the Serbs and Greeks applied every conceivable measure of coercion to compel the Bulgarian Macedonians to disavow their nationality (E.B. 32: 404; B.P. 39–41; C.E. 16, 52–6, 60–3, 160–86), and prepared for war with Bulgaria thus rendered inevitable. Although Russia strove to avert hostilities, the Serbs and Greeks skilfully compelled Bulgaria on the 29th June to take the initiative and precipitate a war in which she appeared the aggressor. They then refused to treat (C.E. 65, 225–6) until Bulgaria, attacked also by Turkey, Roumania, and Montenegro (who declared war to secure her position with Serbia), was obliged to abandon her claims to Macedonia by the Treaty of Bucharest.

There followed the Great War. Serbia considered the prospective acquisition of Bosnia and Slavonia insufficient compensation for sacrifices in Macedonia, and refused to make any concessions to Bulgaria (E.B. 30: 519) unless the Entente Powers guaranteed her the whole of Yugoslavia to Liubliana, to which Italy was opposed; and the Entente statesmen who advocated an arbitrary settlement of the question had to contend with "the unthinking excitement of pro-Serbian feeling" (B.P. 63–98). On the 12th October, 1915, Bulgaria declared war upon Serbia, whereupon Great Britain, France, and Italy declared war upon her. Bulgaria was again crushed, and still further reduced (E.B. 30: 521) by the Treaty of Neuilly (27th November, 1919), while Serbia, whose size had been doubled by the Balkan Wars, trebled it again and became Yugoslavia. The Serb refuses to allow the Bulgarian element to call or feel themselves Bulgarians (N.E. 24.2.27, etc.), allows them no Bulgarian schools, yet conscripts them for the army. What, then, must be the lot of the Albanians of Yugoslavia whose parent State is very much less able to uphold their interests than Bulgaria those of the Bulgarian Macedonians? Indeed, until Serbia recognizes the ethnical principle, there remains in the heart of the Peninsula an ulcer poisoning the European system, and bidding fair to render inevitable a bloody operation. But the Serbs, aware that their overbearing policy may ultimately lead to the secession from the Yugoslav State of their more enlightened compatriots, emancipated by the Great War from Austro-Hungarian rule, have not yet abandoned all hope of obtaining access to the sea through Salonika or Albania, and thus becoming independent of the Yugoslav ports.

During the deliberations over the Greco-Albanian frontier France supported Greece (T. 15.5.13), who resorted to every conceivable subterfuge to prove that "Northern Epirus" was "Greek by religion, by sentiment, and by nationality", while Italy led the way in pressing Albanian claims. Apart from the inability of the Powers to agree, the question was complicated by the adherence of the Christian element to the "Greek" Orthodox Church, the existence of Greek schools, and the profound ignorance of Europe with regard to the Albanian race and her sentimental attachment to Greece. Europe either could not or would not grasp the essential fact that a Greek-speaking Christian of southern Albania is not by any manner of means necessarily a Greek by nationality or by sentiment; and an Albanian who spoke Greek, adhered to the Orthodox Church, and sent his children to Greek schools, was represented as a Greek in sentiment. That the Albanian cares nothing for the religion of his neighbours is a characteristic so unusual that the average European failed to appreciate or believe it; and the diplomat, unfettered by the pressure of public opinion, was free to ignore it.

Apart from a desire for territorial expansion, and an anxiety to increase their male population for military purposes, to counterbalance the growth of their neighbours, the Greeks were aware that their prosperity and even existence were in large measure due to the Albanians of Epirus. "There are in Athens to-day few important institutions which have not been founded and endowed by Epirots" (F.E.). Korcha especially did Greece wish to acquire, although the population, which in 1918 numbered 17,779 Orthodox Christian Albanians and 5,464 Moslems (J.B.; for statistics of *caza* of Korcha compiled by the French, see Q.K. Annex 1), included no Greeks (O.J. June/22. 522; T. 22.4.19). "Its geographical and strategic position render it invaluable to her, and its acquisition essential, while its value to Albania would not be so great now that Janina will undoubtedly remain Greek. . . . Santi Quaranta is indispensable as an outlet for the commerce of the more northern territories which Greece will have. It is the only port for the hinterland, and the natural port for merchandise from Janina destined for Italy and Austria" (H.W.; S.A. 26). Upon similar grounds Greece claimed the Korcha–Ersek road, part of the principal route from Janina to Monastir and Salonika.

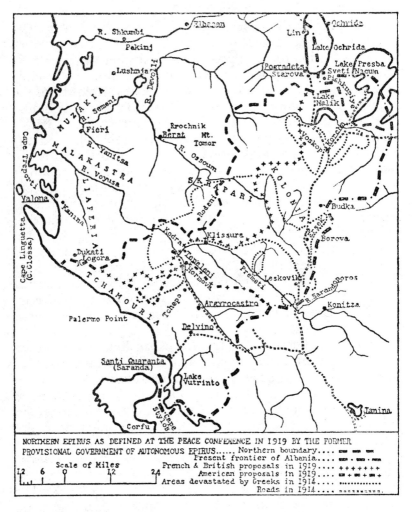

NORTHERN EPIRUS AS DEFINED AT THE PEACE CONFERENCE IN 1919 BY THE FORMER
PROVISIONAL GOVERNMENT OF AUTONOMOUS EPIRUS...... Northern boundary....
Present frontier of Albania....
Scale of Miles   French & British proposals in 1919.... ++++++
12   6   0   12   24   American proposals in 1919....
Areas devastated by Greeks in 1914....
Roads in 1914....

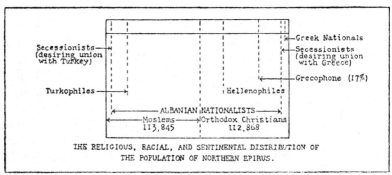

Secessionists—   ⌐Greek Nationals
(desiring union   ⌐Secessionists
with Turkey)   (desiring union
                                                    with Greece)

                                                  ⌐Grecophone (17%)

Turkophiles—   Hellenophiles

            — ALBANIAN NATIONALISTS —
            —Moslems— —Orthodox Christians
             113,845   112,868

THE RELIGIOUS, RACIAL, AND SENTIMENTAL DISTRIBUTION OF
THE POPULATION OF NORTHERN EPIRUS.

The Greeks declared that Korcha and, indeed, the whole of Northern Epirus, was either Greek by nationality or by sentiment, and that its inclusion in Albania would be an outrage upon civilization, in view of the "contrast between the gentle, peace-loving nature of the Greeks and the barbarous and unsettled character of the Albanians." (H.W.) They protested that all the culture which the district could show was the outcome of Greek civilization (H.W.; compare with C.E. 72-3, 90-108, 148), that the Albanian national dress was Greek (F.O. 21), and that "her policy in regard to Northern Epirus shows that the Greeks really believe in their right to the districts which they have occupied"! But the supreme effort of the Greek propagandists was the quotation of Essad Pasha's views. "Essad Pasha, a real Albanian chieftain with all the virtues and defects that this implies, has repeatedly shown, and very wisely too, how little he cares to overburden the new Albanian polity with more Christian inhabited districts than is absolutely necessary" (F.E.)!

Undoubtedly there were in southern Albania a certain number of true Greeks who had filtered into the country for trade purposes, and a number also of Grecophile Albanians, but these formed a very small minority. Even Janina, which had been a centre of Greek propaganda for years, was still more Albanian than Greek, although the Greek element was stronger in the towns, especially around Janina, than in the rural districts. Viscountess Strangford, who travelled in the neighbourhood of Janina in 1863, wrote of the difficulty she experienced in making herself understood, since the inhabitants spoke only Albanian; and the Hon. R. Curzon's account of his travels around Janina and Mezzovo is confirmation of the inherently Albanian character of the land and its inhabitants, which was further demonstrated when it was proposed to cede these regions to Greece after the Treaty of Berlin.

Mr. J. D. Bourchier wrote (E.B. 1 : 483):

". . . Mount Zygos and the Pindus Range—the Great Walachia . . . of the Middle Ages—are inhabited by Vlachs or Tzintzars, who possibly number 70,000. Some Turkish colonies are also found in the southeastern districts. There is a considerable Greek-speaking population in Epirus (including many Mohammedan Albanians) which must, however, be distinguished from

the genuine Greeks of Janina, Prevesa, and the extreme
south; these may be estimated at 100,000. The population of the vilayet of Skutari is given as 237,000, that of
the vilayet of Janina as 552,000."

The Albanians claimed that the Vlachs desired incorporation
in Albania which, in view of the attitude of the Greeks
towards them, is probable. They certainly did not desire
union with Greece (T.E. 377).

In a Memorandum submitted on the 13th January, 1913, to
the Conference of Ambassadors, M. Venizelos quoted statistics
of a Turkish census of Albania, which had been taken in 1908
by direction of Hilmi Pasha. These statistics showed, he
wrote, that in the vilayet of Janina there were (presumably
excluding Vlachs) 477,833 inhabitants, of whom 316,561
were "Greeks", 154,413 were Moslems, and 5,104 were Jews.
Where, then, were the Christian Albanians? It appears that
there were none, unless it be borne in mind that the only
distinction between Ottoman subjects in Turkey was that of
religion, and that all were classified as either "Greeks" or
Moslems. (P.D. 52: 2304; 53: 412). There were certainly few,
if any, Moslem Greeks; and it is eloquent that in 1880 Greece
acquired a Moslem population of 24,165, which in 1908 had
been reduced to 5,000 (E.B. 12: 428; A.S. 27, footnote).

M. Venizelos claimed that in "Northern Epirus" there were
120,000 Greeks and 80,000 Albanians (F.O. 98 and T. 24.1.19).
But in the above-mentioned Turkish census, the figures given
for this area were 120,000 Christians and 170,000 Moslems, in
all 290,000 inhabitants. French statistics, compiled during the
French occupation of Korcha, gave the figures for the area
occupied as 40,000 Christians and 82,245 Moslems, a total of
122,315 (Q.K. Annex 1). Turkish statistics showed that in the
remainder of N. Epirus there were 76,651 Christians and
91,846 Moslems. Although France had always favoured Greek
in preference to Albanian aspirations, a map issued in 1915
by the French Ministry of War, marking the distribution of
races and religions in Albania (see *La Question albanaise*:
Beratti; S.A. 99; text, p. 300), shows that Northern Epirus
was considered overwhelmingly Albanian and preponder-
antly Moslem. This was confirmed by the report of the
Commission of Inquiry (O.J. May/23. 491–502) subsequently
sent to Albania by the League of Nations (see diagram). The

Commission reported that in the Prefeftures of Korcha, Argyrocaftro, and Tchamouria, but excluding the sub-Prefeêture of Pogradets, there were 113,845 Moslems and 112,868 Chriftians; 17 per cent. of the population were Grecophone—but not necessarily Greek or even Grecophile. The Powers were unable to arrive at any decision around the conference table regarding the south-eaftern boundary. Throughout the protraéted negotiations which took place, France sought to limit as far as possible the boundaries and independence of Albania (S.A. 24), and to obtain from Auftria-Hungary and Italy concessions to Greece. France insifted that Greece, if she forfeited her claims to the Adriatic coaft beyond Cape Stylos, should, in addition to retaining Korcha and Premeti, be compensated with the Ægean Islands, with the possible exception of Imbros and Tenedos. But eventually she was compelled to modify her attitude, and "in view of the opposition on the part of the Dual Monarchy, Pichon proposed to Tittoni on the 3rd July that Auftria-Hungary and Italy should conditionally accept Sir Edward Grey's proposal for a commission to delimit the frontier, leaving, however, Argyrocaftro and Korcha to Albania" (S.A. 32).

This proposal was accepted, and on the 11th Auguft the Conference of Ambassadors adopted a resolution (C. 204, M. 125, 1921, VII. Annex 2) proposed by Auftria-Hungary, dealing with the boundary and the work of the Commission. It being eftablished that "the coaft region to Phtelia, including the island of Saseno, the region situated to the north of the Greek line, as well as the old Ottoman *caza* of Korcha with the coaft and south shores of Lake Ochrida . . . shall form an integral part of Albania", the Commission was empowered to operate within limits defined, in the weft, by "the mountains separating the coaftal regions attributed to Albania, as far as Phtelia, from the Valley of Argyrocaftro; to the north-eaft, the frontier line of the old Ottoman *caza* of Korcha. Between these two regions, the line indicated in the Memorandum presented by M. Venizelos to the Conference shall form the northern limit of the province of the Commission, while to the south and south-eaft it shall extend to the line proposed by Auftria-Hungary and Italy".

It was further provided that the Commission should begin its task on the 1ft September, and complete it by the 30th November, 1913, should take account of the "natural conformation of the valleys", and should carry out the delimitation on "ethnographic and geographic bases; for ethnographic determination, the maternal tongue of the population should be ascertained . . . the Commission shall not take account of attempts at plebiscite or other political manifestations". The resolution also stipulated that "one month, at most, after the closing of the work of the Commission, the evacuation by the Greek troops of the territory allotted to Albania shall take place".

The conduct of the Greek troops compelled many of the Moslem inhabitants from the occupied districts to seek refuge in Valona. Every effort was made, but without success, to stir up religious animosity between Christians and Moslems. Mass meetings in the disputed territory were organized by the Greek authorities, which the inhabitants were ordered to attend, and press representatives were invited to witness these demonstrations of loyalty to King Constantine. Resolutions prepared beforehand were read to the assembled crowds, and then dispatched to the Conference of Ambassadors as having been carried unanimously, since those assembled either dared not contradict them, or could not, owing to their inability to understand the Greek language (B.T. 244–6). Petitions for unity with Greece from the towns in the disputed area were submitted also, bearing the signatures of either non-existent persons, or of those of the very small Greek minority which does exist, and which the Greek authorities were careful to locate and employ as demonstrators and delegates! (Compare with methods employed in Macedonia by both Greeks and Serbs: C.E. 55–6, 166–7, 173–6, 182, 197–9, 200, 231). And press reporters conducted hither and thither by the Greeks— of course the country was unsafe for unescorted correspondents—saw only as much as it was thought fit to show them. Korcha, for example, was occupied by some 6,000 troops, the speaking of Albanian in the streets was prohibited, and those unable to speak Greek confined to their homes. Townsfolk were ordered to paint their houses, shops, and signs in blue and white—the Greek national colours—which also became fashionable in wearing apparel. Imprisonment, exile, or beating to death were the penalties prescribed for unfashionable people! And, in case anyone might display originality at the critical moment, the most prominent Albanian patriots were imprisoned: those who were allowed to remain at liberty of necessity, since the towns could not be entirely depopulated, were reminded of the inadvisability of any expression of their personal sentiments (S.S. 307. See also Q.K. Annex 4. Extr. from *l'Illustration*. 20.1.17; B.K. 240). Similar measures were applied throughout the disputed area. Indeed, all possible efforts to convince Europe that Greek claims were justified, and all possible preparations to mislead the Boundary Commission when it arrived, were made, and provoked a warning from Austria-Hungary and Italy (S.A. 36).

The Greeks also determined to provide an armed force other than the Greek regular army, which might masquerade as a force organized by the inhabitants of the disputed areas themselves, to resist their incorporation in Albania.

"Sacred Battalions"—"sacred" in that they pledged themselves to secure the union of southern Albania with Greece— were formed of volunteers ("deserters". P.D. 64: 1897) from the Greek Army, augmented by the importation of Cretan desperadoes and criminals. These "Sacred Battalions" became the terror of the land. M. Casanges wrote (F.E.) that there were 40,000 men, "Epirot" veterans of the Balkan War, well equipped and well trained, who, if the Powers insisted upon the withdrawal of the Greeks, were prepared to defend their land to the last from the Albanians!

The International Commission arrived in October, and its first meeting took place on the 4th, at Monastir. Lieutenant-Colonel Doughty Wylie was elected President of the Commission by the other delegates, who were Commandant C. Thierry (Germany), M. C. Bilinski (Austria-Hungary), M. A. Lallemand (France), S. N. Labia (Italy), and Colonel J. P. Levkovitch (Russia). Neither Greece nor Albania was represented, although Greece protested, on the 13th October, that she should be (G.C.). Among the rules of procedure drawn up, it was agreed that the Commission should refuse to receive any Greek or Albanian deputations, that it should not be escorted by Greek or Albanian officials of any description, that any necessary escort should not accompany it while actually making investigations in villages, that the services of private persons should not be accepted, that a decision as to the next village to be visited should be made only on leaving the last visited, that decisions of a diplomatic nature should be kept secret, and lastly, that the Greek Government should be informed of the above rules.

Throughout the proceedings the French, supported by the Russian delegate, pressed Greek interests, while the German, Austro-Hungarian, and Italian representatives supported the Albanian cause. But the delegates worked, not in the interests of the countries directly concerned, but in those of the Powers which they represented. Austria-Hungary and Italy maintained, from the outset, that the frontier must be drawn at least twelve kilometres south of Argyrocastro, rightly contending, first, that otherwise the coastal region already allotted to Albania would be too narrow: secondly, that the Argyrocastro-Delvino road must remain within Albania in its entirety: and thirdly, that Argyrocastro was the industrial centre for the valley, and Santi Quaranta its natural outlet (S.A. 36).

Upon one point the Commission at once agreed, namely, that the occupation of the area in dispute by Greek troops was prejudicial to an impartial investigation and decision. That the Greeks made every possible endeavour to exploit this advantage, and, indeed, finally compelled the Commission to abandon its task, are facts established beyond dispute by the "Procès Verbaux de la Commission Internationale pour la délimitation de la Frontière Méridionale Albanaise" and by the "Procès Verbaux de la Conférence de Florence, 1913".

The Commission at first attempted to arrive at a decision upon a linguistic basis. Had it been possible to carry out the necessary investigation, a just decision would have been possible only if the Commission had endeavoured to establish the limits within which the Albanian language was spoken among the elder peasantry, since Greek had ever been the language of the commercial and educated classes (owing to the limited scope of the Albanian vocabulary), and Greek propaganda had not been without effect among the younger generation of peasantry, some having been led to believe themselves Greek (S.F. 41). But despite an assurance from Athens that the local authorities had been instructed that the Commission was not to be hindered in its work (S.A. 36), every effort was made to hamper its investigations. When the Greeks found it impossible to seal the mouths of the inhabitants, many of whom succeeded in expressing their actual sentiments to the Commissioners, they detailed a detachment from a "Sacred Battalion" to follow them and prevent such occurrences, to cry at every opportunity "Union or Death", and to make similar demonstrations, and whenever the Commission appeared to be pressing its investigations too closely, to adopt a threatening attitude. A man in plain clothes attached himself to the Commission and directed the operations of the detachment.

The Commission observed, upon approaching a village, that men rushed in ahead of them. Then the church bells rang; and either an apparently hostile crowd or a procession of school children bearing Greek flags met them, while armed men hung about in the background. The principal performers in these dramas were always the same! (P.V.)

The climax was reached at Borova. There, one of the Commissioners knocked at the door of a house in which were confined some townsfolk unable to speak Greek. The attitude of the detachment thereupon became so threatening that the Commissioners were convinced of the futility of attempting further investigation, and informed their respective Governments to this effect.

In view of these developments, Austria-Hungary and Italy acting independently of the other Powers, presented identical Notes to Greece on the 31st October protesting against the attitude of the Greek authorities and their incitement of sections of the population. In threatening terms the two Powers informed Greece that their representatives had been instructed to regard as Albanian all villages where opposition was encountered, and that they adhered to the conditions laid down by the Conference of Ambassadors regarding the duration of the Commission's operations and the evacuation by Greece of territory awarded to Albania (S.A. 37). The action of these two Powers aroused indignation in France and Russia, and to some extent also in Great Britain, where the roots of phil-Hellenism had been well fertilized by classical education.

The Commission carried out no investigation below a line between the points already fixed by the Conference of Ambassadors; and the whole of the unexamined area, including thousands of Orthodox Albanians, a homogeneous population of about 40,000 Moslem Albanians in the southern Tchamouria (F.O. 25), and the Vlachs of the Pindus Range, were handed over to Greece irrespective of their wishes. (For list of British and French authorities who declare, in works published between 1804 and 1876, that S. Albania, to the Gulf of Arta, is a purely Albanian region, see Q.K. Annex 5.)

In view of the situation the British Government proposed

that the delimitation should be completed by means of maps, and that a line drawn arbitrarily between the two points already fixed should be modified only by geographic, economic, and strategic considerations. This proposal was accepted by the other Powers, and the Commission proceeded to Florence, where, in December, 1913, it completed its task with the aid of the Geographical Institute there.

By the Protocol of Florence (17th December) Albania retained the provinces of Korcha and Argyrocastro, but with complete inconsistency a small triangle of the road which was the only line of communication for other than pedestrians and pack-horses between south-eastern Albania and Santi Quaranta was left within the Greek frontier. The frontier intersects this road at a point where it joins the Premeti and Berat or Valona road. The Russian delegate actually proposed that even this road junction should be excluded from Albania, and that the Albanians might construct a fresh road between Premeti and Ersek. This was an undertaking which the new State was in no position to consider, and the proposal was rejected.

Although the Commission had established the indisputably Albanian character of the territory thus allotted to Albania, Greece refused to abandon her claims to Korcha, Premeti, and Argyrocastro, and prepared to obtain them by conspiracy.

CHAPTER V

THE REIGN OF PRINCE WILLIAM

On the 30th May, 1913, was signed the Treaty of London. Thereby Turkey ceded conjointly to the four Balkan Allies all territory weſt of the Enos–Midia line. The Allies agreed to leave the settlement of the Albanian queſtion to the Powers, with the reservation, however, of the right to discuss with them during the course of negotiations "questions pertaining . . . to the definitive fixing of the frontiers" (S.A. 29).

On the 29th July, at its fifty-fourth meeting, the Conference of Ambassadors agreed as follows:

1. L'Albanie eſt conſtituée en principauté autonome souveraine et héréditaire par ordre de primogéniture, sous la garantie des six Puissances. Le Prince sera désigné par les six Puissances.

2. Tout lien de suzeraineté entre la Turquie et l'Albanie eſt exclu.

3. L'Albanie eſt neutralisée; sa neutralité eſt garantie par les six Puissances.

4. Le contrôle de l'adminiſtration civile et des finances de l'Albanie eſt confié à une commission internationale composée des délégués des six Puissances et d'un délégué de l'Albanie.

5. Les pouvoirs de cette commission dureront dix ans et pourront être renouvelés en cas de besoin.

6. Cette commission sera chargée d'élaborer un projet d'organisation détaillé de toutes les branches de l'adminiſtration de l'Albanie. Elle présentera aux Puissances, dans un délai de six mois, un rapport sur le résultat de ses travaux, ainsi que ses conclusions au sujet de l'organisation adminiſtrative et financière du pays.

7. Le Prince sera nommé dans un délai de six mois au plus tard. En attendant sa désignation et la formation du Gouvernement national définitiv, le fonctionnement des autorités indigènes exiſtantes ainsi que de la gendarmerie

formera l'objet du contrôle de la commission internationale.

8. La sécurité et l'ordre publique seront assurées par l'organisation internationale de la gendarmerie. Cette organisation sera confiée à des officiers étrangers, qui auront le commandement supérieur et effectif de la gendarmerie.

9. Ces officiers seront choisis dans l'armée suèdoise.

10. La mission des officiers instructeurs étrangers ne portera pas atteinte ni à l'uniformité du service, ni à l'emploi d'officiers, sous-officiers et gendarmes indigènes.

11. Les traitements de ces officiers pourront être assurés sur les ressources du pays avec la garantie des Puissances (D.W. Annex 1).

The scheme of organization was duly drawn up and signed at Valona on the 10th April, 1914, by the representatives of Albania and the Powers (the International Commission of Control, which arrived at Valona in the autumn; T. 30.9.13), namely, Mehdi bey Frasheri, Winckel (Germany), Kral (Austria-Hungary), Krajewski (France), Lamb (Great Britain), Leoni (Italy), and Petraieff (Russia). Meantime Dutch officers, with General de Weer in command, were commissioned to organize a gendarmerie.

The Serbian withdrawal from Albania was accompanied by a series of atrocities which aroused considerable indignation (P.D. 51 : 1925) in some quarters. At Flet, for example, fifty-two persons, mostly women and children—the men had taken to the hills—were massacred (S.S. 298); cattle and sheep were driven off wholesale, thousands of olive-trees were felled, and much other wilful damage done in pursuance of a deliberate policy. Moreover, the withdrawal was not completely carried out. Serbian troops remained in Mirdita (P.D. 56 : 1935; T. 25.9.13) connected with Prizren by a line of posts, and ignored Admiral Burney's requests—he had no authority to demand—that they should withdraw. Prenk Bib Doda connived at this arrangement (*Auswärtige Politik Serbiens, 1903–1914*, Bogitchevitch). The Serbs, as an alternative to obtaining direct access to the sea, had agreed to support his plan to establish himself as ruler of an autonomous Mirdite principality including Alessio, which was to retain its own church and schools; they provided him with money with which to buy the support of the priests and bairaktars, but in this he ultimately failed.

The Serbs also remained in occupation of "strategic points" in the neighbourhood of Dibra, and it says much for the good sense of the Albanians that they refrained so long from rising, believing that the Powers would eventually secure the evacuation of their lands.

In the Albanian districts ceded to Serbia the inhabitants persistently hoped that the Powers would recognize the legitimacy of their desire to be united with their Motherland. But discontent among them became daily more acute, and "*Le Réglement sur la Sécurité Publique*, published on the 21st September, 1913, and signed by King Peter, proves only too clearly that Serbia was dealing with a completely foreign population, which was ready at any moment to revolt against the Serbian yoke" (A.Q.). This brutal decree (for full text, see C.E. 160–2) called forth cries of horror in the foreign Press, and even in the Serbian Socialist paper, *Radnitchké Noviné*, which expressed the opinion that its ordinances were ". . . such as can only be imposed upon conquered countries by conquerors". The Carnegie Endowment Commission of Inquiry wrote that ". . . if one did not know what Macedonia is, one might guess it from the publication of these ordinances. Clearly, Macedonia was not 'Old Servia' unified, since the population is treated as 'rebels in a perpetual state of revolt' " (C.E. 160).

The climax was reached at the end of September. The events which followed were described in a letter from Elbasan published by *L'Echo de Bulgarie* on the 11th October, and accepted as accurate by the Carnegie Endowment Commissioners, who were themselves prevented by the Serbian authorities from visiting the Albanian regions (C.E. 233):

"On the 20th September last (new style) the Servian army", withdrawing across the frontier in the neighbourhood of Dibra, in reluctant compliance with the reiterated demands of the Powers (T. 20.9.13), "carried off all the cattle of the Malesia [= Maltsia: i.e. mountain land] of Dibra. The herdsmen were compelled to defend themselves and to struggle, but they were all killed. The Servians also killed the two chieftains of the Ljuma clan, Mehmed Edem and Djafer Eleuz, and then began pillaging and burning all the villages on their way: Pechkapia, Pletza, and Dochichti in lower Dibra; Alai Beg, Machi, Para, Oboku, Klobotchichta and Solokitzi in upper Dibra. In all these villages the Servians committed acts of horrible massacre, and outrage on women, children, and old people. In the town of Dibra itself the authorities published an order to the effect that the bazaar was not to be opened on Sunday, or the inhabitants to come out of their houses on that day. Forty-eight notables were arrested. When the Servians saw that the inhabitants of the pillaged villages, of which a list has been given above, had come to reclaim their cattle and were surrounding the town, they had the notables brought out of prison and killed them in the most shameless way. Henceforth terror and despair reigned among the Albanians of Dibra and the neighbourhood, and they rose in revolt. They attacked the Servians with arms, or with hatchets, stones, and sticks; they killed some of them, and drove the rest out of the town. Nearly all of the men who were killed were Servian officials; the soldiers who remained alive fled to the other side of the Radika River" (C.E. 150; also S.S. 312; T. 22 and 24.9.13).

The incident was the signal for a general rising in the Albanian districts annexed by Serbia and Montenegro. Both countries were compelled to remobilize (T. 22, 25, 26.9.13; 4.10.13), and despite a most courageous struggle by the inhabitants (T. 26.9.13; 1.10.13), doubtless assisted by many of their compatriots from over the border, the insurrection was ruthlessly suppressed with fearful barbarity, slaughter, and wanton destruction. Thousands of these unfortunate people sought refuge with their compatriots in Albanian territory, where many died of starvation or cold owing to the inability of their countrymen to provide for them (C.E. 181–4). *L'Echo de Bulgarie*, on the 16th October, reported that

"on entering the village of Portchassie, the regular Servian army led all the husbands outside the village, and then brought the wives thither to exact money from them in the shape of ransom if they wanted their husbands set at liberty. After the ransom had been paid, however, the wretched men were shut up in the mosque,

THE REIGN OF PRINCE WILLIAM 177

which was then blown up with four shells. In the village of Sulp seventy-three Albanians suffered a horrible death, and forty-seven others from the village of Ptchélopek were basely assassinated. Was it not the Prefect of Krouchevo, when the Servian army returned from the Albanian frontier, who openly told them to burn all the villages situated between Krouchevo and Ochrida?"

If further evidence of Serbian atrocities is required, it is supplied by the following letter from a Serbian soldier, reproduced by the *Radnitchké Noviné* on the 22nd October:

"I have no time to write to you at length, but I can tell you that appalling things are going on here. I am terrified by them, and constantly ask myself how men can be so barbarous as to commit such cruelties. It is horrible. I dare not (even if I had time, which I have not) tell you more, but I may say that Ljuma (an Albanian region along the river of the same name) no longer exists. There is nothing but corpses, dust, and ashes. There are villages of a hundred, a hundred and fifty, two hundred houses, where there is no longer a single man, literally *not one*. We collect them in bodies of forty to fifty, and then we pierce them with our bayonets to the last man. Pillage is going on everywhere. The officers told the soldiers to go to Prizren and sell the things they had stolen."

The same paper added:

"Our friend tells us of things even more appalling than this (!); but they are so horrible and so heart-rending that we prefer not to publish them" (C.E. 149).

"Thus the Albanian petitioners", wrote the Carnegie Endowment Commissioners, "who, on the 21st September, addressed themselves to the Great Powers in the name of the populations of Djakova, Ipek, Plava, Gusinje, and the ex-vilayet of Kossovo, did not exaggerate when they stated that 'the Servian and Montenegrin regular troops undertook and did everything, from the first day on which they invaded the Albanian territory, either to compel the inhabitants to lose their nationality or brutally to suppress the Shqipetar race.' *Houses and whole villages reduced to ashes, unarmed and innocent populations massacred* en masse, *incredible acts of violence, pillage, and*

N

brutality of every kind—such were the means which were employed, and are still being employed, by the Serbo-Montenegrin soldiery, with a view to the entire transformation of the ethnic character of regions inhabited exclusively by Albanians" (C.E. 150).

Yet these regions were handed over to those who set themselves to transform their ethnic character, for reasons of political expediency; and atrocities were hushed up lest diplomacy, which had tied Great Britain to the Slav, might be embarrassed by public opinion (B.T. 254). Speaking in the House of Commons on the subject, Colonel Walter Guinness said:

"The war now coming to an end has been a war in which Albania has lost terribly, not only in combatants, but also among the non-combatant population, and there is no doubt whatever that the inaction of the western Powers has done much to allow that war to assume a barbarity which is exceptional even in the Balkans. I think it is a reproach to the civilization of western Europe that atrocities were hushed up which, if they had been fully disclosed, would have raised such a storm as the Allies could not possibly have ignored" (P.D. 52 : 2298).

When compelled by the pressure of the Powers to withdraw from Albania, the Serbs had declared that they "could take no responsibility for the eventual consequences of any frontier disturbances which might occur" (T. 20.9.13), and upon the outbreak of the insurrection presented a Note to the Powers in which they charged Albania with provocation constituting an act of war (T. 25.9.13; 4.10.13). Both Ismail Kemal Bey and Essad Pasha denied complicity (T. 3.10.13). Meantime the Austro-Hungarian and Italian Governments exchanged views on the situation (T. 29.9.13), while the Austro-Hungarian Press assumed a "told you so" attitude (T. 25.9.13). The Serbian Press called for drastic measures, and declared that the trouble was due to the closing of annexed frontier towns to Albanians across the frontier because they had smuggled arms to their compatriots in the annexed districts (T. 26.9.13).

The Austro-Hungarian Government reminded Serbia of the

necessity of respecting the Albanian frontier, and received assurances that no violation was intended (T. 3.10.13). Nevertheless the Serbs carried fire and sword across the border, and re-established themselves at "strategic points" in Albania "in order to prevent fresh raids".

Austria-Hungary at once intervened. Supported by Italy and Germany, she inquired what Serbia's intentions were (T. 16.10.13), and, as she received no satisfactory explanation, followed up her inquiry by demanding, on the 15th October, the immediate withdrawal of the Serbian troops (T. 18.10.13). Serbia refused to comply. Thereupon Count Berchtold dispatched, on the 18th, an ultimatum to the effect that unless the demand was complied with within eight days (T. 20.10.13) Austria-Hungary would be compelled to take military action. In this crisis Russia counselled prudence and moderation in view of "the important events which must make their appearance among the Great Powers" (Bogitchevitch, Annex IV.), assuring Serbia that once Russian preparations for war were completed she might do as she pleased. In accordance therefore with the advice of the Triple Entente, the Serbs reluctantly agreed to withdraw (E.B. 30 : 331), at the same time begging the Great Powers "to enjoin upon their Albanian protégés a respect for the frontiers created for their benefit" (E.B. 32 : 404).

After the capitulation of Skutari, Essad Pasha marched through Alessio (where he received military honours from the Serbian garrison; T. 1.5.13) to Tirana. He was instructed by the Porte (T. 1 and 9.5.13) to disband the Albanian (Redif) Division. The Turkish units joined Djavid Pasha's army, which was repatriated by sea during June, and by the end of October the Greeks alone remained within the borders of the new State.

Essad Pasha's intentions aroused misgivings which led to the dispatch of an Austro-Hungarian and Italian warship to Durazzo (T. 19.5.13), and it was erroneously reported that he had proclaimed himself King. But to the Austro-Hungarian and Italian Consuls who visited him at Tirana he professed his loyalty to the Provisional Government. The fact that he had under his control (although demobilized; T. 12.5.13) some 9,000 men gave him an influence in the country which could not be ignored; and when Ismail Bey returned in June from his mission to Europe, Essad was invited to become

Minister of the Interior (T. 3.7.13), an invitation which he accepted.

The Provisional Government (still unrecognized by the Powers) established local authorities and unified, as far as possible, the administrative system of the country. It had, however, insufficient funds at its disposal for the organization of an effective military or gendarmerie force to uphold its authority or enforce legislation; and for this reason the Dutch Mission was able to do no more than lay plans for a future organization. But the people obeyed it without question; and no single case of brigandage, theft, or rape was reported in the districts it administered (L.S. 9; B.K. 244), an ample refutation of the charge that the Albanians are a lawless and ungovernable people. Referring to their remarkable patience in a most difficult and almost unprecedented position, Miss Durham wrote (S.S. 297) that while on relief work

> "I was always unarmed, was frequently with men I had never seen before, and everyone knew that I had at least £T200 in gold in the bag at my belt. Men by the wayside would call out to me: 'Where are you taking the money to-day? Come to our village next.' But no attempt of any sort was ever made either to take it from me or to force me to change my route. I often wondered whether similar sums could be safely carried through England supposing all police withdrawn. . . ."

Ismail Bey was encouraged by the attitude of the people to attempt a number of reforms. The first problem to which he directed his attention was the religious question, and the necessary measures were carried out with little opposition except from the Moslem clergy. Of the three Churches in Albania, namely, the Moslem, Orthodox, and Roman Catholic, the first was unquestionably the most powerful, not so much through numerical superiority as because of the political power, privileges, and prestige which it had enjoyed under the Turkish régime. Questions of marriage, divorce, inheritance, and loyalty to the State rested entirely in the hands of its priests. Moreover, the highest judicial court for the application of the sacred Law (the Sheriat) of Mohammedans, was composed of Moslems, whose supreme head was the Sheik-ul-Islam. Such religious and political subservience to Constantinople placed Albania in an impossible position and threatened to complicate her status in the eyes of Europe. But Ismail Bey tackled the problem with courage, and it is indeed significant that a Moslem should have initiated such sweeping reforms of his own Church.

The bond of allegiance to the Sheik-ul-Islam was severed by the appointment of a patriotic Albanian Moslem Mufti as supreme head of an independent Albanian Moslem Church. Jurisdiction over civil cases was transferred to the civil courts, which adopted the jury system with remarkable success; and in a case unique in the annals of Islamism, the hitherto all-powerful Mufti was sentenced for some offence by the Civil Tribunal at Valona under the presidency of C. Chekrezi (C.C. 110). This case probably contributed to the outbreak of insurrection in central Albania.

But despite the progress in educational, administrative, and legal matters made by the Provisional Government, circumstances combined to provide fertile soil for the hostile propaganda which was being carried on. These circumstances proved beyond the control of Ismail Kemal Bey, who was too advanced in years to act boldly and with decision. Moreover, he did not enjoy the confidence of the malissori (B.K. 236), and was suspected of being subservient to Italy (D.W.) and of accepting bribes. (That he, as did other Albanians at different times, sought to capitalize the interest shown by foreigners in his country is quite probable, this being regarded as a perfectly legitimate practice; but that he was prepared to betray his country for gold—quite another matter—is not possible.) Lastly, it was widely believed that he aspired to the throne of southern Albania—a belief encouraged by Essad Pasha—and in order to realize his ambition was prepared to betray the remainder of the country. In the circumstances the Provisional Government appealed to the Powers at the end of July (T. 2.8.13) to terminate the existing uncertainty with regard to the political future of the country and secure the withdrawal of the Greek troops.

A section of the public, best described as Radical Nationalists, the majority of whom were Albanian emigrants who had returned from the United States, where they had assimilated advanced democratic ideas, imagined that Albania could become a modern State overnight. They failed to appreciate the international complications which prevented more rapid strides, or to understand that until the south-eastern frontier was delimited, the future ruler of the country selected by the Powers, and financial support forthcoming, it was impossible for the Government to make appreciable progress towards the establishment of equilibrium and prosperity. The impatience of this section, intrigue between rival candidates for the throne, a frantic propaganda carried on by neighbouring States "with the object of provoking trouble" (I.K. 378) and a pretext for intervention, destitution in consequence of the war, the presence of thousands of homeless starving refugees, and discreditable attempts by foreign financial groups to gain concessions, all contributed to the discomfiture of the Government. A series of incidents completed it.

In the first place, while Ismail Bey and his colleagues anxiously awaited the arrival of the International Boundary Commission to delimit the south-eastern frontier, the Wiener Bank Verein and the Banca Commerciale d'Italia sought a concession for the establishment of a National Albanian Bank. It was even intimated to the Government, so it is alleged, that the Commission would not operate until contracts for this and other concessions were signed. The Government accordingly granted a concession for the Bank, and another to the Commercial and Transport Co., of Vienna, for the construction of a railway through Albania from north to south (T. 15.9.13). The concession for the Bank included the right to deal in real estate. This aroused apprehension that advantage might be taken of the poverty of the people to purchase all available land, which would thus become the property of foreigners, and colonies be perhaps established therein. (This eventuality has since been rendered impossible, firstly by legislation introduced by Mehmed bey Konitza which prohibits the purchase of land in Albania by foreigners; secondly by a Bill passed in 1928 limiting the duration of leases to twenty years —see below; and thirdly by the prohibition of immigration except in cases where skilled technical labour is required. This legislation applies to all foreigners without distinction.)

The Bank concession was also opposed by Russia, who maintained that it should be upon a wider international basis (T. 2.1.14). In this attitude she was supported by Great Britain and France, and the three Powers refused to agree to the establishment of the Bank (T. 28.1.14).

The choice of a sovereign prince for Albania from the

formidable list of candidates presented the Powers with a problem to which they had difficulty in finding a solution, each fearing that the other's candidate might bring Albania within a hostile sphere of influence. Aladro Castriota, of the Albanian colony in Italy (who claimed descent from Skenderbeg), Prince Ghika of Roumania, Duke Ferdinand de Montpensier (see above), Prince Karl von Urach, Prince Moritz von Schaumburg-Lippe, the Count of Turin, and Prince Arthur of Connaught, whom the Albanians particularly desired (B.T. 257), were all either rejected on these grounds or refused to accept the throne.

But the main point involved was whether Albania should become in principle an eastern or a western State (I.K. 273). When Ismail Bey had notified the Porte of the declaration of independence, the Grand Vizier had emphasized in reply his belief that Albania could be preserved only as a vassal State of the Ottoman Empire, and had urged the acceptance of a member of the Imperial Ottoman Dynasty. Princes Burhan Eddine, Abdul Medjid, and Ahmed Fuad Pasha of Egypt (a descendant of the Albanian Mehmed Ali Pasha) were all proposed. Russia, it seems, favoured an Ottoman Prince, believing, no doubt, that Albania under Turkish suzerainty would be more easily and unostentatiously partitioned on some future occasion among her protégés.

But Ismail Bey, his colleagues, and indeed the vast majority of Albanians, were resolved that Albania should become a European State, and as such be ruled by a European Prince. Ismail Bey made this clear to the Porte, declaring that Albanians relied on the right to exist and the duty of the Powers to respect nationalities (I.K. 374). Thereupon the Porte, reluctant to lose an element which had for centuries provided its ablest statesmen, administrators, and soldiers, inaugurated an intensive propaganda in Albania in favour of Turkish suzerainty (I.K. 380).

Eventually the choice of a prince was entrusted to Austria-Hungary and Italy. Shortly afterwards rumours began to circulate that Prince William of Wied had been nominated (T. 4.10.13); and these rumours were followed by an intensive propaganda in his favour in the country. But in reply to an inquiry by Ismail Bey, his nomination was emphatically denied, and accordingly the Provisional Government at once took steps to expel the propagandists.

In the meantime Essad Pasha, who was not the man to remain for long content with a subordinate position, and was much distrusted by Ismail Bey, resolved to make a bid for power. He retired to Tirana, demanded the reconstruction of the Cabinet *which, he declared, was hostile to Moslems*, its removal to Durazzo (within his sphere of influence), and the cancellation of all concessions which it had granted. He sent a Memorandum to this effect to the Consuls and Representatives of the Powers, and asked that a decision with regard to a future ruler should be no longer delayed. Ismail Bey refused to comply with his demands, and declared his intention to carry on until the future ruler arrived (T. 19 and 22.9.13). Mufid Libohova and P. Poga were sent to negotiate with Essad; but they failed to reach an understanding.

Essad Pasha now gathered around him the discontented Moslem priests, who were disgruntled by Ismail Bey's reforms which threatened their privileges, his Redifs, and his own personal adherents, proclaimed himself the saviour of Albania and champion of Islam, announced his intention to overthrow the Provisional Government, and declared that central Albania desired a Moslem sovereign. Between Durazzo and Tirana, notably at Bazar Shjak, there were large settlements of Moslem Bosniaks, who, during the two preceding centuries, had for various reasons fled from Bosnia and sought refuge there. Unlike the Albanians, they were fanatical believers, and among them their priests wielded unlimited influence (S.m/s. 21). Moreover, the central Albanian Moslems belonged to the Sunni sect, and were always stricter in their observance of Moslem ordinances than Moslems in any other part of the country. Essad's Redifs were largely recruited from among these elements, whose support he now sought on religious grounds. He formed at Durazzo a Senate of representatives from Tirana, Kruja, Kavaja, Shjak, and Durazzo, describing himself as chief of the executive, and succeeded in establishing his authority pretty firmly between the Mati and Shkumbi Rivers (D.W. Annexes 2 and 3: Nadolny to Bethmann-Hollweg; also T. 16.10.13). By bribery and intrigue he worked to extend his power beyond these limits; and his principal colleagues in intrigue appear to have been the Greek Bishop at Durazzo (B.T. 241), and his secretary, Djurashkovitch (see below), who had been civil prefect of Durazzo during the Serbian occupation (T. 24.9.13).

Pekinj and Elbasan were under the control of Akif pasha Elbasani, who was loyal to the Provisional Government, and fighting (T. 14.1.14) ensued at Elbasan between the Essadists and adherents of the Government. The town itself was defended by a handful of gendarmerie under officers of the Dutch Mission. It was also reported (T. 30.10.13) that the Essadists were defeated during October in Bregumatia by Ded Soko.

In these circumstances Ismail Bey again appealed to the Powers at the end of October. He declared that his Government had maintained order for eleven months only through the patriotism of the people, but that the limit of their patience had been reached; he begged therefore that the future ruler of Albania should be designated and enthroned without further delay, an event which he believed would unite the country (I.K. 378). A month later he was officially informed that Prince William of Wied had been chosen by the Powers (T. 24.11.13); but the Prince wisely declined to proceed to Albania until the political situation had been cleared up (by the resignation of Essad Pasha, etc.) until a loan of £3,000,000 had been guaranteed by the Powers and a proportion of it advanced, and until the Albanian people had signified their approval. The last condition was at once fulfilled by the formality of an election.

Meantime the Young Turks, encouraged by the chaos which prevailed, resolved to restore Turkish suzerainty over Albania, and on the 9th January a conspiracy to this end was discovered which caused great consternation.

A Turkish major, Bekir Agha Grebenaly, a native of southern Macedonia, arrived at Valona with some fifty other men, who explained that they were refugees anxious to return to their homes. Suspicions were aroused. Grebenaly and his companions were arrested and brought before a court martial of which General de Weer was president. It was found that they had been sent to organize an insurrection among the Moslems of Albania and to overthrow the Provisional Government. The conspiracy was also directed against the Greek authorities in Macedonia. It was revealed that Grebenaly had been in correspondence with both Essad and Ismail Bey (T. 16.1.14), both no doubt wishing to turn his activities to the advantage of their respective policies. Arrangements had been made for the dispatch of troops from Conftantinople under Izzet Pasha, who was to have established himself as dictator of Albania. Grebenaly was executed, but apprehension prevailed left further complications should ensue.

In these circumstances Ismail Bey proposed to the Powers that either a High Commissioner should be appointed to govern the whole country until Prince William arrived, or that the International Commission of Control should do so. The latter course was adopted, and on the 22nd January the Provisional Government abandoned its powers in favour of the Commission (I.K. 380). Ismail Bey retired to Nice.

The Commission at once invited Essad Pasha to follow Ismail Bey's example. Essad declined. Thereupon a plan for his eviction was drawn up by Colonel Phillips; but the Commission was reluctant to adopt violent measures, and in the meantime Essad realized that he could not defy both the Powers and the people. On the 3rd February, therefore, he agreed to retire, upon the understanding that the Commission should govern through the Senate he had nominated (S.m/s. 15 and 36). He also insisted upon leading the deputation proceeding to Neuwied formally to offer the crown to Prince William (whose accession he had hitherto opposed).

The Commission appointed an Albanian governor to replace the International Administration of Skutari, but the international military force of occupation under the command of Colonel G. F. Phillips (West Yorkshire Regiment), which had replaced the Naval Brigade (T. 17.10.13), remained. The British detachment consisted of 8 officers and 383 other ranks of the Warwickshire Regiment.

At Alessio, Medua, and in the surrounding district Ded Soko had set up a very creditable provisional administration. He had wished to extend his authority to the Bojana, but this the Commission had forbidden. But the hostility and propaganda of Essad and Prenk Bib Doda—more especially the latter—undermined the confidence of his followers. Prenk, who had contrived the murder of Djeto, Ded's brother, regarded Ded as a usurper in territory which Prenk's family had ruled for generations; moreover, Prenk feared that Ded would frustrate his plan to establish a Mirdite principality which included Alessio and the Zadrima, thereby depriving him of the means of retaining a Serbian subsidy (in return for access to the sea). Eventually Ded's followers declared that they were able no longer to acknowledge the authority of a man who was no better than they (by birth), and asked Colonel Phillips to appoint an authority over them. Phillips, having consulted the Commission, sent Captain Francis, an Austro-Hungarian, and an Italian officer, with a British detachment, to Alessio. Ded Soko at once voluntarily retired, honest patriot that he was, and Francis took over the administration, appointing local councils to assist him (D.W. Annex III).

Prenk Bib Doda continued to rule Mirdita, although submitting to the control of the Commission. The other tribes remained under their bairaktars, who likewise conformed to the Commission's instructions.

Thus was Albania, with the exception of the southern districts under Greek occupation, nominally united under a single administration. But the Commission, by the very nature of its composition, was handicapped in the performance of its functions; and although it was of assistance to Albania at a critical stage of her existence, it might have been of much greater assistance had not the rivalries of the two great alliances been reflected in every decision which the Commissioners made. The delegate of each Power, with the exception of Mr. (now Sir) Harry Lamb, representing Great Britain, was actuated in the making of his decisions by the instructions of his Government, not by his own personal views as to what would be beneficial to Albania. This resulted in a divergence of opinions which retarded constructive and progressive measures.

Meantime the situation in southern Albania was developing. On the 13th December the Powers had reminded the Greek Government of their stipulation that the districts allotted to Albania should be evacuated by Greek troops within one month of the completion of the delimitation. Greece had protested that this period was insufficient.

No further action was taken until the beginning of February, when the Powers united in presenting a Note to Greece in which they affirmed that the majority of the Ægean Islands should be ceded to her provided she withdrew her troops from southern Albania—as delimited by the Protocol of Florence—and pledged herself neither to resist nor to encourage resistance to the incorporation in Albania of the districts in question. Further, it was stipulated that the Greek withdrawal should begin on the 1St March in the *ca$a* of Korcha, and be completed by the evacuation of the *ca$a* of Delvino on the 31St (T. 14.2.14; S.A. 41).

In its reply on the 21St February the Greek Government agreed to bow to the decisions of the Powers, but proposed that "certain villages in the Valley of Argyrocastro should be given to her [Greece] in exchange for an extension of Albanian territory along the coast and the payment to Albania of £100,000" (S.A. 41; T. 16.2.14). A further rectification was proposed in the neighbourhood of Korcha. It was proposed also that the population of the areas to be evacuated should be assured of the safety of its institutions and property (S.A. 41)—a subtle insinuation. It is difficult to reconcile the conciliatory tone of this Note with subsequent events unless one assumes that it was merely bluff.

The Greeks let it be known that should they be compelled to withdraw they would take with them the entire Christian population, that Europe might see how these people feared the Albanians (P.D. 62 : 1259. Also compare with methods in Macedonia: C.E. 204–6). Moslems were advised to emigrate before it was too late, and terrified refugees poured into Valona with tales of Greek threats and brutality. Resistance, in face of the overwhelmingly superior Greek forces, by whom they had been disarmed, would merely have precipitated a massacre and devastation of the country.

The events which followed have been described as an insurrection (S.A. 42–50), but the evidence of impartial authorities and an analysis of facts proves that the "insurrection" was actually a movement promoted and sustained by Greece from across the frontier. Moreover, Argyrocastro, which was the centre of the activities of the so-called "insurgents", was one of the principal centres of Albanian nationalism and of the Bektashi Moslem Albanian sect (P.V.). Over that town Fehim bey Leskovik, who under Ottoman rule had been Prefect, hoisted the Albanian flag in November 1912 (A.R.), whereas had the town been Greek in sentiment, there could have been no opportunity more favourable for a declaration of those sentiments, since the Greek Army was approaching and the Albanian Provisional Government had no means of imposing its authority on any part of the country. Actually what happened at Argyrocastro was that the inhabitants were prevented from leaving the town by Greek troops, and were powerless to resist, since the town was commanded by the guns of the citadel, which was in Greek hands (P.D. 63 : 1259, 1521, 1961). Again, the theory that an insurrection took place is incompatible with the subsequent findings of the League of Nations Commission of Inquiry. Lastly, the "insurgents", who destroyed the property which they claimed as their own, bore none of the characteristics of a national force, and numbered, at most, 10,000 men, of whom the majority (S.A. 47) had served in the Greek Army (see memo by Prince Michel Sturdza, Attaché of the Roumanian Legation: Q.K. Annex 6). There is therefore no doubt that a comparatively infinitesimal proportion of the population of "Northern Epirus" voluntarily (T. 16.4.14) took part in the "insurrection" (for coercive recruitment of volunteers, compare with C.E. 172–3, etc.), although it seems that a large proportion of the Orthodox population adopted an equivocal attitude, torn, on the one hand, by nationalist sentiments, and on the other by phil-Hellenism, the outcome of their association with Greece and Greek propaganda. Among the phil-Hellenic sections— which were by no means politically pro-Greek—the Greeks succeeded also to some extent in creating a fear that a predominantly Moslem Albanian Government would continue to regard the Orthodox element as inferior to the Moslem element, as had been the case under Ottoman rule; and in view of this the "insurgents", in demanding not union with Greece—to which the population of southern Albania was almost universally opposed—but autonomy, which, from the Greek point of view was advantageous in that it would enable them to continue their policy of Hellenization—enjoyed the political support of a proportion of the Orthodox element. Moreover, it was no difficult matter for Greece to throw dust in the eyes of Europe, where the situation had never been appreciated and where phil-Hellenic sentiments had flourished for generations. Such organizations as the Anglo-Hellenic League (S.A. 41) acted as vehicles for Greek propaganda— although doubtless unwittingly—and questions on behalf of Greece were asked in the House of Commons (P.D. 59 : 6. Reference to "Albanian brigands"), while the French Press was violently pro-Greek (S.A. 39) for political reasons.

Thus rumours gained currency that the population of the

disputed areas was opposed to incorporation in Albania, and was preparing to resist. On the 16th February

> "the British Government was asked in the House of Commons 'whether, seeing that the inhabitants of the district are opposed to such inclusion, and are determined to oppose it by force of arms, His Majesty's Government are prepared to assent to their coercion?' [P.D. 58 : 550]. In reply, the Under-Secretary of State for Foreign Affairs referred to communications then being carried on with the Greek Government respecting the settlement of the southern Albanian frontier, and trusted that 'no question of coercive measures will arise'."

Towards the end of February, there being no reply from the Powers to the Greek Note of the 21st (S.A. 42), proclamations of the autonomy of Epirus were issued from the Tchamouria, Argyrocastro, Santi Quaranta, and Delvino, and on the 28th February Durazzo was informed that a "Provisional Government of Autonomous Epirus" had been constituted (P.D. 59 : 852) at Argyrocastro under the presidency of M. Christaki Zographos. On the 2nd March the independence of "Northern Epirus" was proclaimed at Argyrocastro. Ostensibly this "Provisional Government" had been constituted in accordance with the wishes of the people of southern Albania, who were "so thoroughly Greek in sentiment" (J. N. Mavrogordato, E.B. 31 : 304. Compare with Q.K. Annex 17, etc.), that they were determined, so the Greeks declared, to resist incorporation in Albania; ostensibly also these "Epirots" were beyond the control of the Greek Government, which could not possibly be held responsible for their actions. Actually, this "Government", which described itself as "an executive committee acting as a Provisional Government" (S.A. 43), was directly responsible to Athens through its Prime Minister, M. Zographos, a former Minister of Foreign Affairs for Greece, who returned to that portfolio in March, 1915. A member for Arta of the Greek Chamber of Deputies, M. Karapanos, acted as Minister for Foreign Affairs, and Colonel Doulis as Minister for War. In this camarilla was vested the administration of all territory under Greek occupation which Albania had been allowed by the

Powers to retain, and which the Greeks were now required to evacuate.

M. Zographos, prior to his departure from Athens for Argyrocastro, made a declaration in which he stated that

"three means existed for preserving the population from fatal ruin: first, complete autonomy under the sceptre of the Prince of Albania; or, secondly, very large administrative or cantonal autonomy based on a gendarmerie recruited exclusively among the people of the district concerned; or, thirdly, European occupation and administration sufficiently lengthy to clarify the true situation, and lasting until the withdrawal would involve no danger. If Europe wished to avoid the misfortune of leaving to Albanian invaders only smoking ruins, 'she should intervene in time to take measures which, without modifying the bases of the decision of the Powers, would save a people and safeguard the principles of humanity'" (S.A. 43).

"The program for which the autonomous Epirot Government was struggling was embodied in a list of guarantees and privileges demanded, which was presented officially to the Albanian Government. These demands comprised the administration by two governors of Swiss or Dutch nationality, the establishment of a Diet on the model of that of Croatia, the incorporation of Christian elements in the gendarmerie, which should not be sent out of Epirus, complete liberty for Greek schools, complete religious liberty, and the concession to the Tchamouria of all the privileges that district had enjoyed under the Sultan" (S.A. 47).

"Zographos . . . impressed observers with his moderation, and desire to effect a settlement by peaceful means; he insisted only on administrative autonomy, not on union with Greece. His moderation, however, far surpassed that of many of his followers" (S.A. 48).

The reason for this moderation may be explained firstly by a desire to obtain the support of the Orthodox Albanian element, who, although infused with phil-Hellenic sentiments, desired union with Albania rather than with Greece; and secondly, by the certainty that any suggestion that union with Greece was the object of the "insurrection" would

at once lead to the adoption of a wholly uncompromising
attitude by Austria-Hungary and Italy, and in all probability
to the military occupation by those two Powers of "Northern
Epirus" (S.A. 49). Hence M. Zographos's preference for a
peaceful settlement! This moderation was, moreover, mere
bluff. Greece was determined to retain control of "Northern
Epirus", and Zographos, her agent, acted with skill to this
end. With reference to this point, Sir Harry Lamb gave the
writer the following amusing explanation:

> "It is merely a matter of pronunciation," he wrote.
> "I do not know how deeply you are versed in Near
> Eastern languages, but you probably know that in
> most of them many of the longer words (specifically
> *autonomia, ethnologia,* and, I think, *dhemokrateia* amongst
> them) are pronounced with the tongue firmly pressed
> against the left cheek. That is all there is to it. I forget
> what the Greek for 'moderation' is, but if Zographos
> ever mentioned *his,* it was probably pronounced in
> the same way."

In the meantime the Greek Government took every
possible step to conceal its complicity (T. 6.4.14; 17.4.14).
On the 7th March it ostentatiously declared a blockade of
Santi Quaranta (T. 9.3.14), "at present in the hands of the
insurgents" (S.A. 44), but this step did not inflict any hardship
on the "insurgents" (S.m/s. 37) since their supplies from Greece
were conveyed by land through the medium of the Greek
military authorities. It did, however, enable Greece to prevent
the landing of those who might give undesirable publicity to
her activities. Zographos himself did not, of course, omit to
complain bitterly that the Greek Government had

> "strangely misconceived the extent of its obligations
> towards the Powers. . . . It has blockaded Santi
> Quaranta, hindering our supplies and the victualling of
> our soldiers. Orders have been issued prohibiting
> officers, soldiers, and others from coming to our aid.
> Merchants have been warned not to supply us with arms
> and ammunition. Dispatches and even private letters
> have been intercepted" (S.A. 44).

Such orders were ostentatiously issued for the benefit of
the Powers, but not enforced, and were of no greater worth

than the official contradiction by the Greek Minister in London, Gennadius, of the allegation that Greece was encouraging the "revolutionary movement" (T. 20.4.14). That the Powers might be led to believe that their instructions were being complied with, and to give colour to the story that this movement was the outcome of the Greek evacuation, some Greek troops were actually withdrawn. But a large number, stripped of badges (S.m/s. 8) and identity discs were left (D.W. Annex VI), with a liberal supply of ammunition and war material, at the disposal of Colonel Doulis. Thenceforward they were "Epirots". They were reinforced by fresh contingents of Cretan desperadoes (P.D. 65 : 5, 6, 613, and S.m/s. 55), by criminals released from the prisons of Greece and Crete, by Greek immigrants and partisans, and by Albanians who were compelled to join them. The following proclamation is eloquent, the special significance in the Balkans of the word "punished" being borne in mind:

"Tous les citoyens de dix-huit à cinquante-deux ans sont invités obligatoirement à s'enrégimenter dans les rangs des bataillons sacrés jusqu'au premier décembre prochain. Après cette date tous ceux qui ne seront pas inscrits seront punis sévèrement. De même seront punis sévèrement ceux qui, une fois inscrits, ne se présenteront pas aux exercices militaires. Les inscriptions se feront tous les jours au bureau de l'Anagnesis sauf le samedi et le vendredi, depuis une heure jusqu'à trois heures de l'après-midi. Coritza [i.e. Korcha], 22 novembre 1913, émané du bureau de la Commission" (S.m/s. 7).

These "Sacred Battalions" (S.m/s. 29) were commanded by Greek officers who had resigned their commissions (*ad interim*). The Commander-in-Chief was Colonel G. Tsontos Vardhas.

On the 1st March the Greek troops duly evacuated Korcha, which was occupied by fifty Albanian gendarmes under a Dutch officer. The Greeks, however, left in the hospital a number of soldiers upon the pretext that they required further treatment before removal (B.T. 261). They are alleged (C.C. 132) to have buried, before withdrawing, a number of stones bearing inscriptions in ancient Greek, which might, at some future time, be discovered by credulous archæologists, guided no doubt by Greek "scientists", and create a fresh basis for their claims to the town.

Meantime Prince William of Wied had agreed to accept the throne of Albania in the following letter (from Potsdam to the British, French, and Russian Ambassadors in Berlin), dated the 6th February, 1914:

> Messieurs les Ambassadeurs d'Autriche-Hongrie et d'Italie à Berlin viennent de m'informer au nom de leurs Gouvernements qu'un institut de banque austro-hongrois, et un institut de banque italien, agissant sous la garantie de leurs Gouvernements respectifs, sont prêts à mettre immédiatement à ma disposition, pour ле Gouvernement de l'Albanie, une somme de 10 millions de francs comme avance sur le montant total de l'emprunt de 75 millions, à la garantie duquel les autres Grandes Puissances se sont également montrées disposées à adhérer en principe.

> En portant ce qui précède à la connaissance de Votre Excellence j'ai l'honneur de Lui declarer que je me suis décidé à accepter le trône d'Albanie et à me rendre prochainement en Albanie.

He formally accepted the throne from the Albanian deputation led by Essad Pasha at Neuwied on the 21st February. But he hesitated to proceed to Albania until the Greco-Albanian situation was cleared up; and his friends urged him to refuse to do so unless foreign armed forces were placed at his disposal. But Count Berchtold brought pressure to bear on him through the Austro-Hungarian Ambassador in Berlin, believing, no doubt, that Austria-Hungary would be able to uphold him. Berchtold was supported in this matter by the Greek Minister for Foreign Affairs, who probably feared that if the Prince continued to refuse to go to Albania the Powers would be compelled to take action to the detriment of Greek projects (*Reign of Prince William*: Refs. A.m/s., S.m/s.; W.N.; D.W.; B.T. 254–82; C.C.; T.; N.E. 1.1.25; etc.).

Prince William is the third son of William, Prince of Wied, and Mary, Princess of Holland, nephew of Queen Elizabeth of Roumania ("Carmen Sylva") and grand-nephew of the Emperor William I. He was born on the 26th March, 1876, lived at Neuwied in Rhenish Prussia, and married in

1906 the clever, courageous, and ambitious Princess Sophie of Schoenberg-Waldenburg. He has two children, Princess Marie Eleanor (1909) and Prince Charles Victor (1913). He is a tall and imposing figure, with a charming personality. In 1914 he had become, in open competition, a Captain of the German General Staff, and had proved himself to be a very capable soldier. But he had no knowledge of Albania. He never sought the throne, his candidature having been pressed principally by his aunt, and being led to believe by King Charles of Roumania and others (W.N.) that the task was not an impossible one, for no one could foresee the course of events, he accepted it. He is a soldier with a very high sense of honour and duty, had no experience of intrigue and diplomacy, and believed in the good faith of the Powers, which is probably why they agreed upon his designation. In consequence he became the victim of unprincipled politicians and despicable propagandists.

"Prince William", wrote Mgr. Noli, "can be criticized only for being unable to perform miracles" (N.N.).

"The tale of Prince William of Wied", wrote Miss Durham (B.T. 259), "is among the most sordid that the Powers have woven. . . . We may blame Wied for incompetency, but only a man of unusual force of character and intimate knowledge of the land could have made headway against the Powers combined against him" (B.T. 265).

Indeed, Prince William's only fault was his ignorance of diplomacy in its lowest form, which made him incapable of holding his own with the knaves and fools by whom he was surrounded.

In judging Prince William and in criticizing his failure, too little prominence has been given to the part played by Italy, France, Russia, and their protégés in rendering his task an impossible one. First, it should be remembered that only the solidarity of Austria-Hungary and Italy in opposing the access of Russia's protégés to the Adriatic Sea, or their excessive aggrandizement, had made possible the creation of an independent Albania; but once these two Powers allowed their conflicting interests to shake that solidarity, the very existence of Albania became threatened. Moreover, "there can be no doubt", wrote Prince William to the author (W.N.), "that between the time I accepted the Albanian throne, and the month of May, 1914, when the situation became intricate, lies an important moment of European politics. . . . I mean the moment when among the Great Powers the hope to preserve peace was superseded by the fear that war would become unavoidable.

"The institution of the Albanian State and my own designation being connected with the previous policy of peace of the Powers, it is evident that its slow but steady transformation into a policy of war had necessarily to affect very deeply the whole basis of my mission.

"I need not tell you what repercussion it had in Durazzo when Austria-Hungary and Italy, on whose former common policy independent Albania was based, began to disagree, for reasons lying mostly outside the Albanian problem. Russia and France had never been very favourably disposed towards the freedom of Albania, and when Austro-Hungarian-Italian dissension and the other causes foreboding war became evident, it is clear that their policy was not in the least discouraging to the action of Albania's hostile neighbours, nor of some either egoistical or deluded elements within Albania.

"Even at this critical time I had not the least reason to complain about the attitude of Great Britain and her representatives in Albania. As to Germany, it has to be pointed out that her behaviour, which even at the London Conference had not been absolutely phil-Albanian, had become decidedly neutral in the spring of 1914. This was not only due to the embarrassment caused by the discussion between the Austro-Hungarian and the Italian ally, but also to the struggle about Greek neutrality in the coming war, a struggle which had then already begun. The Kaiser himself, perhaps also under his sister's and his brother-in-law's influence, had, at any rate, much more interest for the Greek than for the Albanian side of the questions which arose, and I learned from reliable sources that his dislike for everything concerning Albania went so far that the Berlin Foreign Office avoided placing before his eyes diplomatic correspondence regarding Albania, fearing to incur his Majesty's ill humour.

"These hints on the international situation will show

you the real reasons why my work in Durazzo was bound to fail. Under normal circumstances neither Essad Pasha nor the poor deluded rebels of Shjak would ever have dared to oppose the decisions of united Europe."

Of the selection of a ruler for Albania the ex-Kaiser wrote as follows (*My Memoirs*, 161):

". . . I sought to bring my influence to bear towards the appointment, if possible, of a Mohammedan—perhaps an Egyptian. . . . I was not at all pleased, therefore, when the choice fell upon Prince William of Wied. I esteemed him as a distinguished, knightly man of lofty sentiments, but considered him unfitted for the post. The Prince knew altogether too little about Balkan affairs to undertake this thorny task with hope of success. It was particularly unpleasant to me that a German Prince should make a fool of himself there, and it was apparent from the start that the Entente would place all kinds of obstacles in his path. Upon being questioned by the Prince—my cousin—I told him all my doubts, laying stress upon the difficulties awaiting him, and advised him urgently to decline. I could not command him, since the Prince of Wied, as head of the family, had the final word in the matter."

Throughout Prince William's reign Great Britain and Germany preserved a neutral attitude, although each was bound to her respective allies, and each was influenced by a desire to avoid unduly alienating Greece. That country thus enjoyed an immunity in carrying on her machinations of which she took full advantage. France and Russia had never favoured the creation of an independent Albania, and supported their Balkan protégés. Serbia, Greece, and Montenegro desired the partition of the country. Pašitch declared that "Serbia could not be pleased by the creation of an independent Albania" (T. 6.4.14); and displeasure is seldom passive in the Balkans. The policy of these States was to create anarchy in Albania and convince the Powers that the country was incapable of self-government. Turkey continued to carry on a frantic propaganda in favour of a Moslem Prince and Turkish suzerainty (T. 10.1.14; 5.3.14). Roumania alone supported Prince William disinterestedly, owing to the influence of his aunt. Austria-Hungary alone of the Powers endeavoured throughout to fulfil her obligations towards Albania, but purely as a matter of policy.

Only the co-operation of Italy and Austria-Hungary, who, San Giuliano declared, were resolved to work together to preserve equilibrium in the Adriatic (T. 17.12.13), had made Albanian independence possible. But Italy considered that Prince William was austrophile, essentially the representative of Austro-German interests, and that Albania might, through him, be brought entirely within the Austro-Hungarian sphere of influence; moreover, she sought, by extending her own influence in Albania, to redress her unfavourable strategic position with regard to Austria-Hungary (see below). She therefore selected Essad Pasha as the instrument of her policy, seeking to elevate him and degrade Prince William before the Albanian people.

Meantime Prince William, having paid State visits to the capitals of the six Great Powers, sailed from Trieste on the Austro-Hungarian yacht *Taurus*, with an international squadron led by H.M.S. *Gloucester* as escort. On the 7th March he landed at Durazzo, which he had chosen as his capital. The choice aroused considerable jealousy both in the north and south (T. 11.4.14), where Skutari and Valona respectively were favoured; moreover, Durazzo was within Essad's sphere of influence. On the other hand, it was central, easily accessible, and possessed a building suitable for conversion into a palace. Insufficient notice of his arrival had been given, and therefore the crowd assembled in Durazzo to welcome him was not as representative as it might have been (T.11.3.14). Nevertheless, he was greeted with great enthusiasm, hailed as the successor of Skenderbeg, and at once proclaimed Mbreti (King: the Powers recognized him only as "hereditary sovereign prince").

The festivities in celebration of his arrival lasted for a week. Deputations from Albanian colonies in all parts of the world hastened to swear fealty to their sovereign and accredited representatives of Great Britain, France, Italy, Germany, Austria-Hungary, Russia, Roumania, Serbia, Greece, and Bulgaria to present their credentials. It was anticipated by the ignorant majority that the Prince would provide a panacea for all evils, and that hitherto undreamt-of prosperity would follow instantly: that, as it were, a magic hand would pass over Albania, and that a poverty-stricken people would find themselves in comparative affluence. Tales to this effect had been spread by those over-anxious to ensure the success of his reign, and led to disillusionment and discontent.

Prince William had already appointed Essad Pasha first General of Albania and Minister for War, thinking it expedient to conciliate him (D.W.); moreover, he was under the impression that much of the hostility towards the Pasha was due to jealousy (S.m/s. 40). Essad was widely believed to be the most powerful man in Albania; and so long as he retained the support of his Redifs there is no doubt that he was. On his journey to Neuwied he had been honoured both by Italy and Austria-Hungary, had received the Grand Cross of their respective orders, and had made every effort to ingratiate himself with the Prince. This transference of allegiance was resented both by Turkey and by those central Albanians whom he had previously encouraged to accept only a Moslem prince; on the other hand, it was regarded with the utmost contempt and suspicion by Albanian "Nationalists" and patriots who were unable to forgive his treachery to the Provisional Government. His appointment was therefore regarded with the gravest misgivings.

Power and money were Essad's primary considerations; and it is notorious that he capitalized foreign interest in his country to an almost unlimited degree. As regards the attainment of power he doubtless considered that as he could not be nominal ruler of Albania himself, and as the Powers had insisted upon a European Prince, he would establish himself as actual ruler, and perhaps on some future occasion usurp the throne.

But Essad's unpopularity was not confined only to rivals and patriots. It has already been explained that he was disliked and distrusted both in the north and in the south, and for that reason was not opposed to the satisfaction of Greek and Serbian claims. But he was also hated by the majority of his own tenants on his property around Tirana and Durazzo, who considered him an extortionate tyrant and representative of the feudal Beys. Thus his power actually depended almost entirely upon his authority, and certainly not upon popularity. While a Turkish officer, his authority was upheld by the Ottoman Empire, but in the service of Prince William it depended entirely upon his prestige.

The International Commission of Control at once transferred to the Prince the authority which it had wielded *ad interim* on his behalf. It had been constituted to act in an advisory capacity to the Government of Albania for a period of ten years, but owing to the conflicting interests of the Powers represented upon it, was of very little practical value. Prince William then invited first Omer pasha Vrioni, then Ferid pasha Vlora (former Grand Vizier) to form a Cabinet, but both declined. Finally Turkhan pasha Premeti accepted ·the invitation. On the 17th March he formed a Cabinet as follows:

TURKHAN PASHA PREMETI .	Prime Minister, and Minister for Foreign Affairs.
ESSAD PASHA TOPTANI . .	Minister of the Interior and for War.
MUFID BEY LIBOHOVA . .	Minister of Justice and Religion.
DR. TOURTOULIS BEY . .	Minister of Education.
DR. ADAMIDI BEY FRASHERI .	Minister of Finance.
HASSAN BEY PRISHTINA .	Minister of Public Works.
AZIZ PASHA VRIONI . .	Minister of Agriculture and Commerce.

Turkhan Pasha had concluded a brilliant career in the Turkish service as Ambassador to Russia from 1908–13, but the intrigues of Essad and of the various "interested" Powers and States proved beyond the control of this able but aged diplomat. Essad had supported Turkhan's nomination, being confident that he could influence him as suited his purpose, a confidence which was justified by his acquisition of the Ministry of the Interior, which gave him virtually supreme authority in the country. Prenk Bib Doda, who had acquired during his years in exile a somewhat indolent disposition, preferred the seclusion and safety of Mirdita (A.m/s. vi). It is interesting that at a dinner-party subsequently given by the Prince, he remarked: "If Albania is to be ruled peacefully, three persons ought to be hanged: Ismail Kemal, Essad Pasha, and myself. If all three of us were dead, Albania would fare much better" (W.N.).

The Cabinet was an unpopular one. With the exception of Essad and Aziz, none of the Ministers had been resident in the country for many years. Moreover, it was considered that the landowning class was too strongly represented, and that the Ministers were too deeply steeped in Turkish methods of administration to break with Orientalism, and were under the influence of Essad Pasha (A.m/s. vi).

The Prince had with him his wife and children, a German Controller of the Household—Von Trotha, an Italian adviser—Captain Castoldi, who had escorted the Albanian deputation to Neuwied, an Austrian counterpart to the Italian—Baron Buchberger, a British private secretary—Mr. (now Major) D. Heaton Armstrong, and two ladies-in-waiting to the Princess. His court was completed by Sami bey Vrioni—Chamberlain, Ekrem bey Libohova and Selim bey Vassa—A.D.C.s; and around it revolved the official representatives of Austria-Hungary and Italy—Herr von Löwenthal and Baron Aliotti, ever intriguing the one against the other in the interests of the countries which respectively they represented. The Russian and French representatives hovered in the background.

Expenditure of the advance (£500,000) made by Austria-Hungary and Italy upon the loan to which the other Powers had not decided to subscribe (and never did) was controlled by the International Commission. But the Government, being, it seems, under the impression that the balance would be forthcoming in due course, embarked upon an ambitious programme. A High Court of Appeal was created, and inspectors of public education appointed.

For the gendarmerie, which was Albania's most urgent requirement, the Commission sanctioned only a minimum expenditure; and indeed the Dutch Government ultimately threatened to withdraw the gendarmerie mission unless it received proper support from the Powers (T. 25.7.14). Moreover, the mission itself, which included no N.C.O.s, was inadequate. Being a neutralized State under international guarantee, Albania was not at liberty to dispose of a military establishment—with the exception of mountain artillery units.

It has been said, notably by the Emperor William II (*My Memoirs*, 164–5) that the Prince ought to have toured his country to study conditions and make the acquaintance of his subjects. But it does not seem unintelligible that he should have thought it wiser during the first month to devote himself to the formation of his Cabinet, settlement of the dispute over southern Albania, inauguration of legislation, and study of the characters of those immediately around him. Moreover, events developed so rapidly that unless he had set off directly after landing he would have absented himself while critical diplomatic matters required his attention. He did, however, make two State visits early in May, one to Kavaja and the other to Tirana. At both places he was received enthusiastically. On the latter occasion Essad, by a ruse, succeeded in leaving the Prime Minister in Durazzo and in securing a seat in the Prince's car, hoping thereby to give the impression in Tirana that he, and not Turkhan Pasha, was the most influential Minister! His Redifs lined the streets.

On the 30th March Greece presented another Note to the Powers (P.D. 60 : 1320), "asking whether, at the moment when Hellenic troops were concentrating with a view to evacuation, the Powers would not consider it a suitable occasion to make a reply in regard to the guarantees requested for the Epirot population in the Greek communication of the 21st February" (S.A. 45). The Powers, after negotiations between them, replied to the Greek Government on the 24th April declaring their readiness to support the principle of linguistic and religious equality which the Commission of Control had already recommended, to advise the Albanian Government to consider the proposal regarding enrolment of local elements in the gendarmerie, and to consider minor rectifications of the frontier. This Note deprived Greece of every pretext for delaying further the evacuation, which was ostensibly completed on the 28th April (S.A. 46).

Meantime the small pro-Greek faction in Korcha, headed by the Orthodox Bishop Ghermanos, had done everything possible to create an incident which might afford a pretext for the return of the Greek troops. But the forbearance of the gendarmerie and townsfolk and discretion of the universally respected and patriotic governor, Pandele Evangheli, had been such that these attempts had failed.

During the night of the 6th April, however, the soldiers from the hospital broke loose in the streets and were joined by Greek partisans in the town, while bands of "Epirots" equipped with machine guns descended upon it. The coup was successful, and within a few hours the public buildings and other points of vantage were in Greek hands. So infuriated were the Greeks at the patriotism of the Albanian Christians that they laid waste the Christian quarter, although Europe was led to believe that the Christians of Korcha desired union with Greece (S.m/s. 56). But the townsfolk

rallied in support of the gendarmerie under Commandant
Shnellen and Captain Doorman, and after four days of street
fighting the invaders were expelled and order restored. Ghermanos was carried off to Elbasan.

Guerrilla warfare in other parts of Albania now developed.
At Tepeleni a detachment of Albanian gendarmerie was
treacherously attacked and massacred (S.m/s. 37). Although
the Albanian forces consisted merely of armed civilians and
2,500 gendarmerie under Dutch officers, undisciplined and
with wholly inadequate supplies of war material, the "Epirots"
encountered stubborn resistance (*Plain English*, 3.11.21;
A.m/s., etc.). Although less accustomed to warfare than their
compatriots of the north (many of whom came to their assistance under Prenk Bib Doda and other chieftains), the southern
Albanians, led by Salih Budka and others, fought manfully;
but being without bayonets they were at a great disadvantage
(S.m/s. 62–8). The Dutch officers, although under no
obligation to do so, readily and gallantly fought for the
country in which they had agreed to serve only as instructors;
and many women rallied to resist the invaders. Indeed, the
latter were unable to hold their own (S.m/s. 50), and the
Albanians gradually closed upon Argyrocastro, the "Epirot"
headquarters. On the 12th May they attacked the "Epirot"
position at Tchepo, but were repulsed owing to the intervention of regular Greek infantry and artillery under General
Papoulias (P.D. 62 : 418; B.T. 262).

In the meant me the Albanian Government drew the
attention of the Powers (T. 25.4.14) to the complicity of
Greece in this "regrettable situation", and entreated them to
exert their influence with the Greek Government to bring
it to an end (S.A. 47; S.m/s. 38). Prince Sturdza, as a neutral,
was sent to investigate the situation, and Colonel Thomson,
of the Dutch Mission (who had been appointed Governor
of southern Albania), to negotiate with Karapanos (T. 31.3.14).
But Thomson's proposals were acceptable neither to the
"Epirots" nor the Cabinet. Neither Italy nor Essad Pasha
seems to have been in favour of negotiations; and the latter
is alleged to have been in receipt of a subsidy from the Greeks
to impede effective operations (D.W.). In any case, Thomson
was recalled and his proposals repudiated.

The Albanian Government had purchased from Austria-
Hungary a number of machine and mountain guns, and from

Italy (who insisted that expenditure of the loan should be divided equally between the two Powers) several thousand rifles. But these remained at Durazzo, although the Albanians resisting the "Epirots" were handicapped by inadequate equipment. Naturally the Minister for War was held responsible (S.m/s. 73); moreover, it was reported that bands of northern tribesmen marching to the assistance of their compatriots in the south had been attacked by his Redifs (S.m/s. 31), for which, of course, he may not have been responsible. Nevertheless, he was widely believed to be conspiring against the Prince, except by the Italians, who protested his innocence and alleged that he was the victim of Austro-Hungarian intrigue. There was probably some foundation for both points of view.

Prince William would have welcomed an opportunity to place himself at the head of an army against the "Epirots". But such a step would probably have established at once his prestige in the country, an eventuality which coincided with the plans of neither the Italians nor of Essad Pasha (B.T. 261 and 268; S.m/s. 39). Moreover, the Commission as a whole, and notably Sir Harry Lamb (S.A. 47; T. 6 and 8.4.14), was strongly opposed to military measures in view of the inferiority of the Albanian forces, the state of the country's finances, and the danger of complications with Montenegro (S.A. 48) and other States. Lastly, the Greek Government had intimated that any regular military action by the Albanian Government would lead to war with Greece (i.e. an abandonment by Greece of her subterranean methods). Intervention by Italy and Austria-Hungary, and probably the outbreak of a European war, would have ensued.

Meantime an agitation in favour of military measures and against Essad Pasha grew rapidly. Essad's point of view probably was that if military measures were to be adopted they must be taken entirely under his leadership so that he might compensate himself for the loss of his Greek subsidy by recovering his prestige in the country, an end which would have been acceptable to Italy. Moreover, Italy was probably not averse from an opportunity for intervention against Greece. In any case Essad now declared his intention to raise 20,000 men in central Albania for service in the south. Prince William, although aware of the danger of this plan, dared not oppose it, as, had he done so, he would have been held responsible for the fate of the south, a responsibility which Essad would not have failed to emphasize for his own ends (S.m/s. 42).

Accordingly Essad called for volunteers, and the rifles purchased from Italy were carried inland and diftributed. Fortunately, through the intervention of the Dutch officers, the guns remained at Durazzo.

But the Powers now intervened, and the Commission was authorized to proceed to Corfu to negotiate on behalf of the Albanian Government (T. 8.5.14) with the "Government of Autonomous Epirus". But even while it was on the island men were being shipped across to the mainland to reinforce the "Epirots" (P.D.L. 17 : 229).

The Greeks were not inclined to court an invefligation of the situation by the Powers, or intervention by Italy and Auftria-Hungary, who, it was reported (T. 12.5.14), intended to occupy "Epirus" if negotiations broke down. On the 17th May, therefore, hoftilities were brought to a close by the "Disposition of Corfu". Southern Albania, as delimited by the Boundary Commission, was to be handed over to the Albanians, but the "Epirots" were accorded a measure of autonomy. The Commission was entrufted with the execution and maintenance of the "Disposition" (under the guarantee of the Powers), the organization of public adminiftration, finance, and juftice, and the delimitation of the provinces (of Korcha and Argyrocaftro), composing "Autonomous Epirus". The Albanian Government retained the right to appoint (and dismiss)—in agreement with the Commission—all governors and high officials in proportion to the relative ftrengths of the two religions. On this basis also a local gendarmerie was to be recruited which was to serve outside the province only in times of crisis (as recognized by the Commission). The employment of other than local military units in "Epirus" was prohibited except in time of war or revolution. Among the Orthodox communities religious education was to be exclusively in Greek, which was to be the language of inftruction in their schools, Albanian being, however, taught concurrently in the three elementary classes. Both languages were to be equally valid in all official departments. Provision was made for an amnefty and relief; and the Tchams were assured of all the privileges they had enjoyed while under Turkish rule (S.A. 49–50).

"The World War prevented the Great Powers from giving their formal assent to these provisions . . ." (G.C.), although the Greeks claimed (S.A. 49–50) that the agreement had been ratified by the representatives of the Great Powers at Athens on the 18th June, and by the Albanian Government on the 23rd June.

That the Albanian Government accepted these provisions cannot be interpreted (G.C.: see S.A. 167) as an admission by Albania that the south was entitled to an autonomous administration. It had no alternative but to agree to the arrangements which the Commission made, both because it was powerless to go to war with Greece, and in view both of the international and internal situation. The Greek Government regarded the "Disposition" as a temporary expedient which, while giving complete freedom to Greek propagandists, should last only until an opportunity to annex the area in question presented itself; while Sir Harry Lamb—and no doubt also the other members of the Commission—was aware that in negotiating with the "Government of Autonomous Epirus" he was treating actually with the representatives of the Hellenic Kingdom, and not with those of the Epirots or southern Albanians. The agreement, wrote Sir Harry Lamb, "was based on nothing real, and its ultimate destination seemed to me certain", namely, the scrap-heap. (For pronouncement to this effect by the Under-Secretary of State for Foreign Affairs, see P.D. 65 : 6.)

In the meantime propaganda had borne fruit in central Albania. Agents had been active in dissuading the Albanians from responding to Essad's appeal for volunteers (S.m/s. 42), and as it seems inconceivable that Essad should have worked to stir up an insurrection against himself, those agents were evidently in Greek pay. It would seem that Essad had thought it within his power to retain control of the situation in the districts in which his influence had been hitherto predominant; but that he underestimated the hostility towards him which had grown up even among those to whom he had looked for support. In any case, shortly after the distribution of arms, rumours gained currency in Durazzo that the central Albanians refused to "march against their brothers"—in other words, that they refused to go to the assistance of their Moslem compatriots in the south. Essad visited the disaffected regions and returned after a few days' absence to report that the disaffection was not serious (S.m/s. 74), and due mainly to the tactlessness of certain minor officials. But it was rumoured that actually he had been badly received in the interior and that the country was seething with hostility towards "Essad's tyrannical Government". On the 8th May he tendered his resignation, in an audience of the Prince at which Castoldi acted as interpreter, and offered to emigrate to America! But the Prince refused to accept it, believing him to be less dangerous as a responsible Minister than as a private individual.

On the 17th May an urgent telegram was received from the commander of a detachment of gendarmerie at Bazar Shjak, on the Tirana road, reporting that armed men were concentrating in the neighbourhood. During the preparations which were made to meet an attack Essad Pasha refused to allow Major Sluys—of the Dutch Mission and Commandant of Durazzo—to assume command of the Albanian artillery, which he entrusted to Captain Moltedo, an Italian, and demanded the resignation of Sluys. Whether this manœuvre was the outcome of Italian pressure or of anxiety on Essad's part to remove Sluys, whose sympathies were with the progressive Nationalists, is not clear. In any case, Prince William, at the instigation of Baron Aliotti, sent Mufid Libohova to Sluys to "grant him indefinite leave". Sluys prepared to leave Durazzo, but was persuaded by his friends to interview the Prince before doing so. The outcome of the interview was that Prince William was persuaded that Essad was a traitor, and agreed to his arrest (S.m/s. 75). This was fraught, however, with considerable danger. Whereas everyone else who had previously kept an armed retinue had reduced theirs to two or three men when the Prince had arrived, Essad had retained a considerable bodyguard. At his house were quartered about 30 armed men and at least 100 more elsewhere in the town. On the other hand, there were, at most, 200 armed Nationalists upon whose support the Prince could rely. It was considered, therefore, that unless Essad was surprised, he might resist arrest and seize the town, especially if he had time to call to his aid his adherents in the interior. In view of this eventuality, warships in the bay were warned that disturbances were anticipated, and an arrangement made whereby, at a given signal, naval detachments should be landed to protect the palace (A.m/s. xii. F.).

In the early hours of the 19th May, under the direction
of Major Sluys, a gun was trained upon Essad's house, which
was surrounded by gendarmerie and volunteers. Essad and
his men were then called upon to surrender. They refused
and prepared to resist. Major Sluys subsequently reported that
a shot was fired and one of his men wounded, whereupon, not
wishing to endanger the lives of his men, he ordered the
gunners to open fire. Three shells were fired, one exploding
in Essad's bedroom. Thereupon, so the story goes, his wife
appeared at a window waving a white sheet, and Essad agreed
to surrender. The question then arose whether he should be
imprisoned ashore or upon the Austro-Hungarian cruiser
Szigetvar, which had been placed at Prince William's disposal
for the purpose. Eventually the Prince decided upon the
latter course. Heaton Armstrong, with an Austro-Hungarian-
Italian naval detachment (for which the Pasha, fearing assassination, had asked), and the Dragomans of the Italian and
Austrian Legations, escorted him to the quay by (at his special
request) an indirect route, preparations for his assassination having been made along the route which it was expected
that he would follow. He arrived at the quay in safety, followed by a crowd which howled its disapproval at him, and
was handed over to Captain Schmidt of the *Szigetvar*.

Although everyone of consequence in Durazzo was convinced that Essad had conspired against Prince William, and
everyone except the Italians congratulated the Prince upon
his arrest (D.W.), there was no proof of his guilt, and therefore his trial by court martial would have been the logical
conclusion of the matter. This course was urged by the Dutch
officers, the Austro-Hungarian Minister, and by almost every
impartial person, but Baron Aliotti insisted that he should
be allowed to retire into exile without further investigation
(and brought pressure to bear to this end), which seems to
indicate that the Italians feared the outcome of any investigations. Meantime tension between the Austro-Hungarian and
Italian squadrons in the bay became acute (B.T. 264; also C.C.).
Prince William eventually accepted the advice of the Roumanian Minister, who for some unaccountable reason supported
the Italian proposal (S.m/s. 80). Essad was transhipped to an
Italian vessel on which he left for Bari, having signed the
following undertaking before his departure: "Je m'engage
sur ma parole d'officier de m'éloigner de l'Albanie et de ne

plus y retourner sans autorisation signée personnellement par Sa Majesté le Roi. Je m'engage aussi à me tenir loin de toute agitation intérieure ou extérieure" (D.W. Annex V). Upon his arrival in Italy he was taken to Rome, and there fêted (B.T. 264). No further investigation was ever made; and none of Essad Pasha's papers were examined (A.m/s. xiii; C.C. 146), the Prince being of the opinion that in the circumstances it was better to close the incident.

These events led to the resignation of the Cabinet. But Turkhan Pasha re-formed it as follows:

AKIF PASHA ELBASANI .	. Minister of the Interior and Minister for War.
MUFID BEY LIBOHOVA .	. Minister of Justice and Religion.
DR. TOURTOULIS BEY .	. Minister of Education.
PHILIPPE NOGGA . .	. Minister of Finance.
MIDHAT BEY FRASHERI	. Minister of Public Works.
ABDI BEY TOPTANI .	. Minister for Agriculture and Commerce.

Tourtoulis was subsequently succeeded by P. Poga.

In the meantime Durazzo was in confusion, but no further disturbance took place. The Palace was guarded by foreign naval detachments which had been landed within fifteen minutes of the bombardment of Essad's house. The arrival of two hundred armed men from Kruja, thought to be supporters of Essad Pasha, caused consternation, but having been interned overnight they were released on the 20th and made a demonstration of loyalty before the Palace.

Essad Pasha is generally believed to have brought about the insurrection in central Albania which ensued. But there is no evidence to this effect—in fact, rather to the contrary—unless indeed he actually encouraged a movement which was largely directed against himself and his class in the hope that Turkish power would be restored and with it his own authority. It is, however, probably beyond the power of any living mortal to unravel the tangled skein of intrigue behind the events which ensued.

"La vérité est que toute œuvre est, en ce moment, vouée d'avance en Albanie à un échec certain", wrote Prince Sturdza (S.m/s. 102). "Quelle que soit la méthode choisie, la complicité des voisins, grands et petits, se chargera de la déjouer. Soyez doux, d'innombrables

P

agents prêcheront la violence et l'insurrection, toutes les frontières laisseront filtrer des armes et des munitions, l'argent étranger sera à la disposition des agitateurs. Prenez les armes vous-mêmes, personne ne vous soutiendra, toutes les difficultés vous seront faites, vous resterez bientôt à court de tout."

For the fomentation of insurrection and anarchy everything was favourable. Among the peasantry there was profound disappointment that the Prince had surrounded himself with the landowning Beys (including Essad Pasha), who leased their land upon the most onerous terms to tenants who were little better than serfs, and in most cases were obliged to give their landlords one-third of their produce—frequently more. These wretched people had expected the Prince to perform miracles and instantly to redress their grievances. Their disappointment combined with their ignorance made them readily susceptible to propaganda; and of this fact the disgruntled Moslem priests, Turkish agitators, and the agents of Serbia, Greece, and Montenegro took full advantage. Italy also seems to have contributed to the trouble which ensued, although possibly to the extent only of intriguing to establish her prestige among the insurgent central Albanians in opposition to Austro-Hungarian influence among the northern tribes.

But on the whole the insurrection in central Albania seems to have been brought about by Turkish agitators, of whom Arif Hikmet (T. 25.5.14), an Albanian from Kalkandalen, appears to have been the chief. These agitators had spread reports to the effect that the Prince, who was described as a Jew (S.m/s. 73: a race much despised in Albania), intended to suppress Islamism (A.m/s.; C.C.); and this caused exasperation among the Moslem Bosniaks, which was shared by the Sunni Moslems, who considered such a step would be an infringement of their liberty. Moreover, many Moslems feared that the Prince, as a Christian, would overrule in favour of the Christian elements the social superiority which they, as Moslems, had enjoyed under the Turkish régime; and of this the agitators took full advantage, urging them to demand a restoration of Turkish suzerainty. Of the insurgent leaders, Musa Quasim (Mufti of Tirana) and Mustafa Ndroqa were the principal organizers, and Quamil Haxifeza of Elbasan

the commander-in-chief. It is alleged that Haxifeza was supplied with war materials by the Serbs at Ochrida, and was
assisted and advised by officers of neighbouring States,
including twenty Serbians (A.m/s. xxiv). Moreover, among
them were many of Essad Pasha's Redifs, trained and experienced troops. On the other hand, the Prince was unknown
to his people, and his prestige was entirely dependent upon
the fact that he was the sovereign whom the Powers had
chosen. But the Powers gave him neither moral nor material
support—in fact generally and very decidedly the contrary.
He had at his disposal only a handful of untrained gendarmerie
and undisciplined "Nationalists", and was otherwise entirely
dependent upon those tribesmen who chose to support him,
and foreign volunteers. Probably much of the support which
he obtained from the northern tribesmen (when they were
not preoccupied with the Serbs and Montenegrins) was due
to the arrest of Essad Pasha and the participation of his
Redifs in the insurrection.

On the 20th May serious disturbances were reported from
Tirana, where the loyalists in the town were surrounded and
besieged, but whether by Essadists who were indignant at
his arrest or whether by Essad's Redifs who had joined the
revolt against all Beys, is not clear. Accordingly the Kruja
men, and a body of Kossovons led by Isa Boletin, were
dispatched under Major Roelfsema to occupy the Rasbul
Hills commanding the approaches to Durazzo. (But in the
confusion which prevailed Roelfsema subsequently misunderstood an order and withdrew again to Durazzo. Sluys
allowed the mistake to stand, and in consequence forfeited
all freedom of action for the defence of the town.)
At the same time a detachment under Captain Saar, of 50
gendarmes, 200 Catholic malissori under Simon Doda, and a
machine and a mountain gun in charge of Prince Sturdza
and the Comte de Pimodan, was dispatched to Tirana.

When Bazar Shjak was reached the malissori refused,
despite Doda's entreaties, to go farther, probably because
they expected fighting and a violation of the general *besa*
which had been proclaimed on the arrival of the Prince and
which they had pledged themselves to maintain; probably
also they were reluctant to fight against compatriots with
whom they were not "in blood". They made frivolous excuses.
Saar therefore telegraphed to General de Weer for instructions,

and the latter, anticipating no bloodshed, ordered him to proceed (A.m/s. xiv). Saar pushed on with the gendarmerie and guns, hoping that should hostilities begin Doda's men would support him (S.m/s. 86).

Among the Bosniaks around Shjak the rumour had been spread that the Prince intended to expel them to Turkey on account of their fanaticism; and that he was a bloodthirsty tyrant whose sport it was to kill his subjects!

Shortly after leaving Shjak, Saar met a large body of these misguided Moslems, armed, as a matter of course, in accordance with the custom of the country. It appears that Saar, in ignorance of this custom, and aware that Sluys had prohibited the carrying of arms in the province of Tirana (S.m/s. 74), thought he was about to be attacked, and opened fire (B.T. 265). Thereupon he was attacked. After some sharp fighting against heavy odds he succeeded, with the aid of Sturdza's guns, in beating off his assailants. But he was surrounded, and ammunition for the guns was exhausted. The guns were abandoned and the detachment fought its way back to Shjak. But the bridge there was held in force by the enemy; and Saar, who had lost half his men, was obliged to surrender (S.m/s. 86).

Those who had worked to provoke an upheaval now proclaimed that the universal *besa* given to and by the Prince had been broken, an unpardonable crime; and central Albania rose in revolt with the intention of evicting those responsible for it. Mr. Chekrezi (secretary to the Commission) was sent upon several occasions to negotiate with the insurgents, and stated (C.C. 150) that the violation of the *besa* was the actual cause of the outbreak of the insurrection. At Kavaja, Slinza, Tirana, and elsewhere where the Moslem element had been led to believe that the national flag was a symbol of oppression, the Turkish flag was raised and the loyalists evicted or imprisoned. Many of the refugees from Dibra and Kossovo were led to believe that if the Prince was evicted the Serbs would restore their lands to them (B.T. 265). Thus misled, they threw in their lot with the insurgents who occupied the Rasbul Hills commanding Durazzo.

On the 23rd May the insurgents advanced upon Durazzo and drove in the outposts to the bridge across the marshes just beyond the town, which was held by 70 men under a

young German adventurer, Baron Gumppenberg. There were
in all only 150 men in the firing line, under Gumppenberg
and Roelfsema (who was captured by the rebels), and 100 in
reserve. The ships of the international squadron were forbidden to give any support to the Prince except to protect
his person. Moreover, the Austro-Hungarian Minister refused
to allow the Austro-Hungarian officers who had arrived to
instruct Albanian gunners to take any part unless the Prince
gave a written request to this effect, which he refused to do,
fearing complications with the Italians. The command of the
guns was therefore entrusted to Mr. Walford (a young
Englishman who had come to Durazzo on business), who
had as his subordinates Ekrem bey Vlora, two German commercial travellers (German reservists), and an Austro-Hungarian waiter (also a reservist). Indeed, all the foreign civilians
in the town co-operated gallantly in the defence except the
Italians, who were in force but refused to assist.

During the afternoon Baron Aliotti told the Prince that
the position was desperate, that the Italian detachment
guarding the Palace would be withdrawn, and that the insurgents were infuriated by the presence in Durazzo of
Catholic malissori who ought, in order to avert a massacre,
to be embarked and sent home. He urged the Prince to take
refuge on the Italian warship *Vittor Pisani*.

There is no doubt that this advice was given and a panic
created in order both to destroy Prince William's prestige and
to provide an opportunity for Captain Castoldi to examine
his papers (Heaton Armstrong declares that he saw Castoldi
in the act; A.m/s. xv). The Prince refused to accept Aliotti's
advice, although urged by the Cabinet to do so (D.W.). Von
Löwenthal at first supported the Prince in this, but subsequently supported Aliotti. Moreover, the malissori refused
to embark until he had done so, and the Princess to leave her
husband. In the circumstances the Prince finally decided to
escort his family on board the *Vittor Pisani*, and when the
malissori had embarked, to return ashore. But once he was on
board, the *Vittor Pisani* left her anchorage, despite his wishes,
and joined the remainder of the Italian squadron outside the
roadstead (W.N.).

Those are the details of Prince William's notorious "flight".
His prestige was undoubtedly compromised, as had been
intended, but that he did not lose the confidence of his sub-

jects is proved by subsequent events. The sequel was the
dismissal of Castoldi and (necessarily) Buchberger, who were,
however, compensated with the Order of the Albanian
Eagle.

Some hours after the Prince had become the virtual prisoner
of Italy, the Italian Admiral Trifari told him that the insurgents
had agreed not to enter the town if he would return to the
Palace and receive their spokesmen. This he did. During
the night Captain Saar and Prince Sturdza were sent to him
by the rebels with a demand for an amnesty, and a message
to the effect that unless it was granted and Saar and Sturdza
returned, all prisoners would be shot. The rebels also asked
to see the International Commission. The Prince sent Saar and
Sturdza back to Shjak with a letter granting an amnesty; and
a deputation led by Mehmed pasha Dralla (under the Italian
flag), and the Commission, went out to treat with them.

Meantime relations between the Austro-Hungarians and
Italians were strained almost to breaking-point. The Austro-
Hungarians had lost in the subtle game which had been
played; their squadron in the bay was inferior to that of the
Italians, Durazzo was surrounded by rebels who, consciously
or unconsciously, played the Italian game, and the arrival
of Austro-Hungarian reinforcements would have precipitated
war. Austria-Hungary was not then prepared to go to war,
and therefore, although wishing to support the Prince, was
compelled to act prudently. The Austro-Hungarian Minister
refused to allow any Austro-Hungarian armed men to remain
ashore that night except a machine-gun detachment (for the
protection of Austro-Hungarian subjects), which remained at
the landing-stage ready for immediate action, and the Italians
provided a guard for the Palace. Throughout the night the
rival squadrons lay in the bay, cleared (it is alleged) for action,
while an Albanian gun was laid upon the Italian Legation in
case of further Italian treachery. But the 24th May dawned
without further incident, and the crisis passed.

On the 28th May the Commission again visited Shjak.
It was well received by the insurgents, who demanded,
however, more schools, roads, and gendarmes, and Turkish
suzerainty. Kral, who acted as spokesman of the Commission,
told them that they could not have Turkish suzerainty, but
suggested that they should have the protection of Europe
as represented by the International Commission. This they

PRINCE WILLIAM, WITH PRINCESS SOPHIE AND THEIR CHILDREN,
INSPECTING ALBANIAN ARTILLERY

ESSAD PASHA (LEFT) AT DURAZZO, 1914

accepted, and agreed to release the prisoners and restore the guns captured with Saar; but no transport was sent to bring in the guns; they remained at Shjak, and were subsequently employed against Durazzo.

Some days later the Commission visited Kavaja, where it was well received; but the rebels refused to have any dealings with the Prince or his Government. At the beginning of June it again visited Shjak, but on this occasion was badly received; and the insurgents reiterated their demand that Prince William should leave the country and be replaced by a Moslem. Thereupon the Prince and his Government decided that the rebels—who had employed the amnesty to extend their power in other parts of the country—must be crushed by force. This, it was anticipated, would prove no difficult task. But the reluctance of the vast majority of the populace to take part in civil strife, and the effect of propaganda among the loyalists, were underestimated. Even the malissori who came to Durazzo protested their reluctance to fight compatriots with whom they were not "in blood", while in other parts of central Albania the rebels were allowed to occupy towns and villages unopposed, and junior officials continued to carry out their duties as if nothing had occurred (B.T. 272).

It was decided that operations against the insurgents should be undertaken by five different columns with the object of surrounding them (without bloodshed if possible), and of starving them into submission. Prenk Bib Doda Pasha agreed to operate from Alessio, where he claimed to have 5,000 to 7,000 men (for whom the Government was paying), although it is doubtful whether his forces were ever so strong. Small forces (1,000 to 1,500 men) were concentrated at Berat, Elbasan, and Valona; and Ahmed bey Zogu had 2,000 Moslem tribesmen at his disposal in Mati.

Ahmed Zogu (destined to become King) bore, until March, 1922, the surname Zogolli (Turkish: "olli", or "oly", or "ogli" = son of). He was born at Burgayet in Mati in 1895, the son of Djemal Zogolli, chieftain of Mati. Both his grandfather and father (who died when Ahmed was nine years of age) were Pashas in the Turkish service, and an ancestor had been Grand Vizier. Ahmed was educated at the preparatory school for officers at Monastir and at Galata Serai. When the Balkan War broke out he was at Constantinople, but hastily returned to Mati, where he organized resistance to the invading Serbs, who burnt Burgayet. He was present when the independence of Albania was proclaimed at Valona. Shortly after Prince William's arrival, Ahmed (then nineteen years old) sought an audience of him to make certain proposals regarding the convocation of a National Assembly. The Prince received him well, but his uncle, Essad Pasha, attempted to contrive his arrest (probably because he knew too much). The Prince indignantly intervened, and Ahmed returned to Mati.

On the 1st June 700 well-armed but undisciplined Catholic Mirdites arrived by sea with the courageous Bishop of Alessio. They were nominally commanded by Marco Gjoni (see below), "a close relative of Prenk's, who, however, had very little influence with his men and preferred the café to the trenches" (A.m/s. xvii). Naturally the arrival of these reinforcements displeased the Italians; and Aliotti declared that as their presence would enrage the Moslem rebels (T. 27.5.14) the Italian naval detachments guarding the Palace would be withdrawn unless they were sent away again. But the Prince, now less dependent upon the Powers, declared that unless international forces from Skutari were placed at his disposal (to which the Entente Powers would not agree) they would remain (D.W.).

A body of secret police had been formed in Durazzo of men of unquestionable patriotism. These police reported to Colonel Thomson (then Commandant of the town) that on several successive nights signalling from a house and answering signals from the Rasbul Hills had been noticed. The Austro-Hungarian Minister also reported that he had noticed signalling (S.m/s. 103). Accordingly, on the night of the 5th June, the house was surrounded by police under Captain Fabius, who arrested Colonel Mauriccio, Captain Moltedo, and Professor Chinigo. Aliotti at once and indignantly demanded their release, under the Capitulations (T.E. 117: although Albania was no longer Turkish territory, and therefore the Capitulations no longer applicable), and an apology from Colonel Thomson. Finally he had an audience of the Prince. The latter, in no position to refuse the demands of any Power, and believing therefore that only a conciliatory attitude was possible, advised Thomson to apologize. Thomson refused, and the Minister of Justice declared that he could not be dismissed (since he had been appointed by the Powers) before the Commission had investigated the case. Thomson produced fifteen witnesses to support him; but the Italians brought such pressure to bear against any investigation that the matter was dropped, although very compromising papers had been found in the possession of the arrested men! The Commission did nothing! (D.W.; T. 11.6.14.)

Another notable arrest was that of Djurashkovitch, formerly Essad's secretary (see above), believed to be an agent of Montenegro. The Djurashkovitches, a Montenegrin family, had fled to Albania from Prince Danilo in the middle of the nineteenth century, and had held official posts under the Turkish Government until 1912 (B.T. 31). Through the intervention of Russia the arrested man was released without trial!

This constant interference by the representatives of the Powers on behalf of their agents, and in furtherance of their own particular projects, paralysed the loyalists, and completed the confusion which prevailed in the town and in administrative circles.

Meantime a fresh exchange of views (T. 11.6.14) between Italy and Austria-Hungary had led to a temporary reconciliation (official only) between them. It was agreed that their respective representatives should be instructed to co-operate to maintain Prince William, but "to observe the greatest circumspection" in dealing with the International Commission of Control; also that the other four Powers, who had withdrawn their warships from the International Squadron, should be asked to send back a warship each to Durazzo—presumably to preserve an appearance of unanimity in Albanian affairs—and again to express to Albania's neighbours their determination to uphold the principles of the Conference of London. Accordingly H.M.S. *Defence*, with Admiral Troubridge on board, was ordered to Durazzo from the Bojana (P.D. 65 : 5), and French, Russian (T. 22.6.14), and German ships also arrived.

At dawn on the 15th June the rebels attacked, and fought with some determination. The attack was a surprise to all but the Italians (D.W.), who were so sure it would succeed that accounts of the fall of Durazzo were published in Italian newspapers! But the garrison had been reinforced by some foreign volunteers, among them several German and Austro-

Hungarian reserve officers, who manned the guns and broke the attack. During the fighting Prince William rode along the firing line encouraging his men, and was greeted with much enthusiasm. It was estimated that the insurgents lost some 200 killed, and the defenders 40 officers and men, including the gallant Colonel Thomson. Thomson had been Prince William's ablest servant, and was respected among loyalists and insurgents alike. Indeed, his funeral service, which was conducted by the chaplain of H.M.S. *Defence*, was attended by a number of rebels, who made their way into the town for the purpose! Thomson was succeeded by Major Kroon, the commander of the northern gendarmerie. He arrived by sea from Alessio with 1,000 men, who were inspected by the Prince.

It was now decided that a surprise attack should be made on the Rasbul Hills at dawn on the 18th, and the insurgents driven back to Tirana. There were now in Durazzo some 3,000 men, which was considered adequate for the purpose, since the insurgents were credited with no military organization. Actually the rebels, whose morale had been in no way shaken by their reverses, had entrenched themselves strongly, were equipped with machine guns carefully sited to cover their positions, and were warned of the attack in time to bring up reinforcements; whereas the Prince's force was wholly undisciplined, and the tribesmen quite unable to understand regular methods of attack. Moreover, there was much jealousy between the Dutch officers and the foreign volunteers.

The attack began six hours late, due, it seems, to petty quarrels (probably engineered) between rival Albanian commanders (the most culpable being Gjoni), who resented the interference of the Dutch and volunteers, and preferred to act in their customary leisurely manner in such circumstances. In consequence the attack failed, despite the gallantry of Isa Boletin and his Kossovons. A panic created among the Mirdites led to their precipitate retirement. Gjoni sought refuge in a café! The Mirdites subsequently blamed him for their defeat, and resentment of him became so pronounced that he was sent back to the north in case worse should befall him. The insurgents did not follow up their success. The loyalists sustained some 150 casualties.

Akif Pasha, acting entirely upon his own initiative, now

concluded an armistice with the insurgents. This was much resented by the Dutch, who considered it an admission of defeat, and feared it would enable the rebels to concentrate against Prenk Pasha.

Colonel Phillips, who had arrived on a visit from Skutari, went out to the insurgents, who had asked to speak to a British officer; but they were barely courteous to him. He reported that the five insurgent leaders whom he interviewed were certainly not Albanians, that one of them seemed to be a Greek priest, and another a Young Turk leader. He appealed to the rebels to accept Prince William as the choice of Europe. But the five leaders declared that only the Prince's eviction would satisfy them; and their subordinates, who at first seemed inclined to accept Phillips's proposal, at length decided to support their leaders' views (B.T. 272–3).

Some days later the rebels sent a message to the representatives of Great Britain, France, Italy, and Russia asking them to come to Shjak. (Bearing in mind that the Archduke Francis Ferdinand was assassinated on the 28th June, the fact that the representatives of Germany and Austria-Hungary were not asked is curiously significant). The representatives refused to go to Shjak, but invited the insurgent leaders to interview them on board ship (D.W.). But the leaders refused thus to reveal their identity (B.T. 273).

Prenk Pasha's advance from Alessio was delayed by Serbian and, it would seem, Italian intrigue (S.m/s. 109). Eventually, through the insistence of Major Kroon and Prince Sturdza, he agreed to move. Kroon was recalled to Durazzo (see above); but Sturdza, with Prenk and 1,500 men, advanced to Slinza, while 200 men masked Kruja. Beyond Slinza Prenk refused to advance, entrenched himself, and negotiated with the enemy. The majority of Prenk's bairaktars heartily disapproved of his attitude, but did not care to act against his wishes. Eventually Sturdza, losing patience, pressed on to the old Genoese fortress at Ishmi, which he bombarded and captured with the assistance of Noz Gjoni and Bairam Tsuri. Sturdza was recalled by his Government for interfering in Albanian affairs. Prenk's column eventually fell back to Alessio, and was disbanded (S.m/s. 108–26). Prenk then went to Durazzo to command the Mirdite forces there.

Zogu occupied Kruja and took up a strong position overlooking Tirana. But his men, like the Catholic Mirdites showed reluctance to shed blood in civil strife in which they had no personal interest, so the young chieftain negotiated with the insurgents. But negotiations broke down, and Zogu, too weak to attack Tirana single-handed, retired to Mati.

The Elbasan column advanced upon Tirana; but although it consisted partly of gendarmerie under Dutch officers, it was forced back to Elbasan and dispersed. Two Dutch officers fell into the hands of the rebels, but were subsequently released owing to British representations.

The Valona column advanced through the Muzakia Plain, a loyal district, and appears to have requisitioned supplies and committed acts of pillage which exasperated the inhabitants. While advancing up the Semeni River it was attacked by rebels, sustained a considerable number of casualties, lost its artillery, and retired precipitately whence it had come, pursued by the insurgents and by the now hostile inhabitants of Muzakia.

The column which advanced from Berat under Aziz pasha Vrioni fared no better. It was driven back to Berat, which was called upon to surrender by the rebels, who declared that they were supported by the Entente Powers (B.T. 274). But Berat refused to surrender, and was besieged. There were in the citadel some old British naval guns which Nelson had presented to Ali Pasha, and these were employed in the defence! After some sharp fighting the loyalists were driven from Berat, and retired to Korcha, where they were reinforced by the loyalists and gendarmerie in that town. The insurgents were twice repulsed, whereupon they called upon the Greeks for assistance, offering to hand over the town to them once it was captured. On the 10th July Korcha fell before a combined attack. Part of the garrison escaped with their guns to Valona.

These disasters to the Prince's cause were the outcome of propaganda, treason, indiscipline, and incompetence. Moreover, the Dutch officers and volunteers were ignorant of Albanian character and unable to adapt themselves to it, whereas the rebels were assisted by officers of Balkan States who understood it, and their forces included Essad's Redifs, who were trained and to some extent disciplined. The rebels under arms ultimately numbered at most 15,000, the loyalists perhaps 10,000 men, the vast majority of Albanians being completely bewildered by the situation (B.T. 272).

The loyalists showed no further activity except that on one or two occasions Kavaja was bombarded with one of the ubiquitous mountain guns from a vessel chartered from an Austro-Hungarian shipping company. The rebels made no further attempt to attack Durazzo—perhaps because a yet bigger game was being played by those who had urged them on hitherto.

Early in July the defending force was strengthened by several hundred disciplined Roumanian volunteers. Meantime, Turkhan Pasha toured western Europe (Libohova acting as Prime Minister) to beg proper support for the Prince, who, on the 10th July, addressed a Note to the Powers, asking them to fulfil their obligations in respect of Albania (D.W.).

Encouraged by the anarchy which prevailed, the Greeks had abrogated the "Disposition of Corfu", and resumed their fearful atrocities and systematic destruction in the south (E.B. 30 : 106; P.D. 62 : 418, 898, 1555; 64 : 97, 121-2, 1715; 65 : 5; etc.; Q.K. Annexes 6, 7, 8; S.m/s. 60; B.T. 262, 275; and compare with C.E.—Greek atrocities in Macedonia). Korcha, Klissura, Berat, and Tepeleni were occupied by "organized Greek forces". Speaking in the House of Commons on the 29th June, 1914, the late Colonel A. Herbert said:

"I have had telegrams from all classes and all creeds in Albania with regard to persecution. I have had letters from English and American missionaries. I have also heard—though I do not quote this because the information is not the most recent—from Mr. Bourchier, of *The Times*. Last of all, I have heard from phil-Hellenes who have the welfare of Greece at heart, and their evidence has, perhaps, been the worst of all. I will read it briefly. It is dated from Argyrocastro on the 18th June, 1914:

" 'The village of Kodra has been used as a slaughterhouse where groups of Mussulmans and Albanians were brought on different days, and there butchered. The reported massacre in the Christian Church of Kodra (Hormova) was only the last of the series. Here these poor men were shut up and regular Epirot soldiers climbed on the roof of the church, took off some tiles, and with their army rifles fired upon the defenceless people below. . . . The church we found even now, after two months, bathed in blood; and there were nearly 100 killed. . . . The day before, twenty-two were shot, defenceless shepherds; eleven other shepherds were killed some days before by a guerrilla band during the Greek occupation. Other graves of groups have been found. The Dutch doctor attached to the gendarmerie exhumed, counted, and reburied ninety-odd bodies. I have a list of 205 names of people killed at Kodra, and verified it. We found 30 women and children in the village Hormova, and 151 women and 159 children of Hormova in Tepeleni who had lost all their male relatives. We are told many others are being cared for in other villages. Their wailing and death songs and the cries of the children and babes at breast were the most terrible thing I have ever had the horror of witnessing. The Epirus Government admit nearly all the facts; but I am sure that the guilty parties are also higher up'" (P.D. 64 : 98).

These facts were subsequently confirmed by General de Weer in a grim official report (A.R. January–February, 1919. For text, see Q.K. Annex 6).

"I do not for a moment accuse the Greek Government of complicity in the murders," continued Colonel Herbert. "What I do say, of what I do accuse the Greek Government is this—of complicity in the machinery that has produced these results. There was a great deal more than mere connivance in opening the doors of the prison at Janina, and who was it that gave the criminals who were freed the weapons but the Greek Government? Who was it that allowed hundreds of armed Cretans to go about on their fell work? The Greek Government. . . . Who is it that year in and year out has been waging the most bitter propaganda? The Greek Government. Who had inside knowledge of everything that has happened? The Greek Government."

Almost two hundred villages were completely burnt, mainly in the Tepeleni, Klissura, Ersek, and Korcha districts; while many more, and the towns of Tepeleni and Leskovik, were partially destroyed (for details of destroyed villages, see

Q.K. Annexes 7 and 8; also map p. 164). About 150,000 men, women, and children were driven from their homes, which is proof indeed of their allegiance to Greece (*The Christian Work*, October, 1914). On the 27th November, 1916, Mehmed bey Konitza, then representative in London of the Vatra, presented to Lord Robert Cecil (Under-Secretary of State for Foreign Affairs) a Memorandum (A.Q.: reproduced A.R., October, 1918), in which he stated that

"in order to get rid of the Albanian population with a view to repopulating southern Albania with Greeks, Zographos and his Government ordered his bands to burn the whole region from Tepeleni to Korcha, and hundreds of villages were destroyed . . . and in order to deprive the unhappy population of any means of living, the bands at the same time burnt all the standing corn in the fields. These barbarous acts caused the death of thousands of women and children, who had to face the winter without either food or shelter" (*L'Illustration*, 7.4.27; Q.K. 5).

It is interesting to find that M. Cassavetti wrote in a book published in 1913, that is to say some months before this wanton destruction took place:

"Moreover, what further proof is needed of the non-Albanian character of northern Epirus than the wholesale burning and pillaging of their villages by the Albanian bands? Of the 150 villages in Epirus which have been destroyed, 45 lie in the disputed district of Delvino alone" (H.W.).

As it happens, there was little damage done in the Delvino district; the devastated area was farther north, and it is evident that M. Cassavetti underestimated the prowess of his compatriots, who penetrated very much farther into Albanian territory. But there were some Greeks by nationality settled in that particular neighbourhood, much probably explains why he chose to designate it in particular. His premature statement seems to indicate that this destruction was a premeditated act.

The Greeks endeavoured to terrorize into submission the Orthodox Albanians, and to drive out the whole Moslem population (*L'Illustration*, 20.1.17; Q.K. Annex 4; B.T. 267,

275-8; the majority of the destroyed villages lie in purely Moslem districts). Their intention seems to have been to destroy the influence of the Bektashis, who had largely contributed to their failure to foment religious animosity, and to exterminate those whom they could never assimilate. On the evidence of Colonel Herbert, General de Weer, Mr. F. Williams, United States Minister in Athens (Q.K. 6), and many others, the Albanians were guilty of no excesses.

Albania had few friends and no press. The Greeks were therefore unrestrained; and questions asked in the House of Commons were met by non-committal replies. Sir Mark Sykes inquired the source from which the troops of the "Government of Epirus" obtained machine guns and modern rifles, and whether they did so contrary to the wishes of the Greek Government. Sir Edward Grey replied that he had no information as to the source of supply, and that the Greek Government had "disclaimed all responsibility in the matter" (P.D. 63 : 1961). Mr. Stewart asked whether, in view of the admission of the Greek Minister at Durazzo that Cretan criminals were in Epirus, the Secretary of State for Foreign Affairs could say who was responsible for their release, and whether he would request the Greek Government to withdraw them (P.D. 65 : 5), while Mr. Gibbs asked whether he had any official or unofficial information of the number of Cretans landed at Santi Quaranta. But the reply was: "I have no information upon the subject from any source" (P.D. 65: 613). Mr. Shirley Benn asked the Secretary of State for Foreign Affairs whether he would ascertain whether the Greek Government proposed to hold Colonel Doulis "responsible for past massacres of Albanians", to which the reply was: "I have been informed by the Greek Government that Colonel Doulis has been struck off the list of officers of the Greek Army. He is therefore no longer responsible to them" (P.D. 65 : 7, 613; 63 : 1961).

In reply to a proposal by Colonel Herbert that he should send "Consuls or other qualified persons to the areas in question for the purpose of giving accurate information", Sir Edward Grey replied:

"Though His Majesty's Government are responsible, with the Governments of other Great Powers, for the creation of an autonomous Albania, I cannot admit responsibility for maintaining order there, and I do not wish to assume such responsibility by taking the measure which the Hon. Member suggests" (P.D. 63 : 1963).

Consuls, Sir Edward Grey subsequently explained in qualifying these remarks, could not be sent to Albania without escort, and "we have taken the line that we are not prepared to send British troops into Albania. On the other hand, if you are not prepared to send troops of your own to use force, you must, of course, stand aside when things are very bad and other Powers take a different view, and you must not object to the measures they propose to take. . . . The most I can say is that, while we are not prepared to do things ourselves, we are not going to obstruct the steps other people will take for themselves" (P.D. 64 : 122). Armed intervention by Italy and Austria-Hungary would not then have been opposed by Great Britain.

The question of intervention by Great Britain was debated with some heat in the House of Lords on the 28th July (P.D.L. 17 : 228–36). Lord Lamington said: "I should like to ask whether representations have been made to other Powers that we should join with them in the extension of the system which has operated so successfully in northern Albania. That is the only way that I know of by which you can save Albania." Viscount Morley (Lord President of the Council) replied: "The Albanian question is about as complex as any question that has ever faced a Government or various Governments together, and it cannot be dealt with in this trenchant, off-hand manner." The Marquess of Lansdowne, who was supported by Earl Loreburn, remarked: "I think my noble friend is entitled to ask not only that we should not object, but that we should be glad to co-operate with any Power who will make it their business to see that something is done to arrest the carnage that is going on in this unfortunate region." Viscount Morley replied: "I am willing to suggest that to Sir Edward Grey, but I am not sure that I should back it", where-upon Earl Loreburn exclaimed: "Then I greatly regret it, and I must say that it is a grossly inadequate answer for a Liberal Minister to make, because that is not the spirit in which we as a nation ought to approach these questions, especially in regard to populations where we have most properly undertaken some responsibility. I greatly regret what I would call a decadent answer."

Q

Lord Lamington said (P.D.L. 17 : 229) with reference to the atrocities: "Coming to the subject-matter of my question, which is based on a letter which has been corroborated by a great deal of other evidence, it would, perhaps, be as well if I read *in extenso* the contents of the letter. It runs:

" 'One cannot exaggerate the appalling atrocities that are being enacted by the Greek bands in the south. These bands are composed of Greek soldiers who remained behind when the Greeks nominally evacuated the south. They all wear their uniform with the badges removed, and are under their own officers. Yesterday it was reported that 60,000 Albanian refugees were crowding down to Valona from Berat and Korcha (which have now fallen to the Greeks) and the neighbourhood. An officer of the gendarmerie there, who arrived here to-day, reported that the number was more like 100,000, as the whole country was devastated, and the Albanians were killing their own wives and children to prevent them falling into the hands of the Greeks. They [the Greeks] have literally burned out the whole country-side to cover up all traces of their atrocities. This officer said it was almost impossible to believe what he had seen with his own eyes: streets full of naked bodies of women, each with the mark of strangulation, and little babies literally hacked to pieces with knives, the idea being to utterly exterminate the inhabitants.' "

The Powers could not entirely ignore these atrocities, and found themselves obliged to take some steps to adjust Albanian affairs. In reply to Colonel Herbert, who asked, in the House of Commons, whether the Secretary of State for Foreign Affairs had any information as to the massacres in Epirus, and whether definite steps would be taken by the Greek Government to terminate the unsatisfactory state of affairs therein, Sir Edward Grey replied:

"I have little to add to what I have already told the House on this subject. The accounts of what has occurred in southern Albania are very distressing, but I have received no details in regard to actual excesses or massacres, and such reports as have reached me as to the numbers that have been rendered homeless are from unofficial sources, which cannot all be considered as quite reliable. In Valona itself I hear from a private source that there are now some 12,000 refugees, but I fear that it cannot be doubted that in the country round thousands more are destitute and in urgent need of the necessities of life. Some proposals have been made for their immediate relief. The Italian Government informed me that they were prepared to send maize and other necessaries at once, and His Majesty's Government are ready to bear their share of the cost, if the other Powers do likewise. Furthermore, the Powers are considering the dispatch from Durazzo of an International Mission which will endeavour to elucidate past occurrences, and I trust contribute to the restoration of some sort of order and confidence. Such information as I have received that seemed trustworthy respecting excesses in Epirus I have brought to the knowledge of the Greek Government, pointing out that though I am convinced that M. Venizelos earnestly desires to prevent these occurrences, *the fact of their being due to Greeks*, however irresponsible, must produce a very unfavourable impression" (P.D. 65 : 1091-2; the British Government contributed £5,000 for the relief of the refugees (P.D. 65 : 1089), but it is significant that the latter were reported to have refused supplies offered by Italy (P.D.L. 17 : 232), presumably on account of Italy's complicity in the discomfiture of Prince William).

Although Greece continued to protest that she could be held in no way responsible for the acts of undisciplined bands operating in territory from which her troops had been withdrawn, the Powers now began to consider measures to restore order in southern Albania and strengthen the Government at Durazzo (P.D.L. 17 : 232-6). It is doubtful, however, whether adequate steps would have been taken without provoking a serious international crisis which would have precipitated the inevitable European upheaval. But the *casus belli* between the two great groups occurred beyond the Albanian borders.

Meantime Ismail Bey, having reached an understanding with San Giuliano (I.K. 384), returned to Valona. A few days later he left for Durazzo with fifteen notables of the

diſtrict to discuss the situation with the Prince. In a meeting
of notables over which the Prince presided, "I told him",
wrote Ismail Bey, "the conclusions we had come to and the
measures we deemed necessary." Briefly those were that
Albania should be divided into three cantons upon Swiss
lines, and entailed the withdrawal of the Prince, the dismissal
of the Cabinet, and the resumption by the International
Commission of the government of the country, proposals
which the Prince very naturally refused to discuss and which
were sharply rejected by those present, notably by Isa Boletin
(W.N.). In consequence, Ismail Bey, offended, subsequently
declared that the Prince "seemed incapable of making an
observation or putting a queſtion. . . ."

Ismail Bey returned to Valona, and there formed a "Committee of Public Safety" under his presidency. In an address
signed by thirty delegates of the refugees and inhabitants, the
Prince and Powers were notified of this ſtep, were entreated to
transfer the Government of Albania provisionally to the
International Commission of Control, and to take all steps
necessary in the critical circumſtances. It was added that this
was, in the opinion of the delegates, the only measure

> "that can keep the legitimate Sovereign on the throne,
> ensure national unity and territorial integrity, and save
> from deſtruction more than one hundred thousand human
> beings who, fleeing from fire and sword, have left their
> burnt and devaſtated homes and taken refuge in the only
> corner of Albania which remains free, the town of Valona
> and its neighbourhood" (I.K. 385).

But when Ismail Bey's proposals for tripartition of the
country, which would have entailed its division into Italian
and Auſtro-Hungarian spheres of influence and withdrawal
of the Prince, became more widely known, a ſtorm of indignation arose againſt him. He was declared a traitor, and was
obliged to leave the country secretly by night for Italy (W.N.).
He played no further part in Albanian hiſtory, and died at
Perugia early in 1918.

To check Ismail Bey's propaganda the Prince decided to
visit Valona. At midnight on the 25th July, and with great
secrecy, so that all possibility of a panic might be avoided, he
sailed with the Princess and their suite. They were met by a
guard of honour under Mr. Spencer, an English volunteer.

and were received with great enthusiasm by the townsfolk, whose faith in them remained unshaken. The Prince was met by deputations from all parts of the country which told fearful tales of atrocities, and appealed for aid against the invaders. The surrounding woods and hill-sides were crowded with refugees, whose wretched lot did not prevent them from giving him an enthusiastic reception. But the unfortunate ruler was powerless to justify their faith in him, although he called a conference of the Representatives of the Powers to discuss the situation on his return to Durazzo on the following day.

Meantime Zogu issued a manifesto in the name, he declared, of 150,000 Albanians, in which he proclaimed that the insurgents comprised only a small minority of the people, the majority being loyal to the Prince, and ready to support him; moreover, the insurrection had been promoted by foreign agitators, and consequently no self-respecting Albanian should identify himself with it (A.m/s. xxv). The insurgents, in a counter-proclamation, replied that all patriotic Albanians should join them in driving out the "foreign tyrant", and that they enjoyed the support of the Triple Entente. To what extent this last statement was justified is a matter of conjecture; the Russian Consul in Valona had, however, circulated a message that the Entente Powers did not wish the Albanians to support the Prince (B.T. 272), and evidence that various sections enjoyed respectively the support of Italy and the various Balkan States seems conclusive.

During the last days of July the International Squadron in the Bay of Durazzo gradually melted away, and the Italians soon found themselves the sole representatives of the Powers. But they did not take any immediate advantage of the situation, being anxious to avoid any action which might complicate their relations with Austria-Hungary, their nominal ally, before they came to terms with the Entente. The Prince's funds were almost exhausted, but although almost half the loan of £500,000 guaranteed by Italy and Austria-Hungary remained due, Italy refused to authorize the International Commission of Control to pay down further amounts, unless she was granted certain fishing, forest, and telegraph concessions, a price which the Prince refused to pay (W.N.). Austria-Hungary likewise refused her assistance, fearing to alienate Italy; but she intimated that if Prince William would declare war against Serbia, funds would be forthcoming. "But though I was persuaded," wrote the Prince, "just as all Albanians were, that the purely Albanian territories wrongly attributed and handed over to the Serbians, should be reincorporated with Albania, I was not able to give such assurances in view of the existing situation. For thereby Albania would have violated her neutrality, guaranteed in common by all the Great Powers" (D.W. and W.N.), a neutrality essential to her existence.

Among the refugees from Kossovo, and among the Kossovons in Durazzo, however, a plan to bring about a fresh insurrection in the Albanian regions recently annexed by Serbia was set on foot. Isa Boletin and Hassan Prishtina were among the principal instigators, and the plan was advocated by certain British friends of Albania, who never anticipated the participation of Great Britain in the war upon the side of Serbia (B.T. 277). Prince William, while sympathizing, disapproved of any movement which would involve his country in war on behalf of either side; but he was powerless to prevent it (A.m/s. xxx), and the Kossovons in Durazzo left for their homes to participate in the proposed revolt.

Zogu, despite his manifesto, remained inactive, being afraid perhaps to provoke Italy. Nor did the insurgents show any immediate activity, doubtless because those who had encouraged them hitherto now preferred to await the development of the international situation. In the meantime the garrison of Durazzo dwindled rapidly. The German and Austro-Hungarian volunteers left to join their respective armies. Many of the Albanian irregulars drifted away to their homes, and at the beginning of August the Dutch military mission was recalled to Holland. Durazzo was filled with the wildest rumours, while every night the insurgents indulged in desultory sniping, and occasionally raided the outposts. A committee of defence, consisting of two or three Austrians who had not been recalled, a Roumanian officer, and several bairaktars, was formed; but it was clear that the Prince's position was hopeless. On the 13th August funds came to an end, and everyone, including the German Minister, urged him to leave the country. But this he refused to do, hoping that assistance would be forthcoming from some source, although he sent away the ladies-in-waiting and his children on the 22nd August. Towards the end of August Valona was occupied by the insurgents, who did not, however, cause any disturbance. Upon their approach the Committee of Public Safety, under Osman Haggi, called an assembly of the townsfolk, of whom the majority decided that resistance would be futile; but a considerable number went to join the Prince at Durazzo.

The Prince's reluctance to depart was, however, displeasing to his foes. Accordingly, one night at the beginning of September, a detachment of insurgents brought up a gun, fired several shells into the town, and sent an ultimatum demanding his immediate departure. In the circumstances he saw no other course than to comply with the demand, since neither food nor money nor adequate forces to defend the town remained. Accordingly, on the 3rd September, he issued the following proclamation:

"Albanians!

"When your delegates came and offered me the crown of Albania I answered with confidence the call of a valiant and noble nation asking me to assist them in working for their national salvation.

"I came to you animated by an ardent desire to help you in this patriotic work. You have seen me doing my best from the very beginning to organize your country, and endeavouring to give you a good government. But the war which has broken out in Europe has added to the complications of our position.

"In the circumstances I have decided that in order not to leave unachieved the work to which I have resolved to dedicate my whole strength and my life, it is more useful if for some time I go to the west; but I want you to know that far away, just as while among you, I have no other thought than to work for the progress of your noble native country.

"Given at Durazzo, the third day of September, 1914.
            "(Signed) WILLIAM."

Upon the same day Prince William and the Princess embarked upon the *Misurata*, entrusting the Palace and their private effects to the International Commission of Control, which was then under the Presidency of the Italian Consul Galli, who promised to take care of them. They retired to Lugano, and thence to Germany. The Albanians watched the

Prince depart "with sadness, as if he were a hope that was perishing, a dream fading away" (I.K. 386). Although ruler of a neutral State, and therefore under no obligation to do so, he ultimately rejoined the German Army, probably hoping to retrieve a reputation which relentless and mendacious propaganda alone had shaken. He was attached to a Divisional Staff on the Eastern Front. In view of his attitude with regard to the neutrality of Albania, his return during the Austro-Hungarian occupation (see below) was not favoured.

Prince William never abdicated, reserved his rights, and renounced none of his claims to the throne. Albania remained therefore a Principality. But with regard to his return to his country, he wrote to the author on the 5th August, 1928: "I never intend to provoke dissensions among the Albanians, whose union, progress, and prosperity have been and are still my only aim, and so my return to Albania would necessarily presume a unanimous wish of the population" (W.N.). To that attitude he has firmly adhered since September, 1914.

CHAPTER VI

ALBANIA DURING THE GREAT WAR

THE assassination, on the 28th June, 1914, of the Archduke Francis Ferdinand and his wife at Sarajevo, by two Serb students (Austro-Hungarian subjects), led to a declaration of war by Austria-Hungary upon Serbia, on the 28th July. The late M. Stefan Raditch declared that Serbia *brought on the war* in order to get to the sea (N.E. 5.4.28); and it is becoming widely believed that this is the truth. With the question of war guilt this book is not concerned. It is, however, important that at the beginning of 1909 Russia was not prepared, and therefore induced the Serbian Government, which had almost precipitated war, to declare, on the 31st March, that it would change its attitude of hostility towards Austria-Hungary and in future maintain "good neighbourly relations" (E.B. 30: 329). Nevertheless the activities of the secret societies which worked in Serbia to stir up disaffection in Bosnia, and provoke Austria-Hungary, were redoubled. The most important of these was the powerful military clique known as the Black Hand. At its head was Colonel Dimitrijevitch, one of the regicides of 1903, and in 1914 Chief of the Intelligence Department of the Serbian General Staff. Of the activities of this society in Macedonia the Carnegie Commissioners wrote (C.E. 169):

> "*The worst crimes were committed by this secret organization, known to all the world, and under powerful protection. It was a distinct advantage for the regular Government to have under its hand an irresponsible power which, like this, soon became all-powerful, and which could always be disowned if necessary.*"

Colonel Dimitrijevitch instructed Major Tankositch to train Princip and Cabrinovitch to use their arms for the purpose of assassinating the Archduke, and to arrange for them to cross the frontier into Bosnia. M. Pasitch, the Prime Minister, informed the Cabinet of reported preparations at the end of May or beginning of June, but no adequate steps appear to have been taken to prevent them, or to warn the Austro-Hungarian Government of what was impending. Very naturally

Austria-Hungary addressed a "formidable document" to Serbia; and very naturally did she insist that Austro-Hungarian officials should participate in the investigations she demanded, since without this participation nothing derogatory to Serbia would have been revealed.

That Serbia fought for territorial aggrandizement, not in self-defence, is proved by her subsequent attitude both to Bulgaria and Albania. Had she been willing to gratify Bulgaria's legitimate claims to the newly named "South Serbia", the war would have been brought to a close very much sooner than it was. She regarded, and continues to regard, Albania as an abortive creation which has deprived her of territory, and persisted in an aggressive policy towards the new State (*Recent Revelations of European Diplomacy*, G. P. Gooch, London, 1927; "Is there a Slav Peril?" T. Lothrop Stoddard, *Boston Sunday Globe*, 9th August, 1914; *Causes of the War*, M. Bogitchevitch, Amsterdam, 1919; B.T., etc.).

News of the Austro-Hungarian declaration of war upon Serbia was received with satisfaction throughout Albania. The Serbs had ravaged the land and deprived the Albanians of their most prosperous districts. The latter hoped that the war would cause a diversion which would enable them to set their affairs in order, and some even that with Austro-Hungarian assistance they would be able to destroy the power of the Ottomanized Beys. Among the Nationalist leaders the prestige of Great Britain was, generally speaking, paramount; she was recognized as being the only Power disinterestedly anxious for the welfare of Albania, and responsible for turning the scales in her favour in 1913. The entry of Great Britain into the war against the Central Powers, especially when avowedly for the purpose of fulfilling a moral obligation no greater than that which she had incurred towards Albania, led to hesitation on the part of many who had considered an attack upon the Serbs; and internal affairs finally distracted their attention from Serbia, until that country drew it to herself again.

So much, then, for the general situation at the outbreak of war. But each region of Albania had its own peculiar situation. In the south, whence hailed the majority of the Nationalist leaders, including Ismail Kemal Bey, distrust of France and Russia was outweighed by the prestige of Great Britain. Moreover, Greece was the enemy, and in attempting to resist Greek and central Albanian insurgent incursions, and in providing for the starving and homeless refugees from the devastated areas, the southern Albanians were fully engaged. Central Albania, which was uncompromisingly hostile both to Austria-Hungary and Serbia, was in a state of anarchy, brought about by the causes and events described in the preceding chapter. In the north, the malissori, although they had been at one time within the Austro-Hungarian sphere of influence, were staunchly pro-British, owing to the influence among these primitive and grateful folk of Colonel Herbert, Miss Durham, and Colonel Phillips. The two latter had won their devotion by assisting the refugees from the Serbs and Monte-negrins, while Colonel Herbert had championed their cause in England.

The Albanians were, then, the potential allies of Great Britain. Had that country definitely guaranteed the integrity and independence of Albania, and had the Serbs, with the concurrence of Russia and France, declared themselves prepared to restore to the Albanians Dibra, Prizren, Djakova, and Ipek in return for Albanian support, that support would have been freely given.

Ismail Kemal Bey believed that, provided Albanian independence and a revision of the 1913 frontier were guaranteed, a national call to arms, especially if made on behalf of Great Britain, would meet with an immediate response, might unite the country in a national cause, and eliminate internal strife. He proposed, therefore, that Albania should enter the war upon the side of the Entente Powers, upon the condition that her independence, and a revision of her frontier with Serbia, were guaranteed. He proposed further that Colonel Herbert should undertake the task of organizing an Albanian army. But the integrity and independence of Albania were considered by Russia, France, and their protégé, Serbia, to be too great a price to pay. By those Powers the Treaty of London which embodied that guarantee, and to which they had appended their signatures, was already regarded as a mere "scrap of paper"; and Great Britain, whose scruples with regard to a better-known "scrap of paper" had ostensibly brought her into the war, allowed her allies their way with regard to Albania. Moreover, Greece, whose alliance the Entente Powers sought to obtain, would have been irrevocably alienated by the adoption of any project which entailed a guarantee to Albania of territorial integrity; and the Entente

Allies sought to lead Greece into the war by profuse promises of territorial expansion. These same difficulties presented themselves when in the autumn of 1915 Sir Edward Grey proposed that Miss Durham and others should recruit Albanian malissori, and through the opposition of France and Russia and in view of the existence of the Pact of London, the proposal was dropped (B.T. 284, 290).

Three days after Prince William of Wied left Durazzo the insurgents entered the town. The Turkish flag was raised, cheers given for the Sultan, and the Prince's supporters imprisoned. The Young Turks, the Serbs, and the Greeks had triumphed. The Young Turks imagined that Albania had been reclaimed for Turkey, and the Serbs and Greeks that she would be more easily partitioned if under Turkish rule than under European guarantee.

Once the object of the insurrection was achieved, there were indications of disagreement among the insurgents. A large number of Moslems whose religious fanaticism had been exploited persisted in their demand for a Moslem Prince, insisting, at the instigation of the Moslem clergy, that the sovereign should also be head of the Church; and the people of Shjak and Kavaja even went so far as to proclaim Prince Burhan Eddene King. There were others who were influenced less by religion than by fear that, with the abolition of Turkish rule, would disappear their privileges as Moslems : and, again, others who regarded Turkey as their natural protector against the Slavs. Then there were Essad Pasha's personal supporters, those who were little more than the agents of Italy, Serbia, and other States, and those—among them some of the Beys—who would acknowledge no overlord.

However, a Senate for central Albania, consisting of twenty-nine persons, was formed under the presidency of Mustafa Ndroqa, and the representatives of the Powers officially informed of its formation. A delegation led by Hadji Ali, a member of the Young Turk Committee of Union and Progress, and an enemy of Essad Pasha, was at once dispatched to Constantinople to offer the crown to the Sultan, or, should he refuse to accept it, to request him to nominate a Prince. The French, Austrian, and Italian members of the International Commission of Control who had remained after the departure of Prince William, were informed that their services were no longer required, and thought it discreet to leave.

These steps were regarded with the keenest disapproval both in northern and southern Albania, although at the instigation of Hadji Ali the Senate had definitely pronounced itself opposed to the return of Essad Pasha, a declaration which was appreciated throughout Albania.

Upon the outbreak of war, Colonel Phillips and the international force under his command evacuated Skutari, the various detachments—with the exception of the French, who went to Cettinje—being withdrawn to their respective countries. A Council of the Consuls of the Powers continued, however, to supervise the administration of the town and district, which was carried on by Albanian urban and district councils. Ded Soko returned to preside at Alessio. The remainder of northern Albania relapsed into its old state of local self-government, each bairak under its bairaktar and Mirdita under Prenk Bib Doda. The greater part of southern Albania remained under the scourge of the Epirot bands.

In the meantime Essad Pasha had not been idle. He still enjoyed the confidence of Italy as her agent in intrigue against Austria-Hungary, and probably intimated that provided she would continue to support him in his struggle for power he would suppress Austro-Hungarian intrigue in any territory under his sway and remain indifferent to any action she might take to safeguard her own interests in connection with Valona. It is alleged (D.W.) that he intimated also to Greece, Montenegro, and Serbia respectively his indifference to the fate of southern Albania, Skutari, and north-eastern Albania, provided those countries would acknowledge his sovereignty over central Albania and give him both moral and material assistance (E.B. 30: 106), an arrangement to which Italy does not seem to have been a party.

Essad met M. Pasitch in Nish at the beginning of September, made final arrangements, and was liberally supplied with funds and equipment (E.B. 30: 106). Then, no doubt with the assistance of the notorious Black Hand organization, he collected a considerable force, and arrived in Dibra on the 20th September, where he added to his column a large body of Dibrans, who believed that by assisting him they would be freed from the Serbian yoke.

In the meantime the Essadists in Durazzo, simulating patriotic sentiments, encouraged the Senate to send 4,000 men against the "Epirots", who had advanced northwards and occupied Berat. In their absence, Essad crossed the frontier with 5,000 men, marched rapidly westward, and entered Durazzo unopposed on the 2nd October. On the 5th he compelled the Senate to proclaim him President and Commander-in-Chief, by threatening, so the story goes, to shoot every member of it unless he was elected. Mustafa Ndroqa became Vice-President. Essad took possession of the Palace, and proceeded to sell Prince William's private property (D.W.)

Upon the day that Essad Pasha entered Durazzo, Baron Aliotti returned with Captain Castoldi, and publicly embraced him. Shortly afterwards, M. Krajewski, formerly the French Representative upon the International Commission of Control (a Polish Jew from Sarajevo) likewise returned to contribute to the Pasha's prosperity (B.T. 289).

Essad's *coup* aroused a storm of indignation. The majority of those who had rebelled against Prince William began to realize that the Pasha had duped them. Even among his own tenantry he was regarded as a tyrant; moreover, the minor Beys were fiercely jealous of their own power, and resented his usurpation of it. The central Albanians whom he had outwitted, demanded an explanation of the conditions upon which he had obtained his funds and equipment; and on the 23rd November, a demonstration against him, and in favour of reunion with Turkey, took place in Tirana. It should, however, be emphasized that while the whole population was opposed to Essad, it was by no means unanimously in favour of Turkey, and there is no doubt that much of the pro-Turkish feeling was created by a violent propaganda from Constantinople. Essad sent gendarmerie to arrest the ringleaders, and Quamil Haxhifeza was imprisoned. Thereupon the central Albanians, who had formerly rebelled against Prince William, rose against him. Tirana was seized by the populace and Essad's supporters imprisoned. The insurgents, joined now by many who had fought on behalf of Prince William, then marched upon Durazzo. Essad Pasha sought refuge upon an Italian warship in the bay, where he remained for several nights; but his men, supported by the fire of the Italian squadron (T. 5.1.15), were able to hold the town, which occupies an admirable position for defence against irregulars.

It is difficult to gather reliable information with regard to events at this period. It is, however, clear that the political leader of the insurrection was Musa Quasim, the Mufti of

Tirana, who had played a prominent rôle in the revolt against Prince William; while Haxhifeza's place seems to have been taken by one Hadji Quamil of Tirana, an extortionate and tyrannical upstart, who obtained control of the most fanatical section of the populace—among them many men who had served formerly in the Turkish Army—and terrorized the population of central Albania into submission to his will (N.D. *Recollections of Thanas Floqi*). It appears that, at their instigation, a meeting was convened of delegates from all those districts in insurrection against Essad, which appear to have been known as "the Union of Kruja." The delegates assembled on the 20th December under the presidency of Mehmed Gjinali, at Abdi bey Toptani's farm near Kruja. The articles passed at this meeting are recorded in a proclamation issued on the 29th December, 1914 (N.D. 13).

Therein it is set forth that it was the desire of the population of the Union either to be reincorporated in the Turkish Empire, or to make one of the Ottoman Princes King of Albania, but that the Government of Durazzo—presumably Essad Pasha's Government—had taken measures to prevent the realization of this desire. Accordingly the people had revolted again, with the intention of overthrowing the Government, and electing an Administrative Council "under no single leader", which should protect the rights of the people, and govern through local committees and under the direction of the Porte, until such time as the Turkish Government should appoint an Ottoman Prince as King of Albania, or the country should be reunited with Turkey. Provision was made for the arrival of a Turkish official to direct affairs. The intention to drive Essad from the country and nationalize his property, was declared. Compulsory military service was proclaimed, and, in view of the existence of courts of law to deal with blood debts, drastic legislation against the vendetta passed. The Dibra and Mati districts were boycotted, and no one permitted to pass from them into the territory of the Union. The Union never extended its influence to any of the mountain districts, which took no part on either side.

The districts united against Essad Pasha seem to have been administered through local committees by a "Committee of Public Welfare", with headquarters first at Shjak, and later at Tirana. This Committee, which was apparently controlled from without by he Mufti of Tirana and Hadji Quamil, and frequently changed its composition, was at one time composed as follows:

ABDULLAH RUSHDI (GJINALI)	.	President, and Delegate of Tirana.
MUHARREM NEGIATI .	. .	Delegate of Berat.
OMER LUFTI	. . .	Delegate of Fieri.
HAMID . .	. . .	Delegate of Shjak.
MEHMED HULUSI .	. . .	Delegate of Pekinj.
MEHMED .	. . .	Delegate of Kavaja.
AHMED AINI	. . .	Delegate of Lushnja.
HADJI NIKOLA	. . .	Delegate of Elbasan.

This Committee issued, on the 26th January, 1915, the following declaration of its policy (D.W. Annex VIII):

"To the Consuls of the Great Powers in Skutari.

"The Committee of Public Welfare, having ascertained that certain newspapers are attributing a criminal character to the movement against Durazzo, has the honour to inform the representatives of the Great Powers that the sole aim of the movement is to drive out of Durazzo Essad Pasha and his followers, who have usurped the power of the Government with the intention to make it subservient to their ambitious plans.

"The Committee protests in the strongest manner against the report published in the Press that it has expressed the wish to be placed under the control of the representatives of France and Serbia. Such a desire has absolutely never been expressed. The only object of this report is to deprive the Committee of the good will of Europe, for the enemies of the Committee do not hesitate to employ any means, even treachery and lying.

"The Committee assures the representatives of the Great Powers that on the entry of its soldiers into Durazzo, no attacks or excesses of any kind will be permitted against the lives of foreigners, or of natives who are engaged in their private business, or against their goods and property."

This declaration was signed "in the name of the whole population of Albania" and undoubtedly expressed the views of all but a handful of Albanians. Evidently the rumours which provoked this declaration had been spread by interested parties in preparation for a Serbian occupation of Albania.

The Albanian Committee governing Skutari had already denounced Essad, and forbidden him to enter the town. This Committee, under the presidency of Prenk Bib Doda, also governed San Giovanni di Medua and Alessio, Simon Doda being in command of the gendarmerie. Through the latter's ability, Essad's attempts to extend his authority, by bribery, to Alessio and Medua, were frustrated; but the propaganda of the Union of Kruja was not so easily suppressed, and caused a rising of certain Moslem elements, who believed that their security could only be assured by reunion with Turkey. Accordingly they demanded that the Turkish flag should be raised over Skutari, and some fighting ensued in the spring of 1915; but eventually the dispute was settled by Prenk, who compromised by replacing the national flag by one of red and black stripes.

It appears that at the beginning of May the Italian Consul in Skutari proposed to the Administrative Committee that a National Government should be formed, which should enjoy Italian support, but whether for the whole of Albania or only for Skutari is not clear, as the scheme never materialized. Prenk Pasha favoured the plan, but the Moslems, with the exception of Alush Lohja, an Essadist agent, were opposed to it (N.D. 64).

During February it seems that a meeting of notables was held at Elbasan, and at the instigation of a deputation from Constantinople (Turkey's policy being now identified with that of the Central Powers) drew up the following resolution in anticipation of an assembly which did not then take place:

> "In view of the great difficulties in the way of the appointment of a Prince of the Imperial Ottoman dynasty to be Prince of Albania, the National Assembly, in agreement with the Imperial Ottoman Government, resolves to accept with equal readiness a non-Moham-medan Prince, on condition that he shall be only a German Prince; and it resolves, with the consent of Germany, to request Prince William to accept the crown of Albania again" (D.W. 34).

It would seem that this step did not meet with the approval of the more fanatical elements led by Hadji Quamil and Musa Quasim, and that this incipient revival among the rebels of loyalty to Prince William was suppressed. But it remains

R

impossible to make any definite statement with regard to this incident, and unfortunately the Prince has mislaid documentary evidence which would further elucidate the matter. Turkey had changed her policy in Albania and declared in favour of the Prince in September, 1914; and her activity at this juncture was probably due to the negotiations of the Central Powers for the support of Roumania and Bulgaria (Roumania desired the restoration of Prince William owing to his connection with the Roumanian Royal House, while Bulgaria was opposed to the restoration of Turkish power in the Peninsula). Further, Turkey was probably aware that a Moslem Prince would be unacceptable to the majority of Albanians, who would be alienated by his appointment, and that would have been contrary to her own and her allies' interests in the war with the Entente Powers.

In the early spring Essad Pasha attempted to assume the offensive, and some fighting ensued between his forces and those of the Union. Essad's troops were driven back into Durazzo. Thereupon, in pursuance of some obscure political manœuvre—possibly in connection with Italy's negotiations with Austria-Hungary—Aliotti was withdrawn from Durazzo, and was accompanied by almost the whole Italian colony. Moreover, the Italian Government prohibited the exportation to Essad Pasha of arms from Montenegro. The French Minister, M. de Fontenay, who had been accredited to Durazzo, likewise withdrew. Shortly afterwards, however, presumably when Italy had definitely committed herself to alliance with the Entente Powers under the terms of the Pact of London, the Italians returned, and it was only with their assistance that Essad succeeded in remaining in Durazzo. An Italian torpedo-boat was even placed at his disposal to enable him to move his troops along the coast (D.W.).

Meantime the tide of international affairs engulfed Albania, and she became a battlefield.

During the first year of the war the attitude of the Powers towards the Albanian question was governed principally by their anxiety to win the support of Italy and Greece, then neutral, to their respective sides. During September, 1914, Italy began to consider the advisability of securing her position in the Adriatic by occupying the rocky island of Saseno, commanding the entrance to Valona Bay, the key to the Adriatic. Austria-Hungary sought therein a means of preserving the solidarity of the Triple Alliance by agreeing thereto, provided a public declaration was made to the effect that the occupation had been agreed to by the three Powers of the Alliance. Moreover, Austria-Hungary saw in Italy's uneasiness with regard to Albania a means of compensating her for possible Austro-Hungarian expansion in other parts of the Balkan Peninsula, while she feared that Italy might consider it advantageous, or even necessary, to combine with the Triple Entente for the preservation of Italian interests or security. Italy, on the other hand, feared that either Austria-Hungary or Greece, or both, might forestall her in Albania, and expressed her intention, as the only Power signatory to the Treaty of London who remained neutral, to uphold Albanian integrity and independence (S.A. 53).

In the meantime, the chaotic state to which they had succeeded in reducing southern Albania, proved an irresistible temptation to the Greeks. Accordingly M. Venizelos declared, on the 23rd August, and with full authority, that the place of Greece "was at the side of the Powers of the Entente" (E.B. 32: 305), the guarantors of Greek independence. Thereby he won the agreement of Sir Edward Grey, supported by France and Russia, to a proposal that Greece should send troops into southern Albania, and should occupy Argyrocastro "to preserve order" (T. 27.10.14), provided she agreed to an Italian occupation of Valona, recognized the temporary nature of the concession, and agreed to withdraw whenever the Powers requested her to do so. Sir Edward doubtless considered—if indeed he did consider the matter—that while Greek troops were in occupation, responsibility for outrages could be attributed to the Greek Government, and that, therefore, there would be less probability of their occurrence than if southern Albania remained at the mercy of unofficial Greek machinations, and the ravages of Greek bands; moreover, it was hoped that the concession would induce Greece to act in accordance with the spirit of M. Venizelos's declaration, and of her Treaty of Alliance, concluded at Salonika on the 1st June, 1913, with Serbia, in anticipation of a favourable re-consideration of her claims at the Peace Conference. Signor Salandra, the Italian Prime Minister, when approached in the matter by the British Government, refused to accept the suggestion of a direct understanding with Greece regarding even a temporary occupation of southern Albania, but agreed not to oppose the execution of police duties therein by one Greek regiment, noted M. Venizelos's undertaking to withdraw again when required to do so, and reserved the right to act at Valona as the welfare of the refugees therein required; but he emphasized that these measures and concessions were temporary only, and without prejudice to the inviolability of the decisions which had been made by the Conference of Ambassadors in London (S.A. 53-4).

Once Greece had obtained this concession, the King, supported by a large party, refused to lead his country into the war, being firmly convinced of the ultimately inevitable victory of Germany. On the other hand, M. Venizelos, tempted by profuse promises of territorial concessions made by the Entente Powers, and convinced of their ultimate victory, was anxious, so he professed, that his country should fulfil her moral obligations to them. Greece became divided into two camps, the Venizelists and the Royalists, neither strong enough definitely to establish its ascendancy over the other. And although the Venizelists joined the Entente Powers in September, 1916, she was not finally coerced, cajoled, and led by lavish promises of territorial aggrandizement, to abandon neutrality until the 29th June, 1917, when she officially declared war against the Central Powers.

During the late autumn and early winter of 1914, Greek troops officially reoccupied southern Albania, including the towns of Korcha, Argyrocastro, and Tepeleni, and a military administration was established. M. Venizelos declared to the Greek Chamber that the occupation was effected to preserve order only, that it was not to be regarded as an annexation, and that its primary object was to secure the application of the Corfu Agreement.

Throughout the negotiations conducted by the Entente Powers with Greece, in a fruitless endeavour to wean her from the vacillating and pro-German policy which she pursued, southern Albania, despite the solemn undertakings of 1913, played the part of a pawn, as likewise it did between Greece and the Central Powers; and with a scarcely moral inconsistency, which cannot be excused on the grounds that a group of Moslem Albanians had fallen under Turkish influence, the Triple Entente, while avowedly fighting for the freedom of small nations, showed their readiness to barter away the patrimony of the smallest and most recently emancipated, in the name of expediency. On the 22nd November, 1914, southern Albania, exclusive of Valona, was offered to Greece in return for her immediate participation in the struggle, but fear of Bulgaria was stronger than avarice (S.A. 56). The same area was again employed as a bait in the spring of 1915, but to Greece, who shared with other Balkan countries the opinion that it is difficult to override *le fait accompli*, the bait was not sufficiently attractive now that she already held it! Indeed, M. Venizelos declared to the Greek Chamber in August, 1915, that "only colossal faults" could separate "Northern Epirus" from Greece (S.A. 57), so confident was he that the temporary occupation would become permanent!

In December of the same year the Greek authorities contrived the return by the small pro-Greek minority of "deputies" to the Greek Chamber, with a mandate to secure international recognition of the union of southern Albania with Greece (Q.K. Annex 19). These "deputies" took their seats in the Chamber on the 11th January, 1916, and this step was followed, in February, by the substitution of civil for military officials. In April the signature of a royal decree annexing "Northern Epirus" was announced, while the Greek Prime Minister, M. Skoulidis, declared to the Chamber "his conviction that northern Epirus with its present frontiers constituted an integral part of the kingdom of Greece" (S.A. 62).

But Greece had overestimated the preoccupation of the Entente Powers, who demanded an explanation, to which the Greek Government replied that it had been considered necessary to replace the military by civil authorities. In reply to a second Note from the Entente, which pointed out that the action of Greece was incompatible with the decision of the Powers with regard to southern Albania, the Greek Government protested that it had been considered necessary to give "Epirus" a voice in the Chamber to sanction the taxes imposed to meet the cost of its administration. However, the upshot of this correspondence was that Greece was compelled to exclude the "Epirot deputies" from the Chamber (S.A. 62–3).

In the meantime Italy, although she had agreed to the Greek occupation, which she did not deem it wise to oppose, and thereby isolate herself—since neither the Entente nor Central Powers, being anxious to conciliate Greece, would support her in so doing—could not regard it with equanimity; and her anxiety was accentuated by the international situation, the increasing possibility of a rupture with Austria-Hungary, and the doubtful attitude of Greece.

It was to counteract the growth of Austro-Hungarian influence in Albania that Italy had supported Essad Pasha; and it was to prevent the Austro-Hungarians from establishing themselves at Durazzo that an Italian squadron watched the port. Likewise she feared that the Greeks, "or one of the belligerent Powers, might occupy Valona, which would be a serious menace to Italian security" (E.B. 31 : 621).

As a precautionary measure, therefore, the island of Saseno was occupied by Italian marines on the 30th October. But this step did not provide adequate security either against a possible occupation of Valona by the Greeks, or against the Austro-Hungarians, who enjoyed temporary success in Serbia during November. The Italian Government "called Austria-Hungary's attention to the fact that the invasion of Serbia tended to destroy the balance of power in the Balkans; Art. 7 of the Triple Alliance Treaty gave Italy in these circumstances a right to compensation" (E.B. 31 : 621). But the Austro-Hungarian Government at first rejected the Italian claim, and, accordingly, on the 26th December, 1914, Italian sailors and the 10th Regiment of Bersaglieri (A.A.) landed at Valona, the Italian Government having previously attempted to give a semblance of legitimacy to the act by obtaining from Essad Pasha an invitation to occupy the port (S.A. 54). Both France and Russia approved of the step, regarding it as an act directed against the Central Powers. The occupation was unopposed, and Osman Haggi continued to act as civil governor.

Although technically the occupation of Valona by the Italians was a violation of Albanian neutrality, it is difficult to see what alternative course was open to them, since Albania was in no position to defend her neutrality, and had no Government to define her policy or suppress intrigues within her borders by Powers hostile to Italy. And the possibility of an occupation of the port by the Greeks, especially while they remained benevolent to Austria-Hungary, constituted a menace to Italian security which Italy could not disregard. It seems that at this early stage the occupation was purely a precautionary measure, although Italy was, no doubt, glad of a pretext upon which to assure her possession of Valona, should Albania be partitioned.

While Essad Pasha remained besieged at Durazzo, the

remainder of central and northern Albania enjoyed a period of tranquillity. But it was of brief duration.

The Montenegrins had, on the 5th August, 1914, entered the war against the Central Powers for one purpose only, namely, territorial aggrandizement. They were of no material assistance to the Serbs, nor did King Nicholas ever intend them to be, since he himself aspired to the throne of Great Serbia, and military operations against the Austro-Hungarians were soon brought to an end. The Serbs, on the other hand, had, at the close of 1914, defeated three Austro-Hungarian offensives. These successes were in part due to Putnik's clever strategy, the tenacity of his veterans of the Balkan Wars, and natural topographical advantages which the Serbs enjoyed; and in part to the incompetence of Potiorek, his persistent underestimation of his opponents, and the diversion caused by the Russians, who absorbed the attention of the greater part of the Austro-Hungarian Army.

From January to October, 1915, comparative tranquillity reigned upon the Serbo-Montenegrin front. The opposing forces were exhausted, and their ranks were decimated by typhus. Both sides pressed forward the work of reorganization; and the Central Powers negotiated feverishly for the active support of Bulgaria, to whom the Serbs persistently refused to make concessions, flushed as they were with their successes. Indeed, they actually proposed to attack Bulgaria before she was prepared for war, but were restrained by the Entente Powers.

But the preoccupation of the Entente Powers, and the precedent which they had created in agreeing to the occupation of southern Albania and Valona by Greece and Italy, the fact that the Central Powers who had been mainly responsible for the creation of an independent Albania were the enemy, the equivocal position of Italy between the two belligerent groups, and the chaotic state of the country, tempted Serbia and Montenegro to stake out claims in Albania.

Of the two Serb States, Montenegro was the first to take the initiative, and in so doing she was supported by the French. Russia, indignant at the precipitation of the Balkan War by Montenegro, before she herself was prepared for war, and without her sanction, had withdrawn her military mission from Montenegro, and concentrated upon Serbia as the instrument of her future policy. The Russian mission had been replaced by a Serbian mission under General Yankovitch, the Serbs hoping that through it they might obtain control of the Montenegrin forces, in furtherance of their aspirations to ascendancy in the projected Great Serbia. Meantime France, in opposition to Italy, had been striving to establish her prestige in Montenegro, and when the International Force was withdrawn from Skutari at the end of July, the French detachment was sent to Cettinje to flatter King Nicholas by acting as his bodyguard. Moreover, the French Minister publicly apologized to Nicholas for the participation of French warships in the international naval demonstration off the Montenegrin coast in April, 1913!

King Nicholas, in declaring war against Austria-Hungary, had as his principal object the seizure of northern Albania north of the Drin, and hoped that meantime the attention of the Powers would be distracted by their own affairs.

Beginning on the 24th September, Montenegro sent a series of Notes to the Entente Powers, attempting to establish grievances against the Albanians, an attempt which, being without foundation in fact, signally failed. It was declared that the Albanians, led by Austro-Hungarian officers, were preparing to attack the Montenegrins, while Montenegrin agents were sent into Albania to cause some incident which might afford a pretext for hostilities. An alleged projected attack by 10,000 Albanians under Austro-Hungarian officers upon Djakova was eventually reported as an incident in which two Montenegrins were alleged to have been killed.

The British Government, through Count de Salis, the British Minister, protested strongly against this tendency to ignore the Austro-Hungarians and provoke hostilities with a neighbouring State, and in reply received both from King Nicholas and his Prime Minister, M. Plamenetz, the most definite assurances that Montenegro had no intention of attacking the Albanians. Nevertheless, in the spring of 1915, Nicholas set to work systematically to pick a quarrel with them. He complained that they levied an illegitimate tax upon supplies for the Montenegrin Army, which were brought up the Bojana River; but this charge was pronounced unfounded by the Council of Consuls at Skutari. Thereupon an attack by a notorious band of Albanian outlaws upon a Montenegrin convoy passing up the Bojana was engineered by Montenegrin agents, and employed as the pretext for the invasion of Albania.

On the 11th June, 1915, the Montenegrin Army crossed the frontier. A column operating between Lake Skutari and the sea occupied Mt. Tarabosh, commanding Skutari, and seized strategic points on the Bojana "to ensure free passage". King Nicholas again declared he had no intention of occupying Skutari, but communications between the town and the remainder of Europe were cut. Another column advanced through Kastrati and Klementi, and although fiercely opposed by the tribesmen, succeeded, on the 26th June, in occupying the positions held during the siege of Skutari in 1912–13. On the 27th the inhabitants, being quite unarmed, considered it discreet to surrender, and the Montenegrin Army occupied the town. Nicholas declared that the Skutarenes had petitioned him to enter, but actually, a few days previously, they had addressed an appeal to Sir Edward Grey, begging him to protect them from the undisciplined rabble descending upon them.

On the 28th June, Great Britain, Italy, and Russia, who refused to recognize the occupation of Skutari, lodged an emphatic protest in Cettinje against operations in Albania, which were contrary to the interests of the Allies, in that first they engaged troops which should have been employed against the Austro-Hungarians—a fact of which the latter did not take advantage, in view of secret negotiations in progress for a separate peace—and secondly that they aroused the hostility of the Albanians, and created a fertile soil for Austro-Hungarian propaganda in the Serbo-Montenegrin rear. France did not participate in this protest. Indeed, she did everything possible to obstruct it, and continued secretly to support King Nicholas.

Although, in her reply of the 30th June, Montenegro gave an assurance that she would undertake no further operations in Albania, operations continued with the object of subduing all Albania north of the Drin. Heavy fighting took place throughout July, the Montenegrins being by no means always victorious. Eventually a truce was concluded, but Skutari remained under Montenegrin occupation.

It seems that after the truce, Isa Boletin and his family went to Podgoritza, either to negotiate with the Montenegrins or to seek refuge from the Serbs and Essadists. Possibly he was induced to go there by the Montenegrins, who contemplated gaining his support in their intrigues to establish their predominance in the projected Great Serbia; or, more probably, they treacherously induced him to place himself in their power. In any case they provoked a dispute which led to a fight in the town. Isa, his sons, and two or three others, nine men in all, defended themselves against overwhelming odds for three hours before they fell.

Meantime Serbian troops crossed the frontier on the 12th June. Like the Montenegrins, they seem to have anticipated a separate peace with Austria-Hungary, and were under the impression that she would never again dare to attack them! Ahmed Zogu manned the passes of Mati, but the Serbs did not molest him; and it seems possible that, in view of the fact that his brother Djelal was with Essad Pasha, some understanding to this effect existed. Nor did the Serbs attack Mirdita. But fierce fighting took place between the forces of the Union of Kruja, under Hadji Quamil, and the invaders. The forces of the Union were reinforced by many Nationalists, among them a number who had been imprisoned by the insurgents until a few days previously, who spontaneously rallied to resist the hereditary foe. The Serbs soon, however, occupied Pogradets, Elbasan, Tirana, Kavaja, and Ishmi, but in agreement with Essad, and in view of the complications which might have ensued with Italy, they did not occupy Durazzo. Hadji Quamil, Musa Quasim, Quamil Feiza—an emissary from Constantinople—and several other leaders were captured and sent to Durazzo, where, with Quamil Haxhifeza, they were tried by a court under the presidency of Djelal Zogu, and executed by order of Essad Pasha (W.N.). The forces of the Union were scattered, and Essad established as Dictator of central Albania; but his power was entirely dependent upon the proximity of the Serbs, and was never extended to Mati and Mirdita. Indeed, it was reported (T. 3.9.15) that his troops were defeated with heavy losses by the Mirdites during September.

In view of the violent protests of their allies, the Serbs satisfied themselves with the occupation of a strategic line commanding the coastal plains, and remained in occupation until October, when the Austro-Hungarians resumed the offensive in the north. They then withdrew their troops, which they had so unwisely sent into Albania, and the Albanians harassed them fiercely as they retired, thereby rendering invaluable assistance to the Central Powers (D.W.).

The Serbs had attempted to legitimize their invasion by concluding a Military and Economic Convention with Essad Pasha (O.J. Sept. 1921 : 736). This manœuvre enabled them to claim that they were justified in attacking his opponents, who had declared themselves subservient to Turkey, and deny that they were violating the neutrality of Albania as guaranteed by the Conference of Ambassadors in 1913, because Essad, in concluding the Convention, had repudiated it; and it was on this basis that they subsequently attempted to justify their claims to Albanian territory, both at the Peace Conference and before the League of Nations.

In explanation of their invasion, M. Yovanovitch declared before the Council of the League of Nations on the 25th June, 1921 :

"When the war began in 1914, we noticed a certain amount of agitation in Albania, accompanied by various preparations. The enemy was preparing to attack us from this side. . . . The enemy was eventually successful. In fact, an armed force attacked us in May, 1915, with a view to cutting our communications, these being at that time the only ones which were left to us for keeping touch with our allies at Salonika" (O.J. Sept. 1921 : 736).

The Allies were not, however, at Salonika in May, 1915!

It may, perhaps, be said that Serbia was justified in attempting to open an alternative line of communication with her allies through Albania, in case Greece should close the line to Salonika; but had she abandoned her intrigues with Essad Pasha, there is no doubt that this could have been effected with the aid of a British mission, judicious propaganda, and a conciliatory policy, since the pro-Turkish minority was very small. That preparations, on a scale large enough to justify the invasion, were being made in Albania to attack Serbia, is quite out of the question in view of the chaotic state of the country (N.D. : *Recollections of Thanas Floqi*), and the absence of any means of direct communication between Albania and the Central Powers or Turkey; and if raids by armed bands into Serbia were under contemplation, or, indeed, did take place as alleged (T. 15.2.15), it would have been simpler to repel them, than to violate the principle of economy of force by occupying the land with large forces, and arousing the active hostility of the whole population. If the Serbs were, indeed, attacked by Albanians, those Albanians were their own oppressed subjects of Kossovo under Hassan Prishtina and Isa Boletin, striking once again a blow for liberty. There were no Austro-Hungarian officers with Hadji Quamil's forces, as was alleged (T. 17.6.15).

Meantime Italy, like Greece, Bulgaria, and Roumania, enjoyed a position of which she sought to take advantage. She considered herself absolved from her obligations to the Central Powers, incurred by the Triple Alliance Treaty, because (1) the Alliance being essentially defensive in character, and based on the maintenance of the territorial *status quo*, Italy was not bound to assist her allies in an aggressive policy; (2) Austria-Hungary had failed to come to an understanding with her before taking action, (3) had given her no opportunity to exercise diplomatic action in favour of peace; and (4) she had not been warned of the intentions of her allies in time to take the necessary military measures.

On the other hand, a movement grew rapidly in favour of intervention upon the side of the Entente. Both

> "Signor Salandra and Baron Sonnino were determined that Italy should not emerge from the European conflict without realizing at least a part of her aspirations, acquiring some of the Italian districts of Austria-Hungary, and correcting the inquitous frontiers of 1866, designed to leave the country at the mercy of invasion" (E.B. 31: 621).

Accordingly, Italy demanded extensive concessions as the price of her neutrality. But Austria-Hungary at first refused to make concessions, and then, when she eventually agreed to do so, contested every point of the Italian demands, before she yielded, hoping the while that the military situation would improve and enable her to adopt a more resolute attitude.

In these negotiations the question of Albania played an important part. During January, 1915, Sonnino expressed the opinion "that Italy's interests in Albania consisted solely in preventing others from gaining a foothold there, but not in establishing herself on Albanian soil" (S.A. 58), while Austria-Hungary maintained that in view of the Italian occupation of Valona, she was entitled to compensation. Italy protested that the occupation was merely a provisional measure, which she, as the only neutral European Power, had taken to preserve Albanian integrity, that she adhered to her agreement with Austria-Hungary regarding Albania, and intended to uphold the decisions made by the Conference of Ambassadors. But a large section of Italian public opinion was in favour of the annexation of Valona, and to this view it seems that Sonnino subsequently inclined.

On the 29th March Austria-Hungary made an attempt to secure the benevolent neutrality of Italy, and freedom of action in the Balkans—except in Albania, in regard to which country she confirmed the Italian attitude as outlined above—by an offer to cede the southern Tyrol to Italy. But Italy replied that she could not give Austria-Hungary freedom of action in the remainder of the Peninsula, unless the latter declared her complete disinterestedness in Albania; and, moreover, that in view of the dependence of her industries upon an uninterrupted supply of raw materials, she could only observe strict neutrality, since benevolent neutrality might result in the closing of the Straits of Gibraltar by Great Britain, and in consequence a shortage of supplies. Italy declared that she would remain neutral upon certain conditions, which included the unreserved renunciation by Austria-Hungary of her interests in Albania, and her recognition of Italy's unrestricted sovereignty over Valona, Saseno, and a strategic hinterland. But Austria-Hungary, while declaring her readiness to discuss their respective interests in Albania, protested the impossibility of renouncing her own rights in a country "so very close to the sphere of Austria-Hungary's most vital concerns", and that only by the "concordant will of the Great Powers could the political situation of Albania be modified—an eventuality impossible during the present war" (S.A. 59–60). It was only when negotiations between Italy and the Triple Entente were on the verge of conclusion that Austria-Hungary made a last desperate bid for Italian neutrality; she said she was willing to declare her disinterestedness in Albania, with the sole reservation that provision should be made against the establishment therein of a third Power; and finally, to declare complete disinterestedness without reserve (S.A. 58–60). Italy had, however, conducted parallel negotiations with the Entente Powers, and these were brought to a conclusion on the 26th April, 1915, by the secret Pact of London, by which Italy obtained the assurance of a very much greater extension of territory than she had demanded from Austria-Hungary as the price of her neutrality, and in return agreed to wage war against the enemies of her new allies with every means at her disposal. Secrecy was preserved regarding the terms of the Pact, although most of its clauses soon became known. It was first published by the Russian Bolsheviks in 1917. On the 24th May, 1915, Italy declared war against Austria-Hungary.

Among the clauses of the Pact of London were the following:

"Article 6. Italy shall receive full sovereignty over Valona, the island of Saseno, and surrounding territory of sufficient extent to assure defence of these points (from the Voyusa to the north and east, approximately to the north boundary of the district of Tchamouria on the south).

"Article 7. Should Italy obtain the Trentino and Istria in accordance with the provisions of Article 4, together with Dalmatia and the Adriatic islands within the limits specified in Article 5, and the Bay of Valona (Article 6), and if the central portion of Albania is reserved for the establishment of a small autonomous neutralized State, Italy shall not oppose the division of north and south Albania between Montenegro, Serbia, and Greece, should France, Great Britain, and Russia so desire. The coast from the south boundary of the Italian territory of Valona (see Article 6) up to Cape Stylos shall be neutralized.

"Italy shall be charged with the representation of the State of Albania in its relations with foreign Powers.

"Italy agrees, moreover, to leave sufficient territory in any event to the east of Albania to ensure the existence of a frontier line between Greece and Serbia to the west of Lake Ochrida" (S.P. 112: 975).

The Pact was signed by Edward Grey, Jules Cambon, Imperiali, and Benckendorff, representatives of the very Powers which had only three years previously guaranteed the independence and neutrality of Albania.

It may be said that "victory appeared to be doubtful without Italian assistance . . . and it was under the impression that peace would still leave the Hapsburg Empire a formidable foe to Italy that the Entente agreed to the terms" (E.B. 32: 1078); but that does not explain the provision for the "division of north and south Albania", imposed, apparently, by Russia and France, in order to extend the zones of their influence through their respective protégés. It was certainly not in accordance with Italian policy, which had aimed, and still aims, at the preservation of a substantial strategic buffer between the Adriatic coast and the zone of influence of a third Power; on the other hand, Italy probably accepted it while under a misapprehension—with regard to the fate of Austria-Hungary —which is explained elsewhere.

Once the Central Powers had won the support of Bulgaria, the Austro-German and Bulgarian armies, commanded by Von Mackensen, launched an attack in overwhelming strength against the Serbs. Their principal objective was the Orient railway, of which they were anxious to obtain possession and thus open a direct line of communication between the Central Powers and Turkey.

Although the Austro-German armies operating from the north slowly pressed back the Serbs, the reinforcements under Sarrail, which the Entente Powers began to land at Salonika in October, would no doubt have brought their advance to an end, or at any rate have prevented the Serbian retreat from becoming a rout, had communications with Salonika remained open. In any case the retreat would have been considerably facilitated by the railway and roads. But once the Bulgarians, attacking in the Serbian right rear, reached the line at Uskub, and threatened the Serbs with envelopment, all possibility of preventing a debacle was at an end.

The Serbs now reaped the reward of their folly. Despite a gallant resistance which enabled them to escape the enveloping movement, they were pressed back towards the inhospitable, snowbound, and roadless Albanian mountains, inhabited by a people rendered hostile by the brutality inflicted upon them by their hereditary foes; and with the remnants of the Serbian Army fled the Serbian civil population.

Between the 20th and 25th November the Serbs, upon the Kossovopolje and with their backs to the Albanian wall, made a final effort to restore the situation, then broke up and flowed away through Ipek, Djakova, Prizren, and Dibra, into Albania, fiercely harassed by their Albanian subjects of those districts, who rose in revolt and materially assisted the Austro-Hungarians (W.N.). At this stage, pursuit by the Austro-Hungarians and Germans ceased, and was not pressed by the Bulgarians, whose attention was diverted by the Allied Army under Sarrail. The Austro-Hungarians and Germans were undecided as to the policy to be adopted in regard to Albania, and doubtless expected that the Albanians themselves would complete the destruction of the Serbs. The Austro-Hungarians diverged into Montenegro, where the Montenegrin Army remained, since King Nicholas refused to withdraw it in view of the negotiations which were in progress for the conclusion of a separate peace. But the negotiations broke down, King Nicholas fled, and his army was entrapped. By the end of January Montenegro was completely occupied by the Austro-Hungarians, who then withdrew the greater part of their forces to the Asiago. The German troops were sent to oppose Sarrail operating from Salonika, but he withdrew across the Greek frontier, and for political reasons the Germans and Bulgarians did not follow him. The Germans were then withdrawn to other fronts.

In view of the successful invasion of Serbia by the enemy— a threat to Valona and the Albanian coast which Italy could not disregard—some 30,000 Italian troops, under General Ferrero, were landed at Valona at the beginning of December, 1915. They occupied the area allotted to Italy by the Pact of London—north and east to the Voyusa, and south to Dukati and Logora—and proceeded to fortify Valona. They also temporarily occupied Durazzo—where Essad still remained— and prepared for the arrival of the Serbs.

Through the rugged, wild, and almost trackless Albanian mountains, and through passes choked with snow, struggled the Serbian Army. But the Albanians let them pass almost unmolested! They fought only to preserve their flocks, or when the Serbs committed acts of violence, pillage, or attempted to requisition supplies in return for paper money. Austro-Hungarian agents tried to incite them to attack the Serbs, and had they succeeded the retreating host would probably have been annihilated. (Their failure is interesting when considered in conjunction with the allegations with which the Serbs sought to justify their invasion in May, 1915!) But Austro-Hungarian propaganda was more than counteracted by the influence among the malissori of Miss Durham, Colonel Herbert, Colonel Phillips (who had won their respect while at Skutari), and Admiral Troubridge (who commanded an Inter-Allied Naval Brigade operating with the Serbs). Moreover, the war was not their quarrel, and they remained indifferent to an already vanquished foe in flight; on the other hand, stragglers who sought hospitality received it in accordance with the sacred Albanian law (J.B.).

Of the Serbian Army, 130,000 men, 310 mountain guns, and 81 field guns, together with thousands of civilian refugees, horses, and cattle, reached the coast, where they were given supplies by the Entente Powers and Italians (although the behaviour of General Bertotti, the Italian commander at Durazzo, was deplorable). But more than 100,000 perished during the retreat, and huge quantities of war material were abandoned. They were evacuated to Corfu (which the French had occupied in January), the main body from Durazzo, others from Medua and Valona. They were then reorganized, re-equipped, and dispatched to Salonika.

Essad Pasha, knowing that the Austro-Hungarians would certainly never recognize him, and probably execute him if he remained at Durazzo, ostentatiously declared war against them (T. 4.1.16) to secure his position with the Entente. He, his "Government", and a handful of supporters went therefore with the Serbs, having made a handsome profit by taxing the supplies issued to them by the Allies! At Salonika he posed as a dispossessed ruler of the same class as King Peter of Serbia, wore a uniform of his own design, and decorated himself as he thought fit. France, pursuing a Serbo-Grecophile policy, officially recognized him, her accredited Minister being M. de Fontenay. Eventually, however, he was temporarily repudiated by the Entente Allies and by Italy (M.C.), but Serbia and Greece persisted in upholding him, and spread reports that he commanded an Albanian army of some strength. Actually he was unsupported except by some 500 mercenaries; moreover, he never ventured into the Albanian territory under Allied occupation. At the end of 1916 he came to London, where he attempted to pose as the representative of Albania in opposition to Mehmed bey Konitza, the Nationalist representative. Essad soon found that he "cut no ice" and eventually retired to Paris.

The Allied Expeditionary Force, under General Sarrail, had landed at Salonika in October, 1915, at the invitation of M. Venizelos, to reinforce the Serbs. By the terms of the Serbo-Greek Treaty of the 1st June, 1913, it had been agreed that should either country be attacked—"Viendrait à être attaqué"—the other should support it with all its resources, and to this end Greece should concentrate an army of 90,000 men in the area Pangaion–Salonika–Goumnitza, while Serbia should concentrate 150,000 men in the area Gevgheli–Veles–Kumanovo–Pirot, with the object of presenting a united front to Bulgaria should she attack (H.D. 5 : 118). But Serbia, engaged with Austria-Hungary, had insufficient troops available to fulfil her part of this arrangement, and Venizelos therefore asked the Allies to supply them, to which the Allies agreed, and proceeded to land them at Salonika (H.D. 5 : 200–1), employing a line of communication to which Serbia had been entitled by the terms of her Treaty with Greece. But since Serbia was now in the hands of the enemy, and Monastir, the Serbs' last foothold in their country, had been evacuated on the 4th December, this justification for the presence of Sarrail's troops in Greek territory no longer existed, and would not again exist until the Serbian Army was transported from the Adriatic to Salonika. It was decided, however, that Salonika should be held, but nevertheless Sarrail's army was decidedly in an equivocal position, and was restrained by these political considerations from anything but a purely defensive policy. Fortunately, much the same conditions applied to the enemy.

Although Greece showed a decided tendency towards the Central Powers, she was distinctly hostile to Bulgaria—indeed, fear of that country had been very largely responsible for her persistent refusal to join the Entente Powers — and therefore it was politically impossible for the Bulgarians to cross the Greek frontier in pursuit of Sarrail without a preponderating proportion of German or Austro-Hungarian troops. These were not, however, available.

Thus the beginning of 1916 found the opposing armies on either side of the frontier some twenty miles apart. The Salonika Expeditionary Force occupied a frontage of some eighty miles, from the mouth of the Vardar by Doganzi and Daudli, to Langaza, and thence to the Gulf of Orfano. The Bulgarians aligned themselves along the frontier from the Struma, on their left, to Lake Ochrida, with flank guards at Dibra, and at Elbasan, which they occupied in the early spring.

The surrender by the Greeks to the Bulgarians on the 10th May of Fort Rupel, whereby Sarrail's right was threatened, the action against Greece thereupon taken by Great Britain and

France, and the arrival of the reconstituted Serbian Army, materially altered the political situation, and during the summer Sarrail advanced his line towards the frontier. But pending the conclusion of negotiations then in progress with Roumania, no offensive operations were undertaken until the military convention with Roumania was signed on the 17th August.

On that day, however, the Bulgarians assumed the offensive, with the object of shortening their line by advancing both their flanks, their left to the angle of the Struma, and their right from Monastir through Florina. With this in view they had advanced during June beyond Lake Malik in Albania to the outskirts of Korcha, which was occupied by the Greeks, and which was an important link in the communications between Greece and the Central Powers.

On the 17th August the Serbs, who had also begun an advance on the Allied left, were driven from Florina, and through Banitza to Lake Ostrovo. By the end of the month, however, the Bulgarian attacks had died down, since no offensive on a large scale had been intended. The Roumanians, too, had entered the field and diverted their attention.

The Serbs now counter-attacked, and on the 14th September broke the Bulgarian line at Gornichevo. The Bulgarians thereupon withdrew to Brod, with their extreme right upon Lake Presba. On the 17th Florina was reoccupied by the French, who then proceeded to clear the mountain region towards Korcha.

During January, 1916, the Austro-Hungarians had crossed the frontier from Montenegro and occupied Skutari. Before entering Albania, they issued a proclamation declaring that they came merely to drive out the Serbs and Italians, and calling upon all Albanians, both Christian and Moslem, to join them. Upon the 28th January two proclamations were also issued from Skutari signed by Prenk Bib Doda, Seid Pasha, Feizi Alizoti, Louis Gurakuchi, and Akif Elbasani, who had been banished to Cettinje by the Montenegrins during the previous summer—from which it seems evident that Prenk had abandoned his plans for Mirdite autonomy under Slav suzerainty, and rallied to the national cause. In these proclamations the signatories called upon their compatriots to receive the Austro-Hungarians as liberators, and do everything possible to assist them.

Ahmed Zogu had, since August, 1914, wisely held himself

aloof in Mati (*My Memoirs*, Prince Ludwig Windischgraetz; translation by Constance Vesey, London, 1921, p. 97) from affairs throughout the remainder of the country which he was unable to control. He had, while closely following the course of events, confined his activities to the improvement of conditions in Mati, which became a haven for Nationalists seeking refuge from the insurgents, and to the extension of his influence to other loyal districts (N.D. 96, 126). Encouraged by the flight of the Serbs and Essad Pasha, this daring young man, still only twenty-one years of age, now took the initiative, rallied his tribesmen, called upon Albanian patriots to follow him, and marched with Captain Ghilliardi, Salaheddin Bloshmi, and other partisans, to Elbasan. He entered the town on the 31st January, and there met Akif Elbasani and his colleagues from Cettinje, Midhat Frasheri, Lef Nosi, and others. A company of 23rd Bulgarian Infantry Regiment, under Captain Serafimoff, had occupied Elbasan two days previously, but agreement between them and the Albanians presented no difficulties. During the previous months there had been much intrigue by the Austro-Hungarians and Bulgarians against each other in Albania, Bulgaria being anxious to establish her influence in the country, which would have been a neighbouring State had the Central Powers been victorious; and both countries had sought to win Ahmed Zogu's support. Indeed, Austria-Hungary had sent a mission under Prince Windischgraetz to Zogu for this purpose.

Directly order had been established, Zogu and Irfan bey Ochri (Ochrida) went to Durazzo, which the Italians had evacuated, and on the 14th February telegraphed to Elbasan: "To-day we raised the national flag in our King's Palace at Durazzo, and are returning to Shjak. To-morrow we shall start direct for Elbasan. The army should have no anxiety. Let it await us" (N.D. 182). A fortnight later Durazzo was occupied by the Austro-Hungarians, who subsequently established there a naval base from whence submarines harried Allied shipping until the 3rd October, 1918, when an Anglo-Italo-American squadron bombarded it and destroyed the Austro-Hungarian vessels in the bay.

In the meantime the patriots gathered in Elbasan had constituted themselves a provisional National Assembly, and had elected a Commission of Initiative under the presidency of young Zogu. On the 18th February the Commission, with the

HIS HIGHNESS PRINCE WILLIAM OF ALBANIA, PRINCE OF WIED

unanimous approval of the Assembly, decided that a National Congress of duly accredited representatives should at once be convened; and that in the meantime Akif pasha Elbasani, since he had been Minister of the Interior in Prince William's Government, and had never resigned, should be invited to call his colleagues together again, and continue to govern the country. Akif Pasha was joined by Midhat bey Frasheri—who had also held office in the Prince's Government—by Louis Gurakuchi, and by Kara Seid Pasha; Zogu and Lef Nosi were also nominated, but being on the Commission of Initiative, refused to take office.

On the 18th February, the Mayor of Elbasan, Djafer Hilmi Dardha, telegraphed to Tirana to the effect that in commemoration of the anniversary of the acceptance of the throne by Prince William from the Albanian delegation, a fête would be held in Elbasan, and greeting sent to His Majesty. Dardha asked that preparations for a similar fête should be made in Tirana.

The programme of the proposed Congress was drawn up as follows:

(1) National gratitude should be expressed to those Powers which recognized our right to raise our national flag in every part of Albania, and to govern ourselves.

(2) The national desire should be expressed to His Majesty the King [William] for his return to the country as soon as possible.

(3) The manner in which Albania should be governed until the King arrives should be discussed.

It appears that several unofficial telegrams and deputations were sent to Prince William asking him to return, both by groups in Albania—including those who had previously rebelled against him—and by Albanian colonies abroad.

On the 3rd March, Zogu, in his capacity as President of the Commission of Initiative, announced that the Congress would take place on the 18th March, and that accredited representatives should be sent to Elbasan, in telegrams to the Prefects of Berat, Skrapari, Ballsh, Fieri, Lushnja, Kavaja, Durazzo, Pekinj, Shjak, Tirana, Kruja, Alessio, Skutari, Mati, Dibra, Starova, through Bulgarian Headquarters to Nedjhib bey Draga at Mitrovitza, Bairam Tsuri at Djakova, Hassan bey Prishtina at Prishtina, Mehmed pasha Dralla at Tetovo, to the Albanian colonies in Bucharest, Sofia, and Lausanne, and by

letter to Prenk Bib Doda in Mirdita, and the Toptani at
Tirana. Groups of refugees from the areas under Greek or
Italian occupation appointed representatives for those districts.
Zogu also wrote to Herr Auguste Kral—formerly upon the
International Commission of Control—who had been ap-
pointed civil administrator in Albania, expressing confidence
that the Congress would meet with his approval, and that
Austria-Hungary would assure to Albania "the expansion of
the frontier line in accordance with the principle of nationality".

But the Austro-Hungarians held other views. A few days
later Elbasan was occupied by Austro-Hungarian troops, the
Bulgarians having left for the south; and upon the pretext
that there was danger of spreading an epidemic of cholera,
a military cordon was established round the town. This
cordon was not raised until the 21st March. On the previous
day, in a letter addressed to the Municipality of Elbasan,
Czapek Mjn, Commandant of the Elbasan district, declared
"that assemblies for political purposes are prohibited in
districts occupied by the Imperial Armies, such assemblies
being, in time of war, prohibited even in Austro-Hungarian
territory". He also announced that if a fresh assembly with
a purely economic aim should be contemplated, permission
must be obtained from his headquarters, and that before
permission would be granted a complete programme of the
assembly must be submitted.

The Albanians had no alternative but to bow to this decision. On the 14th April Akif Elbasani (or Bicakciu) announced
his resignation, expressing confidence that the assumption of
the Government of Albania by the Austro-Hungarians was
merely a temporary measure rendered necessary by the military
situation, and advising his officials to carry on their duties in
accordance with the instructions they would receive from
Austro-Hungarian Headquarters at Tirana (N.D.: *Okupacioni
Austriak*, 181–9). Nevertheless Albanian confidence in Austria-
Hungary was shaken to its foundations and grave suspicions
of her intentions were aroused. In consequence, attempts by
the Austro-Hungarians to raise Albanian troops for service
abroad were conspicuously unsuccessful, although numbers
of Albanians enrolled under their own officers, attracted no
doubt by the prospect of pay and possible loot. Some of these
troops took part in operations against the Italians—although
the latter were never a popular foe in view of their hostility to

Greece, and especially after Ferrero's proclamation in June, 1917—while others proved of great value against Montenegrin detachments which harried Austro-Hungarian communications (D.F.) in the mountains.

Zogu at first commanded the Albanian forces co-operating with the Austro-Hungarians (D.M. 22.3.27); but subsequently it was discovered that he was conspiring with the Bulgarians for the re-establishment of Albanian administrative independence. Accordingly he was induced to go to Vienna, and there detained.

An Albanian Civil Administrative Council under Kral was formed at Skutari. The Austro-Hungarians allowed the national flag to be flown; and local administration was carried on by Albanian officials, both in Albania as delimited in 1913, and in those Albanian districts which had been ceded to Serbia and Montenegro. An Albanian gendarmerie was raised and trained, and order was preserved by rigid discipline. Some roads and a Decauville narrow-gauge railway system were constructed, also excellent bridges, which were, however, destroyed during the retreat in 1918. The development of agriculture and stock-raising was specially encouraged, for obvious reasons. The customs and language of the country were respected, and a number of Albanian schools opened both within and beyond the 1913 frontier. Generally speaking, the Austro-Hungarian administration was highly efficient and beneficial; on the other hand, the arbitrary conduct of the military authorities, and especially a proclamation issued on the 29th April, 1916, ordering the surrender of all arms, caused much discontent, and local revolts seem to have occurred (T. 16.8.16; 10.4.17). Moreover, the payment in paper money (instead of in coin) for supplies requisitioned was keenly resented by the peasants, who regarded it with the greatest suspicion, a suspicion which, as subsequent events proved, was fully justified.

Nothing beyond desultory skirmishes took place between the Austro-Hungarians and Italians in Albania in 1916 and 1917. The Italians made no attempt to push northwards, and the Austro-Hungarians did not feel disposed to attack Valona, which had been transformed into a fortress of considerable strength. In the meantime Albanian irregulars under the able leadership of Bairam Tsuri, Themistokli Germenj, Salih Budka, and other guerrilla leaders harried alike the Greeks and the

Allied lines of communication in the south; but in the absence of a definite national cause, they fought without any of the ardour which had characterized their struggle against the Turks, and were inspired only by the possibility of loot or pay. Their activities were directed by Von Falkenhausen, previously German military attaché in Athens, whose headquarters were at Pogradets. By skilful propaganda, which played upon their hatred of Essad and the Serbs, he succeeded to some extent in restraining them from attacking the Greeks, and in stirring them to greater hostility towards the Allies.

Various proposals regarding the future of Albania were discussed in Austria-Hungary (A.H. 103), proposals which did not allay suspicion of her intentions among the Albanians. Although the independence of the country, and restoration of Prince William, were among them, they also included the union of northern Albania, Serbia, and Montenegro under a Montenegrin Prince, the annexation of Albania, Montenegro, and parts of Serbia by Austria-Hungary, and the cession of north and south Albania to Montenegro and Greece respectively, leaving only a small independent central Albania. But it does not seem that any definite policy was decided upon; and this indecision led to abortive attempts to provide a solution, among them the proclamation at Dibra by Hassan Basri of a Provisional Government, with the intention of placing Prince Cyril of Bulgaria on the throne—an enterprise which proved a complete fiasco. The proposals made by Dr. Rizoff, the Bulgarian Minister in Berlin, for the partition of Albania, led to a protest by an assembly at Durazzo on the 26th February, 1918, of delegates from Elbasan, Pekinj, Kavaja, Gramshi, Tirana, and Durazzo, who declared that the troubles brought about by foreign intrigue which had led to the "temporary withdrawal of our King William I, who was recognized by the Powers, and approved by the Albanians" could not be adduced as an argument in favour of partition (N.D. 22).

Dr. Rizoff's proposals do not seem to have expressed the Bulgarian official attitude. This was announced by M. Radoslavoff, the Prime Minister, who declared in the Sobranje that Bulgaria was greatly interested in the formation of an independent Albanian State, and would support all Albanian aspirations in this respect (T. 23.4.18).

That the Austro-Hungarian General Staff was aware of

restlessness and suspicion among the Albanians is indicated by a proclamation issued in January, 1917 (D.W. Annex IX), by the Commander of the Austro-Hungarian troops in Albania. This proclamation stated that Austria-Hungary had always endeavoured to preserve the integrity of Albania, and that Austro-Hungarian troops had entered the country only in the necessary pursuit of the common foe, came as friends, had been joined by many Albanians, and that only a small minority had been bribed to join the enemy. Austria-Hungary desired, it continued, "with full regard for the traditional belief, language, rights, and customs of the people, to give the country an orderly administration, and by this to guarantee the safety of person, honour, and property, to repair the damage caused by wars and turmoils, and to promote the future prosperous development of the nation. By means of this Government the Albanian people shall be so educated that as soon as possible they may, in fact, while avoiding former mistakes, enjoy the right of self-government which is theirs. When the preliminary conditions for the autonomy of the country have been created, Austria-Hungary will proceed without delay to the erection of Albanian self-government, and will also in the future not withhold her actual protection from the country."

But this proclamation did nothing to reassure the Albanians; and in 1917 a delegation went to Vienna to demand immediate autonomy from the Emperor (J.B.). But the position remained unchanged.

When the terms of the Pact of London were made public by the Bolsheviks at the end of 1917, they were translated by the Austro-Hungarians into Albanian, and published throughout the occupied areas. They caused considerable consternation and indignation, but this was more than counteracted first by General Ferrero's proclamation, counter-propaganda by the Italians and French, and the action of the French at Korcha, secondly by the declaration of war aims in January, 1917 (T. 27.4.17), and thirdly by the knowledge that the United States had entered the war and would be represented at the Peace Conference. In the United States were large numbers of Albanian immigrants, and their organizations, especially the Vatra, believing implicitly in President Wilson's declarations (B.T. 291), worked enthusiastically for the Allied cause, while hundreds of them enlisted in the American Army; and their contribution to the Third Liberty Loan was higher than that of thirteen other races. All this naturally reacted in Albania among their relatives and friends, at first in the areas occupied by the Italians and French, from whence the greater number of Albanians then in the United States had emigrated, and then gradually throughout central and northern Albania. There were, too, many people who had returned from America, and understood her political ideals and institutions; they were confident that she would uphold the principle of self-determination, and enable them to regain the Albanian districts torn from them in 1913 when ethnical considerations had been ignored.

During 1918 considerable Austro-Hungarian reinforcements were sent into Albania; and by paying in paper money for the supplies which they requisitioned wholesale, stimulated the growth of discontent and unrest (N.E. 29.4.20).

In southern Albania the war was viewed from a different angle. There the Greek was the foe; and the Italians had declared that they came to protect the Albanians from the Greeks. Moreover, Italy had declared that one of her war aims was to re-establish the independence and integrity of Albania.

In March, 1916, the strength of the Italian Expeditionary Force was raised to 100,000 men, and the defences of Valona greatly strengthened. Indeed, the Austro-Hungarian General Staff was censured by the Austro-Hungarian Press for failing to attack the town before the Italians made it a fortress. The Italians improved the harbour, erected jetties, and built an aqueduct five miles in length to supply the town with water. During the summer they began to extend their occupation southwards and eastwards to establish contact with the Salonika Expeditionary Force, and clear the Santi Quaranta–Korcha road. Moreover, in view of the fear of Greek treachery, which had been aroused by the surrender of Fort Rupel and other acts, it was considered advisable to isolate Royalist Greece, and secure the left flank and rear of Sarrail's army.

On the 9th October Premeti was occupied; and more Italian troops, landing at Santi Quaranta, moved upon Argyrocastro and Leskovik. The Greeks fell back into Thessaly, and the Italian occupation was effected without a shot being fired. The Italians were welcomed. They organized a militia with headquarters at Argyrocastro; and many southern

Albanians enrolled, subsequently serving with distinction, in particular at Ostrovica and Tomori. Communications received attention; and with their customary ability in such matters the Italians began at once to repair existing roads and construct fresh ones, notably from Valona to Santi Quaranta, through the spectacular coastal scenery of Tchamouria.

During the late autumn of 1916 events in Roumania and northern Italy made an offensive upon the Salonika front expedient. Sarrail therefore determined to press forward his left. After some heavy fighting the enemy, threatened with an outflanking movement, withdrew, evacuating Monastir, which was occupied by Allied troops on the 19th November.

Sarrail's left now rested upon Lake Presba. His anxiety to continue the offensive was, however, restrained partly by the weather, partly by the attitude of the Greek Royalists in his left rear, and partly by the demand of Cadorna, supported by Robertson, for a withdrawal. "The idea of a Salonika Front had never had any real support in the British War Office, and the Italian point of view seems to have been that the abolition of an inter-Allied force in the Balkans would give Italy greater freedom of action in Albania" (E.B. 32 : 352). Sarrail therefore compromised, and consolidated upon a defensive line.

In view of the hostile attitude of the Greek Royalists, to which the Venizelist troops were as yet no counterpoise, Sarrail considered it advisable definitely to separate the areas which each party controlled. For this purpose he established, on the 16th November, a neutral zone between five and ten kilometres in width, extending from the Albanian frontier near Leskovik to a point on the Gulf of Salonika between the mouths of the Rivers Vistritza and Peneias; and in the middle of December the Allies demanded the withdrawal of Greek troops from Thessaly.

During the winter steps were taken to effect a junction with the Italians. Hitherto liaison had been maintained by wireless and aeroplane, and latterly there had existed a wide gap between the two armies, from which the Greek Royalist troops had withdrawn, but which was still infested with irregular Greek Royalist and Albanian bands, fighting one another, and both harrying the Allies. During the summer and autumn French cavalry had operated in the Korcha neighbourhood against them, and to sever communications between Athens and the enemy; and at the end of October a patrol of the 1er Regt.

Chasseurs d'Afrique visited the Italians at Leskovik, but communications were again interrupted by the bands.

After the Serbian debacle a small Serbian detachment had joined the Greek garrison at Korcha. But the Greek Prefect determined to evict the Serbs. He therefore brought about the introduction of cholera toxin to the flour supplied to them. His ingenuity produced the desired effect, and the Greeks remained in sole occupation (J.B.). When, in the autumn of 1916, the French approached Korcha, the Royalists evacuated the town, and in agreement with General Sarrail, the Venizelist Provisional Government at Salonika sent a Prefect, M. Argyropoulis, to retain it for Greece. But his arrival merely added to the confusion which prevailed; and the Albanians, who had thought that with the arrival of the French their land would be restored to them, and refrained from active hostilities, hastened to join those already in the field (T. 10.5.17).

These circumstances became known to General Sarrail, and steps were taken to consult leading Albanians in the Korcha district. It seems that in the course of the inquiries, Sarrail discovered that not only was a Greek administration repugnant to the inhabitants, but that a grave error had been committed in according official recognition to Essad Pasha. In any case Essad's eclipse seems to date from this period. Henceforth he was kept in the background, and reappeared only at the Peace Conference as a factor in the destinies of Albania.

Sarrail therefore decided "to allow the population to do what it pleased", as he subsequently explained to the Quai d'Orsay (S.A. 69), and to replace the Greeks by an autonomous administration under French protection, a course which he considered would commit nobody as regards the disposal of the district in the future, and yet win the support of the Albanians, and ensure tranquillity in rear of the troops. To this end Colonel Descoins was sent to Korcha with a French garrison. But before he made his official entry a Protocol was signed, on the 11th December (for text, see Q.K. 8, 9), with fourteen Albanian representatives, proclaiming the existence of an Autonomous Albanian Province of Korcha under French protection. The Albanian flag was raised throughout the prefecture, and the Venizelists left the district.

In the same month considerable French reinforcements began to arrive at Salonika, and Sarrail sent the 76th Division inland to Korcha, where it arrived at the beginning of February,

1917, just in time to prevent the seizure of the town by Austro-Hungarian troops from Pogradets. It then moved forward to clear the Santi Quaranta road of bands, to compel the Austro-Hungarians to withdraw the guns with which they had hitherto commanded it, and to open it up as an alternative line of communication. On the 17th February the French and Italian troops met at Ersek and contact was permanently established, the limit between Sarrail's and Ferrero's troops being fixed at a point a little north of that place. The 76th Division was then concentrated north of Korcha in readiness for a resumption of the offensive.

In the meantime an Albanian Provisional Administrative Council was constituted at Korcha, consisting of seven Moslems and seven Christians, with Themistokli Germenj, an Orthodox Albanian, as President. Germenj had fled from the town when it was occupied by the Greeks. When the Bulgarians followed the Serbs into Albania, he had joined them with other refugees. When the French arrived at Korcha he was in command of a band operating from Pogradets around Lake Malik. He was universally respected and had considerable influence among both Christians and Moslems throughout the Korcha district. He was therefore induced to return, and rendered very material assistance to the French (A.D.).

A representative of the Allies, Major Reynard Lespinasse, attended all meetings of the Council, but never found it necessary to interfere in its deliberations.

As time went on, and as they became convinced of the sincerity of the French, many of the Albanian irregulars who had hitherto fought against the Allies, followed Germenj's example and rallied to their flag at Korcha. Hundreds of Albanians too, from the territory in Allied occupation, offered their services to the French, and an Albanian Rifle Regiment was formed which served with distinction. Both Major Felix Holtz, who commanded the 1st Battalion, and General Henrys, praised these Albanian troops enthusiastically; Major Lespinasse wrote:

"Le Général Henrys, commandant l'armée française d'Orient, cite le 1er bataillon de tirailleurs albanais: 'Après s'être antérieurement distingué dans les affaires de Strelca, de l'Ostrovica, et du Kamja, a, au cours des opérations de la Bofnia, sous l'énergique impulsion de son Chef, le commandant Holtz, montré les plus belles qualités militaires, et s'est révélé corps de troupe de premier ordre. Toujours à l'avant-garde des colonnes, il a frayé partout leur chemin, harcelant l'ennemi sans trêve, lui faisant plusieurs centaines de prisonniers et capturant un matériel important.' Cette haute distinction met le bataillon de tirailleurs albanais au niveau des meilleurs régiments français" (Q.K. Annex 11).

The Albanian troops took over a sector, and participated in the ensuing operations. Their colours, and several Albanian officers and men, were decorated with the Croix de Guerre, and some with the Legion of Honour. Germenj himself won the Croix de Guerre for his services during operations which led to the capture of Pogradets.

Albanian irregulars likewise distinguished themselves, and knowing every inch of the ground, relentlessly harassed the Austro-Hungarians. For some time Spahi cavalry and Albanian irregulars were co-operating in the cause of the Allies (M.P. 12.7.18).

The Greeks had seized and exported food-stuffs to the enemy, causing thereby much suffering to the population (Q.K. 7). When the French arrived a daily bread dole until the following harvest was instituted, and the making of roads gave employment. Roads to Florina, and to Pogradets when that town wsa recaptured, and good mule tracks to all villages, were constructed.

The people of the Autonomous Province co-operated with the Administrative Council with enthusiasm, and rapid progress was made in every direction. A gendarmerie was organized, and law and order prevailed. The Organic Law of Albania was revived. An excellent court of justice, which was said to be superior to those of any other Balkan State (A.R. September, 1918. M. E. Durham), and a post office, were established. Stamps and paper money were issued (for reproductions, see Q.K. Annex 10), bridges built, public buildings repaired, a telephone system, linked with the main line to Valona, laid, and medical and sanitary facilities arranged

But the most phenomenal progress made was in public education. Almost the first act of the Administrative Council was to establish an Albanian Board of Education. The Greeks had closed all Albanian schools, and suppressed education in

Albanian even more drastically than the Turks had done (J.B.). It was now unanimously decided that the Greek schools should be closed. Four Albanian primary schools, and one secondary school, attended by about 2,000 pupils from a population of 23,243 (J.B.), were opened in Korcha alone; and before the French retired, the Autonomous Province, which ultimately included a population of some 130,000 persons, possessed no less than 200 Albanian schools (J.B.).

Considerable progress was also made in agriculture, and a brown coal mine was worked in the hills.

All public works were paid for by the province of Korcha itself. When the enemy were driven from the Pogradets area, which had seldom paid taxes to the Turks, regular taxation was inaugurated successfully; and when the French withdrew from Albania, £100,000 remained in the Korcha treasury (for financial details: Q.K. 11, and Annex 9).

The resentment of the Venizelists at their eviction from Korcha was barely counteracted by French assurances that it was a measure adopted merely to secure Albanian support. They were assured that the establishment of an autonomous administration in no way precluded the eventual cession of the province to Greece; and to reassure both Greece and Italy of the essentially provisional nature of the arrangement, the establishment of French civil institutions was prohibited.

When Greece eventually joined the Entente Powers on the 29th June, 1917, Greek agents again obtained access to Korcha and agitated for the reopening of Greek schools. They were, however, effectually silenced by a proclamation against propaganda signed by General Salle (Q.K. Annex 13) and by a plebiscite through which the people definitely decided that while Albanian schools existed, Greek schools—which had been employed as centres of propaganda for the fomentation of religious animosity between Moslems and Christians—were not required.

But Sarrail's action in "allowing the population to do as it pleased" was not in accordance with French policy towards Greece—once that country entered the war; moreover, the repatriation of the Essadists to Pogradets (A.D.) as a counter-move to Italian policy was under consideration. The French therefore compromised.

The Protocol drawn up by Colonel Descoins was considered too definite, and by a proclamation (for text: Q.K.

Annex 14) issued on the 16th February, 1918, was abrogated. The Albanians were, however, assured that this action in no way threatened their independence, and the Albanian flag continued to fly over the province until replaced by that of France in April, 1919. Despite energetic protests the Greek schools were reopened (J.B.; Q.K. 13–16). Upon a charge of treachery brought by the Greeks, Germenj was arrested, taken to Salonika, and subsequently executed. The Administrative Council was abolished, being replaced by a French commandant assisted by three executive officers, who nominated Albanian councillors to collaborate with them.

The occupation of Albanian territory by the French, who favoured Serbian and Greek aspirations, was regarded with a disfavour in Italy which led to several regrettable incidents between the two Allied armies in Albania (J.B.). Moreover, it seems that the proclamation of Albanian autonomy at Korcha prompted Italy to assert herself.

On the 1st March, 1917, the Albanian flag was hoisted throughout the area in Italian occupation. Essad Pasha was repudiated. A measure of autonomy was granted, and a central administration under the control of General Ferrero established. On the 3rd June, at Argyrocastro, before an assembly of Albanian notables, was read the following proclamation:

"To the whole people of Albania:
"To-day, 3rd June, 1917, which is the memorable anniversary of the establishment of Italian constitutional liberties, I, General Giacinto Ferrero, commander of the Italian Expeditionary Forces in Albania, do solemnly proclaim, in accordance with the orders of His Majesty, King Victor Emmanuel, the unity and independence of the whole of Albania, under the shield and protection of the Italian Kingdom.

"By virtue of this proclamation, you, Albanians, have a free government, an army, courts of justice, all composed of Albanians, and are free to use as you wish your property and the products of your labour, for your own benefit, and for the enrichment of your country.

"Albanians! Wherever you are, whether free in the land of your birth, or in exile in other countries and under foreign domination, we are bringing back to you the civilization of the Romans and Venetians.

"You know the bonds which unite Italian and Albanian interests. The sea divides them, and, at the same time, the sea binds them together. Let all good citizens, then, stand unitedly, having faith in the future of your beloved nation. Come, all of you, under the flags of Albania and Italy, and pledge yourselves to Albania, which is to-day proclaimed independent, in the name of the Italian Government and under its friendly protection" (C.C. 162).

"The recent proclamation of the Commander of the Italian troops in Albania reconfirmed [declared Baron Sonnino (the Italian Foreign Minister, to the Chamber of Deputies on the 20th June: T. 22.6.17)] the special interest which the Italian Government has in the destinies of that brave people, which are intimately bound up no less than our certain and direct possession of Valona and its territory with the general settlement of the Adriatic question, which is a vital one for Italy. We recommend the independence of Albania in conformity with the general principles on which our alliances are founded, and which have been recently so eloquently proclaimed by the United States and by the new Liberal Russia. Italy, in regard to Albania, has no other object than to defend it against any possible interference or intrigues on the part of a third Power. Italy will guarantee to Albania the full right to dispose of herself as regards internal affairs, and will support her legitimate rights and interests in the national assembly [? Peace Conference]. The Powers, meeting to discuss the Peace Treaty, will have the general task of determining the precise boundaries of the State of Albania in regard to neighbouring States. Owing to the war, the entire local government of the country must necessarily be subject to the military command, which, however, is inspired with the greatest respect for existing customs and interests. After the conclusion of peace, the Albanians themselves will decide freely as to their interior régime."

The *Corriere della Sera* declared that "Italy assumes the task of defending Albania against anarchy and Austro-German intrigues, such defence responding at the same time to the exigencies of civilization and our safety in the Adriatic".

T

The *Secolo* pointed out that Italian protection was intended only in the diplomatic and not in the colonial sense (T. 7.6.17).

In France General Ferrero's proclamation caused irritation; but in Russia, Kerensky's Government approved of it on military grounds, maintaining, however, that the ultimate fate of Albania should be regulated by the application of the principle of self-determination. In Great Britain it was received with indifference. Italy had consulted none of the above Powers in the matter (P.D. 94 : 576, 7099, 1585, 1944).

From Sonnino's explicit declaration it is clear that Italy, while adhering to the terms of the Pact of London with regard to Valona and the control of Albanian foreign policy, intended to take her stand upon the "principles . . . proclaimed by the United States and by the new Liberal Russia" in opposing the division of Albania. The declaration of war aims, the collapse of Imperialist Russia, and the entry, in April, of the United States into the war had seemed to ensure that at the Peace Conference the principle "that no nation should seek to extend its polity over any other nation or people" (President Wilson to Congress, on the 22nd of January, 1917) would take the place of the right of annexation irrespective of ethnical considerations, a doctrine of which France became the last line of defence among the Powers.

War with Austria-Hungary had absolved Italy of her obligations towards that country, and Sonnino maintained that Italy was now free to pursue her traditional policy of friendship with and sympathy for the Albanian people, anticipating that thereby he herself would win Albanian sympathy, which, *since the serious inception of the Yugoslav ideal,* had become of very considerable importance to her.

When Albanian independence was recognized in 1913 Italy had intrigued to prevent the new State from falling within the sphere of influence of her Adriatic rival, Austria-Hungary, who already possessed every other strategic advantage; and it was largely to redress her own strategic disadvantage that Italy had entered the war. By the terms of the Pact of London she obtained Valona—and thereby control of the Straits—and Dalmatia to C. Planka. From C. Planka to the Voyusa—except from a point south of the Sabbioncello Peninsula to 10 km. south of Ragusa–Vecchia—the coast was neutralized. Moreover, Italy had envisaged the reduction— but not the extinction—of Austria-Hungary, and the partition of the hinterland of the eastern coast of the Adriatic between a Great Serbia, Croatia, Slavonia, and Montenegro, whom she could play off against each other to ensure her own supremacy.

But the proposed union of these four States in one formidable Power, a proposal encouraged by Entente propaganda to undermine Austro-Hungarian solidarity, and assured of success if the principle of self-determination was to be the predominating note at the Peace Conference, threatened merely to alter the name of Italy's Adriatic rival. Italy's position on the Dalmatian coast would become untenable both morally (on ethnical grounds) and strategically (E.B. 31 : 627; the strip allotted to her would be too shallow for defence against a formidable military Power; and reinforcements would be exposed to submarine attack), the neutralization clause would be difficult to enforce, and a French zone of influence would extend from Liubliana to Monastir (or even to the Morea). Moreover, if the Yugoslavs possessed north Albania (to the Drin, perhaps to the Mati) and a frontier to the west of Lake Ochrida, a surprise attack—perhaps in co-operation with Greece—by troops previously concentrated upon a remote frontier, would bring them to the defences of Valona before Italy could reinforce her garrison; while the co-operation of warships might prevent the transportation of reinforcements and render Valona untenable.

In the circumstances the obvious policy for Italy to pursue was to barter the right which she had acquired by the Pact of London to Dalmatia for advantages upon her eastern frontier, and to strengthen her position in Albania by establishing her prestige therein upon the basis of friendship with the Albanians, and by obtaining for that country as far as possible her natural frontiers (natural geographical defences manned by the warlike malissori), thus securing Valona and the Albanian coast from a Yugoslav attack.

In considering Italy's position in the Adriatic, it should be borne in mind that her eastern seaboard is "hopelessly flat for defensive purposes and *practically harbourless*" (A.R. September, 1918) *from Trieste to Taranto*. Moreover, it is enormously extensive. On the other hand, the Yugoslav coastline is comparatively short, admirably suited for defence (and therefore Italian naval supremacy constitutes no threat to her), honeycombed with natural harbours (the Bocche di

Cattaro alone provides absolute security for the most power-ful fleet) and sheltered by "the strategic curtain formed by the Dalmatian islands" (H.M. 278).

From this coast, providing numerous bases, a Yugoslav fleet, even if composed only of submarines and light craft, would be able to harry Italian shipping and even the Italian coast almost with impunity. If Yugoslavia were co-operating with a Power disposing of a formidable fleet, Italy's security would be threatened; and if that fleet had access to Valona Bay, it would command the Adriatic. On the other hand, if Italy had access to Valona, she would be in a position to dispute with the hostile fleet the passage of the Straits of Otranto, and her own fleet would be based within reach of the Yugoslav bases.

In the circumstances Italy's desire to acquire Valona Bay, establish there a fortified naval base, and thus obtain "the incontestable supremacy of the Adriatic Sea" is, at least, intelligible, although wholly inadmissible. Her desire to secure by treaty the right to use it as a base in time of war deserves sympathy. Her anxiety to ensure that in no circumstances should it fall into the hands of another Power is entirely justified, since her very security is involved.

From June, 1917, until the end of 1918 the Italians assumed in Albania the attitude of a benevolent although somewhat autocratic guardian, and the autonomy enjoyed by the people was very limited. But this state of affairs was accepted as being due to the military situation. Some 200 miles of excellent road and 50 miles of narrow-gauge railway were constructed; Albanian labour was employed and well paid in cash. Hospitals were opened, public works received attention, model farms established, and prices regulated. The Italians paid highly for produce requisitioned, and did their utmost to assist the population of the south, which was starving in consequence of the wholesale exportation by the Greeks of food-stuffs.

Relations between the Albanians and the Italian troops became excellent. The latter made every effort to win the support and co-operation of the people, and by their exemplary conduct succeeded. General Ferrero, too, possessed a per-sonality which won the esteem of the Albanians, and it seems that he was genuinely interested in their welfare. Pro-gress was rapid. National newspapers were circulated, schools established, but everything was regulated by policy.

"Children were everywhere taught to speak Italian
. . . they undoubtedly provided one of the chief
weapons of the general pro-Italian propaganda campaign,
which aimed at impressing the Albanians with a sense of
the beneficial effects of Italian protection. Another means
of fostering these ideas was the introduction of as many
modern improvements as possible into the agricultural
activities of the country . . ." (S.F. 107).

In the meantime the war continued. During the spring of
1917 Sarrail resumed the offensive, but although heavy
fighting took place, it was not very successful. During March
the French 76th Division began an advance from Korcha to
Resna, but little progress was made owing to the snow, and
the harrying tactics of Bulgarian irregulars stiffened by small
Austro-Hungarian forces from Pogradets. During May the
Serbs refused to participate in further offensive operations, and
the morale of the Russians became shaken by events in their
country. Further operations had therefore to be suspended.

During June the Greek question finally came to a head,
and Sarrail was authorized to invade Thessaly. The Italians
co-operated with the British and French, invaded Epirus, and
on the 8th June (T. 11.6.17) occupied Janina. Greece protested; but with the exception of a skirmish at Larissa on the
12th, the Allies encountered no resistance. After the dethrone-
ment in July of King Constantine most of the troops were
withdrawn again. The Italians evacuated Janina and withdrew from Greek territory, except the zone through which
runs the Santi Quaranta–Korcha road.

But the antagonism which existed between the French,
Italians, Serbs, and Greeks, undermined the morale of
Sarrail's cosmospolitan army and produced stagnation. To
counteract this state of affairs, he endeavoured to maintain
a certain military activity by a series of minor operations.
The most important of these began on the 11th September,
when French and Albanian troops under General Jacquemot
captured Pogradets, and advanced almost to Lin. In October
a further advance was made into the upper Shkumbi Valley,
but this was suspended owing to representations by the
Italian Government, which was apprehensive of the occupation by the French of Albanian territory, which they might
subsequently hand over to the Serbs. The French therefore

withdrew to Pogradets, leaving the Albanians to operate
independently in the Shkumbi region.

On the 10th December Sarrail was relieved of his command
for political reasons, and was succeeded by General Guillaumat.
The latter devoted himself to the task of reorganization, and
little military activity took place. In July he was recalled, and
was succeeded by General Franchet d'Esperey.

"Meantime operations in Albania, which for two
years had been in the nature of post and police warfare,
rose for a moment in the summer of 1918 to the level
of major operations.

"In the winter of 1917–18 the posts of the Italian
XVI Corps (General Ferrero) in Albania ran along the
Voyusa from the sea to Memaliadz, where it turned
abruptly north and then north-east facing Glava and
Chafa Glava, Parasboar, Barguzyazi, and Tcherevoda.
Here it joined the French posts which ran in a north
and south line along the mountains to Golik in the
Shkumbi Valley, and thence nearly east to Point 1704
south of Lin on the shore of Lake Ochrida. Early in
July, 1918, a frontal advance of Ferrero's Italians from the
Voyusa and combined with flank pressure by the French
57th Division in the mountains of the Devolli regions,
forced the two Austro-Hungarian divisions (47th and 81st)
of General Können-Hozak's XIX Corps to evacuate the
whole Berat region in haste, with a loss of nearly 3,000
prisoners. By the 20th July, the Italians lay along the
Semeni and the lower Devolli from the coast to Petro-
hondi (with a bridgehead in front of Fieri), and thence in
an east to west line to the foot of the Mali Siloves
Range, which was held by the French. The positions of
the latter formed a marked salient, the apex of which
lay at the confluence of the Holta and Devolli Rivers, and
the right flank of which passed by Kamichan to Golik on
the old front. The importance of this salient lay in the
fact that it kept the right wing of the general line eche-
loned well forward, threatening the rear of the enemy's
lines near Berat, and ultimately the connection between
Elbasan and Lake Ochrida.

"In August the Austro-Hungarians, now commanded
by Generaloberst von Pflanzer-Baltin, and reinforced by

the 45th Division, as well as by the fresh 12th Bulgarian Division in the Ochrida–Shkumbi sector, began a counter-offensive all along the line. Between the 20th August and the 24th they recaptured the line of the Semeni and the Devolli, and drove back the Italians to positions only slightly in front of Fieri and Berat. On the 24th August those towns fell again into their hands, and the Italians then withdrew to a line from just south of Fieri, along the Yanitza, south of Berat, and along the Ossoum to Mt. Tomor. Meantime the French, the left rear of their Devolli salient being thus threatened, had had to fall back in the Devolli and Tomorica Valleys to regain touch with the Italians at Mt. Tomor, while still holding on to their posts between the Devolli and the Shkumbi. These operations are of interest as being the last military success won by forces of the Central Powers in the war. Three weeks after their conclusion the Bulgarian front was in ruins" (E.B. 32 : 355).

The final offensive upon the Salonika front was launched on the 15th September, 1918. On that day the French broke through into the Dobropolje. The Serbs, who had consented once again to participate in offensive operations, pushed through them, and the enemy's line between Lake Presba and Lake Doiran collapsed. The Allies then swept forward, Koprulu was occupied on the 25th, and on the 29th Bulgaria surrendered.

Von Pflanzer-Baltin in Albania began at once to fall back "with, as his only purpose, the maintenance of his Divisions as formed military units" (E.B. 32 : 357). This was, however, difficult. The Austro-Hungarians had aroused the utmost hostility among the malissori and central Albanians, and those who had been in possession of arms had been in revolt throughout the summer. Now they rose throughout the country, and, equipped with arms and ammunition abandoned by the retreating Austro-Hungarians, or supplied by the Italians and smuggled through the lines, precipitated their retreat, and compelled them to abandon almost the whole of their war material. The French, Serbs and Italians followed them up. Elbasan was occupied on the 7th October, Durazzo on the 14th, Dibra on the 15th, and Skutari on the 5th November. On the 11th November the Great War came to an end.

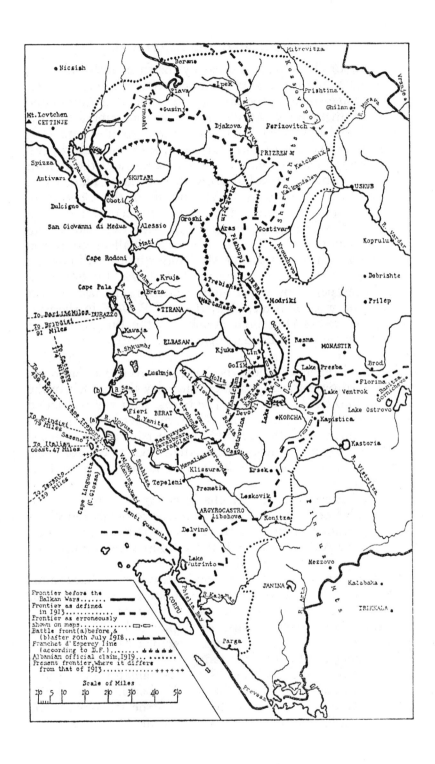

Frontier before the
Balkan Wars......
Frontier as defined
in 1913.............
Frontier as erroneously
shown on maps.............
Battle front(a)before, &
(b)after 20th July 1918...
Franchet d'Esperey line
(according to D.F.).......
Albanian official claim,1919...
Present frontier,where it differs
from that of 1913.............

Scale of Miles

CHAPTER VII

THE ADRIATIC QUESTION

It is notorious that of all the problems which confronted the Peace Conference none was more involved or more difficult to solve than that of the Adriatic; and, by the Pact of London which was the chief obstacle at the Conference, the fate of Albania was inextricably linked with that problem. The Entente Powers had fought, so they had proclaimed, for justice, freedom, and a new diplomacy—namely, the right of self-determination; but they had consolidated their alliance by the old diplomacy which acknowledged the right of annexation, and therefore there arose almost insurmountable difficulties. Even Great Britain refused to commit herself with regard to Albania in any way which might be prejudicial to the decisions of the Peace Conference (P.D. 115 : 565 ; etc.), despite the very definite obligations incurred in 1912–13 and the efforts of the Anglo-Albanian Society to ensure that those obligations were honoured.

The Anglo-Albanian Society was founded on the 28th February, 1918, by the late Colonel Hon. Aubrey Herbert, M.P., who became its President. Among its members were Lord Lamington (Vice-President), Miss M. E. Durham (Hon. Secretary), Lord Treowen, Sir Samuel Hoare, M.P., Mr. C. M. S. Amery, M.P., and Colonel Hon. Walter Guinness, M.P. It did notable service for Albania, and was largely responsible for her admission to the League of Nations. The death on the 26th September, 1923, of Colonel Herbert, who since his first visit to Albania in 1907 had championed indefatigably a cause which appealed to his chivalrous nature, was an irreparable loss to the Albanians.

When the Armistice was concluded, it was decided that Allied troops should remain in occupation of Albania until her fate was settled by the Peace Conference. When during the final advance French troops had approached those Albanian districts annexed by Serbia in 1913, the inhabitants had prepared to resist, fearing that they would be restored to Serbia. On this point, however, they were reassured by the

French, who were allowed to occupy Ipek and all strategic points, which they at once handed over to the Serbs.

It seems that General Franchet d'Esperey, although unauthorized to do so except perhaps by his own Government, agreed that the Serbs should occupy a "strategic line" well within the Albanian frontier of 1913; but whether the line which he agreed that they should occupy corresponded with that which they described as the Franchet d'Esperey or Armistice line (map p. 280; see map D.F.) has never been established. It seems to have fluctuated to cover their subsequent ravages.

The Serbs seized Skutari, but after a brief occupation were relieved by French, British (P.D. 114 : 13), and Italian detachments under the French General (P.D. 116 : 1451) de Fourtou, the international administration being thus revived. The French remained in the Korcha district, while the Italians occupied the remainder of the country. The latter, fearing as Giolitti declared, the growth of Yugoslav influence in Albania, resolved to remain in occupation until the Yugoslavs withdrew (and in March were reported to have demanded their withdrawal: T. 15.3.19), and until their own interests therein had been established. In view of the vast military preparations which Yugoslavia immediately set on foot (E.B. 31 : 628), there was much justification for this attitude; on the other hand, it gave the Yugoslavs a reasonable justification for remaining also.

Italian statesmen now committed a grave error of judgment. They underestimated the strength of Albanian national sentiment and the keen appreciation of the value of national unity which four years of partition under foreign occupation had aroused among the Albanians (W.N.). Moreover, in fearing the growth of Yugoslav influence they overlooked the hostility of the Albanians towards a country which holds in subjection thousands of their race. Had Italy at once declared herself unreservedly in favour of Albanian independence and renounced all claims to Albanian territory including Valona (except perhaps Saseno), her prestige in the country would have been placed upon an unassailable foundation; and Italian security is infinitely greater while a benevolent Albania allied to her on terms of equality possesses Valona than it would be if Italy herself held the port and thereby alienated Albanian sympathy.

"Italy is right", wrote Mehmed bey Konitza (in 1918), "when she wishes to assure herself of the friendship and fidelity of Albania. This may be assured her by Albania's political and geographical position. But the Albanians are ready to assure Italy of their sincerity by more concrete guarantees, provided that these guarantees inflict no injury on Albania's national sovereignty" (A.Q.).

There exist many ties which bind the two countries together. The co-operation of Albanians and Venetians against the Turks in the Middle Ages, commercial intercourse between Italian and Albanian ports where the commercial language is to-day Italian, the existence of a large Albanian colony in Italy, are all bonds which may be strengthened into an unshakeable friendship; and in 1918 the Albanians would have welcomed unconditional Italian assistance. It was not the occupation of their country as a temporary measure which they resented, but the conduct of the Italians, which became arbitrary, their proposed annexation of Valona, and their connivance—rather than abandon their claims to that port (and under pressure)—at the proposal to compensate other States at the expense of Albania.

There were many Albanian Nationalists who were aware, as in 1912, that their country was not prepared for independence; and they were ready to submit to, and indeed would have welcomed the guidance and protection of, a disinterested Power (Great Britain or the United States) until their country had recovered from Turkish misrule, and was prepared for complete independence. They knew that the benevolence of the world, a period of external tranquillity, friendly relations with their neighbours, and protection from foreign aggression, were the only circumstances in which order, tranquillity, and prosperity would be restored to the unhappy remnants of their country. They knew that even were they assured of these circumstances the task before them was no light one; and that years of patient effort were required to eliminate the artificial barriers—historical, topographical, racial, religious, and political—which divided them. But they were not prepared to submit to the dictates of or occupation by any State which sought to deprive them of their territory or their liberty.

Directly after the conclusion of the Armistice the Albanians took steps to reassert themselves, enjoying Italian support in that Italy wished, as her maximum programme, to re-establish Albania—under her control—within the widest possible frontiers.

On the 8th December, 1918, Ismail Ndroqa issued, with the permission and support of the Italian authorities, a proclamation calling a meeting of central Albanian delegates to discuss steps to be taken to preserve national unity, and convene a National Assembly. The delegates assembled at Tirana on the 19th December under the presidency of Abdi bey Toptani. It was agreed that a National Assembly should be held at Kruja on the 11th January, and that the Italian authorities should be asked to allow delegates to attend from all districts under their occupation. Through the Italian authorities the French were to be asked to do likewise, and to arrange for similar facilities to be granted to districts under Serbian occupation. A general *besa* was proclaimed for one year.

In the meantime, however, Mehmed bey Konitza had taken the initiative on a wider scale. A graduate of two foreign universities, Konitza had started his career in the Turkish Consular Service. Sent by the Central Albanian Committee to plead his country's cause in London in 1913, he became subsequently the Albanian representative upon the International Commission of Control, and then Minister to Greece during the reign of Prince William. Thereafter he entered the service of the Vatra, of which his brother Faik subsequently became President, and in 1916 was appointed official Albanian representative in London in opposition to Essad Pasha.

Leaving London directly the Armistice was signed, he hurried to Albania, and in co-operation with Mufid bey Libohova convened a National Assembly at Durazzo to elect a National Executive Committee. On the 25th December there assembled forty-eight delegates, representing all parts of Albania except Pishkopj, Ljuma, Starova, Korcha, Tchamouria, and Valona. It appears that the Italians had refused to allow delegates from the two last-mentioned places to attend, in view of their intention to retain them in full sovereignty. Moreover, in allowing the assembly to take place, the Italian authorities had been influenced largely by the knowledge that obstruction would arouse widespread indignation, unite the Albanians against them, and destroy that appreciation of the benefits of Italian suzerainty which they had striven to cultivate. Nor did they anticipate that anything more than an executive committee would be formed. But, with the exception of four delegates who declared they feared to offend Italy, Albania's only friend, the Assembly unanimously voted the constitution of a National Press (*Organ'i Kombëtar*), and formation of a Provisional Government to defend the independence and integrity of Albania. Turkhan Pasha, who with Adamidi bey Frasheri, Sureya bey Vlora, Ismail Kemal bey Vlora, General Hassan Tahsin Pasha, and others forming a national Albanian Committee, had been working for the national cause from Geneva (T. 18.12.18.), was asked once more to form a Provisional Government, composed of representatives of the three religions, and all shades of Albanian opinion. He formed it as follows:

TURKHAN PASHA . . .	Prime Minister.
PRENK BIB DODA PASHA .	Vice-Prime Minister.
MEHDI BEY FRASHERI . .	Minister of the Interior.
MEHMED BEY KONITZA . .	Minister for Foreign Affairs.
PETER POGA	Minister of Justice.
LOUIS GURAKUCHI . . .	Minister of Education.
FEIZI BEY ALIZOTI . .	Minister of Finance.
SAMI BEY VRIONI . . .	Minister of Agriculture.
MUSTAPHA KRUJA . . .	Minister of Posts and Telegraphs.
LEF NOSI	Minister of National Economy.
DR. MICHAEL TOURTOULIS .	Without portfolio.
MUFID BEY LIBOHOVA . .	Without portfolio.
MONSIGNOR LOUIS BUMCHI .	Without portfolio.
MIDHAT BEY FRASHERI .	Without portfolio.

The Cabinet appointed the following as a delegation to the Peace Conference:

TURKHAN PASHA . . .	Prime Minister.
MEHMED BEY KONITZA .	Minister for Foreign Affairs.
MONSIGNOR LOUIS BUMCHI .	Bishop of Alessio.
MIDHAT BEY FRASHERI .	An eminent political writer.
DR. MICHAEL TOURTOULIS .	A specialist in tropical diseases.

A bureau of expert advisers, and representatives from the Albanian colonies in Roumania, Constantinople, and elsewhere accompanied this delegation. The Vatra was represented in Paris by Rev. C. Telford Erickson. During April Turkhan Pasha and Midhat Frasheri returned to Albania, while Mehdi Frasheri, Louis Gurakuchi, and Lef Nosi joined the delegation.

On the 29th December an Extraordinary Convention of the Vatra—then under the Presidency of Anaśtas Pandele—took place in America to consider the measures necessary to defend the rights of the Albanian nation. The Vatra was composed mainly of emigrants, or refugees, driven from Albania by the ravages of neighbouring States (principally Greece—the Tosks were always more ready to emigrate than the Ghegs), who had generally arrived penniless in America. Ignorant of the language, they had been obliged to earn a living by manual labour side by side with the loweśt local elements. In consequence their outlook was generally very democratic—but intensely patriotic; and the Vatra śtood firśtly for liberty, patriotism, and the defence, cośt what it might, of all that was Albanian: and secondly, for the progress of a democratic Albanian State freed from the shackles of Feudalism and the oppression of Oriental Conservatism.

An appeal was made for subscriptions to a National Fund.

> "It was quite speĉtacular", wrote Mr. Chekrezi (C.C. 233), "to see the faĉtory workmen and small shopkeepers offering two and three months' wages and profits for the national cause. Fifty working men of the Weśtinghouse Electric Company of Eaśt Pittsburg, Pa., subscribed $5,125.50, and one of them gave $210. Two working men of the Fore River Shipyards, of Quincy, Mass., gave $360 each, and two other workmen of Biddeford, Me., gave $650 each. A penny goods seller of Bośton offered $550."

These are indeed śtriking examples both of thrift and of patriotism—yet it is śtill said by the misinformed that the Albanians have no national consciousness!

The point of view of all Albanians was well expressed by Djafer bey Ghinocaśtra at Argyrocastro on the anniversary of General Ferrero's proclamation. He said:

> "The Albanians do not want a small Moslem Albania as some diplomats have planned in secret underśtandings revealed lately, but a united Albania within her geo-

graphical, historical, and racial frontiers. No statesman can justly claim at the Peace Conference that our rights in the provinces of Kossovo, north-eastern Albania, and Tchamouria in southern Albania, are less sacred than the rights of France in Alsace-Lorraine" (A.R. September, 1918).

Had the Peace Conference made any real attempt to effect a settlement upon an ethnical basis, the recognition of the legitimate claims of Greece and Serbia to expansion elsewhere would have been, and ought to have been, made conditional upon their cession to Albania of the Albanian districts they had annexed in 1913 (and financial assistance refused them until this condition was accepted). But although the Albanian delegates were permitted to state their case to Committees dealing with territorial questions (P.D. 112 : 536), Albania was denied representation at the Peace Conference; and although her frontiers were under discussion, she was not considered to have been a belligerent State.

Of the formation of the Albanian Provisional Government (which was never recognized by the Powers) the Italians suppressed all news, and the event was not known to the world until a month after it had occurred, when a telegram transmitted through Yugoslavia by Mehmed bey Konitza to the Vatra was published in the American Press. The arrival of the Albanian delegation in Paris, where Essad and his "Ministers" were misrepresenting Albanian aspirations, caused therefore some surprise. (All correspondence and printed matter were subject to Italian censorship before leaving Albania, and this was not abolished until the 1st July, 1919.)

Italy did not wish her own views upon a settlement of the Albanian question to be complicated by any views which the Albanians might have on the subject. Moreover, she encouraged among the people fear of Serbia and Greece, and distrust between Christians and Moslems, in order that Albanians of every creed might value her protection. On the other hand, General Ferrero and the able officers who had, by their benevolence, paved the way for that friendship between the two peoples so essential to Italian security, were relieved by civilian officials less sympathetic, who regarded Albania more or less as a colony and treated Albanian officials with scant courtesy. The Italians retained directly under their administration the towns and districts of Valona, Delvino, Leskovik, Argyrocastro, and Kolonia.

In these circumstances Italian policy had precisely the opposite effect from that which was intended, and hostility towards the Italians developed rapidly. Several skirmishes between Italian troops and Albanian bands were reported during the year (M.P. & T. 30.4.19; T. 14.7.19), but, if they actually occurred, were not of a serious nature. On the other hand, Essadists, Serbs, and Greeks carried on a frantic propaganda against the Government, its delegation, and the Italians. In consequence the country was rent by intrigue, doubt, suspicion, and fear.

In the meantime, through the tact and ability of the French officers who administered it, the Korcha district remained the most well-ordered and tranquil region in Albania, despite the support which the French Government gave to the Greek claims. But in August, 1919, the Greek command arranged to relieve the French, and this became known to the inhabitants. At once the majority abandoned the district and fled into the Italian zone, while the remainder, the menfolk who possessed arms and ammunition, gathered to resist the Greeks. In the circumstances the French, in answer to an appeal by Turkhan Pasha (S.A. 126: note 49; see also Q.K. Annex. 18), were ordered by the Supreme Council to remain. The Greeks were once again checkmated, whereupon they set themselves to discredit the French administration. Meanwhile the inhabitants gradually returned to their homes; but the incident caused much uneasiness.

In May, 1920, the French began to withdraw from southern Albania, and the Greeks advanced from Florina to carry out the project they had abandoned in the previous August. The inhabitants at once raised the Albanian flag (despite the protests of the French) and rallied to resist them, while volunteers from other parts of the country hastened to the aid of their compatriots. A skirmish took place. But the French and British Governments intimated that a Greek advance into Albania was undesirable since the whole question of the frontiers of Albania was under consideration; and the Greeks themselves wished to refrain from any action which might prejudice the negotiations (then in progress) which led to the Treaty of Sèvres. In the circumstances they concluded with the Albanians, on the 15th May, a Protocol at

Kapistica. Both sides agreed to preserve the *status quo* until the Peace Conference had reached a decision, and to accept that decision; moreover, Albania undertook to allow all Greeks, their schools and churches, complete liberty in the disputed districts which the Greek Army had not occupied. With the exception, therefore, of a small area to the southeast of Korcha, including twenty-six villages, southern Albania remained free of Greek troops. Korcha itself was evacuated by the French on the 21st June.

The inter-Allied occupation of Skutari continued until the 11th March, 1920, when General de Fourtou and the detachments under his command were withdrawn. The Serbs had planned to replace the inter-Allied force, but Zogu, at the head of Albanian forces, forestalled them, and was appointed Governor by the Albanian Government. An Italian detachment under Commander Perricone was authorized to remain to represent inter-Allied control, but General de Fourtou handed over the defences of Tarabosh and the Bojana line to the Serbs (P.D. 128 : 386–8).

The policy followed by the Albanian Provisional Government was to await the decision of the Peace Conference regarding the frontier of Albania, trusting that the principles for which the Allies had avowedly fought, would be applicable in her case as in the case of other small nations; and in the meantime to prevent the occurrence of any incidents between the foreign troops in occupation of Albanian territory and the inhabitants. That for two years it seems to have succeeded, with only one outstanding exception, despite the intrigues of rival States and parties, is indeed remarkable. The exception occurred in 1919, when a young Catholic Albanian officer allowed himself to be drawn into an attack upon the Serbs near Tuzi by Albanians and Montenegrins who were resisting the incorporation by coercion of Montenegro in Yugoslavia. Although the Serbs magnified the incident and attempted to establish Italian complicity, nothing followed.

Between 1918 and 1921 the Albanians of Montenegro and Serbia who had been included in those States by the decision of the Conference of Ambassadors in 1913 made repeated though fruitless appeals for union with their kinsmen in Albania, and emphasized these appeals by fierce insurrections against the Serbs. In January, 1919, the inhabitants of Plava

and Gusinje appealed to Great Britain for protection, whereupon they were ruthlessly and barbarously attacked by
Serbian regular troops with artillery, and either massacred
or expelled. Refugees flocked to Skutari and the surrounding
districts (P.D. 116: 367; 113: 2204 and 1433; 115: 1879;
114: 13), some 35,000 in all (P.D. 133: 1373). It was at this
time that Captain Brodie, who had gone to investigate conditions in these districts, was treacherously fired upon,
arrested, and grossly insulted by the Serbs (P.D. 116: 367),
who feared that he might see too much. Brodie was refused
permission to visit certain villages by the Serbian official
whom he encountered, and was told that it was unsafe for
him to proceed, since the Moslem inhabitants were exasperated
with Great Britain owing to her hostility to Turkey! A
number of the inhabitants were brought before him and
ordered to state whether they preferred to be incorporated
in Albania or Yugoslavia; in the circumstances they could
not, of course, do otherwise than express their preference for
the latter.

When Brodie demanded liberty to proceed, he, with Rrok
Perolli (his interpreter) and his Albanian guides were arrested,
the latter being stated to be Austro-Hungarian agents and
notorious brigands, because they had served in the gendarmerie formed by Austria-Hungary during the war; and
when he proposed that inquiries should be made of British
and Allied authorities regarding his identity and *bona-fides*,
he was told that the "brigands" in his company had previously
cut the telephone and telegraph wires! Brodie was escorted
from the district (D.F. 78 *et sqq.*). He and his interpreter
were released upon representations being made by Great
Britain, but his guides disappeared (P.D. 116: 367 and 1383).

The Albanians of Kossovo were subjected to well-nigh
incredible brutalities at the hands of the Serbs, who adopted
the most drastic measures to suppress their active resentment
of alien rule. On the 14th March, 1919, Colonel Guinness drew
the attention of the House of Commons to the Serbian
attacks upon Albanians in the Ipek and Djakova districts,
which, although allotted to Montenegro in 1913, had never
been subdued or occupied by the Slavs (P.D. 113: 2204 and
1433); but no investigation was made, atrocities continued,
and in retaliation, guerrilla warfare of a most relentless nature
was carried on both in Kossovo vilayet and in Montenegro

against the Serbs (T. 4.3.24). The prevalence of Communism in Europe provided the latter with a fresh label for subject races struggling for reunion with their free compatriots, and the Albanian insurgents were misrepresented as "brigands" and "Communists". In vain did these unfortunate people appeal to the Powers; and in 1919 the Albanian Government dispatched Colonel Redjeb bey Shala to report to the Peace Conference upon the Serb policy of extermination. But he did not obtain a hearing.

It was in these circumstances that a so-called Communist party, but actually a party of oppressed minorities, mostly Bulgarian and Albanian, and "led by a small group of extreme theorists" returned no less than fifty-eight deputies to the Yugoslav Constituent Assembly in November, 1920. But the extremists discredited the party, and outrages gave a pretext upon which was passed on the 1st August, 1921, legislation "of extraordinary severity, for the Defence of the State, terrorist agitation being made punishable by death, prolonged penal servitude, or heavy fines" (E.B. 32: 1122). The mandates of the fifty-eight "Communist" deputies were arbitrarily annulled.

These measures enabled the Government to quell any further attempts by the oppressed minorities to assert themselves, and the most inhuman treatment of Albanians was legalized. Treated as outcasts, they were deprived of their rights, stripped of their belongings, and, under the pretext of agrarian reform, robbed of their land, which was given to Serb colonists. A vigorous propaganda was carried on by the Press, inciting the Orthodox Serbian against the Moslem Albanian peasants, and creating fear among the former of a Moslem menace. For the latter there was no security whatever even against assassination. In short, the million Albanians of Yugoslavia have been subjected to every conceivable outrage and systematic persecution, in an attempt to change the ethnographical features of the land.

In July, 1921, a petition was submitted to the League of Nations by the Albanians of Kossovo vilayet, renamed "South Serbia", begging for reunion with their compatriots. The petition covered seventy-two closely printed pages, describing the atrocities which the Serbs had committed, with the name and address of each sufferer. It stated that throughout the vilayet of Kossovo 12,371 persons had been killed, about 22,000 imprisoned, and 625 seriously mal-treated.

That there was a considerable measure of truth in these statements is shown by the fact that on the 24th August of the same year, the United Committee of Kossovo and Tcha-mouria issued from its headquarters at Boston, U.S.A., a "Memorandum and Appeal to the League of Nations", signed by Rushit Dedan, Bako Hajredin, and Anastas Pandele. The Memorandum briefly outlined conditions in these two districts, and asked, not that they should at once, and without further question, be handed over to Albania, in the same way as the Yugoslavs demanded northern, and the Greeks southern, Albania, but that an International Commission should be appointed by the League to investigate conditions and the alleged atrocities. A similar appeal was submitted inde-pendently by Tchamouria on the 25th June.

The United Committee of Kossovo and Tchamouria has been said to be a Communist organization. This allegation was unfounded; but if, indeed, it had at any time availed itself of the aid so freely given by Moscow to all revolutionary organizations throughout the world, it would not be sur-prising, since its appeals to constitutional States have been ignored. Anastas Pandele is an undoubted patriot: he may perhaps be impetuous, but he is certainly no agent of Moscow.

Although Serbia had increased her population from three and a half to fourteen millions, and had realized her every legitimate aspiration, including union with the Slavs of Montenegro, Bosnia, the Hertzegovina, Dalmatia, Carniola, Croatia, Slavonia, and the Banat, and access to the sea through the magnificent natural harbours of Dalmatia, she adopted a policy of "the Balkans for Yugoslavia". Already holding in subjection a million Albanians and almost as many Bul-garian Macedonians, she threatened to deny her small neigh-bours the very right to exist. It must be said, however, that this discreditable attitude was entirely due to the Serbs, and not to the kindred peoples with whom they are incorporated.

"The Pan-Serb section of opinion in Belgrade", wrote Professor Seton-Watson, "encouraged in this instance by some of the army chiefs for strategic reasons", and led by Pasitch, the protagonist of aggressive imperialism (N.E. 28.10.20), "has always coveted northern Albania: and the Montenegrin Unionists, led by Radovitch, made every effort to secure the adoption of their full claim by the Yugoslav delegation. This was opposed by Trumbitch and all the more progressive elements in the new State, *who realized that the claim to Skutari knocked the bottom out of the whole Yugoslav case against Italy and Austria-Hungary*" (E.B. 32: 1121; also N.E. 4.3.20).

At first the Serbs prevailed, and on the 18th February, 1919, the Yugoslavs demanded northern Albania. "The sole justification for such a claim lay in the terms of the Treaty [Pact] of London, *which the Yugoslavs could not adopt as a basis without stultifying their whole position against Italy*" (E.B. 32: 1120). Possession of northern Albania would not have compensated them for the loss of Yugoslav territory allotted to Italy by the terms of the Pact. Eventually this had to be admitted, albeit reluctantly (and through no zeal for the welfare of Albania, as is sometimes alleged), "the advocates of an unscrupulous 'deal' on the lines of 'Skutari for Fiume' failed to assert themselves, and Yugoslavia pronounced in favour of an independent Albania, merely reserving her right to share the spoils if it came to a general partition" (E.B. 32: 1121). Nevertheless the Serbs remained in occupation of the districts they had claimed, and once they had obtained those other territories which, had they persisted in their claim to northern Albania, they would have forfeited to Italy, they sought by every conceivable means to acquire the coveted Albanian territory for strategic reasons. (See below.)

To the complicated situation created by the irreconcilable claims of Italy and Yugoslavia, Greece, encouraged by the short-sighted policy of Italy, the Pact of London, and Mr. Lloyd George's inexplicable partiality for her, made another bid for southern Albania "as a guarantee against further Italian encroachments". In M. Venizelos she had an asset of inestimable value. Supported by his Foreign Minister, M. Politis, he succeeded in capitalizing his friendship with the Allies, especially with Great Britain, whose support he determined from the outset to obtain.

On the 18th February, 1919, a Commission of experts (*sic*) assembled to consider the claims of Greece. Great Britain was represented by Sir Robert Borden and Sir Eyre Crowe; France by MM. Jules Cambon and Jean Gout; Italy by Signor di Martino and Colonel Castoldi; and the United States by Dr. W. L. Westermann and Mr. Clive Day. To this Commission were referred the Albanian claims, after the Albanian representatives had been heard by the Council of Ten on the 24th February (T. 23.2.19).

With regard to southern Albania, Greece employed every conceivable device to influence public opinion, and the decisions of the Conference, in her favour; and in this game Albania, unestablished and impoverished, was hopelessly out-matched. While the latter country relied upon the justice of her claims, Greece placed reliance upon "vilification of opponents, magnification of self, imagined or cunningly distorted statistics, personal pressure of every sort, adultera-tion of news, skilful identification of present mediocrity with past genius, reiteration of the false till it seemed to be true" (*Journal of International Relations*, April, 1920, pp. 404–24; *The Balkan Situation*, A. H. Lybyer; see S.A. 77). Through the press, notably *Le Temps*, through pro-Greek societies, notably the Pan-Epirotic Union of America—organized in 1918 under the presidency of N. J. Cassavetes "for the general purpose of enlightening American public opinion on the national aspirations of the people of northern Epirus to be united with their mother-country, Greece"—and through the medium of endless pamphlets, petitions, and other litera-ture, Greece resurrected her old claims to possession of northern Epirus, attempting to prove that the district was inhabited by an overwhelming Greek majority, and that even if a minority of the "Epirots" were Albanian by nation-ality and language, they were Greek in sentiment!

In her official Memorandum submitted to the Conference, Greece claimed that "Northern Epirus" was inhabited by 230,000 persons, of whom 150,000 were Greeks; and that if those parts of the *cazas* of Tepeleni and Premeti lying north of the Voyusa, and the *caza* of Starova, were excluded, there remained a region inhabited by 120,000 Greeks and 80,000 Albanians, inextricably mixed. Thus once again "Greek" and "Orthodox" were held to be synonymous. It was just, it was contended, that the Albanian "minority" should be included in Greece owing to her "superior civilization". In reply to the objection that the element described as Greek spoke Albanian, it was contended that although many prominent Greek public men, in addition to the rank and file of the Greek Navy—and, it may be added, Greek Army—spoke Albanian as their native language, this did not signify that

they were Albanian by nationality or sentiment. This contention was again raised by M. Politis before the Council of
the League of Nations in 1924; he said: ". . . Greece could
claim Monsignor Noli, who speaks the same language as myself,
and Albania could carry off the President of the Greek Republic, Admiral Condouriotis, who in the intimacy of his own
home speaks nothing but Albanian" (O. J. October, 1924: 1354).
But because an Albanian minority which, it would appear,
constitutes the mainstay of the Hellenic State, is includ.d in
Greece, is surrounded by an overwhelming Greek majority,
and therefore could not reasonably claim union with Albania, is
attached to Greece by sentimental ties cultivated while both
suffered from Turkish oppression, and serves loyally the
country in which, by force of circumstances, it finds itself,
it does not follow that further Albanian elements, forming
part of a homogeneous Albanian population, should be
incorporated in Greece.

Lastly, the Pact of London, by which Italy was to obtain
Valona, was employed as a justification of Greek claims.

Arguments embodied in unofficial memoranda were even
less convincing. The Italians were represented as oppressors
of a people who desired union with the gentle and cultured
Greeks. The "Epirot" fiasco of 1914 was cited as an indication of this desire; and it was alleged that in constituting the
government of Autonomous Korcha, Sarrail had been the
dupe of political adventurers! "A further line of attack consisted in showing that Albania is Moslem, hence Turkish,
hence an enemy of the Allies, and therefore deserved no
consideration, but rather partition, at the hands of the Conference" (S.A. 90), and in support of this view were quoted
the opinions of Essad Pasha and his adherents, notably
Basri Bey, who wrote: "Thanks to her large Moslem majority,
Albania considers herself still as a little Turkey" (S.A. 90).
The basis of Albania's national policy had always been a
desire to prove her Occidental tendencies, and to eradicate
Orientalism.

An example of the methods employed by the Greeks is
given by the action of the Pan-Epirotic Union, which *con-
fidentially* submitted a *printed* document to the Peace Conference, demanding for "Epirus" union with Greece. To this
document were appended the names of 1,756 persons in the
United States who were supposed to be natives of the Korcha-

Kolonia diſtriĉt. The names, it was found, were either fictitious or forged; and the Vatra submitted at once a counter-
declaration bearing the *original signatures* of 3,250 *Chriſtian*
Albanians of the diſtriĉt who did not desire the union of their
country with Greece, at the same time disproving the names
upon the "Epirot" ſtatement (A.R. Auguſt 1919).

Albanians have frequently proposed that the "Greek"
charaĉter of "Epirus" should be atteſted by a plebiscite,
and had there been any foundation for the claims of Greece, she
would have supported this proposal. "Though various sug-
geſtions for a plebiscite occurred in the pro-Greek literature"
—produced by those who had been led by propaganda to
believe that the Greek claims were juſt—"the official Greek
Memoranda were silent on the matter; Albanian delegation
propaganda, on the other hand, made repeated efforts to
obtain one" (S.A. 103).

In 1918 Mehmed bey Konitza wrote:

> "As for those Albanian territories which are disputed
> by their neighbours, the Albanians are quite prepared
> to accept, when the time comes, the decision of a Com-
> mission nominated by President Wilson or by the
> British Government, which shall make inquiries on the
> spot after due measures have been taken to ensure that
> the said populations may freely express their feelings
> and wishes, and that no aliens shall be temporarily
> imported for the purpose of falsifying faĉts" (A.Q.).

The Albanian official claims included only those diſtriĉts
in which Albanians were inconteſtably in an overwhelming
majority, and had they been admitted, would have given
Albania a chance to become a prosperous State, free from
foreign influence.

In the north and east, the frontier proposed by the Albanian
delegation left to the Yugoslavs all territory in which there
was any doubt as to the preponderance of Albanians, Bulgarians, or Serbians, and much also in which the Albanians
had been, in 1912, in an overwhelming majority. In the south
it included no territory in which there was a subſtantial
minority of Greeks, or which was inhabited by Vlachs; but
on the other hand, left to Greece territory inhabited by thousands of Orthodox Chriſtian Albanians (map p. 280).

The Albanian delegation presented their claims to the

Conference in a series of Memoranda. The firSt of these, dated the 12th February, 1919, briefly reviewed paSt hiStory, invoked the principle of self-determination, for which the Allies avowedly had fought, and claimed the reStoration to Albania of the Albanian territory awarded to Serbia, Montenegro, and Greece, by the Conference of London in 1913. The claims of her neighbours to further extensions of territory at her expense were briefly refuted, and a claim made for indemnification for material damage done by the "Epirots" in 1913. The Paĉt of London, and the possibility of any further mutilation of their country, were ignored. There followed, on the 24th February, a second and more detailed Memorandum, in which special attention was paid to a refutation of the Greek claims to southern Albania which M. Venizelos had succeeded in pressing.

These Memoranda did not receive the attention which the Albanians had anticipated, and the delegation became alarmed by the haSte with which the Commission of experts was aĉting, and its apparently exclusive consideration of Greek claims to Albanian territory. Accordingly, on the 7th March, following the submission of the Commission's report, Turkhan Pasha wrote to M. Clemenceau asking that a disintereSted Power which had not been a signatory of the Paĉt of London, namely, the United States, should be given a mandate under the League of Nations to adminiSter the disputed diStriĉts for a period of from two to five years, and that thereafter, when adequate provision had been made for the proteĉtion of the population from all intimidation and propaganda, their fate should be decided by a plebiscite. This requeSt was reiterated two months later by the Rev. Erickson on behalf of the Vatra, in an appeal to American public opinion; he declared that "America cannot be true to herself and subscribe to such a Treaty of Peace," which placed an Albanian population, unheard and againSt their wishes, under alien rule. This seems adequate proof of the juStice of Albania's claims.

But the proposal was ignored; indeed, no Steps were taken to make any impartial inveStigation, and the Commission of experts "hardly met the hypothetical requirement of impartiality. As each of the Allied Powers was represented on it, any decision reached . . . was likely to be in the nature of a compromise. Such, at any rate, was the case" (S.A. 104).

On the 17th March the Albanian delegation formally protested against the secret Pact of London, the application of
which would be, it declared, " . . . in flagrant contradiction
to the principle of nationality, and the declarations made
on several occasions by the Allied and Associated Great
Powers. . . ." A second protest against the Pact was made
on the 14th April in a Memorandum dealing with the conditions under which Albania would submit to the mandate of
a Great Power; she reserved the right to select that Power,
to preserve her sovereignty and independence by an autonomous administration at home, and representation abroad,
and to prevent any systematic penetration and colonization
(S.A. 98).

The Yugoslavs (and here not alone the Serbs who controlled Yugoslav policy) were in every respect uncompromising. They claimed a frontier to the Isonzo, which would
have deprived Italy of even Trieste. Thus with the exception
of Venice (unless she acquired Valona), she would have had
no naval base in the Adriatic, and her vulnerable eastern coast
would have been defenceless against attacks from the many
secure natural harbours of the Yugoslav coast. Thus, desiring
to strengthen her position both on her eastern frontier and
in Albania, Italy intimated her readiness to agree to certain
modifications of the Pact in other directions, especially in
Dalmatia.

Throughout 1919 various fruitless efforts were made to
find a solution to the problem, while relations between the
two countries rapidly became worse. Yugoslavia was encouraged in her uncompromising attitude both by France,
who supported her unreservedly for strategic reasons, and
by President Wilson, who insisted that his principles should
be applied without consideration for the security of Italy.
Great Britain alone attempted to hold the balance between
the two irreconcilable points of view.

Meanwhile the Commission of experts on Greek Affairs
submitted its report. It had been unable to reach a unanimous decision. The Italians favoured a restoration of the 1913
line; the French favoured extensive concessions to Greece,
for strategic reasons and in opposition to Italy, and were
supported by the British through the influence of M. Venizelos
and Mr. Lloyd George; the Americans seem to have been
influenced either by a misapprehension, or by a desire to

thwart Italy and support France (for Albanian protests against decisions, by majority, of the Commission, see Q.K. Annex 18). Italy was strongly opposed to the cession to Greece of the Albanian coastline opposite Corfu. The Italian case in this connection was contended by Captain Conz, a naval expert. He declared that Greece could desire the Albanian coast opposite Corfu only for strategic reasons, since its possession could not assist her emigration problem, its population was purely Albanian, it was mountainous, poor, and included no good port. Between Corfu and the Albanian coast, he said, lay an extensive and extremely valuable natural naval base, its value being, however, dependent upon the possession of both the island and the coast, and if Greece obtained the coast, since she already held the island, the strategic situation at the entrance to the Adriatic would be for Italy even less satisfactory than before the war, whereas if Albania remained in possession of the coast Greece was not threatened thereby (G.C.: see S.A. 171-2). These views provide the key to the Italian seizure of Corfu in 1923.

The British and French representatives contended that events had proved that the 1913 frontier did not meet with the approval of a large proportion of the population, confessed that they were impressed by the evidence of MM. Venizelos and Karapanos to the effect that a large part of the population was Hellenophile in sentiment—they did not, or would not, it seems, appreciate the difference between Hellenophile and pro-Greek—and thirdly "that for political and strategic reasons it would be unfair to Greece and Serbia to place so vital a point as Korcha under the tutelage and control of another European Power" (G.C.). In view, however, of the overwhelming evidence to the effect that the vast majority of the population of Southern Albania was staunchly nationalist in sentiment, it is clear that these contentions were brought forward in attempted justification of a decision, made, in the case of France, for strategic reasons in connection with her policy towards Italy, and in the British case, because of the favour which M. Venizelos and other Greeks enjoyed in certain circles.

The United States representatives rightly considered the evidence of events which occurred in 1913-14 to be untrustworthy, and based their decision upon the consideration that the construction of the Premeti–Valona road enabled the

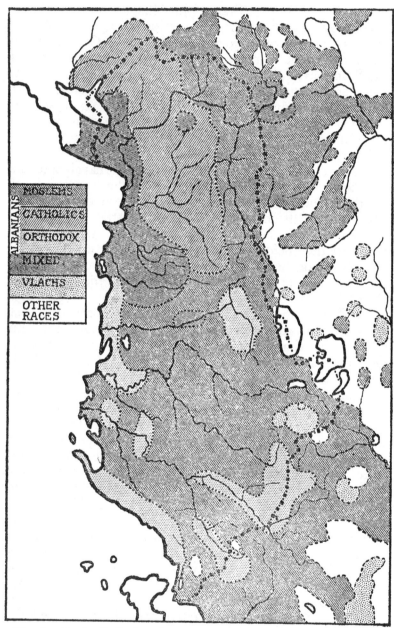

MOSLEMS

CATHOLICS

ORTHODOX

MIXED

VLACHS

OTHER
RACES

ALBANIANS

Map showing the distribution of races and religions in Albania, according to the
French Ministry of War (see opposite)

districts of Korcha and Argyrocastro to be separated without economic injury, that in the district south-west of the Voyusa the majority of the population seemed to be Greek in sentiment and political inclination, and was connected with Greece commercially, whereas the population north-east of the Voyusa was Albanian in every respect, and particularly strongly attached to the Albanian national cause.

The Italian representatives supported their decision by contending that the district was overwhelmingly Albanian in race, language, and sentiment, that Moslems were in a majority, that the atrocities committed by the Greeks in 1914 provided an argument against the annexation of the district by Greece, that the Albanians had proved their national spirit by their insurrections against the Turks to obtain autonomy, that religious differences did not affect nationalism, that propaganda from without found little support, that most of the land was owned by Moslems, that the economic life of the country would be disturbed if deprived of its centres, namely, the principal towns, that the cultural argument could not be advanced against the Albanians, as the Turkish Government had never allowed Albanian educational institutions, and that in 1880 the Greeks had claimed as Greek no territory beyond the Albanian frontier as established in 1913.

"In support of all these arguments the Italian Delegation draws attention to a French publication. The Ministère de la Guerre (Geographical Commission of the Army Geographical Service) brought out in 1915 a pamphlet, entitled *Notice sur l'Albanie et le Monténégro,* which confirms the Italian point of view. A map showing races and religions is appended to it, according to which the Greek inhabitants form only two small groups in the neighbourhood of Argyrocastro and Delvino— which is, in fact, the exact truth of the matter.

"The importance of this testimony cannot be denied. The publication in question has the object of providing military commanders with accurate information, to assist them in the fulfilment of their duties in the districts which are now under discussion by the Commission" (G.C.).

In view of the failure of the Commission of experts to reach an agreement, a deadlock ensued. So inextricably entangled with the Adriatic question was the fate of Albania that further deliberations upon the subject were useless until the differences between Italy and Yugoslavia were adjusted, and therefore, on the 14th May, the Albanian question was adjourned. Meanwhile Signor Orlando's Cabinet resigned, and was succeeded by a fresh Cabinet headed by Signor Nitti, who considered that conditions in the interior of Italy rendered an early settlement of the Adriatic question essential, even if sacrifices were entailed. He at once reversed Italian policy with regard to southern Albania, and reluctantly (T. 10.6.20), but in order to purchase Greek support of Italian claims elsewhere, and despite the conclusive arguments which Italy had previously advanced in favour of the preservation of the 1913 frontier line, concluded with Greece on the 29th July, 1919, the secret Venizelos-Tittoni Agreement.

The terms of this Agreement were as follows (D.T. 9.8.20; S.A. 114):

1. Italy bound herself to support at the Peace Conference Greek claims to eastern and western Thrace.
2. Italy bound herself to support also the Greek demand for the annexation of southern Albania, retaining, however, for fifty years a share in the port of Santi Quaranta, and the right to construct a railway thence into the interior if the Greek Government did not do so. The neutralization of the Straits of Corfu, as stipulated by the Conference of London, was confirmed.
3. Greece bound herself to support before the Conference Italian claims to a mandate for the remainder of Albania, sovereignty over Valona, and a strategic hinterland; she agreed also to refund to Italy the latter's expenditure upon public works, the amount to be determined by an Italo-Greek Commission.
4. If Greece received satisfaction on these points, she agreed to renounce in favour of Italy her claims in Asia Minor.
5. Italy was prepared to cede to Greece the islands of the Dodecanese in the Ægean Sea, with the exception of Rhodes.
6. Italy and Greece undertook to respect religious liberty

reciprocally in the regions which each should thus acquire.

7. Each side was entitled to resume its liberty of action if the above claims, after a certain time and under certain conditions, had not been satisfactorily realized.

It should be noted that although the above Agreement entailed a reversal of Italy's previous policy, Italian support for Greek claims to southern Albania was made conditional—by the last clause—upon the realization of Italy's claim to Valona, a strategic hinterland, and a mandate for the remainder of Albania.

In the meantime the wave of extremist reaction to which Russia had given birth, and which swept through Europe, finding support everywhere among the discontented, spread like a contagious disease among the war-weary Italian people. Anarchist agitation had begun directly the war had ended and censorship restrictions were removed, and Socialist-Communist propaganda spread like wildfire even among the troops. With the exception of one Division, the Italian troops who had served in Albania during the war had been withdrawn, and many of those who remained were prostrated by malaria, while in certain cases fresh troops in Italy, detailed to relieve or reinforce them, mutinied, and refused to proceed to Albania, which was an unpopular station. Strikes paralysed communications, and riots occurred with increasing frequency. These circumstances filled Italian statesmen with alarm, and made it expedient that all possibility of war with Yugoslavia—in which Italy might have lost very much more than by adopting a conciliatory attitude—should be avoided. The immediate and peaceful settlement of all outstanding questions was essential to Italy, that she might be free to restore order and tranquillity within her frontiers.

On the 9th December, 1919, Sir Eyre Crowe (Great Britain), Mr. Polk (United States), and M. Clemenceau (France) addressed a Memorandum to Italy, in which they proposed as a solution of the Adriatic *impasse* that Zara should choose for itself which country should represent it diplomatically, Pelagosa, Lissa, and Lussin should go to Italy, also Valona in full sovereignty, and a mandate in Albania under the League of Nations. On the other hand, Italy should abandon her claims to the Island of Lagosta, and the eastern part of Istria—the

Pact had given her the whole of it—while Fiume should be autonomous within a free buffer State. Had Italy accepted this proposal, Trieste and Pola would have been scarcely less vulnerable—and therefore worthless as naval bases— than Valona if Albania was partitioned in accordance with Art. 7 of the Pact, or the harbours of Dalmatia, because the frontier proposed lay only eleven miles from Trieste and fourteen miles from the defences of Pola: both would have been therefore within artillery range of the frontier.

Although those clauses which referred to her eastern frontier made it impossible for Italy to accept this Memorandum as a whole, the proposals therein which referred to Albania were as satisfactory to her—with minor alterations (G.B. 17)—as they were unsatisfactory to the Yugoslavs. The representatives of the three Powers expressed the opinion that the independence of Albania should be recognized, and that no material alteration of her northern and eastern frontiers should be made, although she should be free to negotiate with Yugoslavia "regional rectifications"; the southern frontiers, on the other hand, definitely excluding Argyrocastro and district, which it was proposed should go to Greece, should be the subject of further negotiations, to which Italy had already signified her assent by the Venizelos-Tittoni Agreement. They were, however, of the opinion that Albania required "administrative advice and assistance", and that in view of Italy's geographical position and economic capacity she should be entrusted with the task. By the terms of the proposed mandate (see G.B. 8 and 17), Italy was authorized to occupy the country with troops for a period of two (she proposed that it should be for five) years; thereafter, it would be demilitarized, and completely independent, except that the higher commissioned ranks of the gendarmerie to be organized in the meantime would be filled by Italian officers. The Yugoslavs were to be accorded a concession to construct a railway from Prizren along the Drin Valley to Skutari and San Giovanni di Medua upon which they were to be guaranteed freedom of transit. (These concessions were offered to Yugoslavia by Albania during 1919. See letter from the President of the Albanian delegation to Clemenceau, the 26th December, 1919.) The control of navigation upon the Bojana between the sea and Lake Skutari was to be entrusted to the League of Nations, which would be at liberty to delegate its power in the matter alternately to Italian or Yugoslav committees of control (Q.A.). A Commission of three persons, representing Italy, Albania, and the League of Nations, the Albanian representative to be designated by the Allies, was to be appointed to elaborate the terms of the mandate and organic law of Albania, and to submit its recommendations at the end of five months, but final decisions were to be made by the Council of the League acting by a majority vote (G.B.). Italy subsequently proposed that the Italian Government, in consultation with the Albanian authorities, should fulfil the task for which it was proposed to constitute the above-mentioned Commission.

Although these proposals were unsatisfactory from the Albanian point of view, they removed every legitimate foundation for the Yugoslav claims to northern Albania. In the first place the Yugoslavs complained that their frontier with Albania was wholly dominated by the Albanian positions; this was provided for by the clause referring to "regional rectifications". Secondly, they protested that Albania, virtually in the hands of Italy, would constitute a menace to them; but whatever foundation existed for this assertion was removed by the same clause, by the limitation of the period of Italian military occupation, and by the stipulation that at the end of five years Albania should be demilitarized. The control by Italian officers of the gendarmerie constituted a threat to Yugoslavia only to the extent that it precluded prospective intrigues in the country. Thirdly, the Yugoslavs claimed the Drin Valley, as being the most direct route from South Serbia—of which they are in illegitimate possession—to the sea, but the concession to build a railway removed all foundation for further claims upon this basis. Fourthly, they asserted, as the Montenegrins had done in 1913, that since the Bojana was choked, had in consequence flooded Montenegrin territory at the northern end of Lake Skutari, and was not navigable except by small craft, it should be wholly included in Yugoslavia; but this difficulty was effectually overcome by the proposed control by the League of Nations. But these proposals did not satisfy the Yugoslavs, although they removed every pretext for their claims to northern Albania except the fundamental one provided by offensive strategy, which seems likewise to supply the only reasonable explanation of their refusal to agree to the neutralization of their coastline.

x

The Italian attitude at this juncture with regard to the frontiers of Albania was clearly expressed in Section VI of her official Memorandum, of the 10th December, in reply to the Memorandum of the previous day:

> "Le Mémorandum des Gouvernements alliés propose au No 8 qu'une discussion devrait se faire au sujet des frontières de l'Albanie. La Délégation italienne ne doute pas que, dans la pensée des Alliés, cette discussion devra se borner aux frontières de l'Albanie méridionale, étant déjà établi qu'au nord et à l'est, les frontières fixées en 1913 ne pourraient subir des restrictions qui mettraient le futur État albanais en condition de ne pouvoir subsister.
>
> "A ce sujet, il semble opportun de rappeler qu'en 1913 les régions albanaises de Ipek, Djakova, et Dibra ont été annexées à la Serbie et au Monténégro" (Q.A.).

As regards the proposed cession of territory to Greece, Italy contended, in accordance with the spirit of the Venizelos-Tittoni Agreement, that the proposals made by M. Venizelos on the 26th February, 1919, should be taken as the basis of negotiations, but that the most satisfactory settlement would be arrived at by an examination by representatives of the four Powers of the claims of Greece and Albania, as set forth by one representative of each; and that the representatives of the Powers should make a decision upon the evidence set forth, or alternatively, submit all or any part of the disputed area to a plebiscite (G.B. 16). Since the Powers did not seem disposed to accept Italy's counter-proposals to the Memorandum of the 9th December, Signor Nitti, on the 6th January, 1920, demanded the fulfilment of the terms of the Pact of London, with certain modifications. These were that Fiume should be independent within the proposed "buffer" State—whose south-western frontier should correspond with that proposed by the Pact—but connected by a strip of territory with Italy. The latter should acquire Cherso and Lagosta as well as Pelagosa, Lussin, and Lissa. The coast from Fiume to the Voyusa should be neutralized, and the civil rights of the Italian element in Dalmatia guaranteed. Italy had renounced her claims in Dalmatia in return for advantages in Albania and for Fiume.

On the 8th January Yugoslavia submitted her reply to

the Memorandum of the 9th December, which satisfied her no more than Italy. With regard to Albania, she declared that the re-establishment of Albania as a completely independent State, *but with a rectified frontier*, was, in her opinion, the most satisfactory solution of the Albanian question. She stated further (which is especially interesting in view of the allegations which were made subsequently) that:

"Nous considérons que l'Albanie possède des éléments suffisants pour s'administrer elle-même, et qu'elle saura s'administrer au points de vue économique et politique d'une manière plus appropriée que si elle était soumise à une administration étrangère quelconque."

If, however, the Powers did not agree to the re-establishment of Albania as a completely independent State, and decided to give a mandate to a foreign Power, then in those circumstances she demanded northern Albania.

In support of this demand the Serbs marshalled all those pretexts of which they had been completely deprived by the Memorandum of the 9th December, again claimed Skutari upon obscure historical grounds, and added that they had shed torrents of blood for the town in 1913. They did not, however, mention the blood which the Albanians had shed upon more than one occasion in its defence! In brief, the whole basis of the Yugoslav claim was that, since they already possessed three-quarters of northern Albania proper, they should possess the whole of it.

After some further correspondence, an agreement was reached on the 14th January between Signor Nitti, Mr. Lloyd George, and M. Clemenceau, but in the absence of Mr. Polk, the United States representative. The terms of this Agreement were that the whole of Istria and Fiume should go to Italy, but Susak to Yugoslavia—the port and railway under the League of Nations; Lussin, Lissa, and Pelagosa should go to Italy, but should be demilitarized; Zara should be independent and free to choose its own diplomatic representative. Italy should have a mandate in Albania under the League of Nations, but Yugoslavia should acquire northern Albania—including the Drin Valley, Skutari, and San Giovanni di Medua—which should be granted a special autonomous régime. As regards the Greco-Albanian frontier, the line proposed by the British and French representatives on the

Commission of experts on Greek Affairs (see map, p. 164) was adopted; this line gave Argyrocastro and Korcha to Greece.

Italy was undoubtedly reluctant to agree (T. 9.2.20) to the above concession to Yugoslavia in Albania. It seems, however, that she accepted this arrangement rather than forfeit the security of her eastern frontier, or prolong a dispute which threatened to provoke armed conflict at a time when she was paralysed by civil unrest. M. Clemenceau's readiness to make concessions to Yugoslavia at Albania's expense is intelligible, but Mr. Lloyd George's acquiescence can be attributed only to an anxiety to add an Adriatic feather to his cap. He showed a profound indifference for that moral obligation which Great Britain had incurred, which he himself acknowledged, and which had been confirmed by Mr. (now Lord) Balfour when on the 5th December, 1917, in reply to Commander Wedgwood, who asked whether "H.M. Government will see to it" that Albania "be not used as a pool or a consolation prize", he said: "H.M. Government have the warmest sympathy with the Albanian people, and would welcome any solution which, accompanied by adequate security against future strife, was of a nature to safeguard the full exercise of their national rights" (P.D. 100: 400); and again, on the 18th February, 1918, "the arrangements come to in 1913, to which Albania was not a party, have ceased to have binding force, as all the signatory Powers are now engaged in war. . . . As regards the future . . . His Majesty's Government would be glad to see the principle of nationality applied as far as possible to this as to other difficult questions which will have to be settled by the Peace Conference" (P.D. 103: 454. See also P.D.L. 32: 319).

Yugoslavia, however, objected to the proposals. She did not consider that the Albanian districts offered her were so valuable as the eastern part of Istria, Fiume, and Zara, and to these places maintained her claim. But above all, she was aware that, did she accept Albanian territory, she would be unable to protest against the occupation by Italy of the remainder. She therefore reiterated her pronouncement in favour of an independent Albania—and continued to do so until the Treaty of Rapallo was signed on the 12th November, 1920.

President Wilson likewise objected to an agreement which had been arrived at in the absence of the United States Representative; he also objected to its terms, and on the 10th February stated precisely what these objections were. First, they gave to Italy the whole of Istria and Fiume. Secondly, he wrote:

"The Memorandum of the 9th December maintained in large measure the unity of the Albanian State. That of the 14th January partitions the Albanian people, against their vehement protests, among three different alien Powers."

To President Wilson's criticism Lloyd George and Clemenceau replied that they had merely endeavoured to find a basis for settlement acceptable to all parties. With regard to Albania, they maintained that the proposed lines of partition corresponded approximately with religious divisions, that partition upon these lines would tend to remove the religious differences which divided the race, and did not preclude the eventual realization by the Albanians of national unity and independence! Briefly, "the Entente statesmen explained that they did not mean to do what they had announced, and then went on with their plans" (Gibbons: *Europe Since 1918*: see S.A.). This attempt to justify an unscrupulous deal reveals either a criminal indifference to the admitted principles of justice, or an abysmal ignorance of Balkan affairs. Fortunately, President Wilson did not share their opinion, and expressed his belief that partition would merely accentuate any religious differences which did exist; and on the 6th March the United States closed the controversy with a Note which stated that

"Albanian questions should not be included in the proposed joint discussion of Italy and Yugoslavia, and the President must reaffirm that he cannot possibly approve of any plan which assigns to Yugoslavia in the northern districts of Albania territorial compensation for what she is deprived of elsewhere" (P.C. and Q.A.). Thus "Italy and Yugoslavia were left to settle their differences, if they could, by separate negotiations, with the proviso that they must not come to terms at the expense of Albania" (E.B. 32: 46).

In emphasis of this point of view M. Constantine Chekrezi was recognized as Albanian Representative in the United States (N.E. 29.4.20).

The destiny of Albania was thus at last disentangled from other issues; it was not, however, settled. Italy was still determined to hold Valona and a mandate in Albania, and while she did so the Yugoslavs had a foundation for their claims to Albanian territory, which, once the United States had withdrawn from interference in European affairs, might have been admitted by Italy, despite Mr. Wilson's pronouncement, in the same way as the Greek claims had been admitted. This danger was accentuated when in April the Yugoslavs proposed that direct negotiations would be more likely to produce an amicable settlement than further attempts in conjunction with the representatives of other Powers! The Italians accepted the proposal, and on the 10th May Signor Scialoja, M. Pasitch, and M. Trumbitch met at Pallanza. But a Cabinet crisis in Italy interrupted the proceedings, Nitti was succeeded as Prime Minister by Giolitti, and direct negotiations were not resumed until the 8th November. In the meantime the Albanians settled their own destiny. The remaining points at issue between Italy and Yugoslavia were settled by the Treaty of Rapallo. Italy abandoned her claims to any part of the Yugoslav coastline, but obtained a most favourable eastern frontier.

Italy's resolve to retain Valona, the basis which that resolve gave to Greek and Yugoslav claims in Albania, and reports that Italy was prepared to admit those claims (T. 10.6.20), combined with the failure of the Albanian delegation in Paris to gain recognition of Albania's just claims, naturally aroused the wildest indignation in the country and turned patience to impatience and alarm. An agitation—which the Serbs certainly did not discourage—began in the north in favour of active measures against the Italians; and the Provisional Government, which had been inclined to co-operate with them (on the basis of General Ferrero's proclamation) lost the confidence of the people.

The Italians, who had every reason to avoid a conflict in Albania, had permitted, in an attempt to stem the rising tide of unrest, the Provisional Government to take over the administration of the Kolonia, Leskovik, Argyrocastro, and Delvino districts. This did not, however, counteract the tactlessness of the Italian officials, who spoke freely of their resolve to remain at any rate at Valona.

On the 28th November, 1919, during the celebration at

Valona of Albanian independence day, incidents occurred which still further aroused popular indignation; rumours too began to circulate that an Agreement had been signed between Greece and Italy, which were substantiated by the withdrawal of the Italians from certain points in southern Albania on the Santi Quaranta–Korcha road. Shortly afterwards the Greek Press divulged the existence of the Venizelos-Tittoni Agreement, and soon afterwards came news of the Agreement of the 14th January.

These circumstances united the whole country, and a National Congress was convened at Lushnja on the 28th January, 1920, under the presidency of Suleiman bey Delvino. The assembled delegates concluded that the position of their country was desperate, that they had been mistaken in believing that the principles of justice and self-determination would be applied in their case, wrong in trusting to the benevolence of the Powers. They decided that while representations to the Powers should continue, they themselves must take active steps both to free their land from foreign troops and influence, and to demonstrate to the world their determination to preserve the independence and integrity of their country (S.A. 123 : note 41); and for this purpose they decided that a general election must take place, a National Legislative Assembly be called, and a fresh and more active Government (P.D. 128 : 386–8), which was ready to act without hesitation upon these lines, must be formed.

Accordingly a *besa* was proclaimed throughout the country, feuds ceased, and despite the presence of Italian troops a general election took place. The deputies elected by the people—including representatives from Korcha, Pogradets, and Valona, the refugees from the areas under Serbian occupation, and even from districts beyond those frontiers delimited in 1913—assembled at Tirana on the 27th March, 1920, and the following Cabinet was formed:

SULEIMAN BEY DELVINO	. Prime Minister.
AHMED BEY ZOGU . . .	Minister of the Interior.
MEHMED BEY KONITZA .	. Minister for Foreign Affairs.
KADRI BEY PRISHTINA .	. Minister of Justice.
SOTIR PETSI	. Minister of Education.
L. COBA	. Minister of Finance.
ESHREF FRASHERI . .	. Minister of Public Works.

Thus began the Parliamentary life of Albania. In the proclamation which opened the proceedings, the desire was expressed that the Albanians might be permitted to live in harmony with their neighbours and the hope that Italy would abandon her former policy and champion Albanian independence. Gratitude was expressed to President Wilson, and a plea for justice made (N.E. 22.4.20).

A further problem had confronted the deputies assembled at Lushnja, namely, whether the country should declare itself a Republic or remain a Principality. The return of Prince William, certainly at that critical stage, was precluded firstly by the artificial antipathy which propaganda had aroused among the victorious Powers and their allies (upon whom Albania was now dependent for her existence) against the German races (and especially German royalty), on whose side the Prince had fought; secondly, by the effect which unjustifiable Entente propaganda had had upon his reputation among some sections of the Albanian people; thirdly, by the fact that, as in 1914, he would have become the powerless axis of unlimited intrigue which would have rent the country; fourthly, by the mutual hostility which had arisen between the Prince and Italy (in consequence of Italy's attitude and policy in 1914) and the Prince's resolute attitude with regard to the absolute independence of Albania (he had protested against General Ferrero's proclamation as an infringement of it); and lastly, a court was at that stage an expense which Albania was in no position to bear. (Should the present King die, the return of Prince William would not seem to be precluded; and in view of the fact that he possesses the inestimable advantage of being beholden to no Power, is a European Prince (now) speaking the Albanian language, and has (now) an intimate knowledge of Albanian affairs, his restoration in those circumstances, and under the auspices of the League of Nations, might prove of inestimable advantage both to Albania and to the cause of European peace.)

The National Assembly resolved that until the integrity of Albania was assured, foreign influence eliminated, and a Constituent Assembly convened to make a decision, the whole question of the constitution of the country should be held in abeyance, but that in the meantime, since she was still nominally a Principality, a High Council of Regency representing the four religious divisions of the country should be elected by the deputies to fulfil the functions of the Prince. Its powers were practically limited to the convocation and dissolution of Parliament.

The High Council of Regency was composed as follows:

AKIF PASHA ELBASANI	President of the Council of Regency—*Bektashi* Moslem.
MONSIGNOR LOUIS BUMCHI	Bishop of Alessio—Roman Catholic.
DR. MICHAEL TOURTOULIS	Albanian Orthodox Christian.
ABDI BEY TOPTANI	Of the family, but in no way connected with the intrigues of Essad Pasha—*Sunni* Moslem.

The delegation in Paris was also reconstituted. Turkhan Pasha had become too old for the arduous task of claiming justice from the consummate jugglers with principles in Paris, and retired to Rome. He died at Neuilly on the 18th February, 1927. Monsignor Bumchi and Dr. Tourtoulis were recalled to the Council of Regency.

The reconstituted delegation was composed as follows:

MEHMED BEY KONITZA	Minister for Foreign Affairs—unchanged.
MIDHAT BEY FRASHERI	Unchanged.
PANDELE EVANGHELI	Of the Albanian colony in Roumania.
MR. C. TELFORD ERICKSON	An American citizen of Scandinavian origin.

Mr. Erickson went first to Albania as a Congregational missionary. In 1913 he retired from this profession that he might serve Albania, being convinced of the justice of her cause.

The choice of a capital presented grave difficulties. Some favoured Skutari, others Korcha, and others Durazzo; but the two first were too close to the frontier, and subject to any disturbances which their neighbours might create, while Durazzo could be commanded by the Italian fleet. Tirana (thus named when founded in 1600 to commemorate a Turkish victory at Teheran), a small town in the interior with some 12,000 inhabitants, connected with the coast at Durazzo, 31 miles distant, by a good road, was therefore selected. The decision seems to have been a wise one, although keenly resented by those whose prosperity, and even existence, largely depended upon the development of Skutari.

The first essential was to organize armed forces. A Committee of National Defence was formed of ex-officers who had served in the Turkish Army, or with the French, Austro-Hungarians, or Italians, and a National Militia organized. A Government loan was floated, to which Albanians throughout the country, and abroad, generously subscribed.

Apart from foreign affairs, and the preservation of integrity, many problems confronted the Albanian Government. The first was to eliminate, as far as possible by peaceful means, foreign influence in the country, and to this end, in all districts which were under its control, any Prefects appointed by the Provisional Government who had become to any degree subject to the control of the Italian authorities were replaced by others who were instructed to act only as directed by the Minister of the Interior.

Although the Government was anxious to establish a uniform and Western system of administration, it was aware that this could not be accomplished overnight, especially while neighbouring States sought every opportunity to foment discontent. In the country there were but two classes, namely, those who owned land and claimed semi-feudal rights, and those who did not. The landowners had always held the principal ruling posts in central and southern Albania, but many of them were steeped in the antiquated Oriental Conservatism which had allowed the Turkish Empire to drift to ruin. These men now expected that they would continue to enjoy precedence over sheer ability. Any attempt at once to overrule their claims would have given rise to endless jealousy, of which Albania's neighbours would have taken advantage. It was therefore impossible to consider merit alone in nominating officials, and this caused some dissatisfaction among the Liberals.

As the majority of the landowning class were Moslems, and as the majority of the trained and experienced administrators and officials at the disposal of the Government were Moslem Albanians, who had obtained their training and experience in the service of Turkey, the majority of the administrative posts were consequently filled by Moslems. The religious, as distinct from the social, aspect was a matter of indifference to the Albanians themselves, but it gave their foes an opportunity to misrepresent Albania as a Moslem State which would be for ever subject to the influence of

Constantinople, and to propagate among the Christians a fear that Moslems would always, as they had done under Turkish rule, receive precedence.

In southern Albania, among the more progressive Tosks, the French and Italians had established a Western administrative system which, when they withdrew, the Albanian Government retained, replacing French and Italian officials by Albanian Prefects and sub-Prefects. This system was extended, ,as the opportunity occurred, into central Albania, where the semi-feudal system of administration still remained intact. In northern Albania, Skutari and its neighbourhood—where the French had established a similar administrative system to that at Korcha—was the only part which was directly controlled by the Government. The malissori, including the Mirdites, were nominally answerable to the Government, but the old tribal organization endured. As when Albania was under Turkish rule, the Church was the principal link between Tirana, through Skutari, and the tribesmen; and in most cases administrative communications were addressed to the priests for circulation among their parishioners.

Progress in every direction was slow, since the requirements of the country were far beyond its financial resources, and could not be otherwise while foreign occupation, propaganda, or intrigue, prevented foreign capital from developing its natural resources; but progress was none the less sure in every direction in which much expenditure was not necessary.

In one respect Albania had an advantage over her neighbours—she had practically no national debt. (Austria-Hungary and Italy appear to have recovered by taxation during the war the amounts advanced upon the credit they had accorded to Prince William's Government.) Had she been granted, therefore, adequate protection by the Powers against hostile machinations, she would have been able to organize her administration and develop her resources. But a prosperous Albania her neighbours did not desire.

The progress made by Delvino's Cabinet, and its failure to plunge recklessly into a struggle with the Italians, found no favour among the Yugoslavs, especially the Serbian adherents of Pasitch, who had hoped that a readiness to make concessions to them, and a desire for their support, would be the corollary of hostility towards Italy. Neither did Essad

Pasha regard it with favour; and there is no doubt that he had very largely contributed to the difficulties which the Albanian delegation had experienced. Liberally financed by interested parties, he lived luxuriously in Paris, and strove to impress upon all and sundry that he, and not the Provisional Government, represented the Albanian people (*Globe*, 28.2.19). He and his partisans supplied both Yugoslavs and Greeks with abundant remarks and expressions of opinion upon which to base their claims; and he worked assiduously for the dismemberment of a country which would not accept him as ruler. It is alleged that the Serbs had agreed to support his pretensions to the throne of central Albania provided he supported their claims to the north (D.T. 12.6.20; 14.6.20); and to him adhered some Albanians who either considered him a sound financial proposition or feared that in a united Albania their privileges as Moslems would be curtailed by the Christians of the north and south.

Essad dared not set foot in Albania; but through his agents Osman Bali and Halid Lleshi he attempted to restore his power. With, it appears, Serbian financial support and the connivance of Colonel Castoldi, who had been sent to Durazzo as Italian "Commissioner", these men rallied in insurrection Essad's few supporters, and the discontented element which always exists where distress is acute (as it was in Albania) and is ready enough to support anyone who pays it. But a Government official at the last moment dissuaded Lleshi from taking up arms; and a handful of the most resolute insurgents were routed by Bairam Tsuri after a skirmish at Breza. Seventy-four of them (including Hamid and Fuad Toptani—formerly Prefects respectively of Durazzo and Tirana, Mytesim Effendi—deputy and Mufti-Kadi of Tirana, Veli bey Kruja—Essad's nephew, and Mazar and Omer Shjak, respectively deputy and commandant of gendarmerie at Shjak) were imprisoned at Argyrocastro.

Essad's attempted *coup*, following his intrigues, aroused widespread indignation; and accordingly a young Albanian student in Paris, Avni Rustem, shot him dead on the 13th June, as he was leaving the Hotel Continental (M.G. 18.6.20).

Essad's death (aged fifty-six) deprived the Serbs of their "chief supporter in Albania" (E.B. 32: 1121); and he was described by their Press as a great benefactor of the Serbian and Albanian peoples! But he died unregretted by any of his countrymen. On the other hand, the trial in Paris of Avni Ruŝtem aroused widespread intereŝt, and Albania spared no effort or expense to secure his acquittal. Ably defended by M. de Monzie, he was at length acquitted upon the grounds that his act was prompted by patriotism and political motive. He returned to Albania, very rashly since Albanian honour demanded that the blood even of Essad Pasha should be avenged by his family, where he was welcomed as a public benefactor. He became a prominent member of the Liberal party.

Incidents between Italian troops and Albanians occurred with increasing frequency, and one in particular exasperated the Albanians. In pursuance of the national programme, a league was formed in Valona with the object of bringing the adminiŝtration of the diŝtrict directly under the control of the Government; but the Italians deported fifteen of the leaders, and at the same time publicly proclaimed their intention to remain at the port.

Relations, too, between Italians and Yugoslavs were the worŝt possible. It seems that the Serbs advocated hoŝtilities, but were reŝtrained by M. Trumbitch's prudence.

The Italian troops in Albania were either suffering from malaria, or demoralized by Communism which was paralysing their country (and in consequence had been reduced in numbers to a minimum). This circumŝtance, combined with the possibility of a conflict with Albanians or Yugoslavs, the political crisis in Italy, the proteŝts of the Albanian colony in Italy againŝt any proposal to partition Albania (N.E. 20.5.20), and President Wilson's attitude, at length convinced the Italian Government that the beŝt course was to withdraw, while negotiating with the Albanian Government for a protectorate over the country and pressing for the confirmation of Albania's frontiers as defined in 1913.

Tirana, Medua, and Durazzo were evacuated at the end of May (the detachment at Skutari remained, being there in special circumŝtances), but the withdrawal was carried out with lamentable tactlessness. The Italians made no secret of the fact that they were retiring to Valona only; and this, coupled with several unfortunate acts, brought Albanian indignation to a head. It was in these circumŝtances that the arreŝt by the Italians of the newly appointed Prefect of

Tepeleni—because, it was alleged, he refused to sign a declaration in favour of an Italian protectorate—convinced the Albanians that it was necessary to resort to force.

The events which led to the outbreak of hostilities were set forth by Suleiman bey Delvino in the following report, dated the 10th June, 1920 (M.G. 23.7.20 and T. 31.7.20):

"After we had petitioned the Italians many times on the question of Valona, and had received only evasive answers with the object of gaining time, finally they sent an answer as follows: 'When we have received from the Paris Conference sovereignty over Valona, we shall be prepared to treat with you concerning the administration of the city. The question of Valona is a European question, just as is that of Gibraltar.' Thus we Albanians were given to understand that only upon that basis were the Italians willing to discuss the matter with us.

"As a result, a great meeting of the men of Valona was held at the mountain of Barcalla, in which they pledged themselves to die to the last man, if need be, in order to secure the evacuation of Valona by the Italians. This meeting was held on the 29th May. On the 3rd June the following ultimatum, with a demand for a reply within twenty-four hours, was delivered to General Piacentini:

" 'The Committee of National Defence appointed by the people of Valona, assembled at Valona, the 29th May, 1920, have the honour to make to your Excellency the following declaration:

" 'When the Italian Army landed at Valona in 1914 the Italian commander in his official capacity gave the assurance on the honour and in the name of the Italian nation that free Italy had no intention to take possession of Valona, and that the only reason for the landing of troops was to secure for them a strategic base in view of the possibility of war between Italy and Austria-Hungary.

" 'The Albanian people therefore refrained from resistance, and for their part bound themselves on their word of honour to permit the Italians to exercise their authority over them, yielding submissively to the Italian military occupation. For five years they have endured this unjust and unrighteous subjection which was forced upon them by the Italian Government, in Valona and throughout Albania, which has prevented their independence, has treated them as if they were the most contemptible of colonies, and has restricted their language, their administration, and their flag with conditions more cruel than those which the Turk imposed when he dominated the land.

" 'But that which casts the greater stain and reproach upon the so-called liberty-loving Italian Government is the dismemberment of Albania for which it provided in the secret Pact of London, thus compromising its honour by violating the Treaty of London which it signed in 1913.

" 'We are not blind to the fact that it is possible for a Great Power like Italy to coerce by arms a small people like the Albanians. But the Italian Government, however powerful it may be, cannot prevent a small people like the Albanians from giving their lives for their ideal of liberty.

" 'In connection with the plan to dismember Albania in accordance with the secret Pact of 1915, Italy, with her imperialistic programme, proposed to hold Valona permanently as a colony under her yoke.

" 'To-day the Albanian people, like others, are not minded to submit to being sold like cattle in the European markets as the spoil of Italy, Serbia, and Greece. They prefer to take up arms, and demand of Italy the administration of Valona, Tepeleni, and Tchamouria, and to place them under the administration of the Tirana Government.

" 'The Committee of National Defence assembled here request that your Excellency will give your answer to this demand of the people of Valona and of all Albania by to-morrow at 7 p.m. The Committee will not be responsible for what may happen in the event of failure to give a favourable answer.

" 'Signed and sealed for the Committee of National Defence.

" ' OSMAN NURI.
" 'QASIM.' "

General Piacentini replied to the Albanians by gunfire.

On the 5th June Albanian volunteers assisted by militia attacked the Italians. Valona itself was held, but most of the outlying detachments, including Colonel Cavallo, Lieut.-Colonel Gotti, and thirty-five other officers, were made prisoners; and on the 12th June the garrison of Tepelini, 400 strong, was compelled to surrender. On the 11th the inner defences of Valona itself, held by some 3,000 Italians, were attacked and the town almost captured; but the Albanians were driven back with heavy losses by a desperate sortie supported by the gunfire of Italian warships in the bay. An attempted rising in the town itself was quelled, and those implicated interned upon the island of Saseno.

But from every part of Albania flocked volunteers, both Moslems and Christians (J.B.), highlanders and lowlanders, under Bairam Tsuri, Salih Budka, and other leaders, to the assistance of the irregulars already before Valona, equipped with guns which the Italians had abandoned; and the town remained closely beleaguered (by some 10,000 Albanians), but protected by the guns of Italian warships in the bay. The Albanian Government unofficially connived at hostilities, and everything which it could do without openly identifying itself with the movement was done for the Albanians in the field. Zogu was particularly active, and indeed seems to have been one of the principal instigators of the movement. But in reply to a protest by Colonel Castoldi, the Government pointed out that "since we have not control over that region we cannot be held responsible for what happens there. Give us the administration and we will guarantee order". Moreover, it is said that the Serbs assured the Albanian tribesmen that if the Italians were evicted, they would also withdraw beyond the 1913 frontier, and the Greeks probably gave similar encouragement. In any case, both wished the Italians to be driven out, and wish and deed in the Balkans are generally closely allied in such cases!

It is very difficult to gather reliable and impartial information with regard to events in Albania at this period. (The contemporary Press is hopelessly unreliable.) The British Government persistently refused, despite its very definite obligations, to adopt an independent attitude or express any definite opinion with regard to Albania which might prejudice the deliberations of the Supreme Council (P.D. 125: 216;

128: 386–8; 132: 1977; 133: 1373); and presumably to
facilitate this attitude the British Representatives in Albania
—Colonel Phillips and Mr. Morton Eden—were withdrawn
in January, 1920 (P.D. 128: 386–8). Information obtained
through the British Minister in Athens "and from other
sources" was considered adequate (P.D. 131: 1624). Thus
reports appeared in the Press that anarchy reigned as opposed
to the actuality of a national movement: and of atrocities
perpetrated upon Italian prisoners, doubtless spread to arouse
popular indignation in Italy. It subsequently transpired,
however, that Italian prisoners were very well treated (T. 2
and 8.7.20).

In the meantime Giolitti had returned (on the 16th June)
to power in Italy supported by a substantial Liberal majority.
On the 24th June he said: "I have no hesitation in declaring
that the Government is not in favour of a Protectorate in
Albania, but wishes for the independence of that country"
(T. 25.6.20). On the 27th he added that Italy would withdraw
from Albania, but that "Valona is a strategic point which, if
occupied by a Power unfriendly to Italy, would constitute
a grave danger; Albania was at present incapable of defending
it, but *when she was consolidated and reorganized, there would be
no difficulty in reaching an agreement with her about it.* Therefore
Italy must retain control of Valona" (T. 30.6.20; P.D. 132:
1977).

There was, indeed, no alternative but to withdraw. The
Communist upheaval had paralysed communications and
demoralized the army. The protracted occupation of Albania
had caused much dissatisfaction in Italy among the Socialists,
and when hostilities began violent agitation took place
against the sending of reinforcements to Valona, and in
favour of an evacuation. Troopships with reinforcements
detailed for Valona were held up by the Italian Federation of
Seamen; railwaymen refused to transport troops; and in
many cases the troops themselves refused to proceed to
Albania in support of an unjust cause (T. 12, 14, 28.6.20;
1.7.20). The Italian Minister for War, Signor Bonomi, replied
to the appeal of the Italian Commander-in-Chief in Albania
for reinforcements in the following terms: "Internal conditions of country [Italy] do not permit sending of troops
to Albania. Attempt to do so would provoke general strikes,
popular demonstrations, gravely injurious to solidarity of
Y

Army, which must not be exposed to such hard tests." These points should be borne in mind by Albanians, who are too prone to congratulate themselves that their irregulars, by mopping up the handful of Italian regular troops, who had no stomach for fighting, accomplished a great achievement, and that therefore a well-trained and well-disciplined regular army is a superfluity to Albania. Had circumstances been otherwise, and had the Italians been determined to remain in the country, all the prowess and valour of the whole Albanian nation could not have prevented them from so doing.

Towards the end of June, Baron Aliotti and Colonel Castoldi were sent to Tirana to negotiate an agreement with the Albanian Government. But Aliotti was unpopular on account of the part he had played in the Italian conspiracy against Prince William; moreover, his proposals appear to have included the permanent occupation of Linguetta and Treporti Points, commanding Valona Bay. The Albanian Government, assured of popular support, refused to consider any agreement upon this basis, especially while the Venizelos–Tittoni Agreement endured. On the 16th July, therefore, negotiations broke down; and Valona was again fiercely attacked on the 23rd (T. 24 and 26.7.20).

Italy was, however, in no position to become involved in a struggle to impose her will upon the Albanians, which, almost certainly, would not have been confined to Albania alone; and already there were indications (see below) of impending complications between Albanians and Serbs. Accordingly, the Venizelos–Tittoni Agreement was rescinded on the 22nd July, by Count Sforza, in a Note to M. Venizelos (Italy declared that Greece had failed to preserve secrecy with regard to its terms, and, moreover, had encouraged the Albanians to attack Valona). Meantime Count Manzoni was sent to Tirana with instructions to propose more reasonable terms, and to secure the most favourable settlement, without further arousing Albanian hostility; and on the 2nd August an Agreement was signed by Manzoni and Suleiman Delvino.

The following statement was issued by the Stefani Agency:

"On the 2nd August an Agreement was signed at Tirana between the Governments of Italy and Albania providing for the settlement of outstanding questions. The Agreement is inspired by the traditional sentiments of cordial friendship existing between the two Governments and the two peoples, and is destined to consolidate anew their mutual good relations. The Italian Government, in conformity with these sentiments, has already provided for the repatriation at an early date of the Italian troops actually stationed at Valona and on the littoral and of those still remaining in other parts of Albanian territory, with the exception of the island of Saseno. Nevertheless, the Skutari detachment [which had not been attacked: T. 19.6.20] will remain in that town. The Protocol also contains provisions concerning certain particular questions, such as the handing over of the administration of the town of Valona to the Albanian Government within a very short time, as well as of its territory, the settlement of outstanding points concerning the private interests of Italian and Albanian subjects, the liberation of arrested persons, a general mutual amnesty, and others."

It is said that the text of the Agreement has never been published. (The author asked for it from the Albanian Foreign Minister, the Italian, and British Foreign Offices, but in each case was informed that the request could not be complied with. He was, however, authoritatively informed that it had been published in Albania in 1920, but was unable to verify this. Apparently Italy is sensitive on the subject!) The substance of it seems, however, to have been that Italy acknowledged the independence of Albania within the frontier defined in 1913. She agreed to evacuate the whole of Albania including Valona, but with the exception of the island of Saseno, which commands Valona Bay. She undertook to use all her influence to obtain full and unreserved recognition of the independence of Albania within the 1913 frontier by the Powers, but reserved freedom of action in the event that any nation should threaten Valona itself or the integrity of Albania. An agreement to the above effect was reported from Milan as early as the 3rd July (T. 5.7.20), and probably represented the Albanian proposals. The *Giornale d'Italia* declared (T. 5.8.20) that Italy had obtained Saseno, the right to fortify Linguetta and Treporti Points, economic privileges, and mining concessions; but this version probably represented what was under contemplation in Italy. It is emphatically denied in Albania (both by officials and by those in a position to speak with authority who are no longer connected with the Government) that there was any agreement respecting Treporti and Linguetta Points or the island of Saseno (one of the Ionian group ceded to Greece by Great Britain on the 17th March, 1864, and by Greece to Albania on the 18th June, 1914, S.P. 107: 889). Italy remains in possession of Saseno, her position there being very similar to that of Great Britain at Gibraltar. A submarine base has been established there, and heavy guns which, in conjunction with others upon the Italian coast forty-seven miles distant, are capable of bringing effective fire to bear upon any vessel passing the Straits of Otranto.

On the 2nd September the last Italian troops left Valona.

The Italian withdrawal considerably strengthened the prestige of the Albanian Government, but met with much adverse criticism in Italy. It was not so much the withdrawal which Italian public opinion resented, as the manner in which it was carried out—it seemed a capitulation, rather than a matter of policy, whereby Italian prestige in south-eastern Europe might be lowered.

> "It is very sad", wrote one critic, "to witness this débâcle after so much noble and generous Italian blood has been given, and so many millions have been expended for a great work of civilization and for the security of our frontiers" (S.A. 125).

Speaking on the 6th August, Count Sforza gave the following explanation of the Italian withdrawal:

> ". . . seeing that a clever propaganda from north and south had induced the Albanians to believe that, but for our military occupation of Valona, Albanian integrity would have been respected by everyone, we have withdrawn our troops from Valona, retaining in our power, adequately provided with artillery and troops, the island of Saseno, which commands and neutralizes the Bay of Valona.
>
> "I am fully aware that the decision does not meet with unanimous approval, but, without denying that four years of war count for more than twenty years of formulæ—and everybody knows of what real service

Valona has been to us during the war—we must yet recognize that without an impossible contradiction we could not elect to remain indifferent and pacific at Valona, and at the same time excite the discontent and dislike of the Albanians, on account of international compacts which were supposed to be secret, and were not.

"It was perhaps at that time [April, 1915, when the Pact of London was signed] not possible to foresee the reawakening of national feeling among the Albanians, which is now reaching the masses and stirring them in a way which quite transcends the old authority of the Beys.

"This new factor is now present. It will operate in our favour. What else could we have done? Incur the enormous expense of an expedition altogether out of proportion to the problematic benefits to be derived from it? By so doing *we should also, in all probability, have been playing the game of other people, and we should have seen the Albanians going off to throw themselves into the arms of their neighbours on the north and south.*

"The necessity for military occupations having come to an end with the war, we will not and cannot pursue towards the Albanians any policy but one of friendship" (*The New Europe*, 26.8.20).

The Italo-Albanian Agreement brought to an end a series of lamentable misunderstandings between two nations whose interests and destinies are inextricably linked together. In agreeing to the partition of Albania, Italian diplomacy had failed to take Albanian nationalism into account; and Italian statesmen were so preoccupied in attempting to forestall and outwit Yugoslavia that they failed to understand that a firmly re-established, independent, and benevolently neutral Albania gives Italy immeasurably greater security than the possession of territory therein, inhabited by, and surrounded by, an intensely hostile and warlike race. Very naturally, the short-sighted policy which Italy had pursued had aroused the greatest suspicion of her intentions among the Albanians; and indeed a certain amount of suspicion remains. But by a policy of co-operation and benevolence, Italy will regain her prestige, with mutually beneficial results. Italy has learnt by

experience that the Albanians will resist any act which com-
promises their independence or violates their territorial integrity, and although there may still exist a small and irresponsible section of the Italian public which believes that
Italian interests can be served only by planting the Italian
flag in Albania, the possibility that Italy will ever again attempt
to annex any part of that country is extremely remote. The
reasons may be summarized briefly as follows:

(i) Yugoslavia and Greece—supported by France—would
either resist any such attempt, or would demand—and
if necessary fight to obtain—northern and southern
Albania respectively in compensation. The remainder
would be vulnerable, difficult to defend, and insecure
unless permanently occupied by Italian troops in
strength.

(ii) The annexation or occupation of any part of Albania
would at once arouse the hostility of the Albanians,
who would resist the Italians. Their resistance and
hostility would prevent Italy from enjoying commercial advantages in Albania which, while she
retains Albanian good will, she can.

(iii) The interests of both Yugoslavia and Greece conflict
with those of Italy. Aggressive action by Italy in
Albania would facilitate the growth of their influence
among the Albanians, since Italy would be the common foe.

(iv) A struggle between Italy and Albania would sap the
strength of two races whose interests are coincident.

(v) By bringing about the partition of Albania (i), or by
sapping the strength of the Albanian race (iv), Italy
would destroy the "buffer" which lies between the
Albanian coastline and Yugoslavia; and *any threat to the
Albanian sea-coast constitutes a threat to the security of
Italy.*

CHAPTER VIII

THE STRUGGLE WITH YUGOSLAVIA

WHILE Trumbitch was reiterating his wish that the independence of Albania should be confirmed, the Serbs recked not of prudence or policy. They were determined to acquire northern Albania. Part of it they had occupied since General Franchet d'Esperey authorized them to advance to a "strategic line" in 1918. It cannot be supposed that their anxiety to obtain northern Albania was actuated by a mania for symmetry in cartography, nor because these rugged highlands offered any economic advantages—which could not be acquired by Treaty—commensurate with the expenditure both in blood and money necessary to subdue and retain it. Their determination was undoubtedly based upon strategic considerations, although there was certainly also a political consideration, namely, a desire to prevent the growth of Albania into a potential rival.

The "strategic line" was ostensibly one of defence against Albanian attacks. Now apart from the absurdity of occupying a strategic line of defence against a country which possessed no army, this pretext falls flat when it is remembered first that the line *included almost half northern Albania* as delimited in 1913, inhabited by approximately 126,000 Albanians: secondly, that the districts occupied—therefore in no way separated from Yugoslavia by any line—were inhabited chiefly by Moslem tribesmen intensely hostile to the Slavs, their hereditary foes: and thirdly, that irregular bands, the only armed forces which Albania possessed, will penetrate any line in a mountainous country with equal facility unless it follows a river—which the 1918 line did not do, except for a quarter of its length (map, p. 280).

That it was a defensive line against the Italians while they remained in Albania would have been a more plausible pretext, had the Yugoslavs withdrawn to the 1913 frontier when the Italians left Valona and renounced their mandate in Albania. This, however, they did not do, but protested that it was essential to their security that the Franchet d'Esperey line should be accepted as the frontier of Albania. Why? Apart from the fact that if ethnology is to give place to strategy as the primary consideration in determining the frontiers of States, then the majority of frontiers throughout the world should be demarcated afresh, it is inconceivable that Yugoslavia, with a population of fourteen millions, fears the attack of Albania with a population of rather less than one million; further, Yugoslavia acquired in 1913 quite enough Albanian territory within which to constitute a dozen defensive lines against incursions by Albanian bands. One must therefore presume that she feared the attack of an Italian army operating through Albania; but a brief analysis of essential facts renders even this theory untenable.

Albania, especially her northern and eastern frontier districts, is extremely mountainous. She constitutes therefore a natural protection to southern Yugoslavia. Even Cattaro, which is a prospective Yugoslav port of importance, is adequately defended by high mountain ranges and the barrier constituted by Lake Skutari, which together should provide ample security in any eventuality. Mountains themselves are valueless and even dangerous in defence. Their true value lies in the manner in which they break up, and hamper, the communications of an army operating offensively, rendering it disorganized, and therefore vulnerable upon debouchment from the passes into low country. Much the same applies to a river—in this case to the Drin—which constitutes a grave danger to an army upon the defensive if it lies in rear, but is a source of strength if it lies to the front, provided it is regarded merely as an obstacle to the advance of the enemy, and not as a defensive line.

Let it be supposed for a moment that an Italian army landed in Albania, and, based upon Valona or Durazzo, attempted to advance across country to invade southern Yugoslavia (South Serbia). When the army reached the Drin, its lines of communication would be extended over about eighty miles of almost roadless, and principally rugged, rocky, and precipitous, country. The River Drin is a formidable obstacle, crossings are few, and in many places it runs through deep gorges. To advance to, and effect a crossing of, the Drin would take time even supposing the Italians had, with the connivance of the Albanians, made preparations before the outbreak of war. Yugoslavia would have ample warning of the Italian

advance, and her armies, concentrated within her own territory along the 1913 frontiers of Albania, would be in a
position either to deliver a crushing blow at the Italians as
their columns crossed the Drin, and penetrated the mountains
to the north or east of it, or to push forward covering troops
to dispute with them the passage of the passes leading to the
river.

If, however, the frontier lay along the river, or to the south
or west of it, a defensive campaign would entail a retirement
therefrom of all but covering troops that the geographical
features might be employed to the best advantage. Strategically
therefore the situation would be precisely the same wherever
the frontier lay, except that did it coincide with the Franchet
d'Esperey or any other line less favourable to Albania than
the 1913 frontier, the latter country would be the more inevitably the whole-hearted ally of Italy, actuated by the hope
of re-establishing her frontier as delimited in 1913, or even
further to the east.

If, on the other hand, the Yugoslavs at any time declared
war upon Italy, assumed the initiative, and attempted to
advance through Albania from the line of the 1913 frontiers,
they would find themselves at precisely the same disadvantage
as would the Italians if they attempted to invade Yugoslavia
from the Albanian coast. Their advance would be opposed
by the Albanians, and once they reached the coastal plains
their lines of communication, extending over eighty miles of
difficult country, would be exposed to the attacks of the
intensely hostile Albanian highlanders. In the circumstances
their advance would take time, and this would enable the
Italians to effect a landing; they would therefore be confronted upon debouchment from the highlands with an
Italian army with a short and secure line of communication,
a safe line of retreat to its transports, and supported by the
guns of the Italian fleet. But if the Albanian frontier was
coincident with the Franchet d'Esperey line, or lay farther
to the south and west of it, this disadvantage to Yugoslavia
would disappear. She would be able to subdue, expel, deport,
or otherwise dispose of, the hostile highlanders, and so prepare her lines of communication in time of peace that immediately upon the outbreak of war her troops would be able
to sweep down into the Albanian coastal plains, perhaps
before the Italians could effect a landing in any strength.

With Skutari or Mirdita in her hands, she would hold the last barriers between herself and the Albanian coastline from the Bojana to the Shkumbi, while the possession of Pogradets and district would give her an invaluable *point d'appui* for an advance upon Valona (n.b. See also Art. in T. 23.6.28 by "A Military Correspondent"). In the latter case it is natural for this very reason that she should wish to hold any point of strategic importance in this neighbourhood, as, for example, Sveti Naoum.

From the above analysis it is clear that while the frontiers of Albania remain as delimited in 1913, it would be very difficult for either Italy or Yugoslavia to carry out offensive operations against the other in Albania. It has been explained that even did Italy hold the Albanian coastline, this would not constitute a threat to Yugoslav security; only if Italian troops occupied the whole of Albania before the outbreak of war —which the Albanians themselves would never tolerate— would Yugoslavia have any foundation whatever for anxiety. Any roads through Albania might be used no less advantageously by the Yugoslavs than by the Italians. On the other hand, if the Albanian frontier lay farther to the south or west, the security of the Albanian coast from seizure by the Yugoslavs would be no longer assured—the farther south or west it lay, the greater would be the insecurity—and *any threat by Yugoslavia to the Albanian coastline constitutes a threat to the security of Italy*. It is for this reason that Italy is so readily alarmed by any invasion or threat of invasion of Albania by Yugoslav troops; and one must conclude that it is because she wishes to be in a position to threaten that security that Yugoslavia has consistently endeavoured by every possible means to acquire more and more Albanian territory and to control Albania politically.

The strategic interests of Italy in Albania are defensive only. It is for this reason that since the 2nd August, 1920, she has striven consistently to preserve the integrity of Albania, and to assist that country to become a consolidated State, a barrier between herself and Yugoslavia. The latter country has, equally consistently, striven to destroy this barrier. She pronounced, while it suited her purpose to do so, in favour of an independent Albania, and expressed the opinion that Albania was quite capable of becoming a prosperous and stable State without outside assistance; but once these proteſtations had served their purpose, and the Italians had renounced a mandate in Albania, she redoubled her efforts to deſtroy her ſtruggling little neighbour.

On the 26th July, 1880, Lord Goschen wrote: "I consider that, in proportion as the Albanian nationality could be eſtablished, the probability of European intervention in the Balkan Peninsula would be diminished." It would seem, then, that once the Italians had renounced their claims in Albania—which removed every foundation for Yugoslav claims therein (E.B. 32: 1121)—the Yugoslavs, if their ſtrategic intereſts in Albania had indeed been defensive, at once would have followed their example, withdrawn beyond the 1913 frontiers, recognized the independence of Albania, guaranteed her independence and integrity, and by every possible means have sought to remove every cause for friction between themselves and the Albanians, to assist the Albanians to eſtablish themselves that they might be independent of Italian assiſtance, and to create a basis for the foundation of a cordial friendship and underſtanding between the two adjacent races, upon the lines subsequently proposed by the Albanians themselves. This, however, they did not do, principally because such a course would have entailed the renunciation of their claims to territory in northern Albania; secondly, because they already held in subjection almoſt half the Albanian race, which causes the Albanian patriot to regard the Slav as his worſt foe; and thirdly, because a prosperous Albania would become powerful, and, in alliance with Bulgaria—the other Balkan State which has a very legitimate grievance againſt Yugoslavia—might possibly attempt in the future to regain the territory and compatriots of whom she has been deprived.

In brief, the fundamental principles which have hitherto underlain Yugoslav relations with Albania (as conducted by the Serbs) seem to have been as follows:

(1) To seek to acquire northern Albania.

(2) To prevent the progress to prosperity of the Albanian State.

(3) To promote diſtruſt of Italy, and thus render fruitless her attempts to ſtabilize Albania as a "buffer" State.

(4) To seek to prove that Albania was unable and unfit to govern herself, and by every possible means to prevent her from disproving the allegation.

The methods by which the Serbs have pursued this policy may be summarized as follows:

(a) By gradual and unrelaxing pressure to wear down the strength of the Albanian race.

(b) By hampering relief work, and by closing the frontiers in times of stress, to reduce the race by starvation.

(c) By taking advantage, whenever the opportunity presented itself, of the heedlessness of Europe, to invade or raid northern Albania, devastate the country-side, burn villages, and embarrass the Albanian Government with destitute refugees.

(d) By organizing and promoting comitadji activity, to cause unrest on the frontiers, and alarm in official circles.

(e) By stirring up distrust of the Albanian Government among the ignorant and illiterate malissori.

(f) By diplomatic action to acquire rectification of the frontier in their favour, point by point.

(g) By propaganda, and by taking advantage of the part played by Serbia during the Great War, which prejudiced the Entente Powers in their favour, to win support for their claims.

(h) By propaganda, and by taking advantage of the profound ignorance throughout Europe of Albania and her affairs, to misrepresent facts, to malign the Albanians as ignorant, barbarous, primitive, fanatical Moslems subservient to Turkey, and wholly incapable of governing themselves, and to ridicule Albania by spreading false reports about the crown, etc.

(i) By promoting unrest, and by spreading reports of insurrections and assassinations, to discourage foreign financial enterprises in the country.

(k) By spreading reports of religious disturbances, and atrocities committed by Moslems against Christians, and by attempting to promote such disturbances.

(l) By sending false deputations and forged petitions to Europe, to make it appear that the inhabitants of the coveted districts desired to be incorporated in Yugoslavia.

(*m*) By seizing, whenever the opportunity presented itself, the desired territory, and confronting Europe with *le fait accompli*.

In the circumstances it is scarcely surprising that the repeated attempts made by successive Albanian Governments to bring about an amicable settlement and *rapprochement* between the two countries have been completely unsuccessful. There has never been in recent years a more outstanding example of wanton aggression by a large country against a small one, than that provided by the overbearing attitude of Yugoslavia towards Albania. Only a few years ago Serbia claimed the sympathy of the world when beset by Austria-Hungary. Six years later, and subsequently, she attempted to inflict the same treatment upon an entirely defenceless Albania, which sought only the right to exist, and gave no provocation whatever to Yugoslavia, the aggrandized Serbia, except that she did exist, and was determined to remain in existence!

When in November, 1918, the Yugoslavs had occupied the Franchet d'Esperey line, the Albanians had protested but had refrained from resistance, believing the occupation to be merely a temporary measure. The troops in occupation behaved badly, and treated the Albanians in a frankly hostile manner; but although relations between the Albanian civil authorities and the troops were everywhere strained, except in the Pogradets district (J.B.), the Albanian Government prevented any serious incidents while awaiting the decision of the Peace Conference. But even while negotiations were in progress between the Albanians and Italians at Tirana, there were indications that the Serbs had no intention of withdrawing in any eventuality, and an incident which occurred on the 16th July, when Yugoslav troops in the neighbourhood of Dibra advanced beyond the Franchet d'Esperey line to occupy another strategic point, convinced the Albanians that only drastic measures would drive the Slavs from their country.

Accordingly Bairam Tsuri was appointed Minister for War at the beginning of August; and Yugoslavia was officially invited to withdraw her troops beyond the 1913 line. She replied by occupying the Kastrati district, and by advancing towards Tirana from the east. Thereupon preparations to drive out the invaders were made, instructions being, however, issued that Albanian forces were on no account to cross the frontier.

On the 13th August the tribesmen of Dibra and Mati, supported by Albanian militia, attacked the Yugoslav detachments in those districts and drove them over the frontier; but although the Yugoslavs evacuated Dibra, the Albanians refrained from occupying it. A company of Serb regular troops (with two officers and two machine guns) and a battalion of Croatians who declined to participate in unnecessary fighting in an unjust cause, were reported to have surrendered.

A few days later Hassan Prishtina evicted the enemy in the Skutari region.

But Yugoslav reinforcements were rushed to the scene of operations, and the Albanians, although offering a stubborn resistance, were driven back. In the north the enemy were reported to have occupied Alessio (on the 19th August), although Skutari, being still occupied on behalf of the Powers by an Italian detachment, was not attacked. In the east they occupied Martanesh and threatened Chafa Tuglaver (P.D. 139: 2214; 143: 52; etc.). In a report subsequently submitted by Midhat bey Frasheri to the League of Nations (O.J. July–August, 1921, 474) it was stated that no less than 6,603 houses, 113 mills, 101 shops, 50 mosques, and 18 convents were totally destroyed; 738 Albanians were killed—238 (including 78 women and children) were shot, 200 executed, 300 (including 146 women and 91 children) burned alive; 37,072 small domestic animals, 6,228 head of cattle, 1,635 horses, and 11,052,750 kilograms of cereals were carried off. Between 30,000 and 40,000 destitute refugees fled from the ravaged districts to the plains, where they proved a source of the utmost embarrassment to the Government. The author subsequently rode through the Dibra district, and saw everywhere blackened ruins.

Colonel Hon. A. Herbert (*New Statesman*, 5.2.21) gave the number of villages destroyed as 120. A certain British Serbophile indignantly denied that there are 120 villages in the district in question upon the Austro-Hungarian staff map, upon which all existing maps of Albania were based. But this map is notoriously inaccurate (T. 4.3.14), was plotted in the roughest possible manner—much of it by eye from a distance—

and villages and tracks were, except in easily accessible districts, plotted from information gathered from the inhabitants!

Mr. H. A. L. Fisher, before the Assembly of the League of Nations on the 17th November, 1921, gave the following conclusive evidence. He said: "I am bound to state that the Albanian account is confirmed by a dispatch from the British Consul at Durazzo, who visited the spot. This is what he writes:

" 'When we reached the top of the range (Chafa Rounes) overlooking the Drin Valley, a magnificent panorama was spread out before us, and we could see from beyond the town of Dibra to Ljuma in the north, some 600 square miles of one of the (formerly) most prosperous and fertile valleys in Albania. With the naked eye and with the aid of glasses we perceived nothing but burnt and ruined villages on all this vast expanse; lands untilled and the valley depopulated, with the exception of one village—Suhodol—which, for some unexplained reason, the Serb had spared.' "

And then again:

" 'I have no longer any doubt whatever that the number of destroyed villages given by the Albanian Commission of Inquiry—namely 157—is correct. I should have supposed it to be under the mark. That evening we stayed at the village of Muhri on the Drin, where some 25 houses were more or less undamaged out of a total of 300. The next day we rode to Aras, which was entirely destroyed, and during six hours' travelling every village and house we came across was burnt. Not till we reached Luria did we find a village intact.'

"There are many further details of this character which only deepen the general impression of the very serious character attaching to the Serb invasion" (O.J. December, 1921, 1185).

This is not, however, all. Of the luckless refugees who fled from the Slav scourge, M. Marcouard, of the International Red Cross of Geneva, estimated that no less than 10,000 died of exposure, sickness, or starvation *during 1920 alone* (O.J. December, 1921, 1191; P.D. 148: 439).

On the 27th January, 1921, the Yugoslav Government
issued a proclamation calling upon the refugees from the
devastated areas to return to their ruined homes, presumably
in anticipation of the investigations made subsequently by
impartial observers, and the adverse reports—such as that
above quoted—which would be the inevitable consequence
unless the refugees returned and the damage was successfully
attributed to Albanians; indeed, it was attributed to the
Albanian troops by the Yugoslav delegate before the Council
of the League in November of the following year, but with
a conspicuous absence of success! (O.J. December, 1921, 1204).
The proclamation was accompanied by an intimation that
unless they returned their houses would be destroyed, and
any of their families who had remained in the district deported.
As, however, there remained little to destroy, and as few of
the inhabitants had ventured to remain, the threat did not
produce the desired result.

In view of the above facts, the following statement, made
by the Yugoslav representative, M. Yovanovitch, to the
Assembly of the League of Nations on the 25th June, is . . .
interesting! It is to be remembered that the Yugoslavs described the Franchet d'Esperey line as a frontier, and accordingly regarded the inhabitants of the Albanian territory which
came thus under their occupation as Yugoslav subjects, and,
if they took up arms, as rebels. M. Yovanovitch said:

"The Royal Government, by its proclamation of the
27th January last, called upon the rebels to return to their
homes, and even promised them an amnesty for the
breaches of the law of the country which they had committed. The period allowed for this return expired on
the 10th March of this year, upon which date it was
prolonged until the 20th March. By this measure the
Royal Government has done all within its power to
induce the rebels to lead a peaceful workaday life" (O.J.
September, 1921, 739).

Comment is superfluous!
It was alleged from Yugoslav sources that Italians partici-
pated in the fighting, but since there were no Italian troops in
Albania with the exception of 200 men at Skutari, the allega-
tion seems unfounded. It is, however, possible that the
Italians in Skutari may have co-operated with the Albanians

in resisting the advance of hostile detachments which approached too near the town. (On the other hand, d'Annunzio offered a consignment of arms and ammunition valued at £800,000, which, however, the Albanian Government rejected.) Doubtless the object of such reports was to justify Yugoslav aggression, and make it appear that Yugoslavia was obliged to defend herself against Albanian attacks instigated by Italy. That Yugoslavia should fear Albania was, of course, ridiculous. Albania's military establishment consisted of 8 battalions of gendarmerie (total, 3,200 men), 3 battalions of infantry (total, 1,200 men), 1 battalion of engineers (for road construction; total, 600 men), and in process of formation 3 regiments of militia (total, 6,000 men), in addition, of course, to the malissori, who, however, could be depended upon only to defend their own localities. (Albania proposed to acquire 6 gunboats for revenue service purposes, and 6 aeroplanes for the postal service; her mercantile marine consisted of 47 vessels, 9 being oil-driven and 5 being steamships; see Report submitted in October, 1920, to the L.O.N. by Mehmed bey Konitza; also L.O.N. *Armaments Year Book*, Geneva, January, 1928.)

In the meantime the Albanian Government sent a representative to Cettinje to negotiate with the Yugoslavs (M.P. 13.9.20); and addressed a Note to the Powers asking that Yugoslavia should be requested to withdraw her troops and that the integrity of Albania should be recognized. Accordingly, on the 16th September, the Italian Government (D.T. 20.9.20) intimated in Belgrade that further hostilities against the Albanians were undesirable, since the whole question of the Albanian frontier was still under consideration; and the British Government made representations (P.D. 140: 1846) on two occasions (D.T. 21.9.20) to the same effect.

In view of the negotiations in progress for the conclusion of the Treaty of Rapallo, and owing to the prudence and moderation of M. Trumbitch (the Foreign Minister), who knew that aggressive action would be prejudicial to a satisfactory settlement of the Adriatic question, Yugoslavia agreed to bow to the will of the Powers. In this attitude she was probably influenced also by the seething discontent and insurrection of the Albanians and Bulgarians of South Serbia, which caused considerable anxiety and embarrassment to the Yugoslav

z

authorities. Accordingly the Yugoslav troops were withdrawn to what M. Boskovitch, before the Council of the League of Nations in November, 1921, described as "their main positions to the east of the Drin".

The Albanians, who sincerely desired the establishment of peace, and friendly relations with their neighbours (and were frankly opposed to military expenditure: A.C.) were aware that some measure of protection against those neighbours was essential. Accordingly, on the 12th October, Pandele Evangheli (of the Albanian delegation) addressed to the Secretary-General a formal request for the admission of Albania to the League of Nations. He pointed out that Albania had been declared an independent State by the Conference of Ambassadors in 1913 and by the Protocol of Florence, and that these declarations had never been rescinded, although the work of consolidating her independence had been interrupted by the Great War. (A further and more detailed memorandum upon the international status of Albania was submitted to the League by Monsignor Fan Noli, President of the delegation sent to Geneva in November.)

There was much opposition to Evangheli's proposal. The Albanian question was hopelessly misunderstood by the majority of statesmen who were entrusted with the responsibility of pronouncing Albania's fate, and their profound ignorance of Balkan affairs was a fertile soil in which Yugoslav and Greek propaganda readily germinated. The principal objections raised were, first, that Albania was not a Christian State; secondly, that until her frontiers were settled and her stability assured, her admission would be premature; and thirdly, that the Government then in office had not been recognized by any Power. France, represented by M. Viviani, in an attempt to turn to her advantage and to the advantage of her protégés Greece and Yugoslavia even the supposedly impartial decisions of the League of Nations, proposed "that the Committee, after having examined the report of the sub-committee, should postpone the admission of Albania to the League of Nations until such time as the international status of Albania should have been decided upon by an Agreement replacing the Agreements drawn up in 1913 and 1914 *which have now lapsed*" (O.J. September, 1921, 733). But Lord Robert Cecil, in a powerful appeal (*Records of the First Assem-*

bly, *Plenary Meetings*, 1920, 645), pointed out that religion was quite outside the question, that the peace of Europe would never be assured until Albania was secured from the pretensions of her neighbours, and that

> "the first recognition brings a State into the comity of nations, and thereafter that State exists, unless it is extinguished by general consent or by conquest; the Governments may or may not be recognized from time to time, but the State remains . . . there is no reason for impugning the good faith of Albania, or her desire and power to fulfil her international obligations".

Accordingly, on the 17th December, 1920, Albania became a full member of the League of Nations, with the proviso that her admission was in no way prejudicial to the forthcoming decision of the Conference of Ambassadors as regards her frontiers. Both Yugoslavia and Greece considered it policy to record their votes in favour of her admission.

This event, which, it was anticipated, would mark the beginning of an era of prosperity and stability, was acclaimed with great joy throughout Albania. Lord Cecil was hailed as a great benefactor of the Albanian people, and it was thought that he had provided a panacea for all those evils from which the Albanians had for so long suffered. But alas! these anticipations and rejoicings proved premature. It was thought that membership of the League would at once ensure for Albania the integrity of her frontier as delimited in 1913, and security from the aggression of her neighbours. Great advantages certainly did follow. She was inevitably, albeit tardily, recognized by the remainder of the world as a State aspiring to the epithet "civilized"—although her Government was not diplomatically recognized until almost a year later—and one by one the nations appointed their representatives to Tirana, foremost among them being Great Britain, who, in January, 1921, appointed Mr. H. C. A. (now Sir Harry) Eyres, formerely Consul-General at Constantinople, as H.M. Representative in Albania. These appointments marked a step in the commercial development of the country, and Mr. Eyres was followed by Englishmen seeking concessions for the exploitation of oil and tobacco.

In the meantime Albanian public opinion considered that Delvino's Cabinet had outlived its usefulness, and disagreement between the Ministers themselves largely contributed to its downfall. It had been essentially a national coalition Ministry—with a Liberal majority—and had been entrusted with the specific task of opposing Italian pretensions. This it had done, and further, had succeeded in reaching an agreement which laid the foundation for the re-establishment of friendly relations, so necessary to the welfare of both countries. It had made great progress in the task of organizing an army and gendarmerie, had established a moderately efficient administrative system throughout the country, and had done much to promote national education by the establishment of schools. But its greatest achievement was the consolidation of Albanian national unity, which alone made possible the entrance of Albania into the League of Nations. On the other hand, although it had brought a brief struggle with the Yugoslavs to a successful issue, by drawing the attention of the Powers to the situation in north-eastern Albania, it had not succeeded in freeing the country from foreign occupation, and the ignorant and destitute refugees from the devastated districts, who were, like the majority of their compatriots, wholly unable to understand the international complications with which the whole Albanian question was fraught, regarded this failure to evict the Yugoslavs as an indication of weakness and incompetence, and accordingly contributed in no small measure to the embarrassment of the Government. On the 20th November, therefore, the Cabinet resigned.

A general election followed, but ten constituencies occupied by Yugoslav troops were unable to participate. The Liberals returned with a reduced majority, and Elias bey Vrioni, a man of moderate views, was entrusted with the formation of a fresh Cabinet. On the 10th December his Cabinet took office composed as follows:

ELIAS VRIONI	Prime Minister and Minister for Foreign Affairs.
FUAD ZAMBRAK . . .	Minister of the Interior.
SALAHEDDIN SHKOZA . .	Minister for War.
DJAFER YPI	Minister of Justice.
KRISTAG FLOQI . . .	Minister of Education.
TEF TSURANI	Minister of Finance.

The election was conducted in the following manner: Each person over twenty years of age, with the exception of military and gendarmerie officers, was entitled to vote, and each 500 electors elected a representative; every 24 representatives (i.e. the representatives of 12,000 persons) elected one deputy. The first problem to which the new Cabinet turned its attention was Albania's relations with Greece. The Greeks still occupied a small area within the 1913 frontier to the south-east of Korcha; but the Kapistica Protocol, and anxiety to avoid giving any pretext upon which Italy might re-occupy southern Albania, or take action under the terms of her Agreement with the Albanian Government, prevented them from taking any official steps to annex those districts which they were determined to acquire. This did not, however, prevent the activities of Greek agitators and Greek comitadji bands. During December some skirmishes took place around Tepeleni between the latter and Albanian forces, and the Greeks were driven back over the frontier.

Greece pursued precisely the same policy with regard to Albania as Yugoslavia did. She was anxious to acquire southern Albania; she feared the growth of Albania into a formidable State, well remembering the leading part which Albanians had played in her own history; she feared the growth of Italian influence in Albania; and she sought to prove that Albania was incapable of self-government, a country inhabited by fanatical Moslems, and a wholly unsuitable neighbour for a State so civilized as herself. Yet "from Byron's days downward", rightly wrote Mr. H. N. Brailsford (*New Republic*, March, 1919), "it would be hard to find a western European who has learned to know the Albanians without admiring them".

Fortunately for Albania, Greece became involved in a struggle with Kemalist Turkey, which absorbed her strength and resources. In December, 1920, too, in consequence of an election in which an overwhelming majority (999,954 to 13,770) of votes were cast in favour of King Constantine's return, Greece was ostracized by the Powers, who hitherto had been unduly favourable to her chiefly through the confidence enjoyed by M. Venizelos, and who availed themselves of the pretext thus afforded to revise the Treaty of Sèvres, which had been signed on the 19th August. In the circumstances Greece refrained from hostilities against the Albanians, which would have brought about an unprofitable guerrilla warfare while her whole resources were required against the

Turks, and no doubt also have provoked the intervention of
Italy, if not of the other Powers; but she made every endeavour to recover the sympathy of the Powers—especially
Great Britain, whose relations with Nationalist Turkey were
strained during the latter part of 1921—by linking Albanian
nationalism with Turkish nationalism. It is noteworthy that
Yugoslavia both officially and unofficially employed precisely the same plan in attempting to justify her subsequent
aggression; and the Yugoslav army vote in 1922 was passed
upon the pretext that she feared Turkish imperialism (M.G.
24.11.22). Both Yugoslavia and Greece alleged that Albanian
troops were commanded by Turkish officers; and the organization of the Albanian Army was misrepresented as preparation
for war in co-operation with Turkey. Turkish officers or
officials took no part whatever in Albanian affairs. But
some foundation did exist for these allegations since many
Albanian officers and officials had been in the Turkish
service, many having held high rank and served with
distinction.

To counteract this propaganda (J.B.) the Albanian Government decreed that no Albanian who had served in the Turkish
services was eligible for the Albanian services until two years
had elapsed from the date upon which he left the service of
Turkey.

An attempt was actually made during 1921 by Turkey to
obtain the co-operation of Albania against Greece, and Turkish
officers landed in Albania to negotiate an alliance; but their
proposals were summarily rejected, and they themselves
hastily evicted. On the other hand, an Albanian mission led
by General Ali Riza pasha Kolonia, which was returning from
Belgrade, was described by the Greek Press as a Turkish
mission to Albania! Ali Riza Pasha had been at one time
in command of a Turkish Army Corps, but had long since
left the Turkish service.

The religious question was, of course, one of the principal spheres of activity of the Greek propagandist, and
reports emanated from Greek sources of massacres by
Moslems of Orthodox Christians in imaginary and sometimes
in actually existing localities. Sometimes, however, these
massacres were reported from districts in which there happened to be impartial eye-witnesses, who were able to contradict the reports. This occurred upon one occasion at

Korcha; it was reported that a massacre had occurred upon the same day that festivities in honour of the arrival of M. Justin Godart took place (J.B.). But these reports reproduced by an irresponsible Press, tended to prejudice European public opinion against Albania, embarrass the Albanian Government, and justify any activity by Greek troops and bands in the coveted districts (n.b.: O.J. July–August, 1921, 469–73. *Propaganda of Pan-Epirotic Union of America;* also 478–80 for Albanian reply).

At the end of February, 1921, the Greeks began to concentrate regular troops and bands on the frontier, which caused considerable alarm in Albania; and the situation was in no way improved when on Good Friday evening the Albanians of Korcha enforced the holding of church services in their own language, instead of, as hitherto, in Greek. The Greek Metropolitan, Monsignor Jakopos—the only Greek by nationality in the town—and a small minority of Grecophile Albanians protested, and it was reported that Moslem Albanian gendarmes had entered a church in which Mass was being celebrated in Greek, a struggle had ensued, and that twelve persons had been massacred. Actually the townsfolk took the matter into their own hands, the gendarmerie had nothing to do with the affair, there were no disturbances, and no one was injured. This was substantiated by the League of Nations Commission (see below).

Albania made every endeavour to arrive at an understanding with her neighbours. These endeavours, and the consistency with which she submitted every matter without reserve to the arbitration of the League of Nations are proof of her very genuine anxiety for peace.

During April, 1921, a mission was dispatched to Athens; and for the third time a mission was sent to Belgrade, under General Ali Riza pasha Kolonia. On the 11th May Ali Riza Pasha presented a Note to the Yugoslav Government, embodying the Albanian Government's proposals for a peaceful settlement and Agreement between the two countries. These proposals are of immense importance, as they prove beyond question that Yugoslavia had every opportunity to arrive at a most satisfactory solution of the matters at issue with Albania, and further, to eliminate every possibility of danger from Italy, whose projects in Albania she has always professed to fear. The proposed Agreement was as follows:

"1. The Yugoslav Government recognizes the independence of Albania with its frontiers as settled by the Conference of London in 1913, and in consequence evacuates all Albanian territory occupied by Yugoslav troops.

"2. The Albanian Government promises the Yugoslav Government to maintain its neutrality (Albania being a country established as a neutral State) *and to sign no defensive or offensive Treaty with any State.*

"3. As soon as diplomatic relations are re-established between the two States, the Albanian Government undertakes that it will conclude with the Yugoslav Government a commercial Treaty and a Customs convention on a basis of reciprocity" (C. 204, M. 125, 1921, VII).

These proposals were ignored.

In the meantime a Memorandum was submitted on the 29th April (C. 37, M. 18, 1921, VII) by the Albanian Government, through its delegation in Paris, to the League of Nations upon the unsatisfactory state of Albania's relations with Greece and Yugoslavia, and requesting investigation, arbitration, and the confirmation of the frontiers assigned to Albania in 1913. At the same time an appeal was made for diplomatic recognition by the Powers of the Albanian Government. It was pointed out that the delay in according recognition and in accrediting Ministers not only made it almost impossible for Albania to make progress in any direction, but also was largely responsible for the unsatisfactory state of her relations with her neighbours. In reply the Secretary-General of the League invited the States concerned to send delegates to Geneva in June, that the questions at issue might be discussed. Accordingly a delegation, of which Monsignor Fan Noli was, as before, President, was dispatched to Geneva.

Before the Council of the League (*Minutes of the Thirteenth Session*, 210–24) on the 25th June, both Yugoslavia—represented by M. Yovanovitch—and Greece—represented by MM. Alexandropoulis and Frangoulis—refused to recognize the competence of the League to interfere with the question of the frontiers of Albania while it remained under consideration by the Conference of Ambassadors, which represented the Supreme Council of the Allies. Actually they knew that a solution favourable to them was more likely to be forthcoming from the Conference of Ambassadors, at which France upheld their interests in pursuance of her own, than from the League of Nations, which was guided by the principles of justice, rather than by the views and wishes of any one country or group of countries. Unfortunately the Council adopted a reticent attitude, and passed on the 25th June the following resolution:

"The Council of the League of Nations is informed that the Conference of Ambassadors has taken up the Albanian question, and that it is discussing it at the present moment. In these circumstances the Council of the League of Nations considers it inadvisable to take up the question simultaneously.

"Pending the solution, which will be communicated to it, the Council recommends the three parties, in conformity with the Covenant, strictly to abstain from any act calculated to interfere with the procedure in course. The question will be most carefully watched by the Council of the League of Nations, which will give to the defence of the people and nation of Albania every possible attention.

"The Council recommends that, in the interests of the general pacification and normal development of Albania, the Conference of Ambassadors should take a decision with the least possible delay" (O. J. September, 1921, 725).

By the recommendation contained in this resolution Albania loyally abided—although she alone held the view that the League, and not the Conference of Ambassadors, should settle the questions at issue—but unfortunately her neighbours did not do likewise.

In short, all that the Albanian delegation were able to accomplish at Geneva was to ventilate the grievances of their country, and repudiate some of the allegations made against her. Basing his appeal for intervention by the League upon the contention that the arrangements arrived at in London and Florence in 1913 "clearly defined the frontiers of Albania", and had not been abrogated, Monsignor Noli stated that despite the sincere desire and repeated attempts of Albania to establish and maintain friendly relations with her neighbours, Yugoslav troops remained in occupation of about one-sixth of the country, the home of 150,000 Albanians, while the Greeks still occupied a small area near Korcha; this occupation paralysed the internal policy of the Albanian Government. "The Albanian people, which has, hitherto, shown unparalleled patience and moderation, may at length find its patience exhausted, in view of such proceedings." With regard to conditions within the country, he said that "internal order in Albania is such that it might be envied by many civilized States," and continued, "what Albania requires to-day is that she should be allowed to develop herself freely within her national frontiers. . . . As soon as the Council shall have pronounced its decision on the vital question of the evacuation of our territory, we think that we shall be anticipating the wishes of the Albanian people if we ask the League of Nations to be good enough to dispatch a Commission to the spot. This Commission would see that the decision of the Council was carried out, and would also make itself acquainted with the general situation of Albania at the present time." This was an effective reply to the oft-repeated charge that Albania's "Moslem, Turko-Albanian" Government was engaged in repressing, and even massacring, Christians. Monsignor Noli, himself an Orthodox Bishop, pointed out that then, as ever, Moslems and Christians were working together, irrespective of creed, for the development of their country, and in confirmation stated that at the previous election many districts where Moslems either preponderated or were —as in the Dibra district—in an overwhelming majority, had returned Christian deputies; also that of the seventy-eight deputies elected no less than thirty-two, and in addition the President of the Chamber, were Christians. He stated further that neither in the Albanian district of Kossovo nor in northern Greece were Albanian schools permitted, whereas the only Serb village in Albania—namely, Vraka near Skutari, with a population of about one hundred—had been permitted to open a Serb school, and that the small Greek minorities in southern Albania enjoyed the same privileges (O.J. September, 1921, 726–9). Indeed, their schools were subsidized by the Albanian Government (O.J.).

M. Frangoulis, speaking on behalf of Greece, took the opportunity to serve up once again the usual Greek claims to southern Albania. He maintained that the decisions made in London and Florence in 1913 were no longer valid, and based his arguments upon the Corfu Agreement, which had lapsed and which the Greeks themselves had violated: upon the Paĉt of London, which had been abrogated by the Treaty of Rapallo: and upon the aĉtion of Essad Pasha in declaring war upon the Central Powers and thereby repudiating Albanian neutrality; but Essad Pasha had been recognized neither by the Albanians as their leader, nor by the Entente Powers as an ally. Frangoulis maintained that by the Kapiŝtica Agreement, by which both Greece and Albania had agreed to await the decision of the Peace Conference with regard to the Greco-Albanian frontier, Albania had acknowledged the competence of the Conference to deal with the matter, a competence which she now denied. To this Monsignor Noli replied that the agreement had been concluded under the menace of Greek guns, that it had been purely provisional, and had been ratified by neither Government, that it only applied to the diŝtriĉt occupied by the Greeks, that it did not mention the League of Nations because Albania was not at that time a member of the League, and that "it did not imply that Albania renounced the frontiers of 1913, nor did it prevent the League from settling the dispute".

M. Frangoulis contended further that at its meeting of the 31ŝt December, 1919, to the 13th January, 1920, the Supreme Council had decided to accept the frontier proposed by the Venizelos-Tittoni Agreement, and had embodied that decision in the Note of the 14th January, 1920, when it was stated that "the southern frontier of Albania shall be the line proposed by the French and British Delegates on the Committee on Greek Affairs. It leaves Argyrocaŝtro and Korcha to Greece". This "decision" was not, however, a decision, but merely a proposal; in any case, the whole Note had been vetoed by President Wilson's timely intervention (S.A. 133–4). M. Frangoulis also maintained that by the Venizelos-Tittoni Agreement Italy had recognized the Greek claims, and that prior to the signature of the Treaty of Sèvres in Auguŝt, 1920, the British delegation had obtained from the Allied Powers, including Italy, a recognition of the validity of that Agreement. Italy had, however, definitely repudiated the Agreement in July, 1920, and proof that she reaffirmed its validity—even the validity of those clauses therein which did not refer to Albania—is conspicuous by its absence (S.A. 134).

In his concluding remarks, M. Frangoulis asserted that

"the admission of Albania into the League of Nations in no way implies an intention to deprive the Great Powers of the task which has been entrusted to them, of determining the frontiers of Albania, nor did it imply a renunciation by the Supreme Council of its powers in favour of another jurisdiction" (O.J. September, 1921, 729–35).

M. Yovanovitch concurred with M. Frangoulis in the opinion that the decisions made in London and Florence with regard to the frontiers of Albania were no longer valid. In support of this view he referred to correspondence upon the Adriatic question, and, more especially, to Article 4 of the Treaty of Sèvres, which laid down with reference to Yugoslavia that "the frontiers with Italy and in the south" should be fixed subsequently. This, he pointed out, proved that the frontier of Albania drawn in 1913 was no longer considered definite. He likewise concurred in the opinion that the Allied Supreme Council, and not the League of Nations, was the body competent to fix the Albanian frontiers, and that the League itself had acknowledged this "last year in giving its decision with regard to the admission of Albania when, although mentioning the fact that the situation of Albania was in this respect very vague (from the point of view of frontiers), it made no further mention of this fact, feeling that it was obviously incompetent to deal with the matter".

Towards the conclusion of his speech, which included a somewhat lame explanation of the occupation of the Franchet d'Esperey line, and an attempt to hold the Albanians responsible for the destruction of their own villages in the Drin Valley, M. Yovanovitch said: "His Majesty's Government has in no way altered its attitude with regard to Albania since the Peace Conference, at which it made the following declaration:

"The Delegation of the Serb-Croat-Slovene Government considers that the general interests of peace and quiet in the Balkan Peninsula demand that the Albanian territory, as it was fixed at the Conference of London, should, in accordance with the spirit of that Conference, form an independent State. Such a settlement would enable the Albanian tribes themselves to work towards

the formation of their State, and would be in agreement
with the principle 'The Balkans for the Balkan peoples',
a principle which is the essential basis for tranquillity
and for the peaceful development of the Balkan peoples.

"During the war the Provisional Government of
Albania, together with the greater part of the Albanian
people, placed themselves on the side of the Entente,
and helped the common cause of the Allies within the
limits of their powers; in acting thus they had a right
to hope that their liberty would be guaranteed.

"Nevertheless, should the Conference not consider
that it is possible to carry out the decisions taken in
London in 1913 with regard to this matter, and, were it
disposed to admit a right of occupation or protectorate
by a foreign State over the whole or part of the said territory, we must declare that we reserve the right to safeguard our vital interests in these countries, which have
been consecrated by thirteen centuries of neighbourhood
and common life with the Albanian tribes, and claim
the same privileges for our State (O.J. September, 1921,
735-9).

The above statement contains some remarkably interesting
admissions, and was in accordance with the policy pursued
by M. Trumbitch at the Peace Conference. But it is difficult
to reconcile its reiteration at this juncture with events which
ensued despite Italy's renunciation of all claims to a mandate
in Albania. It seems that it was merely "window dressing"—
in other words, an attempt to predispose Europe in general,
and the League in particular, to accept the Yugoslav rather
than the Albanian version of subsequent hostilities, to maintain until the last possible moment the Yugoslav case against
Italy, to preclude liability to a charge of inconsistency, and
to preserve Albania from all interference except from Yugoslavia.

At the conclusion of the deliberations, Monsignor Noli
declared with reference to the resolution which the Council
had adopted, and to which the representatives of Greece and
Yugoslavia had assented,

"that the Conference of Ambassadors was not competent
to deal with the question [of the frontiers of Albania].
". . . The League of Nations was the natural suc-

cessor of the European Concert which had regulated the affairs of Albania. He asked that the question of competence might be referred to a committee of jurists. The decision of the League of Nations would be more readily accepted by the people of Albania than that of the Conference of Ambassadors. The prestige of the League would be diminished if the question was referred back to the Ambassadors."

Despite these protestations, Mr. Fisher, the "Rapporteur", declared that

"that afternoon the members of the Council, other than the representatives of the parties to the dispute, had unanimously agreed to a resolution, and in consequence the members of the League, by the mere fact that they were members of the League, and had adhered to the Covenant, were debarred by Article 15 from going to war. It was possible that the Conference of Ambassadors might refer the matter back to the Council, or any question arising out of the present difficulties. As the Conference of Ambassadors was examining the question at that moment, the Council of the League could not intervene. This did not exclude the possibility of an inquiry by the Council at a later stage. For the present the Council would merely forward to the Ambassadors the observations of the Albanian representative" (O.J. September, 1921, 726).

Monsignor Noli "replied that the Conference of Ambassadors had been discussing the question for three years, and that the Albanian people had lost patience. The Albanian Government bowed before the decision of the Council, but it did not recognize the competence of the Conference of Ambassadors", and "reserved to itself the right to appeal to the Assembly" (O.J. September, 1921, 726). This appeal was submitted on the 29th June.

Prior, however, to a consideration by the Assembly of the Albanian question, it was again considered by the Council during its fourteenth session (O.J. December, 1921, 1092–8). At a private meeting on the 2nd September, a report read by Mr. Balfour, representing Great Britain, was adopted, dealing with the status of Albania, her frontiers, and the protection of minorities. As regards the first two points, Mr. Balfour said:

"that the Assembly has been requested by Albania to deal with the determination of the Albanian frontiers, and the Council has been asked to prevent these frontiers being violated by the action of the Serbs. The two subjects are evidently intimately connected, and it seems absurd to send one of them to the Assembly and the other to the Council. I suggest therefore that, as the Assembly has been requested by the Albanians to deal with the determination of the frontiers, they should be also asked to deal with the violation of the frontiers."

As regards the third point, he said, however, that

"it seems advisable not to make the question of minorities the subject of a Treaty between the Principal Allied and Associated Powers and Albania, but to give it the form of a Declaration made by Albania to the League. The reason for this is that Albania is not one of the States brought into existence by the Treaties of Peace, and that its special obligations toward minorities arise out of a resolution of the Assembly of the League. The League therefore deals directly on this subject with the Albanian State, and not through the Allied and Associated Powers."

This statement seems incompatible with the resolution of the 25th June.

It was likewise agreed that the question of sending a Commission of Inquiry to Albania should be referred to the Assembly.

The question of the protection of minorities in Albania was dealt with by the Council at a meeting on the 2nd October. Mr. Fisher, the British Representative, made a report which was adopted by the Council, in which he mentioned that the Albanian Government had stated in Notes dated the 9th and 13th February that it "was taking the necessary steps to ensure the application of the general principles of the Minorities Treaties, and was ready to comply with any recommendations which the Council might make on this subject"; also that it declared that it was "legitimately entitled to ask for

the friendly intervention of the League of Nations in favour
of the Albanians at present under the domination of the
Serbs, Croats, and Slovenes, and the Greeks". Mr. Fisher
continued: "The Greek Government proposes that the right
to inform the Council of any violation, or danger of violation, of any of Albania's obligations, should not be reserved
solely for members of the Council, as under the other Minorities Treaties, but should be granted also to Greece, which is
particularly concerned with the rights of Greeks in Albania."
In reply to this proposal, "the Albanian Government categorically declared that no kind of intervention, open or
disguised, on the part of Greece in the internal affairs of
Albania, will ever be accepted."

By the terms of the Declaration, which was signed by
Monsignor Noli, who pointed out that "the Albanian Government had always granted to minorities the rights stipulated in
the Minorities Treaties" (*Minutes of the Fourteenth Session of
the Council*), it was provided (Art. 2) that "full and complete
protection of life and liberty will be assured to all inhabitants
of Albania, without distinction of birth, nationality, language,
race, or religion." Persons resident in Albania before the
war, with their wives and children, might become Albanian
citizens upon application within two years from the signature
of the Declaration (Art. 3); Albanian nationals should be
"equal before the law and enjoy the same civil and political
rights without distinction as to race, language, or religion"
(Art. 4); minorities were assured liberty to establish and maintain "charitable, religious, and social institutions, schools, and
other educational establishments, with the right to use their
own language and to exercise their religion freely therein"
(Art. 5); and that in districts inhabited by minorities, instruction in the primary schools should be given to the
children "through the medium of their own language, it
being understood that this provision does not prevent teaching of the official language being made obligatory in the said
schools" (Art. 6), and lastly, that the Declaration would be
"placed under the guarantee of the League of Nations"
(Art. 7).

In reply to a proposal made by the Marquis Imperiali,
that "since the Greek Government was not at the moment
bound by the Minorities Treaty which it had signed, it would
be advisable to invite it to make to the Council a Declaration

of its readiness to apply to the Albanian minorities in Greece the principle which the delegate of Albania had accepted in respect of the Greek minorities in Albania", M. Dendramis, the Greek delegate, "stated that he was not in a position to reply on this point, and that his Government entirely reserved its decision and reply" (*Minutes of the Fourteenth Session of the Council*, 115–16; and O.J. December, 1921, 1161–4).

In consequence of the decision of the Council of the League to refrain from attempting a settlement of the Albanian question, the Albanian Cabinet resigned in despair. It refused to accept the responsibility of acknowledging the competence of the Conference of Ambassadors to reopen the question of the Albanian frontiers which had been decided in 1913, and declared, in a telegram to the Council on the 29th June, that the "Albanian people will vigorously oppose any decision involving dismemberment" (O.J. July–August, 1921). It had failed, although it could not well have done otherwise, to obtain diplomatic recognition, the restoration of the frontiers, or to improve relations with Yugoslavia and Greece. During its period of office, considerable progress had nevertheless been made. Miss Durham wrote in May, 1921, that no less than 528 schools for children existed in the country, and that the law was upheld by a smart gendarmerie. The Government had shown its moderation, and anxiety to effect a reconciliation with all parties, by granting an amnesty to political prisoners of the Essadist faction who had participated in the insurrection during the previous year.

Elias bey Vrioni formed a fresh Cabinet, which included three Ministers of the previous one and two of the 1920 Cabinet. It was composed as follows:

ELIAS VRIONI	Prime Minister.
SULEIMAN DELVINO . .	Minister of the Interior.
PANDELE EVANGHELI . .	Minister for Foreign Affairs.
SALAHEDDIN SHKOZA . .	Minister for War.
DHIMITRI KACIMBRO . .	Minister of Justice.
SOTIR PETSI	Minister of Education.
TEF TSURANI	Minister of Finance.
MEHDI FRASHERI . . .	Minister of Public Works and Agriculture.

The attention of the new Cabinet was at once directed to the north, where there were ominous signs that Yugoslavia was once more at work. The account of the events which followed is drawn principally from the official report of the League of Nations Commission of Inquiry (C. 542, M. 387, 1921, VII, and O.J. February, 1922, 149-59), which proceeded to Albania in November, and the official Memorandum upon Albania by the Secretary-General of the League (C. 446, M. 328, 1921).

During 1920 Prenk Bib Doda, hereditary chieftain of Mirdita, had been ambushed and killed in the Bregumatia by Ded Soko, as an act of vengeance for the death of his brother Djeto. Ded was arrested and imprisoned. Prenk had been jealous of the growing power of the Sokos in districts which he considered his sphere of influence. Prenk had no son, and Marko Gjoni, his cousin, was heir to the chieftaincy; but Prenk, aware of his cousin's unpopularity, and believing that the days of chiefs were over, had disinherited him, and left his property to the tribe. Marko Gjoni was exasperated, and enjoyed French sympathy. The Minister of the Interior— of the Cabinet which had demonstrated its benevolence to all parties by granting an amnesty to the Essadists—offered him an administrative post and a salary; but with this he was not satisfied, and on the 28th April, with some sixty supporters, left Mirdita for Prizren to seek Serb support for his claim.

Early in June he returned to Mirdita with large sums of gold, which he distributed freely, and at the same time spread it abroad that the Tirana Government—which was described as being of purely Moslem and "Young Turkish" tendencies—intended to interfere with the religious liberty of the Catholic Mirdites. "It was no difficult task", reported the League of Nations Commission, "to stir up the imagination of this extraordinarily uneducated and ignorant population, living in a district absolutely isolated and cut off from all communication. His success was, however, only partial, for there is no doubt that the vast majority of the Mirdites remained passive during the whole struggle" which followed.

On the 7th July Monsignor Noli lodged a protest with the League of Nations against the repeated attempts of the Yugoslavs to stir up trouble in Mirdita and at Skutari. Upon the same day Yugoslav troops occupied Gashi and Krasnitch, which districts, although within the Franchet d'Esperey line, had not hitherto been occupied by them. These movements of troops the Yugoslavs denied (P.D. 144: 1515). Three days

MONSIGNOR FAN S. NOLI

PRENK BIB DODA PASHA (RIGHT), THE ABBOT OF MIRDITA (CENTRE),
AND SOME OF THEIR MEN, 1914

later Gjoni, who had been completely unsuccessful in his attempts to ſtir up ſtrife in Mirdita—although his propaganda had caused some misgivings among the Mirdites as to the good faith of the Government—retired once more to Prizren.

On the 17th July the Yugoslav Press Bureau circulated a telegram, oſtensibly from Marko Gjoni at Prizren, announcing the proclamation of "the Mirdite Republic" (T. 12.7.21, 3.8.21), his election as President—he could neither read nor write—and the formation of a Cabinet. In the telegram it was alleged that the Chriſtian Mirdites, exasperated by the attempts of the "Young Turkish" Government of Tirana to exterminate them, had determined to conſtitute an autonomous State, and to enter into diplomatic relations as speedily as possible with other States! This mythical "Government" was ſtrangely reminiscent of the "Government of Autonomous Epirus". The Yugoslavs, in an attempt to discredit the Albanian Government, conceal their complicity in the matter, and, by confounding the issues, to delay the arrival of the League of Nations Commission of Inquiry, subsequently asked that a Commission should be conſtituted to inquire whether the Government of Tirana or of the Mirdite Republic truly represented Albania (O.J. December, 1921, 1093). In reply they were informed that the matter was within the sphere of the Commission of Inquiry which already was being conſtituted in accordance with the requeſt of the Albanian Government.

Some weeks later Gjoni returned to Mirdita with Osman Bali, Halid Lleshi, and Taf Kaziu, who had been supporters of Essad Pasha, and were officers (D.F.) of the Yugoslav reserve. The League of Nations Commission subsequently reported that Gjoni succeeded in gathering 1,300 adherents—from among the 30,000 inhabitants of Mirdita. It seems clear, however, that only a ſmall proportion were actually Mirdites, and that the Albanian report that the majority were Serbian comitadjis, and the remainder Albanian renegades, was correct, firſt, in view of the loyalty of the Mirdite leaders and the universal unpopularity of Gjoni—to which the Commission bore teſtimony: secondly, because since the Yugoslavs supplied Gjoni with arms and ammunition, and themselves invaded Albania, it is improbable that they did not reinforce him with their own comitadji bands. In addition, reported the Commission, Gjoni had at his disposal two mountain guns, a number of machine guns, and was well supplied with ammunition, which could have been forthcoming from Yugoslav sources only. Neither mountain guns nor machine guns are kept in action, or effectively handled, by "extraordinarily uneducated and ignorant" irregulars!

On the 25th July a detachment of Government troops proceeding to the frontier was attacked by Gjoni's bands, and suffered a reverse. Reinforcements were, however, brought up, and, supported by Mirdite irregulars, drove Gjoni once more across the Drin on the 9th August. Gjoni's house, and those of his few supporters in Mirdita, some sixty in all, were then burnt, and the crossings of the Drin leading into Mirdita strongly occupied. These crossings seem to have been upon the Yugoslav side of the Franchet d'Esperey line, as described by the Yugoslavs.

At the end of August the Committee which had been appointed at the beginning of July by the Conference of Ambassadors to deal with the Albanian frontier question, at last completed its task; but since the Conference had, in the meantime, adjourned, the decision was not officially reported until the beginning of November. The conflicting interests of the Powers themselves had been responsible for the inordinate delay in reaching a decision so vital to the welfare of Albania; and since August, 1920, Italy alone had consistently maintained that the frontier delimited in 1913 should be restored. The other Powers had, to a greater or lesser extent, supported the claims of Yugoslavia and Greece, principally, it seems, through an anxiety to win their benevolence; and it would appear that for that very reason they refrained from sending an international commission, as was repeatedly proposed by the Albanians themselves, to investigate conditions in the disputed areas before attempting to reach a decision in the matter.

In view of the reports of Yugoslav activity, the gathering of comitadji bands, the movement of troops, and the presence of General Martinovitch in command, Mr. Eyres, the British Representative, carried out a reconnaissance in the Drin Valley. He passed through Aras, a village on the Drin at the entrance to a valley leading into the heart of Mirdita, on the 15th September.

The occupation by the Albanians of Aras and the surrounding positions denied to Yugoslav comitadjis free access to

Mirdita, and three days after Mr. Eyres had departed, the officer commanding the Yugoslav troops on the right bank of the Drin peremptorily ordered the officer in command of the Albanian troops on the left bank to evacuate, within twenty-four hours, Aras and five other points of strategic importance surrounding and commanding it, namely, Muhri, Sinaj, Gruka, Darza, and Mal-i-lures. Possession of these points would have given the Yugoslavs a "bridgehead" upon the left bank, which would facilitate the incursion into Mirdita of comitadjis and constitute a secure base on the Albanian side of the river from whence they could operate.

The Albanian commander refused to withdraw, whereupon, on the 18th September, the Yugoslavs crossed the Drin under cover of artillery and machine-gun fire, occupied Aras and Muhri, and advanced three miles towards Luria. The Albanians were inferior to the Yugoslavs both numerically and in weapons, and were compelled to fall back. The Yugoslavs crossed the river also at Klyeshi, and advanced to Rechi. Albanian reinforcements were, however, brought up, and between the 20th and 23rd the Yugoslavs were driven back across the Drin at all points, with the loss of 4 officers and 57 other ranks killed, and a number of prisoners, including Russians of General Wrangel's refugee army (T. 21, 26, 27, 29.9.21). Units of Wrangel's army played a considerable part in subsequent operations (N.E. 3.11.21); possibly they were considered more reliable than the Croatian troops, who had, upon a previous occasion, shown themselves indisposed to support the programme of the Serbian military party, which was unwilling to sacrifice its own countrymen.

A local operation, which the Yugoslavs had undertaken on the 20th September in the Kastrati district, proved no more successful than their operations on the Drin.

In the meantime the Albanian Government appealed both to the League of Nations and to the Powers, to bring about a cessation of hostilities and the withdrawal of the Yugoslav troops. The Yugoslavs protested that the Albanians had been the aggressors, because the points which the former attempted to occupy were within the Franchet d'Esperey line. That they were within what the Yugoslavs described as the "Armistice line" was true, but since they had previously evacuated them, the Albanians had been fully justified in occupying them, and were equally justified in retaining them, especially as they could be of no value to the Yugoslavs except for offensive purposes.

The League of Nations satisfied itself with an intimation that hostilities were not in accordance with the resolution of the 25th June, and indeed, in view of the procrastination of the Conference of Ambassadors in pronouncing their decision regarding the Albanian frontier, it could do little else.

On the 2nd October, however, the Albanian question was considered by the Assembly of the League. Lord Robert Cecil presented resolutions adopted in Committee No. 6, which were carried unanimously after a debate in which the respective delegates concerned spoke in the usual vein. The resolutions were as follows (*League of Nations: Records of the Second Assembly*, 659–75):

"The Assembly, having considered the appeal of Albania to the Assembly, dated the 29th June, 1921, and the reference by the Council to the Assembly of the allegation by Albania against the Serb-Croat-Slovene State, dated the 2nd September, 1921:

"Recognizing the sovereignty and independence of Albania as established by her admission to the League:

"Taking note of the fact that the Serb-Croat-Slovene State and Greece have recognized the Principal Allied and Associated Powers as the appropriate body to settle the frontiers of Albania:

"Understanding that the Principal Allied and Associated Powers are very near agreement on the question submitted to them:

"Recommends Albania now to accept the forthcoming decision of the Principal Allied and Associated Powers."

"The Assembly, further, taking note of the allegations of Albania against nationals of the Serb-Croat-Slovene State, and of the allegations of the Serb-Croat-Slovene State against certain tribes and individuals in Albania:

"Taking note also of statements made that there is serious unrest in southern Albania and northern Epirus:

"Requests the Council forthwith to appoint a Commission of three impartial persons, to proceed immediately to Albania, and to report fully on the execution of the decision of the Principal Allied and Associated Powers, as soon as it is given, and on any disturbances which may occur on or near the frontier of Albania. The Commission should have power to appoint observers, or other officials being impartial persons, to enable it to discharge its functions."

In asking the Assembly to adopt these resolutions, Lord Robert Cecil, commenting upon the undue procrastination of the Conference of Ambassadors in settling the frontiers of Albania, said:

". . . if I may venture very respectfully to say so, even to such an august body as that, delays in this matter are really criminal to the peace of the world . . . we have no right to play with the lives and happiness of the people in order to serve the methods of the Old-World diplomacy."

In accepting the resolutions, Monsignor Noli said:

". . . in the case of the first resolution I am confident that the Albanian Government would no doubt accept any just decision transmitted to it. With regard to the second resolution, I would ask the Assembly to vote that a Commission be sent immediately to Albania. . . . This Commission would also shed some light on conditions in our country which up to the present have been little known, and it would put an end to the rumours which have been circulated from time to time about us."

In commenting upon the views expressed by M. Spalaiko-vitch, Monsignor Noli said:

"Our honourable colleague from Serbia believes in the advice that the lawyer used to give to his pupils. He used to say: 'When the Law is against you, insist on the facts. When the facts are against you, insist on the Law. When both the Law and the facts are against you, revile the other party.' I do not believe in this policy, and I shall abstain from saying anything unpleasant to our neighbours. . . . In conclusion, let me draw your attention to the meaning of the words 'savage and uncivilized'. In the vocabulary of the oppressors it means those who refuse to bow to foreign oppression and foreign invasion, and in that respect we are all savage here, because I do not see anyone who believes in Christian non-resistance."

In commenting upon a very immoderate speech by M. Casanges, Lord Cecil said:

"The last speaker said, and I think said truly, that the Albanian delegation had attracted a great deal of sympathy from the Assembly. Let me tell him that, if that is so, it is because the spokesman of that delegation has always from this platform and elsewhere shown moderation and fairness in controversy. That is the quality which, I believe I may say, is most admired by this Assembly (applause). It is for the Greek delegation to consider how far they can imitate their neighbours, at any rate in that respect."

On the 6th October, the Council of the League adopted the following resolution (*Minutes of the Fourteenth Session of the Council*, Pt. II, 121–3):

"The Council approves of the appointment of a Commission of three impartial persons to proceed to Albania and to report fully on the execution of the decision of the Principal Allied and Associated Powers, as soon as it is given, and on any disturbances which may occur on or near the frontier of Albania. The Commission shall have power to appoint impartial observers to enable it to discharge its functions.

"The Council, in its great anxiety to see peace preserved, and feeling assured that the decision of the Principal Allied and Associated Powers will be taken without delay, considers that the Commission should arrive in Albania by the 1st November, 1921, but that it should take no action until the decision of the Principal Allied and Associated Powers is given."

Meanwhile the Powers, especially Great Britain and Italy, lodged immediate and emphatic protests at Belgrade; and the Yugoslav Minister for Foreign Affairs, then in Paris, was warned that peace on the Albanian frontier must be preserved (P.D. 147: 234). It was intimated that in view of the forthcoming decision of the Conference of Ambassadors, hostilities against Albania were undesirable, and Yu- slavia was reminded that she herself had admitted the com- petence of the Conference to deal with the matter. Moreover, the Italian Foreign Minister had stated publicly that Italy was "prepared to fight any Power in order to protect the inde- pendence of Albania" (T. 4.8.21).

In view of these representations, hostilities came tem- porarily to a close, although Gjoni and his comitadjis con- tinued their activities, and again but unsuccessfully attempted to cross the Drin on the 8th October. Meantime, however, the Yugoslavs began to concentrate troops in the north- eastern and western frontier districts and to raise the strength of their comitadji bands. It was alleged that bands were raised for the express purpose of entering Skutari (where the Italian garrison still remained), and that they were promised a sub- stantial reward should they succeed; and it was no difficult matter to misrepresent Serb comitadjis as insurgent Mirdites, for whose acts Yugoslavia could not be held responsible. It is significant that at the same time Greek comitadjis and troops began to concentrate along the southern border.

In the meantime the Mirdites had reaffirmed their loyalty to the Albanian Government. While operations were in progress around Aras a few miles distant, the Mirdite leaders had assembled at Oroshi, the principal village of the district, on the 22nd September, and had telegraphed to Geneva de- nouncing Gjoni as a traitor and declaring their loyalty to the Albanian Government. The telegram bore forty-four signa- tures. Nevertheless the "Government of the Mirdite Repub- lic" continued to flourish, and it does not seem to have appeared incompatible to the Yugoslavs (D.F.) that although the Mirdites were supposed to be solidly against the Albanian Government, their own Government remained, not in Mir- dita, but at Prizren! At the end of September Antony Achikou was sent from Prizren as delegate of the "Mirdite Republic" to Geneva, and this aroused great indignation in Mirdita. Dom Joseph Gionali, Primo Dochi's successor, thereupon telegraphed on the 2nd October to the League, denouncing Achikou as a traitor, and a renegade priest who had been expelled from the Franciscan Order in 1920. This telegram was confirmed three days later by the Archbishop of Skutari.

In view of the failure of the Powers and the League of Nations to prevent the continuance of warlike preparations

by the Yugoslavs, and in view of the seeming in
of further and more serious hostilities, there was felt a pre
need for the formation of a coalition war Cabinet for the
express purpose of dealing with any contingency. Further,
the semi-trained troops at the disposal of the Government,
which were sufficient only for frontier-post duty, were wholly
inadequate to oppose an invasion by Yugoslav troops, or even
by large bands of well armed and equipped comitadjis; and
in the circumstances it was thought absolutely essential to
secure the whole-hearted co-operation of the malissori
irregulars, who constituted the principal armed strength of
Albania, by including in the Cabinet the most prominent
guerrilla leaders. In addition, Elias Vrioni was suffering
from ill health, and was therefore unfit to guide his country
through the storm which was brewing. Accordingly the
Cabinet resigned in the middle of October, and Pandele
Evangheli, of the Liberal party, which was represented in
the Chamber by thirty-one deputies, was entrusted with the
formation of a fresh Cabinet.

Evangheli's Cabinet, which was constituted for the express
purpose of defending the integrity of the State, and was
known as the "Sacred Union", included the three foremost
Albanian guerrilla leaders, namely, Ahmed Zogu, Bairam
Tsuri, and Zia Dibra. It was composed as follows:

PANDELE EVANGHELI . .	Prime Minister and Minister for Foreign Affairs.
BAIRAM TSURI	Minister of the Interior.
AHMED ZOGU	Minister for War.
KOTCHO TASSI . . .	Minister of Justice.
HIL MOSSI	Minister of Education.
AHMED DAKLI . . .	Minister of Finance.
ZIA DIBRA	Minister of Public Works.

Pandele Evangheli was trusted by all parties; Ahmed
Zogu had proved his capacity on many occasions; Zia Dibra
was entrusted with a Ministry which would be unable to
function if the country was invaded, and therefore his un-
suitability for the Ministry was of no account; and Bairam
Tsuri, as Minister of the Interior, was placed in direct control
of the malissori in the districts which would be the scene
of operations.

Very naturally the first step taken by the new Cabinet was

to order a general mobilization. The order was enthusiastically complied with, and once again the Albanians exhibited that loyalty to race, in the presence of danger, which seems an adequate refutation of the charge that they possess no sense of nationality. Armed irregulars flocked to the assistance of Albania's little army, and women and children enrolled for auxiliary purposes.

The Albanian mobilization was represented by the Yugoslav Press as an aggressive act! And the opinion was freely expressed in Belgrade that further hostilities were inevitable in consequence! On the 17th October the Yugoslavs occupied Oboti on the Bojana, thus threatening the communications of Skutari with the outside world, and throwing open to them a road to Alessio; and at the same time troops advanced through Maltsia e Djakove towards the Drin. These preliminary movements completed their preparations.

At this time there appeared in the European Press the usual series of false reports, which were spread with the express purpose of predisposing the public of Europe in favour of the originators of those reports, of ridiculing the Albanian cause, and of attempting to show that Albania was unfit for self-government, and should be partitioned. Belgrade and Athens possess an amazing proclivity for the origination of such reports about Albania, and irresponsible newspaper editors possess an equally amazing credulity. Between 1921 and 1925 reports from these sources appeared with extraordinary frequency—their true origin being, of course, in many cases, carefully concealed—of "a Crown which nobody wants", of revolutions, and of internal discord, reports which were readily accepted by a profoundly ignorant and credulous public, and which did irreparable harm to the cause of a little State which had no Press Bureau through which to deny them, and within whose borders there were no newspaper reporters, and few impartial observers, to contradict them.

At the end of October Belgrade resolved to throw caution to the winds, to seize northern Albania, and to confront the Powers with *le fait accompli*. On the 26th October Yugoslav troops, covered by artillery and supported by aircraft, once again launched a sudden attack upon Aras and the surrounding positions, which they carried. The Albanians were compelled to fall back before overwhelming numbers, and four days later were driven from Luria, the strategic key to northern Albania (P.D. 147: 1945). Upon the following day Oroshi fell to the invaders (P.D. 148: 28), and the loss of these places was officially confirmed by Mr. Eyres. A few days later Yugoslav troops and irregulars, advancing from Oboti, occupied Medua and Alessio, isolated Skutari, and approached to within thirty miles of Tirana (see Yugoslav Press).

Both in the House of Commons and in the Press the Yugoslav invasion of Albania was the subject of lively comment. The *Manchester Guardian* (8.11.21) described the attack as a violation of the Covenant of the League of Nations, an outrage upon an inoffensive State, and a challenge to Italy. Colonel Herbert, who championed the Albanian cause in the House of Commons, described the attack as entirely unprovoked. This view was shared by the British Government, which, however, still hesitated, to the intense indignation of Lord Robert Cecil, to take any independent action in fulfilment of its obligations with regard to Albania (P.D. 147: 1924). But not only did Yugoslavia pay not the slightest heed to the British and Allied protests (P.D. 147: 1924, 1945)—especially those of Italy, who made it clear that she could no longer tolerate the truculent attitude of Belgrade—or to those of the Conference of Ambassadors, but she even denied that there had been any aggression whatever upon her part! She maintained that she was merely reoccupying the Franchet d'Esperey line, that Alessio had been seized by the Mirdites, and that Oroshi was destroyed by Albanian troops (D.F.)!

Contemporary statements in the Yugoslav Press quoted by Mr. Fisher before the Council of the League on the 18th November (O.J. December, 1921, 1191) and reproduced by the *Daily Telegraph* (19.11.21), do not, however, bear out her protestations of innocence. "Our troops have passed the Albanian frontier" (*Salo*, the 3rd November). "The first Albanian prisoners have arrived, and say that our troops have completely taken the Albanian forces by surprise" (*Pravda*, the 5th November). . . . "We are in a state of war with Albania; our General Smiljanitch has taken positions which we must hold" (*Sloviniski Narod*, the 6th November). "Our Army has occupied Alessio and Medua. Our troops are near Tirana" (*Sloviniski Narod*, the 10th November). These are not extracts from the Press of a country "more sinned against than sinning"!

But Yugoslavia had overestimated the preoccupation and apathy of the Powers, and if she imagined that she could ignore their protests with impunity, she was abruptly disillusioned. The patience of the British Foreign Office has limits, and those limits had been reached. Early in November Great Britain recognized "the Government at Tirana as the *de jure* Government of the whole of Albania" (P.D. 148: 29); and on the 7th, Albania having addressed a further appeal to the League (P.D. 148: 28), the following telegram (O.J. December, 1921, 1182) was dispatched to Sir Eric Drummond, the Secretary-General of the League at Geneva:

"Continued advance of Serb-Croat-Slovene forces into Albania being of nature to disturb international peace, His Majesty's Government desire to call the attention of the Council thereto, and request that you will take immediate steps to summon a meeting of the Council to consider the situation and to agree upon measures to be taken under Article 16 in the event of the Serb-Croat-Slovene Government refusing or delaying to execute their obligations under the Covenant. Ambassadors' Conference has now decided frontiers of Albania, which will at once be notified to interested parties.

"(*Signed*) D. LLOYD GEORGE."

Article 16 of the Covenant of the League of Nations provides that

"if any member of the League, in contravention of its agreements resorts to arms, such a member is *ipso facto* 'deemed to have committed an act of war against all other members of the League,' and the other members are obliged to prevent all financial, commercial, or personal intercourse between the nationals of the Covenant-breaking State and the nationals of any other State. . . . Article 16 only comes into force in the case of a State insisting on going to war without waiting for any attempt at peaceful settlement such as is provided for in Articles 12, 13, and 15, or where the agreed tribunal or a unanimous Council have given a decision which has been accepted by the other party. In other cases ultimate resort to war is envisaged as possible. . . . Article 16 further lays down that in addition to the blockade, which is an automatic obligation of all the members of the League, the Council shall consider and shall recommend to the several Governments concerned what effective military, naval, or air forces members of the League shall severally contribute to the armed forces to be used to protect the Covenant" (E.B. 31 : 738).

The unprecedented step taken by the British Government, rendered necessary by the aggressive attitude of Yugoslavia, who had placed herself in the unenviable position of being the first country deliberately to shelve her obligations under the Covenant of the League, kindled a smouldering hostility towards Great Britain.

On the 9th November the Conference of Ambassadors, under the presidency of M. Cambon, at last pronounced its decision regarding the frontiers of Albania. The Protocol signed on that day by the representatives of the British Empire, France, Italy, and Japan, was as follows (O.J. December, 1921, 1195):

"Whereas the tracing of the frontier of Albania, as it was established in 1913 by the Conference of Ambassadors in London, is to be confirmed;

"Whereas, moreover, the southern frontiers of Albania have been delimitated on the spot by the Delimitation Commission, which drew up the final Protocol of its work at Florence on the 17th December, 1913; and whereas the Commission entrusted with the delimitation of the northern and eastern frontiers was obliged to interrupt its work in 1914 on account of the outbreak of hostilities;

"The British Empire, France, Italy, and Japan decide:

"1. The Governments signatory to the present Decision recognize the Government of Albania constituted as a sovereign and independent State.

"2. A Commission composed of four members appointed by the Governments signatory to the present Decision shall be entrusted as soon as possible with the duty of tracing on the spot the northern and north-eastern frontier line of Albania under the conditions laid down hereafter.

"3. In order to assure good neighbourly relations between the States situated on the one and the other side of the frontier line which is to be traced, the Commission referred to shall take into account, as far as possible, the existing administrative limits and the local economic interests. It shall in particular rectify the line fixed in 1913 by the Conference of Ambassadors in London:

"(a) In the region to the north-east of Skutari it should be traced in such a way that, while ensuring the protection of that town, the means of access to, and the protection of, Podgoritza shall be assured, and that free passage shall be guaranteed to the neighbouring Albanian population through this region with their live-stock, their furniture and their effects.

"(b) In the region west and south of Prizren, in such a way as to leave to the territory of Prizren its natural approaches. The new frontier, which shall be fixed on the spot, shall start from point 729, south of Godeni and east of Chafa Prusit, shall run from north to south and shall join the frontier line of 1913 south of Vad, running through the points 1996 (Baistriku), 2381 (Koritnik), 2512 (north-east of Vad), leaving to the east the border of the territory occupied by the Gora clan (according to the scale 1/200,000 map of the Austrian General Staff, dated the 23rd January, 1911, reproduced by the Geographical Institute of the Italian Army).

"(c) In the region to the west and south-east of Dibra, so as to leave entirely outside the Albanian territory the road from Dibra to Struga and thus to assure the liberty of the economic communications of Dibra.

"(d) In the region of Lin, so as to attribute to Albania the town of Lin, and thus to assure, on the borders of Lake Ochrida, the economic communications between Elbasan and Korcha.

"4. The Commission shall be authorized to appoint, in an advisory capacity, members nominated respectively by the States situated on the one and on the other side of the frontier line to be traced. It may take into consideration the requests formulated on behalf of the Governments of these States, ensuring, however, that any rectifications which may be made shall not involve the transfer of more than a minimum of the population.

"5. At the end of its work the Commission shall draw up a Protocol which shall be submitted for approval to the Governments signatory to the present Decision.

"Done at Paris, the ninth of November, nineteen hundred and twenty-one.

> "(*Signed*) HARDINGE OF PENSHURST.
> JULES CAMBON.
> BONIN.
> K. ISHII."

What untold suffering and bloodshed might have been avoided had this decision been made eighteen months earlier!

The revised frontier gave Lin, upon Lake Ochrida, and its environs to Albania. On the other hand, Yugoslavia obtained a small concession in the Kastrati district, and the remainder of the Dibra–Struga–Lin road, which deprived Albania of the remainder of her sole communication between the north-east and south-east; and in view of the nature of the country to the west of the revised frontier, the construction of a fresh road within Albanian territory will prove an extremely difficult and costly undertaking for a State so deficient financially. Those who are in a position to appreciate the extreme value of roads in Albania, where few exist, and where the difficulty and expense of construction are almost prohibitive, will understand the injustice—apart from ethnical considerations—thus inflicted upon the little State.

The decision satisfied none of the States concerned. The Albanian Government had never admitted the competence of the Conference of Ambassadors to deal with the matter, but "being of the opinion that foreign invasion endangers the existence of the country, finds itself compelled to submit to the decision taken by the Conference of Ambassadors at its meeting on the 9th November with regard to the Albanian frontiers, while protesting against the alteration of the boundary to the prejudice of Albania" (Midhat Frasheri, President of the Albanian Delegation to the President of the Conference of Ambassadors, the 16th November, O.J. December, 1921, 1210). Greece and Yugoslavia likewise protested, both to the Conference of Ambassadors and to the League, whose competence to deal with the matter they had, on the 25th June, refused to acknowledge (O.J. December, 1921, 1207-9)!

Upon the same day that the Ambassadors reached the above decision, they concluded the following momentous Agreement (League of Nations: Treaty Series):

"The British Empire, France, Italy, and Japan, recognizing that the independence of Albania, and the integrity and inalienability of her frontiers, as fixed by their decision of the 9th November, 1921, is a question of international importance,

"Recognizing that the violation of these frontiers or of the independence of Albania might constitute a danger for the strategic safety of Italy,

"Have agreed as follows:

"(1) If Albania should at any time find it impossible to maintain intact her territorial integrity, she shall be free to address a request to the Council of the League of Nations for foreign assistance.

"(2) The Governments of the British Empire, France, Italy, and Japan decide that, in the above-mentioned event, they will instruct their representatives on the Council of the League of Nations to recommend that the restoration of the territorial frontiers of Albania should be entrusted to Italy.

"(3) In case of a threat to Albania's integrity or independence, whether territorial or economic, owing to foreign aggression or to any other event, and in case Albania has not availed herself within a reasonable time of the right provided for in Art. 1, the above-mentioned Governments will bring the situation before the Council of the League of Nations.

"If the Council considers intervention necessary, the above-mentioned Governments will give their representatives the instructions stipulated in Art. 2.

"(4) If the Council of the League of Nations decides, by a majority, that intervention is not expedient, the above-mentioned Governments shall reconsider the question in conformity with the principle enunciated in the preamble to this Declaration, namely, that any modification of the frontiers of Albania constitutes a danger for the strategic safety of Italy.
BB

"Done in Paris, on the ninth of November, nineteen hundred and twenty-one.

"(*Signed*)   HARDINGE OF PENSHURST.
JULES CAMBON.
BONIN
K. ISHII."

The propriety of this declaration *vis-à-vis* the Covenant of the League remains a controversial matter (*Survey of International Affairs, 1927*, 167). Its importance, made by four Powers who constitute almost half the membership of the Council of the League, lies in the facts, first, that the preservation of the integrity of Albania was recognized as a matter of international importance: secondly, that the right of Italy to preserve that integrity was acknowledged: and thirdly, that Italy was *ipso facto* precluded from attempting herself to violate that integrity, even did she wish to do so despite the considerations already laid down. By the above Declaration, the peace of Europe was inextricably linked with the preservation of the territorial integrity of Albania; and the means by which Yugoslavia could pursue her policy in Albania was confined to methods (*b*), (*d*), (*e*), (*h*), (*j*), (*k*) (see p. 332).

The Yugoslavs had no alternative but to agree to withdraw their troops from Albania. On the 14th November, that is to say, three days before the Council of the League, summoned in accordance with Mr. Lloyd George's telegram, assembled, M. Pasitch sent a telegram to the Conference of Ambassadors in which he protested angrily against their action in reaching a decision regarding the frontiers of Albania without the consent of Yugoslavia, and against the action of the British Government, which, he complained, had acted upon "the unfounded accusations of the Tirana Government". M. Pasitch seems to have ignored the presence in Albania of Mr. Eyres, who was able to confirm the truth of those "unfounded accusations". M. Pasitch likewise protested against the threat contained in Mr. Lloyd George's telegram to the League, and continued:

"Placed in this position, the Royal Government states with the greatest regret, and under protest, that it bows to the decision of the Conference of Ambassadors in order to avoid the dangerous consequences of non-acceptance, *while remaining firmly convinced that subsequent events connected with order and peace in the Balkans will vindicate the anticipations of the Royal Government.*"

And most consistently has Yugoslavia striven to make sure that that prophecy should come true!

In reply the Ambassadors intimated that the frontier question was closed. At the same time they defined a "zone of demarcation" along the frontier, which should be evacuated by both Yugoslav and Albanian troops, that the Inter-Allied Boundary Commission, which, however, did not arrive in Albania until the following March, might be assured of complete freedom of action when performing its task.

In the meantime the Council of the League of Nations assembled on the 17th November (O.J. December, 1921, 1182–1214). Mehmed Konitza and Midhat Frasheri were the Albanian representatives, Yugoslavia being represented by MM. Boskovitch, Yovanovitch, and Popovitch. Before the Council Mr. H. A. L. Fisher stated (O.J. December, 1921, 1182–6) the facts of the case briefly and bluntly. In the first place he reviewed the events which had led up to the crisis to which the attention of the League had been called, and commented at length upon the grave abuse by the Yugoslavs of the privilege granted to them of occupying the "line of demarcation" in Albania. He dealt with the question of the "Mirdite Republic", which had been proclaimed and existed only in Yugoslavia, and stated that the British Government was satisfied that it was nothing but an instrument of the Yugoslav Government. He then quoted the Belgrade paper (*Sloviniski Narod*) which, on the 10th November, stated:

"Our Army has occupied Alessio and Medua. Our troops are near Tirana" (O.J. December, 1921, 1192; D.T. 19.11.21).

"The British Government", said Mr. Fisher (O.J. December, 1921, 1184), "infers from the facts of which it has been placed in possession, that a plan is on foot for detaching the north of Albania—and by the north of Albania I mean that portion of Albania which lies north of the Mati River—from the Tirana Government . . ." and that "this attempt is supported by the regular forces of the Serb-Croat-Slovene Army."

In reply to Mr. Fisher, M. Boskovitch said:

"The British Government alleges that Serbian troops have advanced beyond the line of demarcation; I must therefore declare that our troops have never been the first to pass that line as it has existed since the end of the war. . . . The Albanians have always been the aggressors, and we have only defended ourselves. I hope, after the explanation which I shall give at a future meeting, the Council will agree that the British Government's proposal is not justified. . . . Our Government thought . . . that it was its duty, in the circumstances, to avoid all risk of conflict; in spite of the objections which it has formulated . . . it has stated that it would bow to the decision of the Conference of Ambassadors. While protesting against the decision of the Conference, it is about to order its troops to withdraw to the line of demarcation given by that Conference, despite the fact that it is not exactly known, since certain portions of the frontier have still to be fixed. . . . With regard to the movement among the inhabitants of northern Albania, I must make reservations. There the point at issue is the desire of Christian tribes not to submit to the rule of the Government of Tirana, in which Mohammedan influence is predominant. We cannot disguise our sympathy for these Christian populations, nor our desire to see them obtain the independence necessary for their development" (O.J. December, 1921, 1186-7).

He reserved the right to make a further declaration at a subsequent meeting.

Midhat Frasheri, who also reserved the right to speak again at a subsequent meeting, said:

"I am glad to hear the delegate of the Serb-Croat-Slovene State declare that the territories given to Albania at the last meeting of the Conference of Ambassadors will shortly be evacuated, but our unfortunate experience in the past makes it necessary for us to act cautiously. We accordingly suggest that the Council should set up a permanent Frontiers Commission composed of a representative of Albania, of the Serb-Croat-Slovene State, and a delegate of the League of Nations, entrusted with the duty of watching over the frontier and preventing any occurrence likely to disturb the peace."

This wise proposal seems to be the only satisfactory method of securing the inviolability of wild and remote frontiers, and might constitute a measure applicable by the League upon the appeal of any State which desired international surveillance of her frontiers. The State which feared aggression would doubtless contribute its share of the expense entailed gladly enough; and the potential aggressor, to avoid the inference which would be deduced if it refused, would perforce contribute likewise. Presidency of the Commission would be in rotation, and the President would indicate the direction in which the Commission would operate during his presidency.

Midhat Frasheri's proposal was not adopted, since the League of Nations Commission of Inquiry had already proceeded to Albania, and this was considered an adequate step for the time being. Why, however, it was not subsequently adopted is obscure, since the expenses entailed might have been negligible; and in any case expenditure in that direction—a peace assurance premium—would have been more beneficial than in the construction of architectural extravagances at Geneva.

"The unjust and unprovoked Serbian attack", continued Frasheri, "has cost the Albanian Treasury seven million gold francs, without taking into account the destruction of property. The Albanian Government reserves the right to have this property valued and to reclaim the amount. . . . This line, which is called the 'armistice line', has . . . never been officially communicated to us. I should like to point out that an 'armistice line' is always drawn up by two belligerents in the form of a Protocol which they agree to respect, whereas we have never been at war with Serbia. . . . Even according to the statements of the Serbian delegate [before the Sixth Committee of the Assembly] the line follows the Drin. Luria, Aras, Darza, etc., which are towns on the left bank of the river, are therefore on the Albanian side of the armistice line. . . . These villages were administered by Albania, and had taken part in the elections of the Albanian legislature. . . .

The Serb-Croat-Slovene delegate alleges that Albania has always been the aggressor. I should like to know how he can justify that statement when confronted with the destruction by the forces of the regular Serbian Army of 150 villages situated in Albanian territory. . . . Our Government is one created spontaneously and freely by the population itself" (O.J. December, 1921, 1187–8).

At the second public meeting of the Council, on the following day, M. Boskovitch made a lengthy, complicated, and contradictory statement, by which he attempted to prove that the Albanian Government "had violated the line of demarcation and was constantly violating it. . . . This line was not the same as the one which that Government had just pointed out to the Council on a map—i.e. it did not follow the course of the Black Drin; this line was the one which the Serb-Croat-Slovene delegate had indicated to the Council of the League of Nations on the 25th June, 1921" (O.J. September, 1921, 735–40). With reference to the Mirdite fiasco, he declared that "in proceeding in this manner, the Royal Government was actuated only by the sympathy which our people feel for that valiant little people which is imbued with the love of liberty", and with regard to the devastation of the Drin Valley, "that the devastations, burnings, murders, and deportations (40,000 refugees) were the work of the invading troops of the Tirana Government" (O.J. December, 1921, 1197–1204).

In reply to these statements, Midhat Frasheri said that

"the whole argument of the Serb-Croat-Slovene delegate was based on the hypothesis of a fixed armistice line. . . . Even if one admitted the necessity of an armistice line for military reasons of any kind, such a line would have to be a fixed one. In reality, the line mentioned by the Serb-Croat-Slovene Government had moved its position on the map, and was essentially elastic. It was first inflated, then depressed; it moved in either direction. . . . The aggressions and attacks had always been begun by the Serbs, and had always been premeditated. The havoc wrought by the Serbs was terrible. . . . The anxiety of the Serb-Croat-Slovene Government on behalf of the Catholics of Mirdita was quite recent. A short while ago this concern had been manifested in favour of the Mussulmans of the Government of Essad Pasha. It was shown for any traitor to his country."

In conclusion, Mr. Fisher said that "the main concern of the Council should not be with the past but with the future". As regards M. Boskovitch's criticism of the British Government, he said that it "was obviously bound, under Article 11 of the Covenant, to draw the attention of the Council to the grave situation which had arisen in Albania. The gravity of the situation was shown by the statements which had appeared in the Serbian Press" (O.J. December, 1921, 1190–1).

At the third public meeting of the Council of the League, held on the 19th November, the President read the following draft resolution:

"The Council of the League of Nations,

"Having heard the statement concerning the information which led the British Government to request, in its telegram of the 7th November, the immediate convocation of the Council 'to study the situation created by the advance of the Serb-Croat-Slovene troops into Albania and to agree upon measures to be taken';

"Having heard the explanations given by the representatives of the Serb-Croat-Slovene and Albanian Governments;

"Considering that the Assembly of the League of Nations recognized on the 3rd October, that the Principal Allied and Associated Powers were responsible for fixing the definite frontiers of Albania;

"Considering that the Conference of Ambassadors decided on the 9th November, 1921, that it was necessary to confirm with certain specified alterations the line of the frontiers of Albania established in 1913 by the Conference of Ambassadors in London; and considering that the frontiers of Albania are consequently now fixed and must be respected in accordance with the guarantees assured to the members of the League of Nations by the Covenant.

"The Council notes the declaration of the Prime Minister of the Serb-Croat-Slovene State, in which he affirms that the Serb-Croat-Slovene State is taking, in accordance with the above decision, all steps to assure the immediate evacuation of its troops from all territory belonging to the Albanian State. The Council notes also the assurance given by the representatives of the two States that they intend to live as neighbours maintaining good relations with each other, which implies that neither shall take, either directly or indirectly, any action to provoke or encourage any movement which might disturb the internal peace of its neighbour.

"The Council is glad to note the conciliatory attitude adopted in its presence by the Albanian and the Serb-Croat-Slovene Governments, which augurs well for the future.

"The Council decides to give the Commission of Inquiry sent to Albania in accordance with its resolution of the 6th October, the following instructions:

"1. The Commission shall keep the Council informed of the retirement of both the Serb-Croat-Slovene and Albanian troops from the provisional zone of demarcation provided for in the decision of the Conference of Ambassadors of the 18th November, 1921; it shall keep in touch with the Delimitation Commission whenever necessary, and shall place itself at the disposal of the local authorities to assist in carrying out the evacuation so as to avoid incidents.

"2. The Commission shall satisfy itself that no outside assistance is given in support of a local movement which might disturb internal peace in Albania. The Commission shall examine and submit to the Council measures to end the present disturbances and to prevent their recurrence."

The resolution was unanimously adopted by the Members of the Council, and was accepted by the representative of Albania, who said, however, that "he would have liked the draft resolution to state that it applied not only to regular troops but also to irregular bands". The representative of the Serb-Croat-Slovene State said that he accepted the resolution subject to the reservation "that it should be clearly understood that its [the Commission's] field of activity should be limited to Albania". This reservation is interesting! (O.J. December, 1921, 1192-3).

Albania received no compensation whatever for the damage she had sustained at the hands of the Slavs. She had been involved in war since 1910 almost without respite, and it is scarcely surprising therefore that, deprived of the flower of her manhood, her initial steps towards stability and prosperity have been slow. The survivors of those luckless refugees from the devastated areas were left to return to their gutted homes and ruined villages, assisted only by the meagre relief which the Albanian Government was able to give them, and by a few charitable people in Europe and America. Many more died of exposure and starvation, and it is indeed surprising that the remainder did not seek relief by lawless proceedings to a greater extent than they did. In southern Albania, too, the inhabitants had by no means recovered from the consequences of Greek ravages and destruction, which had been completed by severe earthquakes in 1919 and 1920. The Commission of Inquiry subsequently reported that much distress prevailed.

On the 19th November the League of Nations Commission of Inquiry arrived in Albania. It consisted of Colonel Schaefer (Luxemburg), Major Meinich (Norway), and M. Thesleff (Finland)—the latter subsequently replaced on account of ill health by Professor J. J. Sederholm—with Count H. de Pourtalès as Secretary. The Commissioners reported that they were enthusiastically received at Tirana, that the Government placed a house at their disposal and facilitated their work in every possible way (C. 542, M. 387, 1921, VII). They were deeply impressed by the prestige enjoyed by the League of Nations, by the universal and implicit faith in it which prevailed, and by the anxiety of all classes for its assistance not only during the existing crisis, but in economic matters in the future. Some days later they proceeded to Skutari, and reported that they had observed Yugoslav outposts on Tarabosh within rifle range of the town.

On the 9th December the Commissioners arrived in Mirdita. They reported that Gjoni, with fifty adherents, had fled to Prizren on the 20th November—that is to say on the day after the Commissioners had arrived in Albania, and when the Yugoslav troops withdrew; this seems conclusive evidence that very few of his 1,300 adherents were Mirdites. They confirmed a telegram sent by Colonel Schaefer on the 2nd to the effect that no incident had occurred, and no shot had been fired either in Mirdita or any other district occupied by Albanian troops. Ahmed Zogu, they stated, had been sent to Mirdita to investigate the situation, and on the 28th

November—Albanian independence day—the Government had granted a general amnesty to all political offenders, including those implicated in Gjoni's activities (C. 542, M. 387, 1921, VII).

On the 17th December the Commission sent from Valona the following telegram to Geneva:

"Commission returned to Tirana the 15th December. Communication impossible during journey. . . . Perfect calm prevails in Mirdita. Have consulted all the chiefs of the Mirdite tribes and priests of the district of Oroshi. Any idea of an independent Mirdite Government baseless and absurd, for all repudiate Marko Gjoni, who can only count on a few families, all refugees in Prizren. Mirdite chiefs have expressed to us their desire to form part of an independent united Albania, and are at present at Tirana to take oath of fidelity to Central Government. . . . . Commission being anxious also to consult Serbian authorities, asked permission to enter Dibra. Military Governor replied impossible without instructions from Belgrade Government, which would involve a delay of several days. . . . Commission. Albania."

The Commission also stated that the evacuation of the "zone of demarcation" was proceeding satisfactorily, and, on the 22nd: ". . . If the Yugoslav Government insists, we are ready to hear Marko Gjoni, but we consider his presence in Albania to be imprudent, as he is very unpopular everywhere, and in Mirdita. . . ." Subsequently, of the Drin Valley, the Commissioners reported: "All the villages in the plain of the Drin have suffered heavily. In most villages all but a few houses are destroyed. It is, however, probable that most of this damage dates back to the Serb occupation of 1913 and 1920, and that only a slight proportion was done this year" (O.J. February, 1922, 152). It seems improbable, however, that the greater part of the damage done in 1913 was not repaired during the seven years which ensued.

On the 7th December the "Sacred Union" Cabinet resigned. Although its specific task had been accomplished, the immediate cause of its resignation was a difference of opinion between Evangheli and the Council of Regency regarding a Ministerial nominee. Evangheli was universally respected, and public opinion held that the interference of the Regency, whose power, never clearly defined, had always been more or less fictitious, was unwarrantable. It fell, therefore, into disfavour. Thereupon, in the absence abroad of two members of the Council, Akif pasha Elbasani, unable to find anyone else willing to undertake the task of forming a Cabinet, took it upon himself to nominate as Prime Minister and Minister for Foreign Affairs the deputy Hassan Prishtina, who enjoyed the support of a very small section only of the public. Prishtina's virtual usurpation of power aroused widespread indignation, since he was extremely unpopular, and, in addition, was thought to have been irregularly elected, since the constituency from which he had been returned had been under Yugoslav occupation when the election took place. He was a Kossovo irredentist, and a member of the Kossovo Committee which advocated the continuance of the struggle for the reunion of Kossovo with Albania; but the majority of the Albanians recognized the futility of this course, which would have involved them in further unprofitable strife, perhaps in disaster, when all desired peace. In consequence demonstrations took place against him, and Ahmed Zogu appeared with some thousands of adherents to dispute his unconstitutional step (O.J. February, 1922, 152 and 156). In the circumstances, Prishtina, who had held office for four days only, was compelled to resign. Akif pasha Elbasani and Dr. Tourtoulis were invited to leave the country, an invitation which they thought it discreet to accept. The Council of Regency temporarily ceased therefore to exist.

Yugoslavia and Greece took advantage of the occasion to spread reports of disturbances and revolution, and doubtless the public of western Europe exclaimed "Another revolution in Albania!" It was declared that the partisans of Essad Pasha overthrew the Tirana Government and imprisoned all the Ministers! But the Commission of Inquiry reported that there had been demonstrations, but unaccompanied by any violence or bloodshed, and on the 18th December telegraphed from Valona: "Can vouch for fact that change in Government was carried out calmly and without violence. Tirana absolutely quiet."

M. Kostouris was appointed Prime Minister *ad interim*, with the Under-Secretaries of Departments as Ministers *ad interim*. Meantime Djafer Ypi, a former Minister of Justice, formed a fresh Cabinet, which took office on the 25th December, composed as follows:

DJAFER YPI	Prime Minister.
AHMED ZOGU	Minister of the Interior.
MONSIGNOR FAN S. NOLI	Minister for Foreign Affairs.
ISMAIL HAKKI TATZALI.	Minister for War.
HUSSEIN VRIONI . . .	Minister of Justice.
REDJEB MITROVITZA . .	Minister of Education.
KOL THACHI	Minister of Finance.
SPIRO KOLEKA . . .	Minister of Public Works.

M. Spiro Koleka acted as Minister for Foreign Affairs until the end of January, when Monsignor Noli accepted the portfolio. The Cabinet, which was predominantly Liberal, received a vote of confidence. It reconstituted the High Council of Regency as follows:

OMER VRIONI . . .	Bektashi Moslem.
SOTIR PETSI	Orthodox Christian.
ANTOINE PISTULI . . .	Roman Catholic.
REFIK TOPTANI . . .	Sunni Moslem.

In the meantime the Commission of Inquiry proceeded, at the end of December, to the Korcha district. During the previous October the Albanian Government had reported the concentration of Greek troops and bands upon the frontier (P.D. 154: 807). The Albanians had feared a recrudescence of the ravages of 1914 (*Plain English*, 3.11.21), while they were preoccupied with the Yugoslavs, and although in reply to a protest by the British Government the Greek Government denied all knowledge of the matter, there is little doubt that the attitude of the Powers, especially Great Britain and Italy, in regard to the Yugoslav invasion, coupled with the fluctuating fortunes of Greek arms in Asia Minor, alone deterred the Greeks from making another bid for "Northern Epirus".

The Commissioners were enthusiastically received, and first visited the Monastery of Sveti Naoum, a point of strategic importance commanding the Korcha–Pogradets–Lin road, and also the strip of land connecting Albania with Yugoslavia between Lakes Ochrida and Presba. The frontier in this neighbourhood had never been demarcated in detail, since the work of the International Boundary Commission had been interrupted by the Great War; and although the Monastery had been allotted to Albania, the Serbs had occupied it, and had established a military post close by, which was held, so reported the Commission, principally by Russians.

The Commissioners visited the twenty-six Albanian villages of which the Greeks remained in occupation. It seems that these villages had been included in the old Turkish *caza* of Korcha, the whole of which had, in 1913, been allotted to Albania. Through a cartographical error, however, the boundary of the *caza* (see map: O.J. March, 1922, 265), and in consequence the frontier of Albania, had been misrepresented! The Commissioners stated that the Greek and Albanian outposts were everywhere on friendly terms, and expressed their appreciation of the courtesy of the Greek military authorities.

The Commission then proceeded to Korcha. In its official reports of the 18th January (O.J. March, 1922, 261–5) and the 12th May (O.J. June, 1922, 572–82), it stated that although the population is entirely Albanian, there existed a small Grecophile party consisting of the Conservative Orthodox element, a relic of the days when Albania was under Turkish rule, and the Albanian Christians looked to Greece as a potential liberator and a country in which they, as Christians, would not be regarded as inferior beings. These—folk soaked in Greek propaganda, who feared that the proposal to establish an Albanian Autocephalous Church would cause an open rupture with the Patriarch at Constantinople—and in addition a few traders who were interested in the maintenance of good relations with Greece, composed the Grecophile minority.

"These differences of opinion", reported the Commission, "are the cause of a certain amount of excitement which, though in no way dangerous in itself if there is no outside interference—*for the minority wishing to be under Greek domination is extremely small*—possibly helps to encourage hopes cherished on the other side of the frontier. The influence of the clergy, and especially of the Greek Metropolitans, who, as we have pointed out, are working openly for the detachment of southern Albania and for its union with Greece, might make itself felt here.

"Monsignor Jakopos, Bishop of Korcha, of Greek nationality, and the mouthpiece of Hellenism in Albania, was the most zealous of these Metropolitans. He appeared to be as much interested in politics as religion, and used his influence with the Grecophile minority to institute propaganda for Greece. The result of his action was that, when Albania was recognized by the Great Powers [9th November, 1921], and its frontiers were traced, the Nationalist element, carried away by its patriotic enthusiasm, resolved to be rid of this foreign priest whom it regarded as an intruder.

"The Government of Tirana, at that time presided over by M. Pandele Evangheli, in order to avoid any incidents, gave formal orders—the Commission can confirm this statement—that any disorder or hostile manifestation was to be suppressed by force.

"In view, however, of the ever-increasing force of public opinion in Korcha, the Government was finally obliged to order the Metropolitan to leave the town within three days.

"A motor-car was placed at his disposal, and he was left free to choose his destination. A foreigner in Albania, who witnessed his departure, assured us that it gave rise to no manifestation, either hostile or in his favour" (O.J. March, 1922, 263).

In celebration of the recognition of Albania by the Powers, the Albanian Government granted, on the 28th November, a general amnesty to all political offenders, provided they returned to their homes within forty-five days. The Greeks immediately reported to the League of Nations that the amnesty had been accompanied by a threat that unless these offenders returned within the stipulated time, their homes would be burned and their property confiscated. The Commission reported that it was unable to discover the origin of these rumours!

The Yugoslavs, who had agreed with an ill grace to withdraw, took advantage of the absence of the Commission in the south to renew their attempts to discredit the Albanians. On the 21st December they reported to the Conference of Ambassadors that Albanian troops had violated the "zone of demarcation", that Albanian bands were concentrating therein, that these bands were attacking the Christian Serb inhabitants and driving off their cattle, and that these inhabitants were fleeing before the Albanians and taking refuge in the Yugoslav lines! They maintained that in the circumstances their prophecy of the 15th November was proving correct, and intimated that if these occurrences continued they would reoccupy the "zone of demarcation". This, however, the Ambassadors abruptly forbade.

On the 9th January the Commission reported that it had information from *non*-Albanian sources to the effect that 80,000 Yugoslav troops were massed on the frontier ready for all emergencies, but that the Albanian troops, which were commanded by General Ali Riza pasha Kolonia, had been instructed by the Government to fall back without fighting should the Yugoslavs advance (O.J. February, 1922, 157). It stated further, that in regard to the allegations which had been made by the Yugoslavs, and which it subsequently proceeded to investigate, it was at a loss to understand them, since, upon its previous visit to the districts in which the alleged outrages had been committed, it had encountered no Serb peasants, and that the only Christian non-Albanian inhabitants of the area were Bulgarians.

In their report of the 15th February the Commissioners wrote:

"When this district was occupied by Yugoslav troops, the Albanian local authorities were forced to flee or to resign their offices, and were partly replaced by notables of the Christian minority.

"It appears certain that these persons were often guilty of acts of violence against Mussulman Albanians, which accounts for the fact that, on the evacuation of these villages by the Serbian troops, a great number of Bulgarians, fearing reprisals, abandoned their dwellings and followed the troops to Dibra."

This report, which gives details of the careful manner in which the Albanians dealt with the property and dwellings abandoned by those Bulgarians, is striking evidence of their honesty and forbearance, despite the extreme provocation which they had suffered (O.J. April, 1922, 324–6).

The Commissioners also reported that certain unimportant and inadvertent violations of the "zone of demarcation" had occurred on both sides, due to the inexactitude of maps and misinterpretation of orders, but that both the Albanian and Yugoslav authorities seemed anxious to avoid any such violations. Further, the Commissioners proposed that a Yugoslav-Albanian military Commission should be appointed to deal with any further incidents in the zone, to which both sides at once agreed.

Open warfare between the Albanians and the Yugoslavs thus came to a close. At the beginning of March Yugoslavia officially recognized the Albanian Government, and appointed a Minister to Tirana.

At the beginning of March the Inter-Allied Boundary Commission arrived in Albania, and met the Commission of Inquiry at Skutari on the 7th March; it was composed of the representatives of Great Britain, France, and Italy, namely, Colonel Giles, Commandant Perret, and General Tellini. The Commission of Inquiry shortly afterwards withdrew from Albania, despite the protests of the Albanian Government, which, on the 25th March, addressed the following telegram to the Secretary-General of the League of Nations:

"The Albanian Government recognizes the successful work accomplished by the Commission of Inquiry, which has helped to remove the dangers which threatened the peace of the country. Considering, however, that these dangers have not yet entirely disappeared, it believes it to be essential to the interests of Albania that the Commission should continue its work for a further period. The Albanian Government therefore begs the Council to take the necessary steps to this end. Moreover, the Albanian Government, convinced that political development depends above all on the economic progress of the country, begs the League of Nations to extend its support to the economic sphere, by appointing experts to proceed to Albania, and after having made an inquiry on the spot, make proposals as regards the suitable steps to be taken to encourage employment of foreign capital in the development of the natural resources of the country" (O.J. June, 1922, 583).

In short, Albania desired publicity, and for publicity she has consistently begged. *A State which has anything to conceal, and whose claims are unfounded, does not seek publicity!* Her neighbours and their friends, on the other hand, knowing how unfounded were their allegations against her, have consistently sought to discourage tourists—Albania, a land which compares very favourably with Scotland or Switzerland, has actually been described as dreary and bleak—and by the methods already set forth to prevent the employment of foreign capital for the development of her considerable resources.

In compliance with the request of the Albanian Government, reiterated by Mehdi Frasheri before the Council of the League on the 12th May (O.J. June, 1922, 521–3), and in accordance with the recommendation of the Commission of Inquiry, the Council adopted a resolution (O.J. June, 1922, 535) to the effect that one member of the Commission— Professor Sederholm's services were accepted—should return to Albania and should remain there until the Financial Adviser arrived. It was decided further that the Economic and Financial Committee should be requested "to send experts to Albania to make a report on the measures necessary to encourage investment of foreign capital in Albania", and that Albania's request for a Financial Adviser should be submitted to the same Committee, which should be asked to propose to the Council at the following session suitable candidates for the post. It was also resolved that in view of the unsatisfactory state of affairs on the Greco-Albanian frontier, the attention of the Conference of Ambassadors should be drawn to this matter.

In accordance with the above resolution, Professor Sederholm, with Count H. de Pourtalès as his secretary, returned to Albania on the 20th June. The latter was, however, succeeded some days later by Count Frederik Moltke (Denmark).

CHAPTER IX

A STATE IN EMBRYO

In their General Report (O.J. June, 1922, 572–82) of the 12th May, 1922, the League of Nations Commissioners wrote as follows:

"Unquestionably there is an Albanian problem, and it is one which will continue for a long time to occupy the attention of Europe. . . . The argument is still put forward that the Albanians are not inherently a nation, that they will always be unable to exist as an independent modern State, and that sooner or later the country is certain to be divided up among its neighbours.

"This argument in itself constitutes a serious menace to the independence of the country. The Commission, after thorough study of the whole Albanian question, was led to the conclusion not only that an Albanian nation exists, but that its existence is a necessity."

The Albanians "are united by common customs, age-long traditions, and even language, the difference between the Gheg and the Tosk languages being at bottom nothing more than a difference of dialect.

"Although differences in religion occasionally have some effect upon the domestic politics of the country, the fanatical manifestations so frequent in other countries which are divided in religion are very rare in Albania. On the contrary, the general rule is a remarkable tolerance; for the adherents of the various creeds are often closely related by ties of blood, by tradition, and even by common national and religious festivals. The clergy of the three religions (Catholic, Orthodox, and Mohammedan) have been known to visit together both the Mosque and the Christian Churches to celebrate solemn services, which proves that the sentiment of patriotism is stronger than religious divergences. Moreover, the sufferings endured in common during the Balkan Wars and the World War, in all of which Albania was a theatre of operations, gave a new impulse to Albanian nationalism which has extended to all the classes of the population.

"It seems certain that any attempt to stifle these legitimate [Nationalist] feelings would not only be destined in advance to failure, but would have disastrous consequences for the peace of the Balkans, for the Albanians would then become zealous partisans of every revolutionary movement. On the other hand, if the national sentiment is allowed to develop, there is every reason to believe that the qualities of the Albanian race, its traditions, its high intelligence, and its artistic taste, will enable this little people to contribute profitably and at no distant date to world culture. . . ."

With reference to relations between Albania and Yugoslavia, the Commissioners wrote:

"There are many causes of friction in addition to an hereditary hostility which can only be removed by great good will and extreme prudence on the part of both Governments.

"In the first place, and this is a point upon which the Commission has insisted on every possible occasion, the Albanians must give up all irredentist ambition.

"As a general rule, public opinion in the country understands the danger of such a policy. . . . It may be hoped that the economic development of Albania will render possible a rapid increase of population.

"Relations between Greece and Albania," continued the Commissioners, "will always be difficult so long as the former has not fully recognized the frontiers laid down by the Conference of Ambassadors, and the rights of Albania over the region called Northern Epirus. This region, on account of its more advanced culture and its prosperous economic situation, will certainly be called upon to play a most important part in the development of the country.

"In the opinion of the Commission there can be no doubt that the great majority of the population is in favour of the present régime, and constitutes an important factor in the Albanian Nationalist movement."

With reference to Italy, the Commissioners wrote:

"As Albania has at present no maritime policy, there seems to be no point upon which the interests of the two countries are likely to conflict. On the contrary, as the southern provinces of Italy have a considerable Albanian population, Italy will assuredly have an important share of influence on the future economic and social development of the newly recognized country.

"In a word, Albania should endeavour to refrain as far as possible from any active foreign policy. The essential point is that Albania should enjoy complete neutrality, in order to devote herself entirely to her constitutional, economic, and social development.

". . . The Commission is convinced that a free and independent Albania is an essential condition of tranquillity and peace in the Balkans. This report will have shown that Albania possesses all the moral and material elements which go to form the basis of an independent State.

"The country has, however, not yet attained the degree of political stability and economic development sufficient to obviate all risk of internal disturbances and foreign complications. In order to do so it will need disinterested advice and economic support. The League of Nations, which enjoys an indisputable prestige in Albania, would appear to be the organ best fitted to give this support.

"The Commission considers that the required assistance should not be organized by countries having direct interests in Albania, but by an international body.

"To sum up, it seems clear that the essential elements of a prosperous Albania exist, that this little country possesses all the conditions necessary for the formation of a politically and economically independent State, and that there is every reason to hope that the day is not far distant when Albania, forgetting her warlike past, and setting herself energetically to constructive work, may by her culture and wealth render appreciable services to Europe.

"We must not, however, delude ourselves so far as to believe that this result is already achieved. On the contrary, the country is still in a similar situation to that of several Balkan countries immediately after their liberation from Turkish domination. Its social organization is, indeed, only beginning."

In short, there was everything to be done; and it was in these circumstances that the Albanians began, in the spring of 1922, to construct their State. The endless difficulties which confronted them have never been fully appreciated. Within their borders there were adherents of four religious doctrines, dialectal differences which made it difficult for Albanians from different parts of the country to understand each other, natural obstacles which made intercommunication a matter of extreme patience and endurance, an alien Oriental atmosphere which would be eliminated only in course of time, roads to be constructed, bridges to be built, schools to be opened, and resources to be developed. There was no bank, no railways, no modern port, and no efficient military force. The future form of Government remained to be settled, and while it so remained, it was difficult for the country to acquire stability. Then again the peasants were beginning to dispute the control of the landed aristocracy of central and southern Albania, and this agrarian problem threatened grave difficulties.

Though Greece officially recognized the independence of Albania during June, she did so subject to a reservation regarding the frontiers, did not appoint a diplomatic representative until the end of the year, and continued to cause trouble whenever the opportunity presented itself; while Yugoslavia, now unable to enjoy the contents of the Albanian pot, did everything possible, nevertheless, to keep it boiling, and by ruthless oppression of the 800,000 Albanians of Serbia and Montenegro, rendered remote a satisfactory *rapprochement* between the two countries. The frontier, too, was the cause of much unrest, since it deprived the inhabitants of the north-eastern districts of their markets, and "frequently cuts off towns from their hinterland, and even separates men of the same feudal tribe" (O.J.). Last, but by no means least, there was the problem of bringing into line the northern tribesmen—without doubt one of the greatest of all Albanian problems while the Yugoslavs chose to make it so.

The northern and eastern districts of Albania, wrote
the League of Nations Commissioners, "which are only
with difficulty accessible to civilization, are peopled by
tribes of an independent and headstrong temperament,
whose social organization recalls that of the clans of the
Scottish Highlands in the Middle Ages. . . . In a
country where there is no Press, and where the great
majority of electors are illiterate, the elections always
depend upon a small number of influential persons.
Accordingly, political struggles are almost always personal rivalries, which, owing to the customs and character
of the Albanians, are often likely to degenerate into
armed conflicts. The power of the politician is still
measured less by the number of his electors than by the
number of armed men at his disposal. The first thing he
looks for is assistance from the chiefs of the warlike tribes
of the northern and eastern frontier regions, who are
always ready to take any opportunity of winning glory or
money. He can, with their support, impose his will upon
a Government which sometimes has only very limited
resources at its disposal. . . . *The character and importance of these struggles have often been misrepresented by
foreign propaganda.*"

Despite these difficulties, Djafer Ypi and his colleagues
tackled their formidable task with courage and resolution;
and the chivalrous character, traditional loyalty, and more than
average intelligence (O.J.) of their compatriots enabled them,
in the space of two years, to produce truly remarkable results.

One of the first acts of Djafer Ypi's Cabinet was to request
Italy to withdraw her troops from Skutari, and this request was
complied with at the end of March. The Ministry of Finance
appreciated the expediency of drastic economy, and to
redress the unfavourable trade balance and conserve the
gold reserves of the country during the period of reconstruction, a high customs tariff was imposed (on the 5th
February). The Ministry of Public Works directed its attention to the improvement of communications, Austrian, Hungarian, and Italian engineers being engaged for this purpose.
Preference was given to Austrians and Hungarians, both for
reasons of economy, and also because Austria and Hungary had
no longer any interests in the country. Diplomatic relations with

HIS EXCELLENCY MEHMED BEY KONITZA, FIRST ALBANIAN MINISTER
PLENIPOTENTIARY TO GREAT BRITAIN

other States were opened, and Legations were established in Rome, Constantinople, Paris, and Vienna. On the 24th January, Mr. (now Sir Harry) Eyres, presented his credentials as British Minister Plenipotentiary; and on the 28th March Mehmed bey Konitza presented his credentials as Albanian Minister Plenipotentiary in London.

In the meantime Ahmed Zogu, although under thirty years of age, proved himself an able and courageous Minister of the Interior. He resolved to disarm all civilians throughout the lowlands, a task both dangerous and formidable, when it is remembered that the right to carry arms was a traditional custom. Throughout central and southern Albania he was successful, and thereafter it became illegal to bear arms without a licence. Among the malissori, however, matters were very different. "Adet" was the foundation of their existence, and any attempt, or even threat, to change the traditional customs of an illiterate people, especially when those people are warriors from birth, is invariably fraught with grave consequences. To the malissori, too, the Yugoslav menace was ever present, and not only did this make it even more improbable that they would surrender their arms without a struggle, but also unwise to deprive these irregular troops of the means with which to defend themselves or their country. A conciliatory policy, entailing the gradual super-imposition of modern for mediæval ideas, was acknowledged the wiser policy.

Perhaps Zogu's policy was, although necessary, a little premature; and in some quarters it was misconstrued as an indication that he was following in the footsteps of Essad Pasha, and favoured Slav aspirations, especially as he was opposed to irredentism. He was, too, inclined to be arbitrary in his methods. He is a mountain chieftain, and Bairam Tsuri, Zia Dibra, and others, with whom personalities counted for more than principles, and who either failed or refused to acknowledge his undoubted natural ability, were jealous of the power he had obtained in the land. These men, at bottom honest patriots, regarded him merely as an ambitious rival who wished to impose his authority upon them. In addition, Bairam Tsuri and Zia Dibra, both irredentists of the Kossovo Committee, had held portfolios in the "Sacred Union" Cabinet, and resented his inclusion in Djafer Ypi's Cabinet, while they themselves were excluded. Lastly, they were indignant at the establishment of the capital at Tirana instead of at Skutari, the commercial centre of the north. To what extent Yugoslav agents and propagandists through devious channels aggravated causes of discontent is a matter of conjecture.

It seems that it was the above circumstances which, in February, induced Bairam Tsuri to begin in Puka to organize an insurrection with the purpose of overthrowing Zogu, and forcing an election. The movement spread to the Dibra area, and Elez Yssuf, whose influence there was predominant, allied himself with it. At the same time Hamid Toptani raised a considerable force at Bazar Shjak, with which, at the beginning of March, he seized Durazzo and marched upon Tirana, while Bairam Tsuri and Elez Yssuf advanced upon the capital from their respective districts. Halid Lleshi took advantage of the occasion to cross the frontier from Yugoslavia with some comitadji followers, but was routed by Government troops before he had penetrated far into the interior. Subsequently he abandoned the Yugoslav cause, and espoused nationalism.

In the meantime the Cabinet—with the exception of Zogu, who remained to defend the capital—retired to Elbasan. Monsignor Noli took the opportunity to resign, and dissociated himself from Zogu and his colleagues, not wishing to identify himself further with their policy. He was succeeded as Minister for Foreign Affairs by Djafer Ypi, who at the same time remained Prime Minister. Two members of the Council of Regency—Omer pasha Vrioni and Antoine Pistuli—likewise resigned, and in consequence the power of the Regency became even less than before. The vacancies were not filled until December.

The Government imprudently scattered the few troops at its disposal, and sent separate columns against the three insurgent forces. In the course of his advance, however, Bairam Tsuri discovered that public opinion as a whole was opposed to the unconstitutional course which he and his colleagues were pursuing. True patriot that he was, he retired therefore whence he had come without causing bloodshed. But Elez Yssuf, a gallant but illiterate old warrior who was exasperated by the sufferings his people had endured at the hands of the Slavs, pressed forward with a few hundred men and encountered a company of Government troops near

Kruja commanded by Major Melek Frasheri. The troops were defeated and Frasheri killed. Yssuf thereupon seized the outskirts of Tirana, and during the night severe street fighting took place, in which the rebels sustained some fifty casualties, and the losses of the Government troops reached much the same figure.

At this juncture Mr. Eyres arrived upon the scene from Durazzo. He obtained an interview with Yssuf, and

> "succeeded in persuading this patriotic but misguided old mountaineer that he was but the instrument of a conspiracy which boded no good for his country, promising him at the same time a safe pardon if he retired from the scene. The advice was accepted, the capital was saved. . . . Ahmed Zogu holds, in fact, that Mr. Eyres thereby saved his life; and thenceforth he always gave the British Minister his confidence" (N.E. 8.10.25),

of which Mr. Eyres was able to take advantage with beneficial results for Albania.

Ahmed Zogu, who, throughout the crisis, had displayed the utmost presence of mind, was now able to concentrate against Hamid Toptani, who had failed to arrive in the neighbourhood of Tirana until after Yssuf had agreed to retire. In a night action the Government troops were entirely successful, and a considerable number of rebels were captured. Toptani himself escaped abroad by sea. So ended a revolt which, although of comparatively insignificant dimensions—the total killed was estimated at eighty only, of whom sixty were rebels—might well have proved disastrous, solely in view of the inadequacy of the military forces at the disposal of the Government. In some respects, however, it produced a salutary effect, since it brought large numbers of malissori into contact with their lowland compatriots, and also with what had been to them hitherto an unintelligible phenomenon, namely a constitutional Government legislating in the interests of the country as a whole.

Zogu's predominant influence was now undisputed, and he at once set about the task of restoring order, in which he was entirely successful. A military court was constituted, those who had been most seriously implicated in the revolt were court-martialled, and nine were executed. But neither Bairam

Tsuri nor Elez Yssuf suffered punishment; their action had been merely the outcome of a misunderstanding, no doubt largely fomented by interested parties beyond the border. The League of Nations Commissioners subsequently wrote with reference to the revolt:

> "In every attempt of this kind there is a rumour that one party or other is subsidized by foreign money. It is difficult to prove the truth of these allegations, but it seems certain that these movements can hardly be carried out with the always limited resources existing within the country."

A period of much-needed tranquillity throughout Albania now ensued. An American representative—Mr. Maxwell Blake—arrived during June to report upon the political situation; and his report was followed by the recognition, in July, of the Albanian Government by the United States, and by the appointment, in October, of Mr. W. Grant-Smith as United States Minister at Tirana. Zogu's influence, predominant in the Cabinet, was unrestricted by the now impotent and discredited Regency, and under his guidance the country bade fair to become a flourishing State (*Graphic*, 23.4.22). "The energy with which the Albanians are preparing for a new era of freedom and progress is worthy of all praise," reported the *Liverpool Daily Courier* (30.10.22). . . . "If only there were more money . . . Albania would forge ahead under a democratic Government to peaceful prosperity." Unfortunately, a request made to the League during May for a loan was not granted, although as a peace assurance premium in the Balkans it might have proved a very sound speculation, had Albania been subjected to temporary financial control by the League, as the Albanians themselves proposed. But it was considered that reform of internal economy and administrative organization was a necessary prelude to financial assistance, which otherwise would merely temporarily alleviate Albania's difficulties and saddle her with the burden of a national debt. "Without security, no money; without money, no security"—thus did Professor Sederholm describe the position. Money was required to enable the Albanians to provide adequate security; and until that was forthcoming, progress could be but slow and with many a retrograde step. But despite the shortage of money the Albanians made remark-

able progress, and would have succeeded in reassuring even
the most sceptical of those who hesitated at once to provide
financial assistance, had they enjoyed the benevolence of their
neighbours.

Some proposals were made by certain foreign banks in
connection with the establishment of a National Bank; but
these proposals were so circumscribed with impossible conditions that both the League of Nations' financial expert and
commissioner advised the Albanian Government to have
nothing to do with them (O.J.). In the meantime the Government spared no efforts to stimulate commercial development
—as indeed the very considerable excess of imports over
exports demanded—and Chambers of Commerce were established throughout the country. Every possible step was taken
to effect economy, and, as an example, marriage festivals which
hitherto had frequently lasted for a week, attended by an
unlimited number of guests, were restricted in duration by
law to twenty-four hours, and the number of guests limited
to twelve. But this anxiety for economy was not allowed to
interfere with any measure calculated to develop nationalism.
A national library and museum were established at Tirana, and
national education progressed at an astonishing rate in view
of the many difficulties with which the educational authorities were confronted. In September, 1922, there were 548
elementary schools in Albania, with a course of six years'
instruction (A.C.). "Most schools are crowded to such an
extent", wrote Professor Sederholm with reference to southern
Albania (O.J. May, 1923, 491–502), "that the class-rooms
could not contain any more pupils. As to the quantity of
educational work performed, no previous administration has
been more successful." He stated that in the north, likewise,
the schools which had been organized by the Jesuits and
Franciscans were "quite satisfactory". Children of all three
religions everywhere attended the same schools without distinction, except during a temporary misunderstanding which
arose at Skutari. Shortage of accommodation in the existing
schools, and shortage of school-books were, however, serious
obstacles, but the Ministry of Education proved itself equal
to them.

There was a more serious difficulty, however. The language, which, through five centuries of alien rule, had been
preserved only in the home and in unofficial Albanian circles,

had not developed with the progress of civilization, and until its reconstruction was completed it was wholly unsuitable for higher educational purposes. In the meantime therefore there was no alternative but to employ some foreign language for the purpose, either French or English, and French was made compulsory from the fourth year (A.C.). Had circumstances been otherwise, the obvious course would have been to have retained the use of the Greek language for the time being, since "Greek has long continued to be the language of religion, of literature, and of commerce, and might thus be regarded as a kind of second mother-tongue for the Christian Tosks of the south". But in view of Greek pretensions, this was out of the question, and the Albanian Government was, very naturally, anxious to eliminate as far as possible all traces of Greek influence. "It is not to be expected", wrote Professor Sederholm (O.J. May, 1923, 491–510), "that the Albanian Government would ever allow Greek schools for the Albanian-speaking population as long as they are used for the purpose of pan-Hellenic propaganda." Schools, however, for the Greek minority continued to exist, subsidized by the Government, which loyally fulfilled its obligations in this connection, and gave the minorities under its jurisdiction no cause for complaint, although the Greeks beyond the frontier continued to make unfounded allegations in the matter. The Albanians "have the quality of tolerance, which is so necessary to those who wish to rule, and which no other Balkan race possesses" (A.D. 19). With reference to this point, Monsignor Noli said (O.J. October, 1924, 1375): "In Albania there are 28 schools for 32,000 citizens who speak Greek, whereas at Skutari there are only 24 schools for a population of 110,000 which is exclusively Albanian. In Greece the Albanian minorities have no schools at their disposal."

The assistance rendered to Albania by the American Red Cross must be placed on record. This organization carried out invaluable work by opening schools and hospitals at Durazzo and Tirana, and its officials worked indefatigably to relieve those rendered destitute by the ravages of the Yugoslavs. A Vocational School was opened at Tirana under its auspices, which is proving a great success.

During May Albania became involved in a dispute with Italy (O.J. January, 1923, 113), which is important in that it shows that the Albanians were ready to brook no infringement by any country of their rights as an independent people. The Italians, who withdrew their military post office, which had been established when they occupied Durazzo, replaced it by a civil Italian post office. To this the Albanian Government objected, and in so doing was supported by public opinion. The establishment of a civil Italian post office was regarded as an attempt by Italy to retain a measure of control over an essential public service, and an infringement of the sovereignty of Albania.

Anti-Italian demonstrations took place in Durazzo, and in the circumstances the acting-Prefect gave instructions that the Royal Italian coat-of-arms displayed over the post office should be torn down. His instructions were carried out, and were endorsed by the townsfolk—who resented any trace of foreign influence—which is significant since their prosperity depended, for commercial reasons, upon the preservation of friendly relations with Italy; and therefore they might have been expected to be more amenable to a prevalence of Italian influence than inhabitants of any other part of the country— except perhaps Valona.

A protest was at once lodged at Tirana by the Italian Minister, and at one moment relations between the two countries became strained. But a conciliatory spirit prevailed on both sides, and eventually the matter was settled without further incident, the Italians agreeing to withdraw their telegraphic and postal service at the end of the year.

During August by-elections throughout the districts which had been evacuated by the Yugoslav troops since the general election, took place, and the new deputies took their seats in Parliament. In the same month the League's financial expert, Professor Albert Calmès (Luxemburg), arrived to investigate and report upon the economic and financial situation in the country prior to the arrival of the financial adviser. He reported that the disturbed state of the country was due to Albania's neighbours, to delay in the final settlement of her boundaries, to the existence of a neutral zone which was a rendezvous for the scum of the Peninsula and disaffected tribesmen, and to the results of thirteen years' ravages and devastations. The redeeming features were, he wrote, "the good sense of her inhabitants, their desire for progress, her metal currency, and the development of education" (A.C.).

A congress of representatives of the Orthodox congregations of Albania was held at Berat during August, at which it was decided that an Autocephalous Albanian Church should be founded. A formal application was made thereupon to the Patriarch for his consent, which was readily given—no doubt in view of the obvious futility of a refusal and the loss of prestige which would have been entailed—and the Exarch Ierotheos, of Albanian origin, was sent to arrange practical details. The Albanian Orthodox Church was formally recognized during the following February, and thus was another obstacle to national stability removed.

Although Yugoslavia had appointed a representative to Tirana, the Yugoslavs showed no disposition to avail themselves of Albanian distrust of Italy to win, by a conciliatory and benevolent policy, the good will of the Albanian people. On the contrary they maintained a prohibitive tariff barrier against Albanian goods, and in other ways displayed their ill will.

Greece likewise continued to pursue an unfriendly policy. "The Greek Government", wrote Professor Sederholm (Report, 19.12.22 to 1.2.23), "was persisting in its former attitude of not regarding the provinces of Korcha and Argyrocastro as belonging to Albania." Albanians from these districts travelling in Greece were deprived of their Albanian passports, for which Greek passports were substituted. Albanian landowners in Macedonia were compelled by the Greek authorities to sell their landed properties at short notice at very low prices (about one-fiftieth part of the value of the property, payable over a period of thirty years), and their lands were then allotted to Greek immigrants from abroad or Christian peasants who had previously worked there under the *Chiftlik* system. The delay in determining the frontier of the former Turkish *caza* of Korcha caused grave uneasiness in that district. The Greeks remained in occupation of a part of the disputed area despite the decision of the Conference of Ambassadors that it should be included in the "zone of demarcation", and the inhabitants were separated therefore from Korcha, their market town, while the people of Korcha found much difficulty in communicating with Monastir, their commercial centre. The Greek authorities

even refused to allow Professor Sederholm to enter the districts occupied.

The Greeks alone were responsible for the delay in the
delimitation of the frontier.

"The Greek Government", wrote Professor Sederholm, "has only reluctantly and under protest taken part
in the work of the Boundary Commission, and that
has made it impossible for it to delimitate the boundary
between Greece and the former Turkish *caza* of Korcha
belonging to Albania before the winter set in, thus
hindering the continuation of the work."

When eventually they did appoint a representative, the
Greeks attempted, through him, to revive the Corfu Agreement of 1914, and unceasingly distracted the Commissioners
with charges against the Albanians of infringements of the
rights of minorities and violence against the Greek clergy
(O.J. January, 1923, 113–18).

Despite these difficulties, Albania forged ahead towards
stability. But a prosperous and stable Albania was precisely
what her neighbours did not wish. They had prophesied
chaos, and chaos there must be. In any case, the Press of
Europe must report chaos, otherwise the truth about Albania
and her people might become known, tourists would arrive,
enterprising capitalists would follow, and there would be an
end of their machinations. An insurrection was therefore
essential that these unpalatable possibilities might be precluded; and if no actual disturbances could be fomented,
fictitious ones must be reported. Probably most of the false
reports which emanated from Italy were Yugoslav and Greek
exports, although it is equally probable that Italian financial
groups employed the subtle weapon of false news to discourage
rivals.

During September Yugoslav and Italian newspapers reported that Bairam Tsuri was in revolt with 2,000 men, and
that the Government had fled to Berat. In December the
Greek delegation at Lausanne complained that ten Turkish
officers and several hundred irregulars had landed at Durazzo
to take part in irregular warfare against the Greeks.

"All these rumours", wrote Professor Sederholm,
"were devoid of foundation. At the present time the

strongest desire of Albania, represented by her Government, is to realize her national ideals on the basis of a western political and cultural organization, and to remain absolutely neutral" (O.J. January, 1923, 117).

Those who sought to discredit and ridicule Albania were ably assisted by credulous newspaper reporters and editors. Ludicrous reports appeared to the effect that Albania was seeking, and even advertising, for a king! And it was alleged that the throne had been offered to all manner of people. These reports produced the most incredible applications for the crown, from even distinguished naval and military officers, and from many obscure persons, including a naval cadet and an instructress of classical dancing! Editors should refrain from publishing such reports, which discredit not only their newspapers but also the country or cause concerned, and discourage commercial enterprise in a State which is thus misrepresented as being hopelessly unstable. It is said that Colonel Aubrey Herbert, who was largely responsible for the existence of Albania and had worked indefatigably in the cause of Albanian independence, was asked quite unofficially whether, if the throne were offered to him, he would accept it; but certainly it was offered to no one else, except perhaps by propagandists wishing to discredit Albania or by journalists as a practical joke!

Reporters allowed their imaginations to run riot when dealing with "unknown Albania". For example, one well-known paper announced (on 23.5.22) that the staff of the Albanian Legation would appear at a forthcoming lévée "in uniforms quite unfamiliar here". The staff consisted of M. Konitza and a Scottish lady secretary, neither of whom ever appeared in anything but perfectly normal British civilian clothes! But perhaps the most grotesque story ever told in connection with Albania or any other country was that of "Princess Krytzchka", the daughter of a British colonel (T. 17.5.22). It appears that she met in Italy an adventurer describing himself as "Prince Radomirko Krytzchka" destined to become "the ruling Prince of Albania", that they married and went to Albania (such was her story), that there she found he was an impostor, and he that as a financial proposition she was a failure, and that they agreed to part. She returned to England (with the title) and reported that her husband had been assassinated before her eyes. Incredible as it may seem, even *The Times* in all seriousness duly reported the ridiculous story (for reasons of its own it apparently never inquired of the Albanian Legation whether there ever had been a "Prince Radomirko"); and a portrait of the "Princess" and her Alsatian wolfhound at a dog show appeared in the Press and on the screen so recently as February, 1925!

Towards the end of October the Albanian Government successfully withstood a violent onslaught by the Opposition—the Liberal Democrats, whose principal characteristic was impatience—supported by the irredentist section. The former derived their strength from the Vatra, which in turn was supported principally by the Orthodox Albanians of southern Albania, who were impatient for agrarian and other reforms, while the latter found support in the north-eastern districts which had suffered from the ravages of the Yugo-slavs, and were in contact with their oppressed kinsmen of Kossovo. Both sections desired a more liberal régime, and were opposed to a continuance in office of the Conservative element, which consisted principally of the landowners and ex-officials of the Turkish service, who, although generally possessed of more experience than the Democrats in the art of administration, were inclined to adhere to the old Turkish order of things. The Democrats pressed for immediate and drastic reforms, which, at so early a stage in the development of the country, would have tended to react unfavourably against the work of consolidating it. Certainly the majority of the reforms for which the Democrats pressed were extremely desirable, and were already included in the programme of the Government, but the latter appreciated that hasty steps by inexperienced legislators spelt disaster.

The principal leaders of the Opposition, which included more moderate men such as Faik and Mehmed Konitza, were Louis Gurakuchi, Monsignor Fan Noli, Suleiman Delvino, D. Kacimbro and K. Tassi. Despite their attacks, Djafer Ypi's Cabinet obtained a vote of confidence.

During September Djafer Ypi had resigned as Minister for Foreign Affairs, and had been succeeded by Pandele Evangheli. On the 2nd December he resigned also as Prime Minister, and was appointed to one of the vacancies in the Council of Regency, created by the resignation, earlier in the year, of Omer Vrioni and Antoine Pistuli. The other vacancy was filled at the same time by M. Gjoni Tchoba. Djafer Ypi was succeeded as Prime Minister by Ahmed Zogu, who temporarily retained the portfolio of Minister of the Interior, subsequently held by Sefi Vlamasi.

In view of these changes it is as well to give the reconstituted Council of Regency and Cabinet in tabular form.

The High Council of Regency:

DJAFER YPI	Bektashi Moslem.
SOTIR PETSI	Orthodox Christian.
GJONI TCHOBA . . .	Roman Catholic.
REFIK TOPTANI . . .	Sunni Moslem.

The Cabinet:

AHMED ZOGU	Prime Minister and
(SEFI VLAMASI) . . .	Minister of the Interior.
PANDELE EVANGHELI . .	Minister for Foreign Affairs.
ISMAIL HAKKI TATZALI .	Minister for War.
HUSSEIN VRIONI . . .	Minister of Justice.
REDJEB MITROVITZA . .	Minister of Education.
KOL THACHI	Minister of Finance.
SPIRO KOLEKA . . .	Minister of Public Works.

One of the young Prime Minister's first acts was to ask the Commission of Inquiry (Professor Sederholm) to ask the League of Nations to appoint foreign advisers for Justice, Education, Gendarmerie, and Public Works.

In his speech in the Albanian Parliament on the 2nd December Zogu announced that it was the intention of his Government to pursue a democratic and constitutional policy, and to acknowledge the freedom of the Press. He mentioned the difficulty presented by the differences which existed in cultural development in different parts of the country, and expressed the intention to give each full liberty. He remarked that an Albanian Orthodox Church had been successfully established, and stated that similar measures would be taken with regard to the reform of the Albanian Moslem Church. He announced that a Constituent Assembly would be convened, probably in September, that the Government would remain neutral during the election of deputies to the Assembly, and that the task of the Assembly would be to deliberate upon the form of the permanent constitution which the country was to adopt. The Government hoped, he said, to make a grant for the purpose of fighting malaria—which

is a great drawback to Albania and accounts for the lethargy
which afflicts numbers of the inhabitants of the lowlands—
and for improving the sanitation of the country generally;
for this purpose foreign experts from abroad would be
engaged. The Budget, he said, would be cut down, the
number of officials reduced, the reorganization of the administrative system begun, and prefects appointed with experience
of the districts with which they were entrusted. The Army
would be reduced, and a foreign organizer appointed; and the
services of a foreign legal expert would be obtained to assist
in reforming the legislature, and an adviser to assist the
Minister of Education. With regard to Public Works,
he stated that three battalions of recruits would be detailed
for road construction, instead of one as hitherto. (In addition,
all male inhabitants were compelled to give six days' labour
to road construction unless able to pay a tax of 20 gold francs
for exemption: A.C.) The estimates, he said, amounted to
17,000,000 gold francs, whereas the anticipated revenue was
19,000,000. Above all, he declared, the Government proposed
to do everything in its power to develop trade and attract
foreign capital.

Zogu had indeed a stupendous task before him. The position of his country when he became Prime Minister was
summarized by Professor Sederholm in his Final Report
(O.J. May, 1923). He wrote:

"Albania has achieved her independence at a time
when the whole world is impoverished, and she finds
herself therefore *financially at a disadvantage* in comparison
with the situation in which other Balkan States found
themselves when they achieved independence. In their
case *they generally found some Great Power able and willing
to befriend them and to afford them financial assistance.*

"Albania depends on the League for impartial political
support and has not to complain of the difference, *but
as regards financial help she must depend on presenting herself
in the financial market in a favourable light, offering opportunities of profitable trade to investors, and affording the
ordinary legal guarantees of a modern and ordered State.*"

The passages in italics provide a key to Albania's subsequent relations with her neighbours. Yugoslav policy has
been to prevent Albania from "presenting herself in the

ALBANIA: THE RISE OF A KINGDOM

financial market in a favourable light", and from "affording
the ordinary legal guarantees of a modern and ordered State".
That being the case, the Albanians, being "financially at a
disadvantage", found ultimately that they had no alternative
but to seek "some Great Power able and willing to befriend
them and to afford them financial assistance", since, without
such assistance, rapid progress and development were impossible. The Yugoslavs had every opportunity themselves to
afford that assistance; they might, with little difficulty, have
obtained the advantages in northern Albania which it had
been proposed in the Memorandum of the 9th December,
1919, that they should enjoy, and which they had been offered
by the Albanian Government in May, 1921. The Yugoslavs
profess to fear Italy, yet instead of attempting to strengthen
Albania as a defensive barrier against her, they sought to
destroy that barrier. If they have thrust an unwilling Albania
into the arms of Italy, they have no one to blame but
themselves.

Nevertheless, at the beginning of 1923 the relations between
Albania and her neighbours appeared to be tolerably satisfactory. During January General Ali Riza Kolonia was
appointed Albanian Minister in Belgrade, and Midhat Frasheri
was appointed to Athens during March.

In the absence of danger, it was but natural (until national
unity had been consolidated, which could be effected only
in the course of time and with the development of the language, communications, commerce, and culture) that domestic
differences should once more appear. The fundamental cause
of the revival of these differences was impatience, and this
was especially marked among the Orthodox inhabitants of
southern Albania, whose contact with Greece, where Christians had enjoyed priority over Moslems—whereas in Albania
under Turkish rule the reverse had been the case—and connection with those emigrants to the United States who had
become imbued with the democratic ideas of that country, had
made them even more eager than their compatriots to call
into existence at once a new and progressive Albania untrammelled by any vestige of the old régime.

"Moreover also", wrote Professor Sederholm (O.J.
May, 1923, 491–510), "a certain political disillusion is
discernible. The Nationalists of Korcha hoped that, as

the result of the foundation of an independent Albania,
a new State would be created which, from the beginning,
would be something very unlike the Turkish province
which Albania had previously been. But, as usual, the
difficulties have been much greater than was anticipated,
and the optimists therefore feel deceived in their hopes."

It has been said that religion was never a direct, and seldom
an indirect, cause of friction among the Albanians. It may then
seem contradictory to say that in the absence of foreign
danger there grew up a marked divergence between Moslems
and Christians, especially in southern Albania. Actually,
however, there is no contradiction, since the cause was purely
a social one. Under Turkish rule the distinction between
Moslems and Christians was principally a matter of class, the
former being the landowners, officials—in short, the ruling
class, while the latter were regarded as inferior beings, whose
right to own land was not admitted. Indeed, the majority
of Albanians who became Moslems abjured the Christian
faith to escape from the latter category and share the privileges enjoyed by the former. They and their descendants
became the owners of land, or officials of experience, while
their Christian compatriots remained at a hopeless disadvantage. In consequence, when Albania obtained independence,
the latter numbered within their ranks few experienced
legislators and administrators, but many Liberal theorists
whose education in Greek and American schools had been
essentially more western, and therefore more democratic,
than that of their Moslem compatriots.

The contact of the Orthodox Christian Albanians with
Greece had led to the growth among them of Hellenophile
sentiments. Here again there may seem to be a contradiction
of former statements, whereas actually there is none. The
majority of the Orthodox population of southern Albania—
that is to say, about one-third (diagram, p. 164) of the population of "Northern Epirus", since Orthodox Christians and
Moslems therein were roughly in equal numbers (O.J.)—were
Hellenophile to the extent that they preferred Greek to
Turkish culture, and cherished an affection for the land which
had afforded them a sanctuary from Turkish oppression, and
in which dwelt so many of their kinsmen. Beyond this, however, their Hellenophile sentiments did not go, and only

an infinitesimal minority were in favour of the union of southern Albania with Greece. This small section may perhaps be described as Grecophile, which bears a more political and less cultural meaning than the term Hellenophile.

> "It results from the foregoing", wrote Professor Sederholm, "that the Hellenophile sentiments of the majority of the Orthodox population of southern Albania are not to be described as Greek nationalism. *Among the most eager Hellenophiles, even among those who have settled in Greece and have fought for her, there often remains a strong feeling in favour of Albania,* although they prefer to call it Northern Epirus and not southern Albania, and they take a pride in belonging to the race of the Shqipetars" (O.J. May, 1923, 500).

These Hellenophiles were Albanian patriots in the first place, and any attempt by Greece to interfere with their new-found political freedom, or to wrench them from their Motherland, aroused their hostility towards her. Their

> "feelings for Greece are not those of an irredenta, but only those for a country which has been the source of their culture and the enemy of the hated Turkish régime. . . . If insurrectional movements should begin, they could only be started from the other side of the frontier, where certainly organizations of 'pan-Epirots' exist, who have openly declared their intention to conquer Northern Epirus for Greece" (O.J. May, 1923, 501).

Conversely, any indication that their Moslem compatriots sought to perpetuate the old order of things, aroused misgivings among the Hellenophiles as to the advantages of a régime which seemed to deny them that freedom and equality which nominally was theirs; and naturally their eyes turned to Greece as a possible alternative to further subservience. Professor Sederholm recorded the following remark by an Orthodox Albanian which he said he had heard indirectly through reliable channels, as indicating the point of view of these Hellenophiles: "Most of us want an Albania, but we want a good Albania; if we cannot get a good one, we prefer Greece." The Orthodox Christians expected that within an independent Albania they would enjoy equal rights with their Moslem compatriots; but if they were not to do so, then their position was no better than under Turkish administration, and union with Greece was the obvious alternative, for geographical, economic, and cultural reasons.

When Ahmed Zogu became Prime Minister, there was much discontent among the Christian population, principally of southern Albania. But this was the result, not of any inclination for Greek rule or of religious animosity, as Professor Sederholm was careful to emphasize, but of an impatience for social and agrarian reforms. Southern Albania, being the most developed, prosperous, and commercially active part of the country, suffered more than any other part from the general economic depression which followed the war. Taxes had to be paid nevertheless, and high taxes and customs dues were placed even on necessities. Matters were made worse by the irregularity of communications with Salonika and Monastir owing to the political situation. The economic depression led to idleness, and in consequence, as is inevitable in the Balkans, to a renewed interest in politics. It followed that the political situation was held responsible for the economic one, and the Government responsible therefore for both.

One cause of dissatisfaction among Moslems and Christians alike was that while Korcha and Argyrocastro paid a great part of the State Budget, only a small proportion thereof was expended in southern Albania, the greater part being used to pay the central administration, army, etc. But the principal cause of discontent, which affected only the Orthodox Christians, was a resentment against the advantages enjoyed by the Moslem landowners and the precedence given to former Turkish officials, who frequently took advantage of their position for personal ends. The Orthodox Christian Albanians had expected, somewhat unreasonably in view of their inexperience, to obtain influence in the country, from the beginning, in proportion to their culture and economic importance; but they had proportionately less to say in State affairs than either Moslems or Catholics. This was, however, largely their own fault, since considerable numbers of them had refrained from voting during the previous election, being led to believe by interested parties that the Government had the intention to interfere. Zogu's Cabinet gave assurances that at the next election it would not attempt to influence a free vote.

The continuance in authority of the landowning Beys

and ex-officials of the Turkish service, who in many cases continued to regard themselves as belonging to a superior class to their Christian compatriots, aroused among the latter unpleasant memories of the past and a fear that the old order of things would continue. The majority of the educated and most intelligent Orthodox Albanians refused to assist the Government by taking office, on the pretext that their commerce paid them better—actually as a protest against the attitude of the Moslems. The Moslem officials were inclined to be arbitrary, especially and not unnaturally in the face of any indication of Hellenophile sentiments, and to imprison the Christians on the slightest provocation, and sometimes through personal motives. The Christians complained that they could not be assured of impartial justice in disputes with Moslems. In some cases the Moslems resisted the law, believing they stood above it, while in others Christian officials who proceeded too firmly against Moslems were forced to resign. Professor Sederholm reported, however, that justice in Albania was no worse than in other Balkan countries at a similar stage in their development. The Beys, on the other hand, frequently attempted to take advantage of the undeveloped character of the legislation to extend their ownership of land, by oppression or arbitrary measures, to property which had hitherto been held in common by communities, and in many cases the land which they already possessed had been obtained by similar measures during Turkish domination. In many of them, especially in those of central Albania, the sense of nationality was weak and patriotism completely overshadowed by interest; above all things they feared the partition of their estates or other measures of agrarian reform (T. 4.9.26), of which Ahmed Zogu was in favour, the ownership and tenancy of land being upon an extremely unsatisfactory basis.

Although much discontent was undoubtedly fomented by Greek agitators of the "pan-Epirot" organizations which existed beyond the frontier, there certainly were many causes for complaint. Abuses and malpractices were to be expected, however, in a land which had for so long stagnated under Turkish rule. Misappropriation and corruption had been rife in the Turkish Empire during its latter days, and however praiseworthy the Albanian race may be, it was but natural that the Albanian Moslem officials and landowners had become

tainted with that corruption (T. 4.9.26). There were many
notable exceptions. Nevertheless, with the achievement by
Albania of independence passed the usefulness to her of the
majority of these officials. Although they played a leading
part during the struggle for autonomy and independence, as
indeed their privileged position within the Turkish Empire
enabled them to do, they have now become relics of the past
—and of all traces of her connection with the Orient must
Albania cleanse herself before she can resolutely go forward
upon Occidental lines. This cannot, however, be done overnight, as the Orthodox Albanians and returned émigrés from
the United States imagined. Indeed, the latter proved themselves very much less suited for positions of responsibility
than the Turkish-trained Albanian officials whom they would
replace. The Albanians must await in patience the maturity of
men bred within the borders of a consolidated Albania, where
blood is free from either artisan American or Oriental taint.
This transition stage, from the old to the new, must take
time—at least a generation; with every other resurrected or
new-born State unfettered from an alien yoke, whether in the
Balkans or elsewhere, it has taken time. In the meantime one
implores both the Albanians themselves and their foreign
critics to learn patience and forbearance.

Ahmed Zogu and his Cabinet were well aware of the
urgent need for drastic reforms in every direction, and despite
the many difficulties in their path and the opposition of
vested interests, set about the task with resolution. The
question of agrarian reforms was discussed, and no insuperable difficulties presented themselves. As a preliminary step
the title of "Bey" was abolished by decision of the Albanian
Parliament; and the expulsion by landlords from their property of tenants who continued to fulfil their normal obligations, no matter of what race, religion, or sentiments they
might be, was declared illegal. The importance of improving
communications as a means of consolidating the country
was appreciated, and work in this direction was pressed
forward. An interesting measure was passed by which all
boys between the ages of twelve and eighteen years were
compelled by law to belong to a Boy Scouts group. The
Scout system had been introduced into Albania in 1920 by
Miss Mosley Williams, of the American Red Cross, who
organized a detachment at Tirana; and at the beginning of

1927 the Albanian Scouts were placed under the control of an English scoutmaster. Indeed, in every direction the Government made progress towards the stabilization of the internal situation.

Professor Sederholm, in his Final Report (O.J. May, 1923, 504), stated that the habit of carrying arms had practically ceased—except, of course, in the highlands—that the blood feud, even in the mountains, was rapidly vanishing, and that public security had made immense strides.

> "For the first time for centuries", he wrote, "a Government has possessed uncontested power all over the territory of Albania, being able to call in conscripts and levy taxes even from remote regions in the mountains which, during the Turkish régime, retained a state of practical independence."

He emphasized the urgent need for reforms and the difficulties of the Government's task, especially as there were few men with sufficient experience to put reforms into practice.

> "I am convinced", he wrote, "that the task is not beyond the patriotism or ability of the Albanian race. Whenever they have had the chance they have held their own, and more than their own, in foreign lands. It has been their unfortunate fate that they have never been able to show their qualities in their homeland. . . . The race is a gifted one, but at present lacks experience and knowledge."

He advocated a strong Central Government, and at the same time a certain measure of local autonomy, but mentioned that to find the proper balance between the two would be a difficult problem. He expressed the opinion that in any case the Government must go forward resolutely under the guidance of men possessed of the necessary strength of purpose and will-power, otherwise stagnation would be the result. "Such stagnation", he continued, "would be the greatest danger to the maintenance of the independence of the country", since "Albania is geographically in and of Europe", and Europe will not permit any part of herself to remain conspicuously and permanently backward. "*The fate of Albania*", he concluded, "*lies in an intelligent use by her people and elected rulers of experienced experts in administrative, educational, and economic affairs."*

During January, 1923, Bairam Tsuri thought fit again to cause trouble, actuated partly no doubt by personal jealousy of Ahmed Zogu, exasperation at the establishment of the capital at Tirana instead of at Skutari, and resentment against the power enjoyed by the Moslem landowners (although the insurgent leaders were themselves Moslems), but principally by irredentist motives. He, Hassan Prishtina, and Mustapha Kruja, leaders of the Kossovo Committee, which maintained that the Government had betrayed the Albanians under the Yugoslav yoke by turning their backs upon irredentism, gathered around them a number of malissori, and also some five hundred "refugees from the Kossovo region of the Kingdom of the Serbs, Croats, and Slovenes" (O. J. May, 1923, 506), who had sought refuge in the "zone of demarcation" from Serb persecution.

The insurgents seized Krouma, the headquarters of a subprefecture in the mountains, but were subjugated with very little bloodshed after two skirmishes with gendarmerie. The total killed on both sides did not exceed ten, and the incident would be unworthy of record were it not that Belgrade spread lurid reports of heavy fighting, and closed the frontier.

Whether Yugoslav agents assisted to stir up the revolt is a matter of conjecture. That the revolt was largely due to a hostility towards them is immaterial. Professor Sederholm, commenting upon the incident, wrote:

> "If no money is available for paying men wishing to partake in such adventures, their repetition will be more and more rare, and it will be easy for the Government to subdue them with the aid of a good gendarmerie."

On the 3rd February the Financial Committee of the League of Nations submitted to the Council of the League, in accordance with the resolution of the 13th May, the name of an Englishman, Mr. R. S. Patterson—proposed, at the request of the Albanians, by Colonel Herbert—as being a suitable financial adviser to the Albanian Government. At once M. Viviani, the French representative, protested (P.D. 160: 1294; 163: 1646) that France had not had an opportunity to consider the matter, and asked that in view of Albania's oil resources a decision should be postponed. Thereupon M.

Blinishti, the Albanian representative, remarked "that Albania was not asking for a financial controller but for a financial adviser to assist in the financial administration of the country. Albania was an independent State, which naturally retained the right to dispose of its economic and financial concessions" (O.J. March, 1923, 241). It is this jealousy between the Powers with regard to Albania—of which the above incident is an example—that has been one of the principal obstacles in the way of her development. Eventually this particular difficulty was overcome by the appointment, during April, of Herr Hunger, a Dutchman, as financial adviser.

During February Lieut.-Colonel W. F. Stirling, British Governor of Jaffa, who had previously served with Colonel T. E. Lawrence in Arabia, was asked by the Albanian Government to become adviser to the Minister of the Interior. He possesses that exceptional gift of being able to grasp and sympathize with a foreign point of view. He accepted the appointment, and proceeded to investigate conditions throughout the country. He subsequently wrote to the British Press denouncing the false reports which continued to appear regarding Albania, originated, he said, for the purpose of discrediting her. He testified to the tranquillity of the country, to public security therein—which he described as remarkably good—and to the desire for foreign capital with which the country might be opened up.

During March the attention of the Government was much occupied by various British, American, Italian, and French companies—including the Anglo-Persian, Standard, and Sinclair Oil Companies—competing for oil-boring concessions. In 1921 the Anglo-Persian Oil Company had obtained a concession, but it required the ratification of Parliament, and to prevent its ratification the Standard Oil Company, the Italians, and French strove by every conceivable means. In addition there were applications for many other concessions. A number were granted, but the Government was obliged to act with extreme circumspection, and in consequence slowly, in the matter, in view of the number of companies with inadequate capital, adventurers, and groups actuated by political rather than commercial motives, who attempted to take advantage of the country's financial need. Indeed, one cannot altogether blame the Albanians if, at times, they are apt to assume an attitude of *Timeo Danaos et dona ferentes*.

On the other hand, the Albanians proved, in some cases, unreasonable, and demanded impossible terms from *bona fide* companies which sought concessions. They were slow to appreciate that the development of their country, and the employment to this end of their labour, are a more certain assurance of ultimate prosperity than any temporary relief afforded by the sale of concessions upon such exorbitant terms that the companies which obtain them are able to expand only slowly, and to make but a precarious profit. Private enterprise is not philanthropic—it seeks profit; and that profit must outweigh apparent risk. Any enterprise in Albania is fraught with apparent risk—owing to the propaganda of her neighbours—and until that apparent risk is proved negligible the Albanians must be prepared to override their suspicion and make liberal concessions. They must judge the value of their resources to the foreign financier not in terms of actual but of apparent risk, until the latter has satisfied himself that the risk exists only in the columns of the Press and not in actuality.

In the meantime Meissner Pasha, the German engineer who had constructed the Hedjaz railway, became temporarily attached to the Ministry of Public Works, an Italian expert was placed in charge of the agricultural school at Lushnja, Signor Menzinger was appointed legal adviser, and an Austro-Hungarian general (Mirdasth) was entrusted with the reorganization of the army. A medical expert appointed by the League of Nations visited the country to investigate hygienic and sanitary conditions and recommend measures to improve them.

During the same month a Congress of representatives of the Albanian Moslem Church was convened at Tirana, on Zogu's initiative, to consider reforms. The Congress broke with the Khaliphate, expressing the opinion that there had been no Khaliph since Mohammed, and that Moslem Albanians owed allegiance primarily to their native land. Thus was severed the last tie between Albania and Constantinople. The same Congress decided that among other reforms monogamy should be enforced by law—polygamy had existed hitherto in principle, although seldom in practice (S.m/s. 25); and the compulsory use by women of the veil—few malissori women had ever worn it—was abolished (T. 9.4.23).

The provision of relief for the inhabitants of the districts

laid waste by the Yugoslavs presented a serious problem
to the Government, in view of the limited resources at its
disposal. Albania may be numbered among those small States
which suffered most, both during and after the Great War,
from the havoc created by belligerent forces and their re-
quisitioning, while she received no compensation, and least
assistance towards recovery. Two successive maize crop
failures had deprived the malissori of their staple food, and
blackened ruins were all that remained of their homesteads.
The ranks of these unhappy people were swelled by refugees
both from Yugoslavia and Greece, and some 80,000 persons
were thus destitute, many of them dying of starvation and
exposure. On behalf of these unfortunate folk an appeal was
made by Mr. Robert Parr, Secretary of the British Legation
in Albania, and a fund was raised by Miss Durham, Lady
Carnarvon, and Mrs. Aubrey Herbert for their relief. Mr.
Ramsay MacDonald contributed a large sum on behalf of
the British Government. The subsequent work of distributing
the supplies purchased was carried out by Mr. Morton Eden,
Mr. and Mrs. Parr, and Mrs. Stirling. The Yugoslavs
obstructed the work by raising objections to the admission
of supplies from their territory.

Both in Yugoslavia and in Greece Albanians were being
subjected to every indignity and injustice, and in consequence
many were returning to their native land, where they might
dwell in comparative tranquillity, if in poverty. The sufferings
of Albanians under Yugoslav rule were confirmed by Mr.
H. V. R. Milne (Oakfield, Leamington Spa: *The Times*, the
6th March, 1924), who was himself arrested, taken to Ochrida,
and imprisoned for several days during October, 1923, for no
other reason than that he had crossed the frontier from
Albania. Upon the pretext that the country was dangerous,
the visa he had obtained from the Yugoslav Consul at Tirana
was ignored, and he was released only because he could be
convicted of no offence. The writer heard these details from
British sources in Albania.

The Greeks pursued much the same policy of boycott and
persecution towards the Moslem Albanian inhabitants of the
territory acquired by the Balkan Wars, with the intention to
drive them from their flourishing properties in Epirus to
the remote regions of Anatolia, and replace them by Greek
emigrants from Turkey. With this policy, that pursued by the

Albanian Government with regard to the Greek minority in southern Albania is a notable contraſt. Speaking before the Council of the League of Nations on the 17th September, Midhat Frasheri said:

"The country which I have the honour to represent has granted the racial minorities within her frontiers all religious, educational, civil, and political rights; in this reſpect Albania is the moſt liberal State in south-eaſtern Europe. The attainment of this end has not entailed any sacrifices of a moral nature for her, as the freedom and equality which she has granted her minorities did not require any effort on her part; she has, however, accepted heavy material sacrifices in order to do juſtice to the ſtranger within her gates" (O.J. November, 1923, 1312).

When the Convention for the exchange of Greek and Turkish populations was signed at Lausanne on the 30th January, 1923, the Greek delegate had declared that Greece had no intention to proceed with an exchange of Moslems of Albanian origin who inhabited a diſtrict well defined, namely Epirus. This undertaking was confirmed by M. Venizelos in a letter to the League of Nations dated the 6th Auguſt, 1923. Moreover, the Greek Chargé d'Affaires at Tirana had, on the 3rd October, assured the Albanian Government that Greece had no intention to endeavour to escape from her solemn undertakings. Nevertheless, Moslems of Albanian race—with the exception of those who had been, or whose fathers had been, born within the exiſting frontiers of Albania, who, Greece declared, comprised only nine families —were said to be Turks and treated as such. A law was passed that all landed property in Epirus would be expropriated, and since almost all the rural eſtates were owned by Moslem Albanians, was in practice aimed at the latter.

Before the Council of the League of Nations on the 17th December (O.J. February, 1924, 365), M. Blinishti, Chief of the Permanent Albanian Secretariat accredited to Geneva, said that the property of Moslem Albanians was confiscated, their harveſt was requisitioned, they were prohibited from sowing their corn or from selling or letting their property to foreſtall its expropriation, Greek refugees were inſtalled in their houses, and their right to vote was suppressed. The

Council of the League of Nations therefore resolved to draw the attention of the Mixed Commission for the Exchange of Greek and Turkish Populations to the facts, requesting it to hear any evidence which the Albanian Government might wish to lay before it.

M. Blinishti begged that the League should constitute a special Commission to investigate the case of the Moslem Albanians, but this proposal was opposed by the Greek representative, M. Caclamanos, who contended that the League would be acting beyond its power in so doing, in view of the existence of a Mixed Commission constituted, in accordance with the Convention of Lausanne, to deal with the whole question of exchange. The Mixed Commission had been constituted to supervise the exchange of populations in accordance with the interests of Greece and Turkey, and was therefore composed of Greek and Turkish representatives with a neutral chairman. Greece was anxious to be rid of the Moslem Albanian minority within her frontiers—the Christian Albanian element she could to some extent assimilate—that the Albanian claims to Albanian territory which she had acquired in 1913 might be silenced. Turkey, who had favoured the exchange, was anxious to restore her population, depleted by the war with Greece, and was not to be expected to refuse Moslems; moreover, the property which they left behind became an asset in her account with Greece. The task of the neutral chairman was limited to holding the balance between the Greek and Turkish points of view; he frequently allowed the delegates to tour alone, merely acting as arbitrator when disputes arose. But since, as regards Moslems, their points of view coincided, Albania was assured of no impartiality before the Commission, the neutral chairman being easily deluded and always outvoted. The repeated appeals of the Albanian Government for the inclusion of an Albanian representative were, of course, rejected by the Commission, and Greece succeeded in expelling thousands of Moslem Albanians.

In view of the League's request, the Mixed Commission agreed to postpone the departure of any person who appeared to lay proper claim to Albanian origin, and sub-commissions of Greek and Turkish representatives with a neutral chairman were constituted to investigate the question. These sub-commissions were instructed by the Mixed Commission to be guided principally by place of origin, language, and national consciousness. In the circumstances it was no difficult matter for the Greek authorities to coerce the inhabitants into making any sort of declaration regarding their origin and sentiments, and to hoodwink commissions which, by the very nature of their composition, were already hopelessly prejudiced in favour of the Greek point of view. Indeed, so well did they succeed that the sub-commission appointed to operate in Epirus reported on the 2nd June, 1924 (quoted by Monsignor Noli before the Council of the League on the 29th September: O.J. October, 1924, 1353):

> "The Minutes referred to will make it quite clear that the vast majority of Moslem-Greek subjects inhabiting Epirus and Macedonia state, without hesitation, that they are of Turkish origin, and consequently desire to be included in the exchange. Only very limited minorities in various localities say that they are Albanian in origin and desire, in consequence, to be exempted from compulsory exchange."

This the Commissioners wrote despite the well-established fact that almost the whole Moslem element in Epirus is of Albanian origin, and further, regardless of M. Caclamanos's declaration on the 19th January, 1923, at the Lausanne Conference—its outcome was described, by M. Politis, as a "convention which hurt the Greek conscience"—that "the Albanians inhabit a district perfectly well defined, namely, Epirus". Even the majority of the Moslem Tchams of the Tchamouria, who are acknowledged by every impartial authority to be no less certainly of Albanian origin than the Christian Suliots, were included among those Moslems to be exchanged.

"No State", wrote M. Blinishti, "has the right to drive out autochthonous inhabitants from its territory like a herd of cattle." Yet this is precisely what the Greeks attempted to do, and to effect this purpose employed every possible method to coerce the helpless inhabitants to declare themselves in favour of exchange, to sign declarations to that effect, and to send deputations to ask that they should be exchanged (O.J. February, 1925, 237). It is unnecessary to describe these methods, which were much the same as those employed to delude the International Boundary Commission in 1913. Nor need Greek denials, and official orders against the employment of coercion, be taken into account. Any doubt in the matter is easily dispelled by a consideration of motive. The Greeks were in favour of the expulsion of the Moslem Albanian population, and to this end described them a of Turkish origin; the Albanians, on the other hand, wished only to protect their co-nationals, and it was in no way to their advantage to extend their protection to Turkish Moslems or to claim them as Albanians. The only possible means of determining the nationality of these people in the circumstances, and that not a wholly satisfactory means, was by the language spoken in their homes.

The Albanian Government appealed to the League to constitute a special commission to examine the question on this basis, but the League did not see its way clear to do so while the Mixed Commission continued to exist. Eventually the Albanian Government was obliged to inform the League during August, 1924, that in view of the decision of many Moslem Albanians to emigrate to the Albanian frontier districts inhabited by Greek-speaking minorities, and in view of the exasperation of the Albanian public at the conduct of the Greeks, it would accept no responsibility for a situation created by the failure of the Greek authorities to observe an international obligation (O.J. February, 1925, 237), and would be compelled to expel the Greek minorities in southern Albania to make place for the refugees.

In these circumstances the Council of the League decided, on the 30th September, to request the Greek Government to avoid creating any *fait accompli* which might prejudice a final solution of the matter. No further steps were taken until December, when at last the League determined to ask the neutral members of the Mixed Commission to act as its mandatories for the protection of the Albanian minorities. These mandatories, when acting as Presidents of Sub-Committees, were each to have at their disposal a person of Albanian origin, selected by themselves, to assist them in obtaining information.

Throughout the summer of 1923 perfect tranquillity reigned in Albania, and the Government made much progress. Athens and Belgrade continued nevertheless to spread mischievous reports.

"In June and July", wrote Herr Hunger, "various European newspapers published information to the effect that there had been risings and even a revolution in the north of Albania. These reports were all false, there having been no trouble whatsoever. Rumours of this nature do considerable damage to a young country like Albania. Proof of this has already been given by the fact that a commercial company which intended to acquire interests in Albania withdrew as a result of these reports" (O.J. January, 1924, 164).

Towards the end of August there began a series of incidents which profoundly affected south-eastern Europe. While the Inter-Allied Boundary Commission was travelling on the 27th August in two cars, some distance apart, between Janina and the Albanian frontier, General Tellini, the Italian representative and chairman of the Commission, who was travelling in the second car, was attacked by unknown persons, and, with his interpreter and three other Italians, murdered.

That the crime was the outcome of a prearranged plot, with the collusion of the local Greek authorities, there was never any doubt. The occupants of the first car were unmolested, but when the second car did not arrive at the prearranged rendezvous, and they attempted to make inquiries by telephone regarding the whereabouts of their colleagues, they were prevented from doing so. Circumstantial evidence is overwhelmingly against the inference that the Greek higher authorities were implicated, since the consequences of such an act were inevitably disastrous for Greece. On the other hand, the Commission, under Tellini's chairmanship, had confirmed to Albania the remaining fourteen—of the original twenty-six—villages near Korcha, which the Greeks claimed and still occupied, and the Greek Press had conducted a violent campaign against Tellini personally, declaring him prejudiced in favour of Albania. In the circumstances it was maintained in some Albanian circles that the Greeks considered that they themselves could not possibly be held responsible for a crime committed upon the "turbulent Albanian border", but that on the other hand it might lead to a revision of the frontier in their favour and a mandate to "restore order" in southern Albania. Greece certainly did everything possible to saddle the Albanians with responsibility for the murder, and her Press declared that Albanians had committed the crime upon Greek soil with the deliberate intention to inculpate her. There was, however, absolutely no motive for such an act by Albanians, since the Commission had acted throughout in favour of Albania within the limits of its jurisdiction.

Whatever the motive, subsequent investigation by the Commission of Inquiry which was constituted left no doubt that the crime was of a political nature in the interests of Greece. Upon the day on which it was committed the Albanian gendarmerie, hearing rumours, asked the adjoining Greek authorities to supply them with details so that they might take steps to apprehend the assassins should they cross into Albanian territory. The Greeks refused the necessary information. It seems that a band did cross into Albanian territory, where its leader admitted the crime; it was pursued by Albanian gendarmerie, and fled back across the border.

The Italian Government was under no misapprehension as to the responsibility of Greece for the crime, and on the 29th delivered in Athens an ultimatum; but the Greek Government rejected the majority of the Italian demands and repudiated responsibility, whereupon the Italians seized the Island of Corfu.

On the 31st August the Conference of Ambassadors intervened to avert a grave international crisis, expressing the opinion that Greece was both morally and materially responsible for an assassination committed upon her soil, demanded the immediate initiation of an inquiry, reserved the right to consider penalties, and took the view that the crime had been directed against itself, on whose behalf the Boundary Commission had been acting.

In the meantime Greece appealed to the League, but the deliberations of this body degenerated into a dispute between the Greek and Italian representatives as to the competence of the League to interfere in the matter.

On the 13th September the Conference of Ambassadors demanded of Greece an unreserved apology, a memorial service in Athens for the victims, the payment of honours by the Greek fleet to the warships of the three Allied Powers, the payment of honours to the bodies of the victims, and the constitution of a Commission of Inquiry under the control of the representatives of the Powers, to begin work at Janina four days later. The Italians agreed to withdraw from Corfu, but the Powers reserved the right to take, if necessary, other punitive or coercive measures. The Commission found that the Greek authorities had been guilty of culpable negligence, and Greece had no option but to pay the indemnity demanded by Italy. Thus closed an incident of which Italy had availed herself to re-establish her prestige in south-eastern Europe; it is possible that this was salutary—but that depends on whether Italy justly uses or abuses that prestige; and this time alone will show.

The Greeks attempted to establish their own innocence, and the complicity of Albanians, by publishing reports of attempts upon the lives of their own officers and by various other means. Eventually the Albanian Government directed the Press Bureau at Tirana to repudiate certain allegations which the Greek Press had made against Albania in connection with the affair. The Bureau published a pamphlet upon the subject which caused great indignation throughout Greece. It seems that the Director of the Bureau went farther than the Government had intended. In any case the Greek Government charged Albania with "openly insulting the Greek people and army, and holding them responsible for the murders", and demanded that the Albanian Government should publish an official refutation of the offending statements. This the Albanian Government refused to do, although it dissociated itself from the offending passages; thereupon Greece, during December, temporarily withdrew her Minister, M. Panourias, as a "strong protest", leaving her Legation in charge of a secretary. This incident did not improve Greco-Albanian relations, already strained over the Minorities question.

During the autumn session of Parliament, which ended on the 30th September, the protracted nature of the debates, and the insignificant details which were brought up for decision, prevented the discussion of more than a part of the agenda, and many pressing matters remained unsettled. This led to another violent attack, during the last days of the session, by the Opposition upon the Government, which was accused of doing very little during its two years in office. "In view of the large number of Bills which the Government has brought in, this imputation is unfounded. . . . Albania will always owe a debt of gratitude to the present Government for all that it has done," wrote Herr Hunger. The

ALBANIA: THE RISE OF A KINGDOM

Opposition, inexperienced in the art of administration, was unable to appreciate the difficulties with which the Government had to contend—difficulties which it subsequently displayed a conspicuous inability to overcome — and despite its attack, Parliament ultimately passed a vote of confidence.

The elections for the Constituent Assembly, which had been postponed principally in view of the friction with Greece, took place at the beginning of January, and the Assembly, which undertook the functions of an ordinary Parliament in addition to its extraordinary duties, met at Tirana on the 21st of the same month. Of the ninety-five seats therein, thirty-five were held by the Democratic party led by Monsignor Fan Noli and Louis Gurakuchi. Ahmed Zogu found himself supported by twenty-six Conservatives and by fourteen Independents led by Elias Vrioni. The Popular party or Clique, led by Sefi Vlamasi, Minister of the Interior, and by Pandele Evangheli, Minister for Foreign Affairs, held the remaining seats. No party therefore obtained a clear majority, and Zogu's Cabinet remained in office.

In the Assembly, which began its session by discussing, but without arriving at any very definite conclusions, amendments to the Lushnja Constitution, and the question of whether Tirana should or should not remain the capital, Zogu found himself in a hopeless position. The Democrats, frequently supported by the Popular party, which included two of his Cabinet, did nothing but embarrass him, and he soon found resignation inevitable. For more than two years he had served his country with distinction, first as Minister of the Interior and then as Prime Minister. During his tenure of office scarcely a case of vendetta had occurred, and the country had made appreciable progress towards stability. He had proved himself an energetic ruler, possessed of the strong hand requisite for the consolidation of a new State, especially of a "buffer" State so encompassed, as is Albania, with difficulties created by conflicting foreign interests; he had established law and order as it had never been established before, had disarmed large sections of a population bred to the carrying of arms, and had made the possession of arms without a licence illegal. But he had lost the support of both the army and the greater part of the gendarmerie, which were inclined to regard the defeat of the Italians in 1920 as a success for which Albanian prowess alone was responsible, and argued therefore that the rights of the State should be asserted by force of arms. He had, too, failed to do much to improve the administration, to introduce agrarian reforms, or to adjust the finances, and the budget for 1924, despite considerable economies, threatened a deficit of £360,000.

Herr Hunger reported (O.J. January, 1924, 164) that the financial situation was extremely unsatisfactory, and that unless further drastic economies were effected, the complete disorganization of the country's financial system and the serious decline of its credit were inevitable. Among the measures to redeem the situation which he proposed were an increase of the existing graduated income tax, which the richer classes were well able to bear: a very considerable increase in the number of days—six was the original number —upon which those who did not pay income tax were compelled to work for the State without payment, principally upon the roads (also advocated by Professor A. Calmès: A.C.), a reduction in the number of officials and deputies—in the case of the latter the fact that no deputy might be, at the same time, an official, was a further reason for a reduction of numbers, since there was generally a difficulty in filling vacancies created by the election of officials as deputies: and the abolition of the army. The latter, as it existed, was too small and too inefficient to prove effective against foreign invasion; there were no funds available to reorganize, train, and equip it, and its existence for the purpose of preserving order within the country would no longer be necessary once the reorganization, then in progress, of the gendarmerie was completed. On the other hand, he advocated the establishment of an Audit Office, and emphasized the need for a State Bank. With regard to the latter, proposals had been drawn up with the assistance of the League of Nations Financial Committee, but extravagant references in the Press with regard to Albania in connection with the murder of General Tellini had led to an indefinite postponement of this matter.

Among the Democrats feeling against Zogu ran high. On the 23rd February, while entering the Assembly, he was fired at by a young student, Bekir Valter, and slightly wounded in three places. His secretary told the writer that Zogu, quite

unperturbed by the incident, calmly walked about directing
the pursuit of his assailant, who was arrested and sentenced
to three years' penal servitude.

Among the last acts of Zogu's Cabinet was the completion
of a commercial Treaty with Italy, signed at Rome on the 19th
February. Italy obtained most-favoured nation status in
Albania, and it was agreed that neither country should grant
concessions to a third which could operate in any way to
the disadvantage of either. But the Treaty remained unratified until the spring of 1925. It should be noted that at
this time Zogu was thought to be pro-Yugoslav in sympathy
because he believed a policy of friendship, if that was possible,
with Yugoslavia was a wiser course than an indulgence in
irredentist dreams.

At the end of February the Cabinet, recognizing that its
position was untenable, resigned. It had remained in office
for no less than two years and two months. If it had failed
in many respects—largely owing to the financial handicap—
it had at least given the country a respite both from external
and internal strife. Zogu advised the Regency to invite his prospective father-in-law, Shevket Verlazi, the biggest landowner
in the country, to form a Cabinet, and in the meantime the
resigning Cabinet continued to act.

As a result, it seems, of the insistent demands of the
Assembly for economy, Pandele Evangheli wrote, on the
29th February, to Herr Hunger, denouncing his contract. It
seems that Hunger shared with the resigning Cabinet the
displeasure of the Assembly at the failure of both to improve
the financial situation, and that the Cabinet accordingly made
Hunger the scapegoat. In any case the Assembly regarded,
with much reason, the salary of which Hunger was in receipt
as wholly out of proportion with the resources of the country,
and in the circumstances the Government was perfectly
entitled to cancel the contract. Hunger, on the other hand,
maintained that the Albanian Government had failed to give
effect to any of his recommendations, which, if they had been
adopted, would have more than reimbursed the Treasury
for his salary, and that he had not been given the facilities and
support for which his contract had provided.

On the 5th March Shevket Verlazi's Cabinet took office,
and obtained a substantial vote of confidence. It was composed
as follows:

SHEVKET VERLAZI . . .	Prime Minister and Minister of the Interior.
ELIAS VRIONI	Minister for Foreign Affairs.
MUSTAPHA ARANITASSI . .	Minister for War.
MUFID LIBOHOVA . . .	Minister of Finance, and Minister of Justice *ad interim*.
M. FAKHRI	Minister of Education.
KOTCHO KOTTA . . .	Minister of Public Works and Agriculture.

It was anticipated that in Zogu's absence the fresh Cabinet would prove sufficiently acceptable to the country to enable the Assembly to complete its labours. But the Opposition considered it merely as a continuance of the old régime, and the Assembly accomplished little, in addition to further discussion of the future Constitution and capital, beyond the adjustment of the salaries of deputies. Politics became an obsession, and the atmosphere was charged with intrigue. Discontent became rife, both in the south, where agrarian reform was the pressing need, and in the north, where irredentism and the failure of the Government to make more rapid progress towards an improvement of conditions had bred dissatisfaction among a famine-stricken population.

Conditions in the north were indeed extremely serious, and had not been improved by the Yugoslavs, who had closed the frontier to the export of maize—the staple food of the malissori—into Albania, and had erected a prohibitive tariff wall (M.P. 14.4.24), upon the pretext that Albanian bands had made raids across the frontier. That raids took place is probable, since the destitution of many mountaineers was due to previous Yugoslav ravages; a blockade would not, however, prevent, but tend rather to increase, them, by rendering more acute the famine which caused them, and the Albanian Government was obviously powerless to do much to restrain starving people, deprived of their market towns and burnt out of their homes, whom it could not assist. Moreover, it is not surprising that irredentism, and exasperation with a Government which had resolutely turned its back upon aspirations which it was impossible to realize, found support among these elements.

The Albanian Government had endeavoured to provide relief, but that which it had been able to give, together with the amount raised by voluntary subscriptions in Europe and

America, had proved wholly inadequate to improve the fearful conditions brought about by a succession of misfortunes since 1912, the ravages of war, droughts, plagues of locusts, floods, and crop failures, which affected some 200,000 people. On the 13th March M. Blinishti appealed to the League for relief for the luckless malissori, mentioning that while every other Balkan State had enjoyed financial assistance during the initial stages of its development, Albania had received none. Lord Parmoor supported the appeal, proposed that the League should act without delay, and read the following extract from a letter from a correspondent whose competence and impartiality were, he said, beyond question:

> "What has particularly struck me is the dignity, courage and resignation with which these poor mountaineers have met their hard lot. They have died by scores of want, misery, and cold, and have suffered without complaint. They have not raised their voices, neither have they asked for alms. The Government of course was aware of the situation, and did as much as lay in its power to alleviate the distress. It spent 10,000 napoleons last year for this purpose, but the sum has been entirely insufficient even to prevent deaths by starvation"
(O.J. April, 1924, 528).

Lord Parmoor intimated that the British Government was willing to contribute a sum not exceeding £5,000 provided other Powers would do likewise. In the meantime it was agreed that 50,000 Swiss francs should be set aside by the League for immediate relief work, and the voluntary services of Professor Pittard—Professor of Anthropology at Geneva University—were accepted to supervise the purchase and distribution of supplies. Professor Pittard initiated the work, but was unable to complete it, and was succeeded during June by M. H. Cuénod, who arranged with the Yugoslav authorities for the exportation of maize from Yugoslavia (O.J. October, 1924, 1506).

The Greeks still remained in occupation of the fourteen disputed villages in the Korcha neighbourhood. They had appealed against the decision of the Boundary Commission, and the assassination of General Tellini had led to a postponement of a settlement. During April, 1924, however, a fresh Inter-Allied Boundary Commission, under the presidency of

General Gazzerra, including Lieut.-Colonel A. B. Clough (Great Britain) and Colonel J. A. Ordioni (France), was sent to Korcha to confirm the decision of the previous Commission, and to erect boundary marks when the Conference of Ambassadors made a final decision. The Conference finally awarded the villages to Albania, but it was not until October, and after repeated representations, that Greece "bowed to the inevitable", withdrew her troops, and enabled the Boundary Commission to complete its task.

CHAPTER X

THE ALBANIAN REPUBLIC

On the 6th April, 1924, occurred an event which caused consternation throughout Albania. While motoring along the Tirana–Skutari road some twenty-five miles from Tirana, two American tourists, Mr. G. B. de Long and Mr. R. L. Coleman, were ambushed and shot by a band of Albanians. The Government adopted very energetic measures to bring the murderers to justice, and on the 9th two of them were killed and one captured in a skirmish with gendarmerie near Kruja. The United States Government proposed to demand a heavy indemnity, but Mrs. de Long generously protested, asking only that her husband's personal effects should be restored to her. Mr. Coleman's relations were equally generous, and the incident closed internationally.

The main facts of the crime are that the murderers, who lined a ditch by the roadside, signalled to the travellers to stop, but as the latter did not comply they were fired upon. None of the valuables on the persons of the murdered men were removed (that coin appears to have been taken proves nothing, since that might have been done to give to a political crime the appearance of brigandage). The arrested man is alleged to have declared that the victims had been mistaken for certain Albanian officials who had been expected to pass at the time the crime was committed.

Fresh rumours had appeared in the contemporary western press to the effect that the throne of Albania was at the disposal of anyone willing to accept it; and it was at first maintained by the Albanian Government that the murder was a political crime financed by an unfriendly country with the intention to destroy the reputation for law and orderliness—compared by *Le Temps* (18.6.24) to that which existed in Switzerland—which Albania had acquired in informed circles (M.P. 14.4.24), and to prejudice the Conference of Ambassadors in its deliberations regarding those parts of the frontier still in dispute (N.E. 17.4.24). This was a reasonable theory, as the instigators of such deeds well cover their tracks; and many considered it an attempt by Greece to throw doubt upon the justice of her conviction in the Tellini murder case. Moreover, acts of hostility against foreigners in no way connected with political intrigue were unknown in Albania, and regarded as a stain upon national honour and violation of the tradition of hospitality. The foreigner is regarded by the Albanian as a guest, and enjoys the protection of the *besa*.

But the Albanian Government subsequently declared that it was purely an act of brigandage committed by one of those bands of outlaws and criminals who roam the Balkan mountains regardless of frontiers and live precariously by violence; and however excellent may be the state of law and order in any country, such men exist, Albania being no exception. On the other hand, Monsignor Noli's clique declared that Zogu was responsible, and that the assassins had been hired to murder some of his political opponents.

There occurred in Tirana a month later another crime. One day early in May, Avni Rustem was attacked outside the House of Parliament, and mortally wounded. Rustem had become a prominent member of the Democratic party, and had been returned to the Assembly at the previous election; he had organized a "Union of Young Albanians"—inspired with progressive ideas—of which Bekir Valter, Zogu's assailant, was a member, and it is believed that Rustem was assassinated in revenge by some of the ex-Prime Minister's followers, since Mati was, of all the tribes, most prone to blood vengeance.

The Opposition were exasperated. They alleged that the incompetence of the Government was responsible for these murders. Some alleged that the Government, under the influence of Ahmed Zogu, was implicated. To these charges Zogu replied, in a somewhat ill-advised speech, when it would have been wiser policy temporarily to efface himself (*Le Temps*, 18.6.24). This completed the rift. The Democrats, with some of the Popular party, forty-four deputies in all, withdrew from the Assembly, declaring that they would not again meet at Tirana, which was too close to Mati, Zogu's native district. As a result the Assembly was reduced to constitutional impotence, being deprived of the quorum necessary for the purpose of passing legislation. The majority of the Opposition deputies, led by Monsignor Noli and Colonel Kassim Kiafzezi—commander of the troops in southern

Albania—assembled at Valona, where a mass meeting and
demonstration took place, nominally to celebrate the funeral
of Avni Rustem. At the meeting it was declared that the
Government was but the instrument of Ahmed Zogu—which
was to some extent correct—and that no deputy of the
Opposition was safe in Tirana; it was demanded that the
Assembly should meet elsewhere, and that Zogu, with certain
of his supporters, should leave the country.

Although the Government was still supported by a majority
of deputies, and was therefore entitled to remain in office,
it appreciated the seriousness of the situation, and adopted
a conciliatory attitude. There was some indication that the
greater number of those who had so impetuously registered
their protest against the Government regretted their ill-
advised act, which was merely injurious to the reputation of
the country, and were willing to return to Tirana. In these
circumstances, Elias Vrioni was dispatched to Valona to
negotiate.

In the meantime, however, Gurakuchi, in northern Albania,
had drawn up a manifesto which was signed by the northern
deputies of the Opposition and countersigned by Colonel
Redjeb Shala, commander of the troops in northern Albania,
inviting Parliament to meet at Skutari. Shala, a northern
chieftain, was one of those who considered that Skutari
should replace Tirana as the capital, both because of its
importance and for commercial reasons. The Government
at once and very properly dismissed Shala; but he ignored the
Government, and declared martial law throughout his zone,
while Elez Yssuf, Bairam Tsuri—who had been condemned
to death in consequence of his escapade in January, 1923,
and had sought refuge with Albanians across the border—
and others, called their followers to arms, and attacked the
Government troops around Krouma.

These events encouraged the southern section of the
Opposition, who considered that matters had now gone too
far for compromise, and Vrioni's mission proved fruitless.
Colonel Kiafzezi declared martial law throughout his zone,
Shevket Korcha, Commandant of the Gendarmerie, joined
him, and the majority of the troops under their command,
together with irregular supporters, began to concentrate
at Valona and Berat. The Government thereupon proclaimed
general mobilization in central Albania, which remained

loyal. In the meantime the northern insurgent forces drove from Skutari, after some desultory fighting, a handful of gendarmerie which remained loyal to the Government, and advanced upon Tirana.

A certain activity by Greek and Yugoslav bands was reported from the frontier; but Italy intimated to both countries that any interference in Albania would be considered an unfriendly act, and despatched a warship to Durazzo. On the 27th January there had been signed between Italy and Yugoslavia a Pact of Friendship and Cordial Co-operation, and although there was no reference therein to Albania, or even to south-eastern Europe—there was an undertaking only "to communicate to each other, after previous consultation, such agreements as affect their policy in central Europe" (Supplementary Protocol, Art. 1)—there was an obligation to exchange views in the circumstances. At the same time the representatives of Great Britain, France, and the United States, invited the Yugoslav Government to express its opinion with regard to the situation. In reply it expressed the view that the disturbances were purely a domestic matter, and that the Government would be able to restore order without difficulty; moreover, Yugoslavia would not interfere provided no other Power did so. Possibly she considered the existing régime preferable to that of the Democrats and Irredentists. In any case, in view of the attitude of the Powers she could not interfere openly, and on the 7th June both she and Italy declared that neither would do so. Greece, mindful of the Corfu incident, adopted the same attitude. That both Yugoslavia and Greece seem to have restrained their hotheads on this occasion proves that they can be restrained upon other occasions.

In view of the increasing gravity of the situation, Shevket Verlazi resigned on the 1st June, and was appointed to command the Government forces, many of whom were his own tenants, at Elbasan. Elias Vrioni succeeded him as Prime Minister, while remaining Minister for Foreign Affairs, and Abdurrahman Dibra took Verlazi's place as Minister of the Interior. Otherwise the Cabinet remained unchanged. In the meantime the United States Minister, Mr. Grant-Smith, who alone of all the representatives of the Powers had preserved a very reserved attitude towards Zogu, and therefore was in a better position than others to act, proposed that the League of Nations should be asked to arbitrate in the dispute. Here again, however, matters had gone too far, and neither side would accept the proposal without reservations unacceptable to the other.

Some sharp skirmishing took place around Alessio, which fell to Colonel Shala after a temporary success by the Government troops; Kiafzezi issued an ultimatum to the Government demanding unconditional surrender, and in the meantime ordered his troops to advance on Tirana and Elbasan. Vrioni, on the other hand, made one more bid for a compromise. Mufid Libohova was sent to treat with Kiafzezi, M. Fakhri with Shala. Neither of them returned. A Military Directorate was constituted at Valona, and in the meantime the advance continued in a leisurely manner. Some skirmishing took place both before Elbasan and in Bregumatia, but there seems to have been, on both sides, except in isolated cases, a reluctance to shed much blood. Moreover, contemporary reports indicate that, at most, 12,000 Democrats and 4,000 Government supporters took part in the struggle—if, indeed, it may be described as such. There is no doubt that contemporary reports of fighting emanated chiefly from imaginative journalists, and that the vast majority of the population took no part on either side.

"A revolution in Albania affects trade no more seriously than a General Election in England, and, in fact, involves a very much smaller proportion of the population", said M. Konitza. Those who are dissatisfied with the Government hasten to swell the ranks of the insurgent forces; those who have no axe to grind leave it to work out its own salvation. Thus it is that many insurrections in such countries may be termed "National Movements", when actually they are but uprisings of the active and disgruntled minority against a legislation satisfactory to the peaceful and law-abiding majority.

So it is in Albania. In face of foreign aggression there is fervent patriotism, but in its absence there is no inclination for civil strife and blood-letting, unless the dispute be a personal matter or affair of honour. The Albanian has fought, through the ages, for existence; and now, the greatest benefit which a Government of Albania can confer upon the people is peace—with liberty.

The revolt of June, 1924, did, however, enjoy a large

measure of popular support—in any case moral support—both in the south, where the failure of the Government to curtail the power of the Beys and introduce sweeping agrarian reforms, was a cause of discontent, and in the north, where jealousy of Ahmed Zogu, the claim of the Skutarenes that their town should be the capital, the desperate plight of the people, and the irredentist aspirations of the Kossovo Committee, all contributed to stir up hostility towards the Government. The Yugoslav Press misrepresented the Kossovo Committee as a separatist organization, and the revolt as a struggle between Moslems and Christians! The Kossovo Committee existed to achieve unity of the Albanian race—it was the *United* Committee of Kossovo and Tchamouria—and was led principally by Moslems. Nor was the revolt a struggle between Monarchists and Republicans, nor between pro-Yugoslavs and pro-Italians. The Cabinet, with the exception of Zogu, sought refuge in Italy; the Democrats (although enjoying sympathy in some Italian circles) held no particular brief for Italy—indeed, they had led the movement against her in 1920—although a writer in a British Socialist organ discovered a mare's nest in a letter from the Democrats, diplomatically expressing appreciation of the above-mentioned sympathy. The fundamental cause of trouble was an impatience for progress and sweeping reforms, untempered by an appreciation of the difficulties entailed.

On the 9th July the insurgent forces closed in upon Tirana, and Vrioni fled precipitately for the coast with Shevket Verlazi and a number of their colleagues. They sailed for Bari, where they were met by a hostile crowd of Albanians, who held them responsible for the state of their country, and some of the Beys were roughly handled before the police intervened. During the afternoon of the 10th Ahmed Zogu called a public meeting in Tirana and asked the people whether they preferred resistance or surrender; they decided in favour of the latter course, and accordingly white flags were hoisted upon prominent buildings. In the evening Colonel Kiafzezi's troops occupied the capital. Ahmed Zogu retired with some five hundred adherents, and after some further skirmishing with Bairam Tsuri and Elez Yssuf, fled into Yugoslavia.

The country was now in the hands of the Democrats, and the Military Directorate, which had become the Supreme

National Council, temporarily replaced the Government. Monsignor Noli was asked by the Council of Regency to form a Cabinet, which took office on the 17th, composed as follows:

MONSIGNOR FAN S. NOLI	Prime Minister.
COL. REDJEB SHALA	Minister of the Interior.
SULEIMAN DELVINO	Minister for Foreign Affairs.
COL. KASSIM KIAFZEZI	Minister for War.
STAVRO VINYAU	Minister of Justice and Education.
LOUIS GURAKUCHI	Minister of Finance.
KASSIM KOTSULI	Minister of Public Works.

Noli emphasized that the revolt had only an internal significance, and that the attitude of Albania towards her neighbours would remain unchanged. He issued the following manifesto and programme of reform:

"The destructive policy of the last Governments has created such despair in the country that insurrection and fratricide were at last the outcome. The results of the late Ministers' administration are a ruined budget with a large deficit, disorganization of the State in all its departments, insecurity throughout the country, anarchy among the organs of the State, the creation of personal powers outside, and above those of the State, together with assassination and attempted assassination of citizens and foreigners. These uncontested facts had endangered the foundation of the country, discredited us at home and abroad, and cast a doubt in the mind of both Albanians and foreigners as to the capacity of our State to live. In order to crown the salutary work of the insurrection, and relying upon the confidence placed in us by the people, we accepted the heavy burden of directing the affairs of the State, entrusted to us by the High Council of Regency, and hereby do promise to our people by an application of the following programme the gradual recovery from the critical state created by the destructive work of our predecessors:

1. The general disarmament of the population without exception.
2. The establishment of tranquillity, order, and sovereignty of the law.

3. To exalt the authority of the State over any personal and extra-legal power.
4. To uproot feudalism, free the people, and establish democracy definitely in Albania.
5. To introduce radical reforms in all branches of the administration both civil and military.
6. To simplify the organization of the administration, and to retrench and purify it; besides ability and morality, the patriotism of the individual employees shall be taken into account.
7. The security of the rights of the employees, and the determination of their responsibilities shall be established by a special law.
8. To organize the Prefectures, so as to improve the condition of villages and villagers, granting to the latter wide powers in local affairs.
9. To balance the budget by radical economies.
10. To modify the system of collecting taxes in a manner favourable to the public.
11. To ameliorate the condition of the farmers so as to ensure their economic independence.
12. To facilitate the introduction of foreign capital, protect and organize the wealth of the country.
13. To raise the prestige and the credit of the country abroad.
14. To grant full municipal freedom to each town.
15. To introduce judicial reforms.
16. To construct new roads and bridges, and take special care of means of communication throughout the country.
17. To organize the sanitary conditions of the country in order to combat the diseases which ravage the population.
18. To organize the department of education on modern and practical lines so that the schools should produce capable citizens, good patriots, and able workers.
19. To entertain friendly relations with all States, and particularly with neighbouring countries.

"On the return of normal conditions we shall appeal to the country at a General Election; and by secret, and direct, and entirely free, vote, the people shall give their verdict in regard to our action, to which verdict we are prepared to bow.

"We do not deny the difficulties attached to the fulfilment of our promises, nor do we say that this programme could be executed at once in its entirety, but we are convinced that with the help of the Almighty, and the support of the people, we shall be able to carry it through gradually.

"*(Signed)* FAN NOLI."

It was an admirable programme, compiled by men who had every intention to carry it out, and were actuated by the highest motives. Unfortunately it was beyond the power of either party to give effect to these desirable reforms and necessary undertakings with greater rapidity than the other, except perhaps in the matter of agrarian reform, where there had been a natural hesitation among the members of the former Cabinets to deprive, except by gradual reform, either themselves, or their colleagues, of their privileges and property. Moreover, there was little in Noli's programme that had not been included in similar programmes by former Governments, and which had not been already initiated or considered.

The new Government committed an unpardonable blunder by constituting a political court to dispose of political opponents. This court passed sentence of death upon Ahmed Zogu, Shevket Verlazi, Elias Vrioni, and others, should they ever come within the jurisdiction of the Government. Their property was confiscated and nationalized. This unstatesman-like act was merely provocative of further trouble, and an incentive to those thus sentenced and in exile to endeavour to restore the *status quo* (N.E. 29.9.24). A general amnesty and a contrast by better government would have proved the *bona fides* of this "Democratic Government", which actually was much more autocratic and short-sighted than the former Governments of which it was so contemptuous.

Monsignor Noli's Government usurped power in a wholly unconstitutional manner, and took no steps to legalize its position by a general election, which would have been the natural course, had it enjoyed the confidence of the people. Moreover, a rigid censorship was exercised. In the circumstances no western Power could be expected to recognize it, and Great Britain naturally did not do so. Italy followed her example. It is difficult to obtain unprejudiced information of events during Monsignor Noli's régime, but it seems clear that the Prime Minister himself was an idealist who enjoyed the whole-hearted support neither of his Cabinet nor party. He is a cultured man, clever politician, and undoubted patriot, but of these attributes an ability to govern is by no means a necessary complement.

Before the Assembly of the League on the 10th September, Monsignor Noli delivered a speech which was not precisely conducive to the inspiration of confidence among his audience in Albania's democratic Prime Minister. If only, however, on account of its wit, rare in so austere a gathering, it deserves quotation:

> "In reviewing the work which has been accomplished by the League of Nations during its five years of active life," he began, "I am afraid that even the most exalted pacifist will throw up his hands in despair, and exclaim: 'Let us rather have war than such a tedious talk about peace.' . . . What has been done in the past five years lies in peace—in eternal peace—locked tightly in the dead files of the Secretariat. . . ."

Nevertheless, he paid a tribute to the assistance given by the League to Albania, which he described as a "hard nut to crack".

> "But do tell me, Mr. Secretary-General," he continued, "why you refuse to give Albania a loan to enable her to get on her feet."

He thought it might be because his Government was a revolutionary Government without a Parliament.

> "But do you know what a Parliament is?" he asked. "Of course you do. But the matter will be clearer when I tell you what I think of it. A Parliament is a hall where heartless politicians meet to vivisect their own race, a hall full of poison gas, of asphyxiating gas, of tear-producing gas, of laughter-producing gas, and of all the other gases with which the last war was fought to end all wars and establish peace, the peace we are talking

about. But since you insist, we are willing to have new
elections, and to convoke that pest, that calamity, that
abominable superstition, the Parliament, after, say, two,
or rather three, years of paternal government. . . .
What are we doing now in this Assembly? The answer
is very easy to give. You will find it in Shakespeare:
'Words, words, words!' and that is to say, in plain
English, hot air, that's all. Oh! 'It is a tale told by an
idiot, full of sound and fury, signifying nothing.'

"What is the result of all these learned and deep
discussions about disarmament and arbitration Treaties?
The questions have been referred to a Committee, which
will refer them to a Sub-Committee, which will report
back to the Committee, which will submit its conclusions to a Conference to be held some time in the near
future. This Conference will refer these same questions
again to a Committee, which will refer them to a Sub-
Committee, which will report back to the Committee,
which will report in turn to the Conference. The Conference will pass a unanimous resolution, which will be
referred to the Council of the League of Nations. The
Council, in its turn, will refer the resolution to the next
Assembly of the League of Nations, which will express
a unanimous vow to Almighty God in Heaven. After
the questions have gone through this poetic cycle of
references and counter-references, of reports and counter-
reports, and advisory opinions, they will be finally
referred to the Secretary-General of the League, who
will lock them up carefully in the dead files of the
Secretariat, and keep them there for generations to come.
Thus the whole thing will have ended in the same way
as all soap-bubbles do."

There was much justification for this cynical criticism of
the League's Committee methods. Had that organization
acted with less trepidation and caution, and with more practical activity, Albania would have been not a danger point, but
a pillar of security and stability in the Balkan Peninsula.

The two outstanding matters affecting Albania's relations
with her neighbours with which Monsignor Noli's Cabinet
was occupied, were the question of minorities in Greece and
the three disputed points on the frontier. These three points

were: (i) the fourteen villages near Korcha still occupied by Greek troops, and only evacuated in October; (ii) the district of Vermoshi—some thirty miles N.N.W. of Skutari—which had been awarded to Albania by the Conference of Ambassadors, but, owing to Yugoslav protests, the matter had been reopened, and held over for further investigations; and (iii) the Monastery of Sveti Naoum, on the southern shore of Lake Ochrida. The protracted negotiations with regard to these places cost Albania approximately 1,000,000 gold francs, a heavy drain upon the resources of a country so embarrassed financially.

Speaking before the Council of the League on the 25th September, Monsignor Noli gave a graphic description of Albania's struggle to preserve the integrity of her frontiers.

"The question of the frontiers of Albania," he said, "which was already under discussion before the World War, eleven years ago, still awaits a final solution—a solution which has been postponed every winter until the following summer. Must we look forward to a further adjournment this coming winter—with all the conflicts and complications that it will bring in its train? This is the question which the Albanian people ask with an ever-increasing anxiety. This torture has lasted too long; this undesired burden weighs too heavily upon a people which only wishes for peace.

"Allow me to give a short account of this tragedy. Its final act is waiting in vain for a suitable summer.

"In 1913, after the Balkan Wars, the Conference of Ambassadors in London, after long and wearisome negotiations, traced upon the map the frontiers of Albania, leaving more Albanians outside the boundary of Albania than inside it. An International Commission was instructed to trace the frontier on the spot, and this Commission began its work in September, 1913. The first winter brought the first adjournment. In the following summer the World War disturbed the work of the Commission, and from 1914 until 1920 we could not count either the winters or the summers which followed. We were too busy counting the invasions, counter-invasions, and the foreign military occupations which succeeded one another in a country which belonged to no one.

"Moreover, during this unhappy period, there was no question of defining Albania's frontiers, but only of abolishing Albania. The frontier question was taken up again in 1921 after the admission of Albania into the League of Nations—an event the importance of which it is impossible to exaggerate.

"In 1921 the situation was as follows: Almost all the territory assigned to Albania in 1913 was in the hands of the Albanians themselves, except for some twenty villages to the east of Korcha, constituting a neutral zone and occupied by Greeks, as well as a fairly extensive area from Lake Ochrida to Lake Skutari, occupied by the Serbs in accordance with a line of demarcation traced by the Allied troops during the Armistice. This line was a very elastic one. It had a spasmodic tendency to move westwards, and more than once reached the very suburbs of Tirana, the capital of Albania. The Albanians did not appreciate the movements of this vacillating line: hence the periodical frontier fighting and the intervention of the League of Nations" (O.J. October, 1924, 1335).

Having referred to the events of 1921, Monsignor Noli besought the Council and the Conference of Ambassadors to settle before the following winter the question of Albania's frontiers.

Of the three points in dispute between Albania and her neighbours, the Orthodox Monastery of Sveti Naoum was the most fiercely contested. Its importance is evident from the map. It and its immediate surroundings command both the Korcha–Pogradets–Elbasan road, and the head of the Devolli Valley, an important route to the coast. That it was a place of pilgrimage from the surrounding country improved the claims of neither Serbs nor Albanians.

When the frontier was delimited in 1913, the Protocol stated that it should run to and from Sveti (Saint) Naoum, but whether Sveti Naoum was to be inclusive to Albania, or exclusive, was not specified. The frontier was never demarcated by the International Boundary Commission in that neighbourhood, as the Great War began when the demarcation was in progress, and the Serbs had remained in occupation of the Monastery.

The Inter-Allied Boundary Commission in 1922 was unable to reach a decision in the matter; the Yugoslavs brought forward a variety of ingenious but generally worthless pleas for a decision in their favour, which were supported by the French delegate. On the 6th December, however, the Conference of Ambassadors assigned Sveti Naoum to Albania for geographical, strategic, ethnical, and economic reasons; but on the 6th April, 1923, the Serb-Croat-Slovene Government demanded that the decision should be reconsidered, claiming that the discovery of fresh documents proving that the Monastery had been assigned to them in 1913, gave them a vested right to it, which was further substantiated by fresh information which had been obtained. The Albanians, on the other hand, contended that if the 1913 frontier was to be upheld in particular cases, then it should be upheld throughout, whereas Yugoslavia had already obtained considerable rectifications in her favour. After much correspondence the Conference of Ambassadors eventually entrusted the matter to a Committee, which was, however, unable to reach a unanimous conclusion. After further correspondence and procrastination, the British Government proposed that the matter should be laid before either the Council of the League of Nations or the Permanent Court of International Justice at The Hague, and on the 4th June, 1924, the Conference decided upon the former alternative. The Council of the League then considered the matter, and decided to ask the Permanent Court of International Justice to express its opinion on the question whether the Principal Allied Powers, as represented by the Conference of Ambassadors, had, by the decision of the latter in 1922, exhausted, in regard to Sveti Naoum, their mission of delimiting the frontier.

On the 4th September the Court informed the Council that the Conference had "exhausted . . . the mission". It expressed the opinion that the decisions of the Conference of 1921—by which it had confirmed the frontier of 1913 with certain specific modifications which did not affect the Sveti Naoum region—and 1922, were definitive; and further, that since, in its opinion after a careful examination of all relevant documents, the decisions of 1913 and 1921 had left the frontier in the region of Sveti Naoum in doubt, it followed that there could be no vested rights in favour of Yugoslavia under these

decisions, and therefore the Conference was at liberty to
decide the question. As regards the fresh information produced by Yugoslavia, the Court found that it consisted merely
of documents to which members of the Conference had
access, and which, moreover, did not prove that the Monastery
had been originally assigned to Serbia.

On the 3rd October the Council of the League decided
that this reply gave the answer to the inquiry made by the
Conference of Ambassadors, and submitted this decision to
the latter despite the attempts of the Yugoslav delegate to
reopen and contest the question upon equivocal legal grounds.
There, for the time being, the matter rested. In consequence
of this decision it was suggested in some Yugoslav circles
that Yugoslavia should withdraw from the League!

In the same day there came before the League an appeal
from Albania with regard to a frontier incident, which
accentuated the need for an immediate decision with regard
to the disputed points. It seems that an Albanian band led
by Islam Galia raided the Albanian-Montenegrin districts
of Kuchi, Triepshi, and Vasojevich, and carried off two or
three hundred head of cattle. The Yugoslav delegate added
that two girls had also been carried off. The raiders were,
however, attacked before they recrossed the frontier, and
deprived of most of their spoil. The raid was merely an inter-
tribal affair. The tribesmen, bred for centuries to inter-tribal
feuds, failed to appreciate the sanctity of an international
frontier, and this led on occasions to incidents which were
of local, but were frequently misrepresented as of international,
importance.

In this case there was organized a counter-raid, but by
whom remains a matter of conjecture. It seems evident that
the raiders received support from Yugoslav troops and local
authorities. They invaded the districts of Vermoshi, Tamara,
Gryka, Vukli, and Seltze, which they sacked. The Albanian
Government sent reinforcements, and ordered a partial
mobilization, while the people of Skutari swore to protect their
native land. The Albanian Government attempted to persuade
the invaders to retire, but eventually was obliged to employ
force, and some sharp skirmishing occurred before the
frontier was restored.

Before the Council of the League the Yugoslav delegate
minimized the incident, declared that the Albanians were

entirely responsible, and denied the complicity of Yugoslav officials or troops. In reply, Monsignor Noli said (O.J. October, 1924, 1374):

"Listening to the representative of the Serb-Croat-Slovene State makes one feel that this is all a bucolic idyll, in the best taste. Sheep and oxen are grazing before the attentive eyes of two young ladies, when suddenly Albanian gallants arrive and carry them off with their sheep and oxen. The parents of these charming ladies, and the owners of the sheep and oxen, dash off in pursuit, but strangely enough, the parents and proprietors choose as the point of their invasion into Albanian territory, just the mountain of Vermoshi, the controversial point on the frontier. And then comes the sad end of this ridiculous opening scene. The alarm is sounded in Albania. Reinforcements are sent; mobilization is carried out; blood is spilt; the invaders are repulsed."

The Council agreed not to discuss the merits and demerits of the conflicting statements, but concluded its memorandum to the Conference of Ambassadors as follows:

"The Council therefore most earnestly urges the Conference of Ambassadors, and the Powers represented on it, to complete the delimitation of the Albanian frontier at the earliest possible moment, and in any case before the beginning of the forthcoming winter."

In the meantime both sides were urged to refrain from any act which might provoke a conflict.

Monsignor Noli's Government remained sufficiently long in office to prove to both its supporters and its adversaries that it was incapable, at so early a stage in the evolution of Albania, of holding the reins. There was an absence of harmony—later an acute friction—between members of the Cabinet, which was conclusive evidence that one strong hand must grip the Albanian helm. Noli, who possessed little real influence except in the south, and was himself an avowed Republican, found himself at loggerheads with many leading Nationalists, including Elez Yssuf, Akif Elbasani, Bairam Tsuri, Louis Gurakuchi, Ali Klissura, and Sami Vrioni, who favoured a constitutional monarchy, and maintained that their oath of allegiance to the Prince of Wied still bound them. On the other hand, "by insisting on the agrarian reforms", wrote Monsignor Noli (to the author),

"I aroused the wrath of the landed aristocracy; by failing to carry them out I lost the support of the peasant masses. My Government colleagues, and the majority of the army officers, were either hostile, or at best indifferent to these reforms, although they had declared themselves in favour of them previously. Mr. Sotir Petsi, the Regent, opposed them violently and openly. Mr. Eyres succeeded in persuading everybody around me that agrarian reforms were a dangerous Bolshevist innovation."

One achievement Monsignor Noli's Government did, however, accomplish, principally through the ability of M. Louis Gurakuchi, who adopted many of the recommendations made by Herr Hunger—it balanced the budget. That was no inconsiderable achievement, and a tribute to the honesty of a Government which, with considerable justification, accused its political opponents of peculation. But it accomplished little else, and, apparently convinced of its own popularity, even neglected the elementary precaution of reorganizing and strengthening the army. In view of the Prime Minister's scepticism with regard to the competence of the League, this is surprising. Monsignor Noli might have aspired to something more than a mere move in the game of "ins and outs"—no doubt he did—but the theory and practice of Government proved two wholly different matters.

In the meantime Ahmed Zogu and his colleagues did not remain idle. It was no difficult matter for them to spread among their supporters a propaganda against an ineffectual Government, especially when they enjoyed something more than mere moral support in Yugoslavia. The Yugoslavs were determined to acquire Sveti Naoum and Vermoshi, Monsignor Noli equally determined that they should not acquire them; further, an Albanian Government restored to power with their assistance would, they imagined, remain more or less dependent upon them, and accede to their demands. But Ahmed Zogu proved no mere pawn, neither did he prove an Essad Pasha, although he allowed them to imagine that he would, until it suited his purpose to disillusion them. The

Yugoslavs were beaten at their own game, and great was their chagrin.

During the autumn the Yugoslav General Staff, probably working through the White Hand Society, that it might disclaim any responsibility should the need arise, began to concentrate on the frontier the following forces which were to support Zogu directly the right moment arrived (these figures, which are approximate only, and details, were obtained from an unquestionable British source):

> 1,000 volunteers from the Yugoslav regular army, mostly Montenegrin and Albanian conscripts.
> 1,000 reservists from Krouchevo, Tetovo, Gostivar and Dibra.

The above were dressed in their native costumes. The Albanians were led to believe that the success of the movement in which they were about to participate would lead to their reunion with their Motherland, and the Albanian flag was displayed freely.

> 500 malissori of Mati, who had fled with Ahmed Zogu.
> 800 men of General Wrangel's refugee army, which had found asylum in Yugoslavia.
> 40 officers of General Wrangel's refugee army.
> 16 officers (in uniform) of the Yugoslav regular army.

The following units of the Yugoslav regular army were also placed at Zogu's disposal (see photographs in *The Graphic*, 17.1.25):

> 2 Batteries of mountain artillery, Austrian model, range 9,000 metres, with gunners.
> 10 Heavy machine guns with gunners.
> 20 Light machine guns with gunners.

These mercenaries were highly paid. A plentiful supply of ammunition, and Yugoslav military motor transport units to convey supplies to the base, were also placed at Zogu's disposal. The force was no larger than was considered necessary to overcome the opposition anticipated, yet large enough to ensure success before any Power should intervene.

The Yugoslavs were careful to protest their inability to prevent such activities in the remote frontier districts, but quite apart from the fact that international law recognizes no such excuse, they themselves were ever ready to protest loudly against the occurrence of the most insignificant frontier incidents, purely local affairs, generally caused by inter-tribal feuds, or by the activities of outlaws, and to accuse the Albanian Government of complicity.

In this case Yugoslavia prepared the world for forth-coming disturbances by reporting the activity of Soviet agents in Albania, and on the 26th November drew the attention of the Powers to the fact that a Russian representative, M. Krakovietsky, was being sent to Albania. Monsignor Noli, in establishing diplomatic relations with Russia, had merely fol-lowed the example of Great Britain, and the step had been taken while Mr. MacDonald's Government was in power. When it fell, Monsignor Noli endeavoured to postpone the exchange of representatives, but the Albanian Consul in Vienna had already visaed M. Krakovietsky's passport, and he arrived in Albania at the beginning of December. The allegation that Albania was drifting towards Bolshevism because Noli's democratic instincts had led him to recognize the U.S.S.R. was nonsense, although in view of that country's mania for interference in the affairs of other States, it was probably a dangerous act. It was subsequently reported that Noli's Cabinet and likewise the Kossovo Committee had been in receipt of money from Moscow; if this was the case, it was accepted either in ignorance of its origin, or for the furtherance of patriotic intentions, although given for a different purpose.

It seems clear that it was by design that at the beginning of December M. Ninchitch travelled to Rome to see Signor Mussolini, and among other matters discussed—in accor-dance with the Pact of Friendship concluded in the previous spring—and reached an agreement with regard to Albania, by which both countries agreed not to interfere therein.

The Albanian Government had been aware for some months of the formation of bands on the Yugoslav frontier. But personal jealousies, and the indecision of the Government, prevented the appointment to supreme command of the energetic Shevket Korcha, the only man who might have saved the situation (N.E. 22.1.25). With the return to power in Yugoslavia of M. Pasitch, whose object it was to stamp out Albanian nationalism by every possible means, violent measures were anticipated in informed Albanian circles, yet Monsignor Noli's Cabinet seems to have done little or nothing to prepare for them. It made, however, various representations in Belgrade, and received assurances that no organization or activity by bands would be tolerated; but the preparations continued nevertheless. Eventually the attention of Great Britain, France, and Italy was drawn to the continued preparations, but of course the Yugoslavs denied them; and in reply to representations made by the British Minister in Belgrade, who, on the 9th December, called "the attention of the Government of the Serbs, Croats, and Slovenes to the possible dangers of the situation which was then developing", M. Pasitch gave assurances "that orders would be sent to the frontier authorities not to countenance any preparation for invasion" (P.D. 179: 803). There the matter rested.

Early in December the Albanian Minister in Belgrade, General Ali Riza Kolonia, reported that the invasion of Albania by Ahmed Zogu's bands, supported by Yugoslav troops, was due to begin on the 10th, and on that day Belgrade reported the existence of much dissatisfaction in Albania among Zogu's supporters, and the approaching arrival of M. Krakovietsky, the Soviet envoy. The invasion did not, however, begin until the 13th (P.D. 179: 803), when an attack was launched from Prizren against Bairam Tsuri, who was holding the north-eastern sector of the frontier. Simultaneously, in the Dibra region, the main attack was launched against the Pishkopj sector—commanded by Elez Yssuf— by irregulars, but was repulsed by the Albanian frontier troops. Thereupon the Serbian Governor of Dibra, which the Serbs had originally acquired principally upon the pretext that possession of it would facilitate the prevention of raids in and out of Albanian territory (N.E. 22.1.25), ordered the regular troops of the Yugoslav garrison to drive back the Albanian frontier posts, and clear the way for the irregulars, it being Yugoslavia's policy to throw Zogu's army into Albania with the least possible delay, and close the frontier behind it. Accordingly the Yugoslav troops attacked, supported by artillery, while irregular forces under Tsena Kryeziu made their way through the Korab Range towards Pishkopj to turn the position. The Albanian frontier troops, 700 strong in that sector, were reinforced by 200 irregulars under Yssuf Geleli, Elez's nephew, and some sharp fighting took place on the Kenok Ridge. Geleli fell, and eventually, in view of the development of the enemy's turning movement, the Albanians withdrew to their main position round

Pishkopj, which was occupied by 500 irregulars under Elez Yssuf. Further fighting ensued, and Elez Yssuf shared the fate of his nephew. The fall of this gallant old chieftain, whose hospitality the writer had enjoyed only nine months previously, brought to an end all resistance in that sector. Indeed, further resistance was useless, the majority of the irregulars made good their escape, and the regular troops surrendered, some of them joining forces with the invaders. The Albanian battalion at Homesh was surrounded, and surrendered at discretion on the 17th December.

Bairam Tsuri, having beaten off the attack in the Prizren sector, and having counter-attacked successfully in the direction of Kukes, Chafa Bicai, and Kalai Dodes, was hurrying to Yssuf's aid when he heard of his death and the disasters at Pishkopj and Homesh. Deciding that all was lost, he and his men retired to the mountains behind Krouma.

The Yugoslav regular troops, and part of the artillery which had been employed during the initial stages of the invasion, were withdrawn to Dibra in Yugoslav territory, while the main body of the invading force, under Zogu, advanced upon Tirana. The Albanian company stationed at Bulchises fell back on Guri Bardh, where 1,000 Albanian regular troops occupying a strong position were attacked on the 19th by the invaders, strongly reinforced by disaffected tribesmen. The position was held, but was turned by Zogu's malissori, who made their way through the mountains, crossed the Mali Fourcetes, and engaged the company at Chafa Murices. Thereupon Major Shevket (Melchani of) Korcha, who commanded the Albanian troops defending the approaches to Tirana, telegraphed to the troops at Guri Bardh to retire on the Shkala Tunyanit (gorge), which they did, having lost one-third of their number.

The remainder of the troops in central Albania at the disposal of the Government were concentrated at Tirana or Elbasan. At Elbasan there were 1,800 men, but owing to the shortage of ammunition they were powerless; and the Italian Government refused to allow fresh supplies, purchased in Trieste, to be sent to Durazzo.

On the 20th the attack upon the Shkala Tunyanit began, and continued throughout the 21st and the following night. The position proved, however, impregnable; but meantime an enemy column made its way round to Chafa Priskes, held

LEAVING THE SHKALA TUNYANIT, ON THE TRACK FROM TIRANA TO DIBRA, 1924

by a battalion of Government troops. The battalion was out-flanked and compelled to surrender, only 3 officers and 60 men making good their escape. The fate of Tirana was now sealed.

In the meantime Great Britain showed anxiety with regard to the situation, but both Yugoslavia and Italy gave assurances that they had no intention to interfere in Albania; and Yugoslavia, as a further proof of her *bona fides*, closed the frontier after the invaders had crossed it. Italy sent destroyers to Durazzo and San Giovanni di Medua, but an announcement made in startling headlines in the Press that British warships had been sent to Albanian waters was without foundation; General Ali Riza Kolonia presented a Note in Belgrade charging the Yugoslavs with complicity, but the Yugoslav Government refused to accept it.

On the 18th December Monsignor Noli telegraphed (O.J. May, 1925, 640) to the League that during the last ten days bands had attacked the Albanian frontier at several points, supported by artillery, had been repulsed, but had returned with reinforcements, and that Yugoslav officers were directing operations. In the Dibra sector he said that the Yugoslav commander had ordered the Albanian commander to give free passage into Albanian territory to 500 armed men; and that general mobilization, and a state of siege in the threatened prefectures, had been proclaimed. He begged that the League would take immediate steps to preserve Albania from further aggression. The League communicated Monsignor Noli's telegram to the Yugoslav Minister at Berne, who presumably communicated with his Government, and six days later M. Ninchitch telegraphed:

> "The Tirana Government is fully aware that the present troubles in Albania are entirely due to the discontent of the population, and it is with a view to concealing the real and only reason that it has brought these grave and unfounded accusations against a neighbouring State."

How "unfounded" were these charges was subsequently revealed by M. Ninchitch, who acknowledged that Zogu had enjoyed the support of Yugoslavia (*Temps*, 15.4.27).

In the meantime, of course, Monsignor Noli's Government had fallen.

It would be difficult to find a more glaring example of the worthlessness of the League in matters of this nature. Although Zogu's return to power may have been desirable, the means which he employed to reinstate himself were deplorable; and by a tacit condonation of them—by what appears to have been deliberate inaction—the League created a dangerous precedent. Monsignor Noli's appeal was left to follow the slow and tedious, though normal, channels of procedure, examination of it was postponed until the following session, and it had not been dealt with when on the 12th February M. Blinishti withdrew it. Yugoslavia has always placed reliance in the immutability of *le fait accompli*, and it seems, so far as the League is concerned, that her reliance is well justified. If the League is to be of assistance to Albania, it must devise a more expeditious method of dealing with such incidents.

Zogu seems to have encountered very little opposition in the interior—although of course there were the usual lurid accounts in the Press of bloody strife—and his return dislocated the everyday life of the country little more than his eviction in the previous June. The casualties were heavy on neither side. Indeed, it seems that the majority of the people ignored the Government's general mobilization order, and many—in addition to his own tribesmen of Mati—threw in their lot with Zogu. Moreover, the report had been spread, and was undoubtedly correct, that the British Government was in favour of his return, a report which counteracted the indignation aroused by his association with Yugoslavia.

On the 23rd Monsignor Noli and his Cabinet fled to Durazzo, whence they sailed to Valona, declaring their intention there to "continue to fight until the last drop of blood is shed". But when Mufid Libohova, who had crossed the frontier from Greece, gathered around him a number of irregulars, occupied Argyrocastro and Tepeleni, and advanced on Valona, they fled to Italy.

When the Cabinet left Tirana, the Shkala Tunyanit and the capital were evacuated, but only a handful of troops reached Lushnja, where they were disbanded. Some 300 officers, fearing that through having served under Monsignor Noli's Government they would be condemned as rebels, fled to Italy or Greece.

Zogu entered Tirana on Christmas Eve. Colonel Stirling

reported that although he brought with him 9,000 men, the occupation was effected without disturbance, and that no case of looting, theft, drunkenness, or outrage was recorded. This was not, however, the case at Skutari, where some of Zogu's mercenaries behaved very badly before they were disbanded.

Bairam Tsuri, with some 500 men, continued for some weeks to defy Zogu in the Krouma district, and the latter, wishing to avoid further bloodshed, hesitated to take active measures against him. Otherwise, tranquillity was quickly restored.

Immediately he had entered Tirana Zogu sent a cordial message to the Italian Minister in Durazzo, assuring him that in no circumstances would the eviction of Noli affect Albania's attitude towards Italy. It seems incompatible in some respects with Italian policy that Italy did not, in view of the undeniable complicity of the Yugoslavs, intervene on Noli's behalf; and the latter, upon his arrival in Rome on the 30th, expressed "surprise and regret" at the failure of Italy to support him, probably because the commercial Treaty concluded with Italy by Zogu had remained unratified.

Zogu at once assumed supreme power as Dictator and Commander-in-Chief, while the country remained under martial law pending the restoration of a Constitutional Government, which he proceeded to form. The fresh Cabinet took office on the 15th January, and was composed as follows:

AHMED ZOGU	Prime Minister and Commander-in-Chief.
TSENA KRYEZIU . . .	Minister of the Interior.
MUFID LIBOHOVA . . .	Minister of Finance and Minister for Foreign Affairs *ad interim*.
PETER POGA	Minister of Justice.
KOTCHO KOTTA . . .	Minister of Public Works.

The Ministry for War was abolished, being replaced by a General Headquarters. The Ministry of Education was reduced to a department of the Ministry of Public Works.

On the same day the "rump" of the National Assembly reassembled at Tirana, and after deliberating for a week, unanimously voted, on the 22nd January, the proclamation of a Republic. It was agreed that the day should be commemorated as a national festival.

On 31st January Ahmed Zogu was elected first President of the Albanian Republic for a period of seven years, and after some further deliberations a form of Constitution modelled upon that of the United States was adopted. This Constitution provided for a Senate of eighteen members, twelve elected, and the remainder nominated by the President, who was also Prime Minister, and, by virtue of Art. 75, "has the general command of the armed forces". The President of the Senate became, *ipso facto*, Vice-President of the Republic, and this office was filled by M. Eshref Frasheri. There was, in addition, a Chamber of 57 elected deputies. The President's powers were extremely wide, which is, of course, an advantage in a newly constituted State, so long as that office is filled by a man qualified to exercise them, and it seems that on the whole, Zogu was so qualified. They included the right to veto without appeal, the right to decree fresh elections, and the sole right to initiate changes in the Constitution.

The National Assembly also decided that Tirana should be the permanent capital of the country.

There was nothing remarkable in the programme of the new Government. Its specific tasks were to assure the benevolence of neighbouring countries, the security of the new régime, and to restore complete tranquillity in Albania. To this end Zogu, directly he was elected President, telegraphed to Signor Mussolini expressing confidence that the benevolence and moral assistance of Italy would continue to aid him. Signor Mussolini replied that he hoped Albania would continue to merit that assistance. At the same time Mufid Libohova telegraphed to the Secretary-General of the League of Nations as follows:

"Monsignor Fan Noli submitted to your Excellency in December, 1924, a complaint against the Royal Government of the Serbs, Croats, and Slovenes. I have the honour to make the following statement on this matter. Last June two Commanders of Regiments, who were incited to mutiny by the Opposition in the National Assembly, which had met to draw up the Constitutional Charter of Albania, had compelled the Albanian Cabinet, presided over by Elias bey Vrioni, who enjoyed the confidence of this Assembly, to leave office. As a result of this act of violence, the Government of the country passed into the hands of the revolted officers and leaders of the Opposition. To crown these illegal proceedings, the National Assembly was dissolved, and a reign of terror and unrest was established. This state of affairs lasted until Ahmed bey Zogu, ex-Prime Minister and Commander of the National Forces, came to Tirana to restore the legal Government and re-establish national representation. Since then the Assembly, which was invited to meet at Tirana in order to exercise national sovereignty, has voted unanimously for a Republican form of government in Albania, and elected Ahmed bey Zogu as President of the Republic.

"His Excellency the President of the Republic, in accordance with the rights conferred on him by the new Constitutional Charter, has formed a Government which at present holds the legal power in the name of this Government. I have the honour to request you to be so good as to inform the Honourable Members of the League of Nations that the accusations brought by Monsignor Noli against the Government of the Serbs, Croats, and Slovenes are unfounded, and that we do not share them" (O.J. May, 1925, 642)!

Another important step taken during February was the ratification by the Assembly of an Agreement with the Anglo-Persian Oil Company, concluded in 1922. This Agreement had originally given to the Company exclusive rights over Albanian Oilfields, which had aroused much indignation in France, the United States, and especially in Italy. These countries had made official representations in the matter, and although they had failed to reap any benefit thereby, the Anglo-Persian Oil Company had thought it wise to modify the Agreement in favour of the Albanian Government, increasing the royalties and omitting certain areas. In its final form the Agreement gave the Anglo-Persian Oil Company a "restricted prospecting commission" over 80,000 acres, while the Company pledged itself to offer participation to Italian capital. It seems that when the Agreement was eventually ratified in February, 1925, Signor Mussolini, with more haste than grace, protested to Great Britain before he was aware of its terms in final form, and while under the misapprehension that it gave the Anglo-Persian Oil Company a monopoly. His anxiety is quite intelligible, in view of the advantage which Italy would derive from the exploitation of oilfields so close to her shores; and indeed he claimed priority of right, since the Italians had begun prospecting operations during the war, although this proceeding was wholly illegitimate. However, the British Government explained that the concession obtained was by no means a monopoly, and the incident terminated. The granting of this concession to a company so renowned was of great importance to Albania, as it encouraged other financial groups to interest themselves in the country. Moreover, Ahmed Zogu, by granting the concession, had assured himself of British diplomatic support.

In the meantime conditions in the interior were rapidly restored to normal. Monsignor Noli and his most compromised supporters were declared outlaws, and Noli himself convicted of misappropriation of State funds, since his Government had been recognized neither by Parliament nor by foreign countries, had usurped power in an illegitimate manner, and carried off a considerable sum of public money when it fled. Troops which had supported him were disarmed and disbanded. Zogu retained several Russian officers and a well-equipped body of his most loyal supporters under arms, but the remainder were disbanded, and the miscellaneous bands of deserters, criminals, and other broken men which, solicited or unsolicited, had given him their support, were made aware that their presence in the country was no longer desirable, and were expelled to the remote regions whence they came. An irregular force of about 5,000 men, recruited principally from the Dibra and Mati districts, was organized, and the period of compulsory military service throughout the country was reduced from eighteen months to six. The irregular force was subsequently disbanded at the end of October, 1926. Drastic steps were taken to suppress the Kossovo Committee, which, apart from the danger which it constituted to the maintenance of good relations with Yugoslavia, had degenerated into a revolutionary organization in many respects. The gallant but misguided Bairam Tsuri was rounded up and slain; and Zia Dibra was arrested, and "shot while attempting to escape".

An even greater tragedy was the assassination, outside a café in Bari on the 2nd March, of Louis Gurakuchi. He had been the outstanding personality of the Opposition, and head and shoulders above the remainder of the Cabinet in ability. His assassination was therefore thought to have been inspired by Zogu. When the assassin, Ubaldo Stamola, was brought up for trial at the beginning of September, he was acquitted.

"The defence consisted in evidence to the effect that the assassin was a degenerate, though not insane; that the crime was altogether unpremeditated, and that the shots that killed the ex-Minister of Finance were due to uncontrolled spontaneous resentment, when, after obtaining an interview with him with a view to procuring some means of livelihood, Stamola was offered help only on condition of his returning to Albania to act there as a political agent or spy on behalf of the Opposition against the present régime.

"The accused was acquitted by an independent jury in accordance with the usual practice in similar cases—and, it should be added, the Italian judiciary has a very high reputation for independence and incorruptibility. Whether or not it may be true that as a matter of fact the assassination was indeed ordered by superior authority is another matter. Those who know the Balkans are at liberty to draw their own conclusions. It should be noted, however, that not one shred of evidence was forthcoming to this effect" (N.E. 17.9.25).

The means which Zogu had employed to restore himself to power had alienated the sympathies of the majority of the moderates of the Popular and Independent groups. Elias Vrioni in particular had refused to associate with Zogu, or to accept a portfolio in the Cabinet, and had retired to his estates; Mehmed Konitza, Minister in London, a moderate of the Opposition, had resigned. As time went on, however, it became clear to these men, and the factions to which they belonged, that although the means employed by Zogu were undesirable, the end was, on the whole, salutary, and that Zogu was by no means a second Essad Pasha, an instrument of the Yugoslavs, but a patriot whose intention it was, and is, whatever his personal ambitions may be, to govern in the interests of his country. Elias Vrioni agreed, in May, to become Minister in London and Paris, and Mehmed Konitza decided in favour of reconciliation, being convinced that his country needed peace above all things.

In the cause of reconciliation worked, too, M. Eshref Frasheri, who made a determined effort to revive the Popular party (or Clique), which had been split between Zogu and Noli in the spring of the previous year. His idea was that revival of the party would effect a reconciliation between the supporters of Zogu and the moderates of the Opposition. His efforts proved fruitless, and in the early autumn a large group of the latter, led by S. Petsi, A. Suma, Ali Klissura, and K. Bushati, representing the four religious divisions, constituted themselves a "National Union", and issued a violent manifesto denouncing Zogu as a traitor. On the other hand, the programme of the "National Union" was moderate, and it dissociated itself from the extreme Democratic faction led by Monsignor Noli and Mustapha Kruja (N.E. 9.9.26 and 16.12.26).

This uncompromising attitude was the more unfortunate since Zogu did everything possible to conciliate his opponents. During August, Fazli Frasheri was sent to Boston to confer with Faik Konitza, President of the Vatra, and although this move did not produce immediate results, it demonstrated the President's anxiety to acquire for the State the services of all competent Albanians, irrespective of party differences. His good will in the matter was further demonstrated by the proclamation during October of a general and unconditional amnesty of all political refugees, who were invited to return to the country provided they ceased to intrigue against the existing régime. It is unfortunate that the patriotism of many of them was not sufficiently strong to enable them to appreciate that a continuance of intrigues against their country would have none but disastrous consequences for the land they professed to serve. The majority of the refugees, however, gladly availed themselves of the opportunity to return, and in many cases were restored to their former posts.

A further statesmanlike act calculated to check the activities of foreign propagandists was the appointment by the President, shortly after he returned to power, of Colonel Stirling—the Adviser to the Minister of the Interior—as Inspector-General of Albanian gendarmerie. Colonel Stirling was authorized to engage nine British officers to serve under him as sub-inspectors (P.D. 188: 349). Unfortunately, in the very limited time at his disposal, he was unable to make a very careful selection; and shortly after their arrival, several of the officers selected seem to have assumed a very improper attitude towards him, which entailed their dismissal and unfortunate consequences for British prestige in the country.

Another event of importance was the establishment during March of an air service for passengers and mails between Tirana, Skutari, Korcha, and Valona, by the Adria Aero Lloyd, a German company, which obtained a monopoly of air routes in Albania. It proved very successful, and contributed to the improvement of communications.

During April a general election took place with every appearance of tranquillity. The Government was victorious, and thereby legalized its position. This was, however, a foregone conclusion, since in the absence in exile of all the principal leaders of the Opposition, it was not to be expected that any of the lesser fry would venture to contest seats with the Government supporters. In these circumstances the election was contested solely on the question of personalities, and it is not surprising therefore that only a small proportion of the electors troubled to vote. The Senate and Chamber of Deputies assembled on the 1st June with the specific task of studying and ratifying various economic agreements and concessions, and with the specific intention of giving every facility to foreign enterprise in the country.

The President's opening speech contained a bitter reference to the continued occupation by Yugoslav troops of the Sveti Naoum district, which seems to disprove a popular belief that Zogu had agreed to cede Sveti Naoum and Vermoshi to Yugoslavia in return for her assistance in the previous December. There is no doubt that Zogu had allowed the Yugoslavs to believe he would do so, but it does not seem that he had definitely committed himself in the matter.

The Yugoslavs continued to base their claims to the disputed points on the inviolability of the decision of 1913, but persistently refused to acknowledge that their claims on that basis had been invalidated by the rectification in their favour which they had already obtained.

Throughout February and March the Conference of Ambassadors considered the matter, twice postponing a decision, while the Yugoslav Press vituperated, pleaded, and threatened. For example, the newspaper *Vreme* said: "If the Conference of Ambassadors should now allocate Sveti Naoum to Albania, the Belgrade Government could not accept such a decision." During July, however, the two Governments concerned entered into direct negotiations, and the Albanian Government, considering the protracted dispute more detrimental to Albania than a sacrifice, acting upon the advice of the Powers, and yielding to what the Yugoslav Minister in Tirana described as "the grip of the stronger force" at length agreed to cede Mt. Vermoshi and Sveti Naoum in return for the village of Pishkupiye, south of Sveti Naoum, and other small concessions. The completion of this Agreement—which was ratified by the Chamber of Deputies on the 14th October, and the demarcation, were entrusted to the Conference of Ambassadors. The Inter-Allied Boundary Commission under General Gazzerra did not complete its task until the following year. The matter was, however, finally closed on the 30th July, 1926, when in accordance with Art. V of the Protocol of the 9th November, 1921, a further Protocol confirming the frontiers of Albania was signed in Paris by M. Jules Cambon, Lord Crewe, Baron Avezzana, Viscount Ishii, M. Karapanos, M. Spalaikovitch, and M. Elias Vrioni (*Temps*, 2.8.26; T. 3.8.26). Thus at last did Albania cease to be a mere "geographical expression", fourteen years after she became independent!

The most outstanding matter which occupied the attention of Ahmed Zogu's Government during 1925 was the formation of a National Bank, and the raising of a loan for the development of the country. Ever since her independence had been reaffirmed at the end of 1921 by the Conference of Ambassadors, Albania had appealed persistently to the League of Nations and elsewhere, but in vain, for financial and economic assistance. Every other Balkan State had received such assistance during the early stages of its existence, but Albania had received none beyond the loan to Prince William's Government.

Zogu knew well that until a bank was established, and a loan floated, there could be no stability in his country; but he likewise knew that the hostile propaganda of his country's neighbours had so prejudiced the world against her that a loan could be obtained only from one of the countries whose interests in Albania conflicted, namely, Italy or Yugo-slavia, or through the League of Nations, Greece being in no position to give assistance even had she wished to do so. To which of them should he turn? Clearly, to the League, which had espoused the cause of Albania and had been ready enough to make recommendations; it was not, however, so ready to give practical assistance to its protégé, and continued to turn a deaf ear to her entreaties (N.E. 9.6.27).

There remained Yugoslavia and Italy, and to choose between them was not difficult. What had been the policy of Yugoslavia? To prevent the growth of Albania into a strong and wholly independent country, which would bar her way to the shores of the Otranto Straits—to stifle the young State in the "grip of the stronger force"—and eventually to eliminate the Albanian race as a political factor in the Balkans.

Contiguity of territory made it no difficult matter to pursue this policy, and while so doing it would have been incompatible with that policy to grant a loan to Albania. Yugoslavia had every opportunity (N.E. 6.10.27; 10.11.27; 17.11.27; 1.12.27; and M.G. 27.4.27) to establish her prestige in Albania and a permanent understanding between the two countries; but that would have entailed an amelioration of the lot of the Albanians of South Serbia, a relaxation of that unrelenting pressure against the Albanian frontiers which she had maintained, and an end of all political interference in Albania. This was too great a price to pay for Albanian friendship.

Ahmed Zogu had been returned to power through the agency of Yugoslavia, principally in anticipation of the satisfaction of her claims to Sveti Naoum and Vermoshi. Whether or not these claims were satisfied, he knew that sooner or later he would incur her displeasure unless he remained her puppet—which he was not prepared to do—and would be ousted by another through her agency, in pursuit of some further advantage—and so on *ad infinitum* (T. 19.3.27). The League of Nations had proved its inability to prevent this eternal cycle, but Ahmed Zogu was determined that it should be prevented. His only course in the circumstances was to turn to Italy (who, apart from political considerations, was better able to grant financial assistance than Yugoslavia, who required all her resources for her own development), and at the same time conciliate Yugoslavia by acknowledging her claims to Sveti Naoum and Vermoshi, and by other means.

Italy had repudiated territorial aspirations in Albania and, divided by sea from her, was unable to interfere in her affairs by the organization of comitadji bands and by Balkan methods in general. Any such attempt would become at once public knowledge; and while the independence and integrity of Albania remain guaranteed by the League of Nations and by the Powers, they are in those circumstances assured. The Powers had acknowledged that "the violation of these [the Albanian] frontiers or of the independence of Albania, might constitute a danger for the strategic safety of Italy", and in accordance with that acknowledgment it is to the advantage of Italy, bound by the Agreement which embodies that acknowledgment, to respect the independence and integrity of Albania, and to consolidate Albania by every possible means. Yugoslavia, on the other hand, to whose advantage it would be to do likewise, has done everything to impede that consolidation. Further, the greater part of Albania's trade (approximately two-thirds) is with Italy; while until the summer of 1926 Yugoslavia had done everything to prevent commercial intercourse across her frontiers. Again, the existence of large Albanian colonies in Italy, which, unlike the Albanians in Yugoslavia, enjoy equal rights with the natives, constitutes a bond of friendship between the two races.

It was through no intention to sell his country to Italy —as his enemies declare—that Ahmed Zogu turned to her. "Believe me," he said to Sir Harry Eyres, "never will I fall into the arms of Italy." That he sought Italian assistance was merely the natural outcome of circumstances—he sought from Italy that assistance which every other Balkan State had enjoyed from a protagonist. If Yugoslavia has misgivings regarding the intentions of Italy in Albania, let her pursue a policy of friendship with Albania (N.E. 19.5.27)—who is herself ready enough to pursue such a policy if only to counterbalance the advantages within her boundaries which Italy enjoys—and as surely as the sun rises will Albania turn to Yugoslavia should Italy threaten at any time her integrity or independence. But if Yugoslavia continues to remain hostile towards Albania and persists in her "aggressive folly" (T. 19.3.27), the latter will be the more easily brought permanently to the Italian heel, which is preferable to the Yugoslav bayonet.

Negotiations for the establishment of a bank and the

raising of a loan were initiated during the spring of 1925, and were brought to a successful issue chiefly through the efforts of Mufid Libohova and his brother, who had succeeded Tewfik Mboria as Minister in Rome. It seems, however, that their efforts were stimulated by anticipation of personal profit, which detracted from the credit they would otherwise deserve.

At the end of June a Bill was passed granting a concession to *Il Credito Italiano* to form a National Bank of Issue and Credit, which should act as the Albanian Government's Treasury. The National Bank, with a capital of 12,500,000 gold francs, was formally constituted in Rome on the 2nd September in the presence of Signor Volpi and M. Libohova —the Italian and Albanian Ministers of Finance—M. Antonevitch—the Yugoslav Minister in Rome, and Signor Alberti, of the *Credito Italiano*, the principal foreign shareholder. The *Credito Italiano*, the *Banca Commerciale Italiano*, the *Banca Nazionale di Credito*, the *Banca di Roma*, the *Banque Commerciale* of Basle, the *Banque Belge pour l'Etranger*, the *Zadruga Banque* of Belgrade, the *Banque Serbe* of Zagreb, the *Banque Adriatique Danubienne*, and the *Banque Serbo-Albanaise*, participated to the extent of 51 per cent., the remainder of the shares being allotted to Albania. Signor Raimondo di Liguoro, of the *Banca d'Italia*, was appointed first managing director. The head office of this Bank is in Rome, the chief office in Albania at Durazzo, and branches at Tirana, Valona, Skutari, and Korcha. The credit of first operating in Albania went, however, to the Bank of Athens, which opened a branch at Durazzo at the end of August.

The Bank remains, however, an essentially Italian concern, with its headquarters in Rome, and with the exception of an Albanian representative, M. Tef Tsurani, the board of directors is composed entirely of Italians. Even the currency notes, placed in circulation by the Bank to the value of (on 1.3.27) 2,657,000 gold francs, did not bear the signature of an Albanian official. Nevertheless, it proved even more successful than had been anticipated. Albania was given a national currency—in place of the dozen different currencies which previously circulated in the country—and for this purpose notes of value 100, 20, 5, and 1 gold francs (the last were subsequently withdrawn) were issued, kept their value as against gold, and circulated in the country, thanks to the confidence placed in them by all Albanians. Despite the stability of the exchange, however, the peasants at first avoided retaining paper money—partly because it is inconvenient in wet weather—and exchanged it against gold at the first opportunity. (Note: The exportation of gold from Albania —in any form—is prohibited.) Coins were also circulated to the value of (on 31.3.27) 455,000 gold francs. During the first eighteen months the business of the Bank enabled the distribution of a dividend of 5 per cent. on the ordinary shares, 5 per cent. to the board of directors, and a bonus of 10 per cent. to the personnel, 24,259 francs being carried forward (N.E. 9.6.27).

The loan amounted to £1,500,000 in cash, issued in the form of a £2,000,000 loan at 7.5 per cent. It was advanced to Albania through an Italian commercial group, constituted to develop commercial relations between the two countries, the S.V.E.A. (*Società per lo Sviluppo Economico Albania*), by a group of Italian banks and the Institute of Exchanges. The annual charge for interest and amortization which began to run in November, 1925, was £224,000, "which, though high, is not extravagant, considering the extreme dearness of money in many countries, such as Italy herself, where it is easy to obtain perfectly safe investments yielding 8 per cent." (N.E. 10.12.25). It might seem that it was beyond the resources of Albania to pay so large a sum in interest, as her annual budget does not exceed £900,000. Actually, however, it was specifically provided that the expenditure of the loan should be spread over a number of years, and in the meantime it was deposited in the Albanian National Bank in Italy—less the amount set aside for current expenditure—bringing in an annual interest of 6⅞ per cent., which reduced the amount of interest payable by Albania to £86,500—increasing as the loan was expended. Moreover, the Albanian Government, acting on the advice of the Italian Government, converted the loan, advanced in gold francs, into lire at a moment when the lira was worth 140 to the £, thereby increasing the amount to its credit to about £2,800,000, which increased the interest brought in by the loan to £192,000, and reduced the balance of interest payable by Albania to £32,000—increasing as the loan was expended.

In November, 1927, the amount of the loan expended did not exceed £400,000. The amount of interest payable by

Albania was not therefore beyond her resources. Moreover, on the 1st March, 1927, by "Decree-Law No. 521" the Italian Government authorized the Italian Minister of Finance to advance to the S.V.E.A. the amount of interest then due on the loan. This procedure enabled Albania to reap the benefits of the loan, and thereby, provided its expenditure was wise, to pay the interest from its productivity. The interest was guaranteed by the Albanian customs dues.

It was provided that the loan should be spent on public works calculated to increase the general wealth of the country, and in many cases to produce immediate income for the State. The objects on which the loan was to be expended, as specified in the Albanian *Official Gazette* of the 2nd April, 1926, and the 27th June, 1927, were as follows:

	£
Railways	92,000
Roads	560,000
Bridges	264,000
Ports (jetties, etc.)	284,000
Buildings	200,000
Drainage and canalization	320,000
Agriculture	200,000
Sundries	80,000
Total	£2,000,000

In view of various allegations which have been made, it should be noted that no provision was made for military expenditure. The sum set aside for railways was a contribution towards the cost of the Durazzo–Tirana line, which the Albanian Government had begun to build with its own resources, and against the advice of the Italians, who attempted at first to prevent any part of the loan from being thus expended (N.E. 24.6.26). But as the line was already begun a part of the loan was eventually assigned to the completion of it.

The sum allotted to road construction was the largest item, since Albania's greatest need was roads—of which in 1921 there were only 695 km.—not only for commercial purposes, but also to knit the country together as a political and cultural unit. For example, a road from the coast to the Dibra region was a most pressing need of the destitute inhabitants of eastern Albania.

General Maglietta, Director-General of the Italian Military Engineers, was commissioned to lay down a scheme of road construction, and the supervision of its execution was entrusted to Captain Gorbino. As might have been anticipated, the scheme, especially when the drawing up and execution of it had been placed in the hands of Italians, was misrepresented by Yugoslavia as being of an essentially military character, and primarily intended to provide communications for an Italian army advancing through Albania. This theory was even seriously believed to be correct by a certain American writer, who might have been expected to be less easily misled. There was nothing whatever in the scheme to which Yugoslavia was justified in taking exception. The projected system of roads was governed solely by geographical features, and commercial needs—existing or anticipated. Under Turkish suzerainty the Albanian leaders had persistently demanded of the Turks roads in the mountains—although some of the tribesmen were opposed to their construction because they would admit artillery to the mountains—and it was but natural that the Albanians took the first opportunity to provide themselves with those roads which the Turks had never given them. Likewise it was natural that small ports lying close to the main coastal trunk road should be connected with it, in anticipation of a development of commerce and fisheries. Lastly, the eastern portion of any road to the Yugoslav frontier might be employed, in the event of war, by Yugoslav troops long before the Italians were able to take advantage of it, and would facilitate a Yugoslav invasion of Albania rather than an Italo-Albanian invasion of Yugoslavia.

Second in importance only to roads was drainage of the marshes, 1,722 square miles in extent (A.C.), which infected the inhabitants of the lowlands with malaria, and in consequence were responsible for the inertia which prevailed in these districts. Moreover, much of the land to be drained is of great value agriculturally—and the development of agriculture, as Professors Sederholm and Calmès and Herr Hunger pointed out, is of the utmost importance to Albania. Almost all Albania's exports (which include maize, beans, linseed, oats, barley, olives, lemons, oranges, milk, cheese, butter, eggs, hay, leaf tobacco, wool, hides, furs, poultry, fish, sheep, pigs, cattle, mules, asses, horses, firewood, charcoal, bitumen, canes, and rice) are agricultural products; and with the adop-

tion of proper methods of cultivation, drainage, and irriga-
tion of the very fertile lowlands, agriculture will become a
source of great wealth to the country.

In connection with these public works, the Albanian
Government made a contract with an Italian Geodetic Mission
for a survey of the country, to be completed within ten
years (N.E. 25.8.27). The Yugoslavs declared that this was
yet another step preparatory to an Italian invasion of Yugoslavia through Albania! Actually, in view of the absence of
any accurate map of Albania, it was a natural and necessary
measure; and if there was any ulterior motive, it was to
facilitate and encourage the development of Albania's (alleged
considerable) mineral resources, a step which Professor
Calmès had advocated very strongly (A.C.) five years
previously.

For some years Albania may experience difficulty in paying
the interest upon this loan, but eventually the economic
development of the country, facilitated by it, should so increase her revenue that she will have no difficulty in doing so.
In the meantime, of course, if the interest is allowed to
accumulate, it will constitute a "powerful instrument for
pressure in the hands of the Italian Government, a point that
is probably not lost sight of by the Consulta" (N.E. 24.6.26).
The Albanians, however, could not (A.C.), and, including
Ahmed Zogu, did not (*Temps*, 13.10.28) expect financial
assistance unless accompanied by some measure of economic
control, and provided that control is exercised to a point
only, it will doubtless prove salutary. *If exercised beyond that
point, Albania may turn to the League, or to Yugoslavia, and of
this Italy is aware; she is not therefore likely to exercise that control
to an extent which would produce inevitably disastrous consequences.*

Although the concessions to Italy were opposed in some
Albanian circles as placing too much power in her hands,
foreign capital was essential to the development of the country;
and Italy, whose strategic interests in Albania the Albanians
themselves admit, undoubtedly had a priority of right to the
principal voice in any national undertaking with foreign
capital as its basis, unless that capital was obtained from a
wholly disinterested Power; and no wholly disinterested Power
was sufficiently interested to supply the requisite capital.

The S.V.E.A., which was formed simultaneously with the
Bank, was given the option of undertaking, at competitive

HH

prices, various public works, such as roads and bridges, for which the expenditure of the loan was earmarked.

In the middle of September the approaching ratification of the frontier agreement with Yugoslavia—which was regarded by many as an unjustifiable surrender of Albania's rights and interests—also some dissatisfaction with the Government with regard to the concessions to Italy (especially with M. Libohova, who, it was alleged, had accepted a commission for the part which he had played), brought about the resignation of the Cabinet and of several senators, including Eshref Frasheri, President of the Senate, and *ex-officio* Vice-President of the Republic. He was succeeded by Pandele Evangheli.

A Parliamentary Commission was subsequently constituted to inquire into Libohova's alleged malpractices, which, however, had in no way detracted from the soundness of the statutes of the Bank, or the provisions governing the concession granted to the S.V.E.A. "In virtue of Article 83 of the Constitution, the President of the Republic presides over the Council of Ministers, while Article 74 stipulates that the President of the Republic is irresponsible [except for high treason or for acts not countersigned by the competent Minister or Ministers]. That means, in practice, that all Ministers, however contrary to the interests of the country their actions might be, are also above responsibility" (N.E. 23.9.26). Thus it came about that Mufid Libohova eventually escaped trial.

Ahmed Zogu formed a fresh Cabinet, which took office on the 28th September, and was composed as follows:

MUSA YUKA	.	.	.	.	Minister of the Interior and Minister of Public Works.
HUSSEIN VRIONI	.	.	.		Minister for Foreign Affairs.
MILTO TUTULANI	.	.	.		Minister of Justice.
SULEIMAN STAROVA		.	.	.	Minister of Finance.

Early in November M. Tutulani was obliged to resign through ill health. The portfolio of Justice thereafter remained vacant until the following August, when it was accepted by Sif Kedhi.

The new Cabinet was able to obtain the ratification of the Agreement with Yugoslavia after an acrimonious debate and in the absence of many deputies, including those whose constituencies were adjacent to the ceded districts, in which there was much indignation.

Another step taken towards an improvement of relations with Yugoslavia—upon the initiative of Albania—was the conclusion of a convention providing for collaboration between the Albanian and Yugoslav authorities for the suppression of comitadjis on their common frontier. This convention proved its value at the beginning of November, when a Yugoslav prefect and priest were captured by an Albanian band. The Albanian Government, acting in co-operation with the Yugoslav authorities, was able to obtain their release and settle the matter satisfactorily, whereas before the incident might have given rise to international complications.

During November and December the vexed question of her minorities in Greece again occupied the attention of Albania.

The appointment by the League of the neutral members of the Mixed Commission as its mandatories did not improve matters very much, since the Greeks adhered to their former policy, and in many cases prevented Albanians from appealing to the mandatories. Nevertheless, in their fifth report to the Council of the League of Nations dated 3.8.25 (O.J. September, 1925, 1218), the latter made some interesting statements. They wrote:

"According to the statistics furnished by our Epirus agent, the Moslem population of this province [Epirus] amounted on the 11th July, 1925, to 20,160 inhabitants, occupying 2,511 houses, and distributed throughout 63 towns and villages, while on the same date 2,993 persons had been declared exchangeable and had left the territory (850 from Prevesa and 1,182 from Janina in June and July, 1924; 561 from Parga and 400 from Konitza in April, 1925). . . .

"The general result of the evidence and information thus obtained confirms previous impressions as to the complexity of the problem of the protection of the Moslem minority of Albanian origin in Greece. In addition to the difficulties which arise from the conflict of interests—resulting from the fact that the Greek Government is counting upon the departure of as many Moslems as possible under the system of exchange, and that the population of Albanian origin is entitled to remain in their homes in full enjoyment of their property —there are several obstacles of a technical character which serve to complicate the work of the Mixed Commission's organization, and, *a fortiori*, that of our agent.

"In spite of the desire expressed *by a large part of the population to remain in the country*, it soon became overwhelmingly evident to us that, contrary to theoretical presumptions, the persons concerned have no idea of their origin" (which was very natural since they were autochthonous, illiterate peasantry who had never been called upon to consider the matter), "and, if questioned on this point, frequently confine themselves to proclaiming their Moslem faith. Furthermore, the measures to which their property—and more particularly their immovable property—is still subject, appear, in a relatively high proportion of cases, to influence the declarations of the persons in question, many of whom regard emigration to Turkey under the system of exchanges as a means of obtaining land; in such cases they make no mention of their Albanian origin, or even go so far as to claim some other origin."

To this Mehdi Frasheri, who had replaced M. Blinishti at Geneva, added: "It is not to be forgotten that, when an individual was asked his nationality, and found an armed gendarme beside him, his reply would be influenced by that gendarme. He would in those conditions be ready to declare himself a Hottentot if called upon to do so."

In their supplementary instructions to the Epirus Sub-Commission, dated 3.8.25, the Mixed Commission wrote:

"1. The fact that a person had been born, or that his paternal ascendants had been born, in a place included in any of the regions specified below, *while it should be regarded as a presumption in favour of the Albanian origin of such a person*, does not constitute proof unless corroborated by the other factors enumerated in the instructions already issued. Absence of any or all of such factors constitutes presumption to the contrary, the weight of which must be judged by the Sub-Commission.

"2. The following are the regions referred to in 1:—

(a) The territory included in the political frontiers of
Albania as now defined.
(b) The province of Epirus, exclusive of the towns of
Janina and Prevesa and of any other district in
which populations of non-Albanian origin are
generally known to have settled as the result of
immigration."

The question of the Albanian Moslem minorities in Greece
was reopened at Geneva by an intimation from the Albanian
Government that it had received information that the Greek
and Turkish delegates of the Sub-Commission in Epirus had
decided, acting in collaboration with the Greek authorities,
to exchange 5,000 Moslem Albanians of Tchamouria for
5,000 Greeks from Constantinople, and had asked for ships
to carry the first batch of 800 persons to their destination.
The Albanian public, the Secretary-General of the League
was informed, was extremely indignant, and threatened
reprisals against the Greek minority in Albania.

On the 7th December Mehdi Frasheri wrote (O. J. February,
1926, 309) to the Secretary-General to the effect that the
Albanian Government had been obliged to inform the Greek
representative at Tirana that if Greece persisted in her intention to drive out the Moslem Albanians of Tchamouria, it
would expel the Greek minority in Albania in retaliation; the
Greek Government had replied that should this happen,
Greece would take suitable measures. Frasheri appealed to
the League to intervene without delay, aptly remarking:
"We are now living in the twentieth century, and religion
should not be confused with race, as was the case in the
Middle Ages."

Fortunately a change of policy in Greece towards Albania
had been initiated. Greece, it seems, has begun to realize that
the Slav menace is no less dangerous to herself than to
Albania, and that it is to her advantage to establish cordial
relations with her small neighbour, especially as there are in
Greece so many of Albanian race, origin, language, and
sentiment. This change of attitude was reflected not only at
Geneva, but in the Greek Press, and at the end of 1925 the
Eleftheron Vima drew attention in a special article to the

good treatment of the Christian element in Albania by Ahmed Zogu's Government (T. 9.3.26). Moreover, during the spring of 1926, General Pangalos made a statement in which he referred to the once current belief that all Orthodox Albanians were Greeks as "an erroneous and exploded idea", and added: "Since this theory has gathered speed downhill, and has reached the depths of tiresomeness, I have proceeded to dissolve the north Epirot societies, which have, so to speak, touched bottom in this sort of mental aberration." He continued, with a humorous cynicism: "Everyone recognizes the services which the north Epirotes have rendered to the Greek hypothesis, but super-patriotism is as dangerous as patriotism is beneficial" (T. 9.3.26).

Thus Greece adopted a conciliatory attitude with regard to the Moslem Albanians whom she had proposed to deport, and agreed not to demand their departure, while the Mixed Commission reported on the 9th March, 1926, that Moslems in Epirus would not be liable to exchange except in isolated cases. This understanding was followed by the conclusion during the summer, at Tirana, of a Treaty of Extradition, and between the Greek Government and an Albanian delegation sent to Athens for the purpose, of a convention concerning the nationality of the inhabitants of the two countries. Negotiations were also begun with regard to the conclusion of conventions relating to Commerce and Navigation, Consular affairs, Transit, Telegraphic and Postal Communications, and other matters, but the overthrow of General Pangalos interrupted them, and they were not finally and satisfactorily concluded until October.

During the early summer of 1926 the Patriarchate at Constantinople sent, at the instance of Greece, the Metropolitan of Trebizond, Monsignor Chrysanthemos, to Tirana, to adjust with the Albanian Government certain matters which had remained outstanding in connection with the recognition of the autocephalous Albanian Orthodox Church. His mission proved entirely successful, and the outstanding points were settled to the satisfaction of all parties.

The Albanian Government was much embarrassed by the influx of refugees, both direct from South Serbia and from Asia Minor. The latter had been either driven out by Yugoslav oppression, while prevented from emigrating direct to Albania, or had been included in the Greco-Turkish exchange of populations, and, destitute and broken, were gradually making their way back to their native land.

During 1925 Colonel Stirling drew up a carefully considered scheme providing for their settlement upon the land, and on the 14th December Mehdi Frasheri formally asked the League of Nations to grant a loan of £120,000 to enable the scheme to be carried into effect. Since a much larger loan for a similar purpose had been granted to Greece, Albania had every reason to anticipate that her request would be granted (N.E. 14.1.26; 11.2.26; 2.9.26). The Albanian Government proposed to provide the land; the loan was to be expended under the direction of the League in providing houses, stock, seed, and so on, until the first harvest. The Government offered the land itself as a security; it was considered that after three years the proceeds of taxation and rent would provide an adequate interest on the amount advanced, together with a percentage for a sinking fund. The League referred the request to its financial experts, and with them, it seems, the matter rested. An explanation of the League's reluctance to give financial assistance to Albania would be interesting.

In the meantime, however, the Albanian Government took the problem in hand, and in January, 1926, a Central Commission was constituted at Tirana to control funds—provided by voluntary subscription, by philanthropic societies and from other sources—and the local committees, which had hitherto operated independently and without much success. Provision was also made for the granting of five acres of land to each family, a sum of money for the purchase of agricultural implements, and material for the construction of houses.

In connection with this work the assistance rendered by Lady Carnarvon—mother of the late Colonel Hon. Aubrey Herbert—and by Mrs. R. V. Pennington, should be mentioned. Lady Carnarvon had interested herself in the welfare of the refugees since 1924, and in addition had organized a medical mission with headquarters at Valona for the purpose of fighting the malaria scourge. She built for the refugees a village—named Herbert—which is almost self-supporting, and equipped a hospital at Valona, providing an English matron and nurse. Mrs. Pennington worked as an honorary member upon the Central Commission for the settlement of the refugees.

Early in 1926 Sir Harry Eyres was succeeded by Mr.
O'Reilly, who, however, did not remain long in Albania, and
was succeeded at the end of the year by Mr. William Seeds.
Among other diplomatic changes which took place during
the course of the year were the resignation of Midhat Frasheri,
Minister in Athens, who was succeeded by M. Stavri. The
latter had succeeded General Ali Riza Kolonia at Belgrade
when Ahmed Zogu returned to power; his successor at
Belgrade was Tsena Kryeziu. Ekrem Libohova was withdrawn from Rome, and was succeeded by Djemal Dino.

The intransigence of Monsignor Noli and his small following of extreme Democrats, and their refusal to reconcile
themselves with Ahmed Zogu's régime, had their sequel
during the summer. A special tribunal was established at
Tirana to deal with all cases of treason against the State, and
person of the President, and Monsignor Noli, Sotir Petsi,
Ali Klissura, Kemal Bushati, Angjelin Suma—a junior ex-
official of the Ministry of Finance—were condemned to death
in contumaciam; Dr. Michael Tourtoulis was sentenced to
ten years' hard labour, and others to similar sentences, also
in contumaciam.

Zogu made every effort to regularize Albania's relations
with Yugoslavia, and to place them upon a cordial basis. To
this end an Albanian delegation led by M. Tutulani was sent
to Belgrade at the beginning of April; and during May a
Treaty relating to Commerce, Consular matters, Navigation,
and Extradition, was signed by Tutulani and M. Ninchitch.
An attempt, however, to conclude a Pact of Friendship and
Security (N.E. 30.12.26) does not seem to have been appreciated in Belgrade, where it was protested that such was
unnecessary while Albanian independence was guaranteed by
the League of Nations (D.M. 2.5.27). But an agreement was
reached with regard to the deepening of the Bojana and
reclamation of land; and the Albanian tribesmen of the
frontier regions were accorded access to their natural market
towns from which the frontier had separated them (N.E.
15.7.26), a concession which Yugoslavia described as a
"great financial sacrifice" (N.E. 30.9.26).

Commercial conventions were also concluded with Germany
and Czechoslovakia on the most-favoured nation basis; and a
Treaty of Extradition with Great Britain was signed at
Tirana on the 22nd July.

The assassination on the 8th September at the door of his house in Tirana of Osman Bali (see above), Major commanding Ahmed Zogu's bodyguard, caused a sensation in the capital. It was, however, an event of no political significance, and was undoubtedly merely the outcome of a feud.

It was reported in September that much consternation had been caused in Albania and elsewhere by the action at the end of June of the Italian Minister, Baron Aloisi. It was alleged that he had presented to the Albanian Government, in a manner which was interpreted as a virtual ultimatum, proposals which were briefly as follows:

(1) To place the Albanian army and gendarmerie under Italian instructors.
(2) To accept the control of Italy in matters of finance and national economy.
(3) To place the whole of Albania under the protection of Italy.

It was further reported that the Albanian Government had categorically rejected these proposals. It was also alleged that Zogu had communicated them to Mr. O'Reilly, who had reported the matter to the British Government; and that to an inquiry by the British Foreign Office the Italian Government had replied that "its Representative in Tirana had misunderstood, and, consequently, exceeded his instructions, and that there had been in addition a misconception of the purport of Baron Aloisi's communication on the Albanian side" (T. 4.9.26; M.G. 19.10.26; N.E. 9.9.26). The withdrawal of Mr. O'Reilly from Albania was alleged to have been brought about through Italian representations to the British Government in consequence of his attitude during the above incident. This allegation seems to have been unfounded. It appears that Mr. O'Reilly had exceeded his duty in connection with the dismissal of certain British gendarmerie officers.

It is denied in Italian official circles that any definite proposals were made at this period, although negotiations were in progress in connection with the Treaty subsequently concluded. While, therefore, it is notorious that "an official denial may frequently be considered as confirmation of the facts denied", the Italian explanation is a very plausible one. Moreover, the whole circumstances may have been exaggerated by those who reported them. On the other hand, the possibility that Italy may have sought to stampede Albania into an Agreement (which she subsequently accepted in consequence of a revolt fomented in Yugoslavia) cannot be altogether dismissed.

As regards the proposals themselves, the services of Italian officers as army instructors were subsequently accepted (foreign military instructors being very necessary), Italy already exercised a degree of financial control (as, indeed, in view of the loan, she was entitled to do), and Albania subsequently placed herself, by Treaty of Alliance (a perfectly normal instrument) under the protection of Italy. With regard to the gendarmerie, its condition was very unsatisfactory, and reorganization under foreign supervision was expedient; but Zogu, probably in deference to Yugoslav sensitiveness and in order to avoid the inference which would be drawn if he accepted only Italian assistance, preferred to strengthen the existing British Mission. Colonel Stirling—who found it impossible both to carry out his duties in connection with the Ministry of the Interior and to reorganize the gendarmerie—resigned, and was succeeded as Inspector-General, during August, by Major-General Sir Jocelyn Percy.

But the true significance of the above proposals was that they gave Yugoslavia ample warning of what was under contemplation, and one would have thought that she would have sought in the circumstances an immediate *rapprochement* with Albania—which Albania was already seeking with her—had she had any genuine apprehension, from the defensive point of view, of Italian intentions. But she pursued a very different policy.

Albania had made much progress since the return to power of Ahmed Zogu, who had conferred upon his country an inestimable blessing, namely peace. Throughout 1925 and 1926 there had appeared periodically rumours of insurrection and bloodshed, "based, no doubt, on a knowledge of what was under contemplation" (N.E. 2.12.26), but all of them had been without foundation. These reports, emanating from Belgrade, became particularly frequent during the summer and autumn of 1926 (M.P. 28.8.26), and corresponded with a growing hostility towards Italy, culminating in a vitriolic outburst against her in the Yugoslav Shkupstina at the beginning of November.

On the 20th November a revolt, of which Dom Loro

Tzaka was reported to be the leader (T. 24.11.26), did break out among the Catholic tribesmen of the frontier regions to the north and north-east of Skutari. The rising was of a much more formidable nature than would have been the case had it been the spontaneous outcome of local unrest, and was so well organized and cleverly handled that the Government was taken by surprise. The rebels advanced on Skutari—driving before them five companies of Government troops—and had they done so with rather more speed they would have been able to occupy the town. As it was, they did not encounter serious opposition until within eight kilometres of Skutari, when, on the 22nd, the Government troops, reinforced from the town, succeeded in checking them, inflicting heavy casualties (T. 26.11.26). A comitadji band which attempted to cross the frontier near Podgoritza was thrown back by gendarmerie.

Troops were hastily sent to the scene of operations from central Albania, and the irregulars—disbanded a few weeks previously—mobilized. Within five days the Government had concentrated 10,000 men and several batteries of mountain guns in the disaffected area. After a second engagement the rebels were driven back into the highlands, and within a fortnight the revolt was crushed with ruthless severity. The houses of those who had participated were burnt, and a number of those most compromised arrested, tried, and executed or imprisoned. The majority seem, however, to have escaped (*Temps*, 24.1.27).

The origin of the revolt remains a mystery, but an Englishman, who is, perhaps, in a better position than anyone to express an opinion, believes that "Yugoslav complicity was apparent to everyone". Those who sought to take a charitable view of the matter have suggested that it was the outcome of local unrest, caused by the economic stagnation of Skutari, which could no longer absorb local produce as it had done during the period of Turkish rule, when it was an administrative centre of some importance. The weakness of this suggestion lies in the fact that some years had passed since the economic downfall of Skutari, while so recently as the previous May the lot of the frontier tribesmen had been ameliorated by a convention which gave them economic access to Yugoslav frontier towns. The inference is irresistible. The tribesmen went to market across the border and were incited or bribed to revolt. The usual procedure of closing the frontier (behind them) was followed by the Yugoslavs, who doubtless intended the step to "imply that the outbreak was expected to serve the interests of Yugoslavia less than those of Italy" (*Survey of International Affairs*, 1927, 168 and 172).

The Yugoslav Press sought to implicate Monsignor Noli, and his followers of the extreme section of the Opposition, in the insurrection, and to insinuate that Italy had financed the enterprise. Apart from conclusive evidence, subsequently provided, that the Albanian Government did not share this view, Monsignor Noli had never ceased to complain of the failure of Italy to support him against Zogu. Indeed, in February, 1927, it was reported (*Temps*, 25.2.27) that his supporters in Italy had been interned. Italy did not then intervene, and there was even less reason for her intervention in 1926, when Ahmed Zogu had proved himself independent of Yugoslavia; she had no wish to drive him back under Yugoslav influence. Since Monsignor Noli had fled from Albania, he had lived in Vienna in—to the writer's certain knowledge, and contrary to allegations which have been made—very straitened circumstances. He certainly had no resources with which to finance any revolutionary outbreak— and the insurrection could not have taken place unless financial assistance had been forthcoming from some source. It is possible that other members of Noli's faction, notably Prishtina and Mustapha Kruja, may, as reported by Belgrade, have participated; but that does not explain the origin of the insurgents' resources.

That Italy provided them in order to stampede Albania into the conclusion of the Pact of Tirana is an explanation which, although unsupported by circumstantial evidence, cannot, of course, be entirely ignored; moreover, there seems no doubt that the insurrection, by reawakening in Albania fears of Yugoslavia, was considered to have provided a favourable opportunity for the signature of a Treaty already drafted, but calculated to meet with opposition.

As regards the National Union, which had its headquarters at Bari, and had officially repudiated Noli, there was certainly no connection between it and the insurgents. Its members had repeatedly complained of the strict supervision which was exercised in their respect by the Italian police; and furthermore, negotiations between them and the Albanian

Government had been opened at Bari some weeks previously, had been continued at Corfu, and had been on the point of leading to a *rapprochement* in view of certain concessions which Zogu had agreed to make, when the insurrection broke out (N.E. 16.12.26).

The following facts seem, however, definite. The insurrection, whether directed from Zara—as the Yugoslav Press alleged, in an attempt to implicate Italy—or from Podgoritza, was organized on Yugoslav territory; and many Yugoslav subjects—whether Albanians or Serbs is immaterial—participated. Further, the insurgents were equipped in most cases with rifles of a pattern which had not been available in Albania, and were financed from some source. Lastly, the whole country—beyond the very restricted disaffected area— including the (Catholic) Mirdites, remained loyal to the Central Government; and demonstrations against the insurgents, and in favour of the Government, took place at Skutari, Tirana, and Korcha.

In the circumstances it would seem that the insurrection was fomented by Serbs (T. 30.3.27) of the Yugoslav military party, who saw in the growth of Italo-Albanian friendship a threat to the ultimate success of their strategic aspirations, and hoped that the movement would find support in other parts of Albania; but whether or not official Yugoslavia was implicated, it is impossible to say. Official Yugoslavia had, however, refused to conclude with Albania a Pact of Friendship and Security which would have precluded the realization of the military party's aspirations.

Briefly, and in conclusion, Yugoslavia had resolutely refused to grasp Albania's hand. Both in 1925 and 1926 did Albania offer to join the Little Entente, only to be rejected. Meanwhile, within Yugoslav territory, hostile intentions against Albania were nurtured. To what extent the insurrection in November was a translation into action of these hostile intentions is immaterial, but their existence was a constant menace to the *status quo*, and created an intolerable atmosphere of apprehension. In the circumstances Albania had but two alternative courses—to continue to roast upon the Yugoslav spit, or to accept the assistance of Italy.

Very naturally she turned to Italy, who, both for strategic and economic (N.E. 23.9.26) reasons, was anxious to see Albania stabilized and prosperous. Italy gave financial assistance, accompanied, of course, by a certain measure of economic control. Financial assistance did not, however, guarantee immediate stability and security. It was necessary for Albania to assure herself of armed assistance, if need be, for the preservation of the *status quo*, until financial assistance had enabled her to consolidate herself. Again she turned to Yugoslavia, and again was she rebuffed; and an armed insurrection, organized in Yugoslav territory, followed. The Pact of Tirana was the logical and inevitable outcome (N.E. 6.10.27; 10.11.27; 17.11.27; 1.12.27; and M.G. 27.4.27). "The perpetual fear of Serbian imperialism pushed Albania into the arms of Italy" (*La République*, Turkey, N.E. 26.5.27).

The terms of the Pact of Friendship and Security between Italy and Albania, signed at Tirana on the 27th November, 1926, are as follows:

"Italy and Albania, with a view to re-enforcing their mutual relations of friendship and security, having regard to their geographical position, and with a view to contributing to the consolidation of peace, animated by the desire to maintain the political, juridical, and territorial *status quo* of Albania within the framework of the Treaties to which both parties are signatories, and of the Covenant of the League of Nations, have decided to conclude the present Pact of Friendship and Security, and for this purpose have designated as their plenipotentiaries the following: For His Majesty the King of Italy, Baron Aloisi, Minister of His Majesty in Albania; for His Excellency the President of the Republic of Albania, M. Vrioni, Minister of Foreign Affairs of the Albanian Republic, who, having exchanged their full powers, found in good and due form, agreed as follows:

"*Art*. 1. Italy and Albania recognize that any disturbance directed against the political, juridical, and territorial *status quo* of Albania is opposed to their reciprocal political interest.

"*Art*. 2. To safeguard the above-mentioned interest, the High Contracting Parties undertake to give their mutual support and cordial collaboration. They likewise undertake not to conclude with other Powers political or military agreements prejudicial to the interests of the other Party as defined in the present Pact.

"*Art.* 3. The High Contracting Parties undertake to submit to a special procedure of conciliation and arbitration questions which may arise between them, and which cannot be settled through regular diplomatic channels.

"The conditions of this procedure of peaceful settlement will be the object of a special convention to be concluded as soon as possible.

"*Art.* 4. The present Pact shall remain in force for five years, and may be denounced or renewed one year before its expiry.

"*Art.* 5. The present Pact shall be ratified, and afterwards registered with the League of Nations. The ratifications shall be exchanged at Rome.

"Done at Tirana, the 27th November, 1926."

In some Albanian circles there existed doubt as to whether Italy had obtained the right to intervene in Albania whenever she pleased, or only upon being asked to do so by the Albanian Government. Accordingly Hussein Vrioni asked Baron Aloisi for an official assurance on this and other points. In reply he received the following Note dated the 5th December, 1926:

"You have asked me to explain, for the benefit of certain Albanians, the exact interpretation by the Italian Government of certain phrases contained in the Pact of Friendship and Security (which is essentially one of peace) signed by us on the 27th November last. You have particularly asked me whether the Italian Government, like the Albanian Government, intended that the phrase '*i trattati di cui ambedue sono firmatarie*' should refer only to Treaties concluded and published since the admission of Albania into the League of Nations. In conformity with the verbal assurances which I have already given you, I herewith confirm that such is also the intention of the Government of Rome.

"Next, you have drawn my attention to the phrase contained in the second part of the first sentence of Art. 2 of the text: '*il loro mutuo appoggio e la loro collaborazione cordiale'.* This phrase, according to the intention of the Royal Government, cannot be a matter for doubt. Mutual support and cordial collaboration can be interpreted only as a collaboration resulting from proposals made by one of the Parties, and voluntarily accepted by the other. Consequently, it is evident that this support and collaboration can come into operation only if one of the two Parties so request.

"I have the honour to renew my assurances that, according to the instructions of my Government, I am now at the entire disposal of the Albanian Government to begin negotiations for the establishment of a special procedure of conciliation and arbitration as provided in Art. 3 of our Pact of Friendship and Security of the 27th November last.

"These explanations confirm the loyal intention of the two contracting Governments; that is why I flatter myself, Excellency, that they will show in still more clarity the good faith and the disinterested spirit with which the Royal Government has met all the wishes expressed by the Albanian Government on the occasion of the conclusion of the Pact."

The Albanian official attitude is made clear by the following telegram received by the Albanian Legation in London on the 15th December (also published in Paris: *Temps*, 17.12.26):

"The Pact of Friendship which has been concluded between Albania and Italy cannot, and ought not to be, regarded as other than a diplomatic act which brings confirmation in regard to the independence and sovereignty of Albania and her territorial integrity. Far from favouring any interference on the part of Italy in the external and internal affairs of Albania, and far from substituting the neighbouring Great Power in the rôle of international guarantee which the high institution of Geneva assures to all its members, this Treaty, which is also a Treaty of Arbitration, is inspired solely by the principles of the Covenant of the League of Nations—where it will be deposited—and thus it does but increase the authority of the League of Nations in the international domain. This Pact is not followed by any secret clause or annex which would be in flagrant contradiction to the principles upon which it is founded. In short, the Treaty of Friendship concluded between Albania and Italy is a Treaty of Peace and is not directed against any State. The anxious commentaries of part of the foreign Press are therefore based upon nothing but conjecture" (N.E. 23.12.26).

The Pact was presented to the Chamber of Deputies on the 8th December, and, in view of the explanations given by Baron Aloisi, was passed without protest, although five deputies refrained from voting. It was then returned to the Foreign Affairs and Juridical Commissions, and on the 10th was ratified by the Senate. Ratifications were exchanged in Rome on the 24th January, and on the 8th February it was registered with the League of Nations (T. 9.2.27).

The Pact marks the completion of Albania's evolution; but it aroused the utmost indignation in Belgrade, and its repercussions were not long delayed.

Note:—The text of the Pact of Tirana, in Albanian and Italian, with translations in English and French, and the annexed letter of explanation, are published in the *League of Nations Treaty Series*,† Vol. LX, pp. 16-21.

CHAPTER XI

ALBANIA AND ITALY

"On the question of Albania Signor Mussolini averred that, while Italy was greatly interested in that country, she was chiefly anxious that Albania should be reserved for the Albanians, and that they should be left as far as possible to conduct their own affairs without interference from their more immediate neighbours" (T. 22.11.22).

THE signature of the Pact of Tirana raised a storm of indignation throughout Yugoslavia (N.E. 9.12.26), although no grounds for a formal protest against it could be discovered. The Pact was equivalent to a declaration by Italy that she was prepared no longer to allow Yugoslavia, either officially or unofficially, to retard the progress of Albania towards stability and prosperity. In the circumstances it was natural that Yugoslavia should declare that Italy intended to pursue in Albania the policy which she herself had endeavoured to pursue. That this accusation found much credence in Great Britain and elsewhere is likewise intelligible, since the Fascist régime in Italy is generally regarded as being almost as nefarious as the Soviet régime in Russia, and Fascist policy as imperialism unbridled.

Belgrade immediately discovered a mare's nest in the supposition that Italy was entitled to interfere in Albania upon any and every occasion; it was contended that "situations calling for intervention . . . can even be engineered to occur at suitable moments" (N.E. 6.1.27; M.G. 22.1.27), and the hackneyed slogan "the Balkans for the Balkan peoples" again revived. Yugoslavia declared that Italy had played false by the Treaty of Friendship between the two countries, and that the Pact of Tirana was aimed at "the very State which she professed to regard as friendly". To emphasize this standpoint, and to draw the attention of Europe thereto (N.E. 16.12.26), M. Nintchitch, the Yugoslav Minister for Foreign Affairs, who had pursued a policy of friendship with Italy, resigned, and his resignation was followed by that of the whole Yugoslav Cabinet. Three days later occurred the sudden death of M. Nikola Pasitch. Had this statesman lived,

A BRIDGE OVER THE DRIN, IN LJUMA, 1924

IN OLD TIRANA, 1924

his country might again have threatened the peace of Europe over the Albanian question, since he had ever been Albania's most uncompromising foe. Actually, the Pact seems momentarily to have restored Yugoslavia to sanity.

Yugoslavia's objections to the Pact were undermined by the supplementary letter of the 5th December, which was confirmed by an official assurance to Great Britain that no Italian troops would be landed in Albania except at the request of the Albanian Government (M.G. 24.3.27). Moreover Yugoslavia elected to ignore the character of the Albanian people, who would never agree to any limitation of their sovereignty by Italy (Statement by Ahmed Zogu, D.M. 4.4.27), and would resent any Italian "penetration" of their country (N.E. 30.12.26). Of this Italy was aware, and appreciated the fact that estrangement of Albanian sympathy would react favourably for Yugoslavia. Further, Albania, by her geographical conformation, is more or less a place apart from the remainder of the Balkan Peninsula, and by no means a gateway to it. Therefore, if Yugoslavia's intentions had been pacific, the Pact of Tirana should have caused no misgivings (N.E. 16.12.26). It merely confirmed the declarations made by the Powers in November, 1921, and, contrary to some assertions (M.G. 24.1.27), threatened the security of Yugoslavia no more than did that declaration.

That the Pact ensured the maintenance of Ahmed Zogu's authority—the *status quo*—in Albania, *unless and until he was overthrown by constitutional means*, was nothing more nor less than a guarantee that Albania might enjoy, undisturbed by her neighbours, a period of tranquillity in which to organize her resources, and acquire political stability (Statement by Ahmed Zogu, D.M. 4.4.27). That it was denounced by Monsignor Noli (*Temps*, 16.3.27) was natural, since that worthy prelate was opposed to everything done by his political antagonist, regardless of intrinsic values. But his opposition is interesting in view of the supposition that he was Italophile and enjoyed Italian support.

Speaking of the Pact, Zogu said (*Giornale d'Italia*, 21.1.27):

"I have concluded the Pact because I was convinced that it is and will be a guarantee for peace in the Balkans, and that it will have historical consequences," while Mussolini, when presenting it for ratification, declared that "Italy

considers the independence and territorial integrity of
Albania as a guarantee of her own position in the Adriatic."

"Italy", declared the *Lavoro d'Italia*, "wants a united
and independent Albania. Ahmed bey Zogu is the only
man who at the present moment can give guarantees of
a continued and solid government. By protecting him
against eventual *coups* and insurrections of comitadjis,
Italy is performing a peaceful work. . . . Any direct or
indirect Yugoslav initiative in Albania would find us
ready to answer back. It is just as well that all this should
be known by all the Powers, so that they may accomplish
their duty for the tranquillity of Europe" (T. 22.3.27).

The intangibility of Albania has always been a principle
of Italian policy (T. 21.3.27), and the Treaty was a declaration
that this principle should stand. The official British attitude
was defined by Sir Austen Chamberlain in reply to questions
by Mr. Moseley in the House of Commons on the 1st June,
1927 (T. 2.6.27). Mr. Moseley (Labour) asked: "Was the
question of Albania discussed at the meeting between the
Rt. Hon. Gentleman and Signor Mussolini, and did the Rt.
Hon. Gentleman give an assurance of support to the project
subsequently embodied in the Treaty of Tirana?" Sir Austen
Chamberlain replied: "The subject of Albania was mentioned
in passing on that occasion. Signor Mussolini said then,
as he had said before and since, that the policy of Italy in no
way menaced the integrity or independence of Albania."
Mr. Moseley then asked: "Did the Rt. Hon. Gentleman
approve of that statement?" Sir Austen Chamberlain: "Yes,
I entirely approved of that statement that it was the object of
the Italian Government to preserve the integrity and independence of Albania." (Ministerial cheers.) The British attitude caused dissatisfaction in Yugoslavia, and in some circles
the possibility of a *rapprochement* with Russia was considered
(N.E. 10.3.27; *Foreign Affairs*, April, 1927).

But the most effectual reply to the fulminations of the
Yugoslavs (T. 6.12.26; M.G. 10.12.26; *Temps* 9.12.26) was
the action of Albania in expressing readiness to conclude
with them a similar Pact (C.S. 7.1.27). This attitude was
supported by Signor Mussolini, who declared that nothing
would give him greater pleasure than if Albania signed a
similar Pact with Yugoslavia (N.E. 6.1.27). During February

the Albanian Minister in Belgrade approached the Yugoslav Foreign Office on the subject, and at the same time the Albanian Minister in Athens made similar proposals to the Greek Minister for Foreign Affairs, M. Michalakopoulos (N.E. 24.2.27; T. 19.2.27; and 5.4.27). But nothing came of these overtures, and nothing more was heard of them. Why? The news of the conclusion of the Pact had been received in Greece with indifference and even benevolence, the indignation of Yugoslavia being interpreted as "the disappointment of one imperialism forestalled by another" (*Survey of International Affairs*, 1927, 172).

The stir which the conclusion of the Pact caused in Yugoslavia lasted ostensibly but a few days, and reflection seemed to show that protestations against a Pact which was innocuous so long as Yugoslavia refrained from interference in Albanian affairs, was useless. The Yugoslavs continued, however, to complain that Italy should have notified Belgrade before the conclusion of the Pact became public knowledge (N.E. 23.12.26 and 10.3.27); but Italy maintained that it was none of Yugoslavia's business. It was even suggested that Rome should have notified Belgrade while negotiations were in progress, but "to anyone who knows the Balkans, let alone fallen human nature generally, such an idea can only be described as a joke" (J. S. Barnes, N.E. 6.1.27).

Once the stir which was caused by the Pact had subsided, Albania relapsed for three months into obscurity once more. On the 17th December severe earthquakes wrought considerable damage, and caused some distress in central Albania, and the Italian Red Cross at once sent doctors and supplies. This assistance from Italy was subsequently misrepresented by Belgrade as a landing by Italian officers detailed to reorganize the Albanian Army (T. 3.6.27).

On the 11th February the Albanian Cabinet resigned, owing, it was reported, to a dispute over the Budget. Ahmed Zogu nominated a fresh Cabinet, which was as follows:

PETER POGA . . .	President of the Council of Ministers and Minister of Justice.
ABDURRAHMAN DIBRA .	Minister of the Interior.
ELIAS VRIONI . . .	Minister for Foreign Affairs.
FEIZI ALIZOTI . . .	Minister of Finance and Education.
MUSA YUKA . . .	Minister of Public Works and Agriculture.

Parliament opened on the 1st March. The programme formulated by M. Poga had two primary objects, namely, at home to balance the budget and effect economies, and in foreign affairs to cultivate friendly relations with all States. The budget threatened a considerable deficit owing to the Army estimates, which amounted to 11,695,000 gold francs out of a total expenditure of 29,314,042 gold francs (N.E. 19.5.27).

During the early days of this month Monsignor Chrysanthemos, Bishop of Trebizond and delegate of the Patriarch, again visited Tirana, bringing, it was thought, official recognition of the Albanian Orthodox Church, which actually had existed since 1923. But much surprise was caused when it was found that he came only with fresh proposals, the acceptance of which would have perpetuated Hellenic influence. Needless to say, his mission was unsuccessful.

Other events of note which occurred at about the same time were the purchase on the 4th February, 1927, by the Italian Government, of the German "Adria-Aero Lloyd" Company (C.S. 27.7.27; T. 15.6.27)—an action justified by Mussolini on political grounds (C.S. 3.9.27); a Bill brought forward in the Chamber of Deputies to limit the duration of land leases to foreigners to a maximum period of ten—subsequently extended to twenty—years, which was passed; and the assassination in Tirana of Yssuf Dibra by a Bulgarian—a personal affair.

Although, as it seemed, the Pact of Tirana had been accepted in Yugoslavia as innocuous, there was a determination that it should not stand; and in the Balkans, especially among the Serbs, there has prevailed hitherto a belief that *le fait accompli* —accomplished by force—is the only means of achieving an end. Although in Yugoslavia the fear was widely expressed that Italy intended to find a pretext under the Pact to flout the League of Nations, and expand into Albania, the expressed fear by no means tallied with the prevalent conviction that Italy would never be permitted by the other Powers, especially by France, to land troops in Albania, and therefore that there was little danger in attempting by subterranean methods to replace Ahmed Zogu by another, more ready to lend himself to the machinations of Belgrade. Moreover, Yugoslavia seemed obsessed with the idea that she could continue to play the old Balkan game, which consists of warfare by

irregulars while nominally there is peace—similar to the
game played by Philip II of Spain and Queen Elizabeth.
That Italy definitely had refused, by concluding the Pact
of Tirana, to play that game, or to allow it to be played at
the expense of Albania, was the actual cause of Yugoslav
resentment against the Pact, which, for the moment, put a
check upon the rashness of Belgrade; "but the check was
only momentary" (T. 30.3.27).

That trouble was anticipated by the Albanian authorities,
once the snows melted in the passes, seems clear, since at the
beginning of March, 240 bairaktars and notables of the
border tribes were called to Tirana, invested with military
rank as officers of the Reserve, placed on half-pay during
peace time (N.E. 19.5.27), and equipped with uniforms.
Rumours became rife that preparations were on foot in
Yugoslavia for another "insurrection" to overthrow Ahmed
Zogu, on the lines of that of the previous November (T.
19.3.27 and 26.3.27). It was reported that Yugoslav officials,
members of the White Hand organization, notably the
Governor of Monastir and General Martinovitch, were
organizing this "insurrection", that comitadji leaders had
been instructed to enrol men on pay at the rate of £4 per
month, that the rumour was being spread that 65,000 Italians
had landed in Albania, and Albanians in Yugoslavia were
being called upon to assist the Slavs in resisting the invaders
(D.M. 31.3.27), that when the passes were clear of snow the
comitadjis were to invade Albania, avoiding if possible any
fighting until they were well within the frontier, that the
impression might be created in Europe that the movement
was of a domestic nature only (T. 30.3.27), and that the
Yugoslav Government would declare neutral a frontier zone,
and disclaim responsibility for whatever occurred. As a prepa-
tory step the Belgrade Press duly reported, as it had done
before the overthrow of Monsignor Noli, that a grave situation existed in Albania, and that a revolt was brewing; also
that a general mobilization had been ordered, and was being
directed by Italian officers (T. 28 and 30.3.27; *Temps* 28.3.27).
Moreover, meetings of the Albanian Revolutionary Committee, held from time to time in Yugoslavia, had been
attended by Yugoslav officials (T. 19.3.27). The Albanian
Government was satisfied "that the Yugoslav authorities
were carrying out an elaborate scheme for setting comitadjis

in motion. The frontier zone, so the reports ran, had been divided into sectors under committees and sub-committees, and each unit was in close touch with officers of the regular army" (N.E. 12.5.27). In short, there was a movement on foot in Yugoslavia to evict Zogu in the same way as the latter, with Yugoslav assistance, had evicted Monsignor Noli in December, 1924 (Statement by Lieut.-Colonel W. Stirling, D.M. 3.5.27); and it is idle for Yugoslavia, who never hesitates to hold the Bulgarian Government responsible for the activities of Bulgarian comitadjis, to disclaim responsibility for the activities of frontier officials, or of the White Hand organization, which in March, 1927, included a number of Generals and two Cabinet Ministers (J. S. Barnes, N.E. 7 and 21.4.27).

It seems more than a coincidence that while this movement was being prepared, the Yugoslavs elected to strengthen their troops in the frontier areas (N.E. 31.3.27), and that military preparations almost upon the scale of a mobilization were taking place (for details of mobilization orders, as reported by the *Giornale d'Italia*, see M.G. 14.4.27), presumably to enable the Yugoslavs to be the first in the field should Italy decide to intervene (N.E. 24.3.27 and 7.4.27). Had Italy intervened, doubtless Yugoslavia would have declared that her own intervention had been rendered necessary by Italian aggression. These preparations were "represented as steps taken in the ordinary course of army reform" (Sir Austen Chamberlain, P.D. 204: 368; T. 24.3.27). That Yugoslavia had been strengthening her army was an open secret (T. 30.3.27). Supplies of munitions had been pouring into the country from France and Belgium. The air force was being strengthened. Communications were being improved, and the development of the arsenal at Kraguyevatz pushed ahead. But a partial mobilization of the Yugoslav II and III Armies based on Uskub and Sarajevo, on the pretext that Albanian bands had collected opposite Prizren, does not seem compatible with "steps taken in the ordinary course of army reform".

The Albanian Government knew that an appeal to the League of Nations would be no less vain than Monsignor Noli's appeal had been, and that its machinery might be clogged by France—who had just initialled a Treaty of Friendship with Yugoslavia—in the same manner as it had been on that occasion (M.G. 25.3.27). Likewise, it knew that direct representations to Belgrade would be either ignored or met by a denial, as had been Monsignor Noli's representations; and in criticizing Ahmed Zogu for allowing Italy to act as his spokesman, it should be borne in mind that he himself had profited by the machinery which was again about to be set in motion to overthrow him. Therefore it drew the attention of Italy, pledged by the Pact of Tirana to maintain the *status quo*, to the situation (D.M. 4.4.27); and on the 19th March the Italian Government passed on the information to Great Britain, France, Germany, and other countries (T. 25.3.27), at the same time intimating that, in accordance with the Pact, Italy "would not remain indifferent" to any attempt to upset the *status quo* in Albania (T. 19.3.27). Yugoslavia was immediately asked to explain the significance of the preparations which were on foot (M.P. 21.3.27). There seems no doubt that this "timely action" (T. 21.3.27), for which Albania, through her Minister in Rome, Djemal Dino, officially expressed her gratitude (T. 24.3.27), averted a grave international crisis.

The Italian Government was severely censured in some circles, particularly in France and the French Press (T. 21.3.27), for its action, which was characterized as "alarmist". Moreover, it was suggested that Italy had created a "scare" with the object of providing a pretext for intervention in Albania in accordance with the provisions of the Pact of Tirana (N.E. 24.3.27; etc.). The landing of Italian troops on the island of Saseno, presumably as a gesture of her intention to fulfil her obligations under the Pact of Tirana, and in reply to Albania's appeal for protection against Yugoslav troops on the frontier (*Foreign Affairs*, April, 1927), or perhaps to forestall a naval Power friendly towards Yugoslavia, was regarded as the first step towards the exploitation of this pretext. The fact that Italy could gain nothing whatever by intervention (M.G. 23.3.27) was ignored.

On the 5th April Major-General Sir Jocelyn Percy, who was already in command of the Albanian Gendarmerie with a staff of five British officers, was appointed to command the Albanian troops in the north-eastern frontier regions (T. 7.4.27). Not only did this step produce an excellent effect upon public opinion in Albania, especially upon the frontier tribesmen, but it removed all foundation for any genuine misgivings in Yugoslavia regarding Italo-Albanian intentions, since General Percy would never assume command in a region in which provocative action entailing the gravest consequences was contemplated. On the other hand, it precluded any attempt by Yugoslavia to act provocatively, except with the full knowledge of Europe, which would accept the credible evidence of General Percy and his staff (T. 10.6.27; D.M. 12.5.27).

It was contended with regard to the reported comitadji activity that Italy should merely have called the attention of the Yugoslav Government thereto, and in the case of the movement of troops, asked for an explanation. But comitadji activities can be denied, and in case inquiries are pressed too closely, the bands "can dissolve into peaceful industrious peasants" (N.E. 31.3.27). Movements of troops can be explained in various plausible ways. In the case in question the Yugoslav Government explained that at the beginning of the year a "test mobilization" had been ordered to determine the efficiency of the country's military organization, whereupon the Albanian Government took the precaution to strengthen its forces on its northern and eastern frontiers. "Alarmed in turn by this concentration, the Yugoslav Government is reported to have instructed its frontier commands to mobilize sufficient reserves to bring their units up to adequate strength in case of emergencies on the Albanian frontiers" (N.E. 14.4.27).

On the 21st March the British and Italian Ministers in Belgrade asked the Yugoslav Government to take steps to prevent the organization upon Yugoslav soil of Albanian revolutionary bands (*Temps* 22.3.27 and N.E. 28.4.27), and the French Minister was instructed by his Government to counsel prudence. Great Britain likewise counselled prudence in Rome. In Yugoslavia, Great Britain was regarded as "the villain of the piece", second only to Italy (T. 22.3.27), presumably because she did not make unqualified acceptance of the assurances of innocence with which Belgrade flooded Europe. This attitude was shared by Russia (*Temps* 26.3.27), and the French Press took much the same view. The Italian Press declared that France encouraged Belgrade, a statement officially denied by M. Briand, who protested against it during an interview with the Italian Ambassador, Baron Avezzana (D.M. 22.3.27). The German attitude was dispassionate and strictly neutral.

Yugoslavia declared that Italy merely sought a pretext to intervene in Albania, while she had always favoured her independence (M.G. 23.3.27)! M. Peritch, Yugoslav Minister for Foreign Affairs, proposed that a Commission of Inquiry should investigate the situation to disprove the allegations which Italy had made. He even declared his readiness to permit the Military Attachés of the Powers at Belgrade to make full investigations. This attitude had in some circles precisely the effect that M. Peritch had intended, and it was seriously maintained, notably in the French Press (T. 24.3.27), that it weakened Italy's case (N.E. 31.3.27). Actually it seems to have been mere bluff. In the first place Italy had acted before military preparations in Yugoslavia had advanced beyond the stage at which they could readily be explained away. Secondly, an investigation, however prompt, by the Military Attachés at Belgrade, would have failed to produce any evidence of the organization of comitadji bands. Miss Durham wrote (T. 26.3.27):

"Wars in the Balkans begin by intensive comitadji work. The comitadjis are always dressed as peasants. During the preparations for the Balkan War of 1912 . . . a vast number of peasants were enlisted and secretly armed by night. They came over the Montenegrin border in the guise of poor peasants coming to market, and received rifles. . . . Not all the military experts in Europe would have detected signs of the coming war there . . . merely peasants at work. In these rough lands there are places in plenty where arms and munitions can be cached. And into cache those arms would go when the 'experts' were expected. Nevertheless, a week or two after they had left, having seen nothing, a large body of armed men could be thrown over the frontier. That they were not in uniform would not make them less soldiers. It however permits the Government to say it knows nothing about the affair. A flying visit to any Balkan frontier is merely a waste of time" (see also C.E. 169).

In the third place, M. Peritch knew well that an effective investigation could be carried out only by a commission of Balkan experts, and that by the time these were assembled all traces of preparations could be obliterated. Lastly, it would seem that he never had the intention actually to permit a Commission to operate; and two days after the proposal had been made, and while steps to give effect to it were being considered by the Powers, he withdrew it (T. 24.3.27). He compromised, however, by declaring his readiness to receive a Commission of Inquiry appointed by the League of Nations, knowing that several weeks would elapse before such a Commission could arrive, and moreover, that none of the Powers were in favour of calling for the intervention of the League.

Meanwhile the proposal that the Military Attachés at Belgrade should be instructed to carry out investigations was rejected by the Powers, the futility of the scheme being, it seems, recognized; and at the instigation of Great Britain, a scheme was drawn up whereby a Commission of Inquiry, composed of experts representing Great Britain, France, and Germany, should be constituted. Yugoslav and Italian delegates were to be attached, but were not to act as members of the Commission (T. 26.3.27). This Commission was to carry out investigations on both sides of the frontier. Italy at first favoured these proposals, but upon further consideration expressed the view that any inquiry unless made by experts within a few days of the publication of her Note to the Powers, would be useless, and would prove nothing (*Temps*, 26.3.27). Moreover, she considered, no doubt, that should the proposed Commission fail to find any evidence in support of the accusations against Yugoslavia which she had made—which in all probability would have been the case—the view that she had created a scare with some ulterior motive would be adopted, to the advantage of Yugoslavia, and to the detriment of her prestige. On the other hand, public opinion in Yugoslavia, especially the Yugoslav Opposition and "other very influential circles" (T. 26.3.27) was very strongly opposed to any inquiry. But M. Peritch, having proposed an inquiry, could not very well prohibit one; he therefore proposed that the whole matter should be referred to the League of Nations, and the Pact of Tirana brought up for examination by the Council.

In view of this opposition from both sides of the Adriatic, the Powers abandoned their intention to carry out an inquiry in Yugoslavia and Albania (M.G. 18.4.27), and before the end of March it was proposed alternatively that the whole question of Italo-Yugoslav relations should be reviewed by direct negotiations between those two Powers. Meanwhile it was arranged, in agreement with the Italian, Yugoslav, and Albanian Governments, that should any further incident occur, the British and French Military Attachés, and a representative of the German Legation, should be available to carry out immediate investigations (T. 13.4.27; P.D. 206: 576; 204: 1436). Italy expressed her readiness to enter into "conversations with the object of clarifying the general relations between the two countries", upon the condition that Yugoslavia ratified the Nettuno Conventions—dealing principally with the economic interests of the two countries in the northern Adriatic—which had been drawn up some time previously but remained unratified owing to the obstruction of the Yugoslav Opposition.

At this stage Great Britain, France, and Germany found themselves in agreement, but France was unable to restrain her protégé, who now clamoured for an examination of the Pact of Tirana and a review of the whole Albanian question by the Council of the League of Nations. In this attitude Yugoslavia was supported by certain sections of the western European Press, but with it official France could not agree. In the first place she was a signatory of the Agreement of the 9th November, 1921, which acknowledged Italy's special interests in Albania, and was obliged to recognize that the Pact of Tirana was, in accordance therewith, perfectly legitimate. Secondly, she was reluctant to place Herr Stresemann, Sessional President of the Council, in the position of arbiter in the dispute. And lastly, she was aware of the *dangerous precedent which would be created should a Treaty between two countries which was directed against no third party be submitted for examination to the Council of the League merely because a third party objected to it* (T. 30.11.27; *Temps*, 1.12.27). What Yugoslavia hoped to gain at Geneva it is difficult to say. Perhaps she hoped that a means might be found to induce the members of the Council, innocent of Balkan intrigue, so to limit Italy's freedom to act in accordance with the Pact of Tirana, that its effect would be nullified, and the original position restored.

At the beginning of April Sir Ronald Graham, British Ambassador in Rome, communicated to Signor Mussolini Sir Austen Chamberlain's views, which were that the whole question of Albania would best be solved by direct negotiations between Italy and Yugoslavia, especially if the latter should prove accommodating with regard to the ratification of the Nettuno Conventions; and that perhaps it would be advisable, in order to avoid further friction, to review the whole situation created by the Pact of Tirana (T. 25.4.27). Mussolini replied that while facts had justified the allegations which Italy had made with regard to preparations in Yugoslavia for aggressive action against Albania, there remained nothing to discuss; that relations between Rome and Belgrade had suffered no interruption, and that any statement which the Yugoslav Minister desired to make would be received in the most friendly spirit. But the Pact of Tirana, he added, had been concluded between Italy and Albania in full exercise of their sovereign rights, its inferences had been fully explained before its ratification by the Albanian Parliament, and as it was in no way directed against any other State, the question of its reconsideration could not arise (T. 28 and 16.4.27).

The official British attitude was made clear by Sir Austen Chamberlain when speaking in the House of Commons on the 2nd May (P.D. 205: 1277). With reference to the Pact he said that he had been informed by Signor Mussolini on the 1st December—the day before its publication—that it had been signed, and that naturally he had had no criticism to offer. H.M. Government had, he declared, "nothing to do with its inception, its negotiation, or its terms". With regard to the crisis in March, he said that H.M. Government had no direct interest in the question, but had done everything possible to facilitate direct conversations.

> "We believe that it is by such direct conversations that a friendly settlement will be most easily reached, and I certainly should not advise in this or any other case that recourse should be had to League intervention before the parties have met and discussed their differences [see also P.D. 204: 2039]. . . . It has been agreed among the Powers concerned that it is unnecessary, and would, indeed, be useless at this date, to conduct an inquiry into the past, but that should fresh occasion arise while the conversations are in progress, representatives of Great Britain, France, and Germany will be

available to carry out an immediate inquiry. . . . I do not think that the publication of papers would add anything material to this full ſtatement, and I fear that it might prejudice the success of conversations between the two Governments by reviving controversies which, I hope, are paſt.

"Finally," concluded Sir Auſten, "as regards the Resolution of the Ambassadors' Conference of the 9th November, 1921, there seems to be some misunderstanding. The Resolution is binding on H.M. Government, but it does not affeft the rights of Albania as a member of the League of Nations, and contains nothing inconsiſtent with the general obligations of the signatories as members of the Council. . . . The contingency contemplated in the Resolution has not yet arisen, and I truſt never will arise."

Although the Yugoslav Miniſter in Rome had an interview with Signor Mussolini during the early part of April (P.D. 205 : 1277), his country now declared that Mussolini's refusal to discuss the Paft of Tirana, and also the revelations which had been made through the Italian Press—of the details of the Yugoslav plot againſt Albania—rendered impossible direft *pourparlers*, and that Geneva was the only remaining medium for negotiations (*Temps*, 18.4.27). But Italy remained adamant, both as regards the intangibility of the Paft, and the League of Nations, to which she refused to refer the matter; and legislation passed by the Shkupſtina reſtrifting the property rights of Italians in Dalmatia was not calculated to induce her to modify her attitude—indeed, it was regarded as a reprisal (M.G. 18.4.27).

On the 18th April the Yugoslav Cabinet resigned, and a Coalition Cabinet was formed. This event brought about a remarkable change of front by the French Press, which hitherto had been inclined to encourage Belgrade. Alarm leſt Yugoslavia should precipitate a further crisis now became evident, and Belgrade was exhorted to exercise moderation (M.G. 19.4.27). Sir Auſten Chamberlain was made the scapegoat, and it was maintained that his conversations with Signor Mussolini at Rapallo and Leghorn had led the latter to suppose that Great Britain would support his policy in Albania (M.G. 21.4.27). Italy's special rights in Albania were admitted, but it was still emphasized that it should be established that those rights did not include the right to interfere at will in Albania's internal affairs.

On the 26th April, by an exchange of Notes, the Albanian and Italian Governments, "desirous of solemnly affirming the solidarity and complete agreement existing between them on all questions which may arise out of the Pact" of Tirana, agreed upon the following declaration:

> "The Governments of Italy and Albania declare that, if requested either jointly or separately by one or more Powers to enter into negotiations which relate to the interpretation or application of the Pact of Tirana, or the participation in it of third States, or which in any way affect the relations between Italy and Albania, neither of the two Governments will take part in such negotiations without previous consultation on the subject between Italy and Albania, or without a perfect agreement and a simultaneous participation of both countries in such negotiations" (C.S. 15.5.27; T. 16.5.27).

The absence from Rome of Signor Mussolini, and other causes, prevented the opening of conversations between Italy and Yugoslavia before the occurrence of a further incident. It had been hoped that in the course of direct conversations the Italian Government would find an opportunity to stress the harmless character of the Pact of Tirana, although refusing to discuss it, but it was generally acknowledged that if Yugoslavia desired an improvement of relations with Italy and Albania, she could achieve it by adopting a more reasonable and friendly attitude towards the latter country. The incident which occurred proved that conciliation formed no part of her policy.

M. Vuk Djurashkovitch (see above; an Albanian subject: *Temps*, 14.6.27) was again suspected of treason, and it was believed that he was at the head of an organization carrying on espionage on behalf of Yugoslavia. Accordingly, on the 27th May, his house at Durazzo was surrounded and searched—but not, as reported, burnt (T. 25.6.27)—a number of papers of an incriminating nature, including two letters addressed to the Yugoslav Legation, seized, and he himself arrested with three other suspects (T. 1.6.27). Verbal protests were at once made against the arrest by M. Sakovitch, the

Yugoslav Chargé d'Affaires, whereupon the Albanian Government requested the Yugoslav Government to state precisely what was Djurashkovitch's official connection with Yugoslavia.

On the 30th May M. Sakovitch handed a Note to the Albanian Government, in which he declared that Djurashkovitch had been employed as dragoman of the Yugoslav Legation since the 30th August, 1923, and had been arrested without reference to the Legation. He drew the attention of the Albanian Government to the "exceedingly painful impression which will be made on the mind of my Government by this act of violence on the part of the Albanian authorities", and demanded the immediate release of Djurashkovitch and restoration of the documents seized. He requested the Albanian Minister for Foreign Affairs to inform him in writing of the decision of the Albanian Government "on the question of satisfaction which it is ready to accord us over this brutal act in contravention of international rights", and reserved the right to explain what would be the reparation and satisfaction demanded by his Government.

Upon receipt of this document, the Albanian Government telegraphed to Tsena bey Kryeziu, the Albanian Minister in Belgrade, explaining the arrest of Djurashkovitch, and stating that documents "of a compromising nature and extreme gravity" had been found in his possession. The note received from M. Sakovitch, continued the telegram, was couched in terms contrary to international usage; moreover, the Albanian Government had never been notified of the employment by the Yugoslav Legation of Djurashkovitch, who lived at Durazzo, never worked at Tirana, had never acted in any official capacity whatever (*Temps*, 16.6.27), was not mentioned upon the list of members of the Yugoslav diplomatic corps, and could be regarded only as an Albanian subject. In conclusion, Kryeziu was instructed to explain these facts to the Yugoslav Minister for Foreign Affairs, M. Marinkovitch, to inform him that the Albanian Government was convinced that M. Sakovitch had acted without the knowledge of the Yugoslav Government; and lastly, to explain the situation to the British and Italian Ministers.

On the 1st June the Albanian Minister for Foreign Affairs replied to M. Sakovitch to the effect that the Albanian Government had never been notified of the appointment of M.

Djurashkovitch as dragoman, and therefore had never given its necessary consent for an Albanian subject to fill such a post. If, continued the Note, the Yugoslav Legation possessed any document recognizing Djurashkovitch as its dragoman, the Albanian Government asked to see it, "while reserving to itself the right to apply the laws of the country to one of its own subjects". Needless to say, no documentary evidence to prove Djurashkovitch's position was forthcoming, although it was declared in Yugoslavia that such documents existed in the archives of the Yugoslav Foreign Office—but were never produced—and that the Albanian Government had been notified of his appointment (T. 6.6.27; *Temps*, 11.6.27).

On the same day Kryeziu was instructed by Zogu to inform M. Marinkovitch that, although no direct reply with regard to the official status of Djurashkovitch had been forthcoming, "yet in order to show friendship to the person of the Yugoslav Foreign Minister, and also being desirous to bind more closely the existing ties between the two countries", he had already ordered the release of Djurashkovitch when the Yugoslav Note arrived. Nevertheless, "in order to prove how far we are from showing ourselves intransigent", he declared his readiness to release Djurashkovitch if the Yugoslav Foreign Minister would order M. Sakovitch to modify the tone of his Note.

In reply to this communication, M. Marinkovitch, while thanking Zogu for his expression of friendship, declared that the Note had been written upon his instructions, that it would be neither modified nor withdrawn, and reiterated the demand for the immediate and unconditional release of Djurashkovitch.

On the 3rd June M. Sakovitch handed a further Note to the Albanian Government, demanding the immediate release of Djurashkovitch, or, alternatively, visas for the passports for himself and the staff of the Yugoslav Legation.

In reply to this Note upon the following day, the Albanian Minister for Foreign Affairs stated that since Djurashkovitch was an Albanian citizen, his case "constitutes an affair of a purely internal character, and thus the Albanian Government cannot entertain on this matter conversations with foreign diplomatic representatives". Nevertheless, continued the Note, for the sake of the preservation of friendly relations, the Albanian Government "has suggested in this connection a solution satisfactory for the two parties", regretted that Yugo-slavia took views on "this incident, of an abusively demon-strative character", and while granting the request for visas, expressed the hope that "on better consideration of the circumstances you will not ask for these visas" (T. 8.6.27).

The Albanian Government had adopted a conciliatory attitude which can be described only as exemplary (*Temps*, 7.6.27; *La République*, Turkey, N.E. 14.7.27), but to no purpose. Yugoslavia, who "has been seized with a great desire to walk into the shoes of the fallen Empire [Austria-Hungary] in the Near East" (*La République*, Turkey, N.E. 26.5.27) resented the action of the Albanian authorities in taking steps to eliminate her intrigues—although their action was perfectly legitimate—especially as no previous warning of the arrest had reached the Yugoslav Legation, and Djurashkovitch had been unable to dispose of incriminat-ing documents in his possession. In the circumstances Yugoslavia characterized the Albanian attitude as provocative, refused to reconsider her decision to break off diplomatic relations, and on the 4th June the Yugoslav Chargé d'Affaires and staff left Tirana. On the 5th June the Albanian Govern-ment telegraphed a full statement of the situation to the Secretary-General of the League of Nations (C.S. 7.6.27).

In the meantime the Powers had intervened. The Italian Minister at Belgrade had counselled a conciliatory attitude, but the Yugoslav Government had refused to consider the proposals which he had made (*Temps*, 8 and 9.6.27). Great Britain likewise urged moderation and prudence. In France there had been a tendency in the Press to characterize the action of Albania as unjustifiable, but the severance of diplo-matic relations, and reference of the affair by Albania to the League, brought about a complete change of front.

"Yesterday the Paris Press, with its usual unanimity, was proclaiming Yugoslavia's innocence, and denouncing Signor Mussolini as the real culprit behind the scenes. To-day there is silence about Italy, and even a tendency to rebuke Belgrade for its excessive precipitancy and lack of reflection. 'We are fond of our Yugoslav friends,' writes M. Jacques Bainville in the *Liberté*, 'but like everyone else they have the defects of their qualities. They are bitter, obstinate, and intransigent, and it must not be forgotten that it was they who brought about the war of 1914. It was they who gave Austria-Hungary a reason for making war, and by so doing gave Germany a pretext. The Serbs are our friends, well and good, and their friendship is dear to us. But we do not forget that these friends of ours are violent of character and temperamentally explosive' " (M.G. 8.6.27).

Le Soir remarked that "to the Black Shirts of Rome there is the counterpart in the military party at Belgrade".

France showed considerable alarm and anxiety to prevent the dispute from developing further, or being submitted to the League of Nations, and it was declared that the Albanian telegram should be regarded as having "merely informative value". An explanation of this attitude is probably to be found in a fear that the issue of the Pact of Tirana might be raised, and a precedent created prejudicial to French policy in the Balkans and elsewhere. Moreover, it was thought that the slightest incident upon the Albanian frontier might lead to Italian intervention in Albania in circumstances in which France would find herself bound by the Agreement of the 9th November, 1921, to support Italian intervention. The action of Yugoslavia in severing diplomatic relations was described as unjustified, and a way by which she could change her attitude without loss of prestige sought. French concern in the affair caused some surprise in London, where it was held that the rupture would have serious consequences only if its importance was exaggerated. In Italy the situation was not regarded as serious, it being thought that while the Powers co-operated, and while it was known that Albania did not stand alone, Yugoslavia would not venture to take any rash step. Thus Yugoslavia's precipitancy still further cemented the ties between Italy and Albania, and still further embittered relations between herself and Albania (N.E. 16 and 23.6.27).

The settlement of the dispute proposed by the Powers to Yugoslavia was that of the Albanian Government, namely, that Djurashkovitch should be released and that the terms of the Note should be modified (T. 24.6.27). On the 11th June M. Marinkovitch wrote to the Secretary-General of the League of Nations stating that he would agree to modify M. Sakovitch's Note provided the Albanian Government first released Djurashkovitch, and that the expressions to which the Albanian Government objected were found to refer to it, which, it was maintained, was not the case. The Albanian Gendarmerie, not the Albanian Government, were the intended recipients of M. Sakovitch's abuse, declared the Yugoslav Government! Yugoslavia, continued M. Marinkovitch, did not consider the existing dispute of sufficient importance to justify its discussion under Art. 12 of the Covenant, but held itself at the disposal of the Council if the latter wished to inquire into the whole Albanian problem—meaning, of course, the Pact of Tirana (T. 13.6.27).

In the meantime recriminations continued, and neither Government would agree to take any action until the other had done so. On the 14th June Tsena Kryeziu applied for a visa, and left Belgrade, withdrawn, it would seem, principally on account of the manner in which he allowed his own views to take precedence over those of his Government (T. 15.6.27). That he had not received his passport from the Yugoslav Government before his application for it may be explained partly by the pressure brought to bear by the Powers to prevent the completion of the rupture, and partly by the fact that, being a recognized Serbophile, he was *persona grata* in Belgrade. On the 15th June the Yugoslav Consuls at Valona, Skutari, and Korcha, were withdrawn from Albania. The frontier was not, however, closed. Yugoslav interests in Albania were entrusted to the French Minister—the Baron de Vaux—and Albanian interests in Yugoslavia to the representative of the Vatican—the *doyen* of the Diplomatic Corps at Belgrade.

The situation was now extremely grave. Neither side was prepared to make any further concession, and the slightest incident might have brought about a dangerous international crisis (D.M. 6.6.27). But the representations of the Powers, acting in complete accord for the preservation of peace and the achievement of a reconciliation, had not been unavailing. Albania had preserved a conciliatory attitude throughout, while Yugoslavia, through the pressure brought to bear upon her, had become less truculent, and, although refusing to act upon her own initiative to reach a settlement of the dispute, was ready to follow a line of retreat dictated by the Powers, which would enable her to withdraw without loss of prestige. In these favourable circumstances, the representatives of the

Powers, acting independently, presented on the 23rd June identical Notes at Belgrade and Tirana proposing that the Yugoslav Government should modify M. Sakovitch's Note, and that simultaneously Djurashkovitch should be released by the Albanian authorities.

These proposals were accepted by both Governments (T. 24, 25, 27.6.27). On the 3rd July the French Minister in Albania, acting on behalf of Yugoslavia, withdrew M. Sakovitch's Note in exchange for another, in which the passages to which the Albanian Government had taken exception were omitted. Simultaneously Djurashkovitch was released. Thus was burst yet another Balkan bubble. Tsena Kryeziu was ordered to return to Belgrade until the arrival of M. Tahir Shtylla, appointed to succeed him. The Yugoslav Consul at Skutari, who was *en route* for Belgrade, was instructed to return to Albania as Chargé d'Affaires until the arrival of M. Miltitch, appointed to succeed M. Sakovitch.

The tension in Europe over the Albanian problem now relaxed, although no steps were taken to alter the situation. During June Signor Mussolini again received the Yugoslav Minister in special audience (*Temps*, 26.6.27), but whether the interview was of any consequence it is impossible to say. There were indications in the Italian Press that a *rapprochement* with Yugoslavia was considered possible, although always with the reservation that Italy was prepared to forgo none of her rights. In Albania tranquillity and security existed (T. 16.7.27), although the usual series of false reports of unrest (M.G. 15.7.27), persecution (M.G. 2.4.27), conspiracy (*Temps*, 14.5.27), assassination (*Temps*, 18.6.27), and insurrection (*Temps*, 31.8.27) continued to emanate from Belgrade and other sources. For some months no outstanding event occurred. Although Greece had remained indifferent to Yugoslav fulminations against the Pact of Tirana and its repercussions, her relations with Albania were still unsatisfactory, owing to the persecution to which the Albanian Moslems who remained in Epirus and Macedonia were still subjected (N.E. 17.11.27).

During August the President and Cabinet paid state visits to Durazzo and Skutari. During his visit to the latter town, Zogu granted an amnesty in favour of seventy persons under sentence for participation in the revolt in the previous November, which created a very favourable impression. In the same month Colonel Kassim Kiafzezi, who had been a refugee since the eviction of Monsignor Noli, returned to Albania, having been granted a special pardon (N.E. 15.9.27), together with three hundred other political prisoners and refugees (T. 21.9.27). The list of these persons, published in the *Official Gazette* of the 21st September, included the names of MM. Sotir Petsi, Suleiman Delvino, Redjeb Mitrovitza, and Dr. Michael Tourtoulis, but the names of some twenty prominent persons who continued to preserve an uncompromising attitude, notably Monsignor Fan Noli, Kassim Kotsuli, Ismail Hakki Tatzali, and Shevket Korcha, were not included (N.E. 13.10.27). Indeed, Zogu took every step compatible with national security to conciliate his opponents and enable them to participate in the building up of the Albanian State; but the Yugoslav authorities endeavoured to place difficulties in the way of those who had sought refuge in Yugoslavia, and who now wished to avail themselves of the amnesty (T. 5.11.27). The Cabinet was strengthened by the re-establishment of the Ministries of Education and Agriculture, filled by Djafer Ypi and Sif Kedhi respectively.

On the 15th September the autumn session of Parliament opened. In his opening speech (T. 19.9.27; N.E. 6 and 13.10.27) before the Senate and Chamber of Deputies, Ahmed Zogu stressed his desire to establish complete friendship with neighbouring countries. With reference to the Pact of Tirana, he declared that it

"was not directed against any Power, but only reaffirms and consolidates the integrity and independence of Albania. I avail myself of this opportunity", he continued, "to state that all the comments which describe the Pact of Tirana as a limitation of Albanian independence are nothing but insinuations. The Pact, indeed, respects Albanian sovereignty; and the Albanians, who have suffered so much to gain their freedom, would never place themselves under the yoke of any nation. . . . It is therefore untrue that the Pact of Tirana encroaches on Albania's independence. On this occasion I should like to send greetings and thanks to the Royal Italian Government for its political co-operation, and for the help that it has given us in the organization of our army. I would convey also a cordial greeting to our great friend, Signor Mussolini, for the sincere friendship which he has shown us on every occasion. This genuinely sincere policy, and this friendship subsisting between the two neighbouring States, will inaugurate a new era of progress for our nation. . . . Our programme is to maintain friendly relations with all States, and to conclude Agreements and Treaties with a view to consolidating not only our political relations, but also the development of our economic life. We are on the point of concluding a Commercial Treaty with Great Britain, towards whom the Albanian nation entertains very special gratitude on account of the effective support which she has given us in respect of our independence."

He expressed a hope that similar Treaties would be concluded with France, Egypt, Turkey, and Japan, and a Concordat with the Holy See, with which there existed the most cordial relations. The recent rupture with Yugoslavia had been honourably solved, which, he said, was proof of Albania's desire for friendly relations. In conclusion he expressed satisfaction with the internal situation, and stated that the work of internal reconstruction was progressing satisfactorily.

On the 14th October Tsena Kryeziu, appointed Albanian Minister to Czechoslovakia, was shot dead in the Café Passage at Prague by an Albanian student, twenty-three years of age, named Alcibiades Bebi, a native of Elbasan, who believed that it was Kryeziu's intention to deliver his country to Yugoslavia (N.E. 20.10.27; T. 3 and 17.10.27). Kryeziu, who was thirty-two years of age, hailed from Djakova, and came of a well-to-do family; his father had been A.D.C. to Abdul Hamid, and had taken part in the Albanian insurrection in 1912. Tsena had married Ahmed Zogu's sister, to whom, no doubt, his meteoric rise was partially attributable. He had become Governor of Skutari, then Minister of the Interior, but had disagreed with his brother-in-law's policy with regard to Italy (Temps, 17.10.27). He was a zealous partisan of Yugoslavia (N.E. 17.11.27; M.G. 25.10.27), and seems to have been guided by his personal attachment to that country rather than by the interests of his own (N.E. 23.6.27). Indeed, so inexplicable had been his conduct (M.G. 22.3.27), that his assassin had a reasonable justification for the crime, which merely reflected the widespread suspicion of Yugoslavia which existed in Albania, and for which Yugoslavia alone was responsible (N.E. 20.10.27). The deed evidently was premeditated, and Kryeziu had been warned by Tahir Shtylla that his life was in danger, but had disregarded the warning. His body was sent for burial to Tirana.

The assassin refused to reveal the source from whence came the funds which had enabled him to travel to Prague, and the Yugoslav Press at once accused Italy of complicity (M.G. 17.10.27), an attitude deprecated by the *Temps* (20.10.27), and by the European Press in general. Then followed reports that Kryeziu's supporters in Albania had risen in insurrection against Ahmed Zogu, who was held responsible for the murder, that troops had been called out and Italian assistance invoked (*Temps*, 25.10.27), all of which were equally untrue and officially denied.

On the 20th October the Albanian Cabinet resigned (T. 24.10.27) at the instigation of the President, certain changes having become necessary. Peter Poga had become too old to be sufficiently active. Feizi Alizoti was unpopular in the capacity of Minister of Finance, and was considered excessively Italophile (N.E. 10.11.27), a trait which, it was feared, might enable Italy to obtain an undesirable amount of control over the finances of the country and influence in the Cabinet. His successor was notoriously watchful in this respect (N.E. 17.11.27). Musa Yuka was an ardent Moslem, who had been charged with corruption and the commission of grave abuses (N.E. 19.5.27 and T. 5.11.27). His successor, a man of undoubted integrity, was ordered to investigate these charges and to adopt rigorous measures against "graft" (T. 5 and 19.11.27).

The new Cabinet was composed as follows:—

ELIAS VRIONI	Minister for Foreign Affairs and Minister of Justice *ad interim*.
ABDURRAHMAN DIBRA . .	Minister of the Interior.
DJAFER YPI	Minister of Education.
SULEIMAN STAROVA . . .	Minister of Finance.
HIL MOSSI	Minister of Public Works.
FERID VOKOPALA . . .	Minister of Agriculture.

Presumably as a further measure against abuses, Colonel Stirling, Adviser to the Minister of the Interior, was appointed Inspector of Government offices, and made directly responsible to the President. This, or a similar measure, was long overdue. Ahmed Zogu himself, ignorant of financial matters, had failed to suppress corruption—a legacy from the Turks—which was admitted by Albanians to be one of the chief curses of the country (T. 4.9.26). Especially did this apply to the gendarmerie, a state of affairs which the British Mission (increased in April, 1929, to eight inspectors with the rank of Major, in addition to General Percy and his Chief of Staff, Colonel Marten), while acting in a purely advisory capacity, was powerless to rectify.

The Italian Military Mission, under General Pariani, was strengthened by the arrival of a further twenty-five officers. Unlike the British Gendarmerie Mission, which is composed of ex-officers of the British Army in no way responsible to the British Government, and paid by the Albanian Government, the Italian officers are seconded for service in Albania from the Italian Army, and in consequence continue to draw their pay from their own authorities. This arrangement is, of course, the normal one, similar missions from other European Powers having served from time to time in the Balkans on the same basis. In April, 1929, the strength of the Italian Mission was forty-two officers (this figure does not include physical training instructors, surveyors, agricultural experts, and engineers, whose services Albania has been obliged to obtain in order to expedite development), acting as instructors in the Albanian Army (T. 5.11.27). In no case are they permitted to assume command of the units to which they are attached—except during actual training—and any attempt to place them in command would arouse the utmost indignation throughout the army (T. 23.6.28).

The standing strength of the Albanian Army, composed of conscripts who serve for eighteen months, and are drawn principally from the lowlands—the authority of the Government being still insufficient to enforce conscription rigidly in the most inaccessible districts—is approximately 8,000 men. It comprises three groups (quartered respectively at Tirana, Skutari, and Berat), each composed of three battalions, 500 strong, and three mountain artillery batteries. To each group an Italian colonel is attached, and an Italian officer to each battalion, battery, medical, veterinary, and transport unit. There is also at Tirana a guards battalion, 350 strong, four frontier "battalions" of mountaineers, classed as reservists, and commanded by their bairaktars, tanks of the whippet type, and armoured cars. In addition there are large reserves of malissori, untrained, but none the less the finest fighting material in Albania, who, in the event of war, would rally in defence of their country. There is a machine-gun and bombing school, and a cadet school at Tirana, an Italian instructor being in charge of each. A large reserve of officers is assured by the compulsory training at the cadet school of every young Albanian with a higher education.

Sir Harry Eyres declared that the Italian officers have preserved a perfectly correct attitude and have participated in no intrigues whatever. With regard to any misgivings which may be felt in connection with their presence in Albania, it should be remembered that as Albania's own military forces become more efficient and more capable of defending their soil against comitadjis, disguised Serbian troops, and insurrections fomented from without, so the contingency in which Albania would be obliged to seek the assistance of Italian troops becomes more remote. Once Albania is in a position to defend herself, except in the event of a declaration of war by Yugoslavia, there will be no pretext for Italian intervention. Moreover, Italy is fashioning a powerful weapon with which she herself would have to contend, should her policy towards Albania arouse resentment in that country.

That the Italian Mission is benefiting the Albanian Army is unquestionable, and that military service benefits the Albanian is equally so. The conscript is disciplined, taught to read and write, which enables him to grasp wider issues than those of his own locality, and, moreover, is drafted to different parts of the country, which enables him to meet compatriots with other problems than his own. That approximately 50 per cent. of the Albanian Budget is expended upon the army is, at first sight, alarming, but in consideration of the above benefits which military service confers, it may be justifiable.

During 1927 some 20,000 rifles, 40 mountain guns, 120 machine guns, and other military supplies were purchased from Italy—a quantity far in excess of the requirements of an army of 8,000 men; and upon this subject *No More War* (March, 1929) published an alarmist article. The writer evidently forgot that the peace establishment of a conscript army is but a proportion of its strength upon mobilization, and that if it is to be effective equipment for the whole must be available. Only when the League of Nations alone disposes of armed forces will such preparations be unnecessary in Albania. Lest in the "Albanian fleet" a threat to the peace of the world be discovered, it is as well to mention in passing that it consists at present (June, 1929) of two motor launches!

In March, 1926, there had been drawn up and initialled between France and Yugoslavia a Treaty of Friendship and Arbitration (T. 8 and 12.11.27). It had been provided that this Treaty "should be signed whenever one of the two parties expressed the desire", but M. Nintchitch had postponed its signature until a settlement between Italy and Yugoslavia had been reached. Moreover, he proposed to Mussolini in February, 1926, that Italy should be included in a Tripartite Pact. While one doubts the sincerity of M. Nintchitch no more than one does that of M. Trumbitch towards Albania in 1919–20, it must be admitted that Mussolini had every reason to consider that while the Serbian military party remained a factor in Yugoslav politics, the conclusion of a Pact with France and Yugoslavia would give that party an immeasurable advantage over Italy in Albania; and no doubt it was in these circumstances that Mussolini declared (on the 15th December, 1927, to the Council of Ministers, M.G. 16.12.27) that "for obvious reasons the proposal could not be accepted".

The Franco-Yugoslav Treaty was signed in Paris on the 11th November, 1927, by MM. Briand and Marinkovitch, at the instance of the latter. There was nothing in its terms to which exception could be taken by any country, and it covered no ground that was not already covered by the League of Nations. It merely confirmed the part which France is playing with regard to Yugoslavia, as the Pact of Tirana had confirmed Italy's policy with regard to Albania, both Powers taking parts previously played by Russia and Austria-Hungary. It contained nothing more than a mutual pledge of friendship and an undertaking by each contracting party not to make war upon the other, to submit any differences between them to arbitration, and, in the event that either should be attacked, to take counsel together (N.E. 17.11.27). As the Treaty had no other *raison d'être* than as a measure of protection against any aggression by Italy, the latter country had no cause for alarm unless she contemplated aggressive action, but on the other hand, it was feared that its existence might tend to encourage the irresponsible element in Yugo-slavia to fresh acts of defiance and aggression (T. 12.11.27). This view was shared in some French circles (N.E. 17.11.27; M.G. 8, 9, 10.11.27), where a true appreciation of the Yugo-slav character had been formed.

The signature of the Franco-Yugoslav Treaty seems to have been thought by Italy a favourable opportunity for the con-clusion of a fresh and more definitive Treaty with Albania; and at Tirana, on the 22nd November, was signed a Treaty of Defensive Alliance. This Treaty was as follows:

"Italy and Albania, wishing solemnly to reaffirm and develop the bonds of solidarity which happily exist between the two States, and to devote all their efforts to the elimination of causes that might disturb the peace between them mutually and with other States, recog-nizing the advantages that may result from close col-laboration between the two States, and once more affirming that the interest and security of the one are reciprocally bound up with the interest and security of the other, have resolved to conclude by this Treaty a Defensive Alliance of which the sole object is to stabilize the natural relations happily existing between the two States with a view to ensuring a policy of peaceful development, and have for that purpose named as their plenipotentiaries: H.M. the King of Italy, His Excellency Signor Ugo Sola, Italian Envoy Extraordinary and Minister Plenipotentiary in Albania: and the President of the Albanian Republic, His Excellency Elias bey Vrioni, Albanian Minister for Foreign Affairs: who, after the exchange of their full powers, found in good and due form, have agreed as follows:

"*Art.* 1. All former Treaties between the High Con-tracting Parties after the admission of Albania into the League of Nations shall be fully and faithfully observed in accordance with the terms of the said Treaties in such a manner as to assure complete amity between the two peoples and Governments. Each of the High Contracting

Parties shall support the interests of the other with the same zeal as each supports its own.

"*Art.* 2. There shall be a Defensive Alliance between Italy and Albania for twenty years. This Alliance may, however, be denounced during the eighteenth or nineteenth year of its life. Unless this be done the Alliance shall be automatically renewed for a further period of the same length. The two High Contracting Parties shall devote all their energies to guarantee the security of their States and to mutual defence against any attack from abroad.

"*Art.* 3. In consequence of the engagements undertaken in the preceding articles, the High Contracting Parties undertake to work together for the maintenance of peace. In the event of one of the two Parties being threatened by a war not provoked by it, the other Party shall use all means at its disposal not only to prevent hostilities, but also to secure just satisfaction to the threatened Party.

"*Art.* 4. When all efforts at conciliation have failed, each of the High Contracting Parties undertakes to throw in its lot with the other, and to put at the disposal of its ally all the military, financial, and other resources at its disposal if such aid is requested by the threatened Party.

"*Art.* 5. In all the eventualities foreseen by Art. 4, the two High Contracting Parties undertake not to conclude or to enter into negotiations for a peace, armistice, or truce, without mutual agreement.

"*Art.* 6. The present Treaty is signed in four original texts, two of which are in the Italian language and the other two in Albanian, all of which are equally authoritative.

"*Art.* 7. The present Treaty shall be ratified and then registered with the League of Nations. Ratifications shall be exchanged in Rome.

"Concluded at Tirana, the 22nd day of November, 1927.
"(*Signed*) UGO SOLA.
ELIAS VRIONI."

The following correspondence was annexed to the Treaty:

1. "A son Excellence Elias Vrioni, Ministre des affaires étrangères d'Albanie, Tirana.

"Monsieur le Ministre,

"En relation avec le traité d'alliance défensive signé aujourd'hui par nous-mêmes, et notamment dans l'éventualité regrettable que l'article 4 du traité même dût entrer en application, il est du vif désir du gouvernement italien de donner au gouvernement albanais les assurances et les éclaircissements suivants:—

"Dans le cas où ayant épuisé toutes les possibilités de conjurer par les moyens de conciliation une menace d'un tiers Etat contre un des deux Etats alliés, celui-ci se trouvait en présence d'une attaque non provoquée par lui-même, attaque qui rendrait nécessaire la demande du concours militaire du pays allié pour la défense de la Partie attaquée, le commandement en chef des forces interalliées serait donné en Albanie au commandant suprême des forces Albanaises, et en Italie au commandant suprême des forces italiennes.

"Au moment de la signature de la paix, les forces alliées venues au secours de l'autre Etat devront être rapatriées par leurs propres moyens dans un délai qui aura été établi par le commandant suprême sous les ordres duquel elles auront servi en territoire allié.

"Cette lettre forme une partie intégrante du traité d'alliance défensive italo-albanais, et sera ratifiée et ensuite enregistrée par la Société des Nations avec le traité même.

"Veuillez agréer etc.,

(*Signé*) Ugo Sola,
Ministre italien."

2. "A son Excellence Ugo Sola, envoyé extraordinaire et ministre plénipotentaire d'Italie à Tirana,

"Monsieur le Ministre,

"J'ai l'honneur de prendre acte de la lettre datée d'aujourd'hui, par laquelle Votre Excellence a bien voulu donner au gouvernement albanais quelques éclaircissements et assurances au sujet du traité d'alliance défensive signé aujourd'hui par nous-mêmes, et notamment au sujet de l'éventualité regrettable où l'article 4 du traité même dût entrer en application. En vous remerciant vivement pour ces déclarations spontanées faites par vous au nom du gouvernement royal, je suis heureux de donner au gouvernement italien, au nom du gouvernement albanais, les mêmes assurances.

"Veuillez agréer, etc.,

(*Signé*) Elias Vrioni,
Ministre des affaires étrangères albanais."

It would seem that the Italo-Albanian Treaty of Alliance had been drawn up some time previously, but that its signature had been postponed until the Franco-Yugoslav Treaty had been signed, so that the one might counterbalance the other (T. 26.11.27). Indeed, the existence of a military agreement had been rumoured at the time of the conclusion of the Pact of Tirana. It was reported that Ahmed Zogu had, prior to the signature of the Treaty of Alliance, informed the Yugoslav Minister of what was contemplated, but that Yugoslavia had not made any satisfactory alternative proposals (T. 25.11.27). The Yugoslav Government declared that its Minister in Tirana had been instructed to inform the Albanian Government that the conclusion of a Treaty of Alliance was considered unnecessary as no danger threatened Albania, that it would impose upon Albania fresh and unnecessary liabilities in excess of her economic capacity, and that it might prove dangerous politically (T. 26.11.27 and *Temps*, 27.11.27).

The conclusion of the Treaty was regarded in Italy with satisfaction. It was maintained that Italy's policy with regard to Albania was precisely similar to British policy with regard to Belgium and Portugal (T. 26.11.27), and indeed Signor Ugo Sola stated that the Treaty had been modelled upon the Treaty of Alliance existing between Great Britain and Portugal (M.G. 30.11.27 and *Temps*, 1.12.27) concluded on the 16th May, 1703 (S.P., Vol. I, Part 1). Italy pointed out that in the Treaty there was absolute reciprocity, and that she was the first Power to treat with Albania on an equal footing. The Treaty assured to Albania absolute security for twenty years, and to Italy free passage of the Straits of Otranto. If Albania was not assured of security, declared Signor Mussolini, she would become a second Macedonia (*Temps*, 5.12.27).

In France the opinion was widely expressed that the Treaty in no way altered the status of Albania, placed within the Italian sphere of influence by the Agreement of the 9th November, 1921, and whose independence was guaranteed by the League of Nations (T. 26.11.27). It would seem that the expression of this view was the outcome of fear lest any undue resentment of Italy's action might lead to a review of the situation by the League of Nations and the creation of a precedent for an examination of French policy in the Balkans. Should the League proceed to discuss the Italo-Albanian Treaties, a precedent, it was pointed out in the Fascist Party Order Sheet, would be created which would necessitate the discussion of all Treaties concluded since 1919, "many of them of a typical political and military character" (T. 30.11.27; and *Temps*, 1.12.27). For this reason France restrained Yugoslavia from any precipitate action or attempt to raise at Geneva the question of Italian policy in Albania (M.G. 26.11.27); and an attempt on the 2nd December by M. Marinkovitch to protest against acceptance, for registration, of the Treaty by the League, on the grounds that it presupposed a lack of faith in that body (*Temps*, 3.12.27) proved fruitless. In consequence of French restraint, the conclusion of the Treaty was received calmly in Yugoslavia, and there seemed to be a synchronization of the views expressed in the Press of both countries.

The Treaty was ratified by the Albanian Chamber of Deputies on the 26th November, by the Senate—which acclaimed Ahmed Zogu the "Saviour of the Nation" (N.E. 22.12.27)—on the 30th, and signed by the President on the 2nd December. It was ratified by the Italian Chamber of Deputies on the 4th December, and by the Italian Senate on the 14th December. It was received in informed circles in Albania with satisfaction, and demonstrations in its favour took place (N.E. 8.12.27), although there were some who received the news of its conclusion with misgivings, resenting, with that independence which is characteristic of the Albanian, a Treaty which tied them to Italy, in the same way as they would resent any Treaty binding them to any country.

There should be no misgivings. Albania needed support, economic, diplomatic, and military, to precisely the same extent and perhaps even more than Greece, Serbia, or Bulgaria had done during their infancy as independent States, and a careful examination of Albanian history since her admission to the League of Nations proves that the guarantees and support which that organization is under an obligation to afford her are wholly inadequate. Something more specific than the League's guarantees was needed, and that was supplied by the Pact of Tirana and its natural complement the Treaty of Alliance. There is nothing aggressive in either of them. They merely safeguard Albania against the perpetual interference of an aggressive neighbour whose policy alone made them necessary. Fear of Yugoslavia impelled Albania to grasp the hand of friendship—admittedly "friendship for interest"—extended to her by Italy (N.E. 1.12.27). It is to be hoped that Yugoslavia may now realize that the overbearing policy which she has pursued consistently since the conclusion of the Great War towards all her southern neighbours has a more profitable alternative.

Note:—The text of the Treaty of Tirana, in Albanian and Italian, with translations in English and French, and the annexed correspondence, are published in the *League of Nations Treaty Series*,† Vol. LXIX, pp 342-53.

CHAPTER XII

THE ALBANIAN KINGDOM

New Year's Day, 1928, found Albania definitely committed to a close Entente with Italy as the only alternative to perpetual anarchy or instability. But there was widespread apprehension in Europe, encouraged by a skilful propaganda, lest in seeking Italian protection from Yugoslavia Ahmed Zogu had forfeited Albanian independence to Italy. It was therefore expedient that, while reaping the benefits of Italian friendship, Albania should lose no opportunity of reasserting both for her own satisfaction and for that of those who shared these apprehensions, her sovereignty and independence, a policy which Italy, her vital interests secured, had no reason to oppose. These circumstances seem to provide at the same time the keynote of and justification for the culminating event in Albania's renaissance.

But in the interval between the signature of the Treaty of Alliance and the occurrence of the above event, various incidents and events worthy of record took place.

On the 1st January, 1928, the new Albanian Penal Code, based almost without variation upon that of Italy, came into force and replaced the modified Ottoman Code formerly in use (N.E. 19.1.28). This was followed by the adoption of a new Civil Code (modelled upon that of France), designed to give every Albanian subject equal status; it passed the Chamber of Deputies, which assembled on the 1st March, unopposed, and the Senate by a large majority. (It came into operation on the 1st April, 1929.) Opposition to the Code emanated chiefly from some Catholics who resented the recognition therein of marriage as a civil matter and the provision made for divorce. During the same session a Bill was passed replacing the Turkish tithe system by a land tax.

The opposition to the divorce facilities provided for all Albanian subjects of whatever denomination led to the failure of an attempt to negotiate a Concordat with the Vatican. There being five Roman Catholic bishoprics in Albania, MM. Yuk Koci (a deputy) and Demetri Poppa (of the Foreign Office) had been dispatched to Rome for this purpose in the middle of December, but returned unsuccessful during February (N.E. 29.12.27 and 16.2.28).

During February MM. Djafer Villa (Secretary-General of the Ministry of Foreign Affairs) and Milto Tutulani (a deputy) were sent to Athens to induce the Greek Government to fulfil the obligations incurred by the Treaty signed on the 13th October, 1926, especially with regard to the rights of the Albanian minorities in Greece and the expropriation of their property, which continued. But the delegates returned to Tirana during March without achieving practical results (N.E. 16.2.28 and 29.3.28), and the question of Albanian minorities continued to cause friction between the two countries. The Greek Government even refused to allow the Albanian Red Cross to send maize to the starving Tchams (N.E. 12.2.28).

Eventually the Albanian Government appealed to the League of Nations under Art. 11 for its intervention on behalf of the Albanian minorities, some 35,000 Moslem Albanians of Epirus still being subjected to persecution by the Greek authorities.

At its Fiftieth Session, in June, 1928, this appeal was considered by the Council. M. Politis, the Greek delegate, maintained that Albanian interference in Greek internal affairs was unjustified, that Art. 11 should not be invoked in minority disputes, and that only a State member of the Council was entitled to raise minority questions; he maintained that the Agrarian Law under which expropriation of Albanian property was carried out was applicable to all Greek subjects, although in practice it seems that it applied only to Albanians, who were the principal landowners. The Albanian Government, on the other hand, maintained that Albanian minorities in Greece should enjoy the same privileges as Greek minorities in Albania; moreover, M. Roufos, then Greek Minister for Foreign Affairs, had admitted before the Council in March, 1926, that the Albanian complaints were reasonable and had undertaken to rectify them, but the promise had remained unfulfilled and the Council failed to insist upon its fulfilment.

Sir Austen Chamberlain declared that since the Albanian minorities themselves had the right to appeal to the League— whether, in fact, they could do so is doubtful—the Albanian

HIS MAJESTY ZOG I, KING OF THE ALBANIANS

Government's appeal should be rejected on principle; its consideration would create a dangerous precedent for the raising of small grievances, which would thus acquire an exaggerated importance. Accordingly the appeal was rejected (N.E. 21.6.28).

A further cause of friction with Greece was the pressure which that country had brought to bear to prevent the Patriarchate from regularizing the position of the Albanian Orthodox Church created at the Congress of Berat in 1922, the outcome of an unfriendly attitude only modified during General Pangalos's régime. To clear up matters in this connection which remained outstanding, four Albanian Orthodox Bishops met at Tirana during May (N.E. 24.5.28).

Despite these causes of friction, the Greek Government granted in January a subsidy to the Yannoulatos S.S. Co. for the inauguration of a regular coastal service between Peiræus and the Albanian ports (T. 11.1.28), thereby showing a desire to develop commercial intercourse. In the same month the Mazurana Co. of Trieste obtained a concession for the construction of the port of Durazzo at an estimated cost of £320,000 (N.E. 19.1.28). Provision was also made for the canalization of the Bojana, but a proposal by Yugoslavia that she should share the expense of this undertaking with Albania was reported to have been rejected (N.E. 24.5.28), presumably because acceptance would have given the Yugoslavs an undesirable measure of control in the enterprise.

Failure of crops, and economic difficulties, again caused a famine in the Dibra and Skutari regions during the winter of 1927–8, and relief work was entrusted to a commission under Senator Hafiz Khemal. The Italian Government contributed large supplies of food and clothing.

Considerable satisfaction was given by the visit to Valona from the 20th January to the 3rd February of a British squadron of nine destroyers and the supply ship *Sandhurst*, under the command of Captain Cyril Benson, D.S.O., of H.M.S. *Broke*. In an interesting football match between the British and a combined Tirana and Valona team, the British won by seven goals to five.

Three diplomatic changes of importance took place during the early part of the year. In January M. S. Mihajlovitch was appointed Yugoslav Minister in Albania; a report of his assassination in July was without foundation. During March

Ekrem bey Vlora, appointed Albanian Minister to Great Britain and France, arrived in London, and established his Legation at 116 Inverness Terrace. And in April Sir Robert Macleod Hodgson, K.B.E., C.M.G., formerly Chargé d'Affaires in Moscow, was appointed to succeed Mr. William Seeds, who had been appointed British High Commissioner for the Rhineland. During April also the United States Government submitted to Faik bey Konitza, Albanian Minister to the United States, the draft of a proposed Treaty of Arbitration (*U.S. Daily*, 26.2.28), which was eventually signed in October.

When in March the question of Albania's payment of the interest due upon the loan from the S.V.E.A. again arose, a further postponement of the date for payment of the first instalment was arranged, this time until the end of 1930.

Relations between Albania and Yugoslavia, which during the remainder of the year pursued an even tenor, due perhaps to internal discord in the latter country, were, however, disturbed at the beginning of April when the Albanian Government closed the frontier in the Ochrida–Pogradets region in view of an alleged epidemic of typhus. The Yugoslav Government protested that there was no epidemic, but merely a few isolated cases, and within three days the frontier was re-opened. The incident would be unworthy of mention were it not for the undue prominence given to it by the Yugoslav Press, which drew all manner of alarmist and unfounded inferences, notably that the frontier had been closed to conceal preparation supported by Italy for a comitadji raid from Albanian soil. Actually the Albanian Government had taken special precautions to prevent the occurrence of such raids.

A report in May that Italy intended to declare a customs union with Albania—a report which was without any foundation—led to a heated debate in the Shkupstina which proved that Yugoslav hostility towards Italy had in no way abated (N.E. 3 and 17.5.28). But the murders in the Shkupstina on the 20th June, and their consequences, distracted Yugoslav attention from foreign affairs, except in the case of the ratification of the Nettuno Conventions, which was eventually carried out on the 13th August.

On the 9th May the Albanian Cabinet resigned, ostensibly owing to a difference of opinion between the Ministers of Public Works and the Interior over a law regulating the toll tax for the maintenance and construction of roads. Actually, no doubt, the President's desire for a reconstituted Cabinet led to the resignation. On the 11th the following Cabinet took office:

Hiqmet Delvino . . .	President of the Council of Ministers, and Minister of Justice.
Kotcho Kotta	Minister of the Interior.
Elias Vrioni	Minister for Foreign Affairs.
Djafer Ypi	Minister of Education.
Milto Tutulani . . .	Minister of Finance, and Minister of Agriculture *ad interim*.
Salih Vucheterni . . .	Minister of Public Works.

The Ministry of Agriculture was filled in September by Musa Yuka, whose return to office despite his well-known faults, seems to have been due to his outstanding ability and energy. That while recalling him to power the President had no intention to condone malpractices is proved by the arrest and trial of Colonel Kassim Sejfedin, Commander-in-Chief of the Albanian Gendarmerie. To preside over this court, constituted to try officials charged with corruption, General Sir Jocelyn Percy was recalled during June from command of the troops in northern Albania.

Delvino, in announcing the Government's programme, declared that

"the Treaties and Conventions in force will be strictly observed, especially the Treaty of Defensive Alliance concluded with Italy. In this way, inspired by the ideas and the principles of the League of Nations, Albania will endeavour in every way possible to show to the civilized world that she is truly an element of peace in the Balkans, while always safeguarding her independence."

The importance of physical training was specially stressed, and nine Italian officers were appointed to introduce the Balilla system into the schools. This raised the number of Italian officers serving in Albania to 62, including 20 doctors and technicians (*Temps*, 13.10.28).

Elias Vrioni, Mehdi Frasheri, and Djafer Villa were nominated to represent Albania before the Council of the League of Nations on the 5th June. The proceedings at this meeting have been discussed.

Shortly after the formation of the new Cabinet, the President issued a decree proclaiming that elections for a Constituent Assembly to meet at Tirana on the 25th August would be held during July and the first half of August. The Assembly was called to effect certain modifications of the Albanian Constitution, and it was freely rumoured that these modifications were rendered necessary by Ahmed Zogu's intention to proclaim himself King—a rumour which proved entirely correct.

This rumour gave rise to a wave of monarchical enthusiasm which seems to have been spontaneous, although the manner in which the principal enthusiasts organized demonstrations led to some doubts as to their entire spontaneity (T. 2.9.28). Ahmed Zogu was called upon to accept the throne as the saviour of the nation by a grateful people.

Meantime the Albanian Government approached certain Powers, and ascertained that the proposed change of status of the country would be recognized, provided it was acceptable to the Albanian people.

On the 25th August the Constituent Assembly met under the Presidency of Pandele Evangheli, whose patriotism had ever been beyond question. On the same day the Assembly acclaimed the proposed change of the Constitution, and a committee was appointed to draw up the necessary amendments. On Saturday, the 1st September, these amendments were approved by the Assembly, and Ahmed Zogu proclaimed "Zog I, King of the Albanians".

In the afternoon of that eventful day the new King was escorted to the Parliament House through streets lined with troops and packed with Moslems and Christians from all parts of Albania, among them enthusiastic bands of Catholic Mirdites, and there took the following oath to the revised Constitution:—

> "I, Zog, King of the Albanians, on the occasion of ascending the throne of the Kingdom of Albania and taking into my hands royal power, swear before Almighty God to maintain the national unity, independence, and territorial integrity of the State. I will faithfully adhere to the Constitution and act in conformity with its provisions and the laws in force, keeping always before my eyes the will of the people. May God help me."

In his speech to the Assembly the King declared that he accepted the throne because he believed it to be the will of the people, and that should he not prove worthy of their expectations he would yield place to a better man. That elaborate precautions were taken to prevent an attempt being made against his life does not indicate that any section of the population was opposed to him; but in a land where the blood feud had been the custom of the country there were many who would have availed themselves of any opportunity to be avenged for some well-deserved punishment or the execution of a relative. Moreover, Monsignor Noli's handful of fanatical and uncompromising adherents still sought vengeance for their discomfiture by a régime which they described as tyrannical (N.E. 14.6.28), and declared that the proclamation of Zogu as King was "an odious crime" against the Albanian people.

Among Noli's associates there were certainly some who believed that the Prince of Wied was still their legitimate sovereign, and therefore supported Noli's protests in good faith and through loyalty to their oath of fidelity to Prince William. The latter might still enlist the active support of a number of Albanians—among them some whose disloyalty to Zogu rather than loyalty to himself would induce them to ally themselves with any revolutionary movement—if he departed from the honourable policy which he has hitherto pursued; but he merely registered a formal protest, while reaffirming his intention to take no steps which were not supported by the Albanian people.

Italy was the first Power to recognize the change in the status of Albania, and Italian recognition was announced by the Italian Minister directly the King had taken the oath to the Constitution. This prompt recognition led to a wave of enthusiasm in favour of Italy. In a subsequent exchange of correspondence between Elias Vrioni and Ugo Sola, the Italian official attitude was expressed as follows:—

"The Royal Italian Government considers the establishment of the monarchical régime in Albania as a happy event which, while further strengthening the bonds existing between the two countries, will ensure the continuity of their common policy which finds in the Treaty of Alliance its highest expression. Italy will therefore always remain profoundly faithful to that intimate entente whose brilliant results in general policy it has pleased Your Excellency to emphasize. I can assure you that the Italian Government will never fail to consult the Albanian Government in every matter which may concern our common interests, and to act in agreement with it in all questions pertaining to the situation in the Balkans."

A cordial exchange of telegrams between Zogu and King Victor Emmanuel and Signor Mussolini also took place. Congratulations from the majority of European rulers, including Admiral Condouriotis, President of the Greek Republic, followed. Great Britain officially recognized the new king on the 22nd September, the United States on the 13th, and the majority of the other Powers before the end of the month. Baron Gaston de Vaux, the French Minister, was received in audience by the King on the 16th October; and a Consular Convention with France was ratified early in November. Yugoslavia alone of European Powers betrayed pique over the change, attributing her annoyance to Zogu's assumption of the title "King of the Albanians"; but the internal situation seems to have prevented her from taking diplomatic action in the matter (T. 17.8.28), and following an interview between the Acting Minister for Foreign Affairs and the British Minister in Belgrade, she recognized Albania as a kingdom on the 17th September.

Zogu's assumption of the title "King of the Albanians" may be considered a provocative act towards Yugoslavia; but apart from the legitimacy of irredentist claims, however dangerous or futile they may be, it was a concession to the irredentists and therefore a step towards the consolidation of the King's position. Moreover, Albanian minorities do not exist alone in Yugoslavia, and the Greeks, aware of the Albanians in their midst whose existence they had so frequently denied, also betrayed some displeasure at the King's title. On the other hand, there exist large Albanian colonies in the United States, Italy, and elsewhere, and the Albanians who comprise them regard Albania as their Motherland and her King as their King; so that the title appears to be perfectly legitimate if somewhat audacious, and was whole-heartedly supported by Albanian public opinion, although unfavourably criticized in many foreign circles.

The proclamation of Zogu as King was, firſt and foremoſt, a reassertion of Albanian sovereignty, and as such was endorsed by all those who regarded Italian policy in Albania with suspicion and misgivings. Italy seized the opportunity, by giving the change of Conſtitution her unqualified support, to demonſtrate the sincerity of her friendship and loyalty to the principle of Albanian independence. To Italy, as indeed to all thoughtful people, it appeared that a sovereign is less easily dislodged by foreign intrigue or by revolution engineered beyond the frontier; moreover, he is less liable personally to foreign influence than a President with a limited period of office. A monarchy avoids rivalry between chieftains during presidential elections, and provides an element of ſtability that an eaſtern or Balkan Republic muſt ever lack. In short, an Albanian Republic was an anomaly, whereas a monarchy with its pomp and ceremony is underſtood by the Albanian, accuſtomed through the ages to owe allegiance to a chieftain. Therefore Zogu, disciplining his independent and spirited subjects through the medium they understand beſt—military service in an army owing allegiance to a sovereign—may reasonably anticipate the consolidation of his position and the independence of his Kingdom.

There remains only the personal element. Zogu shares with all those who rise to power the actuating force of ambition. But ambition does not exclude patriotism. Zogu's ambition has been rewarded by the crown of Albania, and it is but human nature that it should have been gratified. Is the throne of Albania the goal of his ambition, or does he aspire to a more enduring fame? Will he be content with a life of luxury and ease, squandering his country's resources —but of this there is as yet no indication—or does he aspire to the gratitude of his people? Is he a mere adventurer, or is he the greateſt of Albanian patriots?

.   .   .   .   .

Thus, in the space of fifty years, did Albania rise from a mere "geographical expression" to a Kingdom. From a remote region of a ramshackle Empire, she has become an independent State with every prospect of prosperity, a ſtabilized exchange, a reasonable foreign policy, a powerful ally, and a capable sovereign. But the hiſtory of the Albanian Kingdom has yet to be written—it has yet to be made.

BIBLIOGRAPHY

(Authors mentioned in the text are marked *. Books contained in the Library of the Royal Institute of International Affairs or the London Library are marked †, those in the Library of the Royal Geographical Society ‡.)

N.B.—In order to save space and footnotes, index letters have been used in the text when it has been necessary to make frequent reference to the same source of information. These letters appear below, on the right of the works to which they refer, and represent as far as possible the initials of the book referred to or those of its author. (For example, references to the *Encyclopædia Britannica*, from which much subsidiary information has been drawn, are shown thus: E.B. 1 : 659 = Vol. 1, page 659; and in the case of Parliamentary Debates, P.D. 62 : 418, 898, 1555 = Vol. 62 : pages 418, 898, 1555). The Bibliography is arranged in six sections in Alphabetical order, Sections I, II, and III being in the Alphabetical order of the index letters. *The Author's comments in Sections III and IV refer only to the value of the works to a student of Albanian history, and NOT to their intrinsic value.*

SECTION I

UNPUBLISHED MATTER.

(Manuscripts and Correspondence)

Albania: The Six Months Kingdom. D. Heaton Armstrong *	Manuscript. The writer was Private Secretary to H.H. Prince William of Wied.	A.m/s.
Denkschrift über Albanien.† Von Wilhelm Fürst von Albanien, Prinz zu Wied *	Privately printed in Berlin.	D.W.
Dokumenta Historike për t'i Shërbye. † *Lef Nosi* *	Published in Albanian in 12 parts, at Elbasan, 1924. Partial translation † (m/ss) by Q. E. Kastrati.	N.D.
Correspondence with Mgr. Fan Noli *	Mgr. Noli very kindly answered a questionnaire, and corresponded on various matters.	N.N.
L'Aventure Albanaise. Prince Michel Sturdza *	Manuscript. The writer is now Councillor of the Roumanian Legation at Washington. A spirit of adventure induced him to take part in the events of 1914.	S.m/s.

Letters and Notes from H.H.   H.H. very kindly read through   W.N.
  *the Prince of Wied **   the original draft of the chap-
                                   ter dealing with his reign,
                                   based his notes upon it, and
                                   discussed it at length, includ-
                                   ing certain adverse criticisms
                                   contained in it.

SECTION II

NEWSPAPERS AND PERIODICALS FROM WHICH INFORMATION WAS DRAWN
   (BEYOND THAT FROM THOSE ARTICLES AND REPORTS TO WHICH
   SPECIFIC REFERENCES ARE GIVEN IN THE TEXT. THE MAJORITY OF THE
   ARTICLES REFERRED TO MAY BE FOUND IN THE FILES OF PRESS CUTTINGS
   AND PERIODICALS OF THE ROYAL INSTITUTE OF INTERNATIONAL
   AFFAIRS).

The Adriatic Review. Sep-   Published monthly by the Vatra   A.R.
  tember 1918–22   from September, 1918; Edi-
                                   torial Offices: 97 Compton
                                   Street, Boston, U.S.A.

Corriere della Sera   C.S.

Daily Mail   D.M.

Daily Telegraph   D.T.

Le Matin   Matin.

Manchester Guardian   M.G.

Morning Post   M.P.

The Near East and India,†   A very valuable weekly paper   N.E.
  formerly *The Near East*   dealing with Near Eastern
                                   affairs. A section is devoted
                                   to each Balkan State.

The Times †   Very valuable for the periods   T.
                                   1909–14 (inclusive) and
                                   1925–9 (inclusive), especi-
                                   ally the former.

Le Temps   Temps.

Reconstruction. April, 1921–   A Journal published fortnight-
  June, 1923   ly, in English, dealing with
                                   Balkan and Central Euro-
                                   pean affairs. Editorial and
                                   Publishing Offices: Burg,
                                   Michaelertor, Vienna, 1.

SECTION III

Books, Pamphlets, and Specific Articles to which reference is made in the text.

Geographical Review. Art.: "The Awakening of Albania."‡ Brig-.Gen. G. P. Scriven, U.S.A. — U.S., Aug., 1919.Vol. 8. pp. 73–83. Interesting, but of no value. A.A.

Economic and Financial Situation of Albania. Professor Albert Calmès * (Luxemburg). — London, Sept., 1922. Important pamphlet. A.C.

Albania: Its Discontents and their Origin.† Morton F. Eden * — Lovejoy, London, 1921. 23 pp. Very valuable. A.D.

Austrian Foreign Policy, 1908–18.† A. F. Pribram — Allen & Unwin, 1923, 128 pp. Important. A.H.

The Albanian Question.† Mehmed bey Konitza * — Williams Lea, London, 1919. 27 pp. Very valuable. A.Q.

Albanais et Slaves.† "Lumo Skendo" (Midhat Frasheri *) — Librairie Centrale des Nationalités, Lausanne, 1919, 62 pp. Exhaustive bibliography, and 9 extremely valuable ethnographical maps. A.S.

Albania's Reply to the Demands of M. Venizelos — Pamphlet published by the Anglo-Albanian Society. Interesting. A.V.

Die Kriegsschuldfrage. Art.: "Albaniens Werdegang."† Alfred Rappaport — Sept., 1927. pp. 815–44. Numerous references to official documents. Important. A.W.

The Burden of the Balkans.† M. E. Durham* — Thos. Nelson, London, 1905. 384 pp. Very valuable. B.B.

Causes of the War.† M. Bogitchevich, LL.D., former Chargé d'Affaires of Serbia in Germany — C. L. Van Langenhuysen, Amsterdam, 1919, 135 pp. Interesting revelations. Bogitchevich

Ben Kendim: A Record of Eastern Travel.† Hon. Aubrey Herbert, M.P.* — Hutchinson, London, 1924. 380 pp. Interesting. B.K.

Balkan Problems and European Peace.† N. Buxton * and C. L. Leese. — Allen & Unwin, London, 1919. 135 pp. Deals mainly with Bulgaria. B.P.

Twenty Years of Balkan Tangle.† M. E. Durham * — Allen & Unwin, London, 1920. 292 pp. A valuable record of events in the Balkans which culminated in the Great War. B.T.

Albania, Paſt and Present.† Constantine Chekrezi * — Macmillan, New York, 1919. 255 pp. Valuable, but superficial, and occasionally inaccurate. Bibliography. — C.C.

Report of the International Commission to Enquire into the Causes and Conduct of the Balkan Wars † — Carnegie Endowment for International Peace. Washington, 1914. 418 pp. Contains useful maps. Effectively lifts the veil of propaganda for the pre-war period of Balkan history. — C.E.

Documents Diplomatiques; Les Affaires Balkaniques, 1912–14.† 3 Vols. — Ministère des Affaires Etrangères. Imprimerie Nationale, Paris, 1922. Interesting. — D.D.

A Difficult Frontier.† Henry Baerlein — Parsons, London, 1922. 155 pp. Interesting as an echo of Serbian propaganda, but otherwise quite worthless. — D.F.

The Danger Zone of Europe.† H. Charles Woods — Fisher Unwin, London, 1911. pp. 87 to 119 deal with the Albanian revolts of 1909–11. Important. — D.Z.

Abdul Hamid.† Sir Edwin Pears — Conſtable, London, 1917. 365 pp. Interesting, but of little value. — E.P.

Asiatic Review. Art.: "The Queſtion of the Greco-Albanian Frontier in Epirus."‡C.P. Casanges* — Vol. 3, 1914, 15 pp. The Greek point of view. Propaganda. — F.E.

Albania. Foreign Office handbook No. 17† — H.M. Stationery Office, London, 1920. 100 pp. Important. — F.O.

L'Albania. Artruro Galanti — Biblioteca Italo-Albanese, Vol. I, Societa Editrice Dante Alighieri, Rome, 1901. 252 pp. Exhauſtive bibliography. Valuable for period before 1880, especially for Skenderbeg, Ali Pasha, and the Bushati. — G.A.

Correspondence Relating to the Adriatic Queſtion.† Miscellaneous. No. 2 — H.M. Stationery Office, 1920. 32 pp. Valuable. — G.B.

Report of the Committee on Greek Territorial Claims. 6th March, 1919 — All references are drawn from S.A. Important; but the conclusions set forth were formed by biased (or misinformed) representatives to serve political ends. — G.C.

Geographical Journal. Art.: "The Future of the Albanian State."‡ J. S. Barnes — Vol. 52. 18 pp. London, 1918. Interesting. G.J.

The Greek Operations in Epirus.† Capt. A. Trapmann — Lecture delivered at the United Services Institution, 5th March, 1913. Keliher, London. 16 pp. The Greek point of view, reflecting Greek propaganda. G.O.

High Albania.† M. E. Durham * — Arnold, London, 1909. 348 pp., and valuable map. Deals fully with organization and customs of the Albanian tribes, and includes some important historical notes. H.A.

Harmsworth's Countries of the World. Art.: "Albania." Henry Baerlein — Amalgamated Press, 1924. 16 pp. Wholly misleading, and exceptionally bad taste. H.C.

Histoire Diplomatique de la Grèce.† É. Driault and M. Lhéritier — 5 Vols. Presses Universitaires, Paris, 1925–6. Of little value. H.D.

The Hapsburg Monarchy.† H. Wickham Steed — Constable, London, 1913. 304 pp. Interesting. H.M.

Hellas and the Balkan Wars.‡ D. J. Cassavetti, M.A.* — Fisher Unwin, London, 1913. 368 pp. The Greek point of view. Propaganda. H.W.

Memoirs of Ismail Kemal Bey † — Edited by S. Story, Constable, London, 1920. 410 pp. A section reprinted from the *Quarterly Review*, July, 1917 (Article: "Albania and the Albanians"), deals with the Albanian declaration of independence, etc. Important.

L'Albanie et les Albanais.† Jacques Bourcat — Bossard, Paris, 1921. 264 pp. The author writes from personal experience of Albania during and immediately after the War. Very valuable. J.B.

Les Albanais chez eux et à l'Étranger.† "Lumo Skendo" (Midhat Frasheri*) — Preface by M. Eugene Pittard.* Lausanne, 1919. 27 pp. Bibliography. Interesting. L.S.

The Macedonian Campaign.† Luigi Villari — Allen & Unwin, London, 1922. 285 pp. Interesting. M.C.

MM

A History of the Peace Conference of Paris.† Edited by H. W. V. Temperley	6 Vols. Issued by the Royal Institute of International Affairs. Oxford University Press, London, 1921. Important.	P.C.
Parliamentary Debates (1908–28)		
House of Commons †	Most important.	P.D.
House of Lords †	Most important.	P.D.L.
The Secret Treaties of Austria-Hungary.† A. F. Pribram Vol. 1. Texts of the Treaties and Agreements	Harvard University Press, Cambridge, U.S.A. 308 pp. References in text to Vol. 1 only. Most important.	Pribram.
Vol. 2. Negotiations leading to the Treaties of the Triple Alliance	271 pp.	
The Peaks of Shala.† R. W. Lane	Chapman & Dodd, London, 1922. 224 pp. Interesting sketch of the Albanian tribes, but of no political value.	P.S.
Procès-Verbaux de la Commission Internationale pour la Frontière Méridionale Albanaise ‡	Florence, 1913. Tip. Barbera Alfani e Venturi prop. An official document of great interest dealing with the Greco-Albanian frontier question in 1913.	P.V.
La Question Adriatique.† Adriaticus	Imprimerie Typographique, Paris, 1920. 158 pp. Valuable	Q.A.
La Question de Koritza.† Demètre Kolovani	Dieval, Paris (undated). 95 pp. Bibliography. Very valuable.	Q.K.
*Southern Albania or Northern Epirus in European International Affairs,*1912–23.† Edith Pierpont Stickney	Stanford University Press, U.S.A., 1926. 191 pp. A very valuable book with useful maps, but misleading for period 1912–14. Deals only with southern Albania. Exhaustive bibliography.	S.A.
The Salonika Front. Capt. A. J. Mann, M.A.	Black, London, 1920. 209 pp. Interesting.	S.F.
British and Foreign State Papers †	H.M. Stationery Office. Important.	S.P.
The Struggle for Scutari.† M. E. Durham *	Arnold, London, 1914. 320 pp. Deals fully with events in northern Albania in 1912 and 1913. Most important.	S.S.
Négociations relatives au Traité de Berlin.† Adolphe d'Avril	E. Leroux, Paris, 1886. 474 pp. Valuable.	T.B.

Turkey in Europe.† Sir Charles Eliot, K.C.M.G.	Valuable chapter on the Albanians (pp. 348–70) and Vlachs (370–9).	T.E.
Albania, the Foundling State of Europe.‡ Wadham Peacock. (One-time British Consul-General in Albania)	Chapman & Hall, London, 1914. Interesting, but of little political value. 264 pp.	W.P.
The Nineteenth Century and After. Art.: "Albania."‡ W. R. Stirling *	April, 1926. Vol. 99. pp. 495–501. Interesting.	W.S.

SECTION IV

BOOKS, PAMPHLETS, AND ARTICLES CONSULTED, BUT TO WHICH NO REFERENCE IS MADE.

Les Albanais et les Grandes Puissances.† Dr. Vladan Georgevitch*	Calmann-Lévy, Paris, 1913. 332 pp. The Serbian point of view.
Albania and Illyria.‡ Edward Lear	Bentley, London, 1852. 416 pp. Of no value.
Albania and Her Neighbours.† By an Australian	London, 1921. 16 pp. A useful sketch of the situation of Albania.
L'Albanie en 1921.† Justin Godart *	Les Presses Universitaires de France, Paris, 1922. 334 pp. Interesting.
L'Albanie et Napoléon, 1797–1814.† A. Boppe.	Hachette et Cie, Paris, 1914. 276 pp. Interesting.
Albania. The Problem of the Adriatic †	Foreign Policy Association. Information Service. Vol. III, No. 8, 22nd June,1927.14 pp. Interesting.
The Cradle of the War.† H. Charles Woods	Murray, London, 1919. 360 pp. Valuable chapter: "Albania and the Albanians."
Discovery.‡ Art. "Tribes of Northern Albania." M. E. Durham.*	Vol. VI, 1925. 5 pp. Interesting.
Economic Conditions in Albania. Maxwell Blake * (U.S. representative in Albania)	Trade Information Bulletin No. 83. Published by the Bureau of Foreign and Domestic Commerce, Government Printing Office, Washington, 1923. Valuable.
Epirus and Albania, 1919; question of Northern Epirus at the Peace Conference.† N. J. Cassavetes *	Published for the Pan-Epirotic Union of America by the Oxford University Press, New York, 1919. 172 pp. The Greek point of view.

European Economic and Political Survey

Paris, Fortnightly.

    Art.: "The Agreement of 26th April, 1927, between Italy and Albania." †

Vol. II, No. 18. 31st May, 1927. Facts only.

    Art.: "Albania"

Vol. IV, No. 1, 15th Sept., 1928. 15 pp., incl. extensive bibl. Valuable.

Foreign Affairs

New York. Monthly.

    Art.: "Albania and her Protectress."† W. Miller

April, 1927. 8 pp. Misleading.

    Art.: "Italy, Yugoslavia, and Lilliputia." † H. Fish Armstrong

Jan., 1928. 12 pp. Extremely foolish.

The Fortnightly Review

    Art.: "The Situation in Albania and in Macedonia."‡ H. Charles Woods

May, 1912. 14 pp. Important.

    Art.: "Albania—Yesterday and To-morrow." † H. Charles Woods

Aug., 1927. 12 pp. Interesting.

Italy, Greece, and the League.† H. Wilson Harris

League of Nations Union Pamphlet No. 125. 31 pp. Discussion of the League's attitude with regard to the Corfu incident of 1923.

The Janina Murders and the Occupation of Corfu.† George Glasgow

The Anglo-Hellenic League, London, 1923. Contains report of the investigations of the Inter-Allied Control Commission in Epirus.

Macedonia. Its Races and their Future.† H. N. Brailsford

Methuen, London, 1906. 340 pp. Interesting.

Memorandum and Appeal to the League of Nations †

United Committee of Kossovo and Chameria [Tchamouria]; Boston, U.S.A., 24th Aug., 1921. 8 pp.

My Memoirs, 1879–1918.† Ex-Kaiser Wilhelm II *

Cassell, London, 1922. 334 pp. References of value, to Albania (p. 159), and the Prince of Wied (p. 161).

My Mission to London, 1912–14.† Prince Lichnowsky *

Doran, New York, 45 pp. Interesting.

The New Balkans.† H. Fish Armstrong

Harper & Bros., New York, 1927. 179 pp. Of no value.

New York Times Current History, Jan., 1923

    Art.: "The Betrayal of Greece by Lloyd George " †

Interesting as a defence of King Constantine and indictment of M. Venizelos by an impartial authority. 4 pp.

Pour l'Albanie.† "Lumo Skendo" (Midhat Frasheri *) — Lausanne, 1919. 8 pp. Plea for the re-establishment of Albanian independence. Of no importance.

Le Statut Constitutionnel de la République Albanaise — Bureau de la Presse, Tirana, 1925. 35 pp.

Visits to Monasteries of the Levant.‡ Hon. R. Curzon — H. Milford, London, 1916. 424 pp. Interesting account of a journey in southern Albania in the first part of nineteenth century.

SECTION V

LEAGUE OF NATIONS: DOCUMENTS AND JOURNAL.

(From 1920. Specific references are given only for the most important matter and for documents published separately.)

Official Journal of the League of Nations † — O.J.

Official Reports of the League of Nations Commission of Inquiry.†

Report dated 19.11.21–20.12.21 = C. 542. M. 387. 1921. VII.
Report dated 29.12.21– 18.1.22 = C. 93. M. 48. 1922. VII.
Report dated 19.12.22– 1.2.23 = O.J. May/23. 491.
Report dated 1.2.23– 1.4.23 = O.J. May/23. 503.
Final Report = O.J. May/23. 504.

Reports (four) of the Financial Adviser to the Albanian Government † = O.J. Jan./24. 162–8; April/24. 727–8; May/24. 762–3.

The Admission of Albania to the League of Nations † = A. 38.; 20.48.71.

Report presented by the Sixth Committee † = A. 151. 1921.

Telegrams dated Sept. 25th, 1921, from the Albanian Minister for Foreign Affairs † = A. 154. 1921. VII.

Appeal to the Council of the League by the Albanian Government † = C. 36. M. 152. 1921. VII.

Recognition of Albania and Resumption of Diplomatic Relations † = C. 37. M. 18. 1921. VII.

Dispute between Albania on the one side, and Greece and the Serb-Croat-Slovene State on other. Memorandum by the Albanian Delegation † = C. 204. M. 125. 1921. VII.

Protest by the Albanian Government against the activities of the Serb-Croat-Slovene Government in N. Albania † = C. 257. M. 191. 1921.

Memorandum by the Secretary-General = C. 446. M. 328. 1921.
  on Albania, 17.11.21.†

Note sur le délibérations de la Con- = C. 293. M. 94. 1924. VII.
  férence des Ambassadeurs au sujet
  de l'attribution du monaſtère de St
  Naoum.†

SECTION VI

12th Edition.

Albania. J. S. Barnes, F.R.G.S.   30 : 104

Austrian Empire (Foreign Policy). A. F. Pribram, Ph.D.   30 : 327

Balkan Peninsula. Jovan Cvijic and Yves Chataigneau. (The map   30 : 368
accompanying this article should be compared with that
accompanying the article upon the Balkan Peninsula in Vol. 3.
Professor Cvijic's ability to manipulate ethnographical
features to suit Serbian aspirations is now notorious.)

Balkan Wars. Maj. C. F. Atkinson.   30 : 373

Bulgaria. Elinor, Lady Grogan.   30 : 516

English History (The War Period). G. Earle Buckle, M.A.,   30 : 1004
Hon. LL.D.

Europe. J. W. Headlam-Morley, M.A., C.B.E.   31 : 18

Greece. J. N. Mavrogordato, M.A.   31 : 300

Italy. Luigi Villari, M.C.   31 : 615

League of Nations. Rt. Hon. Lord R. Cecil, M.P.   31 : 735

Montenegro. A. H. E. Taylor, B.A.   31 : 978

Roumania. Marcu Beza, L. ès L.   32 : 302

Salonika Campaigns (unsigned).   32 : 345

Serbia. R. W. Seton-Watson,* D.Litt. (Oxon), Hon. Ph.D.   32 : 398
(Prague and Zagreb).

Serbian Campaigns. Maj. C. F. Atkinson, T.D.   32 : 408

The World War (Political History). A. F. Pollard, M.A., Litt.D.,   32 : 1075
F.B.A.

Yugoslavia. R. W. Seton-Watson.*   32 : 1112

Albania. Albert Calmès.*   New Volumes† (13th Edition).   1 : 86

INDEX